P9-DET-895

New Worlds

An Introduction to College Reading

FIFTH EDITION

Janet Elder

Emerita, Richland College
Dallas County Community College District

The McGraw·Hill Companies

NEW WORLDS

Published by McGraw-Hill, a business unit of The McGraw-Hill Companies, Inc., 1221 Avenue of the Americas, New York, NY, 10020. Copyright © 2014 by The McGraw-Hill Companies, Inc. All rights reserved. Printed in the United States of America. Previous editions © 2011, 2008, 2004, and 2000. No part of this publication may be reproduced or distributed in any form or by any means, or stored in a database or retrieval system, without the prior written consent of The McGraw-Hill Companies, Inc., including, but not limited to, in any network or other electronic storage or transmission, or broadcast for distance learning.

Some ancillaries, including electronic and print components, may not be available to customers outside the United States.

This book is printed on acid-free paper.

1 2 3 4 5 6 7 8 9 0 RJE/RJE 1 0 9 8 7 6 5 4 3

ISBN 978-0-07-351350-8 (Student edition)
MHID 0-07-351350-4 (Student edition)

ISBN 978-0-07-753144-7 (Instructor's edition)
MHID 0-07-753144-2 (Instructor's edition)

Senior Vice President, Products & Markets: *Kurt L. Strand*
Vice President, General Manager: *Michael Ryan*
Vice President, Content Production & Technology Services: *Kimberly Meriwether David*
Managing Director: *David Patterson*
Director: *Paul Banks*
Executive Brand Manager: *Kelly Villella*
Senior Director of Development: *Dawn Groundwater*
Editorial Coordinator: *Dana Wan*
Senior Marketing Manager: *Jaclyn Elkins*
Market Development Manager: *Suzie Flores*
Director, Content Production: *Terri Schiesl*
Senior Production Editor: *Carey Eisner*
Full Service Project Manager: *Melanie Field, Strawberry Field Publishing*
Senior Buyer: *Laura Fuller*
Designer: *Matt Diamond*
Cover/Interior Designer: *Laurie Entringer*
Cover Image: *© James Kirkikis*
Content Licensing Specialist: *Jeremy Cheshareck*
Photo Researcher: *Ira Roberts*
Digital Product Manager: *Janet Smith*
Media Project Manager: *Angela Norris*
Typeface: *10.5/12 Times Roman*
Compositor: *MPS Limited*
Printer: *R.R. Donnelley & Sons*

Photo Credits: p. 1: © James Kirkikis; **p. 3:** © AP Photo/Lsa Billings; **p. 13:** © Purestock/SuperStock; **p. 29:** © The Baltimore Sun/Algerina Perna, photographer; **p. 40:** © GILKIS-Damon Hyland/Getty Images; **p. 37:** © Rubberball/Getty Images; **p. 52:** © Bill Aron/PhotoEdit; **p. 63:** © Royalty-Free/Corbis; **p. 66:** © MIXA/Getty Images; **p. 119:** © MGM-UA/Photofest; **p. 129:** © Gregg DeGuire/PictureGroup via AP Images; **p. 139:** © James Kirkikis; **p. 141:** © Wilfred Krecihwost/Getty Images; **p. 144:** © Pixtal/AGE Fotostock; **p. 163:** © JGI/Blend Images LLC; **p. 174:** © George Pimentel/WireImage/Getty Images; **p. 183:** © Reuters/Lucy Nicholson; **p. 191:** © Comstock; **p. 194:** © The McGraw-Hill Companies, Inc.; **p. 214:** © Andrew D. Bernstein/NBAE via Getty Images; **p. 225:** Photo from Olson, DeFrain, & Skorand: *Intimacy, Diversity, and Strengths, 7/e,* p. 279. Copyright © by The McGraw-Hill Companies, Inc. Reprinted with permission of The McGraw-Hill Companies, Inc.; **p. 234:** © Allen Kee/Getty Images; **p. 243:** © Photodisc/Getty Images; **p. 270:** © Brand X Pictures/Punch Stock; **p. 271:** Paul Margolies © 1996 NAMES Project; **p. 297:** © Royalty-Free/Corbis; **p. 300:** © Tetra Images/Getty Images; **p. 333:** © Kurt Scholz/SuperStock; **p. 343:** © AP Photo/Khampha Bouaphanh; **p. 353:** © Pixtal/SuperStock; **p. 403:** © Rubber Ball/SuperStock; **p. 412:** Library of Congress, #LC-DIG-ggbain-02466; **p. 420:** © Jeff Greenberg/PhotoEdit; **p. 427:** © James Kirkikis; **p. 429:** © Masterfile/Royalty-Free; **p. 475:** © Kristi A. Rines; **p. 481:** © Photodisc/Getty Images; **p. 491:** © The McGraw-Hill Companies, Inc./Gary He, photographer; **p. 525:** © ThinkStock/SuperStock; **p. 534:** © Digital Vision/PunchStock; **p. 543:** © Peter Dazeley/Getty Images; **p. 551:** © James Kirkikis; **p. 553:** © The McGraw-Hill Companies, Inc./Christopher Kerrigan, photographer; **p. 568:** © Photodisc Collection/Getty Images; **p. 569:** © Bettmann/Corbis; **p. 607:** © Pixtal/AGE Fotostock

All credits appearing on page are considered to be an extension of the copyright page.

Library of Congress Cataloging-in-Publication Data

Elder, Janet.
New worlds : an introduction to college reading / Janet Elder. — 5th ed.
p. cm.
Includes bibliographical references and index.
ISBN-13: 978-0-07-351350-8 (alk. paper)
ISBN-10: 0-07-351350-4 (alk. paper)
ISBN-13: 978-0-07-753144-7 (alk. paper)
1. Reading (Higher education) 2. College readers. I. Elder, Janet. II. Title.
LB2395.3.C68 2014
428.6—dc23

2013043312

The Internet addresses listed in the text were accurate at the time of publication. The inclusion of a website does not indicate an endorsement by the authors or McGraw-Hill, and McGraw-Hill does not guarantee the accuracy of the information presented at these sites.

www.mhhe.com

About the Author

Janet Elder

Reading changes lives. Hardly a new thought, but one I know from experience and believe with all my heart. If I didn't, I wouldn't have spent such a large part of my life teaching college reading courses and writing textbooks. I had the good fortune to teach for nearly three decades at Richland College in the Dallas Community College District, the best professional experience a teacher could ask for: a large, open-door college that drew students locally and from around the world. I took early retirement from teaching to move to Santa Fe, New Mexico, a place my husband and I love. It was not an easy decision but, happily, has turned out to be a good one. I continue to write college reading improvement textbooks and I am the co-author of another highly successful reading textbook, *Opening Doors,* which is now in its seventh edition. I'm also the author of McGraw-Hill's *Exercise Your College Reading Skills: Developing More Powerful Comprehension* and was the lead writer for its Connect Reading 2.0 program.

If you're wondering about my own education, I graduated summa cum laude from the University of Texas in Austin with a BA in English and Latin. I'm a member of Phi Beta Kappa. I received a government fellowship for Southern Methodist University's Reading Research Program for my master's degree. My PhD is in curriculum and instruction in reading. I earned it at Texas Woman's University, where the College of Education presented me with the Outstanding Dissertation Award. I could always relate to my own students who juggled working, school, and family responsibilities. It took me six years to complete my doctorate: I was teaching full-time and attending graduate school part-time during the academic year and full-time during the summers.

I went from being in college to teaching, a profession I loved, which is something I think my students knew. At Richland, I twice received the Extra Mile Award from disabilities services students, was twice a nominee for Richland's Excellence in Teaching Award, and twice received the Excellence Award from the National Institute for Staff and Organizational Development. I've made countless presentations at professional conferences: They were learning experiences both for me and, I hope, for those who attended my sessions!

My own education has meant a great deal to me and has enriched my life immeasurably in every way. Teaching and writing are ways I can give back and help those who are on their way to becoming formally educated. I write a great deal of the year, but when I'm not writing, I enjoy working out, hiking, spending time with my husband and friends, and—you guessed it—reading!

Brief Contents

Contents

CHAPTER 2 Developing a College-Level Vocabulary: A New World of Words 63

CONNECT Reading 2.0 Personalized Learning Plan CORRELATION GUIDE		
Unit	**Topic in PLP**	**Relevant Learning Objectives**
Unit 1: Vocabulary Skills	Vocabulary: Context Clues	• Understand the skill of using context clues • Recognize 6 types of context clues • Recognize clue words and signals for 6 types of context clues • Use context clues to determine a word's meaning • Use context clues to select the appropriate dictionary definition
Unit 1: Vocabulary Skills	Vocabulary: Word-Structure Clues	• Understand the skill of using word-structure clues • Identify and know the meaning of common prefixes • Identify and know the meaning of common roots • Identify and know the meaning of common suffixes • Use one or more word parts to unlock a word's meaning
Unit 3: Interpreting	Author's Tone and Figurative Language	• Understand 4 common figures of speech and the skill of interpreting them • Interpret 4 common figures of speech

CONNECT Reading 2.0 Personalized Learning Plan CORRELATION GUIDE

Unit	Topic in PLP	Relevant Learning Objectives
Unit 2: Understanding	Main Idea	• Differentiate between the stated and implied main ideas • Understand the skill of formulating the implied main idea of a paragraph • Formulate the implied main idea of a paragraph • Formulate the overall implied main idea of a longer selection

CONNECT Reading 2.0 Personalized Learning Plan CORRELATION GUIDE

Unit	Topic in PLP	Relevant Learning Objectives
Unit 2: Understanding	Supporting Details	• Understand the connection between main ideas and supporting details • Understand the types of information in supporting details • Apply the skill of identifying supporting details • Use signal words to identify supporting details • Distinguish between major and minor details

CONNECT Reading 2.0 Personalized Learning Plan CORRELATION GUIDE

Unit	Topic in PLP	Relevant Learning Objectives
Unit 2: Understanding	Patterns of Organization	• Understand the skill of identifying organizational patterns • Understand 6 common organizational patterns • Recognize clue words and signals for 6 organizational patterns • Identify the organizational pattern in a paragraph
Unit 2: Understanding	Sentence Relationships	• Understand the skill of identifying within-sentence relationships • Understand common types of within-sentence relationships and their clue words • Interpret within-sentence relationships • Understand common types of between-sentence relationships and their clue words, and the skill of identifying between-sentence relationships • Interpret between-sentence relationships

CONNECT Reading 2.0 Personalized Learning Plan CORRELATION GUIDE

Unit	Topic in PLP	Relevant Learning Objectives
Unit 4: Reading Critically	Author's Point of View	• Understand the skill of author's point of view • Understand clues that reveal the author's point of view • Identify the author's point of view in passages
Unit 2: Understanding	Author's Purpose and Intended Audience	• Understand 4 common purposes and the skill of identifying author's purpose • Understand how to identify or reason out the author's purpose • Apply the skill of determining the author's purpose in paragraphs • Understand 3 types audiences and the skill of determining author's intended audience • Understand clues to identifying the author's intended audience • Apply the skill of identifying the author's intended audience
Unit 3: Interpreting	Author's Tone and Figurative Language	• Understand the skill of author's tone and clues that reveal it • Understand common types of tone and the words that signal them • Identify the author's tone in passages

CONNECT Reading 2.0 Personalized Learning Plan CORRELATION GUIDE		
Unit	**Topic in PLP**	**Relevant Learning Objectives**
Unit 4: Reading Critically	Fact and Opinion	• Understand fact and opinion • Understand the skill of distinguishing facts from opinions • Identify facts and opinions in paragraphs • Distinguish well-supported opinions from poorly-supported and unsupported opinions
Unit 3: Interpreting	Inferences and Conclusions	• Understand the skill of making inferences and drawing conclusions • Apply the skill of making inferences • Find the faulty inference • Apply the skill of drawing conclusions • Identify stated conclusions and the words that signal them

CONNECT Reading 2.0 Personalized Learning Plan CORRELATION GUIDE

Unit	Topic in PLP	Relevant Learning Objectives
Unit 5: Study Techniques	Using Textbooks Effectively	• Understand the skill of using the SQ3R study technique • Understand the skill of using textbook features • Understand 4 types of graphic aids and how to interpret them • Understand 4 types of visual aids and how to interpret them

CONNECT Reading 2.0 Personalized Learning Plan CORRELATION GUIDE		
Unit	**Topic in PLP**	**Relevant Learning Objectives**
Unit 5: Study Techniques	Study Skills	• Understand the skill of marking and annotating textbooks • Recognize correctly marked and annotated textbook passages • Understand the skill of outlining textbook information • Recognize a correct outline of a passage • Understand the skill of mapping • Recognize a correct map of a passage • Understand the skill of summarizing • Recognize a correct summary of a passage • Understand the Cornell note-taking method and its advantages

Preface

New Worlds . . . Introducing Students to College Reading

NEW WORLDS PAIRED WITH CONNECT READING 2.0 OFFERS PERSONALIZED LEARNING

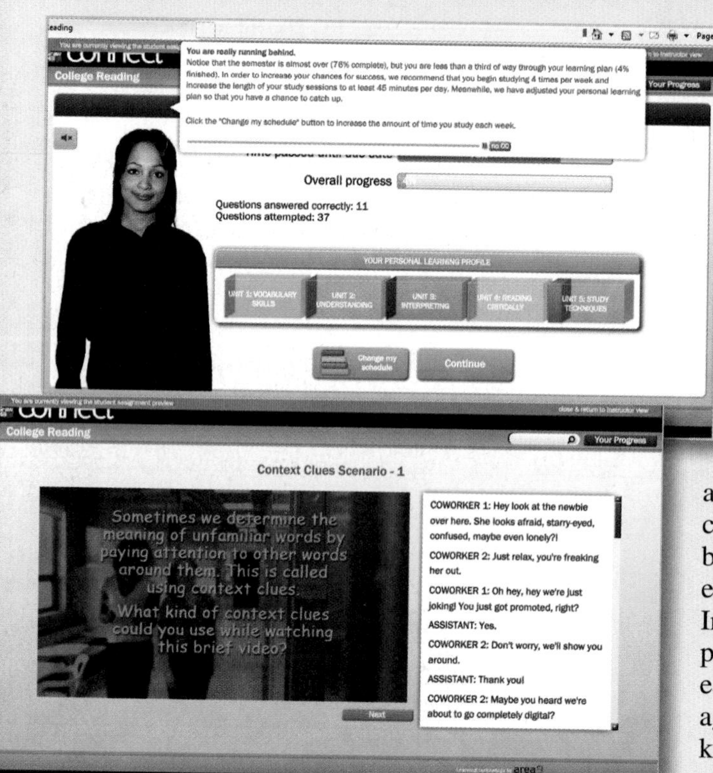

Powered by Connect Reading, students gain access to our groundbreaking personal learning plan, which supports differentiated instruction. With a simple diagnostic test that assesses student proficiencies in five core areas of Vocabulary Skills, Understanding, Interpreting, Reading Critically, and Study Techniques, students' responses generate a self-guided, adaptive plan of contextualized reading lessons, videos, animations, and interactive exercises tailored to their specific needs.

Embedded reading selections across the academic disciplines prepare students for future coursework, and real-world videos and examples bring relevance to the students' work to further engage them and generate in-class discussion. Informed by metacognitive learning theory, the personal learning plan continually adapts with each student interaction, while built-in time management features make students more productive, keep them on track, and ensure they progress steadily to achieve course goals.

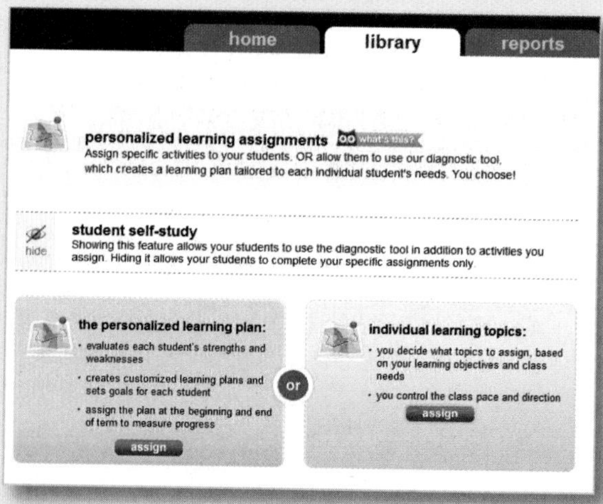

Built around common national learning objectives and designed to increase student readiness, motivation, and confidence, Connect Reading may be used in conjunction with any course material. This flexible content and format works well in traditional course settings, hybrid and online courses, or redesign models including accelerated courses, supplemental instruction, non-course-based options, and emporium/lab-based environments. Instructors may assign individual learning topics in the personalized learning plan for weekly coursework or the

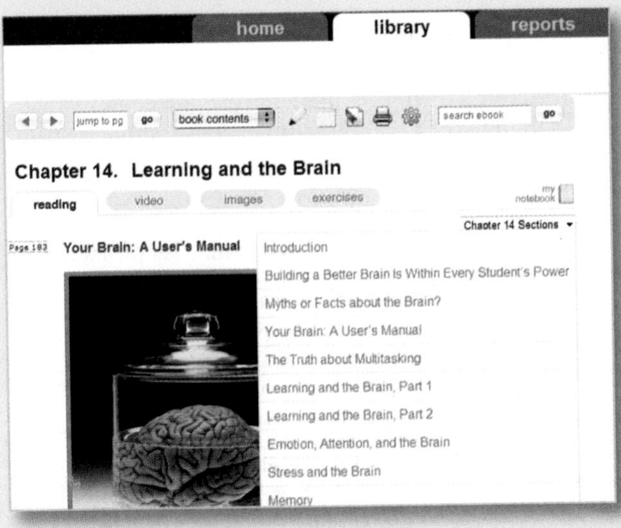

holistic personalized learning plan for individualized instruction.

Additionally, the Connect Reading eBook contains 12 modules on learning and the brain in Chapter 14.

In *New Worlds*, personalized learning plan icons appear next to the first heading of any chapter with related content.

The detailed table of contents for this book includes Connect Reading 2.0 Personalized Learning Plan Correlation Guides for each chapter. These guides beneath each chapter title provide instructors with a list of units, individual learning topics, and learning objectives in the personalized learning plan that relate directly to content in the chapter.

NEW WORLDS EMPHASIZES PRACTICE

This new edition of *New Worlds* contains ample practice with college textbook excerpts and other relevant material. The new Checkpoint feature in Chapters 3–9 allows students to gain experience and practice with skills before they move to the Test Your Understanding sections. Ten new Essential Skills Review Tests allow students to apply multiple skills to 3- to 5-paragraph passages.

For every chapter reading selection, Annotation Practice Exercises and Respond in Writing exercises integrate writing and reading by calling for written responses and the formulation of the selection's overall main idea.

CHAPTER 4 CHECKPOINT
Locating the Stated Main Idea

Directions: Read each paragraph to determine the topic. Write the topic in the space provided. Then locate and underline (or highlight) the stated main idea of the paragraph.

1. This paragraph comes from a human sexuality textbook.

The possibilities for promotion sometimes are greater for men than for women. Parenting and household responsibilities still often fall to women. This can limit the time and energy available for their careers. Many institutions and employers are trying to create equal employment opportunities for women. There are still differences in how well women and men fare in their jobs, but there are signs things may be improving. Among married couples who both work, over 30 percent of the wives earn more money than their husbands. Also, in increasing numbers of families the woman is the primary breadwinner, while the man stays home to take care of the household responsibilities and children.

Source: Adapted from Gary Kelly, *Sexuality Today*, 10th ed., p. 117. Copyright © 2008 by The McGraw-Hill Companies, Inc.

Topic: ______________________________

2. This paragraph comes from a criminal investigation textbook.

When people place their outstretched arms in front of their bodies, with palms up, this is known as the *rogatory* (or "prayerful") display. Those who worship turn their palms up to God to ask his mercy. This behavior is also seen in individuals who say something that they want the investigator to believe. Since rogatory behavior can indicate deception, a criminal investigator should watch for it. When a person makes a declarative statement, note whether the hands are palms up or palms down. People who are telling the truth do not have to plead to be believed. They make a statement and it stands. During regular conversation in which ideas are being discussed and neither party is deeply committed to a particular point, the investigator can expect to see both palms-up and palms-down displays.

Source: Adapted from Charles Swanson, Neil Chamelin, Leonard Territo, and Robert Taylor, *Criminal Investigation*, 11th ed., p. 149. Copyright © 2012 by The McGraw-Hill Companies, Inc.

Topic: ______________________________

3. This paragraph comes from a psychology textbook.

We work to build social and romantic relationships because we need acceptance and love from others. We strive to reach for goals because we need to experience self-esteem and a sense of competence. The point is, our needs motivate much of our conscious behavior.

Source: Adapted from Denis Waitley, *Psychology of Success: Finding Meaning in Work and Life*, 5th ed., p. 263. Copyright © 2010 by The McGraw-Hill Companies, Inc.

CHECKPOINT CHAPTER 4 Locating the Stated Main Idea

Copyright © 2014 The McGraw-Hill Companies, Inc. All rights reserved.

201

NEW WORLDS EMPHASIZES ENGAGING READINGS

Reading selections were chosen for their excellence, student relevance, and value in helping students expand their knowledge base in a variety of academic subjects and on a variety of topics. Chapters 1–9 each contain three reading selections. Chapter 10 contains a single, longer selection.

READING

SELECTION **4.3**

Health

Concussions: Don't Shrug Them Off!

From *The Dana Foundation and the Sports Concussion Institute websites*
Compiled by Janet Elder

Motor vehicle accidents are the primary cause of traumatic brain injuries, and falls also account for a large number. Brain injuries can happen at any age, but young adults between the ages of 15 and 24 are at greatest risk.

Traumatic brain injuries are a leading cause of death and disability. It is estimated that a head injury occurs every seven seconds. In light of that, it is no surprise that each year hospital emergency rooms treat one million people for head injuries. Any brain injury is a potential threat, and anyone who experiences a head injury should see a doctor—even if the person feels fine.[1]

Concussions are often described as "mild" brain injuries, but many experts believe it is a mistake to describe any brain injury as mild. During the last few years, public awareness of the seriousness of concussions has increased. The reason is research on the growing number of former pro football players whose lives have been forever altered by their multiple concussions.

1 According to the Sports Concussion Institute, the term **concussion** refers to a brain injury that can be caused by a direct blow to the head, or by an indirect blow to the body. It is a misconception that the person always loses consciousness. In fact, only a small percent lose consciousness, and when this does happen, it is usually brief—perhaps only a few seconds. There may be no symptoms, but the symptoms can be so subtle that they go unrecognized. For example, the person may be temporarily confused, disoriented, have difficulty concentrating, or experience memory problems. Physical symptoms can include nausea, vomiting, and headaches. There can be sleep disturbances. There may be changes in energy levels or appetite. The person may also show changes in moods, such as sadness or irritability.[2]

2 The human brain weighs about three pounds. It has a custard-like texture, and this delicate organ floats in fluid inside the skull. The fluid inside the skull is designed to cushion the brain, but when there is an impact or a whiplash, a concussion can result. It occurs when the brain moves too quickly inside the skull. Upon impact, the brain receives two jolts: the initial one, which sets the brain in motion, and a second one when it hits the opposite side of the inner skull. In a case in which the brain rotates too rapidly from one side to the other, its tissue can be strained or even torn.[3]

3 Many concussion victims do not see a doctor because after a short period of time, they feel fine. Feeling fine, however, does not mean that an injury hasn't occurred. Other victims go undiagnosed because their symptoms are subtle, or they do not associate their symptoms with a head injury. It is no wonder concussions have been described as a "hidden epidemic."[4]

4 A concussion can be dangerous at any age, but it poses a special threat to developing brains. They are more vulnerable. Recovery takes longer. Moreover, many youngsters and young

Annotation Practice Exercises

Directions: For each exercise below, write the topic of the paragraph on the lines beside the paragraph. Then locate the stated main idea of the paragraph and underline or highlight it.

Practice Exercise

Topic of paragraph 1:

____

____

Determine the *stated main idea* and underline or highlight it.

Practice Exercise

Topic of paragraph 2:

____

____

Determine the *stated main idea* and underline or highlight it.

Practice Exercise

Topic of paragraph 3:

____

____

Determine the *stated main idea* and underline or highlight it.

Copyright © 2014 The McGraw-Hill Companies, Inc. All rights reserved.

WHAT IS NEW IN THIS EDITION

In addition to incorporating correlations to the Connect Reading personalized learning plan, expanding the exercises, and updating the reading selections, *New Worlds* includes the following changes:

- **More than 150 new and updated example and exercise paragraphs** throughout the book.
- A new, short feature in Chapter 1 that tells **how to locate and evaluate material online.**
- **Three additional Test Your Understanding vocabulary exercises in Chapter 2,** one each on using context clues, using word-structure clues, and interpreting figurative language.
- **Seven new Checkpoint exercises,** one each in Chapters 3–9 that check to be sure students understand the chapter skills before applying them in the Test Your Understanding exercises.
- **Eleven new chapter reading selections** with accompanying activities, exercises, and quizzes:

  2.1: "Overcoming Obstacles" *(Student Success)*
  2.2: "Autism: A Public Health Emergency" *(Public Health)*
  2.3: Excerpt from Temple Grandin's *Thinking in Pictures (Nonfiction)*
  3.3: "State-of-the-Art and High-Tech Ways of Dealing with Death" *(Health)*
  4.2: "Parent-Arranged Marriages" *(Marriage and Family)*
  4.3: "Concussions: Don't Shrug Them Off!" *(Health)*
  5.2: "Companies Struggle with 'Inside Jobs' and Outside Threats" *(Management Information Systems)*
  7.1: "Viruses: Easily Spread and Ever Evolving" *(Health)*
  7.3: "Are You Shopping Smart?" *(Personal Finance)*
  9.1: "Taboos and Myths about Conflict and Anger" *(Marriage and Family)*
  9.3: "For Better or Worse: Divorce" *(Human Development)*

- **Nine updated chapter reading selections** with accompanying activities, exercises, and quizzes:

  1.2: "Fire Up Your Memory with Proven Strategies" *(Student Success)*
  1.3: "The When and How of Preparing for Tests" *(Study Skills)*
  3.1: "Parenting Style: Does It Matter?" *(Human Development)*
  3.2: "Giving a Speech? If You're Nervous, You're Normal!" *(Speech)*
  4.1: "Who's the Boss? Leaders, Managers, and Leadership Styles" *(Business)*
  5.1: "Two Artistic Tributes: The Vietnam Memorial and the AIDS Quilt" *(Art Appreciation)*
  6.1: "'Hold It! You Can Recycle That!' Recycling: A Twenty-First Century Necessity" *(Environmental Science)*
  7.2: "The Right to Vote: Valued but Underutilized" *(Government)*
  8.3: "You? A Millionaire? Yes!" *(Business)*

- **All new examples of the chapter features** presented in Chapter 10.
- **All new and updated graphics in Chapter 10** on interpreting visuals and graphic aids and in the chapter's Test Your Understanding exercise.

- **Many new photographs, graphics, and other visuals** throughout the rest of the text.
- **Ten new Essential Skills Review Tests** at the end of the text. These 10-item quizzes over short, multiparagraph selections target a variety of reading skills. They can be used for practice, as homework, for extra credit, or as collaborative exercises.
- **New Assignment Sheet and Progress Record** at the back of the book, which allows students to record due dates for assigned activities, note whether they have completed them, and record their scores.
- **New Reading Skills and Competencies Chart** at the beginning of the book so students and instructors can quickly locate the instructional pages in *New Worlds* and related exercises for each skill.

HALLMARK FEATURES

The following hallmark features of *New Worlds* have been retained:

- **Clear explanations** of each skill **and understandable examples.**
- **Scores of textbook excerpts** for application of reading and study skills.
- **"It's Your Call"** feature in Chapter 1 that refers students to more complete discussions of study skills and test-preparation skills that appear later in the book, should they wish to explore them in depth at the beginning of the semester.
- An extensive, thorough, seven-chapter **Comprehension Core:** basic comprehension skills (Chapters 3–7) and critical reading and thinking skills (Chapters 8 and 9).
- Approximately **50 brief embedded exercises** for on-the-spot application of new skills presented in the chapters.
- **Other Things to Keep in Mind,** a short section in each chapter that presents additional pointers and supplemental information related to the chapter skill(s).
- A **Chapter Review Card activity** for every chapter.
- **Twenty-one Test Your Understanding Exercises** in Chapters 2–10. Some contain objective (multiple-choice) items; others require fuller written responses.
- **Twenty-seven full-length Reading Selections** (three in each of the first nine chapters).
- **A chapter-length Reading Selection** in Chapter 10 and one online (Chapter 11).
- **Comprehension and Vocabulary Quizzes** for the 27 reading selections in Chapters 1–9.

  These 20-item quizzes contain four sections:

  Comprehension

  Five questions of the type a content-area instructor (such as a psychology professor) would expect students to be able to answer after reading the selection.

  Vocabulary in Context

  Five questions that test the ability to use context clues to determine the meaning of words from the selection.

Word Structure

Five questions that test the ability to use word-structure clues to help determine a word's meaning. Students learn the meaning of a word part (root) that appears in a word in the selection and then use the meaning of that root to determine the meaning of the other words that contain the same root.

Reading Skills Application

Five questions that test the ability to apply various reading skills to material in this selection. These are the types of questions that appear on standardized reading tests, exit tests, and state-mandated basic skills tests.

- For every chapter reading selection, **Annotation Practice Exercises** and **Respond in Writing exercises** that integrate writing and reading by calling for written responses and the formulation of the selection's overall main idea.
- **One or more websites for each reading selection** so students can read more about the selection's topic or author, along with suggested keywords to use with online search engines.
- Presentation of **vocabulary and study skills** as they relate to learning from college textbooks and other college-level materials.
- **Comprehension monitoring questions** for reading comprehension, critical reading, and critical thinking appear throughout the book in the margins.
- Coverage of the **skills typically included on standardized reading tests, exit tests, and state-mandated reading competency tests.**

RESOURCES TO SUPPORT YOUR TEACHING WITH *NEW WORLDS*

Annotated Instructor's Edition (AIE)

The AIE contains the full text of the student edition of the book with answers as well as an Instructor Guide at the front, marginal Teaching Tips, Timely Words, and relevant quotations. The *Instructor's Guide* in the Annotated Instructor's Edition contains three alternative teaching sequences because one of those may better suit a specific course. Some instructors prefer to begin with the study skills (outlining, mapping, summarizing, note taking, and marking textbooks) at the end of *New Worlds*. Only you can determine what is best for your students, but the reason these skills are presented near the end of the book is that students cannot master them without first having a solid grasp of main ideas and supporting details.

Downloadable Instructor Supplements

A revised **Online Learning Center** contains a document listing readings organized thematically and correlating Connect Reading eBook readings, updated PowerPoints for each chapter, updated instructor test bank to use for chapter quizzes, and the following **Supplemental Reading Selections** with questions that may be assigned for extra practice or used as tests:

"Rage on the Road"
"Causes of Cancer"
"Smokers vs. Nonsmokers"

"Why Relationships Develop and What Makes Them Last"
"Achoo! You've Another Cold!"
"Ticket Scalping"
"Whose Grave Is It Anyway?"
"Information Technology, the Internet, and You" (the chapter-length reading selection for Chapter 11)

Full-Length Textbook Chapters and Pedagogy to Customize *New Worlds*

With McGraw-Hill Create™, you can easily arrange your book to align with your syllabus, eliminate chapters you do not assign, integrate material from other content sources, and quickly upload content you have written, such as your course syllabus or teaching notes, to enhance the value of course materials for your students. Now you can also enhance *New Worlds* with content area chapters selected by the author and accompanied by author-developed apparatus.

Through Create™ ExpressBooks, you may choose from the following seven author-selected, full-length textbook chapters from across career-oriented disciplines to customize this text. You may also choose to incorporate any of the three supporting pieces of pedagogy for each chapter: Introduction, Post-Selection Apparatus, and Practice Quiz.

	Textbook/Edition/Author/Copyright/Content Area	Chapter Number and Title	No. of Pages
#1	**Choosing Success in Community College and Beyond,** 1st Ed., 2012 by Rhonda Atkinson and Debbie Longman *(Student Success)*	Ch 12: "Exploring Career Options and Opportunities," pp. 276–95	20
#2	**Business and Administrative Communication,** 10th Ed., 2013 by Kitty Locker and Donna Kienzler *(Business)*	Ch 1: "Succeeding in Business Communication," pp. 2–24	23
#3	**Emergency Medical Technician,** 2nd Ed., 2011 by Barbara Aehlert *(Allied Health)*	Ch 16: "Scene Size-Up," pp. 310–23	14
#4	**Computing Essentials 2013: Making IT Work for You,** Introductory Ed. by Timothy O'Leary and Linda O'Leary *(Information Technology)*	Ch 1: "Information Technology, the Internet, and You," pp. 2–28	27
#5	**Think Criminology,** 1st Ed., 2012 by John Fuller *(Criminology)*	Ch 1: "Thinking Critically about Crime," pp. 2–15	14
#6	**Think: Critical Thinking and Logic Skills for Everyday Life,** 2nd Ed., 2012 by Judith Boss *(Critical Thinking)*	Ch 10: "Marketing & Advertising," pp. 308–37	30
#7	**Connect Core Concepts in Health,** 12th Ed., Brief, 2012 by Paul Insel and Walton Roth *(Health)*	Ch 15: "Conventional and Complementary Medicine," pp. 362–83	22

McGraw-Hill Create™ ExpressBooks facilitate customizing your book more quickly and easily. To quickly view the possibilities for customizing your book, visit www.mcgrawhillcreate.com and enter "New Worlds" under the Find Content tab. Once you select the current edition of this book, click on the "View Related ExpressBooks" button or ExpressBooks tab to see options. ExpressBooks contains a combination of pre-selected chapters and readings that serve as a starting point to help you quickly and easily build your own text. You will find an ExpressBook table of contents for *New Worlds,* 5e that includes all of the textbook chapters and pedagogy listed in the table on page xxii. You may adjust the table of contents to build your perfect course materials.

Go to www.mcgrawhillcreate.com and register today!

ACKNOWLEDGMENTS

The following reviewers contributed to this new edition with their thoughtful, constructive comments and suggestions. They remind me all over again of the talent and collegiality that characterizes the teaching profession. I am indebted to them.

Elise Geraghty, *El Camino College*
Tanya Masso, *South Texas College*
Rick Richards, *St. Petersburg College*
Grace J Richardson, *Mt. Hood Community College*
Mitra Sapienza, *City College of San Francisco*
Amanda C. Sauermann, *Hopkinsville Community College*
Catherine Charis Sawyer, *Johnson County Community College*
Tracey Schaub, *Massasoit Community College*
Renee Wright, *Triton College*

A new edition of any textbook represents the combined efforts of a host of able individuals, and I am privileged to have worked with an abundance of them. I am particularly fortunate to have Executive Brand Manager Kelly Villella-Canton as my new editor. She brings extensive experience and expertise to this role. She is a pleasure to work with, and any project is enhanced by her involvement. I thank Dawn Groundwater, Senior Director of Development, for graciously handling the project during the transition between editors. Development Editor Anne Leung was instrumental in getting the project off to a successful start. It was an honor and a delight to work with an outstanding production duo: Senior Production Editor Carey Eisner and Full Service Production Manager Melanie Field. Nor could I have asked for a more knowledgeable or congenial copy editor than Carole Crouse. Jane Mohr ably shepherded the project through the final weeks of production. Credit for the attractive design and format of this edition of *New Worlds* goes to Senior Designer Matt Diamond and Cover/Interior Designer Laurie Entringer. A tip of the hat also goes to Content Licensing Specialist Jeremy Cheshareck, top-notch photo researcher Ira Roberts, Marketing Manager Jaclyn Elkins, and Editorial Coordinator Dana Wan for their contributions. As always, it's a pleasure to work with Paul Banks, McGraw-Hill's talented and dedicated Director of Developmental English. There are undoubtedly others who have contributed to this edition with whom I have not had the opportunity to have direct contact. I thank them as well.

Janet Elder

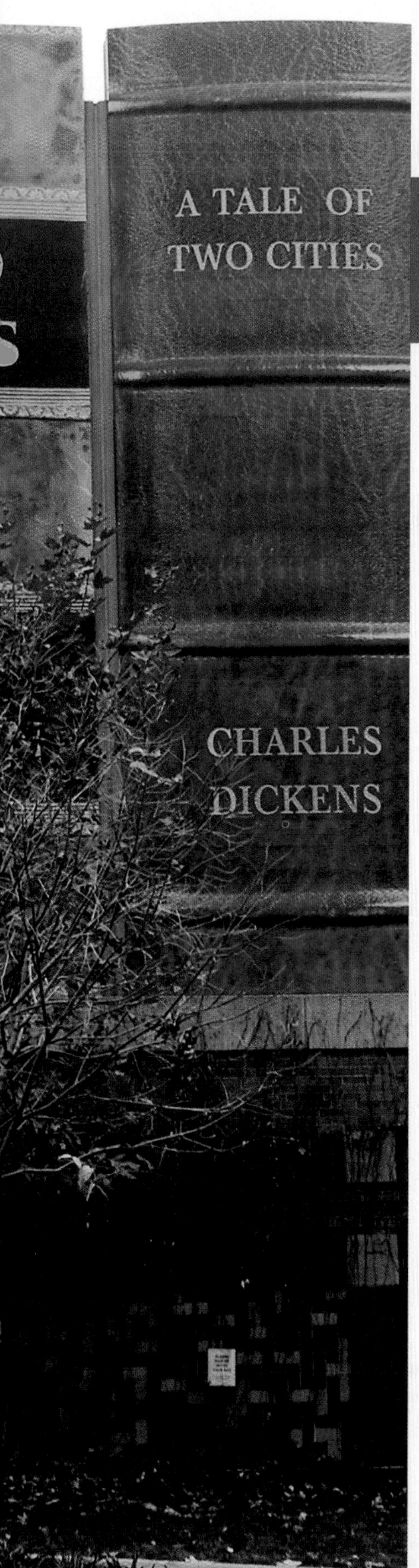

PART 1

A New World of Learning

Reading and Studying in College

CHAPTERS IN PART ONE

CHAPTER 1

Introduction to Reading and Studying

Being Successful in College

LEARNING OBJECTIVES

In this chapter you will learn the answers to these questions:

- What do I need to know about the process of reading and studying?
- What are the keys to studying textbooks?
- What is the SQ3R study system?
- How can I adjust my reading rate when I study?
- What do I need to do to be successful in college?
- Why is it important to set goals for myself?
- What are learning preferences?

NEW INFORMATION AND SKILLS

WHAT DO YOU NEED TO KNOW ABOUT THE READING AND STUDYING PROCESS?

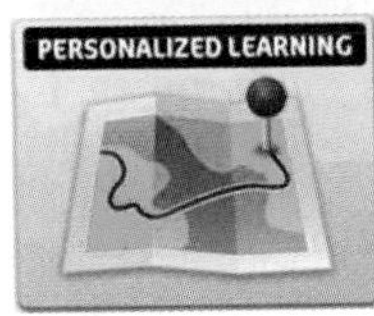

Knowing about the reading process can help you read and study more effectively. Reading is more than just moving your eyes in a certain way and decoding and pronouncing words. It is a form of the *thinking* process, and the goal is to comprehend the author's message. To do this, you must "think along" with the author; that is, you must follow and understand his or her train of thought. Furthermore, you must make connections between what you are reading and what you already know about the topic. This background knowledge—what you already know about a topic—is called **prior knowledge.**

prior knowledge

What you already know about a topic.

Prior knowledge is also known as *background knowledge.*

How can you activate your prior knowledge when you begin reading an assignment? One way is to preview the assignment. **Previewing** means examining material to determine its topic and organization before actually reading it. To do this, look at the introduction, headings, illustrations, and chapter summary. Think about the topic and try to recall anything you already know about it. In other words, activate and assess your prior knowledge. If the material is challenging and you do not know very much about the topic, you may want to learn a little bit more about it first. You might check the dictionary or go online. After you finish previewing, take a few minutes to reflect on this information or jot down a few introductory notes.

previewing

Examining material to determine its topic and organization before actually reading it.

Good readers are active readers. As they read, they constantly ask questions and think about how the material is organized. They use the skill of **predicting** to anticipate what is coming next. Predicting helps them concentrate and read actively.

predicting

Anticipating what is coming next as you read.

Skillful readers prepare themselves to read by previewing and assessing their prior knowledge. Then they ask and answer questions as they read. Finally, they review material by rehearsing the answers to their questions. The reason good readers ask themselves questions as they read is to check their comprehension (understanding) of what they are reading. Whenever they realize they are not comprehending, they take specific steps to fix the problem.

Even good readers have to reread certain things when they are studying, especially when the material is complicated or the topic is new to them. Skillful readers also adjust their reading strategies and reading rate according to the *type* of material they are reading (such as a textbook, a newspaper, a book of poems, a comic strip) and their *purpose* for reading (to gain information, to entertain themselves, to receive inspiration or comfort, and so forth). You will learn more about all these strategies in *New Worlds.*

IT'S YOUR CALL

Want More Information Now about *Reading, Studying, and Memory*?

Information about the reading process and study techniques is presented here to help you get off to a good start. If you would like additional, in-depth information now, you are welcome to look ahead:

Rehearsal and Memory, pages 609–10

Following Directions, page 619

In addition, Selection 1.2, "Fire Up Your Memory with Proven Strategies," on pages 37–41, presents information on studying and memory.

It's Your Call: *If you want or need information about these skills, explore these sections now.*

Copyright © 2014 The McGraw-Hill Companies, Inc. All rights reserved.

WHAT ARE THE KEYS TO STUDYING COLLEGE TEXTBOOKS?

Experienced college students know it can take considerable time to read assignments and learn the material in their textbooks. Beginning students often greatly underestimate the amount of time it takes to read and study their textbooks and prepare for tests. In fact, they may be shocked to discover how much time it actually takes. Or if they are spending a great deal of time studying, they may mistakenly imagine that they are the only ones who have to spend so much time.

Successful studying requires a sufficient amount of time, but simply spending large amounts of time studying does not by itself guarantee success: What you *do* during your study time is even more important.

Looking at the words in a book is not the same as reading and comprehending them, nor is sitting at a desk the same as studying. Some students who think they are "studying" are really sitting there daydreaming. Others read without going back to mark, highlight, or annotate anything. Still others highlight almost everything, only to discover later that they do not understand or remember much of what they marked.

There are proven techniques that make studying more productive. This chapter and Chapters 10 and 11 describe techniques that will help you *learn more as you study.* Often, the difference between being a successful student and a less successful one is *applying these study skills in a systematic way.*

You may already be familiar with some of these study techniques, or they may be new to you. In either case, using them can make you a more effective student. They will help you in all your courses and in a variety of other learning situations as well. There will always be situations in college and in the workplace in which you must read, organize, learn, and remember information.

IT'S YOUR CALL

Want More Information Now about *Taking Notes from Textbooks and Preparing for Tests?*

This brief introduction to techniques for studying textbooks is presented here to get you off to a good start. If you would like additional, in-depth information now, you are welcome to look ahead:

Underlining, Highlighting, and Annotating Textbooks, pages 610–12

Outlining, Mapping, and Summarizing, pages 613–18

In addition, Selection 1.3, "The When and How of Preparing for Tests," on pages 49–55, presents information on studying for tests.

It's Your Call: *If you want or need information about these skills, explore these sections now.*

The keys to effective reading and studying are to:

- Monitor your comprehension.
- Be selective as you read and study.
- Organize the information as you read and study.
- Rehearse the information in order to remember it.

There is nothing magic about these study strategies. They are effective if you learn how to do them and then apply them regularly. If you use them consistently, you will become a better student each semester.

How Can You Monitor Your Comprehension as You Read and Study?

monitoring your comprehension

Evaluating your understanding as you read and correcting the problem whenever you realize that you are not comprehending.

Comprehension monitoring means evaluating your understanding as you read and correcting the problem whenever you realize that you are not comprehending. You should monitor your comprehension whenever you read and study.

As you read and study, monitor your comprehension by periodically asking yourself: *"Am I understanding what I am reading?"* If you do not understand it, try to pinpoint the problem by asking yourself, *"Why am I not understanding?"* If you can determine the reason, you can take steps to correct the problem.

Listed below are some common comprehension problems and strategies for solving them.

Problem:

I am not understanding because the topic is completely new to me. Textbooks frequently present topics that are new to you. Sometimes even a single paragraph can contain a lot of new information.

Solutions:

- Read further to see if the information that confuses you is explained or becomes clear to you.
- Look up the topic online or in another textbook. Read simpler or supplemental materials on the topic.
- Stop and ask for a brief explanation from someone who is knowledgeable about the topic (the instructor, a tutor, or a classmate).

Problem:

I am not understanding because there are words I do not know. College-level material is written at a high level and often contains new words and specialized or technical terms you must learn.

Solutions:

- Try to use the rest of the sentence or paragraph (the context) to figure out the meaning of an unfamiliar word.
- Look up unfamiliar words in the glossary at the back of the textbook, in a dictionary, or online.
- Ask someone the meaning of the unfamiliar words.
- Write down the definitions of the new words you are learning.

Problem:

I am not understanding because distractors are interfering with my concentration. Distractors may be *physical* (such as noise or being hungry) or *psychological* (such as daydreaming or worrying about other things you have to do).

Solutions:

Identify any *physical* distractors that are interfering with your concentration and take steps to eliminate them. For example,

- Move to a quiet room or close the door.
- Do not sit facing a window.
- Turn off the television and background music.
- Do not answer the telephone.
- Take a short break and drink a glass of water or eat a light snack.
- Do not try to study lying down—you will fall asleep.

Identify any *psychological* distractors that are interfering with your concentration and take steps to eliminate them. For example,

- If you are worrying about things you need to do, jot the items down. Then, *after* studying, take care of the items on your "to do" list.
- If you are daydreaming or worrying about a personal problem, refocus your attention by making a deliberate decision to concentrate on what you are reading.

Monitoring your comprehension enables you to determine when you are understanding and when you are not. This, in turn, enables you to take steps to correct the situation when you are *not* understanding what you are reading.

Make comprehension monitoring a habit. After all, if you do not understand what you are reading, you are not really reading. You are just looking at the words.

How Can You Be Selective as You Read and Study?

being selective as you read and study

Focusing on main ideas and major supporting details.

Too many students think that they can (and must) learn and remember *everything* in their textbooks, but this mistaken idea leads only to frustration. **Being selective as you read and study** means focusing on main ideas and major supporting details. If you are selective, you will be less likely to feel overwhelmed by the material, and you will be more likely to remember the most important points the author wants you to learn.

How Can You Organize as You Read and Study?

organizing as you read and study

Arranging main ideas and supporting details in a meaningful way.

Organization is another key to learning and remembering what you read when you study. The reason is simple: Organized material is easier to learn, memorize, and recall than unorganized material. **Organizing as you read and study** means arranging main ideas and supporting details in a meaningful way. This is something that you should do on paper. Organizing material as you read and study is one way to transfer what you are learning to your long-term (permanent) memory.

How Can You Rehearse Information to Remember It?

rehearsing to remember information

Saying or writing material to transfer it into long-term memory.

Rehearsing to remember information means saying or writing material to transfer it into long-term memory. Rehearsal is *not* rereading. It is an active way of reviewing that involves looking at the information you have organized into notes or review cards, saying information out loud several times so that you hear the information, and writing the information several times. Rehearsal is especially important when you are studying complex material.

It is important to realize that comprehending and remembering are two separate tasks. Just because you comprehend textbook material does not mean you will automatically remember it, although material that you understand is much easier to memorize. To *remember* material as well as understand it, you must take an additional step: You must rehearse it. Just as actors begin to memorize their lines long before a performance, you need to rehearse textbook material frequently, and you should start long before a test.

These four keys to studying college textbooks that we have just discussed are interrelated. That is, these techniques complement one another, so *all* of them should be used whenever you study. Monitoring your comprehension as you read helps you be selective as to what is important. Being selective helps you organize information efficiently. Organizing information makes it easier to rehearse it. Rehearsing information helps you remember the information.

WHAT IS THE SQ3R STUDY SYSTEM?

The SQ3R study system is a widely advocated textbook study system developed more than half a century ago. The steps in the SQ3R method, **Survey, Question, Read, Recite, and Review,** offer a simple, systematic way to study textbook material. Using this method of asking and answering questions as you read and study a textbook chapter enhances your comprehension and retention.

SQ3R STUDY SYSTEM

Survey	Get an overview before you begin reading the chapter. Look at headings and subheadings, charts, tables, photographs, and words in special print. Read the preface and the chapter summary.
Question	Ask questions based on your preview during the Survey step. Turn chapter headings into questions. Create at least one question for each subsection or section in the chapter. Read any questions the author includes in the chapter.
Read	Read each section with your question in mind. Read actively and search for answers to the questions you developed in the Question step. Reading with a purpose is essential to comprehension and retention.
Recite	After reading each section, stop, recite your questions, and try to answer them aloud from memory. If you cannot answer a question, go back to the section and reread. Don't go on to the next section until you can recite the answer from memory.
Review	After you have completed reading the chapter using the Question, Read, and Recite steps, review all your questions, answers, and other material from the chapter to transfer the information into your long-term memory.

Copyright © 2014 The McGraw-Hill Companies, Inc. All rights reserved.

IT'S YOUR CALL

Want More Information Now about *Methods for Studying a Textbook*?

Information about the SQ3R method is presented here to help you get off to a good start. If you would like additional, in-depth information now, you are welcome to look ahead:

Three-Step Process for Studying Textbooks, pages 555–59
Interpreting Visual and Graphic Aids, pages 567–84
Textbook Features, pages 559–67

It's Your Call: *If you want or need information about these skills, explore these sections now.*

There are many variations of the SQ3R system, such as the SQ4R system (Survey, Question, Read, Recite, 'Rite [Write], and Review) and the PQ3R system (Preview, Question, Read, Recite, and Review). Chapter 10 of *New Worlds* (pages 555–59) presents a detailed explanation of a three-step study-reading process for reading and studying college textbook material.

HOW CAN YOU ADJUST YOUR READING RATE WHEN YOU STUDY?

You should preview textbook material before you read it and determine your purpose for reading it. Also, ask yourself how much you already know about it. If the topic is new to you, you will need to read more slowly. If you are very familiar with the topic, you may be able to read at a faster rate. The point is to read *flexibly,* adjusting your rate as needed. Continue to adjust your rate *as* you read, slowing down when necessary and reading a bit faster when possible.

When to Slow Down

When you read, slow down when:

- You know very little or nothing about the topic.
- A passage contains complicated or technical material.
- A passage has details you need to remember.
- A passage contains new or difficult vocabulary.
- The material presents directions that you must follow.
- There are charts or graphs to which you must shift your attention as you read.
- The material requires you to visualize something (the digestive system in a biology text, for example).
- The writing is beautiful, artistic, descriptive, or poetic and invites you to linger and enjoy each word. (You may want to read such material aloud to yourself.)
- The material contains ideas you want to consider carefully (such as two sides of an argument) or "words to live by" (such as philosophical, religious, or inspirational writing).

When to Speed Up

When you read, speed up when:

- The passage is easy: no complicated sentences, complex ideas, or difficult terms.
- There is an easy passage in a longer, more difficult section.
- A passage gives an example of something you already understand or merely explains it in different words.
- You are already knowledgeable about the topic.
- You want only main ideas and are not concerned about details.
- The material is not related to your purpose for reading (for example, a section of a magazine article that does not pertain to the topic you are researching).

How Can You Improve Your Reading Speed?

College students often ask, "How can I learn to read faster?" The answer, of course, is to practice reading faster on material that is easy. Although you will never be able to read college textbooks as fast as simpler material, you can probably learn to read them at a faster rate than you presently do. The chart below shows various reading rates and their uses.

Here are tips for increasing your reading rate by practicing on easy material:

1. Practice regularly with easy, interesting material, including newspapers (such as *USA Today*), favorite magazines (such as *People* or *Reader's Digest*), and short, simply-written novels (such as *The Old Man and the Sea* or *Animal Farm*).

FLEXIBLE READING: INFORMATION-GATHERING TECHNIQUES AND READING RATES

Information-Gathering Techniques	Approximate Rate (Words per Minute)	Uses
Scanning	1,000 wpm (words per minute) or more	To find a particular piece of information (such as a name, a date, or a number)
Skimming	800–1,000 wpm	To get an overview of material
Reading rates:		
Rapid reading	300–500 wpm	For fairly easy material; when you want only important facts or ideas; for leisure reading
Average reading	200–300 wpm	For textbooks, news magazines, journals, and literature
Study reading	50–200 wpm	For new vocabulary, complex concepts, technical material, and retaining details (such as material to be memorized, legal documents, and material of great interest or importance)

Copyright © 2014 The McGraw-Hill Companies, Inc. All rights reserved.

2. Read 15 to 20 minutes each day, pushing yourself to read at a rate that is slightly uncomfortably fast. When this rate becomes comfortable, push yourself to read a little faster. (Try using a timer when you practice. Set it for 15 to 20 minutes and see how many pages you can read.) Keep track of the number of pages you read each day.
3. Strive to maintain concentration. If you are momentarily distracted, return immediately to your reading.

As you continue to practice, you will find that you are able to read more pages in the same amount of time. You will also find that you can usually understand the important points in a passage even though you are reading faster. There is another bonus: As you read each day, you will add background knowledge. This will enable you to read related material more efficiently in the future.

WHAT DO YOU NEED TO DO TO BE SUCCESSFUL IN COLLEGE?

You've entered the exciting new world of college reading and studying. It's a world in which you can be successful—if you do the right things. Most students want to be successful, of course, but not everyone knows what to do to succeed. One way is simply to do what successful college students do.

What characterizes successful college students? According to the *Journal of College Reading and Learning,* there seem to be at least six important factors. They are logical and obvious, but they require self-discipline. (So do most things in life that are worthwhile and lead to a feeling of accomplishment!) These success behaviors and attitudes are within the reach of nearly all students. You may already do several of them. If so, keep doing them! However, there may be ones you can improve upon or do more consistently. Begin using them today, and use them consistently, semester by semester. If you do, you will become an even more effective, successful student. In short, anyone who wants to be a successful college student must do the things successful college students do.

The six characteristics are these:

1. **Successful students are prepared for class.** Preparing for class means much more than completing homework assignments. Successful students read assignments carefully, underlining or highlighting main points and taking notes. They also look over the information in their text and notes before class so that they can understand what the instructor will be talking about and so that they can take better notes in class. Being prepared enables students to concentrate, to participate in class discussions, and to ask questions that help them understand the material.
2. **Successful students attend every class and pay close attention.** Not only do they attend every class, but they also arrive early. They sit where the instructor can see them and they can see the instructor. They turn off their cell phones, iPods, and PDAs. They do not text during class. They focus on what the instructor is saying, and they take notes. They participate in class, even if their participation is limited at first to asking questions. They view class as an opportunity to learn more about the important information in their homework assignments. Knowing what the instructor considers important is especially helpful when it is time to prepare for a test. These students "attend" in the sense that they are "attentive": They pay attention, participate, and do not socialize with friends during class.

Becoming a successful student involves behaviors and attitudes that nearly all students can adopt.

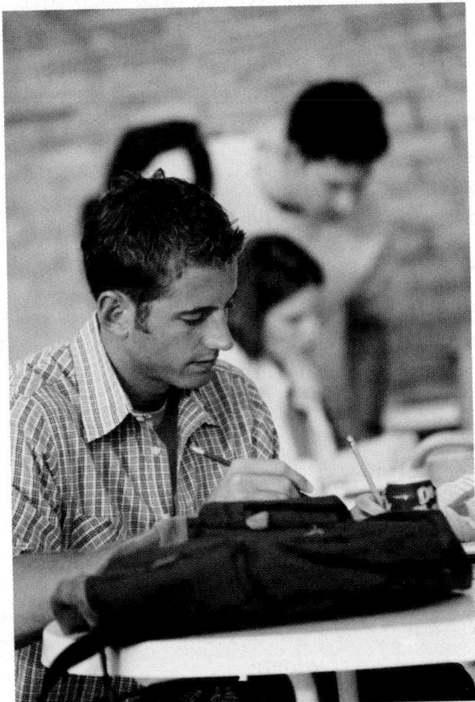

3. **Successful students perceive instructors as experts.** They view instructors as expert resources who want students to do well. They consult the instructor when they need assistance. They do not wait until failure is inevitable before they ask for help. Some students perceive asking for help as an indication of ignorance, but successful students realize that most instructors are pleased when a student is interested enough to seek help.
4. **Successful students follow an organized study routine.** Organized students regularly take time to think about (*a*) the things they need to do, (*b*) which things they need to start working on now, and (*c*) what they can do later. They know when they are using their time well or are wasting it. They establish daily objectives that will help them meet both short- and long-term goals. (Goal setting is discussed later in this chapter.) They often work ahead so that work does not pile up and so that tests and deadlines do not cause undue stress.
5. **Successful students develop a set of study skills strategies.** Successful students constantly review what they are learning. To do this, they develop creative ways to reorganize course material, such as making review cards, summary notes, charts, or diagrams. (Ways of organizing information are discussed in Chapter 11; learning preferences are discussed later in this chapter.) Reorganizing information requires working actively with the information to make sense of it and organizing it in a way that helps them remember it. When preparing for exams, successful students isolate themselves from friends (other than study groups) and other distractions. They start early, review the material, and reread all the important points. They may rewrite some of their notes. They ask for help on material they still do not understand.

Copyright © 2014 The McGraw-Hill Companies, Inc. All rights reserved.

6. **Successful students take responsibility for their own success.** They are realistic about the amount of time it takes to study. They pass up temptations to socialize or to entertain themselves instead of study because they place a higher priority on their schoolwork. They make sacrifices to keep up their grades because they value the long-term rewards associated with completing college. They have a clear idea of why they want to earn a college degree (and it is not simply to make money), and they often know what they want to do once they finish college. (If you are unclear about your major or career interest, talk with one of your college's advisors or career planning specialists.)

The *Journal of College Reading and Learning* article concludes: "Most students attain the maturity to balance their academic and social life. Those who do not know where to draw the line often drop out or fail out of college." The good news, though, is that the characteristics described here are ones almost any student can acquire and use.

Source: Adapted from Robert Nelson, "Using a Student Performance Framework to Analyze Success and Failure," *Journal of College Reading and Learning* 29, no. 1 (Fall 1998), pp. 82–89.

WHY IS IT IMPORTANT TO SET GOALS?

As noted, successful students have a clear idea of why they want to earn a college degree and what they want to do once they finish college. In other words, they have specific goals they want to achieve. Setting goals is a habit that distinguishes not only successful students, but successful people.

Setting goals involves identifying things that you would like to accomplish, writing them down, and making a commitment to achieve them.

There are several benefits from setting goals:

- **Having goals keeps you motivated.** When you set goals, you identify future achievements that are important and meaningful to you.
- **Having goals enables you to make good decisions about how you use your time and energy.** At any given moment, you can ask yourself whether what you are doing is moving you toward achieving one of your goals or away from it.
- **Having clear, written goals enables you to measure your progress toward achieving them.** It is satisfying to accomplish goals and to look back on ones you have achieved.

To be useful, goals must be specific and clear. They should also be realistic, that is, things that you can actually achieve (even though some may require considerable effort). An example of a clear, specific, and realistic goal is "I will complete all my courses this semester and make at least a B average." (An example of a vague goal is "I'll do better this semester." An example of an unrealistic goal is "I'll work 40 hours a week, take six courses this semester, and make all As.")

It is important to put your goals in writing. Goals that are not written down are not much better than wishes. Writing them down helps you make a commitment to them. Keep a copy of them on your desk or some other place where you will see them often. Read them daily and visualize yourself achieving them. Review them on a regular basis, perhaps at the beginning of each month. Update them as needed by modifying them, adding new ones, and removing ones you have attained.

You should designate each goal as a short-term goal, an intermediate goal, or a long-term goal, based on the length of time you think it will take to accomplish it.

short-term goal
Goal you want to accomplish within three to six months.

intermediate goal
Goal you want to accomplish within the next three to five years.

long-term goal
Goal you want to accomplish during your lifetime.

- **Short-term goals** are goals that you want to accomplish within three to six months (or during a semester). Examples: "to learn to use a word processing program," "to find a part-time job," and "to save enough money to take a ski trip during the semester break"
- **Intermediate goals** are those you want to accomplish within the next three to five years. Examples: "to attain my undergraduate degree," "to obtain an entry-level job in my career field," and "to complete a marathon"
- **Long-term goals** are large, often more complex goals that you want to accomplish during your lifetime. Examples: "to establish and run my own software company," "to get married and have a family," and "to travel throughout Europe"

In addition to identifying a time frame for each goal, you will find it helpful to categorize your goals. Use categories such as personal, financial, health, educational, travel, career, and spiritual.

PUTTING YOUR SHORT-TERM, INTERMEDIATE, AND LONG-TERM GOALS IN WRITING

Take a few minutes to write out your goals. Write at least three goals for each category. These are personal and private, and they do not have to be shared with anyone.

What are my short-term goals?

On the lines below, write at least three things you want to accomplish this semester.

1. __________
2. __________
3. __________
4. __________
5. __________

What are my intermediate goals?

On the lines below, write at least three things you want to accomplish within three to five years.

1. __________
2. __________
3. __________
4. __________
5. __________

Copyright © 2014 The McGraw-Hill Companies, Inc. All rights reserved.

What are my long-term goals?

On the lines below, write at least three things you want to accomplish and achieve during your lifetime.

1. ______________________________
2. ______________________________
3. ______________________________
4. ______________________________
5. ______________________________

WHAT ARE LEARNING PREFERENCES?

Being aware of how you learn best can help you become a more successful student. To gain insight into how you prefer to learn, complete the learning preferences inventory that follows. When you have completed the survey and totaled your responses, read the rest of this section.

IDENTIFYING YOUR LEARNING PREFERENCES

To gain insight into how you prefer to learn, answer the following questions. For each item, circle all the answers that describe you.

1. When I go someplace new, I usually
   a. trust my intuition about the right direction or route to take.
   b. ask someone for directions.
   c. look at a map or printed directions.

2. I like to go to places where
   a. there is a lot of space to move around.
   b. people are talking or there is music that matches my mood.
   c. there is good "people watching" or there is something interesting to watch.

3. If I have many things to do, I generally
   a. am fidgety until I get most of them done.
   b. repeat them over and over to myself so that I won't forget to do them.
   c. make a list of them or put them on a calendar or an organizer.

4. When I have free time, I like to
   a. work on a hobby or do crafts, or do an activity such as play a sport or exercise.
   b. listen to music or talk on the phone.
   c. watch television, play a video game, go online, or see a movie.

5. When I am talking with other people, I usually
   a. move close to them so I can get a feel for what they are telling me.
   b. listen carefully so that I can hear what they are saying.
   c. watch them closely so that I can see what they are saying.

6. When I meet someone new, I usually pay most attention to
   a. the way the person walks or moves, or to the gestures the person makes.
   b. the way the person speaks and how his or her voice sounds.
   c. the way the person looks (appearance, clothes, etc.).
7. When I choose a book or article to read, I typically choose one that
   a. deals with sports or fitness, hobbies and crafts, or other activities.
   b. tells me about a topic of particular interest to me.
   c. includes a lot of photos, pictures, or illustrations.
8. Learning about something is easier for me when I can
   a. use a hands-on approach.
   b. have someone explain it to me.
   c. watch someone show me how to do it.

Total your As, Bs, and Cs:

__________ As __________ Bs __________ Cs

If your highest total is As, you have a preference for *tactile* or *kinesthetic* learning.

If your highest total is Bs, you have a preference for *auditory* learning.

If your highest total is Cs, you have a preference for *visual* learning.

learning preference

The modality through which an individual learns best.

visual preference

A preference for seeing or reading information to be learned.

auditory preference

A preference for hearing information to be learned.

tactile preference

A preference for writing information to be learned or manipulating materials physically.

The term **learning preference** refers to the modality through which an individual learns best. The modalities are visual, auditory, and tactile. A person whose learning preference is visual likes reading or seeing, an auditory learner prefers hearing information. Tactile learners prefer a hands-on approach—touching or manipulating materials.

Most students are capable of learning in any of these ways. Even so, most people have a preferred style that makes learning easier for them. For example, one student may prefer to look at a map, whereas another may prefer to listen to directions for reaching the same destination; still another may find it helpful to actually draw the map or trace the route with a fingertip. Some students may be comfortable with any of these ways or prefer a combination of them.

Students who prefer **visual learning** learn best when they see or read material. They benefit from books, class notes, review cards, test review sheets, and the like. Students who prefer **auditory learning** learn best when they hear the material one or more times. They benefit from classes that feature lectures and discussions. They also benefit from reciting material, reading it aloud to themselves, and participating in study groups. Students who prefer **tactile learning** benefit from writing information down or manipulating materials physically. They learn best from laboratory work and other hands-on activities. The following chart summarizes this information on learning preferences. Once you have identified your preferred way of learning, you can choose course formats, classroom settings, and study techniques that let you use your preference to full advantage.

As noted, most students have a way of learning that they *prefer* to use. However, all students will find themselves in situations that require them to learn in other ways. For this reason, it is important to develop and practice a variety of study and learning skills.

In addition to knowing how you prefer to learn, you should think about whether you prefer to work by yourself or with others. If you study more effectively alone, you may need to take steps to protect your study time and your study space. If you find it helpful to study with others, find a serious study partner or form a study group with other motivated students. And remember that being part of a study group is not a substitute for reading and studying on your own. To benefit fully from a study group, every member must prepare by reading and studying alone first.

THREE LEARNING PREFERENCES

If This Is Your Learning Preference...	Then These Strategies Can Help You Learn
Visual (prefers to read or see information)	Reading textbooks and seeing information in print Seeing information on a computer screen, video monitor, or large classroom screen Reviewing class notes and concept maps Reading your chapter review cards Studying test review sheets
Auditory (prefers to hear information)	Listening to class lectures and discussions Reciting material (saying it out loud) Reading aloud to yourself Listening to audio tapes Participating in study groups
Tactile (prefers to write material down or to manipulate materials physically)	Taking notes from lectures and from your textbooks Making concept maps Rewriting lecture notes after class Preparing study cards Doing laboratory work (computer labs, science labs, etc.) Going through steps or procedures in a process Taking hands-on classes (science, computer science, engineering, and other technical or vocational subjects)

CHAPTER REVIEW CARDS

Review cards or *summary cards* are a way to select, organize, and summarize the important information in a textbook chapter. Preparing review cards helps you organize the information so that you can learn and memorize it more easily. In other words, chapter review cards are effective study tools.

Preparing chapter review cards for each chapter of *New Worlds* will give you practice in creating these valuable study tools. Once you have learned how to make chapter review cards, you can use actual index cards to create them for textbook material in your other courses and use them when you study for tests.

Now complete the chapter review cards for Chapter 1 by answering the questions or following the directions on each card. The page numbers indicate the place in the chapter where the information can be found. Write legibly. You will find it easier to complete the review cards if you remove these pages before filling them in.

The Reading Process

What is *reading*? (See page 5.)

What is *prior knowledge*? (See page 5.)

What is *previewing*? (See page 5.)

What do readers do when they *predict*? (See page 5.)

Card 1 Chapter 1: Introduction to Reading and Studying

Keys for Studying Textbook Material

What are *four keys* to studying textbook material? (See page 6.)

1.

2.

3.

4.

Card 2 Chapter 1: Introduction to Reading and Studying

Comprehension Monitoring

Define *comprehension monitoring.* (See page 7.)

Why is it important to monitor your comprehension? (See page 7.)

Card 3 Chapter 1: Introduction to Reading and Studying

SQ3R Study System

Describe each of the five steps in the SQ3R study system. (See page 9.)

Survey:

Question:

Read:

Recite:

Review:

Card 4 Chapter 1: Introduction to Reading and Studying

Flexible Reading Rates

1. List two reading rates appropriate to *information gathering*. Include the purpose and wpm for each. (See page 11.)

2. List three other reading rates, the number of words per minute (wpm), and the types of material each rate is appropriate for. (See page 11.)

Card 5 Chapter 1: Introduction to Reading and Studying

Copyright © 2014 The McGraw-Hill Companies, Inc. All rights reserved.

Doing What Successful Students Do

List the six characteristics of successful students. (See pages 12–13.)

1.

2.

3.

4.

5.

6.

Card 6 Chapter 1: Introduction to Reading and Studying

Setting Goals

List three reasons it is useful to set goals. (See page 14.)

1.

2.

3.

Card 7 Chapter 1: Introduction to Reading and Studying

Three Types of Goals

Describe these three types of goals: (See page 15.)

Short-term goals:

Intermediate goals:

Long-term goals:

Card 8 Chapter 1: Introduction to Reading and Studying

Three Learning Preferences

Define the three learning preferences and describe several helpful activities appropriate for each. (See pages 17–18.)

Visual preference:

Most helpful activities for learning:

Auditory preference:

Most helpful activities for learning:

Tactile preference:

Most helpful activities for learning:

Card 9 Chapter 1: Introduction to Reading and Studying

Copyright © 2014 The McGraw-Hill Companies, Inc. All rights reserved.

HOW TO FIND AND EVALUATE ONLINE INFORMATION

Using Boolean Searches

In the *New Worlds* reading selections, you are encouraged to learn more about the selections' topics online. You can do this either before you read, to enhance your background knowledge, or afterward, to learn additional information about the topic. Each reading selection contains a "Read More about It Online" feature that lists one or two websites to get you started, as well as keywords you can use when seeking more information online.

To find additional information, you can use one or more of the popular Internet encyclopedias and reference sites, such as Wikipedia.com, Yahoo Answers, About.com, Answers.com, eHow, and Reference.com. There are also countless online dictionaries of various sorts.

Internet encyclopedias and dictionaries may not always provide the specific information you need, however. In that case, you will want to do an Internet search. Search engines are designed to help do exactly that: easily locate the information you are seeking. They make it simple because you typically just type in keywords that describe what you want. Among the most popular search engines in the United States are Google, Bing, Yahoo Search, Ask, AOL, and MyWebSearch. Be sure you understand the basis on which the search engine lists the sites. The first entry is not necessarily the best, and is not necessarily the best for what you need.

If using a search engine does not bring up useful results, conducting a Boolean (pronounced BOO-lee-un) search can be the answer. A Boolean search lets you target your search and more quickly locate the information you need. (In fact, most search engines are set up to do a Boolean search using the word AND.) According to About.com, with a **Boolean search,** you "combine words and phrases using the words AND, OR, NOT and NEAR (otherwise known as Boolean operators) to limit, widen, or define your search." The article continues, "Most Internet search engines and Web directories default to these Boolean search parameters anyway, but a good Web searcher should know how to use basic Boolean operators" (http://websearch.about.com/od/2/g/boolean.htm; accessed 22 March 2012).

For an excellent tutorial on how to conduct a Boolean search, go to Internet Tutorials at **www.internettutorials.net**. The website is maintained by Laura B. Cohen, a former academic librarian at the University at Albany, SUNY. Start with "Boolean Searching on the Internet: A Primer in Boolean Logic" (**www.internettutorials.net/boolean.asp**). After you have read it, click on Basic Search Techniques (**www.internettutorials.net/basic-search-techniques.asp**). You can actually try the searches as you go!

In writing and English classes, instructors tell students to "narrow your topic." In other words, they are telling you that before you can begin gathering information, you must narrow the subject to a manageable aspect of a more general topic. For instance, an overly broad topic such as "voter turnout in U.S. presidential elections" would be unmanageable. However, a more precise topic, such as "voter turnout among 18- to 20-year-olds in the 2008 and 2012 presidential elections" would be manageable. Knowing how to conduct Boolean searches can save time and frustration when you need to pinpoint specific information online.

Evaluating Internet Sources

Whenever you gather information from a website, especially if you are doing research, it is a good idea to evaluate the website and the information it contains. For example, you should ask yourself questions such as:

- Who sponsors this website?
- Is the information at this website current (up-to-date)?
- Is the website trustworthy?

Robert Harris, PhD, describes himself as "a writer and educator with more than 25 years of teaching experience at the college and university level. He has written on the use of computers and software in language and literature study, using the Web as a research tool, the prevention of plagiarism, creative problem solving, and rhetoric." At his website, VirtualSalt.com, you can read his clear, complete explanation of how to evaluate Internet research resources. He uses the memory peg "CARS" for his evaluation checklist: credibility, accuracy, reasonableness, and support. This chart from his website summarizes the checklist:

Credibility	trustworthy source, author's credentials, evidence of quality control, known or respected authority, organizational support. Goal: an authoritative source, a source that supplies some good evidence that allows you to trust it.
Accuracy	up to date, factual, detailed, exact, comprehensive, audience and purpose reflect intentions of completeness and accuracy. Goal: a source that is correct today (not yesterday), a source that gives the whole truth.
Reasonableness	fair, balanced, objective, reasoned, no conflict of interest, absence of fallacies or slanted tone. Goal: a source that engages the subject thoughtfully and reasonably, concerned with the truth.
Support	listed sources, contact information, available corroboration, claims supported, documentation supplied. Goal: a source that provides convincing evidence for the claims made, a source you can triangulate (find at least two other sources that support it).

Robert Harris, "Evaluating Internet Research Sources," *Virtual Salt*, November 22, 2012. Web, April 2, 2011, www.virtualsalt.com/evalu8it.htm.

Evaluate Internet sources carefully. As Dr. Harris points out, information is power—but only if the information is *reliable*.

SELECTION **1.1**

Nonfiction

A Mother's Answer

From *The Big Picture: Getting Perspective on What's Really Important*

By Ben Carson with Gregg Lewis

Ben Carson is the director of pediatric neurosurgery at the Johns Hopkins Hospital in Baltimore, Maryland. At Hopkins, where he received his training in neurosurgery, this handsome, calm, soft-spoken man with the "gifted hands" was only 33 when he was appointed the director of his department, the youngest person in the United States to be appointed to such a position. He is internationally known for his success in the intricate, delicate surgeries for separating conjoined twins who are born joined at the head and for hemispherectomies, removing one side of the brain to treat those with extreme seizure disorders.

Carson also specializes in giving young people an inspirational boost. Despite his demanding schedule, he goes out of his way to address groups of schoolchildren. In 1994 Carson and his wife, who have three sons of their own, established the Carson Scholars Fund. By 2012 it had awarded 5,200 college scholarships totaling more than $2 million.

When Carson was a child, no one ever would have predicted that he would become a world-famous brain surgeon. He grew up in an inner city in extreme poverty, came from a broken home, and had a hot, hair-trigger temper. By the middle of fifth grade, he was failing every subject. What changed his life and started him on a path that eventually led to a scholarship to Yale University and then on to the University of Michigan School of Medicine?

Looking back at his childhood, Carson says, "My poor mother was mortified. Here she was with a third-grade education, working two or three jobs as a domestic, cleaning other people's houses, knowing that life didn't hold much for her, and seeing my brother and me going down the same road. She didn't know what to do, so she prayed and asked God to give her wisdom. What could she do to get her two young sons to understand the importance of education so that they could determine their own destiny?" In the selection below, Carson tells about the answer his mother found that helped him and his brother—and ultimately changed his life forever.

1 God gave her the wisdom—though my brother and I didn't think it was all that wise. It was to turn off the television. From that point on she would let us watch our choice of only two or three television programs during the week. With all that spare time, we were to read two books a week from the Detroit Public Library.

2 I was extraordinarily unhappy about this new arrangement. All my friends were outside, having a good time. I remember my mother's friends coming to her and saying, "You can't keep boys in the house reading. Boys are supposed to be outside playing and developing their muscles. When they grow up, they'll hate you. They will be sissies. You can't do that!"

3 Sometimes I would overhear this and I would say, "Listen to them, Mother." But she would never listen. We were going to have to read those books.

4 Sometimes, when I tell this story, people come up to me afterwards and ask, "How was your mother able to get you to read those books? I can't get my kids to read or even turn off the television or Nintendo."

5 I just have to chuckle and say, "Well, back in those days, the parents ran the house. They didn't have to get permission from

Prediction Exercises

Directions: Use the skill of predicting to anticipate what certain paragraphs will be about. At each of the points indicated below, answer the question "What do you predict will happen next?"

Prediction Exercise

What do you predict will happen next?

____

____

____

____

Copyright © 2014 The McGraw-Hill Companies, Inc. All rights reserved.

the kids." That seems to be a novel concept to a lot of people these days.

6 At any rate, I started reading. The nice thing was my mother did not dictate what we had to read. I loved animals, so I read every animal book in the Detroit Public Library. And when I finished those, I went on to plants. When I finished those, I went on to rocks because we lived in a dilapidated section of the city near the railroad tracks. And what is there along railroad tracks, but rocks? I would collect little boxes of rocks and take them home and get out my geology book. I would study until I could name virtually every rock, tell how it was formed, and identify where it came from.

7 Months passed. I was still in fifth grade. Still the dummy in the class. Nobody knew about my reading project.

Prediction Exercise

What do you predict will happen next?

____

____

____

____

8 One day the fifth grade science teacher walked in and held up a big, shiny black rock. He asked, "Can anybody tell me what this is?"

9 Keep in mind that I never raised my hand. I never answered questions. So I waited for some of the smart kids to raise their hands. None of them did. So I waited for some of the dumb kids to raise their hands. When none of them did, I thought, *This is my big chance*. So I raised my hand . . . and everyone turned around to look. Some of my classmates were poking each other and whispering, "Look, look, Carson's got his hand up. This is gonna be good!"

10 They couldn't wait to see what was going to happen. And the teacher was shocked. He said, "Benjamin?"

11 I said, "Mr. Jaeck, that's obsidian." And there was silence in the room because it sounded good, but no one knew whether it was right or wrong. So the other kids didn't know if they should laugh or be impressed.

12 Finally the teacher broke the silence and said, "That's right! This is obsidian."

13 I went on to explain, "Obsidian is formed after a volcanic eruption. Lava flows down and when it hits water there is a super-cooling process. The elements coalesce, air is forced out, the surface glazes over, and . . ."

14 I suddenly realized everyone was staring at me in amazement. They couldn't believe all this geological information spewing from the mouth of a dummy. But you know, I was perhaps the most amazed person in the room, because it dawned on me in that moment that I was no dummy.

Prediction Exercise

What do you predict will happen next?

____

____

____

____

15 I thought, *Carson, the reason you knew the answer is because you were reading those books. What if you read books about all your subjects—science, math, history, geography, social studies? Couldn't you then know more than all these students who tease you and call you a dummy?* I must admit the idea appealed to me—to the extent that no book was safe from my grasp. I read everything I could get my hands on. If I had five minutes, I had a book. If I was in the bathroom, I was reading a book. If I was waiting for the bus, I was reading a book.

16 Within a year and a half, I went from the bottom of the class to the top of the class—much to the consternation of all those students who used to tease me and call me Dummy. The same ones would come to me in seventh grade to ask, "Hey, Benny,

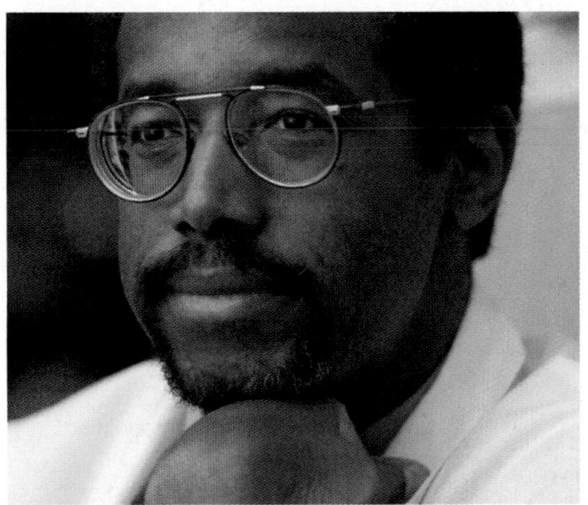

Dr. Benjamin Carson has been director of the division of pediatric neurosurgery at Johns Hopkins since 1984. He is a professor of neurosurgery, plastic surgery, oncology, and pediatrics. He is also the co-director of the Johns Hopkins Craniofacial Center. His practice includes traumatic brain injuries, brain and spinal cord tumors, achondroplasia, neurological and congenital disorders, craniosynostosis, epilepsy, and trigeminal neuralgia. This work includes active research programs.

Dr. Carson has written more than 100 neurosurgical publications. He has been awarded 40 honorary degrees and dozens of national citations of merit. He is the author of several best-selling books, *Gifted Hands, Think Big, The Big Picture, Take the Risk, and America the Beautiful: Rediscovering What Made This Nation Great* (with his wife, Candy).

On June 19, 2008, the White House awarded Dr. Carson the Presidential Medal of Freedom, the nation's highest civilian award. It was awarded for his groundbreaking contributions to medicine and his efforts to inspire and help young people achieve their dreams.

how do you work this problem?" And I would say, "Sit at my feet, youngster, while I instruct you."

17 I was perhaps a little bit obnoxious. But after all those years it felt so good to say that to those who had tormented me.

18 The important point here is that I had the same brain when I was still at the bottom of the class as I had when I reached the top of the class.

19 The difference was this: In the fifth grade, I thought I was dumb so I acted like I was dumb, and I achieved like a dumb person. As a seventh grader I thought I was smart, so I acted and achieved accordingly. So what does that say about what a person thinks about his own abilities? What does this say about the importance of our self-image? What does it say about the incredible potential of the human brain our Creator has given us?

Source: The big picture: getting perspective on what's really important in life by CARSON, BEN; LEWIS, GREGG. Copyright 1999. Reproduced with permission of ZONDERVAN PUBLISHING HOUSE in the format. Textbook via Copyright Clearance Center.

SELECTION 1.1
Nonfiction
(continued)

Comprehension and Vocabulary Quiz

This quiz has four parts. Your instructor may assign some or all of them.

Comprehension

Directions: Items 1–5 test your understanding of the selection. They are the types of questions a content-area instructor (such as a literature professor) might ask on a test. You may refer to the selection as you answer the questions. Write your answer choice in the space provided.

1. The type of rock Ben identified was:
- *a.* lava.
- *b.* obsidian.
- *c.* opal.
- *d.* onyx.

2. Mr. Jaeck's reaction to Ben raising his hand was:
- *a.* joy.
- *b.* anger.
- *c.* shock.
- *d.* disappointment.

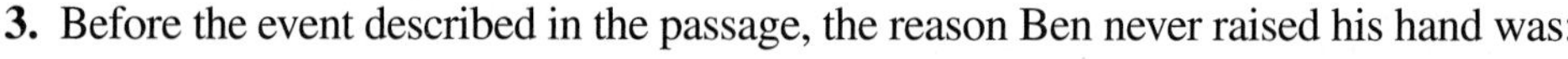

3. Before the event described in the passage, the reason Ben never raised his hand was:
- *a.* he didn't want to show off.
- *b.* he didn't want to embarrass those who didn't know the answer.
- *c.* he was waiting for his big chance.
- *d.* he didn't know the answer.

4. As an adult, Ben Carson probably believes that:
- *a.* parents should set the rules.
- *b.* children should set the rules.
- *c.* parents and children should set the rules together.
- *d.* there should be no rules.

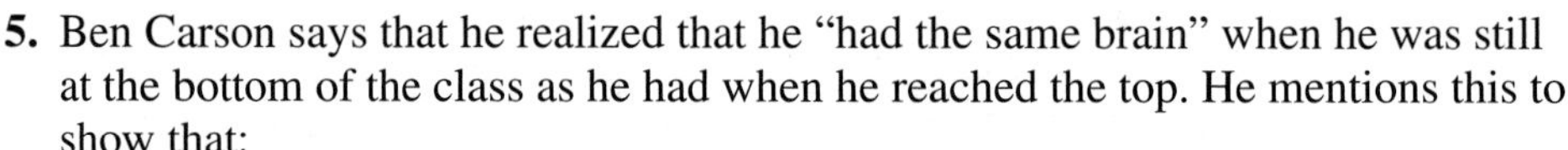

5. Ben Carson says that he realized that he "had the same brain" when he was still at the bottom of the class as he had when he reached the top. He mentions this to show that:
- *a.* he did not expect his brain ever to change in any way.
- *b.* although he was intelligent, his perception of himself had caused him to act as if he were a "dummy."
- *c.* he did not have high enough expectations for himself when he was at the top of the class.
- *d.* more research needs to be done on the human brain.

Vocabulary in Context

Directions: Items 6–10 test your ability to determine a word's meaning by using context clues. *Context clues* are words in a sentence that allow readers to deduce (reason out) the meaning of an unfamiliar word. They also help readers determine the meaning an author intends when a word has more than one meaning. Each item below consists of a sentence from the selection, with the vocabulary word *italicized*. It is followed by another sentence that uses the same word in the same way. Use context clues to deduce the meaning of the *italicized* word. Be sure the meaning you choose makes sense in *both* sentences. Write each answer in the space provided. (Chapter 2 presents the skill of using context clues.)

______ **6.** The nice thing was my mother did not *dictate* what we had to read.

Our company's dress code prohibits nose rings, brow rings, and other facial "jewelry," but otherwise does not *dictate* what we may wear at work.

dictate (dĭk′ tāt) means:

a. like
b. say as an order or command
c. say aloud in order to be written down
d. understand

______ **7.** When I finished those, I went on to rocks because we lived in a *dilapidated* section of the city near the railroad tracks.

The city refurbished the *dilapidated* Civil War mansion and turned it into a museum.

dilapidated (dĭ lăp′ ĭ dāt əd) means:

a. shabby; rundown
b. historic
c. fashionable; up-to-date
d. dangerous

______ **8.** The elements *coalesce,* air is forced out, the surface glazes over, and . . .

Scientists believe that planets may form because great heat and pressure cause particles to *coalesce.*

coalesce (kō ə lĕs′) means:

a. disintegrate; dissolve
b. disappear
c. fly apart
d. fuse; unite

______ **9.** They couldn't believe all this geological information *spewing* from the mouth of a dummy.

My car's radiator hose broke, *spewing* hot water everywhere.

spewing (spyo͞o′ĭng) means:

a. gushing forth; streaming out
b. sending
c. trickling; dribbling
d. gathering

Copyright © 2014 The McGraw-Hill Companies, Inc. All rights reserved.

_______ **10.** Within a year and a half, I went from the bottom of the class to the top of the class—much to the *consternation* of all those students who used to tease me and call me Dummy.

My brother's tattoos caused my conservative parents great *consternation.*

consternation (kŏn stər nā′ shən) means:

a. joy; happiness

b. relief

c. dismay; upset

d. pride

Word Structure

Directions: Items 11–15 test your ability to use word-structure clues to help determine a word's meaning. *Word-structure clues* consist of roots, prefixes, and suffixes. In this exercise, you will learn the meaning of a root and use it to determine the meaning of several words that contain it. If you need to use a dictionary to confirm your answer choice, do so. Write your answers in the spaces provided.

In paragraph 6 of the selection, you encountered the word **dictate.** It contains the root ***dict***, which means "to say" or "to tell." The word *dictate* has many meanings, including "to *say* aloud information that is to be written down," and "to *tell* as an order or command." Use the meaning of ***dict*** and the list of prefixes on pages 72–73 to determine the meaning of the following words.

_______ **11.** **Predictable** means:

a. able to explain what has happened.

b. preventable; avoidable.

c. able to say or tell ahead of time.

d. not able to know in advance.

_______ **12.** When one person **contradicts** another, it means that person is:

a. speaking with anger.

b. saying something with impatience.

c. speaking in defense of the other person.

d. saying the opposite of what the other person has said.

_______ **13.** Speech teachers help students with their **diction,** which means:

a. the quality of their speaking.

b. stuttering.

c. proper breathing.

d. the ability to carry on a conversation.

_______ **14.** A **dictator** is one who:

a. says the opposite of what others say.

b. says what others want to hear.

c. tells others what to do or say.

d. tells interesting stories.

_______ **15.** A religious **edict** is a:

a. ceremony; ritual.
b. document that tells or proclaims a new law.
c. follower of a religion; believer.
d. place of worship.

Reading Skills Application

Directions: Items 16–20 test your ability to *apply* certain reading skills. You may not be familiar with all the skills yet, so some items will serve as a preview. As you work through *New Worlds,* you will practice and develop these skills. These are important skills, which is why they are included on the state-mandated basic skills tests that some students must take. Write each answer in the space provided.

_______ **16.** What is the authors' primary purpose for writing this selection?

a. to prove that self-image affects whether a person uses his or her potential
b. to explain the important role reading can play in a person's life
c. to pay tribute to a mother's wisdom
d. to show that students can be wrong about a classmate they view as a "dummy"

_______ **17.** Which of the following is the meaning of the word *novel* as it is used in paragraph 5?

a. frightening
b. unpleasant
c. familiar
d. new

_______ **18.** Which pattern has been used to organize the information in paragraph 15 of the selection?

a. comparison-contrast
b. cause and effect
c. sequence
d. list

_______ **19.** Which of the following statements best expresses the main idea of paragraph 16?

a. Within a year and a half, I went from the bottom of the class to the top of the class—much to the consternation of all the students who used to tease me and call me Dummy.
b. The same ones would come to me in the seventh grade to ask, "Hey, Benny, how do you work this problem?"
c. And I would say, "Sit at my feet, youngster, while I instruct you."
d. Other students teased Ben and called him Dummy.

_______ **20.** Based on the information in the selection, the authors would most likely agree with which of the following statements?

a. Even slow learners can be successful.
b. Being a good reader is the one key to success.
c. Believing in yourself can be the key to success.
d. A person's mother is the key to his or her success.

Copyright © 2014 The McGraw-Hill Companies, Inc. All rights reserved.

SELECTION 1.1

Nonfiction

(continued)

Respond in Writing

Directions: Refer to the selection as needed to answer the essay-type questions below. (Your instructor may direct you to work collaboratively with other students on one or more items. Each group member should be able to explain *all* of the group's answers.)

1. **Reacting to What You Have Read:** Think of an experience in school—good or bad—that made you see yourself differently as a student. Describe the experience and explain how it changed the way you perceived yourself.

2. **Comprehending the Selection Further:** Even though she herself could not read, Ben Carson's mother required her young sons to read two books each week and write book reports. She pretended to read them and then put check marks on them. Based on her actions, what conclusions can you draw about the importance she placed on reading?

3. **Overall Main Idea of the Selection:** In one sentence, tell what the authors want readers to understand about how seeing himself differently as a learner affected Ben Carson's success as a student. (Be sure to include Ben Carson's name in your overall main idea sentence.)

Internet Resources

Read More about It Online

Directions: Read more about the topic of this selection online. You can read online *before* you read the selection to build background knowledge or *afterward* to extend your knowledge. Start with the websites below, or type **"Dr. Ben Carson"** in the search box of Google, Yahoo, or another search engine. When you visit any unfamiliar website, it is important to evaluate it and the information it contains. If you do not know how to conduct Internet searches or evaluate a website, see pages 24–25.

www.carsonscholars.org
This website includes information about Ben Carson, his Carson Scholars Foundation, and information about the many books he has written. (Go to amazon.com to read more about his books.)

www.tntdrama.com/stories/?oid=44656
The TNT website presents information about the made-for-television movie *Gifted Hands*. The story of Ben Carson's remarkable life, it stars Cuba Gooding, Jr. The website also contains a photo gallery and information about Dr. Carson.

SELECTION **1.2**

Student Success

Fire Up Your Memory with Proven Strategies

From *Peak Performance in College and Beyond*

By Sharon Ferrett

You may have heard people say, "I just don't have a good memory." Do you have a good memory? Do you think some people are simply born with better memories? In reality, memory is a process. As a complex process, memory is not an isolated activity that takes place in one part of the brain. It involves many factors that you can control. How well you remember depends on factors such as your attitude, interest, intent, awareness, mental alertness, observation skills, senses, distractions, memory devices, and willingness to practice. Most people with good memories say that the skill is mastered by learning and continually practicing the strategies for storing and recalling information.

The following selection may look lengthy, but it is clearly written and contains valuable information. It presents valuable strategies that can help you remember information. Keep in mind that the first step of remembering is consciously intending to remember. You must be willing to remember information and be interested in remembering it.

Memory Strategies

1 **1. Write it down.** Writing is physical and enhances learning. When you write information, you are reinforcing learning by using your eyes, hand, fingers, and arm. Writing uses different parts of the brain than do speaking and listening.

- Writing down a telephone number helps you remember it by providing a mental picture.
- Planning your time in a day planner and creating a to-do list can trigger accomplishing tasks later in the day when you may have become overwhelmed with distractions.
- Taking notes in class prompts you to be logical and concise and fills in memory gaps.
- Underlining important information and then copying it onto note cards reinforces information.
- Writing a summary in your own words after reading a chapter helps transfer information to long-term memory.

2 **2. Go from the general to the specific.** Many people learn and remember best by looking at the big picture and then learning the details. Try to outline from the general (main topic) to the specific (subtopics). Previewing a chapter gives you an overview and makes the topic more meaningful. Your brain is more receptive to details when it has a general idea of the main topic. Read, listen, and look for general understanding; then add details.

3 **3. Reduce information.** You don't have to memorize certain types of information, such as deadlines, telephone messages, and assignment due dates. You just have to know where to find this information. Write deadlines and important information in your organizer or student planner or on a calendar, not on slips of paper, which can get lost. You

Prediction Exercises

Directions: Use the skill of predicting to anticipate what the upcoming paragraphs will be about.

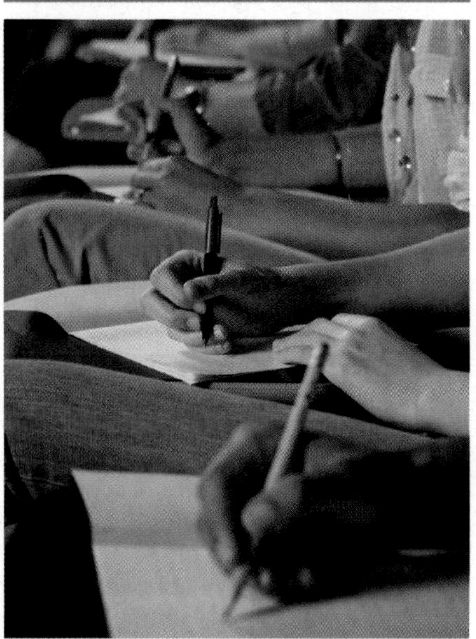

Prediction Exercise

What do you predict paragraph 2 will be about?

____

____

can refer to any of this written information again if you need it.

4 4. **Eliminate distractions.** Distractions keep you from paying attention and remembering what you're trying to learn. One way to avoid distractions is to study in an uncluttered, quiet area, such as a library or designated study room. If it is noisy in class, ask the instructor to repeat information, or move closer to the front. The more effectively you focus your attention, the better you will create associations and recall information.

Prediction Exercise

What do you predict paragraph 4 will be about?

____

____

5 5. **Study in short sessions.** You will use the power of concentration more fully, and the brain retains information better, in short study sessions. After about 40 minutes, the brain needs a break to process information effectively. Break large goals into specific objectives and study in short sessions. For example, if you are taking a marketing course, preview a chapter in your textbook for 20 minutes and mind map the chapter for 20 minutes. Then take a 10-minutebreak. Stretch, drink a glass of water, or treat yourself to a small snack. Then return to complete your goal.

6 6. **Use all your senses.** Memory is sensory, so using all your senses (sight, hearing, touch, smell, and taste) will give your brain a better chance of retaining information.

- *Visualize.* Since much of what you learn and remember reaches you through sight, it is important to visualize what you want to remember. The art of retention is the art of attention. Be a keen observer of details and notice differences and similarities. Suppose you are taking a medical terminology or a vocabulary-building course. You may want to look at pictures and visualize images with the new terms or words. Look at illustrations, pictures, and information on the board.
- *Listen.* You cannot remember a name or information in class if you are not attentive and listening. Actively listen in class, record lectures (ask for the instructor's permission), and play them back later. Recite definitions and information aloud.
- *Move.* Whether you learn best by reading or listening, you will retain information better if you use all your senses and make learning physical. Read aloud; read while standing; jot down notes; lecture in front of the classroom to yourself or your study team; draw pictures, diagrams, and models; and join a study group. Practice reciting information while doing physical activity, such as showering or jogging. The more you use all your senses, the more information you will retain.

Prediction Exercise

What do you predict the bulleted points in paragraph 6 will be about?

____

____

____

7 7. **Use mnemonic devices.** Mnemonic (neh-MON-nik) devices are memory tricks that help you remember information. However, mnemonic devices have limits. Developing a memory trick takes time, and the trick will be hard to remember if it is too complicated. Since mnemonic devices don't help you understand the information or develop skills in critical thinking, they are best used for sheer rote

memorization. Follow up by looking for associations, making connections, and writing summaries. Some mnemonic devices are

- *Rhymes and rhythms.* In elementary school, you might have learned the rhyme "In 1492 Columbus sailed the ocean blue" to remember the date of Columbus's voyage. Rhythms can also be helpful. Many people have learned to spell the word Mississippi by accenting all the *i*'s and making the word rhythmic. This is similar to the technique used in rap music and poetry, in which syllables are accentuated on an established beat.
- *Acronyms.* **Acronyms** are words formed from the first letters of a series of other words, such as HOMES for the Great Lakes (Huron, Ontario, Michigan, Erie, and Superior) and EPCOT (Experimental Prototype Community of Tomorrow).
- *Acrostics.* **Acrostics** are similar to acronyms, but they are made-up sentences in which the first letter stands for something, such as Every Good Boy Deserves Fun for remembering the sequence of musical notes: E, G, B, D, F. Another is My Very Easy Memory Jingle Seems Useful Now, which helps you remember the order of the planets from the sun (assuming you know that the first planet is Mercury and not Mars and that Pluto is no longer considered a planet, can you name the rest with the help of the acrostic?) Acrostics are often used in poetry, in which the first letter of every line combines to spell something, such as the poem's title.
- *Association.* Suppose you are learning about explorer Christopher Columbus's three ships. Think of three friends whose names start with the same first letters as the ships' names: *Pinta, Santa Maria,* and *Niña* (e.g., Paul, Sandy, and Nancy). Vividly associate your friends' names with the three ships, and you should be able to recall the ships' names. Using associations can also be helpful in remembering numbers. For example, if your ATM identification number is 9072, you might remember it by creating associations with dates. Maybe 1990 is the year you graduated from high school and 1972 is the year you were born.
- *Chunking.* **Chunking**, or grouping, long lists of information or numbers can break up the memory task and make it easier for you. Most people can remember up to seven numbers in a row, which is why phone numbers are that length.
- *Stacking technique.* Visualize objects that represent points, and stack them on top of each other. For example, if you were giving a speech on time management, you would start with a clock with a big pencil on it to represent how much time is saved, if you write information down. On top of the clock is a big calendar, which reminds you to make the point that you must set priorities in writing. On the calendar is a Time Log with

the name Drucker on it. This will remind you to present a quote by business writer and management consultant Peter Drucker that you must know where your time goes if you are to be effective in managing your life. You stack an object to remind you of each of the key points in the speech.

- *Method-of-place technique.* As far back as 500 BC, the Greeks were using a method of imagery called loci—the method-of-place technique. (*Loci* is Latin for "place.") This method, which is similar to the stacking technique, is still effective because it uses imagery and association to aid memory. Memorize a setting in detail and then place the item or information you want to remember at certain places on your memory map. Some people like to use a familiar street, their home, or their car as a map on which to place their information. Memorize certain places on your map and the specific order or path in which you visit each place. Once you have memorized this map, you can position various items to remember at different points.

8 8. **Use note cards.** On note cards, the information is condensed and written, so the act of writing is kinesthetic and holding cards is tactile. Note cards are visual and, when the information is recited out loud or in a group, the auditory element enhances learning. Note cards are a great way to organize information and highlight key words:

- Use index cards for recording information you want to memorize. Write brief summaries and indicate the main points of each chapter on the backs of note cards.
- Carry the cards with you and review them during waiting time, before going to sleep at night, or any other time you have a few minutes to spare.
- Organize the cards according to category, color, size, order, weight, and other areas.

9 9. **Recite.** Recite and repeat information, such as a name, poem, date, or formula. When you say information aloud, you use your throat, voice, and lips, and you hear yourself recite. This recitation technique may help when you are dealing with difficult reading material. Reading aloud and hearing the material will reinforce it and help move information from your short-term memory to your long-term memory. Use the new words in your own conversations. Write summaries in your own words and read to others. Study groups are effective because you can hear each other, clarify questions, and increase understanding as you review information. To remember names, when you meet someone, recite the person's name several times to yourself and out loud.

10 10. **Practice, practice, practice!** You must practice information you want to remember. For example, when you first start driver training, you learn the various steps involved in driving. At first, they may seem overwhelming. You may have to stop and think through each step. After you have driven a car for a while, however, you don't even think

Prediction Exercise

What do you predict the bulleted points in paragraph 8 will be about?

___

___

___

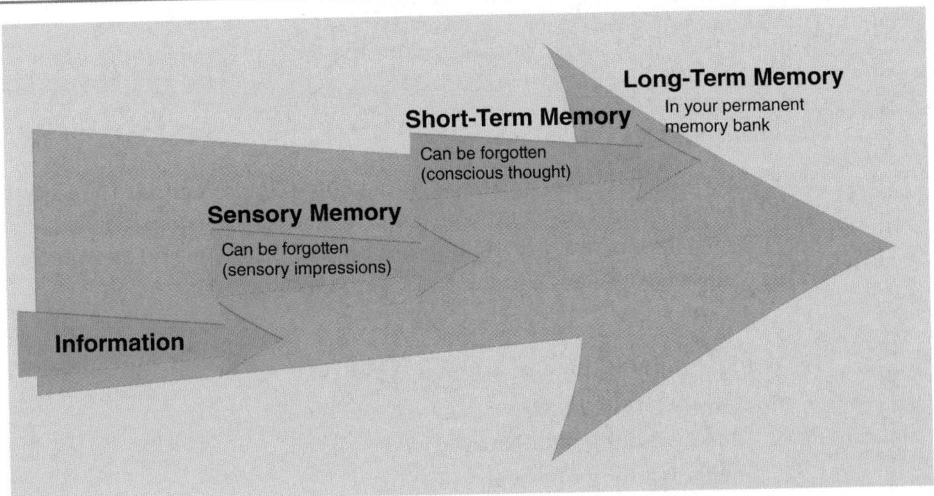

SELECTION 1.2

about all the steps required to start it and back out of the driveway. You check your mirror automatically before changing lanes, and driving safely has become a habit. Through repetition, you put information into your long-term memory. The more often you use the information, the easier it is to recall. You could not become a good musician without hours of practice. Playing sports, speaking in public, flying an airplane, and learning to drive all require skills that need to be repeated and practiced many times. Repetition puts information into long-term memory and allows for recall.

11 These strategies are very effective in strengthening your memory skills. Certain strategies might work better for you than others, depending on your personality and learning styles. Everyone has personal strengths and abilities. You can master the use of memory strategies with effort, patience, and practice. As you build your memory skills, you will also enhance your study habits and become more disciplined and aware of your surroundings.

Prediction Exercise

What do you predict paragraph 11 will be about?

____

____

Source: Sharon Ferrett, *Peak Performance: Success in College and Beyond,* 8th ed., pp. 222, 224–28, 230–31. Copyright © 2012 by The McGraw-Hill Companies, Inc.

Copyright © 2014 The McGraw-Hill Companies, Inc. All rights reserved.

SELECTION 1.2
Student Success
(continued)

Comprehension and Vocabulary Quiz

This quiz has four parts. Your instructor may assign some or all of them.

Comprehension

Directions: Items 1–5 test your understanding of the selection. They are the types of questions a content-area instructor (such as a study skills or student success professor) might ask on a test. You may refer to the selection as you answer the questions. Write your answer choice in the space provided.

_____ **1.** Memorizing information is easier if you:
a. make learning visual.
b. make learning auditory.
c. make learning physical.
d. all of the above

_____ **2.** An auditory learner could memorize information more easily by:
a. writing key words and definitions on note cards.
b. talking aloud when studying.
c. going on field trips.
d. drawing diagrams and models.

_____ **3.** After about an hour of studying, the brain needs:
a. time to process information.
b. to be creative.
c. a healthy snack.
d. reinforcement from a study group.

_____ **4.** Using "ROY G. BIV" to represent the colors of the rainbow (red, orange, yellow, green, blue, indigo, violet) is an example of the mnemonic device known as:
a. an acronym.
b. grouping.
c. association.
d. imagery.

_____ **5.** Previewing a chapter is helpful because it:
a. reduces your anxiety.
b. decreases the amount of information you must learn.
c. gives you a general overview before you read the specific details.
d. helps you stay awake when you actually read the chapter.

Vocabulary in Context

Directions: Items 6–10 test your ability to determine a word's meaning by using context clues. *Context clues* are words in a sentence that allow readers to deduce (reason out) the meaning of an unfamiliar word. They also help readers determine the meaning an author intends when a word has more than one meaning. Each item below consists of a sentence from the selection, with the vocabulary word *italicized*. It is followed by another sentence that uses the same word in the same way. Use context clues to deduce the meaning of the *italicized* word. Be sure the meaning you choose makes sense in *both* sentences. Write each answer in the space provided. (Chapter 2 presents the skill of using context clues.)

______ **6.** Taking notes in class *prompts* you to be logical and concise and fills in memory gaps.

A health scare usually *prompts* people to take better care of themselves.

prompts (prŏmpts) means:

a. prevents

b. hurries

c. moves to action

d. enables

______ **7.** Taking notes in class prompts you to be logical and *concise* and fills in memory gaps.

TV Guide gives *concise* thumbnail descriptions of shows and movies.

concise (kən sīs′) means:

a. informative

b. succinct

c. useful

d. attentive

______ **8.** Your brain is more *receptive* to details when it has a general idea of the main topic.

The committee was not the least bit *receptive* to my suggestion; they didn't even consider it.

receptive (rĭ sĕp′ tĭv) means:

a. ready or willing to receive

b. interested

c. hostile

d. able to understand

______ **9.** This is similar to the technique used in rap music and poetry, in which syllables are *accentuated* on an established beat.

Sherée *accentuated* the second syllable of her name when she introduced herself.

accentuated (ăk sĕn′ cho͞o āt′ əd) means:

a. spelled out

b. sung loudly

c. repeated

d. pronounced with a stress

_______ **10.** Since mnemonic devices don't help you understand the information or develop skills in critical thinking, they are best used for sheer *rote memorization.*

Because I did not understand the quadratic formula, I learned it by *rote memorization.*

rote memorization (rōt mĕm ə rə zā´ shən) means:

a. a memorizing process using physical movement
b. a memorizing process using repetition, often without full comprehension
c. a memorizing process using rhymes and rhythms
d. a memorizing process using visual cues

Word Structure

Directions: Items 11–15 test your ability to use word-structure clues to help determine a word's meaning. *Word-structure clues* consist of roots, prefixes, and suffixes. In these exercises, you will learn the meaning of a word part (a root) and use it to determine the meaning of several other words that have the same word part. If you need to use a dictionary to confirm your answer choice, do so. Write your answers in the spaces provided.

In paragraph 6, bullet 1, of the selection, you encountered the word **visualize.** This word contains the Latin root ***vis***, which means "to see." The word *visualize* means to *see* something in your mind. Use the meaning of the root ***vis*** and the list of prefixes on pages 72–73 to determine the meaning of the following words.

_______ **11.** If you **revise** a paper you are writing, you:

a. look for a different topic to write about.
b. look at it again to see if you need to make corrections or changes.
c. retype it.
d. start over on it.

_______ **12.** **Provisions** for a camping trip consist of:

a. things you see while camping.
b. food and other items you foresee that you will need.
c. the plans you make.
d. the route you plan to drive to get there.

_______ **13.** In the business world, Bill Gates was considered **visionary** because he:

a. told fantasy stories.
b. saw things all wrong.
c. prescribed glasses.
d. foresaw what would be important in the future.

_______ **14.** A **visionless** person:

a. has no imagination.
b. has no glasses.
c. has no sight.
d. wears glasses.

_______ **15.** A bride who is a vision of loveliness is:

a. one that exists only in the imagination.

b. a beautiful sight.

c. one who has foresight.

d. given in marriage by her father.

Reading Skills Application

Directions: Items 16–20 test your ability to *apply* certain reading skills. You may not be familiar with all the skills yet, so some items will serve as a preview. As you work through *New Worlds,* you will practice and develop these skills. These are important skills, which is why they are included on the state-mandated basic skills tests that some students must take. Write each answer in the space provided.

_______ **16.** The overall organization of the selection is a:

a. comparison.

b. sequence.

c. list.

d. contrast.

_______ **17.** According to information in the selection, the method-of-place technique:

a. uses recitation.

b. has been used for centuries.

c. is based on rhymes.

d. involves grouping.

_______ **18.** Does the following sentence represent a fact or an opinion? "These strategies are very effective in strengthening your memory skills."

a. fact

b. opinion

_______ **19.** The author would be most likely to agree with which of the following statements?

a. Mnemonics should be used all the time.

b. Mnemonics are foolproof.

c. Mnemonics are useful, but they have limitations.

d. Mnemonics are difficult to learn.

_______ **20.** Which of the following sentences represents the main idea of paragraph 10?

a. You must practice information that you want to remember.

b. For example, when you first start driver training, you learn the various steps involved in driving.

c. You may have to stop and think through each step.

d. Playing sports, public speaking, flying an airplane, and learning to drive all require skills that need to be repeated and practiced many times.

Copyright © 2014 The McGraw-Hill Companies, Inc. All rights reserved.

SELECTION 1.2 **Student Success** *(continued)*

Respond in Writing

Directions: Refer to the selection as needed to answer the essay-type questions below. (Your instructor may direct you to work collaboratively with other students on one or more items. Each group member should be able to explain *all* of the group's answers.)

1. **Reacting to What You Have Read:** Of the memory strategies mentioned in the selection, which ones do you already use? Describe the courses and/or ways in which you use them. (If you do not use any of the techniques mentioned in the selection, describe the techniques that you use instead.)

___

___

___

___

___

___

___

2. **Comprehending the Selection Further:** Based on information in the selection about learning preferences and memory techniques, check which techniques might work best for each style. For each strategy, place a check mark in the appropriate column. Some strategies may work for more than one type of learner.

	Visual	**Auditory**	**Hands-on**
1. Recite definitions.	_______	_______	_______
2. Draw pictures and illustrations.	_______	_______	_______
3. Read the textbook silently.	_______	_______	_______
4. Write out key terms and important information.	_______	_______	_______
5. Listen to tapes of class lectures.	_______	_______	_______
6. Participate in study groups.	_______	_______	_______
7. Watch a video.	_______	_______	_______
8. Actively listen in class.	_______	_______	_______
9. Build a model.	_______	_______	_______
10. Read the textbook aloud.	_______	_______	_______

3. **Overall Main Idea of the Selection:** In one sentence, tell what the author wants readers to understand about memory. (Be sure to include "memory" in your overall main idea sentence.)

___

___

___

Internet Resources

Read More about It Online

Directions: Read more about the topic of this selection online. You can read online *before* you read the selection to build background knowledge or *afterward* to extend your knowledge. Start with the websites below or type **"memory strategies"** or **"mnemonics"** in the search box of Google, Yahoo, or another search engine. When you visit any unfamiliar website, it is important to evaluate it and the information it contains. If you do not know how to conduct Internet searches or evaluate a website, see pages 24–25.

www.usu.edu/arc/StudySmart/resources.cfm
This site is hosted by the Utah State University Academic Resources Center. Its "Study Smart Starter Kit" contains comprehensive study skills resources, including videos and "Idea Sheets." Explore the section on memory, which also contains information about concentration and mnemonics (memory devices).

www.mindtools.com/pages/main/newMN_TIM.htm
This site provides a wealth of information about the principles behind the use of mnemonic devices, as well as an array of specific techniques.

SELECTION 1.3
Study Skills

The When and How of Preparing for Tests

From *P.O.W.E.R. Learning: Strategies for Success in College and Life*
By Robert S. Feldman

Do you feel uneasy whenever your instructor announces that there will be a test? Do you wait until the last minute to start preparing for tests? Are you usually surprised by the types of questions or type of material on tests? If you answered yes to any of these questions, then this selection is for you! The author, Dr. Robert Feldman, is a psychology professor who has extensive expertise in strategies for academic success.

As Professor Feldman points out, tests are not a measure of your worth as an individual. They are only a measure of how well (and how much) you studied, and of your test-taking skills. They are indirect, imperfect ways of measuring what a person knows.

As noted at the beginning of this chapter, you should start preparing for your final exams from the first day of the semester. In other words, you should learn as you go. In this selection, Dr. Feldman takes this a step further by giving specific strategies for preparing for various types of test questions and for dealing with test anxiety. This reading selection is presented in Chapter 1 of New Worlds *so that you can use the valuable techniques in it from the beginning of the semester. Chapter 11 presents strategies for organizing textbook information so that you can learn it for tests.*

Ready Your Test-Taking Strategies

1 How you do on a test depends on a number of considerations: the kind of test it is, the subject matter involved, your understanding of test-taking strategies, and, above all, how well you prepare for it. Preparation for tests requires a number of strategies. Among the most important are the following:

Remember: Everything You Do in a Course Is Preparation for a Test

2 All the things you do during a course help to prepare you for a test. There is no surer way to get good grades on tests than to attend class faithfully and to complete all class assignments seriously and on time. Preparing for tests is a long-term proposition. It's not a matter of "giving your all" the night before the test. Instead, it's a matter of giving your all to every aspect of the course.

Know What You Are Preparing For

3 Determine as much as you can about the test before you begin to study for it. The more you know about a test beforehand, the more efficient your studying will be. To find out about an upcoming test, ask these questions:

- Is the test called a "test," "exam," "quiz," or something else? As you can see in Table 1, the names imply

Prediction Exercises

Directions: Use the skill of predicting to anticipate what certain sections will be about. At each of the points indicated below, answer the question "What do you predict this section will be about?"

Copyright © 2014 The McGraw-Hill Companies, Inc. All rights reserved.

different things. For simplicity's sake, we'll use the term *test* throughout this chapter, but know that these distinctions exist, and they should affect the way you prepare.

- What material will the test cover?
- How many questions will be on it?
- How much time is it expected to take? A full class period? Only part of a period?
- What kinds of questions will be on the test?
- How will it be graded?
- Will sample questions be provided?
- Are tests from previous terms available?
- How much does the test contribute to my final course grade?

Form a Study Group

4 Study groups are small, informal groups of students who work together to learn course material and study for a test. Forming such a group can be an excellent way to prepare for any kind of test. Some study groups are formed for particular tests, while others meet consistently throughout the term.

5 The typical study group meets a week or two before a test and plans a strategy for studying. Members share their understanding of what will be on the test, based on what an instructor has said in class and on their review of notes and text material. Together, they develop a list of review questions to guide their individual study. The group then breaks up, and the members study on their own.

6 A few days before the test, members of the study group meet again. They discuss answers to the review questions, go over the material, and share any new insights they may have about the upcoming test. They may also quiz one another about the material to identify any weaknesses or gaps in their knowledge.

7 Study groups can be extremely powerful tools because they help accomplish several things:

- They help members organize and structure the material to approach their studying in a systematic and logical way.
- They allow students to share different perspectives on the material.
- They make it more likely that students will not overlook any potentially important information.
- They force members to rethink the course material, explaining it in words that other group members will understand. This helps both understanding and recall of the information when it is needed on the test.
- Finally, they help motivate members to do their best. When you're part of a study group, you're no longer working just for yourself; your studying also benefits the other study-group members. Not wanting to let down your classmates in a study group may encourage you to put in your best effort.

TABLE 1
QUIZZES, TESTS, EXAMS . . . WHAT'S IN A NAME?

Although they may vary from one instructor to another, the following definitions are the ones most frequently used:

Quizzes. A **quiz** is a brief assessment, usually covering a relatively small amount of material. Some quizzes cover as little as one class's worth of reading. Although a single quiz usually doesn't count very much, instructors often add quiz scores together, and collectively they can become a significant part of your final course grade.

Tests. A **test** is a more extensive, more heavily weighted assessment than a quiz, covering more material. A test may come every few weeks of the term, often after each third or quarter of the term has passed, but this varies with the instructor and the course.

Exams. An **exam** is the most substantial kind of assessment. In many classes, just one exam is given—a *final exam* at the end of the term. Sometimes there are two exams, one at the midpoint of the term (called, of course, a midterm) and the other at the end. Exams are usually weighted quite heavily because they are meant to assess your knowledge of all the course material up to that point.

8 There are some potential drawbacks to keep in mind. Study groups don't always work well for students with learning styles that favor working independently. In addition, "problem" members—those who don't pull their weight—may cause difficulties for the group. In general, though, the advantages of study groups far outweigh their disadvantages.

Match Preparation to Question Types

9 Test questions come in different types (see Table 2), and each requires a somewhat different style of preparation.

10
- **Essay questions.** Essay tests focus on the big picture—ways in which the various pieces of information being tested fit together. You'll need to know not just a series of facts, but also the connections between them, and you will have to be able to discuss these ideas in an organized and logical way. The best approach to studying for an essay test involves four steps:

  1. Carefully reread your class notes and any notes you've made on assigned readings that will be covered on the upcoming exam. Also go through the readings themselves, reviewing underlined or highlighted material and marginal notes.
  2. Play professor: Think of likely exam questions. To do this you can use the key words, phrases, concepts, and questions that come up in your class notes or in your text. Some instructors give out lists of possible essay topics; if yours does, focus on this list, but don't ignore other possibilities.

TABLE 2
TYPES OF TEST QUESTIONS

Essay	Requires a fairly extended, on-the-spot composition about some topic, Examples include questions that call on you to describe a person, process, or event, or those that ask you to compare or contrast two separate sets of material.
Multiple-choice	Usually contains a question or statement, followed by a number of possible answers (usually 4 or 5 of them). You are supposed to choose the best response from the choices offered.
True–false	Presents statements about a topic that are either accurate or inaccurate. You are to indicate whether each statement is accurate (true) or inaccurate (false).
Matching	Presents two lists of related information, arranged in column form. Typically, you are asked to pair up the items that go together (e.g., a scientific term and its definition, or a writer and the title of a book he wrote).
Short-answer	Requires brief responses (usually a few sentences at most) in a kind of mini-essay.
Fill-in	Requires you to add one or more missing words to a sentence or series of sentences.

Prediction Exercise

What do you predict this section (paragraphs 9–15) will be about?

____
____
____
____

Study groups, made up of a few students who study together for a test, can help members organize material, provide new perspectives, and motivate members to do their best.

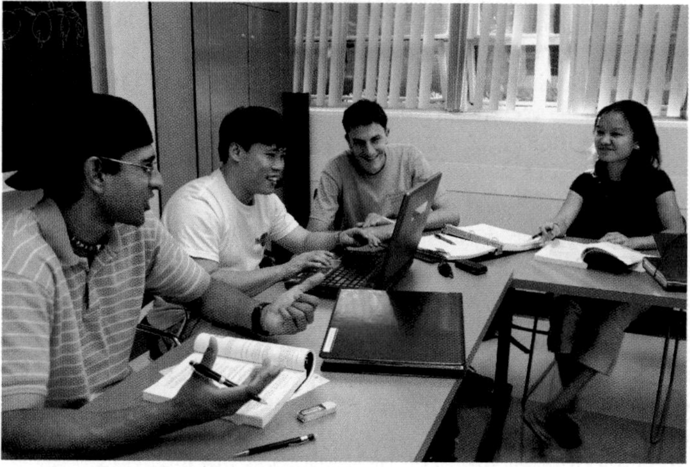

3. Without looking at your notes or your readings, answer each potential essay question—aloud. Don't feel embarrassed about doing this. Talking aloud is often more useful than answering the question in your head.
4. You can also write down the main points that any answer should cover. (Don't write out complete answers to the questions unless your instructor tells you in advance exactly what is going to be on the test. Your time is probably better spent learning the material than rehearsing precisely formulated responses.)
5. After you've answered the questions, check yourself by looking at the notes and readings once again. If you feel confident that you've answered particular questions adequately, check them off. You can go back later for a quick review. But if there are questions that you had trouble with, review that material immediately. Then repeat the third step above, answering the questions again.

11 • **Short-answer and fill-in questions.** Short-answer and fill-in questions are similar to essays in that they require you to recall key pieces of information rather than finding it on the page in front of you. However, short-answer and fill-in questions—unlike essay questions—typically don't demand that you integrate or compare different types of information. Consequently, the focus of your study should be on the recall of specific, detailed information.

12 • **Multiple-choice, true-false, and matching questions.** While the focus of review for essay questions should be on major issues and controversies, studying for multiple choice, true-false, and matching questions requires more attention to the details.

13 Almost anything is fair game for multiple-choice, true-false, and matching questions, so you can't afford to overlook anything when studying. True, these kinds of questions put the material right there on the page for you to react to—Did Columbus land in 1492, or not?—rather than asking you to provide the names and dates yourself (as in the case of the essay question). Nevertheless, to do well on these tests you must put your memory into high gear and master a great many facts.

14 It's a particularly good idea to write down important facts on index cards like those in the figure below. Remember the advantages of these cards: They're portable and available all the time, and the act of creating them helps drive the material into your memory. Furthermore, you can shuffle them and test yourself repeatedly until you've mastered the material.

15 It also can be helpful to write the name of a particular concept or theory on one side of a note card, and then to generate and write an example of it on the other side. Studying the cards will ensure that you fully understand the concepts and theories and can generalize them to different situations.

Political reforms of progressive age:

-direct primaries: people vote for whom they want to run; not appointed
-initiative: people propose laws on their own
-referendum: gov. proposes; people say yes or no
-recall: people can remove politicians from office before they finish term

Endoplasmic reticulum (ER):

Smooth ER—makes fats (lipids)
Rough ER—has ribosomes which make proteins

Together, they make membranes for whole cell (for plasma membrane, mitochondrion, etc.)
Also make more of themselves

Test Yourself

16 Once you feel you've mastered the material, test yourself on it. There are several ways to do this. Often textbooks are accompanied by Web sites that offer automatically scored practice tests and quizzes.

17 You can also create a test for yourself, in writing, making its form as close as possible to what you expect the actual test to be. For instance, if your instructor has told you the classroom test will be primarily made up of short-answer questions, your test should reflect that.

18 You might also construct a test and administer it to a classmate or a member of your study group. In turn, you could take a test that someone else has constructed. Constructing and taking practice tests are excellent ways of studying the material and cementing it into memory.

Deal with Test Anxiety

19 What does the anticipation of a test do to you? Do you feel shaky? Frantic, like there's not enough time to get it all done? Do you feel as if there's a knot in your stomach? Do you grit your teeth? Test anxiety is a temporary condition characterized by fears and concerns about test taking. Almost everyone experiences it to some degree, although for some people it's more of a problem than for others. The real danger with test anxiety is that it can become so overwhelming that it can hurt test performance.

20 You'll never eliminate test anxiety completely, nor do you want to. A little bit of nervousness can energize us, making us more attentive and vigilant. Like any competitive event, testing can motivate us to do our best. You might think of moderate test anxiety as a desire to perform at your peak—a useful quality at test time.

21 On the other hand, for some, anxiety can spiral into the kind of paralyzing fear that makes their minds go blank. There are several ways to keep this from happening to you:

1. *Prepare thoroughly.* The more you prepare, the less test anxiety you'll feel. Good preparation can give you a sense of control and mastery, and it will prevent test anxiety from overwhelming you.
2. *Take a realistic view of the test.* Remember that your future success does not hinge on your performance on any single exam. Think of the big picture: Put the task ahead in context, and remind yourself of all the hurdles you've passed so far.
3. *Eat right and get enough sleep.* Good mental preparation can't occur without your body being well prepared.
4. *Learn relaxation techniques.* You can learn to reduce or even eliminate the jittery physical symptoms of test anxiety by using relaxation techniques. The basic process is straightforward: Breathe evenly, gently inhaling and exhaling. Focus your mind on a pleasant, relaxing scene such as a beautiful forest or a peaceful farm, or on a restful sound such as that of ocean waves breaking on the beach.

Prediction Exercise

What do you predict this section (paragraphs 19–21) will be about?

____

____

____

5. *Visualize success.* Think of an image of your instructor handing back your test marked with a big fat "A." Or imagine your instructor congratulating you on your fine performance the day after the test. Positive visualizations that highlight your potential success can help replace images of failure that may fuel test anxiety.

22 What if these strategies don't work? If your test anxiety is so great that it's getting in the way of your success, make use of your college's resources. Most provide a learning resource center or a counseling center that can provide you with personalized help.

Source: Adapted from Robert S. Feldman, *P.O.W.E.R. Learning*, 5th ed., pp. 118–26. Copyright © 2011 by McGraw-Hill. Reprinted by permission of The McGraw-Hill Companies.

Copyright © 2014 The McGraw-Hill Companies, Inc. All rights reserved.

SELECTION 1.3
Study Skills
(continued)

Comprehension and Vocabulary Quiz

This quiz has four parts. Your instructor may assign some or all of them.

Comprehension

Directions: Items 1–5 test your understanding of the selection. They are the types of questions a content-area instructor (such as a study skills or student success professor) might ask on a test. You may refer to the selection as you answer the questions. Write your answer choice in the space provided.

_____ **1.** A good strategy for preparing for a test is to:

a. find out as much as you can about the type of test, length, grading, etc.
b. match your test preparation to the type of questions that will be on the test.
c. form a small study group.
d. all of the above

_____ **2.** Preparing study cards is an effective way to prepare for multiple-choice test questions because:

a. the very act of creating them helps drive the material into your memory.
b. they allow you to discover different perspectives on the material.
c. they allow you to "play professor."
d. they help you "give your all" the night before the test.

_____ **3.** To prepare for any exam, you should:

a. memorize as many specific details as possible in the order that they were presented in class.
b. eliminate test anxiety completely.
c. test yourself on the material once you feel you've mastered it.
d. all of the above

_____ **4.** Essay questions are similar to short-answer and fill-in questions in that they both:

a. require you to integrate and compare different types of information.
b. require more attention to details when you are studying.
c. require you to put your memory in high gear and master a great many facts.
d. require you to recall key pieces of information.

_____ **5.** Most students benefit from participating in a study group because it:

a. makes it more likely students will not overlook any potentially important information.
b. forces members to approach their studying in a systematic and logical way.
c. helps motivate members to do their best.
d. all of the above

Vocabulary in Context

Directions: Items 6–10 test your ability to determine a word's meaning by using context clues. *Context clues* are words in a sentence that allow readers to deduce (reason out) the meaning of an unfamiliar word. They also help readers determine the meaning an author intends when a word has more than one meaning. Each item below consists of a sentence from the selection, with the vocabulary word *italicized*. It is followed by another sentence that uses the same word in the same way. Use context clues to deduce the meaning of the *italicized* word. Be sure the meaning you choose makes sense in *both* sentences. Write each answer in the space provided. (Chapter 2 presents the skill of using context clues.)

______ **6.** Study groups help members organize and structure the material to approach their studying in a *systematic* and logical way.

Using a *systematic* approach to managing your money can lead you to early financial freedom and security.

systematic (sĭs tə măt′ ĭk) means:

a. related to money

b. methodical in procedure or plan

c. determined by a group rather than an individual

d. difficult and unrewarding

______ **7.** In general, though, the advantages of study groups far *outweigh* their disadvantages.

Our company president took early retirement because he felt the stress of the job had begun to *outweigh* the benefits.

outweigh (out wā′) means:

a. to cancel out

b. to have greater importance than

c. to weigh more than

d. to decrease

______ **8.** However, short-answer and fill-in questions—unlike essay questions—typically don't demand that you *integrate* or compare different types of information.

It took several hours to *integrate* the new files with the existing ones.

integrate (in′ tə grāt) means:

a. to record in written form

b. to puzzle over

c. to bring all the parts together

d. to agree with

______ **9.** A little bit of nervousness can energize us, making us more attentive and *vigilant.*

Vigilant parents would never allow their elementary-school-age children to go to the mall unsupervised or alone.

vigilant (vĭj′ ə lənt) means:

a. selfish and uncaring

b. extremely immature

c. highly emotional

d. alertly watchful

Copyright © 2014 The McGraw-Hill Companies, Inc. All rights reserved.

_______ **10.** Positive visualizations that highlight your potential success can help replace images of failure that may *fuel* your test anxiety.

Scary movies unnecessarily *fuel* children's fears.

fuel (fyōō′ əl) means:

a. support; stimulate
b. diminish; decrease
c. end; stop
d. spread

Word Structure

Directions: Items 11–15 test your ability to use word-structure clues to help determine a word's meaning. *Word-structure clues* consist of roots, prefixes, and suffixes. In these exercises, you will learn the meaning of a word part (a root) and use it to determine the meaning of several other words that have the same word part. If you need to use a dictionary to confirm your answer choice, do so. Write your answers in the spaces provided.

In paragraph 14 of the selection, you encountered the word **portable**. This word contains the Latin root ***port***, which means "to carry" or "to bear." The word *portable* describes something that can be *carried* or *moved about.* Use the meaning of the root ***port*** and the list of prefixes on pages 72–73 to determine the meaning of the following words.

_______ **11.** If someone is arrested for **transporting** illegal goods across a state line, the person was trying to:

a. move illegal goods from one state to another.
b. sneak across the state line.
c. induce others to pursue a life of crime.
d. report a crime to the police.

_______ **12.** Newspaper and television **reporters** gather information and:

a. write it down.
b. bring it to the public.
c. disprove it.
d. speak it into a microphone.

_______ **13.** People who are in the **import-export** business:

a. sell items in a retail store.
b. inspect products brought into a country.
c. bring some products into a country and send out others.
d. produce items to be sold wholesale.

_______ **14.** If illegal immigrants are **deported** from a country, they are:

a. charged with a crime.
b. placed in jail.
c. given citizenship.
d. legally forced to leave the country.

_____ **15.** If there are large beams that **support** the roof of a structure, the beams:

a. angle toward the ceiling.

b. are curved.

c. bear the weight of the roof.

d. are made of wood.

Reading Skills Application

Directions: Items 16–20 test your ability to *apply* certain reading skills. You may not be familiar with all the skills yet, so some items will serve as a preview. As you work through *New Worlds,* you will practice and develop these skills. These are important skills, which is why they are included on the state-mandated basic skills tests that some students must take. Write each answer in the space provided.

_____ **16.** What is the author's primary purpose for writing this selection?

a. to prove that test preparation and test grades are highly correlated

b. to explain how to prepare for tests and deal with test anxiety

c. to explain the different types of tests

d. to prove that working with a study group can enhance test performance

_____ **17.** Which of the following is the meaning of *key* as it is used in paragraph 10, item 2?

a. familiar

b. confusing

c. foreign

d. important

_____ **18.** Which pattern has been used to organize the information in paragraph 5 of the selection?

a. comparison and contrast

b. cause and effect

c. sequence

d. list

_____ **19.** Based on the information in the selection, the author would most likely agree with which of the following statements?

a. If students know more about test preparation, they can improve their performance on tests.

b. Test anxiety is a fact of life and nothing can be done about it.

c. There are test-taking techniques that can make every student successful in college.

d. Study groups are the secret of success when preparing for tests in college.

Copyright © 2014 The McGraw-Hill Companies, Inc. All rights reserved.

_______ **20.** The author has credibility because he:

a. has had experience himself as a highly successful college student.

b. presents the results of interviews with successful students.

c. is an expert on learning and study skills.

d. has conducted extensive research projects on study skills.

SELECTION **1.3**
Study Skills
(continued)

Respond in Writing

Directions: Refer to the selection as needed to answer the essay-type questions below. (Your instructor may direct you to work collaboratively with other students on one or more items. Each group member should be able to explain *all* of the group's answers.)

1. **Reacting to What You Have Read:** "Know thyself," the old saying goes. Through experience, most college students discover techniques that prepare them to do well on tests. List at least three things that you have discovered that help *you* prepare effectively for tests.

____

____

____

____

____

____

2. **Comprehending the Selection Further:** List and explain the five ways to deal with test anxiety.

____

____

____

____

____

____

____

____

____

____

3. **Overall Main Idea of the Selection:** In one sentence, tell what the author wants readers to understand about what you should do when preparing for tests.

(Be sure to include "prepare," "test," and "test anxiety" in your overall main idea sentence.)

____

____

____

____

____

____

Internet Resources

Read More about It Online

Directions: Read more about the topic of this selection online. You can read online *before* you read the selection to build background knowledge or *afterward* to extend your knowledge. Start with the website below or type **"test taking"** or **"test anxiety"** in the search box of Google, Yahoo, or another search engine. When you visit any unfamiliar website, it is important to evaluate it and the information it contains. If you do not know how to conduct Internet searches or evaluate a website, see pages 24–25.

www.usu.edu/arc/StudySmart
Hosted by the Utah State University Academic Resources Center, this site contains valuable information related to test preparation, test anxiety, and test taking.

Copyright © 2014 The McGraw-Hill Companies, Inc. All rights reserved.

CHAPTER 2

Developing a College-Level Vocabulary

A New World of Words

LEARNING OBJECTIVES

In this chapter you will learn the answers to these questions:

- Why is it important for me to develop a college-level vocabulary?
- What are context clues, and how can I use them?
- What are word-structure clues, and how can I use them?
- How do I use a dictionary pronunciation key?
- What is figurative language?
- How do I interpret figures of speech?

CHAPTER CONTENTS

NEW INFORMATION AND SKILLS

Why Is It Important to Develop a College-Level Vocabulary?

What Are Context Clues, and How Do You Use Them?

What Are Word-Structure Clues, and How Do You Use Them?

How Do You Use a Dictionary Pronunciation Key?

What Is Figurative Language, and How Do You Interpret Figures of Speech?

Other Things to Keep in Mind When Developing a College-Level Vocabulary

- Certain punctuation marks in a sentence can signal a definition.
- The most common and helpful roots, prefixes, and suffixes in English come from Latin and ancient Greek.
- A word's etymology (origin and history) indicates the word parts it was created from, including Latin or Greek ones.
- Many words have a connotation as well as a denotation.

CHAPTER REVIEW CARDS

TEST YOUR UNDERSTANDING

Context Clues, Part 1

Context Clues, Part 2

Word-Structure Clues, Part 1

Word-Structure Clues, Part 2

Figurative Language, Part 1

Figurative Language, Part 2

READINGS

Selection 2.1 "Overcoming Obstacles"
from *Peak Performance in College and Beyond*
by Sharon Ferrett (Student Success)

Selection 2.2 "Autism: A Public Health Emergency"
Compiled from Online Sources
by Janet Elder (Public Health)

Selection 2.3 "Thinking in Pictures: Autism and Visual Thought"
from *Thinking in Pictures: My Life with Autism*
by Temple Grandin (Nonfiction)

NEW INFORMATION AND SKILLS

WHY IS IT IMPORTANT TO DEVELOP A COLLEGE-LEVEL VOCABULARY?

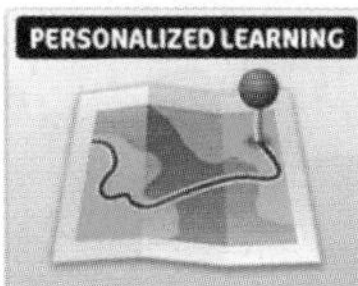

The most important reason to develop a college-level vocabulary is so that you can understand your textbooks, but it can make your college work easier in other ways as well. You will understand more of what others—especially professors—say. Your own speaking and writing will become more precise and more interesting. If all that is not enough, your increased vocabulary may result in a higher salary. Research tells us that the size of a person's vocabulary correlates with how much money the person earns: The larger your vocabulary, the larger your income is likely to be. Thinking of each word you learn as potential "money in the bank" may be an incentive for you to increase your vocabulary! Indeed, developing a powerful vocabulary is a process that takes time and effort, but it is an asset that will benefit you all your life.

How can you develop a strong vocabulary? Read. Every time you read, you have an opportunity to expand your vocabulary. The more you read, the better your vocabulary can become—*if* you develop an interest in words and their meanings.

When you read, there are four strategies you can use to expand your vocabulary. The strategies are:

1. **Use context clues.** Reason out the likely meaning of a word from clues provided by the surrounding words and sentences. The word might be completely new to you, or it might be a common word that has a meaning you are unaware of. Ask yourself, "What would this word have to mean in order to make sense in this sentence?"
2. **Use word-structure clues.** Determine a word's meaning by examining any prefix, root, or suffix it contains.
3. **Use a dictionary.** Determine a word's pronunciation and the precise meaning as it is used in the passage you are reading.
4. **Know how to interpret figurative language.** Understand the nonliteral meaning of words and phrases when they are used in figures of speech.

In this chapter, we will look at each of these skills. To give you ample practice applying them, there are extensive vocabulary exercises that accompany every reading selection in *New Worlds.*

WHAT ARE CONTEXT CLUES, AND HOW DO YOU USE THEM?

context clues

Words in a sentence or paragraph that help the reader deduce (reason out) the meaning of an unfamiliar word.

Textbook authors want you to understand what they have written. When they use words that might be unfamiliar to the reader, they often provide context clues. **Context clues** are words in a sentence or paragraph that help the reader deduce (reason out) the meaning of an unfamiliar word. Such clues are called "context" clues because *context* refers to the setting in which something occurs—in this case, the rest of the sentence and the paragraph in which the unfamiliar word appears.

Context clues can help you figure out the meaning of an unfamiliar word, so think of them as gifts the writer gives you. How can you take advantage of these "gifts"? Simply read the sentence carefully and pay attention to the words and other sentences surrounding the unfamiliar word. When you encounter an unfamiliar word when you are reading, ask yourself, "What would this word have to mean for it to make sense

Copyright © 2014 The McGraw-Hill Companies, Inc. All rights reserved.

Developing a strong vocabulary takes time and effort, but it is well worth it.

in this sentence?" For example, suppose you read this sentence: "My four-year-old nephew Carlos loves cookies, cakes, candy, *churros,* and anything else that is sweet." You can deduce the meaning of the word *churros* from the context: It is some type of dessert or snack food. The context clues in this sentence are the examples of "cookies, cakes, candy" and the words "and anything else that is sweet." For the sentence to make sense, *churros* has to refer to some type of sweet, sugary food. (You may already know that *churros* are sugar-coated, fried-dough snacks that are enjoyed throughout Latin America.)

For words with more than one meaning, context clues can also help you determine which meaning the author intends. You may know that one meaning of the word *consume* is "to eat," as in this sentence: "Americans consume millions of hot dogs every year." Suppose, however, you encounter this sentence: "On average, Americans consume more than 19 million barrels of oil a day." "Eat" makes no sense in a sentence about consuming barrels of oil. You can deduce, therefore, that in this sentence, the word consume means "use." This is the meaning the author intends.

The chart on page 67 lists six common types of context clues. It explains what to ask yourself and what to look for when you encounter each type of context clue. It presents sentences that illustrate each type of context clue. (You also have the opportunity to learn the meaning of any unfamiliar words in the example sentences!)

Using the context is the first strategy you should use when you encounter an unknown word. Remember, however, that context clues enable you to make an educated guess; they do not always allow you to determine the precise meaning of a word. For example, you might read the sentence "He spent the entire weekend visiting used car dealerships, but in spite of his *exhaustive* search he was unable to find a suitable car in his price range." Although *exhaustive* might appear from the context to mean "exhausting" or "tiring," it actually means "thorough" or "complete." (For example, a scientist might do exhaustive research on a topic.) In this case, the context is not sufficient to reason out the meaning of the word.

USING CONTEXT CLUES TO DETERMINE THE MEANING OF UNFAMILIAR WORDS

Example	Type of Clue	What to Ask Yourself	What to Look For
Narcolepsy *is defined as* a sleep disorder in which a person has a recurrent, overwhelming, and uncontrollable desire to fall asleep, often at inappropriate times.	***Definition clue***	Are there *definition clues* and a definition?	Phrases that introduce a definition, such as *is defined as, is called, is, is known as, that is, refers to, means, the term;* a term that is in bold print, italics, or color; certain punctuation marks that set off a definition or a term. (See page 77.)
The old man is a ***recluse***, *or loner,* who lives in a shack deep in the woods.	***Synonym clue***	Is there a *synonym* for the unfamiliar word? That is, is the meaning explained by a word or phrase that has a *similar meaning*? The synonym may be set off by commas, parentheses, a colon, dashes, or brackets. (See page 77.)	Phrases that introduce synonyms, such as *in other words, or, that is to say, also known as, by this we mean, that is.*
Fit people are generally energetic and active, *but* unfit people tend to be ***lethargic.***	***Contrast clue***	Is there an *antonym* for the unfamiliar word? That is, is the unfamiliar word explained by a contrasting word or phrase with the *opposite meaning*?	Words and phrases that indicate opposites: *instead of, but, in contrast, on the other hand, however, unlike, although, even though.*
Most students feel ***discombobulated*** *when the teacher gives a pop quiz.*	***Experience clue***	Can you draw on your *experience and background knowledge* to help you deduce (reason out) the meaning of the unfamiliar word?	A sentence that includes a *familiar experience* (or information you already know) can help you figure out the meaning of the new word.
Because he does not own a car, he ruled out ***itinerant*** jobs, *such as door-to-door sales and restocking coin-operated machines.*	***Example clue***	Are there *examples* that illustrate the meaning of the unfamiliar word?	Words that introduce examples of the meaning of the unfamiliar word: *for example, such as, to illustrate, like.*
It is no wonder the popularity of ***smart cards*** is increasing. *Credit-card sized and password protected,* they can *hold a large amount of* personal, medical, financial and other *information.*	***Clue from another sentence***	Is there *another sentence* in the paragraph that explains the meaning of the unfamiliar word?	*Additional information in another sentence* that may help explain the unfamiliar word.

Copyright © 2014 The McGraw-Hill Companies, Inc. All rights reserved.

EXERCISE 1

Directions: The context clue exercise below presents sentences from college textbooks. Each sentence contains an important word that is *italicized.* Next, there is an additional sentence that uses the word in the same sense. Read both sentences and ask yourself, "What would this word have to mean in order to make sense in *both* sentences?" Use the context from both sentences to *deduce* the meaning of the italicized word. The answer you choose must make sense in both sentences.

______ **1.** We often think that our *affairs,* great or small, must be tended to continuously and with great detail or our world will fall apart.

Balancing your checkbook, keeping an appointment calendar, and using efficient time management techniques enables you to keep your *affairs* in order.

affairs means:

a. romantic relationships
b. financial matters
c. weekly schedules
d. personal business

______ **2.** High levels of stress are *correlated* with health problems.

The number of years of education is *correlated* with the amount of income a person earns in a lifetime.

correlated means:

a. prevented by
b. caused by
c. related to
d. determined by

______ **3.** Although there is no cure for the common cold, there are medications that can *alleviate* its symptoms.

There are many ways to *alleviate* the stresses of everyday living.

alleviate means:

a. to remedy or cure
b. to lessen or make more bearable
c. to increase or enhance
d. to change the form of

WHAT ARE WORD-STRUCTURE CLUES, AND HOW DO YOU USE THEM?

word-structure clues

Roots, prefixes, and suffixes that help you determine a word's meaning.

Word-structure clues are also known as *word-part clues.*

Context clues should be your first strategy in determining the meaning of unknown words, but examining the structure of words can also be extremely helpful. **Word-structure clues,** or word-part clues, consist of roots, prefixes, and suffixes that help you determine a word's meaning. Prefixes and suffixes are called affixes because they are "fixed" (attached or joined) to a root word. Word-structure clues can often be used to confirm the meaning suggested by the context of the sentence.

Word-structure clues can help you in other ways as well. First, they can help you remember the meaning of a word. Second, they allow you to enlarge your vocabulary by learning families of related words that come from the same root (called *cognates*). Finally, knowing prefixes, roots, and suffixes can help you improve your spelling. For instance, if you know the prefix *mis* (meaning "bad" or "wrong"), then you will understand why the word *misspell* has two s's: One is in the prefix and one is in the root word: mis + spell.

The more prefixes, roots, and suffixes you know, the more you can utilize this vocabulary-building strategy. This means that it is well worth your time to memorize common word parts. Of these, roots and prefixes are by far the most helpful. (Lists of common roots, prefixes, and suffixes appear on pages 70–74.)

The three categories of word parts—prefixes, roots, and suffixes—will be discussed in this chapter. Here are their definitions:

Root: Base word that has a meaning of its own.

Prefix: Word part attached to the beginning of a root that adds its meaning to the root.

Suffix: Word part attached to the end of a root word.

To use word-structure clues, examine an unfamiliar word to see if it has a word part that gives you a clue to its meaning. Think of roots and affixes as puzzle parts that can help you figure out the meaning of unfamiliar words. (You increase your chances of figuring out an unfamiliar word's meaning if you are able to use context clues and word-structure clues together.) Now, let's take a closer look at each of the three types of word parts.

root

Base word that has a meaning of its own.

A **root** is a base word that has a meaning of its own. Roots are powerful vocabulary-building tools because entire families of words in English are based on the same root. For example, if you know that the root *aud* means "to hear," then you will understand the connection between *audience* (people who come to hear something or someone), *auditorium* (a place where people come to hear something), *auditory* (pertaining to hearing, as in *auditory nerve*), and *audiologist* (a person specially trained to evaluate hearing). Knowing the meaning of a word's root makes it easier to remember a word's meaning.

prefix

Word part attached to the beginning of a word that adds its meaning to that base word.

A **prefix** is a word part attached to the beginning of a word that adds its meaning to the meaning of the base word. For example, adding the prefix *tele* (meaning "distant" or "far") to the word *marketing* creates the word *telemarketing*, selling goods and services from a distance (in this case, over the telephone), rather than face-to-face. By adding the prefixes *pre* (meaning "before") and *re* (meaning "back" or "again") to the word *view,* you have the words *preview* (to view or see something ahead of time) and *review* (to see or look back at something again).

Remember, however, that a word that begins with the same letters as a prefix does not necessarily contain that prefix. The prefix *mal* means "wrong" or "bad," as in *malnutrition* (bad nutrition). However, the words *mall* and *male* also begin with the letters *mal,* but they have no connection with the prefix *mal*. Nor does the word *rent,* for example, contain the prefix *re,* or the word *pressure* the prefix *pre*.

suffix

Word part attached to the end of a root word.

A **suffix** is a word part attached to the end of a root word. Some suffixes add their meaning to a root, but most suffixes simply change a word's part of speech or inflection. Inflectional endings include adding *-s* to make a word plural or *-ed* to make a verb past tense. Consider these other forms of *predict* (a verb) that are created by adding suffixes: *prediction* and *predictor* (nouns), *predictable* (adjective), and *predictably* (adverb).

Suffixes are not as helpful as roots or prefixes, because many of them have similar or even the same meanings. Also, some suffixes cause roots to change their spelling before the suffix is added. For instance, when certain suffixes are added to words that end in *y*, the *y* becomes an *i*: *sleepy* becomes *sleepier, sleepiness,* and *sleepily*.

A word may consist of one or more of the word parts. For example, the word *graph* consists of a root only. The word *telegraph* consists of a prefix (*tele*) and a root (*graph*). The word *graphic* consists of a root (*graph*) and a suffix (*ic*). *Telegraphic* consists of a prefix, a root, and a suffix.

It is unlikely that you or any other student will learn every word part, but the more word parts you know, the easier it will be to use word-structure clues and, of course, the larger your vocabulary will become. A good place to begin is by familiarizing yourself with the common roots, prefixes, and suffixes on the lists that follow. (You probably already know many of them.) Then watch for these word parts in new words you encounter. Use these word-structure clues to help you confirm the educated guess you made about a word's meaning based on the context.

COMMON ROOTS

Root	Meaning	Examples
1. anthro	man, humankind	anthropology, misanthrope
2. aud	hear	audience, auditorium
3. auto	self	autobiography, automatic
4. bene	good, well	beneficial, benediction
5. biblio	book	bibliography, bibliophile
6. bio	life	biology, biopsy
7. cede, ceed	go, move	precede, proceed
8. chron	time	chronology, chronic
9. cide	kill	homicide, suicide
10. clud, clus	close, shut	exclude, inclusive
11. corp, corpus	body	corporal, corps
12. cred	believe, belief	credible, credit
13. dic, dict	say, speak	predict, dictionary
14. duc, duct	lead	produce, conductor
15. fac	make, do	manufacture, factory
16. fid, fide	faith	fidelity, confidence
17. gam, gamy	marriage	bigamist, monogamy
18. gen	birth, race, origin	generation, genealogy
19. geo	earth	geology, geography
20. graph, gram	write	graphic, diagram, photograph
21. gress	go, move	progression, regress
22. ject	throw, hurl	reject, projection
23. man, manu	hand	manual, manipulate

Root	Meaning	Examples
24. mater, matri	mother	maternal, matricide
25. mem	memory	remember, commemorate
26. meter	measure	thermometer, metric
27. miss, mit	send, sent	mission, transmit
28. mor, mort	death	morgue, mortal, morbid
29. mot, mob	move, go	motion, promote, mobile
30. nov	new	novelty, innovation
31. nym, nom	name	synonym, nominate
32. pater, patri	father	paternal, patriotic
33. pel	push, drive, thrust	repel, compel
34. pend	hang	pendulum, dependent
35. phil, phile	love	philosophy, audiophile
36. phobia	fear	claustrophobia, phobic
37. phon	sound	phonics, telephone
38. photo	light	photograph, photosynthesis
39. pod, pedi	foot	podiatrist, pedestrian
40. port	carry	portable, import, export
41. pos	put, place	pose, position, deposit
42. psych, psycho	mind	psychic, psychology
43. rupt	break, burst	rupture, bankrupt, interrupt
44. scribe, script	write	inscribe, prescription
45. sol	one, alone, only	solo, solitude
46. spec	see, look	spectacle, inspect
47. ten	grasp, hold, stretch	attention, retention
48. therm	heat	thermometer, thermal
49. tempor	time, occasion	temporary, contemporary
50. tort	twist, bend	tortuous, contort
51. tract	drag, pull	tractor, contract, attract
52. ven, vene	come	convention, intervene
53. vers, vert	turn	reverse, convert
54. vid, vis	see	video, vision
55. viv, vive	live, living	vivid, survive
56. voc	voice, call, say	vocal, invocation

COMMON PREFIXES

Prefix	Meaning	Examples
Prefixes That Mean "No" or "Not":		
1. a-	not	atypical, asocial
2. an-	not	anarchy, anaerobic
3. in-, il-, im-, ir-	not	insecure, illegal, immoral, irresponsible
4. non-	not	nonviolent, nonpoisonous
5. un-	not	unhappy, unkind, uneducated
6. dis-	not, opposite of, undo	displease, disservice, disconnect
7. mis-	wrong, bad	mistreat, mistake, misplace
8. mal-	bad, evil	maladjusted, malevolent
9. ant-, anti-	against	antagonize, antivirus, antiwar
10. contra-	against	contradict, contrary, contrast
Prefixes That Relate to Time:		
11. ante-	before	antebellum, antecedent
12. ex-	former	ex-boss, ex-spouse
13. post-	after	posttest, posterior
14. pre-	before	predict, precede
15. re-	again	repeat, recycle
Prefixes That Show Placement:		
16. ab-	away, away from	absent, abnormal
17. circum-	around	circumference, circumlocution
18. co-, col-, com-	together or with	cooperate, colleague, comparison
19. de-	down from, away	descend, depart
20. dis-	away	displace, disappear
21. ex-	out	exit, export, exterior, excerpt
22. in-	in	inside, interior, inhale
23. inter-	between, among	interstate, interrupt, interfere
24. intra-	within, inside	intrastate, intramural, intravenous
25. pro-	forward, ahead	progress, promote
26. re-	back	return, revert, report
27. sub-, sup-	down	submarine, suppress, suburbs
28. tele-	far, distant	television, telepathy, telescope
29. trans-	across	transatlantic, transport
30. hetero-	different, other	heterosexual, heterogeneous

Prefix	Meaning	Examples
Other Prefixes:		
31. hom-, homo-	same	homophobia, homogeneous
32. syn-	same, similar, together	synthesize, synchronize
33. urb-	city	urban, urbanite
Prefixes That Indicate How Many or How Much:		
34. extra-	outside, beyond	exterior, extraordinary, extracurricular
35. hemi-	half	hemisphere, hemiplegic
36. hyper-	too much, excessive	hyperactive, hyperbole
37. hypo-	under, too little	hypothermia, hypodermic
38. macro-	large	macroeconomics, macrobiotic
39. micro-	small	microscope, microorganisms
40. omni-	all, every	omnipotent, omniscient
41. poly-	many	polygamy, polygon
42. pseudo-	false	pseudonym, pseudosophisticated
43. semi-	half	semiconscious, semiformal
44. super-	over, above	supervisor, superlative
Prefixes That Show Number or Quantity:		
45. uni-	one	united, unify, uniform, universal
46. mono-	one	monopoly, monocle
47. bi-	two	bicycle, bisect
48. du-	two	duet, dual, duel
49. tri-	three	triangle, triplet, tripod
50. quad-, quar	four	quadrant, quarter, quart
51. quint-	five	quintet, quintuple
52. penta-	five	Pentagon, pentathlon
53. sex-	six	sextuplet, sexagenarian
54. hex-	six	hexagon, hexagram
55. sept-	seven	septuplets, septuagenarian, septet
56. octo-, oct-	eight	octagon, octopus
57. nov-	nine	novena, November, nonagenarian
58. dec-, deci-	ten	decimal, decade, decimate
59. cent-	hundred	century, cent
60. mill-, kilo-	thousand	millennium, kilowatts, kilometer

Copyright © 2014 The McGraw-Hill Companies, Inc.

COMMON SUFFIXES

Suffix	Meaning	Examples
Suffixes That Indicate a Person:		
1. -er, -or, -ist	one who (does what the root word indicates)	banker, inventor, scientist, pacifist, terrorist
Suffixes That Indicate a Noun:		
2. -ance, -ence, -tion, -sion, -ment, -ness, -ity, -ty, -tude, -hood, -age	state of, quality of, condition of, act of	tolerance, permanence, retention, vision, government, happiness, maturity, beauty, gratitude, statehood, marriage
3. -itis	inflammation of (whatever the root indicates)	sinusitis, tonsillitis
4. -ology	study or science of (whatever the root indicates)	psychology, microbiology, sociology
5. -ism	philosophy of or belief in	terrorism, Buddhism, pacifism
Suffixes That Indicate an Adjective:		
6. -al, -ic, -ish, -ical, -ive	pertaining to (whatever the root indicates)	normal, hormonal, psychic, pacific, selfish, magical, defective
7. -less	without, lacking (whatever the root indicates)	homeless, toothless
8. -ous, -ful	full of (whatever the root indicates)	harmonious, colorful
9. -able, -ible	able to do or be (whatever the root indicates)	comfortable, comprehensible, audible
Suffixes That Indicate a Verb:		
10. -ify, -ate, -ize, -en	to do (whatever the root indicates)	pacify, meditate, criticize, enlighten
Suffixes That Indicate an Adverb:		
11. -ly	in the manner (indicated by the root)	slowly, heavily, peacefully
12. -ward	in the direction of (whatever the root indicates)	eastward, homeward, backward

EXERCISE 2

Directions: The word-structure exercise below presents sentences containing *italicized* words whose word parts give a clue to its meaning. Use the word part that is in **boldface** print to give you a clue to the word's meaning. Refer to the list of roots that begins on page 70.

______ **1.** If you are making a ***spec**tacle* of yourself at a party, other people are likely to:
- *a.* report you to the police.
- *b.* applaud you.
- *c.* watch you.
- *d.* wish they were you.

______ **2.** If protesters *dis**rupt*** a speech the president is giving, they:
- *a.* clap and cheer enthusiastically.
- *b.* link arms and sway from side to side.
- *c.* say and do things that cause the president to temporarily stop speaking.
- *d.* turn their backs on him.

______ **3.** A prisoner who is placed in ***sol**itary* confinement is:
- *a.* assigned to a different prison.
- *b.* put on suicide watch.
- *c.* given restricted food rations.
- *d.* isolated from other prisoners.

HOW DO YOU USE A DICTIONARY PRONUNCIATION KEY?

Most college students know how to locate a word in the dictionary and how to determine which definition pertains to what they are reading. But like many students, you still may not be skilled or confident in using a dictionary pronunciation key. Being able to use a pronunciation key is important when you need to remember a word because one of the most helpful things you can do is learn its correct pronunciation and say it aloud. Checking and practicing a word's pronunciation takes only a moment or two.

Most dictionaries have an *abridged* (shortened) pronunciation key at or near the bottom of each page. An abridged key gives only vowel sounds and the less common consonant sounds, and usually looks similar to this one:

Pronunciation Key: ă **pat** ā **pay** âr **care** ä **father** ĕ **pet** ē **be** ĭ **pit**
ī **tie** îr **pier** ŏ **pot** ō **toe** ô **paw** oi **noise** ou **out** o͝o **took**
o͞o **boot** ŭ **cut** yo͞o **abuse** ûr**urge** th **thin** *th* **this** hw **which**
zh **vision** ə **about** *Stress mark:* ʹ

A complete pronunciation key appears at the beginning of every dictionary. It also gives a familiar word that contains a particular sound, accompanied by the symbol that dictionary uses to represent that sound. For example, the first word above, *pat*, contains the sound of short *a*. That sound is represented in this dictionary by the symbol ă. The pronunciation of words will be written using these phonetic symbols. For example, suppose you read the sentence "Marjorie is an *avid* football fan who hasn't missed a

Dallas Cowboys home game in eight years." When you look up the word *avid,* you confirm what you suspect, that it means having a great interest and enthusiasm for something. You also see that the pronunciation for *avid* is written this way: ăv′ ĭd. To pronounce this word, find the phonetic symbols for ă and ĭ in the pronunciation key. The ă and the ĭ are pronounced the same as the *a* in the word *pat* and the *i* in the word *pit.* When you substitute those sounds in place of the symbols in the pronunciation, you will know how to pronounce the word correctly.

As you work through *New Worlds,* you will have numerous opportunities to practice this skill, because the pronunciation is given for each vocabulary term in the quizzes that accompany the reading selections. To help you interpret the symbols, you can refer to the abridged pronunciation key on page 75. Your instructor can give you further guidance and practice in using a dictionary pronunciation key, if you need it. Also, online dictionaries usually let you hear a word's pronunciation with a click of a button.

WHAT IS FIGURATIVE LANGUAGE, AND HOW DO YOU INTERPRET FIGURES OF SPEECH?

figurative language

Words that present unusual comparisons or create vivid pictures in the reader's mind. Figurative expressions are also called *figures of speech.*

Knowing how to interpret figurative language is yet another way to develop your understanding of words' meanings and interpret authors' messages correctly. **Figurative language** refers to words that present unusual comparisons or create vivid pictures in the reader's mind. Figurative expressions are also called *figures of speech.* Because figures of speech do not literally mean what they say, you must *interpret* their meaning. If you take the words literally, you will misunderstand the meaning. Think about what the author wants to convey by presenting a comparison or creating a vivid mental image.

You use figurative language every day, although you may not know it by this name. When you say, "That homework assignment was a killer!" you mean, "That was a tough assignment!" When you say, "I made such a good grade on my test they'll probably ask me to teach the course next semester!" you mean, "I made a very high grade on the test."

There are four very common figures of speech: *metaphor, simile, hyperbole,* and *personification.* Let's look at each of them.

metaphor

Figure of speech suggesting a comparison between two seemingly dissimilar things, usually by saying that one of them *is* the other.

A **metaphor** is a figure of speech suggesting a comparison between two seemingly dissimilar things, usually by saying that one of them *is* the other (rather than saying it is "like" something else). On the surface, the two things seem very different, yet they are alike in some significant way. The reader must figure out the way in which they are similar.

The author assumes readers will not take a metaphor literally, but will understand that it must be interpreted. That is, the sentence is to be taken *figuratively.* For example, in the sentence "James *is a walking encyclopedia,*" the writer makes a comparison between James and an encyclopedia to suggest that James has a vast amount of knowledge. To interpret this metaphor correctly, the reader must think about the way in which they could be similar: Both have knowledge, a multitude of facts and information. The author, of course, does not mean that James is literally an encyclopedia.

simile

Figure of speech presenting a comparison between two seemingly dissimilar things by saying that one of them is *like* the other.

A **simile** is a figure of speech presenting a comparison between two seemingly dissimilar things by saying that one of them is *like* the other. Whereas a metaphor makes comparisons using the words *is, are, was,* and *were,* a simile is usually introduced by the word *like* or *as.* An example of a simile is "My grandfather's head is as bald as a baby's backside." The meaning (interpretation) is that his head is completely bald.

To repeat: A simile says that one thing is *like* another. (The word *sim*ile suggests a *sim*ilarity between two things.) When you encounter a simile, first determine which things are being compared. Then determine the important way in which the author considers them to be similar.

hyperbole

Figure of speech using obvious exaggeration for emphasis and effect.

A third type of figurative language is **hyperbole,** in which obvious exaggeration is used for emphasis and effect. (The prefix *hyper,* meaning "too much" or "excessive," will help you remember that a hyperbole is an obvious exaggeration. Note, too, that the word *hyperbole* has four syllables and is pronounced: hī pûr′ bə lē.) "If I have to type one more paper this week, *my fingers will fall off!*" is an example of hyperbole. Of course, the student's fingers are not literally going to fall off. To interpret the hyperbole, you must understand the point of the exaggeration: that the student has already typed several papers this week and is extremely tired of typing.

As noted, hyperboles are also used to achieve a particular effect, such as humor. For example, someone might write, "If I eat one more serving of fish on this diet, I'm going to grow fins!"

personification

Figure of speech in which nonhuman or nonliving things are given human traits.

In **personification,** nonhuman or nonliving things are given human traits. (You can actually see the word *person* in *person*ification. Note, however, that the pronunciation is pər sŏn ə fĭ kā′ shən.) For example, consider the human characteristics or qualities in this sentence about a vending machine: "The vending machine *swallowed* my money and then *refused* to give me my candy." Swallowing and refusing to do something are human behaviors. Vending machines, of course, cannot do these things intentionally or in the same sense that a person would. The author wants the reader to understand that the machine accepted the money but did not produce any candy in return. In this case, the interpretation is the machine is broken (it malfunctioned).

The box below summarizes metaphor, simile, hyperbole, and personification and gives additional examples of each.

FOUR TYPES OF FIGURATIVE LANGUAGE

Figures of Speech	Examples
Metaphor: Implied comparison between two seemingly dissimilar things using *is, are, was,* or *were.*	The old witch's face was a *raisin.* My closet is a *disaster area.*
Simile: Stated comparison between two seemingly dissimilar things, usually introduced by the word *like* or *as.*	His eyebrows look like two fuzzy black caterpillars. After we had camped out for a week, the motel seemed *like a palace* to us.
Hyperbole: Obvious exaggeration for emphasis and effect.	It took *forever* to download the movie! The steak they served me *would have fed a dozen people!*
Personification: Giving human characteristics or qualities to nonhuman or nonliving things.	The words *danced* on the page before my tired eyes. Poverty *stole* their dream of a better life.

Skillful readers ask themselves, "Is the author using figurative language?" If the answer is yes, they ask these additional questions:

- "Are two things being compared and, if so, how are they alike?" (metaphor and simile)
- "Is there an obvious exaggeration?" (hyperbole)
- "Are human traits being given to nonliving or nonhuman things?" (personification)

Understanding figurative language helps you interpret an author's message correctly, and it also makes material more interesting and enjoyable to read.

EXERCISE 3

Directions: The sentence below contains a *figure of speech.* Read the sentence and answer the questions that follow.

When you first begin college, getting a degree can seem as distant as the horizon—but before you know it, you're graduating!

______ **1.** What two things are being compared?

a. graduating and beginning college
b. beginning college and the horizon
c. getting a degree and the horizon
d. graduating and the horizon

______ **2.** How are they alike?

a. Both are unusual.
b. Both seem challenging.
c. Both are beautiful.
d. Both can seem very far off.

______ **3.** How should this figure of speech be interpreted?

a. Graduation makes all of the college experience worthwhile.
b. Getting a college degree is nearly impossible.
c. When you start college, getting a degree can seem far off.
d. Beginning college is a difficult time.

OTHER THINGS TO KEEP IN MIND WHEN DEVELOPING A COLLEGE-LEVEL VOCABULARY

Here are four helpful things you should keep in mind with regard to developing a college-level vocabulary:

1. **Certain punctuation marks in a sentence can signal a definition.**

Commas, parentheses, brackets, dashes, and colons can be used to set off definitions in sentences. Each of the sample sentences below presents the statement "Ayurveda is older than Chinese medicine." However, because the author knows that many readers may not be familiar with the term *ayurveda,* he includes the definition in the sentence as well. Notice how the punctuation marks in each example signal that a definition is being given. The definition in each sentence appears in italics.

- *Commas* Ayurveda, *traditional Indian medicine based on herbal remedies,* is older than Chinese medicine.

  or

  A form of medicine that is older than Chinese medicine is ayurveda, *traditional Indian medicine based on herbal remedies.*
- *Parentheses* Ayurveda (*traditional Indian medicine based on herbal remedies*) is older than Chinese medicine.
- *Brackets* Ayurveda [*traditional Indian medicine based on herbal remedies*] is older than Chinese medicine.
- *Dashes* Ayurveda—*traditional Indian medicine based on herbal remedies*—is older than Chinese medicine.
- *Colon* A form of medicine that is older than Chinese medicine is ayurveda: *traditional Indian medicine based on herbal remedies.*

As you can see, there are several ways an author can use punctuation marks to set off a definition. In Chapter 7, "Recognizing Authors' Writing Patterns," you will learn about the definition pattern, a pattern that appears often in textbooks.

2. **The most common and helpful roots, prefixes, and suffixes in English come from Latin and ancient Greek.**

Although English is a Germanic language, it has thousands of words derived from Latin and ancient Greek. Today, the English language contains a considerable number of technological, scientific, and medical terms that are derived from Latin and Greek. If you take college courses in any of these areas, you will benefit greatly from knowing common Latin and Greek word parts.

Incidentally, knowing common Latin word parts also makes it easier to learn Spanish, French, Italian, Portuguese, and Romanian. These languages are referred to as *romance languages,* not because they have anything to do with love, but because they all draw so heavily on Latin. Latin was the "Roman" language because it was spoken in ancient Rome. For that reason, languages derived from Latin came to be known as romance languages. Of course, many Spanish, French, and Italian words such as *rodeo, boutique,* and *galleria* have also become words in English.

3. **A word's etymology (origin and history) indicates the word parts it was created from, including Latin or Greek ones.**

A word's etymology is its origin and history. Dictionaries usually give the etymology of a word in brackets [ ] before or after the definition. An etymology can be helpful because it tells the meaning of the original word parts from which the current word was derived. This can help you understand and remember the word's meaning more easily. For example, the prefix *re* means *back* and the root *ject* means to *throw.* The English word *reject* literally means "to throw back" (that is, not accept) something.

(continued on next page)

Copyright © 2014 The McGraw-Hill Companies, Inc. All rights reserved.

When you look up a word in the dictionary, make it a habit to examine the word's etymology. See if the word contains familiar word parts. Over time, you will expand not only your vocabulary but also your knowledge of word parts. And the more word parts you know, the easier it will be to develop your vocabulary. Below are examples of interesting words that have come into English from other languages. Their etymologies are given in brackets after the definitions.

al•ge•bra (ăl′ jə brə) *n.* A generalization of arithmetic in which symbols represent members of a specified set of numbers and are related by operations that hold for all numbers in the set. [< Arabic: al - jabr, "the (science of) reuniting."] al • ge • bra • ic (ăl jə brā′ ĭc) adj.

bou•tique (bo͞o tē k′) *n.* A small retail shop that specializes in gifts, fashionable clothes, and accessories. [French: from Old French, *botique,* small shop, from Old Provençal *botica,* from Latin *apothēca,* storehouse.]

cor•ral (kĕ răl′) *n.* 1. An enclosure for confining livestock. 2. An enclosure formed by a circle of wagons for defense against attack during an encampment.—*v. -ralled, -ralling, -als.* 1. To drive into and hold in a corral. 2. To arrange (wagons) in a corral. 3. To take control or possession of. *Informal.* To seize; capture. [Spanish: from Vulgar Latin **currāle,* enclosure for carts, from Latin *currus,* cart, from *currere,* to run.]

gal•le•ri•a (gă′lərē′ ə) *n.* A roofed passageway or indoor court usually containing a variety of shops or businesses. [Italian: from Old Italian.]

ro•de•o (rō′ dē ō, rō dā′ ō) *n., pl.* -os. 1. A cattle roundup. 2. A public exhibition of cowboy skills, including riding broncos, lassoing, etc. [Spanish: *rodear,* to surround.]

yen (yĕn) *n. Informal.* A yearning; a longing. [Cantonese: *yan.*]

4. Many words have a connotation as well as a denotation.

A word's dictionary definition is called *denotation*. However, many words also have a *connotation*, an additional, nonliteral meaning associated with the word. These do not appear in the dictionary, but they influence our choice of words. Take for example the word *used.* If a luxury car dealership sells used cars, they may describe them as "pre-owned" because it has a more positive connotation. "Used" has a neutral connotation. Describing a card as "secondhand," however, has a negative connotation. When you add a word to your vocabulary, pay attention not only to its dictionary definition, but also to any connotations it might have.

CHAPTER REVIEW CARDS

Review cards or *summary cards* are a way to select, organize, and summarize the important information in a textbook chapter. Preparing review cards helps you organize the information so that you can learn and memorize it more easily. In other words, chapter review cards are effective study tools.

Preparing chapter review cards for each chapter of *New Worlds* will give you practice in creating these valuable study tools. Once you have learned how to make chapter review cards, you can use actual index cards to create them for textbook material in your other courses and use them when you study for tests.

Now complete the chapter review cards for Chapter 2 by answering the questions or following the directions on each card. The page numbers indicate the place in the chapter where the information can be found. Write legibly. You will find it easier to complete the review cards if you remove these pages before filling them in.

Context Clues

What are *context clues*? (See page 65.)

Describe six types of context clues. (See the box on page 67.)

1. *definition:*
2. *synonym:*
3. *contrast:*
4. *experience:*
5. *example:*
6. *clue from another sentence:*

Card 1 Chapter 2: Developing a College-Level Vocabulary

Word-Structure Class

1. What are *word-structure clues*? (See page 68.)

2. Define each of these terms. (See page 69.)

root:

prefix:

suffix:

Card 2 Chapter 2: Developing a College-Level Vocabulary

Figurative Language

1. What is *figurative language*? (See page 76.)

2. Define each of these figures of speech. (See pages 76–77.)

metaphor:

simile:

hyperbole:

personification:

Card 3 Chapter 2: Developing a College-Level Vocabulary

TEST YOUR UNDERSTANDING
Context Clues, Part 1

***Review*: Context clues** are words in a sentence or paragraph that help the reader deduce (reason out) the meaning of an unfamiliar word. The types of context clues are:

- **Definition clue**—a definition for the word is given in the sentence.
- **Synonym clue**—a word is explained by a word or phrase that has a similar meaning.
- **Contrast clue**—a word is explained by a word or phrase that has an opposite meaning.
- **Experience clue**—the meaning can be understood based on your background knowledge or experience.
- **Example clue**—a word is explained by examples that illustrate its meaning.
- **Clue from another sentence**—another sentence in the paragraph explains the word.

Directions: Items 1–20 present sentences primarily from college textbooks. Each contains an important word or term that is *italicized.* Next, there is an additional sentence that uses the word in the same sense. This sentence provides a second context clue. Read both sentences and ask yourself, "What would this word have to mean in order to make sense in *both* sentences?" Use the context clues from both sentences to *deduce* the meaning of the italicized word. Remember, the answer you choose must make sense in both sentences. Write your answer in the space provided.

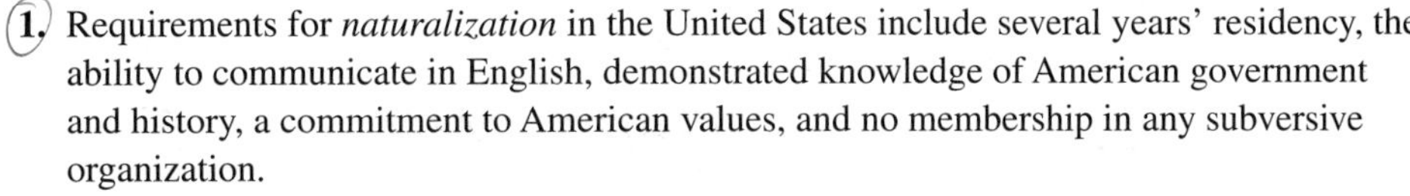

______ **1.** Requirements for *naturalization* in the United States include several years' residency, the ability to communicate in English, demonstrated knowledge of American government and history, a commitment to American values, and no membership in any subversive organization.

Through *naturalization,* millions of immigrants to the United States have become American citizens.

naturalization means:

a. process of becoming an immigrant
b. process of making something more natural
c. process by which a foreigner becomes a citizen of another country
d. process of establishing residency in a country

______ **2.** *Tsunamis,* or seismic sea waves, are often incorrectly called tidal waves.

Tsunamis are produced by underwater earthquakes.

tsunamis means:

a. underwater earthquakes
b. seismic sea waves
c. tidal waves
d. earthquakes

______ **3.** We harbor *stereotypes,* or prejudgments, of college professors, Asians, hairdressers, used car salespeople, the elderly, preachers, Southerners, Democrats, rap singers, and countless other groups of people.

Copyright © 2014 The McGraw-Hill Companies, Inc. All rights reserved.

Stereotypes originally referred to a metal printing plate or mold, but now refers to long-standing, oversimplified, exaggerated, inflexible prejudgments about groups of people.

stereotype means:

a. printing done with a metal plate
b. numerous groups of people
c. an oversimplification
d. a prejudgment about a group of people

________ **4.** The blurring of gender roles is clearly evident in many of today's *androgynous* styles and fashions, such as wearing earrings or having tattoos.

Both the male and the female employees protested their company's new uniforms of khaki slacks and blue shirts; they complained that the uniforms looked *androgynous.*

androgynous means:

a. not clearly masculine or feminine, as in dress, appearance, or behavior
b. wearing earrings or having long hair
c. wearing the styles and fashions of today
d. wearing a uniform

________ **5.** For a special promotion, many retail stores deliberately sell a product below its customary price, or even below cost, to attract attention to it. The purpose of this *loss-leader pricing* is not to sell more of that particular product but, rather, to attract customers in hopes that they will buy other products as well.

Mass merchandisers, such as Target, often sell DVDs at half their customary price because *loss-leader pricing* draws many customers to their stores.

loss-leader pricing means:

a. special promotions to sell videos
b. selling a product below its customary price, or even below cost, to attract customers in hopes that they will buy other products as well
c. retailing technique used by all mass merchandisers
d. attracting customers by selling things half price

________ **6.** *Blues* grew out of African American folk music, such as work songs, spirituals, and the field hollers of slaves.

It is uncertain exactly when *blues* originated, but by around the 1890s it was sung in rural areas in the South and was often performed with a guitar accompaniment.

blues means:

a. African American folk music that originated around the 1890s
b. work songs, spirituals, and field hollers of slaves
c. a form of vocal and instrumental music that grew out of African American folk music
d. music performed in the South

________ **7.** A densely populated area containing two or more cities and their suburbs has become known as a *megalopolis.*

An example of a *megalopolis* is the 500-mile corridor that stretches from Boston south to Washington, D.C., and includes New York City, Philadelphia, and Baltimore—one-sixth of the total population of the United States!

megalopolis means:

a. densely populated area containing two or more cities and their suburbs

b. areas existing in the United States, Great Britain, Germany, Italy, Egypt, India, Japan, and China

c. the 500-mile corridor that stretches from Boston south to Washington, D.C.

d. areas that equal one-sixth of the total population of the United States

______ **8.** Motorists are aware of an increasing sense of aggression on America's *congested* highways.

Malls can become so *congested* with Christmas shoppers that potential buyers give up and go home.

congested means:

a. flowing freely

b. overfilled or overcrowded

c. hostile

d. filled with pollution

______ **9.** New mothers seem more *susceptible* to stress and fatigue because they are now primary caregivers as well as wives, homemakers, and often employees.

Not eating a balanced diet or getting enough sleep can make you more *susceptible* to colds and other infections.

susceptible means:

a. having an unknown effect

b. unaffected by

c. having no effect upon

d. easily affected by

______ **10.** Listing your qualifications on your résumé gives a prospective employer *tangible* clues about the type of person you are.

Many people enjoy volunteer work immensely even though they receive no pay or other *tangible* rewards for their time and service.

tangible means:

a. pertaining to an actual object or something real

b. free; having no cost

c. pertaining to a legal matter

d. expensive; costly

______ **11.** Many states have now prohibited *capital punishment,* but some states still execute those who are convicted of first-degree murder.

Opponents of *capital punishment* cite numerous death-row inmates who have been cleared of crimes as a result of DNA testing that is now available.

capital punishment means:

a. severe punishment

b. the penalty of death for a crime

c. punishment decreed by the government

d. life imprisonment

_______ **12.** The Mississippi River, the longest river in the United States, *meanders* from Minnesota to Louisiana before emptying into the Gulf of Mexico.

The writer described himself as a vagabond who *meanders* through life, open to every new adventure and experience.

meanders means:

a. flows
b. stays
c. wanders
d. visits

_______ **13.** The *façade* of an art deco style building is characterized by the use of chrome, steel, glass and aluminum, geometric patterns, and a rich display of surface decoration.

Over time air pollution has eroded the *façade* of many ancient buildings in Venice, Italy.

façade means:

a. building
b. exterior
c. interior
d. windows

_______ **14.** "Ice cold," "little baby," and "old antique" are examples of *redundant* phrases.

To use time effectively, employees should avoid *redundant* activities such as writing an e-mail message and leaving the same message on voice mail.

redundant means:

a. needlessly repetitive; unnecessary
b. useful; helpful
c. exact; precise
d. boring; uninteresting

_______ **15.** Many art treasures exist today because rulers such as the Roman emperor Augustus and the Byzantine emperor Justinian chose to *glorify* themselves through art.

Throughout the ages cathedrals, hymns, and paintings have been created to *glorify* God.

glorify means:

a. to make larger
b. to give glory, honor, or praise
c. to hide weaknesses
d. to create a portrait of

_______ **16.** In their autobiography, sisters Sarah and Elizabeth Delany, who both lived more than 100 years, attributed their *longevity* to doing what they felt was right for them and to helping others.

Careful eating, regular exercise, sufficient rest, and a positive attitude contribute to a person's *longevity.*

longevity means:

a. intelligence

b. wealth

c. long length of life

d. physical endurance

17. The *Middle Ages,* the period of European history between ancient times and modern times, began with the fall of Rome in the fifth century and ended with the Renaissance in the fourteenth century.

During the *Middle Ages,* life for peasants was difficult, harsh, and short.

Middle Ages means:

a. ancient times

b. the period of time when peasants lived

c. the period in a person's life between the ages of forty and sixty

d. the period of European history between ancient times and modern times

18. The white marble Taj Mahal, a magnificent tomb built in the mid–seventeenth century by a Mogul emperor for his beloved wife, is perhaps the most famous *mausoleum* in the world.

In England, the ancestors of distinguished families are often buried in a *mausoleum* on the grounds of the family's estate.

mausoleum means:

a. a simple, unmarked grave

b. a building designed as a burial vault

c. a building constructed of stone

d. a place where bodies are kept before burial

19. By learning how to reduce conflict, managers and supervisors can help angry employees avoid an *altercation.*

To avoid danger to themselves, police officers receive training in how to break up a violent *altercation.*

altercation means:

a. a loud party

b. loud music

c. a loud argument

d. a loud celebration

20. Strokes can result in paralysis which, in turn, can cause the unused muscles to *atrophy.*

When a broken arm or leg is placed in a cast, the muscles begin to *atrophy* from lack of movement.

atrophy means:

a. to grow stronger

b. to shrink

c. to stretch

d. to disappear

TEST YOUR UNDERSTANDING
Context Clues, Part 2

Directions: Answer the following questions. In some, you will be asked about the *type of context clue* in the sentence. In others, you must *use context clues to determine the meaning* of the underlined word(s).

_______ **1.** Many miners suffer from **black lung disease**, a respiratory condition that results from the accumulation of fine coal-dust particles in their lungs.

The type of context clue in the sentence above is a(n):

a. synonym clue.
b. definition clue.
c. contrast cue.
d. example clue.

_______ **2.** Math is cumulative, building on prior concepts and knowledge.

As used in the sentence above, the word *cumulative* means:

a. hard to understand.
b. successively adding information.
c. unusual; out of the ordinary.
d. sophisticated; cultured; refined.

_______ **3.** Of all the horror-story characters, Frankenstein, with his oversized, oddly shaped head and the bolt through his neck, is one of the most grotesque looking.

As used in the sentence above, the word *grotesque* means:

a. tall and slender.
b. amusing; comical.
c. deformed; bizarre.
d. angry; hostile.

_______ **4.** The vast majority of injuries that occur each year are *unintentional injuries*, such as falls, motor vehicle accidents, drownings, unintentional poisonings and suffocation, fires, and the accidental discharge of firearms.

In the passage above, the type of context clue is a(n):

a. example clue.
b. contrast clue.
c. synonym clue.
d. definition clue.

_______ **5.** *Bankruptcy* is a legal term indicating that a person is financially insolvent and unable to pay his or her debts.

In the sentence above, what are the clue words that indicate a definition is being presented?

a. is a legal term
b. indicating that a person
c. is financially insolvent
d. and unable to pay his or her debts

_______ **6.** Compared with what they do in person, writers using e-mail are more likely to be insulting, swear, name-call, and make hostile statements. *Flaming* is the name given to this behavior.

In the passage above, which type of context clue reveals the meaning of *flaming*?

a. definition clue

b. synonym clue

c. contrast clue

d. clue from another sentence

_______ **7.** In college, elective (nonrequired) courses allow you to explore subjects that simply sound interesting to you.

In the sentence above, what is the meaning of *elective*?

a. college

b. nonrequired

c. interesting

d. required

_______ **8.** *Assertive communication* involves expressing your thoughts, feelings, and desires as your right as an individual, whereas *passive communication* is characterized by an unwillingness to say what you think, feel, or want.

Which type of context clue appears in the sentence above?

a. definition clue

b. synonym clue

c. contrast clue

d. example clue

_______ **9.** When Lola was not chosen homecoming queen, she declared she never really wanted to win. It was sour grapes on her part!

In the passage above, *sour grapes* means:

a. denying you ever wanted something that you did not get.

b. leaving a bitter taste in the mouth.

c. being gracious and courteous.

d. being competitive.

_______ **10.** **Persuasive listening** is hardly listening at all. The "listener" is really looking for an opening to jump in and control the direction of the conversation.

As used in the passage above, the term *persuasive listening* describes someone who is:

a. hardly listening at all.

b. a "listener."

c. not really listening but instead wants to take over the conversation.

_______ **11.** To perform better on tests, get rid of *negative self-talk* ("I'm no good at biology" or "I know I'm going to fail this test").

Which type of context clue appears in the sentence above?

a. definition clue

b. synonym clue

c. contrast clue

d. example clue

_______ **12.** The regular, systematic balancing of income and expenses is called ***budgeting***.

In the sentence above, what are the clue words that indicate a definition context clue?

a. regular, systematic balancing

b. of income and expenses

c. is called

d. budgeting

_______ **13.** Many *viruses*—those rogue programs that can seriously damage your PC or programs—ride along with e-mail as attached files.

In the sentence above, which clues indicate a definition is being presented? *Choose all that apply.*

a. commas

b. hyphens

c. dashes

d. special print

_______ **14.** In 1934 the Federal Communications Commission (FCC) instituted the **equal time rule** to promote equity in broadcasting. The rule requires a broadcast station to provide airtime equally (whether free or paid) to all political candidates if it provides airtime to any.

As used in the passage above, the term *equal time rule* refers to broadcast stations being required to:

a. contact the FCC.

b. promote equity in broadcasting.

c. give all political candidates equal airtime.

d. restrict political candidates' broadcast time.

_______ **15.** Many people use acronyms—for instance, "FACE" to remember the notes of the spaces on the musical staff or "ROY G. BIV" to remember the colors of the rainbow in order.

In the sentence above, which words signal an example context clue?

a. acronyms

b. "FACE"

c. the notes of the spaces on the musical staff

d. for instance

_______ **16.** The topic of the philosopher's thoughtful, well-reasoned treatise is "What Is Truth?"

As used in the passage above, the word *treatise* means a:

a. lengthy written discussion.

b. tale or story.

c. hostile attack.

d. work of fiction.

Copyright © 2014 The McGraw-Hill Companies, Inc. All rights reserved.

_______ **17.** Mistakes are opportunities to learn, so rather than feel dispirited by them, you should feel heartened.

As used in the sentence above, the word *dispirited* means:

a. appreciative.

b. enthusiastic.

c. happy; joyful.

d. disheartened; discouraged.

_______ **18.** One impediment to critical thinking is the tendency to jump to conclusions.

As used in the sentence above, the word *impediment* means:

a. obstacle.

b. skill.

c. aid.

d. benefit.

_______ **19.** Some interest rates are *fixed,* which means that they don't vary from month to month; others are *variable,* which means they change each month.

Which words in the sentence above announce a contrast clue? *Choose all that apply.*

a. interest rates

b. fixed; variable

c. Some; others

d. don't vary; change

_______ **20.** Our self-concept, or view of ourselves, has three parts.

Which word in the sentence above announces a synonym or a restatement clue?

a. self-concept

b. or

c. three

d. parts

TEST YOUR UNDERSTANDING
Word-Structure Clues, Part 1

Review: **Word-structure clues** are roots, prefixes, and suffixes that help you determine a word's meaning. The three categories of word parts are:

- **Roots**—base words that have meaning on their own.
- **Prefixes**—word parts attached to the beginnings of roots that add their meaning to the roots.
- **Suffixes**—word parts attached to the ends of root words.

Directions: Each sentence in items 1–20 contains an *italicized* word whose word parts—roots, prefixes, or suffixes—give a clue to its meaning. Use the word part that is in **boldface** print to give you a clue to the word's meaning. (See the lists of roots, prefixes, and suffixes on pages 70–74.) Some words contain more than one word part; this will give you additional help in determining the meaning of the word. (When possible, use context clues to confirm your answer choice.) Write your answers in the spaces provided.

_______ **1.** Harold is an ***a****typical* student because he started college when he was 16.

a. typical
b. not typical
c. normal
d. ordinary

_______ **2.** It is easy to understand her on the telephone because of her ***dic****tion.*

a. pleasant way of saying things
b. clear, distinct pronunciation
c. use of complex words
d. use of the dictionary

_______ **3.** The serial killer known as Jack the Ripper was a notorious *miso****gyn****ist* who slashed many women to death in London in the late nineteenth century.

a. someone who fails at marriage
b. someone who hates marriage
c. someone who hates women
d. someone who hates adolescents

_______ **4.** The ***biblio****phile* owned more than a thousand volumes and was proud of his extensive book collection.

a. book lover
b. librarian
c. bookseller
d. rare book dealer

_______ **5.** The Vietnam Memorial in Washington, D.C., is a black marble monument that is permanently *inscribed* with the names of all persons in the U.S. armed services who died in the Vietnam War.

a. illustrated
b. engraved
c. painted
d. decorated

_______ **6.** Teenagers who drive recklessly must think they are ***im**mortal.*

a. not able to die

b. above the law

c. impressive

d. susceptible to injury

_______ **7.** Lisa tried to ***con**vert* other members of her family to vegetarianism, but they refused to give up meat.

a. dissuade

b. discourage

c. turn aside

d. turn others to one's way of thinking or behaving

_______ **8.** The lifeguard quickly pulled the child from the bottom of the swimming pool and *re**viv**ed* him with CPR.

a. brought back to life or consciousness

b. expelled water from the lungs

c. made strong again

d. rescued

_______ **9.** The historian ***chron**icled* the events leading up to the Iraq War.

a. disproved

b. discussed

c. presented in order

d. disapproved of

B_______ **10.** *Poly**gamy*** is illegal in the United States.

a. being married to two or more people at the same time

b. being married to two women at the same time

c. being married to two men at the same time

d. being married to two or more people one at a time

_______ **11.** My father has four sisters, and of all my ***pater**nal* aunts, I like Aunt Jane best.

a. pertaining to the father

b. pertaining to the mother

c. pertaining to relatives

d. pertaining to brothers

_______ **12.** Adriana is a ***vers**atile* artist who works in clay, stone, and metal.

a. hardworking

b. able to do many different things

c. beginning

d. outdoor

_______ **13.** We refused to open the front door until the police officers showed us their ***cred**entials.*

a. weapon

b. police car

c. subpoena

d. identification or other evidence of authority

_______ **14.** Professor Howe chose an office on the first floor because she has *acro***phobia.**

a. a fear of earthquakes

b. a fear of heights

c. a fear of work

d. a fear of thunderstorms

_______ **15.** I tell my sister Mary everything; she has been my best friend and *con***fid***ant* all my life.

a. person you trust will keep your secrets

b. relative who is close in age

c. enjoyable companion

d. person who belongs to a religious order

_______ **16.** The surgeon took a ***bio****psy* from the tumor and sent it to the laboratory for analysis.

a. report

b. fluid

c. X-ray

d. sample of living tissue

A _______ **17.** The body of the homeless person was sent to the city ***mor****gue* until an identification could be made.

a. place where dead bodies are kept temporarily

b. place where bodies are cremated

c. place where bodies are prepared for burial

d. place where bodies are maintained in crypts

_______ **18.** Collectors who have ***soph****isticated* taste in art often have their paintings featured in art magazines.

a. too expensive for the average collector

b. unusual

c. knowledgeable and informed

d. modern or contemporary

B _______ **19.** Although spanking used to be a common way to handle disciplinary problems, most school districts now prohibit ***corpor****al* punishment.

a. pertaining to the body

b. pertaining to the military

c. pertaining to schools

d. pertaining to young children

A _______ **20.** The young millionaire was a generous ***phil****anthropist* who paid for a new wing of the children's hospital.

a. one who does things for love of humankind

b. one who has limited financial resources

c. one who has great interest in medical research

d. one who has had a serious illness

TEST YOUR UNDERSTANDING
Word-Structure Clues, Part 2

Directions: Study the following roots and their meaning. Then use these important word parts, along with context clues, to determine the meaning of the underlined word in each sentence.

Root	*Meaning*	*Example Words*
bio	life, living	biology, biography, bionic
chrono	time	chronology, chronometer
flect, flex	bend	reflection, reflex, flex
magn	big, great	magnify, magnificent
manu	hand, make, do	manufacture, manicure, manuscript
mit, miss	send, put	submit, transmit, emission
patri, pater	father	patriotic, patron, paterfamilias
pel, puls	push, drive	repel, compel, expulsion
ven, vene, vent	come	prevent, event, intervention
vid, view, vis	see, look	visible, review, videodisc, vision

_______ **1.** The movie actor selected a well-known biographer to help him with his memoir.

Biographer refers to a person who writes the story of someone's:

a. family.

b. career.

c. life.

_______ **2.** The writing instructor gave students time in class to revise their essays.

Revise means to:

a. do additional research on.

b. discuss with others.

c. look at it again to reconsider and change.

_______ **3.** Diabetes, multiple sclerosis, and cystic fibrosis are examples of chronic illnesses.

Chronic means:

a. related to muscles.

b. continuing over time.

c. requiring medical care.

_______ **4.** In 1863 President Abraham Lincoln emancipated the slaves.

Emancipated means:

a. sympathized with.

b. made free from oppression.

c. supported.

_______ **5.** We put ant repellent in the kitchen cabinets.

Repellent means something that:

a. drives something away.

b. attracts something.

c. looks attractive.

_______ **6.** John gave his two daughters the patronymics Johnna and Johnetta.

Patronymics refers to names that are:

a. derived from the father's name.

b. given to girls.

c. nicknames.

_______ **7.** The satellite continued to emit a faint signal.

Emit means to:

a. record.

b. pick up.

c. send out.

_______ **8.** Because of its magnitude, the tsunami devastated the coast of Japan.

Magnitude means:

a. origin.

b. great size.

c. high speed.

_______ **9.** Flexor muscles are important for lifting and stooping.

Flexor muscles are ones that:

a. are especially strong.

b. stretch farther than most muscles.

c. bend limbs or joints in the body.

_______ **10.** My great-great-grandmother's diary chronicled her family's trip west in a covered wagon in the 1800s.

Chronicled means:

a. evaluated.

b. recorded events in the order they happened.

c. presented an imaginary version of.

_______ **11.** Magnification can be of significant help to the visually impaired.

Magnification means:

a. making something look larger.

b. driving.

c. reading aloud.

_______ **12.** Many companies that care about the environment make products that are biodegradable.

Biodegradable products:

a. are less expensive.

b. meet government regulations.

c. can be broken down by living organisms, especially bacteria.

_______ **13.** The convent is a quiet, peaceful place.

Convent refers to a:

a. very large building.

b. place where women who take religious vows come together to lead a life devoted to God.

c. workshop where things are crafted by hand.

_______ **14.** Typing, knitting, and playing the piano require manual dexterity.

Manual dexterity means skillful use of the:

a. voice.

b. hands.

c. eyes.

_______ **15.** Navy Seals and Army Special Forces are trained to carry out secret missions.

Missions means:

a. military operations done at sea.

b. special assignments a group is sent to do.

c. combat in other countries.

_______ **16.** The country club expelled the two feuding members.

Expelled means:

a. scolded.

b. fined.

c. pushed out.

_______ **17.** The jury will reconvene at 9 o'clock on Monday morning.

Reconvene means:

a. be televised.

b. end.

c. come together again.

_______ **18.** The window was so clean that the glass was invisible.

Invisible means:

a. sparkling.

b. cannot be seen.

c. extremely fragile.

_______ **19.** My wonderful uncle has always taken a paternal interest in me.

Paternal means:

a. special.

b. related to family relationships.

c. like a father.

_______ **20.** The soldier's hands flexed nervously as he spoke to the general.

Flexed means:

a. perspired.

b. clenched.

c. bent repeatedly.

Copyright © 2014 The McGraw-Hill Companies, Inc. All rights reserved.

TEST YOUR UNDERSTANDING
Figurative Language, Part 1

Review: **Figurative language** is the use of words that present unusual comparisons or create vivid pictures in the reader's mind. Four types of figurative language are:

- **Metaphor**—figure of speech suggesting a comparison between two seemingly dissimilar things, usually by saying that one of them *is* the other.
- **Simile**—figure of speech presenting a comparison between two seemingly dissimilar things by saying that one of them is *like* the other.
- **Hyperbole**—figure of speech using obvious exaggeration for emphasis and effect.
- **Personification**—figure of speech in which nonhuman or nonliving things are given human traits.

Directions: Items 1–20 present sentences that contain *figures of speech.* Each figure of speech is *italicized.* Read each sentence. Answer the questions that follow each sentence. Remember that to answer the last question for each item correctly, you must *interpret* the meaning of the figurative language. Write your answer in the space provided.

Fear washed over me *like a tidal wave* when I saw the truck coming toward me in my lane.

_____ **1.** What two things are being compared?

a. a truck and a tidal wave
b. a truck and fear
c. the person and a truck
d. fear and a tidal wave

_____ **2.** How are they alike?

a. Both are unusual.
b. Both are overwhelming.
c. Both are temporary.
d. Both pertain to water.

_____ **3.** How should this simile be interpreted?

a. The driver felt terrified.
b. The driver felt irritated.
c. The driver felt relieved.
d. The driver felt wet.

My supervisor refused to let me have Saturday off to go to my family reunion. Her *heart is a stone*!

_____ **4.** What two things are being compared?

a. a family reunion and the supervisor's heart
b. the supervisor's heart and a stone
c. a stone and a supervisor
d. the supervisor and the family

_____ **5.** How are they alike?

a. Both are hard and unyielding.
b. Both are alive.
c. Both are broken.
d. Both are attending a reunion.

Copyright © 2014 The McGraw-Hill Companies, Inc. All rights reserved.

______ **6.** How should this metaphor be interpreted?

a. The supervisor is hard-hearted.

b. The family reunion is Saturday.

c. The supervisor dislikes family reunions.

d. The speaker is hard-hearted.

If I lived in Switzerland, I'd *spend 24 hours a day skiing.*

______ **7.** What is the hyperbole (exaggeration)?

a. living in Switzerland

b. spending 24 hours a day skiing

c. going skiing

d. knowing how to ski

______ **8.** How should this hyperbole be interpreted?

a. The person loves to ski.

b. The person wants to live in Switzerland.

c. The person has a lot of free time.

d. The person wants to learn to ski.

The tree root *reached up, grabbed my foot,* and sent me sprawling.

______ **9.** What is being given human traits?

a. tree

b. tree root

c. my foot

d. all of the above

______ **10.** How should this personification be interpreted?

a. I ran into a tree.

b. I grabbed a tree.

c. I stepped over a foot-long tree root.

d. I tripped on a tree root and fell.

Mark's little brother was *as still as a statue.*

______ **11.** What two things are being compared?

a. Mark and his little brother

b. Mark's little brother and a statue

c. Mark and a statue

d. all of the above

______ **12.** How are they alike?

a. Both did not move.

b. Both have excellent posture.

c. Both were silent.

d. none of the above

______ **13.** How should this simile be interpreted?

a. Mark did not move.

b. Mark's little brother did not move.

c. A statue does not make any sound.

d. A statue does not move.

The twin sisters are *as alike as mirror images.*

_______ **14.** What is being compared?

a. twin sisters

b. a set of twin sisters and mirror images

c. twins and sisters

d. mirror images

_______ **15.** How are they alike?

a. They have similar personalities.

b. They are identical in appearance.

c. They often behave in the same manner.

d. They have similar beliefs.

_______ **16.** How should this metaphor be interpreted?

a. The twins are identical twins.

b. The sisters are looking in the mirror.

c. The sisters are twins.

d. Mirror images are identical.

After I received an "A" on my history test, I picked up my books and *danced all the way home!*

_______ **17.** What is the hyperbole (exaggeration)?

a. receiving an "A" on my history test

b. picking up my books

c. dancing all the way home

d. all of the above

_______ **18.** How should this hyperbole be interpreted?

a. The person is an excellent student.

b. The person likes history.

c. The person was very excited about the history test grade.

d. The person loves to dance.

***Opportunity knocks* on everyone's door at least once.**

_______ **19.** What is being given human traits?

a. opportunity

b. the door

c. everyone

d. all of the above

_______ **20.** How should this personification be interpreted?

a. Some people never have a good opportunity in life.

b. There are only a few opportunities in each person's life.

c. No one deserves more than one opportunity in his or her lifetime.

d. Everybody receives at least one good opportunity during his or her life.

TEST YOUR UNDERSTANDING
Figurative Language, Part 2

Directions: Identify the type of figurative language (figure of speech) in each sentence below.

_______ **1.** When the fire alarm sounded, the crowd scattered like dice flung across a gaming table.

a. metaphor
b. simile
c. hyperbole
d. personification

_______ **2.** "Reason often makes mistakes, but conscience never does." —Josh Billings, American humorist

a. metaphor
b. simile
c. hyperbole
d. personification

_______ **3.** "I have always imagined that Paradise will be a kind of library." —Jorge Luis Borges

a. metaphor
b. simile
c. hyperbole
d. personification

_______ **4.** If you need me, I'll be there in a heartbeat.

a. metaphor
b. simile
c. hyperbole
d. personification

_______ **5.** "Success is shy—it won't come out while you're watching." —Tennessee Williams, American playwright

a. metaphor
b. simile
c. hyperbole
d. personification

_______ **6.** The fog tiptoed in early this morning.

a. metaphor
b. simile
c. hyperbole
d. personification

_______ **7.** The child's chubby fingers looked like 10 little sausages.

a. metaphor
b. simile
c. hyperbole
d. personification

_______ **8.** My grandfather's snoring is louder than a freight train!

a. metaphor
b. simile

c. hyperbole

d. personification

_______ **9.** "Life is like a box of chocolates: you never know what you're going to get."

—*Forrest Gump* (movie)

a. metaphor

b. simile

c. hyperbole

d. personification

_______ **10.** "Life is a highway." —Rascal Flatts

a. metaphor

b. simile

c. hyperbole

d. personification

Directions: Interpret the *meaning* of the figurative language in each sentence below.

_______ **11.** "'Cause she's bittersweet / She knocks me off my feet." —Click Five, "Just the Girl"

a. She really impresses me.

b. She is angry and bitter.

c. She is skilled at martial arts.

_______ **12.** ". . . With her shoes in her hands, I am watching her dance / As the hem of her dress gently kisses the grass." —Ron Pope, "Fireflies"

a. She is getting grass stains on the bottom edge of her dress.

b. The bottom of her dress is gently brushing against the grass.

c. She is barefooted.

_______ **13.** Lately, my life has been a rollercoaster.

a. Recently, I have had good and bad experiences.

b. Recently, I have started feeling afraid of heights.

c. Recently, I have had a lot of fun.

_______ **14.** "Do you ever feel, feel so paper thin / Like a house of cards, one blow from caving in?" —

Katy Perry, "Firework"

a. Do you ever feel that you are in an emotionally fragile state?

b. Do you ever feel that you would like to forget everything and just play cards?

c. Do you ever feel that you need to lose weight?

_______ **15.** "My mirror speaks. / It never minces words."

—Death Cab for Cutie, "My Mirror Speaks"

a. My mirror is not a reliable indicator of what I look like.

b. My mirror distorts my image.

c. My mirror tells me exactly how I look, even when I look bad.

_______ **16.** Last winter was so cold that even penguins were wearing jackets.

a. Because of global warming, the polar ice caps are melting.

b. Not enough is being done to protect penguins.

c. Last winter was extremely cold.

_______ **17.** When Ed was named the winner, he was out of his seat like a lightning bolt.

a. He was arrogant about winning.

b. He didn't hear his name called.

c. He leaped up very quickly.

_______ **18.** Health is wealth.

a. Health care is expensive.

b. Unless you have your health, you have nothing.

c. You have to be healthy to get a job.

_______ **19.** "You change your mind like a girl changes clothes." —Katy Perry, "Hot and Cold"

a. You are overly concerned about your appearance.

b. You have too many choices.

c. You change your mind frequently.

_______ **20.** "Phillip is just a rhinestone cowboy!"

a. He is a fake, not the real thing.

b. He likes bling.

c. He lives on a ranch.

SELECTION **2.1**

Student Success

Overcoming Obstacles

From *Peak Performance in College and Beyond*

By Sharon Ferrett

Professional basketball player Michael Jordan is considered by most sportswriters and analysts to be the greatest athlete of all time. He once said, "I've missed more than 9,000 shots in my career. I've lost almost 300 games. Twenty-six times, I've been trusted to take the game winning shot—and missed. I've failed over and over and over again in my life. And that is why I succeed."

Babe Ruth was one of the greatest home run hitters in the history of baseball, with a career total of 714. In two different seasons he hit more home runs than any other entire team. Many people forget, however, that Ruth struck out 1,330 times. Said Ruth, "Every strike brings me closer to the next home run" and "You just can't beat the person who never gives up."

Successful people learn to overcome obstacles and keep moving ahead: it is one of the keys to their success. In college, as in life, you will face many obstacles. Read the following selection on the topic of overcoming obstacles.

How Do You Cope with Setbacks?

1 Even peak performers sometimes feel discouraged and need help climbing out of life's valleys. To create and maintain a positive state of mind and learn self-management, you cannot just read a book, attend a lecture, or use a few strategies for a day or two. It takes time and effort. Everyone gets off course now and then, but the key is to realize that setbacks are part of life. Don't allow setbacks to make you feel as if you have failed and can no longer reach your goal. To overcome adversity, you must be resilient. The ability to bounce back or adapt to difficult or challenging life experiences will enable you to thrive under pressure. Find a way to create a positive, resourceful mindset.

2 Figure 1 shows reasons students have given for dropping out of college. Many of these seem out of the students' control, but many may simply be excuses for not persevering. For example, not all classes will be exhilarating and indeed may seem boring at times—but is that a reason to give up? If you think, "I'll be more motivated as soon as I graduate and get a real job," you may never develop the necessary qualities and skills to achieve that. Starting today, you should

- Commit to being motivated and positive.
- Focus on your successes and accomplishments.
- Surround yourself with positive, supportive, and encouraging friends.
- Tell yourself, "This is a setback, not a failure."
- Learn self-control and self-management techniques.
- Make certain you are physically renewed: get more rest, exercise more, and every day do something you love.

Prediction Exercises

Directions: Use the skill of predicting to anticipate what the upcoming paragraphs will be about.

Prediction Exercise

What do you predict the first paragraph will be about?

____

____

____

____

Prediction Exercise

What do you predict paragraph 2 will be about?

____

____

____

____

____

Copyright © 2014 The McGraw-Hill Companies, Inc. All rights reserved.

FIGURE 1

REASONS STUDENTS DO NOT GRADUATE

Juggling the demands of work and school is a major reason why students drop out of college. Besides the reasons cited in this survey, students also struggle with poor study habits, managing their social time, and taking responsibility for their education—including asking for help. *Which "reasons" in the survey are you facing and how are you coping in order to achieve your goals?*

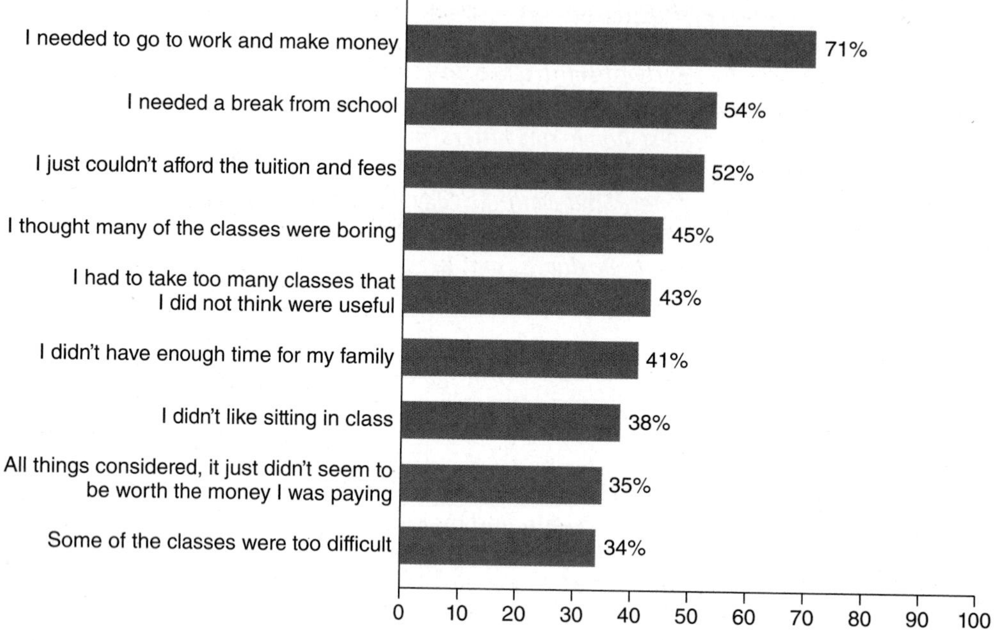

Source: Jean Johnson and Jon Rochkind with Amber N. Ott and Samantha DuPont, "With Their Whole Lives Ahead of Them: Myths and Realities About Why So Many Students Fail to Finish College." A Public Agenda Report for The Bill & Melinda Gates Foundation, December 20, 2009. Reprinted with permission.

- Replace negative self-talk and negative, self-limiting thoughts with affirmations and positive visualization.
- Read about people who received negative "messages," were discouraged, but bounced back.

Prediction Exercise

What do you predict paragraphs 3 and 4 will be about?

____

____

____

____

____

____

Your Beliefs and Expectations Matter

3 Your beliefs and expectations about yourself can either limit or expand your success. Other people's expectations of you may cause you to change who you think you are and what you think you can achieve. You may start to believe negative things you tell yourself or hear from others again and again, and this can limit your thinking and your success.

4 For example, Steve comes from a long line of lumber mill workers. Although they have lived for generations in a college town, his family has never had anything to do with the college. Steve was expected to go to work at the mill right after high school. He never thought about other options. However, during his senior year in high school, he attended Career Day. He met instructors and students from the local college who were friendly and encouraging. His world opened up, and he saw opportunities he had never considered. Steve experienced a major mind shift. Although he had to overcome a lack of support at home, he is now a successful college student with a bright future.

5 College is an ideal time to develop your natural creativity and explore new ways of thinking. What factors can you change in order to overcome obstacles and make yourself more successful?

Prediction Exercise

What do you predict the last paragraph will be about?

____

____

____

____

Source: Adapted from Sharon Ferrett, *Peak Performance: Success in College and Beyond,* 8th ed., pp. 60–63. Copyright © 2012 by McGraw-Hill. Reprinted by permission of The McGraw-Hill Companies.

Copyright © 2014 The McGraw-Hill Companies, Inc. All rights reserved.

Comprehension and Vocabulary Quiz

This quiz has several parts. Your instructor may assign some or all of them.

Comprehension

Directions: Items 1–5 test your understanding of the selection. They are the types of questions a content-area instructor (such as a student success professor) might ask on a test. You may refer to the selection as you answer the questions. Write your answer choice in the space provided.

_______ **1.** Setbacks:

a. can be prevented.
b. cause people to bounce back.
c. are part of life.
d. create a resourceful mind.

_______ **2.** Persevering in college:

a. can help you develop qualities and skills needed for success in a career.
b. is a setback, not a failure.
c. makes you less resilient than you otherwise would be.
d. is exhilarating on a day-to-day basis.

_______ **3.** Your beliefs and expectations about yourself are important because they can:

a. commit you to being motivated.
b. teach you self-control.
c. limit or expand your success.
d. influence other people's opinions of you.

_______ **4.** Steve's life changed after he:

a. talked with his family.
b. dropped out of high school.
c. attended Career Day during his senior year in high school.
d. completed his first year of college.

_______ **5.** An ideal time to develop your creativity and try new ways of thinking is:

a. during your senior year in high school.
b. during college.
c. on the job.
d. tomorrow.

Vocabulary in Context

Directions: Items 6–10 test your ability to determine a word's meaning by using context clues. *Context clues* are words in a sentence that allow readers to deduce (reason out) the meaning of an unfamiliar word. They also help readers determine the meaning an author intends when a word has more than one meaning. Each item below consists of a sentence from the selection, with the vocabulary word *italicized*. It is followed by another sentence that uses the same word in the same way. Use context clues to deduce the meaning of the *italicized* word. Be sure the meaning you choose makes sense in *both* sentences. Write each answer in the space provided. (This chapter presents the skill of using context clues.)

_______ **6.** Even peak performers sometimes feel discouraged and need help climbing out of life's *valleys*.

Although Martin is doing well now, a bankruptcy and the failure of his first marriage were *valleys* in his young adulthood.

valleys (văl′ ēz) means:

a. areas between mountains
b. peaks
c. periods of unemployment
d. low points

_______ **7.** To overcome *adversity*, you must be resilient.

Abraham Lincoln had humble beginnings and faced great *adversity* in life, but he nevertheless became one of the nation's greatest presidents.

adversity (ăd vûr′ sĭ tē) means:

a. hardship; misfortune
b. unpopularity
c. danger
d. achievement; success

_______ **8.** To overcome adversity, you must be *resilient*.

Inventor Thomas Edison was a *resilient* man who never let his failures discourage him.

resilient (rĭ zĭl′ yənt) means:

a. able to recover quickly
b. creative
c. likely to give excuses
d. inclined to daydream

_______ **9.** The ability to bounce back or adapt to difficult or challenging life experiences will enable you to *thrive* under pressure.

To *thrive* in college, you must make attending class and studying two of your top priorities.

thrive (thrīv) means:

a. see possibilities
b. stand up
c. do well
d. study

_______ **10.** Replace negative self-talk and negative, self-limiting thoughts with *affirmations* and positive visualization.

Before she takes any test, Marie calms herself and builds her confidence by quietly repeating *affirmations*.

affirmations (ăf ər mā′ shənz) means:

a. test-taking strategies

b. formulas that have been memorized

c. positive, supportive statements

d. memory pegs

Word Structure

Directions: Items 11–15 test your ability to use word-structure clues to help determine a word's meaning. *Word-structure clues* consist of roots, prefixes, and suffixes. In this exercise, you will learn the meaning of a root and use it to determine the meaning of several words that contain it. If you need to use a dictionary to confirm your answer choice, do so. Write your answers in the spaces provided.

In paragraph 5 of the selection, you encountered the word **factors.** It contains the root ***fac***, which means "make" or "do." In this selection, *factors* refers to something that "makes an active contribution to an accomplishment, result, or process." Use the meaning of ***fac*** and the list of prefixes on pages 72–73 to determine the meaning of each of the following words.

_______ **11.** A **factory** is a place where things are:

a. bought.

b. sold.

c. traded.

d. made.

_______ **12.** To feel **satisfaction** means to feel:

a. content.

b. angry.

c. silly.

d. ill.

_______ **13.** To **manufacture** items is to:

a. produce them.

b. recycle them.

c. collect them.

d. donate them.

_______ **14.** In comic books and cartoons, **malefactors** are characters who:

a. are superheroes.

b. do criminal or evil things.

c. are able to change form.

d. are disguised as animals.

_______ **15.** A **benefactor** is a person who:

a. inherits money.
b. reads widely
c. does good by giving money.
d. grows abundant crops.

Reading Skills Application

Directions: Items 16–20 test your ability to *apply* certain reading skills. You may not be familiar with all the skills yet, so some items will serve as a preview. As you work through *New Worlds*, you will practice and develop these skills. These are important skills, which is why they are included on the state-mandated basic skills tests that some students must take. Write each answer in the space provided.

_______ **16.** According to the bar graph, what percentage of students reported that they dropped out because some of the classes were too difficult?

a. 41%
b. 38%
c. 33%
d. 34%

_______ **17.** In paragraph 2 it says, "Many of these seem out of the students' control, but many may simply be excuses for not persevering." What is the relationship between the parts of that sentence?

a. addition
b. sequence
c. contrast
d. cause-effect

_______ **18.** In paragraph 4 it says, "His world opened up, and he saw opportunities he had never considered." The figurative language "His world opened up" means he:

a. saw new possibilities.
b. faced additional obstacles.
c. refused to give up.
d. sought help from others.

_______ **19.** In paragraph 1 it says, "To create and maintain a positive state of mind and learn self-management, you cannot just read a book, attend a lecture, or use a few strategies for a day or two. It takes time and effort." What is the relationship between the two sentences?

a. The second sentence changes the meaning of first sentence.
b. The second sentence categorizes information given in the first sentence.
c. The second sentence gives a specific example of what is stated in the first sentence.
d. The second sentence clarifies the first sentence.

_______ **20.** Based on information in the passage, it is logical to conclude that:

a. college is the most important way to develop creativity.

b. people who believe in themselves are more likely to be successful.

c. lumber mill workers should go to college.

d. setbacks are the worst type of failure.

SELECTION **2.1**

Student Success

(continued)

Respond in Writing

Directions: Refer to the selection as needed to answer the essay-type questions below. (Your instructor may direct you to work collaboratively with other students on one or more items. Each group member should be able to explain *all* of the group's answers.

1. **Reacting to What You Have Read:** What obstacles have you had to overcome to attend college, or what obstacles do you face in getting a college education? How have you dealt with those obstacles, or how do you plan to deal with them?

2. **Comprehending the Selection Further:** In paragraph 2 the author lists several suggestions that can help you deal with obstacles. Choose two that you are not currently doing. Explain how doing them might help you.

3. **Overall Main Idea of the Selection:** In one sentence, tell what the authors want readers to understand about overcoming obstacles. (Be sure to include "overcoming obstacles" or "to overcome obstacles" in your overall main idea sentence.)

____

____

____

____

____

____

____

Read More about It Online

Internet Resources

Directions: Read more about the topic of this selection online. You can read online *before* you read the selection to build background knowledge or *afterward* to extend your knowledge. Start with the website below or type **"overcoming obstacles"** or **"students overcoming obstacles"** in the search box of Google, Yahoo, or another search engine. When you visit any unfamiliar website, it is important to evaluate it and the information it contains. If you do not know how to conduct Internet searches or evaluate a website, see pages 24–25.

http://mysuperchargedlife.com/blog/ten-top-tips-to-overcome-obstacles-to-success/
My Super Charged Life is a site written by Jeff Nickles, who has had an interesting variety of career steps, travel, and adventure experiences, all of which he says have enriched his life and taught him the value of success. He shares his "good habits for a great life."

Copyright © 2014 The McGraw-Hill Companies, Inc. All rights reserved.

SELECTION **2.2**

Public Health

Autism: A Public Health Emergency

Compiled from Online Sources

By Janet Elder

In the last two years, the national media have given considerable coverage to the topic of autism. One reason was a recent government study showing that this type of neurological problem affects a much larger percentage of the U.S. population than was ever before suspected. Perhaps you, someone in your family, or someone you know has been diagnosed with some form of autism. The selection below sheds light on this little-understood developmental disorder, which means a disorder that arises before adulthood and lasts throughout life.

1 Mention the word "autistic" and the first thing that comes to mind for many people is Dustin Hoffman's 1988 Oscar-winning performance in *Rain Man.* In the movie, Hoffman plays Raymond Babbitt, a gifted, but autistic young man. Ray can remember an astounding amount of information and perform any mathematical calculation in a flash, yet he cannot function normally in everyday life. He insists on following the same rigid schedule every day; he becomes agitated when it is changed. For other people, the word "autistic" brings to mind children who are lost in their own world, who do not respond to others, who do not speak, and who spend long periods of time rocking back and forth or doing other repetitive actions.

2 Only a few decades ago, many people with autism went undiagnosed. They were simply viewed as strange or frustrating or puzzling. Many autistics themselves were aware they were "different," but neither they nor their parents knew why or what to do about it. So what do researchers today know about autism that they and the public didn't know when *Rain Man* was made?

3 According to the National Institute of Child Health & Human Development, "Autism is a complex developmental disability that causes problems with social interaction and communication. Symptoms usually start before age three and can cause delays or problems in many different skills that develop from infancy to adulthood." The symptoms usually show up in a child's first year and a half. They include verbal and nonverbal communication difficulties. For example, autistic children may not talk or make eye contact or respond to others' gestures and smiles. They may exhibit social problems. They have difficulty understanding other people's emotions. Some follow routines obsessively. Some exhibit repetitive behaviors, such as repeating words or actions for hours.[1] People with autism can have very different symptoms, however. For this reason, the term "autism spectrum disorder" (ASD) is now being used instead of "autism." Asperger syndrome, for example, is a form of ASD at the high-functioning end of the spectrum. Some with Asperger's have exceptional abilities in academics, music, math, visual skills, art, or other areas.

An Epidemic in the United States

4 Researchers today know that more Americans are affected than was ever imagined in the past. "Autism is now officially becoming an epidemic in the United States," according to Mark

Prediction Exercises

Directions: Use the skill of predicting to anticipate what the upcoming paragraphs will be about.

Prediction Exercise

What do you predict paragraphs 1–3 will be about?

____

____

____

____

Copyright © 2014 The McGraw-Hill Companies, Inc. All rights reserved.

Identified Prevalence of Autism Spectrum Disorders
ADDM Network 2000–2008
Combining Data from All Sites

Surveillance Year	Birth Year	Number of ADDM Sites Reporting	Prevalence per 1,000 Children (Range)	This is about 1 in X children...
2000	1992	6	6.7 (4.5–9.9)	1 in 150
2002	1994	14	6.6 (3.3–10.6)	1 in 150
2004	1996	8	8.0 (4.6–9.8)	1 in 125
2006	1998	11	9.0 (4.2–12.1)	1 in 110
2008	2000	14	11.3 (4.8–21.2)	1 in 88

Surveillance Year was the year the data were gathered. ADDM sites are the CDC's Autism and Developmental Disabilities Monitoring Network.
Source: www.cdc.gov/ncbddd/autism/data.html.

Roithmayr, president of the advocacy group Autism Speaks. What sparked his comment were the findings of a new study by the Centers for Disease Control (CDC). Their comprehensive, 14-state study investigated the prevalence of autism and related disorders in 8-year-olds. Data revealed that 1 in 88 children—approximately 1 million children and teens—appear to be affected, nearly twice as many as only five years ago. Moreover, autism is five times more common in boys. The number of diagnosed black and Hispanic children is also growing.[2] Geraldine Dawson, chief science officer for Autism Speaks, declares that ASD is "a public health emergency that demands immediate attention."

5 AustismSpeaks.org puts the statistics into perspective. The number of children affected by autism spectrum disorders is greater than those with "diabetes, AIDS, cancer, cerebral palsy, cystic fibrosis, muscular dystrophy or Down syndrome, combined. ASD affects over 2 million individuals in the U.S. and tens of millions worldwide. Moreover, government autism statistics suggest that prevalence rates have increased 10 to 17 percent annually in recent years."[3]

Prediction Exercise

What do you predict the second section will be about?

____

____

____

____

____

Better Diagnosis and More Research

6 The jump in the numbers may be due in part to increased awareness and better diagnosis, however. For example, many black and Hispanic children may have gone undiagnosed in the past. Even now, the diagnosis must be made by observing the child's behavior: there is no medical test for autism spectrum disorders. Nor is there a cure, but treatment that includes intensive behavior therapy can help many children function better.[4]

7 Even though there is better diagnosis nowadays, the cause or causes of autism are not yet understood. The causes appear

Prediction Exercise

What do you predict this section will be about?

____

____

____

____

to be complicated, and they may differ for each child. Autism can show up at birth, or it can show up within a child's first few years. Some children appear normal during the first year or two, but then begin to show signs of autism.

8 During the last decade, more than $1 billion has been spent on autism research, and government funding has increased dramatically. The lion's share of the money has gone to genetics research, since experts think genetics are responsible for approximately 20 percent of autism cases. However, genetics are not the only cause or always the cause: there are studies of identical twins in which only one has ASD. "In many cases, autism can be blamed on both genetic problems that load the gun and other factors that pull the trigger." Recent research has linked genetics and the advanced age of the father at conception as a possibility. Maternal obesity, illnesses and medications during pregnancy may also be factors. Because these factors have been linked with ASD, however, does not mean that they are necessarily causes. For a long time, it was thought that childhood vaccines might be causing ASD, but dozens of studies have found no link.[5]

"A Way of Being"

9 For understandable reasons, people with ASD tend to have difficulty with relationships. On National Public Radio's "Talk of the Nation," guest host John Donovan interviewed Kirsten Lindsmith and Jack Robinson, two young adults with Asperger's syndrome. In general, people with Asperger's are intelligent or have above-average intelligence. They tend to be well spoken. However, they struggle to pick up on other people's social cues, tone of voice, body language, gestures, and facial expressions. All of this interferes with establishing and maintaining relationships. In childhood, they often do not have friends. They may be picked on because they are "weird." They have to learn the social cues and behaviors that most children develop naturally. Donovan explains, "It's missing the joke that everybody else gets. It's not knowing that what you're talking about is boring the life out of everybody else in the room. It's having the tendency to obsess on narrow topics, and maybe having some set routines that cannot be interfered with."

10 Robinson, 21, offers an interesting take on Asperger's. He describes it as "sort of a way of being, rather than a condition you have." Lindsmith, who is 20, concurs: "I would consider it more a type of person rather than a disease."[6] As researchers unravel the mysteries of ASD, we will understand more about this unique "type of person," the ways they can work around the limitations of ASD, and how they can capitalize on their strengths.

Prediction Exercise

What do you predict this section will be about?

____

____

____

____

____

____

Sources:

[1] "Autism Spectrum Disorders (ASD)," http://www.nichd.nih.gov/health/topics/asd.cfm; accessed 24 April 2012.

[2] "More Autism Reported, Likely from Better Testing," by the Associated Press, Atlanta, as reported at http://www.npr.org/templates/story/story.php?storyId=149643884; accessed 23 April 2012.

[3] autismspeaks.org, "How Common Is Autism?", http://www.autismspeaks.org/what-autism; accessed 24 April 2012.

[4] "As More Autism Reported, Doctors Say Check Early," by the Associated Press, Chicago, as reported at http://www.npr.org/templates/story/story.php?storyId=149665068; accessed 23 April 2012.

[5] "Autism Research May Be About To Bear Fruit," Associated Press, Atlanta, as reported at http://www.npr.org/templates/story/story.php?storyId=150289911; accessed 23 April 2012.

[6] "Learning to Love, and Be Loved, with Autism," *Talk of the Nation*, 01/18/12, http://www.npr.org/2012/01/18/145405658/learning-to-love-and-be-loved-with-autism; accessed 23 April 2012.

Copyright © 2014 The McGraw-Hill Companies, Inc. All rights reserved.

SELECTION 2.2
Public Health
(continued)

Comprehension and Vocabulary Quiz

This quiz has four parts. Your instructor may assign some or all of them.

Comprehension

Directions: Items 1–5 test your understanding of the selection. They are the types of questions a content-area instructor (such as a health professor) might ask on a test. You may refer to the selection as you answer the questions. Write your answer choice in the space provided.

______ **1.** Symptoms of autism usually show up:
a. before birth.
b. during the first two months of life.
c. in a child's first year and a half.
d. during adolescence.

______ **2.** The number of U.S. children affected by autism spectrum disorders is greater than the number affected by:
a. diabetes, AIDS, and cancer.
b. cerebral palsy and cystic fibrosis.
c. muscular dystrophy and Down syndrome.
d. all of the above, combined.

______ **3.** The recent increase in data about the estimated number of U.S. children with autism may be due in part to:
a. better genetic testing.
b. increased awareness and better diagnosis.
c. including more children in a major CDC research study.
d. childhood vaccinations.

______ **4.** According to the chart, how many children per 1,000 were estimated to have autism spectrum disorders in 2002?
a. 6.7
b. 6.6
c. 9.0
d. 11.3

______ **5.** According to information in the selection, people with ASD have difficulty:
a. finding a job.
b. graduating from high school.
c. establishing relationships.
d. focusing on narrow topics.

Vocabulary in Context

Directions: Items 6–10 test your ability to determine a word's meaning by using context clues. *Context clues* are words in a sentence that allow readers to deduce (reason out) the meaning of an unfamiliar word in the sentence. They also help readers determine the meaning an author intends when a word has more than one meaning. Each item below consists of a sentence from the selection, with the vocabulary word *italicized*. It is followed by another sentence that uses the same word in the same way. Use context clues to deduce the meaning of the *italicized* word. Be sure the meaning you choose makes sense in *both* sentences. Write each answer in the space provided. (This chapter presents the skill of using context clues.)

_______ **6.** Autism is now officially becoming an *epidemic* in the United States.

The Internal Revenue Service says there is an *epidemic* of tax fraud in the United States.

epidemic (ĕp ĭ dĕm′ ĭk) means:

a. an infectious disease

b. a condition affecting many individuals in a population at the same time

c. a rapid spreading

d. an unexplained phenomenon

_______ **7.** What *sparked* his comment were the findings of a new study by the Centers for Disease Control (CDC).

The firing of the university's head football coach *sparked* a huge protest.

sparked (spärkd) means:

a. set on fire

b. spurred; caused

c. prevented; avoided

d. ended; put a stop to

_______ **8.** Their *comprehensive*, 14-state study investigated the prevalence of autism and related disorders in 8-year-olds.

The *comprehensive* final exam covered everything we had studied during the semester.

comprehensive (kŏm prĭ hĕn′ sĭv) means:

a. carefully planned

b. confusing

c. large in scope and including much

d. done with great skill

_______ **9.** Moreover, autism is five times more *common* in boys.

In tough economic times, homelessness becomes more *common*.

common (kŏm′ ən) means:

a. taking place often

b. quickly recognized

c. upsetting

d. surprising

Copyright © 2014 The McGraw-Hill Companies, Inc. All rights reserved.

_______ **10.** The *lion's share* of the money has gone to genetics research, since experts think genetics are responsible for approximately 20 percent of autism cases.

At a graduation party, the honoree receives the *lion's share* of the attention.

lion's share (lī′ənz shâr) means:

a. largest amount
b. borrowed amount
c. unidentified amount
d. unreasonable amount

Word Structure

Directions: Items 11–15 test your ability to use word-structure clues to help determine a word's meaning. *Word-structure clues* consist of roots, prefixes and suffixes. In these exercises, you will learn the meaning of a word part (a root) and use it to determine the meaning of several other words that have the same word part. If you need to use a dictionary to confirm your answer choice, do so. Write your answers in the spaces provided.

In paragraph 3 of the selection, you encountered the word **emotions.** This word contains the Latin root ***mot***, which means "to move" or "motion." The word *emotions* refers to the *moving* or stirring up of feelings. Use the meaning of the root ***mot*** and the list of prefixes on pages 24–25 to help you determine the meaning of each of the following words that contain the same root.

_______ **11.** If a person in the military is **demoted,** he or she:

a. stays at the same rank for an unusually long period of time.
b. is moved to a lower rank.
c. is moved to a higher rank.
d. is forced to withdraw completely from the military.

_______ **12.** A **remote** control allows you to change TV channels:

a. by pressing buttons on the TV set.
b. through preprogramming the VCR.
c. without having to get up and move to the TV set itself.
d. after consulting the TV schedule.

_______ **13.** If there is a **commotion,** there is:

a. an all-night party going on.
b. agitated movement or a disturbance of some sort.
c. a loud, noisy celebration.
d. a bus or a train going by.

_______ **14.** **Promotion** refers to:

a. moving forward or ahead.
b. moving away from.
c. moving to the side of.
d. moving down.

_______ **15.** A **motive:**

a. prevents an action from occurring.
b. causes an action to stop.
c. slows down a process.
d. moves a person to do something.

Reading Skills Application

Directions: Items 16–20 test your ability to *apply* certain reading skills. You may not be familiar with all the skills yet, so some items will serve as a preview. As you work through *New Worlds,* you will practice and develop these skills. These are important skills, which is why they are included on the state-mandated basic skills tests that some students must take. Write each answer in the space provided.

_______ **16.** In paragraph 8 it says, "In many cases, autism can be blamed on both genetic problems that load the gun and other factors that pull the trigger." The figurative language expressions "load the gun" and "pull the trigger" mean:

a. prevent something from happening before it ever gets started.
b. set something up to happen and then make it happen.
c. destroy something.
d. two things that happen at the same time.

_______ **17.** In paragraph 1 it says, "Ray can remember an astounding amount of information and perform any mathematical calculation in a flash, yet he cannot function normally in everyday life." What is the relationship between the parts of that sentence?

a. addition
b. contrast
c. cause-effect
d. summary

_______ **18.** The authors' primary purpose in writing this selection is to:

a. convince readers that all toddlers should be screened for autism.
b. instruct readers in how to recognize the signs of autism.
c. inform readers about autism.
d. persuade readers to support additional research on autism.

_______ **19.** According to the table, in which year was the incidence of autism spectrum disorders found to be one in every 110 children?

a. 2000
b. 2004
c. 2006
d. 2008

_______ **20.** Based on information in the passage, it is logical to conclude that:

a. the causes of autism disorders will be better understood in the coming years.
b. a cure will be found for autism.
c. the number of children diagnosed with autism disorders will decrease.
d. observation will continue to be the only basis for diagnosing autism.

SELECTION **2.2**
Public Health
(continued)

Respond in Writing

Directions: Refer to the selection as needed to answer the essay-type questions below. (Your instructor may direct you to work collaboratively with other students on one or more items. Each group member should be able to explain *all* the group's answers.)

1. **Reacting to What You Have Read:** What two pieces of new information did you find most surprising or helpful?

____

____

____

____

____

____

____

2. **Comprehending the Selection Further:** The selection mentions several factors that are linked to autism. List at least three of them.

____

____

____

____

____

____

____

____

3. **Overall Main Idea of the Selection:** In one sentence, tell what the authors want readers to understand about autism. (Be sure to include "autism" in your overall main idea sentence.)

____

____

____

____

____

____

____

____

Internet Resources

Read More about It Online

Directions: Read more about the topic of this selection online. You can read online *before* you read the selection to build background knowledge or *afterward* to extend your knowledge. Start with the websites below or type **"autism"** or **"autism spectrum disorder"** in the search box of Google, Yahoo, or another search engine. When you visit any unfamiliar website, it is important to evaluate it and the information it contains. If you do not know how to conduct Internet searches or evaluate a website, see pages 24–25.

www.autismspeaks.org
Funded in 2005, this is "the nation's largest autism science and advocacy group dedicated to funding research into the causes, prevention, treatments and a cure for autism; increasing awareness of autism spectrum disorders; and advocating for the needs of individuals with autism and their families."

www.hhs.gov/autism/
This is the U.S. Department of Health & Human Services website on autism.

www.cdc.gov/ncbddd/autism/index.html
This is the Centers for Disease Control and Prevention website on autism.

SELECTION **2.3** **Nonfiction**

Thinking in Pictures: Autism and Visual Thought

From *Thinking in Pictures: My Life with Autism,* 2nd edition
By Temple Grandin

Temple Grandin, PhD, is an equipment designer for the livestock industry, an author, an inventor, a scientist, and a college professor—who happens to be autistic. Through her books, Grandin has given the public unique insight on what it is like to be a highly gifted person who is also autistic. (If you have not read Selection 2.2 on autism, you may want to read it first.)

The online Encyclopedia of World Biography says this about Grandin:

> *She is a strong advocate for more humane livestock handling, and has designed numerous innovations at such facilities that help to reduce stress in the animals during their final minutes [at slaughterhouses]. Grandin's mission is deeply connected to her autism, and she credits this developmental brain disorder for her success as a scientist. Once she recognized that animals and autistic people share certain traits, such as a reliance on visual clues to navigate their environment, she began to rethink how livestock are handled in the beef and pork industry. (www.notablebiographies.com/newsmakers2/2006-Ei-La/Grandin-Temple.html; accessed 21 April 2012)*

Essentially "concrete and visual" is how this remarkable woman describes herself. She acknowledges that complex human emotions puzzle her. She knows she does not connect with people the same way others do, nor can she "read" people. Autism has given her compensating gifts, however, as she discusses in this excerpt from her book, Thinking in Pictures: My Life with Autism. *She is eminently logical and rational, and as the book title says, she thinks in pictures.*

In 2010 Grandin was chosen as one of the "Time 100" *one hundred most influential people in the world in the category "Heroes." Although she struggled to learn to read and write, she teaches, travels, consults, and lectures (often on autism). Says Grandin, "If I could snap my fingers and be non-autistic, I wouldn't—because then I wouldn't be me. Autism is part of who I am."*

Thinking in Pictures

1 I think in pictures. Words are like a second language to me. I translate both spoken and written words into full-color movies, complete with sound, which run like a VCR tape in my head. When somebody speaks to me, his words are instantly translated into pictures. Language-based thinkers often find this phenomenon difficult to understand, but in my job as an equipment designer for the livestock industry, visual thinking is a tremendous advantage.

Prediction Exercises

Directions: Use the skill of predicting to anticipate what the three subsections of this selection will be about.

Copyright © 2014 The McGraw-Hill Companies, Inc. All rights reserved.

2 Visual thinking has enabled me to build entire systems in my imagination. During my career I have designed all kinds of equipment, ranging from corrals for handling cattle on ranches to systems for handling cattle and hogs during veterinary procedures and slaughter. I have worked for many major livestock companies. In fact, one third of the cattle and hogs in the United States are handled in equipment I have designed. Some of the people I've worked for don't even know that their systems were designed by someone with autism. I value my ability to think visually, and I would never want to lose it.

3 One of the most profound mysteries of autism has been remarkable ability of most autistic people to excel at visual skills while performing so poorly at verbal skills. When I was a child and teenager, I thought everybody thought in pictures. I had no idea that my thought processes were different. In fact, I did not realize the full extent of the differences until very recently. At meetings and at work, I started asking other people detailed questions about how they accessed information from their memories. From their answers I learned that my visualization skills far exceeded those of most other people.

Prediction Exercise

What do you predict the first section will be about?

____

____

____

____

____

Working with Animals

4 I credit my visualization abilities with helping me understand the animals I work with. Early in my career I used a camera to help give me the animals' perspective as they walked through a chute for their veterinary treatment. I would kneel down and take pictures through the chute from the cow's eye level. Using the photos, I was able to figure out which things scared the cattle, such as shadows and bright spots of sunlight. Back then I used black-and-white film, because twenty years ago scientists believed that cattle lacked color vision. Today, research has shown that cattle can see colors, but the photos provided the unique advantage of seeing the world through a cow's viewpoint. They helped me figure out why the animals refused to go in one chute but willingly walked through another.

Prediction Exercise

What do you predict this section will be about?

____

____

____

____

Solving Design Problems in Advance

5 Every design problem I've ever solved started with my ability to visualize and see the world in pictures. I started designing things as a child, when I was always experimenting with new kinds of kites and model airplanes. In elementary school I made a helicopter out of a broken balsa-wood airplane. When I wound up the propeller, the helicopter flew straight up about a hundred feet. I also made bird-shaped paper kites, which I flew behind my bike. The kites were cut out from a single sheet of heavy drawing paper and flown with thread. I experimented with different ways of bending the wings to increase flying performance. Bending the tips of the wings up made the kite fly higher. Thirty years later, this same design started appearing on commercial aircraft.

6 Now, in my work, before I attempt any construction, I test-run the equipment in my imagination. I visualize my designs being used in every possible situation, with different sizes and

Prediction Exercise

What do you predict the final section will be about?

____

____

____

breeds of cattle and in different weather conditions. Doing this enables me to correct mistakes prior to construction. Today, everyone is excited about the new virtual reality computer systems in which the user wears special goggles and is fully immersed in video game action. To me, these systems are like crude cartoons. My imagination works like the computer graphics programs that created the lifelike dinosaurs in *Jurassic Park.* When I do an equipment simulation in my imagination or work on an engineering problem, it is like seeing it on a videotape in my mind. I can view it from any angle, placing myself above or below the equipment and rotating it at the same time. I don't need a fancy graphics program that can produce three-dimensional design simulations. I can do it better and faster in my head.

7 I create new images all the time by taking many little parts of images I have in the video library in my imagination and piecing them together. I have video memories of every item I've ever worked with—steel gates, fences, latches, concrete walls, and so forth. To create new designs, I retrieve bits and pieces from my memory and combine them into a new whole. My design ability keeps improving as I add more visual images to my library. I add video-like images from either actual experiences or translations of written information into pictures. I can visualize the operation of such things as squeeze chutes, truck loading ramps, and all different types of livestock equipment. I'm always making progress because the more I actually work with cattle and operate equipment, the stronger my visual memories become.

Source: Adapted from *Thinking in Pictures: My Life with Autism*, 2nd ed., by Temple Grandin. New York: Vintage Books, 2006, pp. 3–5.

SELECTION **2.3**

Nonfiction

(continued)

Comprehension and Vocabulary Quiz

This quiz has four parts. Your instructor may assign some or all of them.

Comprehension

Directions: Items 1–5 test your understanding of the selection. They are the types of questions a content-area instructor (such as a literature professor) might ask on a test. You may refer to the selection as you answer the questions. Write your answer choice in the space provided.

_______ **1.** Temple Grandin is typical of autistic people in that she:

a. excels at visual and kinesthetic skills.

b. excels at verbal skills.

c. excels at visual and verbal skills.

d. excels at visual skills but not verbal skills.

_______ **2.** How many of the cattle and hogs in the United States are handled in equipment that Grandin has designed?

a. three-fourths

b. two-thirds

c. one-half

d. one-third

_______ **3.** Grandin was able to determine what frightened cows walking through chutes for veterinary treatment by:

a. taking pictures of cows.

b. examining the cows before and after they went through the chute.

c. looking at the chute from the cow's eye level.

d. interviewing veterinarians.

_______ **4.** The helicopter Grandin made as a child:

a. flew straight up on the first try.

b. flew a few feet before crashing.

c. never rose into the air.

d. broke because it was made from balsa wood.

_______ **5.** When creating a new design, Grandin:

a. looks at previous similar designs she has done.

b. constructs and test-runs the design in her imagination.

c. uses a virtual reality computer system.

d. wears special computer glasses.

Vocabulary in Context

Directions: Items 6–10 test your ability to determine a word's meaning by using context clues. *Context clues* are words in a sentence that allow readers to deduce (reason out) the meaning of an unfamiliar word in the sentence. They also help readers determine the meaning an author intends when a word has more than one meaning. Each item below consists of a sentence from the selection, with the vocabulary word *italicized.* It is followed by another sentence that uses the same word in the same way. Use context clues to deduce the meaning of the *italicized* word. Be sure the meaning you choose makes sense in *both* sentences. Write each answer in the space provided. (This chapter presents the skill of using context clues.)

_______ **6.** Language-based thinkers often find this phenomenon difficult to understand, but in my job as an equipment designer for the *livestock* industry, visual thinking is a tremendous advantage.

The ranch owner bought more pasture so he could expand his *livestock* herd.

livestock (līv′ stŏk′) means:

a. pertaining to animals kept as pets
b. pertaining to domestic animals raised for home use or profit
c. pertaining to meat processing
d. pertaining to wild animals that have been tamed

_______ **7.** One of the most *profound* mysteries of autism has been remarkable ability of most autistic people to excel at visual skills while performing so poorly at verbal skills.

Whether the death penalty should be permitted is a *profound* moral issue.

profound (prə found′) means:

a. unimportant; trivial
b. requiring thoughtful study
c. likely to cause arguments
d. questionable

_______ **8.** Early in my career I used a camera to help give me the animals' *perspective* as they walked through a chute for their veterinary treatment.

From my *perspective*, it looked as if the white car caused the accident.

perspective (pər spĕk′ tĭv) means:

a. assessment
b. opinion
c. point of view
d. belief

_______ **9.** To me, these systems are like *crude* cartoons.

The small, *crude* boat was made from a hollowed-out tree trunk.

crude (kro͞od) means:

a. not skillfully made
b. lacking in taste
c. plain
d. immature

_______ **10.** When I do an equipment *simulation* in my imagination or work on an engineering problem, it is like seeing it on a videotape in my mind.

In the lab, scientists conducted a *simulation* of an earthquake to determine the effect on various building materials.

simulation (sĭm yə lā′ shən) means:

a. model

b. pattern

c. computer game

d. example

Word Structure

Directions: Items 11–15 test your ability to use word-structure clues to help determine a word's meaning. *Word-structure clues* consist of roots, prefixes and suffixes. In these exercises, you will learn the meaning of a word part (a root) and use it to determine the meaning of several other words that have the same word part. If you need to use a dictionary to confirm your answer choice, do so. Write your answers in the spaces provided.

In paragraph 7 of the selection, you encountered the word **progress**. This word contains the Latin root ***gress***, which means "go" or "step." In this selection, *progress* means to go or move ahead, or in other words, to advance. Use the meaning of the root ***gress*** and the list of prefixes on pages 72–73 to help you determine the meaning of each of the following words that contain the same root.

_______ **11.** If a young child **regresses** when a baby brother or sister is born, the child:

a. becomes more hostile.

b. goes back to less mature behavior.

c. improves in behavior.

d. remains consistent in behavior.

_______ **12.** You are talking about one thing, *digress,* and then return to your original topic. To **digress** means to:

a. interrupt someone.

b. laugh loudly.

c. stray from your topic.

d. begin talking in a whisper.

_______ **13.** Children who are **aggressive** toward others:

a. go against them in a hostile manner.

b. go around them to get what they want.

c. go backward and act immaturely.

d. go against what their parents have taught them.

_______ **14.** A sign on a door that says "**Egress**" has the same meaning as a sign that says:

a. "Open."

b. "Exit."

c. "Push."

d. "Private."

_______ **15.** If someone plays a **progression** of notes on the piano, the person plays:

a. a chord.
b. three notes.
c. a short song.
d. a sequence of notes.

Reading Skills Application

Directions: Items 16–20 test your ability to *apply* certain reading skills. You may not be familiar with all the skills yet, so some items will serve as a preview. As you work through *New Worlds,* you will practice and develop these skills. These are important skills, which is why they are included on the state-mandated basic skills tests that some students must take. Write each answer in the space provided.

_______ **16.** Based on its word parts, the word *exceeded* in paragraph 3 means:

a. challenged.
b. went beyond.
c. embarrassed.
d. decreased.

_______ **17.** In paragraph 2 it says, "I value my ability to think visually, and I would never want to lose it." What is the relationship between the parts of that sentence? (The second part begins after the comma.)

a. addition
b. example
c. definition
d. summary

_______ **18.** The author's primary purpose in writing this selection is to:

a. persuade readers that having autism is a help in life.
b. instruct readers how to think in pictures.
c. inform readers about her visual thinking and how it is an advantage.
d. persuade readers not to make judgments about people who think in pictures.

_______ **19.** Which of the following is the stated main idea of paragraph 4?

a. I credit my visualization abilities with helping me understand the animals I work with.
b. Early in my career I used a camera to help give me the animals' perspective as they walked through a chute for their veterinary treatment.
c. I would kneel down and take pictures through the chute from the cow's eye level.
d. Using the photos, I was able to figure out which things scared the cattle, such as shadows and bright spots of sunlight.

_______ **20.** Based on information in the passage, it is logical to conclude that:

a. people with autism find it difficult to establish successful careers.
b. animals in this country are treated inhumanely.
c. things that appear to be a disadvantage may also offer an advantage.
d. autism will never be well understood.

Copyright © 2014 The McGraw-Hill Companies, Inc. All rights reserved.

SELECTION 2.3
Nonfiction
(continued)

Respond in Writing

Directions: Refer to the selection as needed to answer the essay-type questions below. (Your instructor may direct you to work collaboratively with other students on one or more items. Each group member should be able to explain *all* the group's answers.)

1. **Reacting to What You Have Read:** Do you think primarily in pictures or in words? What do you think it might be like if you did just the opposite? What would be the advantages and disadvantages of each?

2. **Comprehending the Selection Further:** Describe the process Grandin uses to create new images and designs.

3. **Overall Main Idea of the Selection:** In one sentence, tell what the authors want readers to understand about Temple Grandin and autism. (Be sure to include "Temple Grandin" and "autism" in your overall main idea sentence.)

____

____

____

____

____

____

____

____

Internet Resources

Read More about It Online

Directions: Read more about the topic of this selection online. You can read online *before* you read the selection to build background knowledge or *afterward* to extend your knowledge. Start with the websites below or type **"Temple Grandin"** or **"autism"** in the search box of Google, Yahoo, or another search engine. When you visit any unfamiliar website, it is important to evaluate it and the information it contains. If you do not know how to conduct Internet searches or evaluate a website, see pages 24–25.

www.notablebiographies.com/newsmakers2/2006-Ei-La/Grandin-Temple.html
This Encyclopedia of World Biography tells the life and accomplishments of scientist, inventor, and author Temple Grandin.

www.youtube.com/watch?v=bnI_Y8PyTHM
This You Tube clip includes footage of Temple Grandin herself.

www.hbo.com/movies/temple-grandin/index.html
You may have seen the 2010 HBO movie *Temple Grandin.* It starred Claire Danes, who won the Golden Globe Award for it. At this website, you can watch a trailer for the movie.

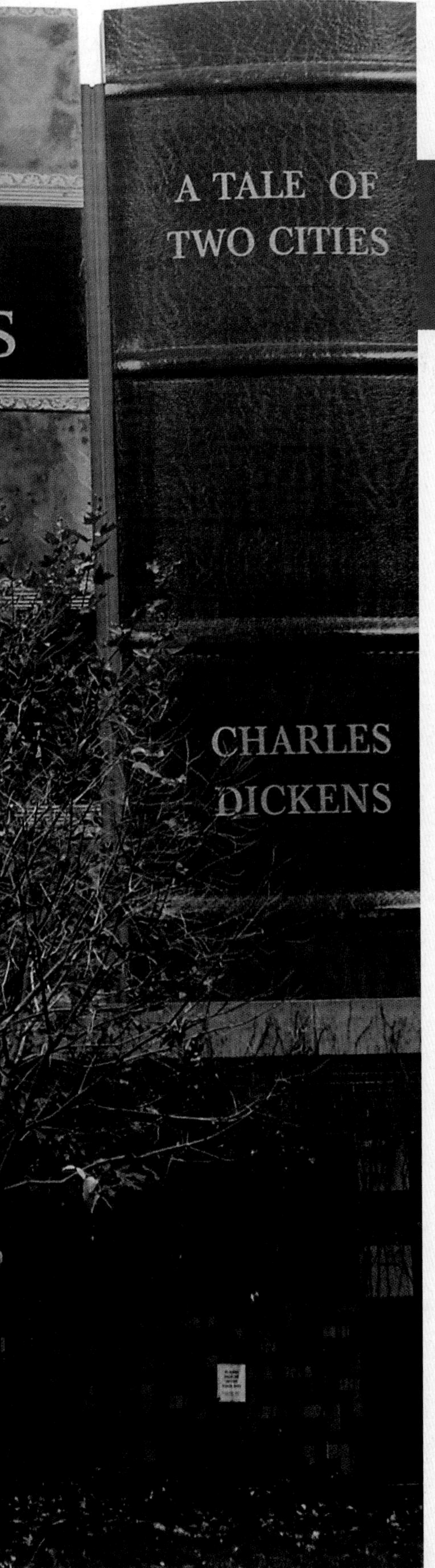

PART 2

A New World of Understanding

Using Core Comprehension Skills When You Read College Textbooks

CHAPTERS IN PART TWO

CHAPTER 3

Determining the Topic

LEARNING OBJECTIVES

In this chapter you will learn the answers to these questions:

- What is a topic of a paragraph?
- Why is it important to determine the topic of a paragraph?
- What are four clues for determining the topic of a paragraph?

CHAPTER CONTENTS

NEW INFORMATION AND SKILLS

WHAT IS THE TOPIC OF A PARAGRAPH, AND WHY IS IT IMPORTANT?

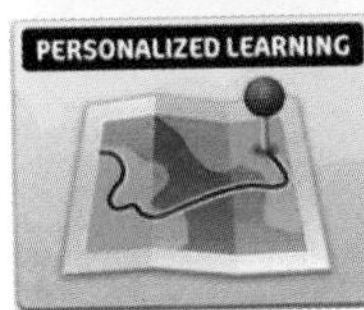

topic

Word, name, or phrase that tells who or what the author is writing about.

The topic is also known as the *subject* or the *subject matter*.

Comprehension Monitoring Question for Topic

"Who or what is this paragraph about?"

Every paragraph is written about something. Whenever you write a paragraph, you have to decide who or what you want to write about. In other words, you have to select a topic. Every paragraph has a **topic:** a word, name, or phrase that tells who or what the author is writing about. All the sentences in a paragraph relate in some way to the topic. The topic may be a name (such as *Jay Leno* or *Seattle*), a word (for instance, *texting*), or a phrase (such as *good study habits* or *advantages of attending college*). In a writing course or an English course, your instructor may call the topic the *subject* or the *subject matter.*

Why is it important to determine the topic of paragraphs you read? It is important because determining the topic is the first step in comprehending a paragraph. (This will become clearer to you as you learn about main ideas in Chapters 4 and 5.) In addition, it helps you focus your attention on what you are reading.

After you have read a paragraph, determine its topic by asking yourself this comprehension monitoring question: "Who or what is this paragraph about?" When you answer this question correctly, you will have determined the topic. Of course, you must make sure you understand the meaning of the word or phrase that tells the topic. In college textbooks, the meaning of the topic is usually defined or explained in the paragraph.

WHAT ARE THE CLUES FOR DETERMINING THE TOPIC OF A PARAGRAPH?

College textbook paragraphs typically contain clues to help you determine the topic. Take advantage of these clues:

- The topic appears as a *heading*, or a *title*.
- The topic appears in *special type* such as **bold print,** *italic*, or **color.**
- The topic is *repeated* throughout the paragraph.
- The topic appears once at the beginning and is then referred to throughout the paragraph by *pronouns* (or other words). (Pronouns are words such as *he, she, it, they*.)

Typically, a paragraph does not have all these clues, but all paragraphs have at least one of them. The following four examples are paragraphs from college textbooks. Each illustrates and explains one of the four clues to the topic of a paragraph.

Clue 1: Look for a Heading or a Title That Indicates the Topic

Pay attention to titles and headings: They often give the topic. This excerpt from a human development textbook illustrates this clue (as well as some others). Read this paragraph and notice that its heading indicates its topic.

Copyright © 2014 The McGraw-Hill Companies, Inc. All rights reserved.

Determining the topic is the important first step in comprehending a paragraph and also helps you focus your attention on what you are reading.

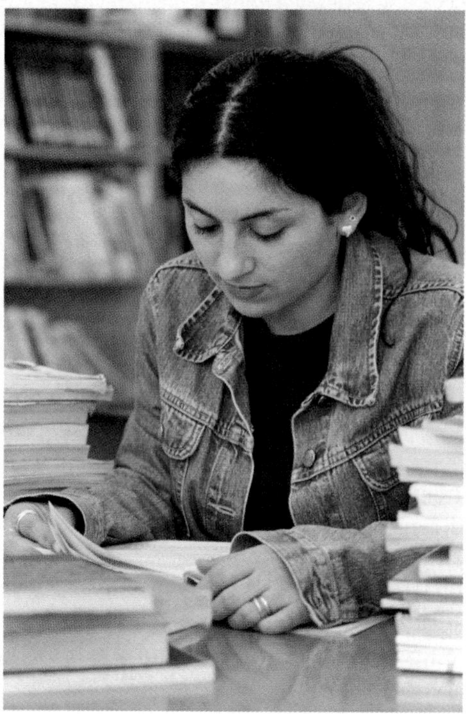

Marriage

In most societies, the institution of marriage is considered the best way to ensure the protection and raising of children. It allows for the division of labor and a sharing of material goods. Ideally, marriage offers intimacy, commitment, friendship, affections, sexual fulfillment, companionship and an opportunity for emotional growth as well as new sources of identity and self-esteem.

Source: Diane Papalia, Sally Wendkos Olds, and Ruth Feldman, *Human Development*, 11th ed., p. 467. Copyright © 2009 by The McGraw-Hill Companies, Inc.

Stop and Annotate

Go back to the textbook excerpt. Underline or highlight the heading, which indicates the topic.

Notice that the heading of this paragraph tells its topic: *marriage*. The term *marriage* indicates the "what" that is discussed in all the sentences of this paragraph. (Also notice that the word *marriage* appears twice in the paragraph.)

Although the heading of a textbook paragraph typically gives the topic, you should read the paragraph carefully to be sure that the heading gives the topic completely and accurately. For example, by itself, a general heading such as *The Crisis* is not complete. The paragraph could be about an earthquake, a stock market crash, a political scandal, or some other type of crisis.

EXERCISE 1

This paragraph comes from a speech communications textbook.

Plagiarism

"**Plagiarism**" comes from *plagiarus*, the Latin word for kidnapper. To plagiarize means to present another person's language or ideas as your own. When you plagiarize, you give the impression that you have written or thought of something yourself when you have actually taken it from someone else.

Source: Stephen E. Lucas, *The Art of Public Speaking*, 10th ed., p. 36. Copyright © 2009, The McGraw-Hill Companies.

Write a word, name, or phrase that tells the topic: ____________________

Clue(s): ____________________

____

Clue 2: Look for a Word, Name, or Phrase in the Paragraph That Appears in Special Print

A second clue to the topic of a paragraph is *italics*, **bold** print, or **color** to emphasize a word, name, or phrase. The paragraph below is from a textbook on public speaking. Read this paragraph and notice that the term in bold print indicates its topic.

Poaching is a major threat to wildlife. It is defined as the illegal taking or possession of game, fish, and other wildlife. Because poaching is a secretive crime committed in the wild, it is believed that wildlife investigators find only 1%–5% of all poached animals.

Source: Adapted from Charles Swanson, Neil Chamelin, Leonard Territo, and Robert W. Taylor, *Criminal Investigation*, 11th ed., p. 501. Copyright © 2012 by The McGraw-Hill Companies, Inc.

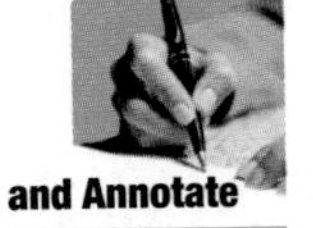

Stop and Annotate

Go back to the textbook excerpt. Underline or highlight the word in *bold print* that indicates the topic.

Notice how the word in bold print indicates the topic: *poaching*. (Notice also that the term *poaching* appears again in the paragraph, as well as the word *poached*. The entire paragraph discusses *poaching*.)

The topic of a paragraph sometimes consists of a combination of words, or a combination of names, or even phrases. For example, a health textbook paragraph might have the words *bulimia* and *anorexia* in special print. Together they would compose the topic: *bulimia and anorexia*. Or a paragraph might repeatedly mention the names of two U.S. Supreme Court justices, Elena Kagan and Sonia Sotomayor. The complete topic would be *Elena Kagan and Sonia Sotomayor*.

Also, be aware that although italic often signals the topic of a paragraph, it is also used by authors merely to show emphasis. For example, an author may put the word "except" or "not" in italic, such as in this sentence: "In general, it is *not* a good idea for college students to work more than 20 hours a week."

Copyright © 2014 The McGraw-Hill Companies, Inc. All rights reserved.

EXERCISE 2

This paragraph comes from an information technology textbook.

How would you feel if someone obtained a driver's license and credit cards in your name? What if that person then assumed your identity to buy clothes, cars, and a house? It happens every day. Every year, nearly 10 million people are victimized in this way. It is called **identity theft**. Identity theft is the illegal assumption of someone's identity for the purposes of economic gain. It is one of the fastest-growing crimes in the country.

Source: Timothy J. O'Leary and Linda I. O'Leary, *Computing Essentials 2013*, p. 297. Copyright © 2013 by The McGraw-Hill Companies, Inc.

Write a word, name, or phrase that tells the topic: ______________________________

Clue(s): ______________________________

____

Clue 3: Look for a Word, Name, or Phrase That Is Repeated throughout the Paragraph

A third clue to the topic is the repetition of a word, name, or phrase in a paragraph. This clue is helpful when there is no heading and the paragraph does not contain any words in special print. (Even though the previous two examples illustrate other clues, they also illustrate this clue.) Read the paragraph below from a business communication textbook. Notice the repeated words that indicate the topic.

A subject line is the title of a document. It aids in filing and retrieving the document, tells readers why they need to read the document, and provides a framework for what you are about to say. Subject lines are standard in memos. Letters are not required to have a subject line. A good subject line meets three criteria: it is specific, concise, and appropriate to the kind of message (positive, negative, persuasive).

Source: Kitty Locker and Stephen Kyo Kaczmarek, *Business Communication: Building Critical Skills*, 5th ed., p. 152. Copyright © 2011 by The McGraw-Hill Companies, Inc.

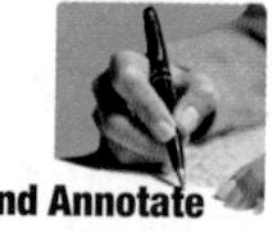

Stop and Annotate

Go back to the textbook excerpt above. Underline or highlight the repeated words that indicate the topic.

Notice that *subject line* appears four times, indicating that it is the topic of the paragraph.

Keep in mind that it is possible to express the same topic more than one way. For example, the topic of a paragraph on *subject lines* could also be expressed as *subject lines giving a document's title* or *subject lines of documents*.

EXERCISE 3

This paragraph comes from a psychology textbook.

At one time or another, almost all of us have difficulty sleeping—a condition known as insomnia. Insomnia could be due to a particular situation, such as the breakup of a relationship, concern about a test score, or the loss of a job. Some cases of insomnia, however, have no obvious cause. Some people are simply unable to fall asleep easily, or they go to sleep readily but wake up frequently during the night. Insomnia is a problem that afflicts as many as one-third of all people.

Source: Robert S. Feldman, *Understanding Psychology*, 8th ed. pp.154–55. Copyright © 2008 by The McGraw-Hill Companies, Inc. Reprinted by permission of the McGraw-Hill Companies, Inc.

Write a word, name, or phrase that tells the topic: ______________________

Clue(s): ______________________

____

____

Clue 4: Look for a Word, Name, or Phrase Referred to throughout the Paragraph by Pronouns or Other Words

A fourth clue to the topic is a word, name, or phrase that appears at or near the beginning of the paragraph and is then referred to throughout the paragraph by a pronoun (such as *he, she, it, they, his, her, its*) or by other words. For example, the topic *smoking* might be referred to later in a paragraph as *this habit* or *this addiction.* Now read this paragraph from a political science textbook and notice how pronouns are used to refer to the topic:

> The State Department (Department of State) is the chief diplomatic arm of the U.S. government. It is responsible for leading and coordinating U.S. representation abroad and for conveying U.S. foreign policy to foreign governments and international organizations. It operates abroad through diplomatic offices and embassies in approximately 80 countries and through mission offices that act as liaisons with international organizations such as the United Nations. Its staff negotiates agreements and treaties on issues ranging from trade to nuclear weapons. Domestically, this department is in charge of issuing passports and visas to U.S. citizens traveling abroad, and, with the Justice Department, for monitoring issuance of visas granted to foreign visitors.
>
> *Source:* Joseph Losco and Ralph Baker, *Am Gov, 2011*, p. 410. Copyright © 2011 by The McGraw-Hill Companies, Inc.

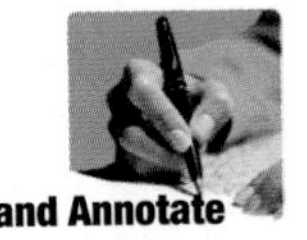

Stop and Annotate

Go back to the textbook excerpt above. Underline or highlight the topic, the pronouns, and other words that refer to the topic.

Notice that State Department appears only in the first sentence, but it is obvious from the pronoun *it* that the rest of the paragraph continues to discuss the State Department. When the authors say, "this department," they are still referring to the State Department. Therefore, the *State Department* is the topic of this paragraph.

EXERCISE 4

This paragraph comes from a science textbook.

> On August 29, 2005, Hurricane Katrina came ashore on the U.S. Gulf coast between Mobile, Alabama, and New Orleans, Louisiana. It was an enormous hurricane, just one of the 26 named storms that hit the Americas in the worst Atlantic hurricane season in history. A few hours after the hurricane made landfall, the combination of the storm surge and the torrential rain falling inland overwhelmed levees that were supposed to protect New Orleans. The storm caused almost 80 percent of the city to flood. Close to 1,000 people died in Louisiana alone, with most of those deaths occurring in New Orleans. Mandatory evacuation orders were issued for New Orleans' 500,000 residents in the days that followed the storm.
>
> *Source:* Adapted from Eldon D. Enger and Bradley F. Smith, *Environmental Science: A Study of Interrelationships,* 12th ed., p. 24. Copyright © 2010 by The McGraw-Hill Companies, Inc. Reprinted by permission of the McGraw-Hill Companies, Inc.

Copyright © 2014 The McGraw-Hill Companies, Inc. All rights reserved.

Write a word, name, or phrase that tells the topic: ______________________________

Clue(s): ____

____

____

One or more of the four clues described above will always help you determine the topic of a paragraph. However, if the topic is still not clear to you, reread the paragraph and ask yourself what all the sentences pertain to. Ask yourself the comprehension monitoring question "Who or what is this paragraph about?"

Determining the topic is the essential first step in comprehending as you read. It is also a key to locating the stated main idea sentence of a paragraph, as you will see in Chapter 4.

EXERCISE 5

Could This Be a Topic?

The topic is a *word, name,* or *phrase* that tells who or what a paragraph is about. Here are some examples of things that could—or could not—be topics:

- Going to college for the first time (*Yes; this could be a topic because it's a phrase.*)
- Barack Obama (*Yes; it's a name.*)
- Happy (*No; this is an adjective, a word that describes, so it could not be a topic.*)
- Happiness (*Yes; this is a noun that tells what a passage is about, so it could be a topic.*)
- Why soccer is popular (*Yes; this is a phrase.*)
- Soccer is popular because it is a fast-moving game. (*No; this is a complete sentence.*)

Directions: Decide whether each item below could be used as a topic that describes who or what a paragraph is about. Write Y for *Yes.* If it could not, write N for *No.* (There are periods after all of them, although not all of them are sentences.)

_____ **1.** Changes in the new tax law.
_____ **2.** The 2012 London Olympics.
_____ **3.** How to text message.
_____ **4.** Benjamin Franklin.
_____ **5.** The war in Afganistan.
_____ **6.** Why biology is a good choice as a college major.
_____ **7.** Washing your hands often can prevent flu and colds.
_____ **8.** The benefits of exercise.
_____ **9.** The effects of sleep deprivation on college students.
_____ **10.** Why hybrid cars make sense.
_____ **11.** Ten tips for passing objective tests.
_____ **12.** Safety measures for airline passengers.
_____ **13.** Yoga is a way to reduce stress.
_____ **14.** Speed kills.
_____ **15.** Starting a new job.

OTHER THINGS TO KEEP IN MIND WHEN DETERMINING THE TOPIC

Here are three helpful things that you should keep in mind about determining the topic:

1. **You should use a *name,* a *word,* or a *phrase,* but never a sentence, to express the topic. This means you must know the difference between a phrase and a sentence.**

   As you know, the topic of a paragraph not only can be expressed as a word or a name but also can be expressed as a *phrase.* A phrase is a meaningful group of words (even a long group of words) that does *not* express a complete thought. A sentence, on the other hand, has a subject and a verb and *always* expresses a complete thought. Phrases can be used to express the topic, but sentences should *never* be used to express a topic.

   The left column below gives examples of phrases that could be used as topics. The right column contains sentences that include the topic. The items in the right column could not be used as topics because they are complete sentences.

Could Be Used as a Topic (because it is a phrase)	**Could *Not* Be Used as a Topic (because it is a complete sentence)**
my tablet computer	My tablet computer was stolen.
my new tablet computer	My new tablet computer was stolen.
my new tablet computer with a bigger screen	My new tablet computer with a bigger screen was stolen.
my new tablet computer with a bigger screen and 5-megapixel camera	My new tablet computer with a bigger screen and 5-megapixel camera was stolen.
traveling by plane	Traveling by plane is the fastest way to travel to distant foreign countries.
fatality rates for passengers traveling by plane	Fatality rates of passengers traveling by plane are significantly lower than fatality rates for passengers traveling by car.
why traveling by plane is the best way to go	There are several reasons why traveling by plane is the best way to go.
how to overcome fear of traveling by plane	Psychologists have several methods to teach people how to overcome fear of traveling by plane.

2. **You must know the difference between "general" and "specific."**

   It is important to be precise when you determine the topic. If you choose a word or phrase that is too general or too specific, you will not be expressing the topic accurately. A topic that is too general goes beyond what is discussed in the paragraph. In other words, it is too broad. On the other hand, a topic is *too specific* if it fails to describe all the things discussed in the paragraph. In other words, it is too narrow.

   Suppose, for instance, that the topic of a paragraph is *causes of voter apathy.* As the following chart shows, the word *voter* or *apathy,* or even the phrase *voter apathy,* would be too general to express this topic accurately. The phrase *lack of interest in candidates as a cause of voter apathy* would be too specific, even though "lack of interest in candidates" might be mentioned in the paragraph as one cause of voter apathy.

Too General (Too Broad)	**Accurate Topic (Precise)**	**Too Specific (Too Narrow)**
voters	causes of voter apathy	voter apathy due to lack of interest in the candidates
apathy		voter apathy due to lack of interest in the issues
voter apathy		voter apathy because one candidate has an overwhelming likelihood of winning

(continued on next page)

3. A longer passage has an overall topic.

Just as every paragraph has a topic, so do longer selections that consist of several paragraphs. In a writing course or an English course, your instructor may call the overall topic the *subject*.

How can you determine the overall topic of a longer selection? First, ask yourself the question "Who or what is this entire selection about?" Then use some of the clues presented in this chapter:

- Look at the title or the heading for the entire selection or section.
- Look for a word, a name, or a phrase that appears in special print.
- Look for a word, a name, or a phrase that is repeated throughout the selection or section.

Once you have finished reading an entire selection or section of a textbook, it is a good idea to reflect on the topics of the paragraphs themselves to see who or what they all pertain to. This will also lead you to the overall topic. For example, five paragraphs of a section in a history book might have these topics: Thomas Jefferson's birth, Jefferson's boyhood, his education, his role in writing the Declaration of Independence, and his presidency. The overall topic of the selection would be *Thomas Jefferson's life.* This overall topic is a general topic that sums up the topics of the five individual paragraphs that comprise the selection.

Directions: Determine the topic of each paragraph. Mark any clues in the paragraph that helped you determine its topic. Then in the space provided write a word or a phrase that tells the topic.

1. This paragraph comes from a marriage and family textbook.

A significant amount of research indicates there is a strong relationship between marital happiness and finances. One large study of over 50,000 couples shows that happy couples have different ways of viewing and managing money than unhappy couples. This study found that the financial management item that most distinguishes happy couples from unhappy couples is how much they agree on how to spend money. Other issues that distinguish happy from unhappy couples include concerns about saving, concerns about debt, control of finances, and the use of credit cards.

Source: Adapted from David Olson, John DeFrain, and Linda Skogrand, *Marriages and Families,* 7th ed., pp. 223, 225. Copyright © 2011 by The McGraw-Hill Companies, Inc.

Topic: ______________________________

____

2. This paragraph comes from an art history textbook.

Following the construction of the Crystal Palace in London, another bold experiment in iron construction came a few decades later, just across the English Channel, in France. It involved a plan that many considered to be foolhardy, if not downright insane. Gustave Eiffel, a French engineer, proposed to build in the center of Paris a skeleton iron tower. Nearly a thousand feet tall, it was to act as a centerpiece for the Paris World's Fair of 1889. Nothing of the sort had ever been suggested, much less built. In spite of loud protests, the Eiffel Tower was constructed. The cost was about a million dollars—an unheard-of sum for those times. It rises on four arched columns, which curve inward until they meet in a single tower rising boldly above the cityscape of Paris.

Source: Adapted from Mark Getlein, *Living with Art,* 9th ed., p. 296. Copyright © 2010 by The McGraw-Hill Companies, Inc.

Topic: ______________________________

3. This paragraph comes from an advertising textbook.

To help managers make marketing decisions, companies develop systematic procedures for gathering, recording, and analyzing new information. This is called **marketing research**. (It should not be confused with *market research*, which is information gathered about a particular market or market segment.) Marketing research does a number of things: It helps identify consumer needs and market segments; it provides the information necessary for developing new products and

Copyright © 2014 The McGraw-Hill Companies, Inc. All rights reserved.

devising marketing strategies; and it enables managers to assess the effectiveness of marketing programs and promotional activities: Marketing research is also useful in financial planning, economic forecasting, and quality control.

Source: William Arens, Michael Weigold, and Christian Arens, *Contemporary Advertising,* 13th ed., p. 229. Copyright © 2011 by The McGraw-Hill Companies, Inc.

Topic: ____

4. This paragraph comes from a health textbook.

Risk factors for burnout include having extreme dedication to work, putting in long hours, taking work home on a regular basis. Other risk factors are taking personal responsibility for all uncompleted work (even if the amounts are unrealistic) and feeling anxiety and guilt about undone work. Although burnout has been studied mostly among service-oriented professionals whose jobs revolve around others, burnout can affect anyone. People who are burned out lose their concern and empathy for those around them and begin to treat them in a detached, mechanical way.

Source: Adapted from Richard Blonna, *Coping with Stress in a Changing World,* 5th ed., p. 164. Copyright © 2010 by The McGraw-Hill Companies, Inc.

Topic: ____

5. This paragraph comes from a science textbook.

Meteors and Meteorites

Comets leave trails of dust and rock particles after encountering the heat of the Sun. Collisions between asteroids in the past have also ejected fragments of rock particles into space. In space, the remnants of comets and asteroids are called **meteoroids**. When a meteoroid encounters Earth moving through space, it accelerates toward the surface. It soon begins to heat from air compression, melting into a visible trail of light and smoke. The streak of light and smoke in the sky is called a **meteor**. The "falling star" or "shooting star" is a meteor. Most meteors burn up or evaporate completely within seconds after reaching a certain altitude. A **meteor shower** occurs when Earth passes through a stream of particles left by a comet in its orbit.

Source: Abridged from Bill Tillery, Eldon Enger, and Frederick Ross, *Integrated Science,* 5th ed., p. 300. Copyright © 2011 by The McGraw-Hill Companies, Inc.

Topic: ____

____

____

CHAPTER REVIEW CARDS

Review cards or *summary cards* are a way to select, organize, and summarize the important information in a textbook chapter. Preparing review cards helps you organize the information so that you can learn and memorize it more easily. In other words, chapter review cards are effective study tools.

Preparing chapter review cards for each chapter of *New Worlds* will give you practice in creating these valuable study tools. Once you have learned how to make chapter review cards, you can use actual index cards to create them for textbook material in your other courses and use them when you study for tests.

Now complete the chapter review cards for Chapter 3 by answering the questions or following the directions on each card. The page numbers indicate the place in the chapter where the information can be found. Write legibly. You will find it easier to complete the review cards if you remove these pages before filling them in.

Determining the Topic

1. What is the definition of the *topic* of a paragraph? (See page 143.)

2. List two reasons it is important to determine the topic of a paragraph. (See page 143.)

3. What comprehension monitoring question should you ask yourself to determine the topic of a paragraph? (Be sure you write a *question*.) (See page 143.)

Card 1 Chapter 3: Determining the Topic

Clues to Determining the Topic

List four clues textbook authors use to indicate the topic of a paragraph. (See pages 143–148.)

1.

2.

3.

4.

Card 2 Chapter 3: Determining the Topic

When Determining the Topic, Keep in Mind . . .

What are the three other things you should keep in mind when you are determining the topic? (See pages 149–150.)

1.

2.

3.

Card 3 Chapter 3: Determining the Topic

TEST YOUR UNDERSTANDING
Determining the Topic, Part 1

Review: The **topic** of a paragraph tells *who* or *what* the author is writing about. Topics are expressed as *words* or *phrases*, but never as sentences. Clues to a paragraph's topic are headings, special print, and repeated words, or are mentioned at the beginning and referred to throughout by pronouns or other words.

EXAMPLE

This paragraph comes from a speech textbook.

Ethnocentrism is the belief that our own group or culture—whatever it may be—is superior to all other groups or cultures. Because of ethnocentrism, we identify with our group or culture and see its values, beliefs, and customs as "right" or "natural"—in comparison to the values, beliefs, and customs of other groups and cultures, which we tend to think of as "wrong" or "unnatural."

Source: Stephen Lucas, *The Art of Public Speaking,* 15th ed., p. 24. Copyright © 2009 by The McGraw-Hill Companies, Inc. Reprinted by permission of The McGraw-Hill Companies.

__c__ What is the topic of this paragraph?

a. customs

b. groups or cultures

c. ethnocentrism

d. values, beliefs, and customs

The correct answer is c. There are several clues that suggest *ethnocentrism* is the topic: The word *ethnocentrism* appears in bold print in the first sentence. The word also appears in the second sentence. And all three sentences in the paragraph pertain to the topic *ethnocentrism.* (Topics are important. Be sure you understand the *meaning* of the topic.)

Directions: To determine the topic of a paragraph, read the paragraph carefully and then ask yourself, "Who or what is this paragraph about?" Mark any clues that helped you determine its topic. Then select the answer choice that tells the topic and write the letter in the space provided.

1. This paragraph comes from a human development textbook.

In 1990, two psychologists, Peter Salovey and John Mayer, coined the term **emotional intelligence (EI)**. It refers to four related skills: the abilities to perceive, use, and understand, and manage, or regulate, emotions—our own and those of others—so as to achieve goals. Emotional intelligence enables a person to harness emotions to deal more effectively with the social environment. It requires awareness of the type of behavior that is appropriate in a given social situation.

Source: Diane Papalia, Sally Wendkos Olds, and Ruth Feldman, *Human Development,* 11th ed., p. 439. Copyright © 2009 by The McGraw-Hill Companies, Inc.

_____ What is the topic of this paragraph?

a. psychologists

b. emotional intelligence

c. understanding and regulating emotions

d. Peter Salovey and John Mayer

Copyright © 2014 The McGraw-Hill Companies, Inc. All rights reserved.

2. This paragraph comes from a music appreciation textbook.

The Major Scale

The **major scale** is the familiar *do-re-mi-fa-sol-la-ti-do.* Sing this scale and you produce seven different pitches and then arrive at the high *do*—the eighth tone—which is really a duplication of the first tone an octave higher. (The octave is the distance or interval between the first and eighth notes of a major scale.) The major scale has a specific pattern of intervals between its successive notes.

Source: Roger Kamien, *Music: An Appreciation,* 10th ed., p. 50. Copyright © 2011 by The McGraw-Hill Companies, Inc.

______ What is the topic of this paragraph?

a. seven different pitches

b. the octave

c. specific patterns of intervals

d. the major scale

3. This paragraph comes from an economics textbook.

For better or worse, most people have unlimited wants. We desire various goods and services that provide utility. Our wants extend over a wide range of products, from necessities (food, shelter, clothing) to luxuries (perfume, yachts, sports cars). Some wants such as basic food, clothing, and shelter have biological roots. Other wants, for example, specific kinds of food, clothing, and shelter, arise from the conventions and customs of society.

Source: Stanley Brue, Campbell McConnell, and Sean Flynn, *Essentials of Economics,* 2nd ed., p. 10. Copyright © 2010 by The McGraw-Hill Companies, Inc.

______ What is the topic of this paragraph?

a. for better or worse

b. unlimited wants

c. goods and services

d. necessities and luxuries

4. This paragraph comes from a human development textbook.

As adolescents spend more time with peers, they have less time and less need for the emotional gratification they used to get from the sibling bond. Changes in sibling relationships may well precede similar changes in the relationship between adolescents and parents: more independence on the part of the younger person and less authority exerted by the older person. As children approach high school, their relationships with their siblings become progressively more equal. Older siblings exercise less power over younger ones, and younger siblings no longer need as much supervision.

Source: Adapted from Diane E. Papalia, Sally Wendkos Olds, and Ruth Duskin Feldman, *Human Development,* 11th ed., p. 410. Copyright © 2009 by The McGraw-Hill Companies, Inc. Reprinted by permission of The McGraw-Hill Companies.

______ What is the topic of this paragraph?

a. changes in sibling relationships among adolescents

b. adolescents

c. siblings and peers

d. older siblings

5. This paragraph comes from an art appreciation textbook.

The **primary colors** or hues (yellow, red, and blue) are the basic, irreducible units that cannot be produced by mixing other colors. The **secondary colors** (orange, violet, green) are made by mixing a different pair of primary colors: orange by mixing red and yellow, violet by mixing red and blue, green by mixing yellow and blue. The **tertiary** or intermediate **colors** are created by mixing adjacent primary and secondary hues on the color wheel. For example, the tertiary hue red-orange is created by mixing the primary color red and the adjacent secondary color orange.

Source: Robert Bersson, *Responding to Art: Form, Content, and Context*, p. 46. Copyright © 2004 by The McGraw-Hill Companies, Inc.

________ What is the topic of this paragraph?

a. primary colors

b. secondary colors

c. tertiary colors

d. primary, secondary, and tertiary colors

TEST YOUR UNDERSTANDING
Determining the Topic, Part 2

Review: The **topic** of a paragraph tells *who* or *what* the author is writing about. Topics are expressed as words or phrases, but never as sentences. Clues to a paragraph's topic are headings, special print, repeated words, or words that are mentioned at the beginning and then referred to throughout the paragraph by pronouns or other words.

EXAMPLE

This paragraph comes from a psychology textbook.

Pressure

Does the pressure of working for good grades ever get to you? If you have been employed, was it a high-pressure job? The term **pressure** is used to describe the stress that arises from threats of negative events. In school, there is always the possibility that you will not perform well and you will fail. Some jobs are loaded with possibilities for making a mess of things and getting fired. Some unhappy marriages are sources of pressure because one spouse always seems to displease the other, no matter how hard he or she tries to avoid it.

Source: Adapted from Benjamin B. Lahey, *Psychology,* 8th ed., p. 503. Copyright © 2004 by The McGraw-Hill Companies, Inc. Reprinted by permission of The McGraw-Hill Companies, Inc.

Write the topic: pressure

Clue(s): The word pressure appears in the heading and in bold print in the paragraph. It also appears several times in the paragraph

Explanation: The topic of the paragraph, pressure, appears in the heading and in bold print. The word *pressure* also appears several times in the paragraph.

Directions: To determine the topic of a paragraph, read the paragraph carefully and then ask yourself, "Who or what is this paragraph about?" Mark any clues in the paragraph that helped you determine its topic. Then in the spaces provided beneath each paragraph, write a word or a phrase that tells the topic, and list any clues you found.

1. This paragraph comes from a public speaking textbook.

For many speakers of English, **articulation**—the production of speech sounds by our vocal organs—is lazy and weak, especially in daily conversations. We slur sounds, drop syllables, and mumble words. While poor articulation may not hurt us in conversation as long as our friends understand what we are saying, it can hinder communication in a speech, especially if English is a second language for some of our listeners. We need to enunciate our words crisply and precisely to make sure that everything we say is intelligible.

Source: Hamilton Gregory, *Public Speaking for College and Career,* 9th ed., p. 280. Copyright © 2010 by The McGraw-Hill Companies, Inc.

Write a word, name, or phrase that tells the topic: ______________________________

____

Clue(s): ____

____

2. This paragraph comes from a business textbook.

In all the markets in which it operates, McDonald's listens to customers and adapts to their culture and preferences. For example, having set up its first franchises in Hong Kong in 1975, McDonald's altered the breakfast menu after realizing customers there liked burgers for breakfast, and chicken or fish for the rest of the day. The company also offers unique products such as curry potato pie and red bean sundaes for its Hong Kong customers. In Israel, all meat served in McDonald's restaurants is 100 percent kosher beef. The company closes many of its restaurants on the Sabbath and on religious holidays. However, it also operates nonkosher restaurants for those Israelis who are not observant Jews. In India, to respect religious sentiments, McDonald's does not include any beef or pork on its menu. Go to www.mcdonalds.com and click on the "I'm Going to McDonald's" link to explore the various Web sites of McDonald's international franchises. Notice how each site blends the culture of the country into the restaurant's image.

Source: William Nickels, James McHugh, and Susan McHugh, *Understanding Business,* 9th ed., p. 68. Copyright © 2010 by The McGraw-Hill Companies, Inc.

Write a word, name, or phrase that tells the topic: ______________________________

____

Clue(s): ______________________________

____

____

3. This paragraph comes from a marriage and family textbook.

Empty-Nest Syndrome

The term empty-nest syndrome describes the feelings of malaise, emptiness, and lack of purpose that parents sometimes experience when their children leave home. Some parents do suffer these feelings, and most go through a period of adjustment when their children leave the nest. But the empty nest is a boon to many parents, giving them more time and energy to invest in their marriage.

Source: David H. Olson, John DeFrain, and Linda Skogrand, *Marriages and Families: Intimacy, Diversity, and Strengths,* 7th ed., p. 384. Copyright © 2011 by The McGraw-Hill Companies, Inc.

Write a word, name, or phrase that tells the topic: ______________________________

Clue(s): ______________________________

____

4. This paragraph comes from a government textbook.

One area in which African Americans have made progress since the 1960s is elective office. Although the percentage of black elected officials is still far below the proportion of African Americans in the population, it has risen sharply over recent decades. There are now roughly 600 black mayors and more than 400 black members of Congress. The most stunning advance, of course, was the election of Barack Obama in 2008 as the first African American president.

Source: Thomas E. Patterson, *We the People,* 9th ed., p. 171. Copyright © 2011 by The McGraw-Hill Companies, Inc. Reprinted by permission of the The McGraw-Hill Companies, Inc.

Write a word, name, or phrase that tells the topic: ______________________________

____

Clue(s): ____

____

5. This paragraph comes from a career-planning textbook.

Communication skills are at the top of the list of most employer surveys conducted by professional associations each year. Employers require good communication skills because they are the foundation for most levels of job functions. Good communication skills are necessary for positions dealing with the public. You need good communication skills to work in teams and to mentor and lead others. In the workplace, you will be judged by the impression you make with how you communicate. Demonstrating that you are polished, professional, and knowledgeable in your communication builds credibility in you and in your company. Developing good communication skills is an ongoing process that includes formal learning in the classroom and practice through work and life experiences.

Source: Donna Yena, *Career Directions: The Path to Your Ideal Career,* 5th ed., p. 52. Copyright © 2011 by The McGraw-Hill Companies, Inc.

Write a word, name, or phrase that tells the topic: ______________________________

____

Clue(s): ____

____

SELECTION **3.1** **Human Development**

Parenting Style: Does It Matter?

From *Human Development*
By Diane Papalia, Sally Wendkos Olds, and Ruth Feldman

To keep her two young children occupied while she fixes their lunch, a mother gives them crayons and paper. When she returns 15 minutes later, she discovers that they have used all of the paper and begun drawing on the bedroom wall. She spanks them and tells them they will not get to have cookies after lunch. Given the same situation, another mother sighs, shakes her head, and ignores the situation. Still another mother in that situation explains to the children why they cannot mark on things other than paper, tells them she expects them not to do it again, and then has them help her clean the marks off the wall. Same situation. Three very different responses. Does the difference matter?

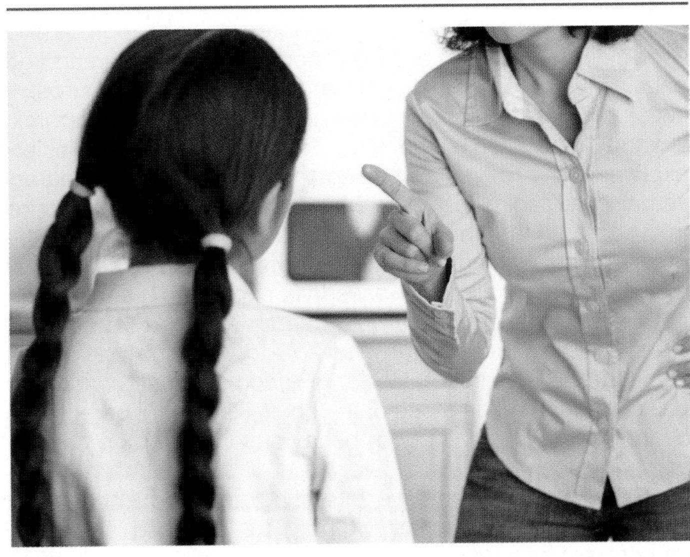

The answer, it seems, is yes. It has been said that "each day of our lives, we make deposits in the memory banks of our children." What does the type of parenting add to children's memory banks and how does it influence their competence to deal with their world? In the late 1960s psychologist Diana Baumrind began investigating this question. She discovered that one style of parenting seems to enhance children's competence more than the other styles.

Diana Baumrind and the Effectiveness of Authoritative Parenting

1 In pioneering research, Diana Baumrind studied 103 preschool children from 95 families. Through interviews, testing, and home studies, she measured how the children were functioning, identified three *parenting styles*, and described typical behavior patterns of children raised according to each. Baumrind's work and the large body of research it inspired have established strong associations between each parenting style and a particular set of child behaviors.

2 **Authoritarian parenting,** according to Baumrind, emphasizes control and unquestioning obedience. Authoritarian parents try to make children conform to a set standard of conduct and punish them arbitrarily and forcefully for violating it. They are more detached and less warm than other parents. Their children tend to be more discontented, withdrawn, and distrustful.

3 **Permissive parenting** emphasizes self-expression and self-regulation. Permissive parents make few demands and allow children to monitor their own activities as much as possible.

Annotation Practice Exercises

Directions: For each exercise below, write the topic of the paragraph on the lines beside the paragraph.

Practice Exercise

Topic of paragraph 1:

____

____

____

Practice Exercise

Topic of paragraph 2:

____

____

Copyright © 2014 The McGraw-Hill Companies, Inc. All rights reserved.

When they do have to make rules, they explain the reasons for them. They consult with children about policy decisions and rarely punish. They are warm, noncontrolling, and undemanding. Their preschool children tend to be immature—the least self-controlled and the least exploratory.

4 **Authoritative parenting** emphasizes a child's individuality but also stresses social constraints. Authoritative parents have confidence in their ability to guide children, but they also respect children's independent decisions, interests, opinions, and personalities. They are loving and accepting but also demand good behavior and are firm in maintaining standards. They impose limited, judicious punishment when necessary, within the context of a warm, supportive relationship. They favor inductive discipline, explaining the reasoning behind their stands and encouraging verbal give-and-take. Their children apparently feel secure in knowing both that they are loved and what is expected of them. Preschoolers with authoritative parents tend to be the most self-reliant, self-controlled, self-assertive, exploratory, and content.

5 Eleanor Maccoby and John Martin added a fourth parenting style—*neglectful*, or *uninvolved*—to describe parents who, sometimes because of stress or depression, focus on their needs rather than on those of the child. Neglectful parenting has been linked with a variety of behavioral disorders in childhood and adolescence.

6 Why does authoritative parenting seem to enhance children's social competence? It may be because authoritative parents set sensible expectations and realistic standards. By making clear, consistent rules, they let children know what is expected of them. In authoritarian homes, children are so strictly controlled that often they cannot make independent choices about their own behavior. In permissive homes, children receive so little guidance that they may become uncertain and anxious about whether they are doing the right thing. In authoritative homes, children know when they are meeting expectations and can decide whether it is worth risking parental displeasure to pursue a goal. These children are expected to perform well, fulfill commitments, and participate actively in family duties as well as family fun. They know the satisfaction of accepting responsibilities and achieving success. Parents who make reasonable demands show that they believe their children can meet them—and that the parents care enough to insist that they do.

7 When conflict arises, an authoritative parent can teach the child positive ways to communicate his or her point of view and negotiate acceptable alternatives. ("If you don't want to throw away those rocks you found, where do you think we should keep them?") Internalization of this broader set of skills, not just of specific behavioral demands, may well be a key to the success of authoritative parenting.

8 Still, Baumrind's model has provoked controversy because it seems to suggest that there is one "right" way to raise children. Also, because Baumrind's findings are correlational, they merely establish associations between each parenting style and a particular set of child behaviors. They do not show that different styles of child rearing cause children to be more or less competent. It is also impossible to know whether the children

Practice Exercise

Topic of paragraph 3:

___

Practice Exercise

Topic of paragraph 4:

___

___

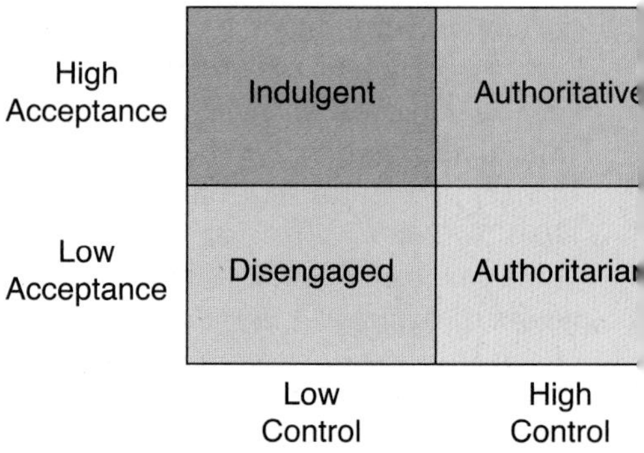

	Low Control	High Control
High Acceptance	Indulgent	Authoritative
Low Acceptance	Disengaged	Authoritarian

Four Primary Parenting Styles: Indulgent (Permissive), Authoritative, Authoritarian, and Disengaged (Neglectful or Uninvolved).

Practice Exercise

Topic of paragraph 5:

___

___

Practice Exercise

Topic of paragraph 6:

___

___

___

___

Practice Exercise

Topic of paragraph 8:

___

___

___

Baumrind studied were, in fact, raised in a particular style. It may be that some of the better-adjusted children were raised inconsistently, but by the time of the study their parents had adopted the authoritative pattern. In addition, Baumrind did not consider innate factors, such as temperament, that might have affected children's competence and exerted an influence on the parents. Another concern is that Baumrind's categories reflect the dominant North American view of child development and may not apply to some cultures or socioeconomic groups.

Source: Abridged from Diane Papalia, Sally Wendkos Olds, and Ruth Feldman, *Human Development,* 11th ed., pp. 272–74. Copyright © 2009 by The McGraw-Hill Companies, Inc.

SELECTION 3.1 **Human Development** *(continued)*

Comprehension and Vocabulary Quiz

This quiz has four parts. Your instructor may assign some or all of them.

Comprehension

Directions: Items 1–5 test your understanding of the selection. They are the types of questions a content-area instructor (such as a human development professor) might ask on a test. You may refer to the selection as you answer the questions. Write your answer choice in the space provided.

_______ **1.** Parents who value unquestioning obedience and control are referred to as:

a. authoritative parents.
b. permissive parents.
c. authoritarian parents.
d. noncontrolling parents.

_______ **2.** Compared with children who experience authoritarian or authoritative parenting styles, preschool children of permissive parents tend to be:

a. more discontented, withdrawn, and distrustful.
b. immature, less self-controlled, and less exploratory.
c. more self-reliant and self-controlled.
d. more content and secure.

_______ **3.** With regard to punishing their children, authoritative parents tend to:

a. withdraw from their children.
b. spank their children often and forcefully.
c. use limited, judicious punishment when necessary.
d. force their children to conform to strict standards.

_______ **4.** Maccoby and Martin are associated with which parenting style?

a. permissive
b. authoritative
c. neglectful/uninvolved
d. authoritarian

_______ **5.** Authoritative parenting seems to enhance a child's competence because authoritative parents:

a. allow children to express their unique personalities.
b. make children conform to a set standard of conduct.
c. allow children to monitor their own activities as much as possible.
d. set reasonable expectations and realistic standards for their children.

Vocabulary in Context

Directions: Items 6–10 test your ability to determine a word's meaning by using context clues. *Context clues* are words in a sentence that allow readers to deduce (reason out) the meaning of an unfamiliar word in the sentence. They also help readers determine the meaning an author intends when a word has more than one meaning. Each item below consists of a sentence from the selection, with the vocabulary word *italicized*. It is followed by another sentence that uses the same word in the same way. Use context clues to deduce the meaning of the *italicized* word. Be sure the meaning you choose makes sense in *both* sentences. Write each answer in the space provided. (Chapter 2 presented the skill of using context clues.)

_______ **6.** *Authoritarian* parents value control and unquestioning obedience.

Nobody likes the new soccer coach because he is as *authoritarian* as a dictator.

authoritarian (ə thôr ĭ târ′ ē ən) means:

a. expecting others to obey without question
b. skilled in leadership
c. pertaining to an author
d. demanding an unreasonable amount of hard work

_______ **7.** They impose limited, *judicious* punishment when necessary, within the context of a warm, supportive relationship.

Because Nadine is *judicious* in her spending, she was able to save $1,000 last year.

judicious (jo͞o dĭsh′ əs) means:

a. harsh; severe
b. showing good judgment
c. legal
d. careless

_______ **8.** *Permissive* parents value self-expression and self-regulation.

The substitute teacher was so *permissive* that she allowed the children to do whatever they wanted.

permissive (pər mĭs′ ĭv) means:

a. asking permission; seeking approval
b. gloomy; expecting the worst
c. lenient; likely to give permission
d. lazy; unmotivated

_______ **9.** *Authoritative* parents respect a child's individuality but also stress social values.

Because the principal was so *authoritative,* the students did not hesitate to follow her instructions during the fire drill.

authoritative (ə thôr′ ĭ tā tĭv) means:

a. proud
b. hysterical
c. deserving scorn or ridicule
d. arising from proper authority

_______ **10.** Baumrind did not consider innate factors, such as *temperament*, that might have affected children's competence and exerted an influence on the parents.

Some breeds of dogs, such as cocker spaniels and Labrador retrievers, make good family pets because of their gentle, calm *temperament.*

temperament (tĕm′ prə mənt) means:

a. typical manner of reacting

b. hostility; anger

c. inability to get along with other people

d. impulsiveness

Word Structure

Directions: Items 11–15 test your ability to use word-structure clues to help determine a word's meaning. *Word-structure clues* consist of roots, prefixes, and suffixes. In this exercise, you will learn the meaning of a root and use it to determine the meaning of several words that contain it. If you need to use a dictionary to confirm your answer choice, do so. Write your answers in the spaces provided.

In paragraph 4 of the selection, you encountered the word **impose.** This word contains the Latin root ***pos***, which means "to put" or "to place." The word *impose* means to *place* or *put* one's own values, beliefs, and so on, on another person. Use the meaning of the root ***pos*** and the list of prefixes on pages 24–25 to help you determine the meaning of each of the following words that contain the same root.

_______ **11.** If you take a picture off the wall and **reposition** it, you:

a. rehang it in a different place.

b. store it away.

c. put it in a closet.

d. clean it.

_______ **12.** If you accidentally **transpose** the letters in a word when you are typing, you:

a. delete the letters.

b. put the letters in the wrong order.

c. capitalize the letters.

d. add extra letters.

_______ **13.** To **compose** a tune means to:

a. place notes in an order that makes a melody.

b. alter the sequence of notes in an existing melody.

c. plagiarize someone else's melody.

d. record the tune you create.

_______ **14.** If a businessperson **proposes** that his or her company develop a new product, the person:

a. builds a model of the product.

b. suggests or puts forth the idea for the product.

c. hires someone to design the product.

d. researches the potential market for the product.

_______ **15.** A safety deposit box is a *repository* for extremely important or valuable items. A **repository** is a place in which items are:

a. stored until they can be sold.
b. left indefinitely.
c. auctioned off.
d. put for safekeeping.

Reading Skills Application

Directions: Items 16–20 test your ability to *apply* certain reading skills. You may not be familiar with all the skills yet, so some items will serve as a preview. As you work through *New Worlds,* you will practice and develop these skills. These are important skills, which is why they are included on the state-mandated basic skills tests that some students must take. Write each answer in the space provided.

_______ **16.** The authors' primary purpose for writing this selection is to:

a. describe three styles of parenting and their effects on children.
b. persuade parents to adopt an authoritarian parenting style.
c. explain how parents develop parenting styles.
d. instruct parents how to change their parenting style.

_______ **17.** Which of the following is the meaning of *conform* as it is used in the second paragraph?

a. cherish
b. create
c. obey
d. ignore

_______ **18.** Based on information in the selection, which of the following represents a logical conclusion about parenting styles?

a. Parents cannot change their parenting styles.
b. All children grow up to have the same parenting style as their parents.
c. Being aware of parenting styles and their effects can help people become better parents.
d. Parenting styles are not well understood.

_______ **19.** Which of the following statements is the main idea of paragraph 6?

a. Children know the satisfaction of meeting responsibilities and achieving success.
b. Authoritative parenting seems to enhance children's competence because authoritative parents set reasonable limits and realistic expectations.
c. In authoritarian homes, children are so strictly controlled that they cannot make independent choices about their own behavior.
d. In permissive homes, children receive so little guidance that they may become uncertain and anxious about whether they are doing the right thing.

_______ **20.** Which of the following best describes the authors' tone?

a. impassioned
b. humorous
c. sarcastic
d. factual

Copyright © 2014 The McGraw-Hill Companies, Inc. All rights reserved.

SELECTION 3.1
Human Development
(continued)

Respond in Writing

Directions: Refer to the selection as needed to answer the essay-type questions below. (Your instructor may direct you to work collaboratively with other students on one or more items. Each group member should be able to explain *all* of the group's answers.)

1. **Reacting to What You Have Read:** Was the parenting style of your parents (or the person or persons who reared you) authoritarian, permissive, or authoritative? Describe some of their actions as parents and their attitudes toward children that cause you to view them this way.

___
___
___
___
___
___
___
___
___
___
___
___

2. **Comprehending the Selection Further:** Put a check mark below the style of parenting that corresponds with each parental action or attitude. (You may refer to the selection.)

Parental action or attitude:	**Authoritarian**	**Permissive**	**Authoritative**
• detached, less warm	______	______	______
• values control	______	______	______
• explains reasoning behind their stands	______	______	______
• views themselves as resources	______	______	______
• makes few demands on children	______	______	______
• imposes limited, judicious punishment	______	______	______
• punishes arbitrarily	______	______	______
• values self-regulation	______	______	______
• stresses social values	______	______	______
• is undemanding	______	______	______

Put a check mark below the style of parenting that corresponds with each of the characteristics of children of these parents.

Children's behavior or attitude:	Authoritarian	Permissive	Authoritative
• have input on policy decisions	_______	_______	_______
• tend to be more distrustful	_______	_______	_______
• participate in verbal give-and-take	_______	_______	_______
• tend to be withdrawn	_______	_______	_______
• feel secure and loved	_______	_______	_______
• are less self-controlled	_______	_______	_______
• cannot make independent choices about their own behavior	_______	_______	_______
• know when they are meeting expectations	_______	_______	_______
• are uncertain and anxious about whether they are doing the right thing	_______	_______	_______
• fulfill commitments	_______	_______	_______

3. **Overall Main Idea of the Selection:** In one sentence, tell what the authors want readers to understand about parenting styles and children's competence in dealing with their world. (Be sure to include "parenting style" and "children's competence in dealing with their world" in your overall main idea sentence.)

____

____

____

Internet Resources

Read More about It Online

Directions: Read more about the topic of this selection online. You can read online *before* you read the selection to build background knowledge or *afterward* to extend your knowledge. Start with the websites below or type **"Diana Baumrind"** or **"parenting styles"** in the search box of Google, Yahoo, or another search engine. When you visit any unfamiliar website, it is important to evaluate it and the information it contains. If you do not know how to conduct Internet searches or evaluate a website, see pages 24–25.

http://pediatrics.about.com/cs/quizzes/l/bl_prnt_style.htm

At this About.com website for pediatrics, you can take the Parenting Style Quiz to see what kind of parent you are or are likely to be.

http://en.wikipedia.org/wiki/Parenting_styles

This Wikipedia entry gives an overview of Baumrind's and Maccoby and Martin's theories of parenting styles, as well as several other parenting styles.

SELECTION **3.2**

Speech Communication

Giving a Speech? If You're Nervous, You're Normal!

From *Public Speaking for College and Career*

By Hamilton Gregory

It has been said that dying is the only thing Americans fear more than having to give a speech! To rank the fear of these two things so closely together indicates the extent to which many adults dread public speaking. Not surprisingly, many college students feel a bit panicky at the thought of having to give an oral report or make a presentation in class. (Some find it difficult even to make a comment or to ask a question in class.) In this selection from a public speaking textbook, the author describes four causes of this nervousness and reassures readers that it is an entirely normal feeling.

If public speaking makes you unusually nervous, consider enrolling in a speech course or joining a group such as Toastmasters. You will be with a supportive group of people who share the same anxiety. You will gain valuable instruction, practice, and–most important–confidence. Being able to speak well in public is an asset that will serve you well in college, in organizations to which you belong, and in your career.

1 After pop singer Kelly Clarkson won the first season of American Idol and became a top star, she received invitations to give speeches, but she declined them all. "I have never been nervous while singing," she said, "but when it comes to public speaking, I stumble on my words, sweat, and pull at my clothes."

2 Only a few months after saying those words, however, she became an official spokesperson for NASCAR, giving presentations throughout the country. Not only was she speaking in public, but she was speaking with confidence and poise.

3 What happened?

4 "A good friend of mine helped me understand that when you give a speech, nothing bad is going to happen to you," she said. "If I open my mouth and make a mistake, people won't look down on me. Actually, they will probably like me because they will see that I'm the same as everyone else."

5 If you experience nervousness as a public speaker, you are not alone. Most people—even performers such as Clarkson—suffer from stage fright when called upon to speak in public.

6 In fact, when researchers ask Americans to name their greatest fears, the fear of speaking to a group of strangers is listed more often than fear of snakes, insects, lightning, deep water, heights, or flying in airplanes.

Reasons for Nervousness

7 Is it foolish to be afraid to give a speech? Is this fear as groundless as a child's fear of the bogeyman? I used to think so, back when I first began making speeches. I was a nervous wreck, and I would often chide myself by saying, "Come on, relax; it's just a little speech. There's no good reason to be scared." But I was wrong. There *is* good reason to be scared. In fact, there are *four* good reasons.

Annotation Practice Exercises

Directions: For each exercise below, write the topic of the paragraph on the lines beside the paragraph.

Practice Exercise

Topic of paragraph 6:

____

____

____

Practice Exercise

Topic of paragraph 7:

____

____

____

Thanks to the insight of a friend, singer Kelly Clarkson is able to speak in public with confidence and poise.

Fear of Being Stared At

8 In the animal world, a stare is a hostile act. Dogs, baboons, and other animals sometimes defend their territory by staring. Their hostile gaze alone is enough to turn away an intruder. We human beings have similar reactions; it is a part of our biological makeup to be upset by stares. Imagine that you are riding in a crowded elevator with a group of strangers. Suddenly you realize that the other people are staring directly at you. Not just glancing. *Staring.* You probably would be unnerved and frightened because a stare can be as threatening as a clenched fist—especially if it comes from people you don't know. That is why public speaking can be so frightening. You have a pack of total strangers "attacking" you with unrelenting stares, while you are obliged to stand alone, exposed and vulnerable—a goldfish in a bowl, subject to a constant scrutiny.

Practice Exercise

Topic of paragraph 8:

____

____

____

Fear of Failure

9 In stressful social situations, most people are afraid of looking stupid. We say to ourselves, "What if I make a fool of myself?" or "What if I say something dumb?"

Fear of Rejection

10 What if we do our best, what if we deliver a polished speech, but the audience still does not like us? It would be quite a blow to our ego because we want to be liked and, yes, even loved. We want people to admire us, to consider us wise and intelligent,

and to accept our ideas and opinions. We don't want people to dislike us or reject us.

Fear of the Unknown

11 Throughout our lives we are apprehensive about doing new things, such as going to school for the first time, riding a bus without our parents, or going out on our first date. We cannot put a finger on exactly what we are afraid of, because our fear is vague and diffused. What we really fear is the unknown; we worry that some unpredictable disaster will occur. When we stand up to give a speech, we are sometimes assailed by this same fear of the unknown because we cannot predict the outcome of our speech. Fortunately, this fear usually disappears, as we become experienced in giving speeches. We develop enough confidence to know that nothing terrible will befall us, just as our childhood fear of riding in a bus by ourselves vanished after two or three trips.

12 All four of these fears are as understandable as the fear of lightning. There is no reason to be ashamed of having them.

Practice Exercise

Topic of paragraph 11:

____

____

____

Source: Hamilton Gregory, *Public Speaking for College and Career*, 9th ed., pp. 24–25. Copyright © 2010 by The McGraw-Hill Companies, Inc. Reprinted by permission of The McGraw-Hill Companies, Inc.

Copyright © 2014 The McGraw-Hill Companies, Inc. All rights reserved.

SELECTION 3.2
Speech Communication
(continued)

Comprehension and Vocabulary Quiz

This quiz has four parts. Your instructor may assign some or all of them.

Comprehension

Directions: Items 1–5 test your understanding of the selection. They are the types of questions a content-area instructor (such as a public speaking or speech professor) might ask on a test. You may refer to the selection as you answer the questions. Write your answer choice in the space provided.

______ **1.** Kelly Clarkson was able to become a successful public speaker once she realized:

a. she needed to pour her heart and soul into reaching her audiences.
b. people wouldn't look down on her if she made a mistake.
c. she must spend more time preparing for her speeches.
d. putting pressure on herself was actually helpful.

______ **2.** Feeling nervous when giving a speech is:

a. caused by strangers in the audience "attacking" you with unrelenting stares.
b. less common than fear of snakes, insects, and lightning.
c. normal.
d. a blow to our ego.

______ **3.** When speaking to a group, our fear of the unknown usually lessens as we:

a. learn to look directly at people in the audience.
b. learn to control our egos.
c. become less afraid of "looking stupid."
d. become more experienced in giving speeches.

______ **4.** The fear of rejection contributes to our nervousness when speaking to a group because:

a. we have a strong need for people to admire us and accept our ideas and opinions.
b. we want to reject the idea of giving a speech.
c. we do not know who will reject us.
d. all of the above

______ **5.** All of the following are good reasons to be nervous about speaking to a group of strangers *except:*

a. we are apprehensive about doing something new.
b. we are afraid of looking foolish.
c. we fear that we have not prepared and rehearsed our speech adequately.
d. we fear that people in the audience won't like us or accept our ideas.

Vocabulary in Context

Directions: Items 6–10 test your ability to determine a word's meaning by using context clues. *Context clues* are words in a sentence that allow readers to deduce (reason out) the meaning of an unfamiliar word. They also help readers determine the meaning an author intends when a word has more than one meaning. Each item below consists of a sentence from the selection, with the vocabulary word *italicized.* It is followed by another sentence that uses the same word in the same way. Use context clues to deduce the meaning of the *italicized* word. Be sure the meaning you choose makes sense in *both* sentences. Write each answer in the space provided. (Chapter 2 presented the skill of using context clues.)

_______ **6.** Not only was she speaking in public, she was speaking with confidence and *poise.*

Even though the waiter spilled wine on her, she maintained her *poise.*

poise (poiz) means:

a. calm state of mind
b. balance
c. sense of reason
d. enthusiasm

_______ **7.** Is this fear as *groundless* as a child's fear of the bogeyman?

The judge ruled that the charges against the defendent were *groundless* and dismissed the case.

groundless (ground′ lĭs) means:

a. severe
b. able to be disputed
c. without basis
d. upsetting

_______ **8.** You have a pack of total strangers "attacking" you with *unrelenting* stares, while you are obliged to stand alone, exposed and vulnerable—a goldfish in a bowl, subject to a constant scrutiny.

Once we entered the grocery store, my children were so *unrelenting* in their demands for candy that I finally gave in and bought them some.

unrelenting (ŭn rĭ lĕn′ tĭng) means:

a. loud; vocal
b. constant; persistent
c. unreasonable
d. hostile; hateful

_______ **9.** We cannot put a finger on exactly what we are afraid of, because our fear is vague and *diffused.*

The patient's anxiety was so *diffused* that the psychiatrist was unable to identify the specific source of it.

Copyright © 2014 The McGraw-Hill Companies, Inc. All rights reserved.

diffused (dĭ fyo͞ozd′) means:

a. intense; focused

b. overwhelming to the point of incapacitating

c. distinct; clear

d. not concentrated on any one thing

_______ **10.** When we stand up to give a speech, we are sometimes *assailed* by this same fear of the unknown because we cannot predict the outcome of our speech.

After the tornado struck the state, the governor was *assailed* with criticism for not responding quickly enough to help its victims.

assailed (ə sāld′) means:

a. attacked

b. frightened

c. praised

d. ignored

Word Structure

Directions: Items 11–15 test your ability to use word-structure clues to help determine a word's meaning. *Word-structure clues* consist of roots, prefixes, and suffixes. In these exercises, you will learn the meaning of a root and use it to determine the meaning of several other words that contain it. If you need to use a dictionary to confirm your answer choice, do so. Write your answers in the spaces provided.

In paragraph 10 of the selection, you encountered the word **rejection.** This word contains the Latin root ***ject,*** which means "to throw." The word *rejection* literally means that someone or something is "*tossed* back" (not accepted). Use the meaning of ***ject*** and the list of prefixes on pages 72–73 to help you determine the meaning of each of the following words that contain this same root.

_______ **11.** If a referee or umpire **ejects** players from a game, he or she:

a. throws them out.

b. cautions them against making future violations.

c. calls a penalty on them.

d. signals to them.

_______ **12.** If you are **dejected,** you are feeling:

a. angry.

b. cheerful.

c. optimistic.

d. downcast.

_______ **13.** If you **interject** your opinion into a conversation your friends are having, you:

a. keep your opinion to yourself.

b. interrupt them by tossing in your opinion.

c. ask them if they would like to know your opinion.

d. decide your opinion is worthless.

_______ **14.** A film **projector** is designed to:

a. throw images on a screen.
b. block images from the screen.
c. blur images.
d. capture images on film.

_______ **15.** If you receive an **injection,** the substance is:

a. given as a pill.
b. dispensed as a cream.
c. pushed beneath the skin.
d. placed in an inhaler.

Reading Skills Application

Directions: Items 16–20 test your ability to *apply* certain reading skills. You may not be familiar with all the skills yet, so some items will serve as a preview. As you work through *New Worlds,* you will practice and develop these skills. These are important skills, which is why they are included on the state-mandated basic skills tests that some students must take. Write each answer in the space provided.

_______ **16.** The information in paragraphs 7–12 of the selection is organized according to which of the following patterns?

a. comparison-contrast
b. problem-solution
c. sequence
d. cause-effect

_______ **17.** The author's primary purpose for writing this selection is to:

a. persuade readers to become more like Kelly Clarkson.
b. instruct readers how to overcome their nervousness.
c. persuade readers to get more practice making speeches.
d. inform readers as to why giving a speech can make a person nervous.

_______ **18.** Which of the following statements best expresses the main idea of paragraph 7?

a. There are four good reasons to be nervous when you give a speech.
b. It is foolish to be afraid to give a speech.
c. The fear of giving a speech is groundless.
d. You can calm yourself by saying, "Relax, it's just a little speech."

_______ **19.** In paragraph 11 it says, "When we stand up to give a speech, we are sometimes *assailed* by this same fear of the unknown because we cannot predict the outcome of our speech." As used in this sentence, *assailed* means

a. troubled; attacked.
b. entertained; amused.
c. punished.
d. confused; puzzled.

Copyright © 2014 The McGraw-Hill Companies, Inc. All rights reserved.

_______ **20.** Based on information in the selection, it can be inferred that:
a. the fear of rejection is stronger in people than the fear of failure.
b. throughout our lives we are apprehensive about doing new things.
c. it is reassuring to know that it is normal to feel nervous about speaking in public.
d. most people eventually adjust to being stared at.

SELECTION **3.2**
Speech Communication
(continued)

Respond in Writing

Directions: Refer to the selection as needed to answer the essay-type questions below. (Your instructor may direct you to work collaboratively with other students on one or more items. Each group member should be able to explain *all* of the group's answers.)

1. **Reacting to What You Have Read:** Have you ever been a victim of "mike fright"? Freezing up when a microphone or camcorder is thrust in one's face is a common experience. Describe a situation when your nervousness or fear interfered with your speaking in the classroom or some other public setting.

2. **Comprehending the Selection Further:** List and explain the four common reasons for nervousness when we are giving a speech.

3. **Overall Main Idea of the Selection:** In one sentence, tell what the author wants readers to understand about being nervous when giving a speech. (Be sure to use "nervous" and "giving a speech" in your overall main idea sentence.)

____

____

____

____

____

Internet Resources

Read More about It Online

Directions: Read more about the topic of this selection online. You can read online *before* you read the selection to build background knowledge or *afterward* to extend your knowledge. Start with the website below or type **"public speaking nervousness"** in the search box of Google, Yahoo, or another search engine. When you visit any unfamiliar website, it is important to evaluate it and the information it contains. If you do not know how to conduct Internet searches or evaluate a website, see pages 24–25.

www.toastmasters.org
This is the official website for Toastmasters International, an organization that promotes effective communication. It contains useful tips on giving speeches and presentations.

SELECTION 3.3
Health

State-of-the-Art and High-Tech Ways of Dealing with Death

From *Understanding Your Health*
By Wayne Payne, Dale Hahn, and Ellen Lucas

Perhaps your experience with funerals is sitting in a place of worship or a funeral home at a service honoring the deceased. Perhaps there was a casket, flowers, and religious music, and one or more people spoke about the person who has died and shared memories of the person. There may have been other traditional rituals. Although many people still choose these, things are changing. Read the selection below to learn more about the options technology is making available.

Annotation Practice Exercises

Directions: For each exercise below, write the topic of the paragraph on the lines beside the paragraph.

1 People cope with death in many individual ways. Collectively, these serve the diverse needs of society. As our society becomes more culturally diverse, funeral directors are becoming more familiar (and accommodating) with rituals used not only by dozens of Christian denominations but also with rituals for Buddhist, Hindu, and Muslim groups.

Unconventional Funerals

2 Increasingly, funeral directors indicate that there is no longer a set "conventional funeral service." Families mourn the loss of loved ones by developing their own customized funerals. For example, soft music, classical music, rap music, folk music, rock music, or ethnic music may be heard at calling hours (body visitation). Food and drinks (including alcoholic drinks) might be served during calling hours or after the service is performed. More and more families are choosing to display collages of pictures of the deceased person to allow the mourners to remember the life of the dead person.

3 One unconventional practice that is gaining popularity is the use of the "drive-through mortuary." Mourners can save time by driving up to a funeral home's drive-through window. Without getting out of their car, they can view the body, sign the guest register, and pay their "respects." Although viewed by many as a callous approach, this option was probably inevitable in a society that seems to value squeezing more activities into less time.

Practice Exercise

Topic of paragraph 3:

____

____

____

4 Other high-tech influences reflect the variety of ways that people cope with death. Many funeral homes now make video recordings that are sold to friends and relatives who cannot

Copyright © 2014 The McGraw-Hill Companies, Inc. All rights reserved.

attend the funeral service. In some cases, digital cameras are used to transmit live video images of a funeral service over the Internet. As the world rapidly changes, so do the ways we handle death rituals.

Unconventional Remembrances and Memorials

5 With cremation on the rise in the United States, some companies are starting to capitalize on ways to use or display the cremated remains (ashes). Some of these approaches can only be characterized as high-tech. For example, one company will rocket into space a small container of your loved one's ashes. Other companies manufacture and sell display urns for ashes. These urns can be shaped into almost anything, including a motorcycle gas tank, a fiddle, a stuffed animal, a heart, or a car. Jewelry artisans are even producing customized "cremation jewelry" that allows you to carry the ashes of the deceased in a pendant around your neck. Some of this jewelry can cost up to $10,000. Ashes can also be compressed into diamonds for jewelry or crushed into balls and placed in the ocean.

Practice Exercise

Topic of paragraph 5:

____

____

____

____

6 Another high-tech approach to death is the use of "electronic" memorials. These are Internet websites that people create to memorialize their deceased loved ones. They usually contain pictures of the person who died, a written life story or family history, and notes and written remembrances from relatives or friends. Some websites allow cybermourners to post condolence messages and share their grief online. "Virtual cemeteries" are websites that feature the posting of pictures and biographical information of the deceased, a chance for mourners to sign the guest book, and the option of leaving "digital flowers." Blogs, MySpace, Facebook, and instant messages are also used to post condolences and pay tribute to loved ones who have died. It is also a way for mourners to connect and gain support.

Practice Exercise

Topic of paragraph 6:

____

____

____

7 Some cemeteries even are offering high-tech choices. Special grave markers store a small video monitor that can display up to 250 pages of information about the deceased person. Thus, while standing at the gravesite, a mourner can study the entire life of the person buried beneath his or her feet.

Sources: Adapted from Wayne Payne, Dale Hahn, and Ellen Lucas, *Understanding Your Health*, 10th ed., p. 102. Copyright © 2009 by The McGraw-Hill Companies, Inc. Drawn from L. A. DeSpelder and A. L. Strickland, *The Last Dance*, 7th ed. (New York: McGraw-Hill, 2005); "New Creations Personalize Cremation," *USA Today*, October 20, 2006.

SELECTION 3.3
Health
(continued)

Comprehension and Vocabulary Quiz

This quiz has four parts. Your instructor may assign some or all of them.

Comprehension

Directions: Items 1–5 test your understanding of the selection. They are the types of questions a content-area instructor (such as a health professor) might ask on a test. You may refer to the selection as you answer the questions. Write your answer choice in the space provided.

_______ **1.** Conventional funeral services are:

a. increasing.
b. decreasing.
c. promoted by funeral homes.
d. disliked by religious leaders.

_______ **2.** At a drive-through mortuary, mourners can:

a. leave flowers for the family of the deceased person.
b. get details about the day and time of a funeral.
c. view the body from their car.
d. visit briefly with the deceased person's family without getting out of the car.

_______ **3.** Today, the ashes of a cremated person can be:

a. launched into space.
b. placed in a custom-shaped urn.
c. turned into jewelry.
d. all of the above

_______ **4.** A way for mourners to connect and gain support from one another is through:

a. virtual cemeteries.
b. social networking websites such as Facebook.
c. video monitors at gravesites.
d. cremation jewelry.

_______ **5.** Many funeral homes make videos of funeral services to:

a. sell them.
b. post them on YouTube.
c. place them at the gravesite.
d. distribute them to those who attend the funeral.

Vocabulary in Context

Directions: Items 6–10 test your ability to determine a word's meaning by using context clues. *Context clues* are words in a sentence that allow readers to deduce (reason out) the meaning of an unfamiliar word in the sentence. They also help readers determine the meaning an author intends when a word has more than one meaning. Each item below consists of a sentence from the selection, with

SELECTION 3.3

the vocabulary word *italicized.* It is followed by another sentence that uses the same word in the same way. Use context clues to deduce the meaning of the *italicized* word. Be sure the meaning you choose makes sense in *both* sentences. Write each answer in the space provided. (Chapter 2 presented the skill of using context clues.)

_______ **6.** *Collectively,* these serve the diverse needs of society.

Everyone liked the idea, and the committee decided *collectively* to approve it.

collectively (kə lĕk′ tĭv lē) means:

a. happily
b. as a whole
c. boldly
d. in part

_______ **7.** As our society becomes more culturally diverse, funeral directors are becoming more familiar (and accommodating) with rituals used not only by dozens of Christian *denominations* but also with rituals for Buddhist, Hindu, and Muslim groups.

Religious leaders of all *denominations* attended the international peace conference.

denominations (dĭ nŏm ə nā′ shənz) means:

a. ethnicities; races
b. large groups of religious congregations united under a common faith
c. churches
d. a set of countries in a particular part of the world

_______ **8.** Although viewed by many as a *callous* approach, this option was probably inevitable in a society that seems to value squeezing more activities into less time.

The coach's *callous* comments hurt the young soccer players' feelings.

callous (kăl′ əs) means:

a. rough
b. lengthy
c. unfeeling
d. impatient

_______ **9.** With cremation on the rise in the United States, some companies are starting to *capitalize* on ways to use or display the cremated remains (ashes).

Toni likes to *capitalize* on the free time between her classes by using it to study.

capitalize (kăp′ ĭ tl īz) means:

a. to turn something to one's advantage
b. to use time productively
c. to be creative
d. to create a new product

_______ **10.** Some websites allow cybermourners to post *condolence* messages and share their grief online.

Several people in the neighborhood paid a *condolence* visit to our neighbor's widow.

condolence (kən dō′ ləns) means:

a. expressing sympathy
b. personal
c. conveying surprise
d. handwritten

Word Structure

Directions: Items 11–15 test your ability to use word-structure clues to help determine a word's meaning. *Word-structure clues* consist of roots, prefixes, and suffixes. In this exercise, you will learn the meaning of a root and use it to determine the meaning of several words that contain it. If you need to use a dictionary to confirm your answer choice, do so. Write your answers in the spaces provided.

In paragraph 3 of the selection, you encountered the word **respects.** It contains the root ***spec***, which means "to look" or "to see." The word *respects* refers to looking back (at a deceased person's life) and expressing esteem and appreciation. Use the meaning of ***spec*** and the list of prefixes on pages 72–73 to determine the meaning of each of the following words.

_______ **11.** If you use **spectacles**:

a. wear glasses.
b. look attractive.
c. see the best in others.
d. look sad.

_______ **12.** If a person wishes in **retrospect** that he or she had finished college, the person wishes this:

a. in vain.
b. as a joke.
c. while looking back at the past.
d. in great frustration and regret.

_______ **13.** A **spectator** at a baseball game is a person who:

a. plays in the game.
b. umpires the game.
c. sells food in the stands.
d. watches the game.

_______ **14.** A **prospector** is a person who:

a. wants free land.
b. looks for mineral deposits or oil.
c. seeks adventure.
d. leads people to new territories.

Copyright © 2014 The McGraw-Hill Companies, Inc. All rights reserved.

_______ **15.** A **specimen** is a sample of tissue or other material that a doctor or scientist:
- *a.* looks at in order to study it.
- *b.* preserves in chemicals.
- *c.* stores in a laboratory.
- *d.* obtains from another researcher.

Reading Skills Application

Directions: Items 16–20 test your ability to *apply* certain reading skills. You may not be familiar with all the skills yet, so some items will serve as a preview. As you work through *New Worlds,* you will practice and develop these skills. These are important skills, which is why they are included on the state-mandated basic skills tests that some students must take. Write each answer in the space provided.

_______ **16.** According to the passage, another term for "calling hours" is:
- *a.* electronic memorials.
- *b.* body visitation.
- *c.* cybermourning.
- *d.* display collage.

_______ **17.** The information in paragraph 5 is organized using which writing pattern?
- *a.* list
- *b.* sequence
- *c.* cause-effect
- *d.* definition

_______ **18.** The authors' primary purpose in writing this selection is to:
- *a.* persuade readers to consider newer options funeral homes offer.
- *b.* instruct readers how to customize a funeral for a person who has died.
- *c.* inform readers about high-tech and societal changes in funerals.
- *d.* persuade readers to feel free to ignore old-fashioned funeral customs.

_______ **19.** In paragraph 5 it says, "Some of these approaches can only be characterized as high-tech. For example, one company will rocket into space a small container of your loved one's ashes." What is the relationship between the two sentences?
- *a.* The second sentence gives the results of something mentioned in first sentence.
- *b.* The second sentence presents a list of something mentioned in the first sentence.
- *c.* The second sentence illustrates something mentioned in the first sentence.
- *d.* The second sentence presents a contrast with information in the first sentence.

_______ **20.** Based on information in the passage, it is logical to conclude that:
- *a.* things have gone too far in this country with regard to funerals and ways of dealing with death.
- *b.* the government should provide guidelines for what is appropriate for funerals and ways of dealing with death.
- *c.* funerals and ways of dealing with death in the United States are likely to continue to change.
- *d.* people no longer have respect for the dead.

Respond in Writing

Directions: Refer to the selection as needed to answer the essay-type questions below. (Your instructor may direct you to work collaboratively with other students on one or more items. Each group member should be able to explain *all* of the group's answers.)

1. **Reacting to What You Have Read:** Which information in the selection were you already aware of? What one piece of new information did you find most surprising? What is your overall reaction to the "high-tech" ways of dealing with death described in the selection?

2. **Comprehending the Selection Further:** The authors present facts about "cremation jewelry." List at least two of them.

3. **Overall Main Idea of the Selection:** In one sentence, tell what the authors want readers to understand about funerals today. (Be sure to include "death," "high-tech," and "funerals" in your overall main idea sentence.)

Copyright © 2014 The McGraw-Hill Companies, Inc. All rights reserved.

Internet Resources

Read More about It Online

Directions: Read more about the topic of this selection online. You can read online *before* you read the selection to build background knowledge or *afterward* to extend your knowledge. Start with the websites below or type "**high-tech death**" in the search box of Google, Yahoo, or another search engine. When you visit any unfamiliar website, it is important to evaluate it and the information it contains. If you do not know how to conduct Internet searches or evaluate a website, see pages 24–25.

http://boston.cbslocal.com/2011/12/29/high-tech-funerals-allow-people-to-attend-online/
CBS Boston reports on high-tech funerals that allow people to attend online. Includes both the video clip and a written version.

www.crainsnewyork.com/article/20120318/SMALLBIZ/303189986
This Crain's New York Business article looks at new digital technologies from the business perspective of funeral homes.

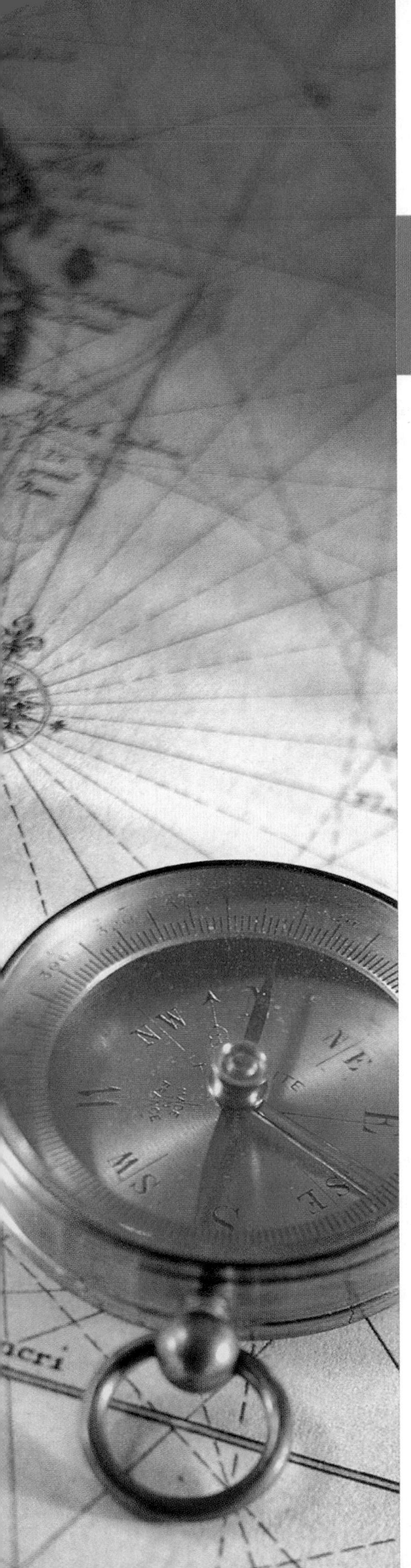

CHAPTER 4

Locating the Stated Main Idea

LEARNING OBJECTIVES

In this chapter you will learn the answers to these questions:

- What is a stated main idea sentence?
- Why is the stated main idea sentence important?
- How can I locate the stated main idea sentence of a paragraph?
- Which sentence can be the stated main idea sentence in a paragraph?

NEW INFORMATION AND SKILLS

WHAT IS A STATED MAIN IDEA SENTENCE, AND WHY IS IT IMPORTANT?

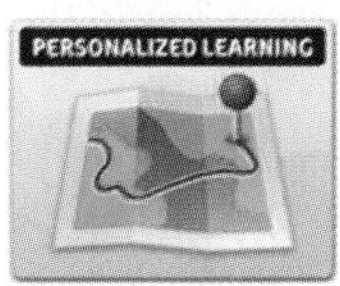

stated main idea sentence

The sentence in a paragraph that contains both the topic and the author's most important point about this topic.

A stated main idea sentence is also known as the *topic sentence.*

You already know that every paragraph has a topic. In addition, every paragraph tells the author's most important point about the topic, the main idea. Frequently, an author states the main idea directly as one of the sentences in the paragraph. A **stated main idea sentence** is the sentence in a paragraph that contains both the topic and the author's most important point about this topic. A paragraph can have only one main—most important—idea.

In a writing or English course, your instructor may call the stated main idea sentence of a paragraph the *topic sentence.* This is because it (1) must contain the *topic,* and (2) must be a *sentence.* When locating a stated main idea, you are looking for the *author's* most important point, not what you think is most important or interesting. (Sometimes the main idea is *not* directly stated by the author as a sentence in the paragraph. This is called an *implied* main idea, and you will learn about it in Chapter 5.)

Here are examples of topics and main idea sentences. In a paragraph whose topic is *Benjamin Franklin,* the author might write this stated main idea sentence: *A Founding Father of the United States, Benjamin Franklin was a genius who achieved remarkable success in a wide range of fields.* Or in a paragraph whose topic is *injuries caused by airbags,* the author might state as the main idea: *To avoid injuries caused by airbags, children under the age of 12 should be buckled in the backseat of a car.* Notice that the topic always appears in the main idea sentence.

Because stated main ideas are so important, authors sometimes draw attention to them by using certain phrases. Watch for phrases such as *The point is; It is obvious that; It is important to understand that; In short; therefore;* and *In conclusion.* These phrases often appear at the beginning of the main idea sentence, but they can appear within the sentence. For example, *Therefore, no U.S. president can serve more than two terms* and *No U.S. president, therefore, can serve more than two terms.*

Understanding the main idea can help you:

- Comprehend more accurately and completely the material you are reading.
- Underline or highlight the most important material in your textbooks.
- Take better notes.
- Organize information into outlines and summaries.
- Locate and memorize more easily the important material for tests.
- Make higher test grades.

Skillful readers underline or highlight stated main ideas in their textbooks. You will find it convenient to mark them, since they are presented as single sentences. Remember to read the *entire* paragraph before deciding which sentence is the stated main idea.

WHAT IS THE METHOD FOR IDENTIFYING THE STATED MAIN IDEA SENTENCE?

To identify the stated main idea sentence, look for a sentence that has the two essential "ingredients": the *topic* and the author's *most important point* about the topic.

The *topic*	+	author's *most important point* about the topic	=	Main idea sentence

Comprehension Monitoring Question for Stated Main Idea

"What is the most important point the author wants me to understand about the topic of this paragraph?"

You must begin, of course, by reading the paragraph and determining its topic. Then, locate the main idea by finding the sentence that answers the comprehension monitoring question, "What is the most important point the author wants me to understand about the topic of this paragraph?" When you find a sentence that contains the topic *and* answers this question (tells the author's most important point about the topic), you have found the stated main idea sentence.

Next, be sure the sentence makes complete sense *by itself.* In other words, it would make sense even if you could not see the rest of the paragraph. For example, this sentence could be a stated main idea because it makes sense by itself: *Franklin Roosevelt is considered one of the greatest U.S. presidents of the 20th century.* In contrast, this could not be a stated main idea sentence because it does not make complete sense by itself: *He is considered one of the greatest U.S. presidents of the 20th century.* We are not told who *he* is. In other words, the sentence does not include the topic, a president's name (which president the author is referring to). Remember, a stated main idea sentence must contain the actual word, name, or phrase that is the topic *as well as* tell the author's most important point about the topic.

Then, be sure the sentence is a general sentence. The main idea sentence is usually the most general sentence in a paragraph, one that "sums up" the details but does not include them. Consider, for example, this main idea of a business textbook paragraph: *There are many important decisions to make when starting your own company.* The words *many important decisions* are very general; the rest of the paragraph (the supporting details) explain specifically what those "important decisions" are. (In Chapter 6 you will learn about identifying supporting details.)

Finally, see if the other sentences explain or tell more about the sentence you have chosen. If you have located the stated main idea sentence, the other sentences—the details—will explain, illustrate, or prove the main idea. Take for example, the main idea *Sexually transmitted diseases present a particular threat to young adults.* The

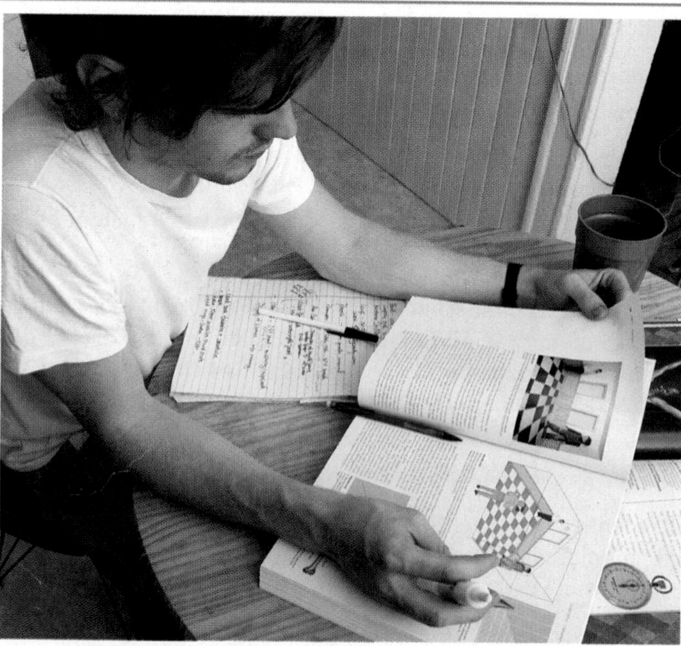

Skillful readers underline or highlight stated main ideas when they study.

supporting details might give examples of specific diseases, such as HIV, hepatitis B, genital herpes, and gonorrhea, and the threats posed by each.

Now let's see the above technique applied to a biology textbook paragraph. Read the paragraph below. The topic is *shingles.*

> *Shingles* is a reactivation of the same virus that causes chicken pox. Once you have been infected with chicken pox, the *Varicella zoster* virus does not leave your body when you recover. Instead, the virus hides within your nervous system, burying itself deep inside a sensory nerve. Later, the virus can reactivate. It travels down the nerve axons to the skin, where it causes a chicken-pox-like rash. The rash is generally found on the chest and lower back, though it can occur anywhere. Unlike the chicken pox rash, this rash is usually found in a broad strip on only one side of the body. It can be very painful and can persist for years.
>
> *Source:* Adapted from Sylvia Mader and Michael Windelsprecht, *Human Biology,* 12th ed., p. 160. Copyright © 2012 by The McGraw-Hill Companies, Inc.

The first sentence contains the topic *(shingles)* and tells the author's most important point about shingles *(that it is a reactivation of the virus that causes chicken pox).* Did you notice, in fact, that the first sentence is the *only* sentence that contains the topic? The first sentence makes complete sense by itself and it is also very general. Finally, we can see that this general statement is explained by the details in the other sentences. (The supporting details all tell more about shingles—its cause and the rash it produces.) Therefore, it is clear that the first sentence is the stated main idea sentence.

WHICH SENTENCE IN A PARAGRAPH CAN BE THE STATED MAIN IDEA SENTENCE?

A stated main idea sentence often occurs at the beginning of a paragraph. The next most likely place is at the end of a paragraph. But the stated main idea sentence sometimes appears within a paragraph. Let's look at three sample paragraphs that illustrate these three placements of a stated main idea sentence.

First Sentence of the Paragraph

Authors frequently begin with a stated main idea sentence because it can make the paragraph clearer and easier to understand. It also draws attention to it. Finally, readers can identify the supporting details more easily if they already know the main idea.

The following excerpt from the same biology textbook shows such a paragraph. Its topic is *cells.* Read the paragraph and ask yourself, "What is the most important point the author wants me to understand about *cells*?" The sentence that answers this question, the first sentence, is the stated main idea sentence.

> A cell is the smallest unit of life. Nothing smaller is able to reproduce, respond to stimuli, or remain homeostatic. Nothing smaller is able to grow and develop, take in and use material from the environment, and become adapted to the environment.
>
> *Source:* Adapted from Sylvia Mader and Michael Windelsprecht, *Human Biology,* 12th ed., p. 44. Copyright © 2012 by The McGraw-Hill Companies, Inc.

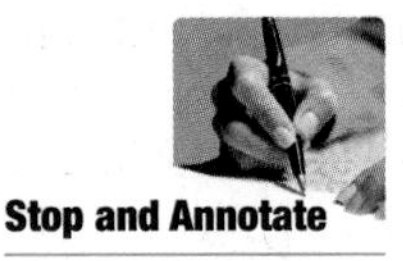

Stop and Annotate

Go back to the preceding textbook excerpt. Underline or highlight the stated main idea sentence, the first sentence of the paragraph.

In this excerpt, the first sentence is a general one that tells the most important point the author wants you to know: *A cell is the smallest unit of life.* The other sentences support the main idea sentence by illustrating and explaining each of the things this smallest unit of life can do. In this paragraph, then, the first sentence states the main idea, and the rest of the sentences are supporting details that tell more about it.

EXERCISE 1

This paragraph comes from a psychology textbook.

Caffeine produces several reactions. One major behavioral effect is an increase in attentiveness. Another major behavioral effect is a decrease in reaction time. Caffeine can also bring about an improvement in mood, most likely by mimicking the effects of a natural brain chemical, adenosine. Too much caffeine, however, can result in nervousness and insomnia. People can build up a biological dependence on the drug. Regular users who suddenly stop drinking coffee may experience headache or depression. Many people who drink large amounts of coffee on weekdays have headaches on weekends because of the sudden drop in the amount of caffeine they are consuming.

Source: Adapted from Robert S. Feldman, *Understanding Psychology,* 8th ed., pp. 169–70. Copyright © 2008 by The McGraw-Hill Companies, Inc. Reprinted by permission of The McGraw-Hill Companies, Inc.

Write one word that tells the topic: ______________________________

Now locate the stated main idea sentence of the paragraph and write it here:

____

____

Last Sentence of the Paragraph

The stated main idea sentence is sometimes the last sentence of the paragraph. This is especially likely when readers need an explanation before they can understand the main idea, or when the author leads up to an important general conclusion (the main idea). Putting the main idea sentence last is also a way authors emphasize or draw attention to it.

Read the following excerpt from a health textbook. As the title suggests, the topic is *eating disorders.* As you read the paragraph, ask yourself, "What is the most important point the authors want me to understand about *eating disorders*?" The sentence that answers this question, the last sentence, is the stated main idea sentence.

Eating Disorders

Problems with body weight and weight control are not limited to excessive body fat. *Anorexia nervosa* is an eating disorder characterized by self-starvation—a refusal to maintain a minimally normal body weight—and an intense fear of gaining weight or becoming fat. *Bulimia nervosa* is an eating disorder characterized by repeated episodes of binge overeating and purging: overeating and then using compensatory behaviors such as vomiting, laxatives, and excessive exercise to prevent weight gain. *Binge-eating disorder* is characterized by binge eating and a lack of control over eating behavior in general. In summary, there are three major eating disorders: anorexia nervosa, bulimia nervosa, and binge-eating disorder.

Source: Adapted from Paul Insel and Walton Roth, *Connect Core Concepts in Health,* Brief, 12th ed., pp. 276, 278. Copyright © 2012 by The McGraw-Hill Companies, Inc.

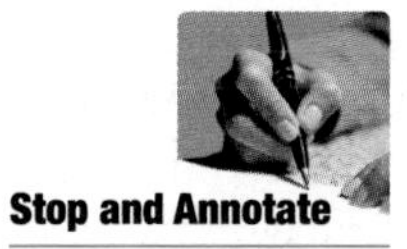

Stop and Annotate

Go back to the preceding textbook excerpt. Underline or highlight the stated main idea sentence, the last sentence of the paragraph.

In this paragraph, the first sentence is an introductory sentence. The second sentence defines anorexia nervosa, an eating disorder. The third sentence defines bulimia nervosa, another eating disorder. The fourth sentence defines binge-eating disorder, a third type of eating disorder. Notice that the last sentence, the stated main idea, contains the topic and is a general statement that tells the authors' most important point about eating disorders. To draw attention to this important sentence, the authors begin it with *In summary.*

EXERCISE 2

This paragraph comes from a speech communications textbook.

Plagiarism and the Internet

When it comes to plagiarism no subject poses more confusion—or more temptation—than the Internet. It's so easy to copy information from the Web, many people are not aware of the need to cite the sources (that is, to give credit to the author) when they use Internet materials in their research papers or speeches. In short, if you don't cite Internet sources, you are just as guilty of plagiarism as if you take information from print sources without proper citation.

Source: Adapted from Stephen Lucas, *The Art of Public Speaking,* 10th ed., p. 41. Copyright © 2009 by The McGraw-Hill Companies, Inc.

Write the topic: ______________________________

Now locate the stated main idea sentence and write it here:

____

____

____

A Sentence within the Paragraph

The stated main idea sentence is not always the first or the last sentence of a paragraph. Sometimes it comes *within* the paragraph.

Authors sometimes begin with an important question and then use the second sentence—the main idea sentence—to answer it. Or authors may begin with an introductory statement or with familiar or interesting examples. At other times, authors begin by stating a widely held misconception they wish to explain and disprove. Or they may begin with a surprising or controversial statement designed to get the reader's attention. Then they present their main idea sentence.

Here is a human development textbook paragraph in which the second sentence is the main idea sentence. The topic is *parenting style and children's popularity.* As you read this paragraph, ask yourself, "What is the most important point the author wants me to understand about parenting style and children's popularity?"

What other family factor plays a role in whether a child is popular? It appears that parenting style can have an effect on children's popularity. Authoritative parents tend to have more popular children than authoritarian parents do. Children of authoritarian parents who punish and threaten are likely to threaten or act mean with other children. They are less popular than children whose authoritative parents reason with them and try to help them understand how another person might feel.

Source: Adapted from Diane E. Papalia, Sally Wendkos Olds, and Ruth Feldman, *Human Development*, 11th ed., p. 336. Copyright © 2009 by The McGraw-Hill Companies, Inc.

Write the topic: ______________________________

Now locate the stated main idea sentence and write it here:

____

____

Stop and Annotate

Go back to the textbook excerpt above. Underline or highlight the stated main idea sentence, the second sentence of the paragraph.

The second sentence contains the topic and tells the authors' most important point about this topic: *It appears that parenting style can have an effect on children's popularity.* Notice that the paragraph opens with a question. The question is designed to lead the reader to the most important point, the *answer* to this question: the second sentence. Therefore, it is the stated main idea. (If you were tempted to select the question as the main idea, remember that a stated main idea *never* appears in the form of a question.) The remaining sentences explain the specific effects of two parenting styles, authoritative and authoritarian.

EXERCISE 3

This paragraph comes from a health textbook.

Would you like to have more variety in your workout routine? Consider joining a club! Health and fitness clubs offer members a wide variety of activities. Fitness clubs offer activities ranging from free weights to weight machines to step walking to general aerobics. Some health clubs have pools, saunas, and whirlpools and lots of frills. Others have course offerings that include wellness, smoking cessation, stress management, time management, dance, Pilates, and yoga.

Source: Adapted from Wayne A. Payne, Dale B. Hahn, and Ellen B. Lucas, *Understanding Your Health,* 10th ed., p. 118. Copyright © 2009 by The McGraw-Hill Companies, Inc. Reprinted by permission of The McGraw-Hill Companies, Inc.

Write a phrase that tells the topic: ______________________________

____

Now locate the stated main idea sentence of the paragraph and write it here:

____

____

OTHER THINGS TO KEEP IN MIND WHEN LOCATING THE STATED MAIN IDEA SENTENCE

Here are four helpful things to remember about locating stated main idea sentences:

1. **All stated main idea sentences have certain characteristics in common. The main idea sentence must:**
   - contain the topic of the paragraph.
   - tell the author's most important point about that topic.
   - make complete sense by itself.
   - be a general one that sums up the details in the paragraph.
   - be supported or explained by the rest of the sentences in the paragraph, the details.
2. **Avoid these three common mistakes when locating the stated main idea.**
   - Do not try to determine the main idea by looking only at the first and last sentences of a paragraph: You could miss a stated main idea sentence that appears within the paragraph. Read the entire paragraph *before* you try to determine the stated main idea sentence.
   - Avoid choosing a sentence merely because it contains familiar or interesting information.
   - Do not select a question as the main idea. Stated main ideas are *never* written in the form of a question. However, the stated main idea is often a sentence that *answers* the question presented at the beginning of the paragraph.
3. **Signal words or phrases can help you locate a stated main idea and locate a stated main idea that is presented as a *conclusion*.**

   Authors sometimes use certain words or phrases to signal the stated main idea sentence, regardless of where it comes in the paragraph. Words and phrases that can signal a main idea include:

It is obvious…	Generally speaking…
To sum up…	The fact is…
The point is…	In summary…
Overall…	In reality…

   Sometimes an author emphasizes a stated main idea by presenting it as a *conclusion* at the end of a paragraph. And often the paragraph itself comes at the end of an entire selection. These signal words and phrases indicate that the conclusion is the main idea:

In conclusion…	As a result…
It is clear, then,…	As one can see…
Consequently…	So…
Therefore…	For these reasons…
Finally…	The point is this…
Thus…	Obviously, then,…

4. **A longer passage often has an overall main idea that is stated, too.**

   Authors sometimes include an *overall* stated main idea to present the general point of an entire selection, such as a section of a textbook chapter, a short reading selection, or an essay. Often, the introductory or concluding sentence of a longer selection expresses the overall main idea of the passage. An overall main idea sums up the main ideas of the individual paragraphs in the selection, just as the main idea of a paragraph sums up the details in the paragraph. Assume, for example, that a passage consists of five paragraphs and begins with this overall main idea stated in an introductory paragraph: *There are several things students can do to make the most of their study time.* The main ideas of the other four paragraphs might be (1) making a study schedule can help

(continued on next page)

Copyright © 2014 The McGraw-Hill Companies, Inc. All rights reserved.

students manage their time; (2) studying at the same time every day is also helpful; (3) using small amounts of free time to study is a useful technique; and (4) studying in the same place each day can also make study time more productive. As you can see, the overall main idea of this passage, *There are several things students can do to make the most of their study time,* is a general statement that sums up the four main ideas in the selection.

In a writing or an English course, your instructor may refer to the overall stated main idea of a selection as the *thesis sentence.* The thesis sentence usually appears at the beginning of a selection.

Directions: Read each paragraph to determine the topic. Write the topic in the space provided. Then locate and underline (or highlight) the stated main idea of the paragraph.

1. This paragraph comes from a human sexuality textbook.

The possibilities for promotion sometimes are greater for men than for women. Parenting and household responsibilities still often fall to women. This can limit the time and energy available for their careers. Many institutions and employers are trying to create equal employment opportunities for women. There are still differences in how well women and men fare in their jobs, but there are signs things may be improving. Among married couples who both work, over 30 percent of the wives earn more money than their husbands. Also, in increasing numbers of families the woman is the primary breadwinner, while the man stays home to take care of the household responsibilities and children.

Source: Adapted from Gary Kelly, *Sexuality Today*, 10th ed., p. 117. Copyright © 2008 by The McGraw-Hill Companies, Inc.

Topic: ____

____

2. This paragraph comes from a criminal investigation textbook.

When people place their outstretched arms in front of their bodies, with palms up, this is known as the *rogatory* (or "prayerful") display. Those who worship turn their palms up to God to ask his mercy. This behavior is also seen in individuals who say something that they want the investigator to believe. Since rogatory behavior can indicate deception, a criminal investigator should watch for it. When a person makes a declarative statement, note whether the hands are palms up or palms down. People who are telling the truth do not have to plead to be believed. They make a statement and it stands. During regular conversation in which ideas are being discussed and neither party is deeply committed to a particular point, the investigator can expect to see both palms-up and palms-down displays.

Source: Adapted from Charles Swanson, Neil Chamelin, Leonard Territo, and Robert Taylor, *Criminal Investigation,* 11th ed., p. 149. Copyright © 2012 by The McGraw-Hill Companies, Inc.

Topic: ____

____

3. This paragraph comes from a psychology textbook.

We work to build social and romantic relationships because we need acceptance and love from others. We strive to reach for goals because we need to experience self-esteem and a sense of competence. The point is, our needs motivate much of our conscious behavior.

Source: Adapted from Denis Waitley, *Psychology of Success: Finding Meaning in Work and Life*, 5th ed., p. 263. Copyright © 2010 by The McGraw-Hill Companies, Inc.

Topic: ____

4. This paragraph comes from a political science textbook.

Public broadcasting got off to a slow start in the United States. Unlike in Europe, where public broadcasting networks (such as Britain's BBC) were created at the start of the radio age, the U.S. government in the 1930s handed control of broadcasting to commercial networks, such as NBC and CBS. By the time Congress decided in the 1960s that public broadcasting was needed, the commercial networks were so powerful that they convinced Congress to assign it second-class status. Public broadcasting was poorly funded. It was denied access to the most powerful broadcast frequencies. In fact, most television sets in the 1960s had tuners that could not dial in the stations on which public broadcast programs were aired.

Source: Abridged from Thomas Patterson, *The American Democracy*, Alternate Ed., 10th ed., p. 270. Copyright © 2011 by The McGraw-Hill Companies, Inc.

Topic: ____

____

5. This paragraph comes from a sociology textbook.

In some cultures, such as that of Papua New Guinea, roast pork is a delicacy reserved for feasts; in other cultures it is a forbidden food. In U.S. culture, genetically modified food is accepted without much question, but in Europe it is banned. Because Swedish people put a great value on natural, organic foods, 99 percent of mothers in Sweden breast-feed their infants—a rate much higher than that in the United States. The foods people eat, along with the customs they observe in preparing and consuming their meals, say a great deal about their culture.

Source: Adapted from Richard Schaffer, *Sociology*, 11th ed., p. 60. Copyright © 2008 by The McGraw-Hill Companies, Inc.

Topic: ____

____

CHAPTER REVIEW CARDS

Review cards or *summary cards* are a way to select, organize, and summarize the important information in a textbook chapter. Preparing review cards helps you organize the information so that you can learn and memorize it more easily. In other words, chapter review cards are effective study tools.

Preparing chapter review cards for each chapter of *New Worlds* will give you practice in creating these valuable study tools. Once you have learned how to make chapter review cards, you can use actual index cards to create them for textbook material in your other courses and use them when you study for tests.

Now complete the chapter review cards for Chapter 4 by answering the questions or following the directions on each card. The page numbers indicate the place in the chapter the information can be found. Write legibly.

Stated Main Idea Sentences

1. What is the definition of the *stated main idea* of a paragraph? (See page 193.)

2. Why is it important to locate and understand the stated main idea of a paragraph? (See page 193.)

3. What question should you ask yourself in order to locate the stated main idea of a paragraph? Be sure you write a *question*. (See page 194.)

Card 1 Chapter 4: Locating the Stated Main Idea

Copyright © 2014 The McGraw-Hill Companies, Inc. All rights reserved.

The Importance of Understanding Main Ideas

Understanding main ideas will enable you to: (See page 193.)

1.

2.

3.

4.

5.

6.

Card 2 Chapter 4: Locating the Stated Main Idea

How to Locate the Stated Main Idea Sentence of a Paragraph

Draw boxes and write the formula that shows the two essential elements of a main idea sentence. (See page 193.)

List three places where the stated main idea sentence may occur in a paragraph. (See page 195.)

1.

2.

3.

Card 3 Chapter 4: Locating the Stated Main Idea

When Locating the Stated Main Idea, Keep in Mind...

The five characteristics of a stated main idea sentence are: (See page 199.)

1.

2.

3.

4.

5.

List three common mistakes students make when locating the stated main idea sentence. (See page 199.)

1.

2.

3.

Card 4 Chapter 4: Locating the Stated Main Idea

When Locating the Stated Main Idea, Keep in Mind...

1. List the signal words or phrases that can give you a clue to locating a stated main idea. (See page 199.)

2. List the signal words or phrases that can give you a clue to locating a stated main idea that is presented as a *conclusion.* (See page 199.)

Card 5 Chapter 4: Locating the Stated Main Idea

Copyright © 2014 The McGraw-Hill Companies, Inc. All rights reserved.

b. The rules are simple.

c. An individual goes outside and in a publicly accessible place hides a waterproof container containing a few items—pens, key chains, small toys, and other inexpensive trinkets—as well as a logbook.

d. Having hidden it, the individual goes online to *geocaching.com* or another website to post the latitude and longitude of the hidden treasure, and perhaps clues to help searchers find it.

4. This paragraph comes from a sociology textbook.

The term *significant other* is used to refer to those individuals who are important to the development of the self. Parents, friends, co-workers, coaches and teachers are often among those who play a major role in shaping a person's self. The point is, as people mature, the self changes and begins to reflect greater concerns about the reactions of others, especially significant others. Many young people, for example, find themselves drawn to the same kind of work their parents engage in.

Source: Adapted from Richard Schaefer, *Sociology: A Brief Introduction,* 9th ed., p. 85. Copyright © 2011 by The McGraw-Hill Companies, Inc.

The topic of this paragraph is *the self's concern about the reactions of others.*

______ What is the stated main idea of this paragraph?

a. The term *significant other* is used to refer to those individuals who are important to the development of the self.

b. Parents, friends, co-workers, coaches and teachers are often among those who play a major role in shaping a person's self.

c. The point is, as people mature, the self changes and begins to reflect greater concerns about the reactions of others, especially significant others.

d. Many young people, for example, find themselves drawn to the same kind of work their parents engage in.

5. This paragraph comes from a *health* textbook.

Athletes are trained in positive visualization to improve their performance and visualize their goals. Positive visualization has also been used in managing pain, especially chronic pain. There are many uses of positive visualization. It has been effective in weight management and insomnia. It is used for smoking cessation and for almost any type of behavior change.

Source: Adapted from Wayne A. Payne, Dale B. Hahn, and Ellen Lucas, *Understanding Your Health,* 10th ed., p. 85. Copyright © 2009 by The McGraw-Hill Companies, Inc.

The topic of this paragraph is *positive visualization.*

______ What is the stated main idea of this paragraph?

a. Athletes are trained in positive visualization to improve their performance and visualize their goals.

b. Positive visualization has also been used in managing pain, especially chronic pain.

c. There are many uses of positive visualization.

d. It is used for smoking cessation and for almost any type of behavior change.

Copyright © 2014 The McGraw-Hill Companies, Inc. All rights reserved.

Review: The **stated main idea** of a paragraph expresses the most important point about the topic. *A main idea is always expressed as a complete sentence,* and it can appear anywhere in the paragraph.

EXAMPLE

This psychology textbook paragraph was used in Chapter 3 to illustrate strategies for determining the topic of a paragraph. The topic is *pressure.* Reread the paragraph and ask yourself, "What is the most important thing the author wants me to understand about pressure?"

Pressure

Does the pressure of working for good grades ever get to you? If you have been employed, was it a high-pressure job? The term **pressure** is used to describe the stress that arises from negative events. In school, there is always the possibility that you will not perform well and you will fail. Some jobs are loaded with possibilities for making a mess of things and getting fired. Some unhappy marriages are sources of pressure because one spouse always seems to displease the other, no matter how hard he or she tries.

Source: Adapted from Benjamin Lahey, *Psychology,* 8th ed., p. 503. Copyright © 2004 by The McGraw-Hill Companies.

Write the topic: pressure

Underline or highlight the main idea sentence.

Explanation: The topic of this paragraph, *pressure,* appears in the heading and in bold print. The word *pressure* also appears several times in the paragraph. The third sentence is underlined because it is the stated main idea. It tells the author's most important point: the definition of *pressure* as it is used in psychology. The remaining sentences give examples of sources of pressure.

Directions: Read each paragraph and then determine the topic by asking yourself, "Who or what is this paragraph about?" In the space provided beneath the item, write the topic (always a word, name, or phrase—never a sentence). Then locate the stated main idea sentence by asking yourself, "What is the most important point the author wants me to understand about the topic of this paragraph?" Then, locate the stated main idea and *underline or highlight* the entire sentence.

1. This paragraph comes from an integrated science textbook.

Aspirin went on the market as a prescription drug in 1899 after being discovered only two years earlier. It is actually acetylsalicylic acid, which inhibits the body's production of prostaglandins, compounds that cause pain. Even primitive humans were familiar with its value as a pain reliever. The bark of the willow tree was known for its pain relief power thousands of years ago: people in many cultures stripped and chewed the bark for its medicinal effect. It is estimated that more than 80 million tablets of aspirin are consumed daily in the United States. The most widely used drug in the world, which we now call "aspirin," has a long history.

Source: Adapted from Bill Tillery, Eldon Enger, and Frederick Ross, *Integrated Science,* 5th ed., p. 446. Copyright © 2011 by The McGraw-Hill Companies, Inc.

Write the topic: ______________________________

Underline or *highlight* the main idea sentence.

Copyright © 2014 The McGraw-Hill Companies, Inc. All rights reserved.

2. This paragraph comes from a government textbook.

Political Apathy

Just as some people would not attend the Super Bowl even if it were free and being played across the street, some people would not bother to vote even if a ballot were delivered to their door. A sense of political apathy—a lack of interest in politics—typifies some citizens: they rarely if ever vote. Many of these citizens regard voting as a waste of time, convinced that government won't respond to their concerns even if they vote.

Source: Adapted from Thomas E. Patterson, *We the People,* 9th ed., pp. 233–34. Copyright © 2011 by The McGraw-Hill Companies, Inc.

Write the topic: ______________________________

Underline or highlight the main idea sentence.

3. This paragraph comes from a psychology of success textbook.

People with a positive self-image realize that they have many more strengths than weaknesses. They accept the weaknesses they do have, but choose not to be bothered by them. They know that they are a unique gift of creation, with skills and personal qualities in a combination that no one else has. The bottom line is that the difference between people who accept themselves and people who reject themselves isn't the number of weaknesses they have, it's their self-image, the way they look at them.

Source: Adapted from Denis Waitley, *Psychology of Success: Finding Meaning in Work and Life,* 5th ed., p. 141. Copyright © 2011 by The McGraw-Hill Companies.

Write the topic: ______________________________

Underline or highlight the main idea sentence.

4. This paragraph comes from a textbook on families.

The family has two aspects. It is, first, the place where we experience much of our private lives. It is where we give and receive love, share our hopes and fears, work though our troubles, and relax and enjoy ourselves. Second, it is a setting in which adults perform tasks that are of importance to society, particularly raising children and assisting elderly parents.

Source: Andrew Cherlin, *Public and Private Families,* 6th ed., Introduction. Copyright © 2010 by The McGraw-Hill Companies, Inc.

Write the topic: ______________________________

Underline or highlight the main idea sentence.

5. This paragraph comes from a critical thinking textbook.

It is largely the public's fault that corrupt politicians have been elected or appointed to public office and high-ranking positions in their parties. Citizens failed to educate themselves about these politicians' activities and ideals. Indeed, in a 1938 poll of Princeton freshmen, Adolf Hitler was ranked first as the "greatest living person"! And in New York City in the mid–nineteenth century, politician William Marcy "Boss" Tweed (1823–1878) conned citizens out of millions of dollars. He also managed to get his corrupt associates, known as the Tweed Ring, appointed and elected to high offices.

Source: Adapted from Judith Boss, *Critical Thinking and Logic Skills for Everyday Life,* 2nd ed., pp. 17–18. Copyright © 2012 by The McGraw-Hill Companies, Inc.

Write the topic: ______________________________

Underline or highlight the main idea sentence.

SELECTION 4.1
Business

Who's the Boss? Leaders, Managers, and Leadership Styles

From *Understanding Business*
By William Nickels, James McHugh, and Susan McHugh

What's the difference between a leader and a manager? In a business setting, what are the major responsibilities of a leader? Is there one best leadership style? This business textbook excerpt answers these questions.

Leaders: Providing Continuous Vision and Values

1 One person might be a good manager but not a good leader. Another might be a good leader without being a good manager. Managers strive to produce order and stability, whereas leaders embrace and manage change. Leadership is creating a vision for others to follow, establishing corporate values and ethics, and transforming the way the organization does business in order to improve its effectiveness and efficiency. Good leaders motivate workers and create the environment for them to motivate themselves. Management is carrying out the leader's vision. It is clear that leaders and managers have different roles and responsibilities, and that a person who is good at one may not be good at the other.

2 Leaders must therefore:

- *Communicate a vision and rally others around that vision.* The leader should be openly sensitive to the concerns of followers, give them responsibility, and win their trust. A successful leader must influence the actions of others.
- *Establish corporate values.* These include concern for employees, for customers, for the environment, and for the quality of the company's products. When companies set their business goals, they're defining the company's values as well. The number one trait that others look for in a leader is honesty. The second requirement is that the leader be forward looking.
- *Promote corporate ethics.* Ethical behavior includes an unfailing demand for honesty and an insistence that everyone in the company gets treated fairly. Many businesspeople have made the news by giving away huge amounts to charity, thus setting a model of social concern for their employees and others.
- *Embrace change.* A leader's most important job may be to transform the way the company does business so that it's more effective (does things better) and more efficient (uses fewer resources to accomplish the same objectives).
- *Stress accountability and responsibility.* If there is anything we have learned from the failures of banking managers and other industry and government managers during the recession of 2008–2009, it is that leaders need to be held accountable and need to

Annotation Practice Exercises

Directions: For each exercise below, write the topic and main idea of the paragraph on the lines beside the paragraph. Then locate the stated main idea sentence of the paragraph and underline or highlight it.

Practice Exercise

Topic of paragraph 1:

____

____

____

Determine the *stated main idea* and underline or highlight it.

Copyright © 2014 The McGraw-Hill Companies, Inc. All rights reserved.

feel responsible for their actions. A key word that has emerged from the crisis is transparency. **Transparency** is the presentation of a company's facts and figures in a way that is clear and apparent to all stakeholders. The Obama administration is trying to make companies (and the government) more transparent so that everyone is more aware of what is happening to the economy and to specific businesses and government agencies.

3 All organizations need leaders, and all employees can help lead. You don't have to be a manager to perform a leadership function. That is, any employee can motivate others to work well, add to a company's ethical environment, and report ethical lapses when they occur.

Practice Exercise

Topic of paragraph 3:

____

____

Determine the *stated main idea* and underline or highlight it.

Leadership Styles

4 Nothing has challenged management researchers more than the search for the best leadership traits, behaviors, or styles. Thousands of studies have tried to identify characteristics that make leaders different from other people. Intuitively, you might conclude the same thing they did: leadership traits are hard to pin down. Some leaders are well groomed and tactful, while others are unkempt and abrasive—yet both may be just as effective.

5 Just as no one set of traits describes a leader, no one style of leadership works best in all situations. Even so, we can look at a few of the most commonly recognized leadership styles and see how they may be effective (see Figure 1):

1. **Autocratic leadership** means making managerial decisions without consulting others. This style is effective in emergencies and when absolute followership is needed—for example, when fighting fires. Autocratic leadership is also effective sometimes with new, relatively unskilled workers who need clear direction and guidance. Coach Phil Jackson used an autocratic leadership style to take the Los Angeles Lakers to three consecutive National Basketball Association championships in his first three seasons. By following his leadership, a group of highly skilled individuals became a winning team.
2. **Participative (democratic) leadership** involves managers and employees working together to make decisions. Research has found that employee participation in decisions may not always increase effectiveness, but it usually does increase job satisfaction. Many large organizations like Wal-Mart, FedEx, IBM, Cisco, and AT&T and most smaller firms have been highly successful using a democratic style of leadership that values traits such as flexibility, good listening skills, and empathy. Employees meet to discuss and resolve management issues by giving everyone some opportunity to contribute to decisions.
3. In **free-rein leadership** managers set objectives and employees are free to do whatever is appropriate to accomplish those objectives. Free-rein leadership is often the most successful leadership style in certain organizations, such as those in which managers supervise doctors,

Former coach of the Los Angeles Lakers basketball team, Phil Jackson has been successful as an autocratic leader. That makes sense, since you don't want basketball players deciding whether or not to play as a team.

FIGURE 1
LEADERSHIP STYLES

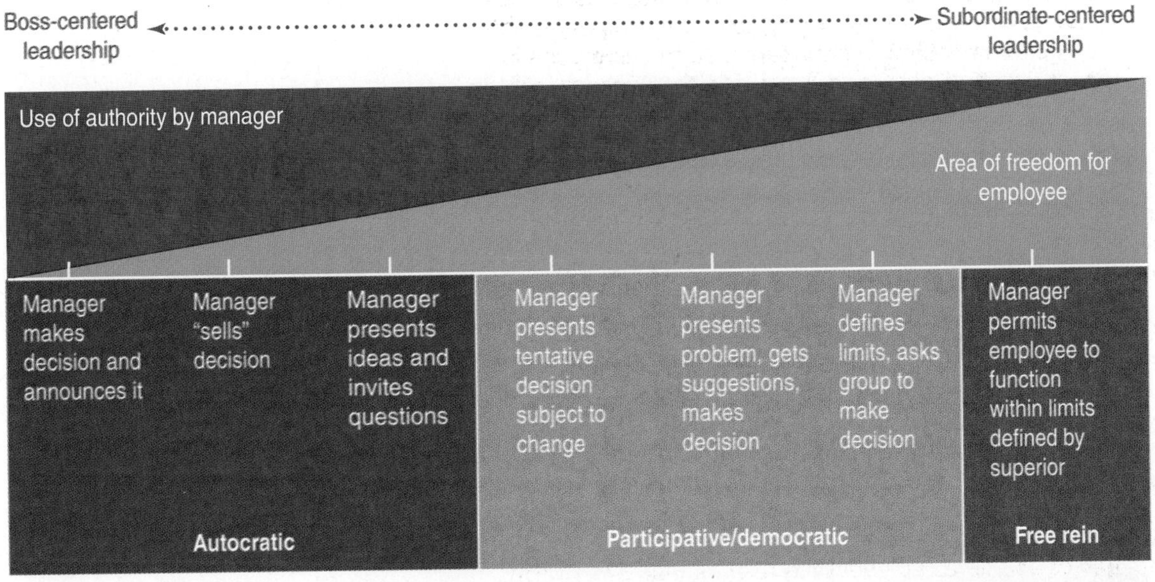

Source: Reprinted by permission of the *Harvard Business Review.* An exhibit from "How to Choose a Leadership Pattern" by Robert Tannenbaum and Warren Schmidt (May/June 1973). Copyright © 1973 by the Harvard Business School Publishing Corporation, all rights reserved.

professors, engineers, or other professionals. The traits managers need in such organizations include warmth, friendliness, and understanding. More and more firms are adopting this style of leadership with at least some of their employees.

6 It might be nice to think that bosses have a single style. The reality is that individual leaders rarely fit neatly into just one of these categories, so we can think of leadership as a continuum. Along this continuum, employee participation varies, from purely boss-centered leadership to subordinate-centered leadership.

7 Which leadership style is best? Research tells us that it depends largely on what the goals and values of the firm are, who's being led, and in what situations. A manager may be autocratic but friendly with a new trainee, democratic with an experienced employee, and free-rein with a trusted long-term supervisor.

8 There's no such thing as a leadership trait that is effective in all situations, or a leadership style that always works best. A truly successful leader has the ability to adopt the leadership style most appropriate to the situation and the employees.

Practice Exercise

Topic of paragraph 6:

____

____

____

Determine the *stated main idea* and underline or highlight it.

Source: Adapted from William Nickels, James McHugh, and Susan McHugh, *Understanding Business,* 9th ed., pp. 189–92. Copyright © 2010 by The McGraw-Hill Companies, Inc.

Copyright © 2014 The McGraw-Hill Companies, Inc.

Comprehension and Vocabulary Quiz

This quiz has four parts. Your instructor may assign some or all of them.

Comprehension

Directions: Items 1–5 test your understanding of the selection. They are the types of questions a content-area instructor (such as a business professor) might ask on a test. You may refer to the selection as you answer the questions. Write your answer choice in the space provided.

_______ **1.** The role of leaders is to:
a. strive to produce order and stability.
b. embrace and manage change.
c. carry out the management's vision.
d. all of the above

_______ **2.** The number one trait that others look for in a leader is:
a. empathy.
b. being forward looking.
c. honesty.
d. warmth.

_______ **3.** With regard to leadership traits and styles of leadership:
a. an autocratic style works best.
b. a participative style works best.
c. a free-rein style works best.
d. no one set or traits or style works best in all situations.

_______ **4.** The leadership style used by Wal-Mart, IBM, and AT&T is:
a. the autocratic style.
b. the participative style.
c. the free-rein style.
d. all of the above

_______ **5.** The leadership style more and more firms are adopting with at least some of their employees is:
a. the autocratic style.
b. the participative style.
c. the free-rein style.
d. a blend of participative and free-rein styles.

Vocabulary in Context

Directions: Items 6–10 test your ability to determine a word's meaning by using context clues. *Context clues* are words in a sentence that allow readers to deduce (reason out) the meaning of an unfamiliar word. They also help readers determine the meaning an author intends when a word has more than one meaning. Each item below consists of a sentence from the selection, with the vocabulary word *italicized*.

It is followed by another sentence that uses the same word in the same way. Use context clues to deduce the meaning of the *italicized* word. Be sure the meaning you choose makes sense in *both* sentences. Write each answer in the space provided. (Chapter 2 presented the skill of using context clues.)

_______ **6.** Managers strive to produce order and stability, whereas leaders *embrace* and manage change.

When the administration proposed a college-wide recycling program, most students were quick to *embrace* the idea.

embrace (ĕm brās′) means:

a. show caution

b. inhibit or prevent

c. request additional information

d. take up eagerly

_______ **7.** Transparency is the presentation of a company's facts and figures in a way that is clear and apparent to all *stakeholders*.

All citizens are *stakeholders* in the outcome of a presidential election.

stakeholders (stāk′ hōl′ dərz) means:

a. people with direct interest or investment in something

b. people who are not responsible

c. people with no knowledge of a situation

d. people who suffer as a result of someone else's actions

_______ **8.** Many large organizations . . . and most smaller firms have been highly successful using a democratic style of leadership that values traits such as flexibility, good listening skills, and *empathy*.

Because Nadine was often picked on as a child, she has great *empathy* for children who are bullied.

empathy (ĕm′ pə thē) means:

a. a sense of fairness

b. feelings of hostility

c. understanding what someone else is feeling

d. lack of concern

_______ **9.** Employees meet to discuss and *resolve* management issues by giving everyone some opportunity to contribute to decisions.

To *resolve* the lack of parking in the business district, the city government is introducing shuttle service from the surrounding areas.

resolve (rĭ zŏlv′) means:

a. remove doubts

b. deny responsibility for

c. solve a difficulty

d. talk over

Copyright © 2014 The McGraw-Hill Companies, Inc. All rights reserved.

_______ **10.** A truly successful leader has the ability to *adopt* the leadership style most appropriate to the situation and the employees.

The company announced it is going to *adopt* a new policy of drug-testing job applicants.

adopt (ə dŏpt′) means:

a. choose and use

b. give up

c. refuse

d. pay no attention to

Word Structure

Directions: Items 11–15 test your ability to use word-structure clues to help determine a word's meaning. *Word-structure clues* consist of roots, prefixes, and suffixes. In this exercise, you will learn the meaning of a root and use it to determine the meaning of several words that contain it. If you need to use a dictionary to confirm your answer choice, do so. Write your answers in the spaces provided.

In paragraph 5, item 1, of the selection, you encountered the word **autocratic.** It contains the root ***auto,*** which means "self." The word *autocratic* describes someone who has all of the power to him*self* or her*self* (such as a dictator or a very controlling boss). Use the meaning of ***auto*** and the list of prefixes on pages 72–73 to help you determine the meaning of each of the following words.

_______ **11.** If a hot iron shuts off **automatically** after 15 minutes of nonuse, the iron shuts off:

a. when the person picks it up again.

b. by itself.

c. only if it is set on a low temperature.

d. when the person using it turns it off.

_______ **12.** If an airplane is flying on **autopilot,** it is flying:

a. in circles.

b. in the wrong direction.

c. without the pilot controlling it directly.

d. at a high altitude.

_______ **13.** Most teenagers like to think that they are **autonomous.** In other words, they like to think that they are:

a. independent and self-governing.

b. selfish and self-centered.

c. extremely mature.

d. smarter than their parents.

_______ **14.** "Didactics" is the art of teaching or instruction. An **autodidact** is someone who is:

a. currently enrolled in school.

b. receiving tutoring.

c. uninterested in learning.

d. self-taught.

_____ **15.** If you write an **autobiography** someday, you will write:

a. an adventure story.

b. a mystery.

c. the story of your life.

d. the story of someone else's life.

Reading Skills Application

Directions: Items 16–20 test your ability to *apply* certain reading skills. You may not be familiar with all the skills yet, so some items will serve as a preview. As you work through *New Worlds,* you will practice and develop these skills. These are important skills, which is why they are included on the state-mandated basic skills tests that some students must take. Write each answer in the space provided.

_____ **16.** Paragraph 5 is organized using which pattern?

a. definition

b. list

c. sequence

d. contrast

_____ **17.** In paragraph 5, item 3, it says, "Free-rein leadership is often the most successful leadership style in certain organizations, such as those in which managers supervise doctors, professors, engineers, or other professionals." What is the relationship between the parts of that sentence?

a. The second part presents a contrast to something mentioned in the first part.

b. The second part continues a sequence started in the first part.

c. The second part gives an effect of something mentioned in the first part.

d. The second part gives an example of something mentioned in the first part.

_____ **18.** The authors' primary purpose in writing this selection is to:

a. persuade readers to adopt a participative leadership style.

b. instruct readers how to determine if they are better suited to be managers or leaders.

c. persuade readers to identify their one best leadership style.

d. inform readers about leaders, managers, and three leadership styles.

_____ **19.** In paragraph 3 it says, "You don't have to be a manager to perform a leadership function. That is, any employee can motivate others to work well, add to a company's ethical environment, and report ethical lapses when they occur." What is the relationship between the two sentences?

a. The second sentence changes the meaning of first sentence.

b. The second sentence categorizes information given in the first sentence.

c. The second sentence clarifies the first sentence.

d. The second sentence gives a specific example of what is stated in the first sentence.

Copyright © 2014 The McGraw-Hill Companies, Inc. All rights reserved.

_______ **20.** Based on information in the passage, it is logical to conclude that the leadership style of Adolf Hitler was:

a. autocratic.
b. participative.
c. democratic.
d. free rein.

SELECTION **4.1**
Business
(continued)

Respond in Writing

Directions: Refer to the selection as needed to answer the essay-type questions below. (Your instructor may direct you to work collaboratively with other students on one or more items. Each group member should be able to explain *all* of the group's answers.)

1. **Reacting to What You Have Read:** Think of a boss, a coach, or a teacher you have had. What leadership style did that person have? Did you like or dislike that person's style? Explain why.

____
____
____
____
____
____

2. **Comprehending the Selection Further:** Using the leadership terminology in this selection, describe your primary leadership style. Explain circumstances in which you have had a leadership role (at your job, in an organization you belong to, as a member of a team, etc.). Explain the behaviors you used that are characteristic of your primary style.

____
____
____
____
____

3. **Overall Main Idea of the Selection:** In one sentence, tell what the authors want readers to understand about leadership style. (Be sure to include "leadership style" in your overall main idea sentence.)

____
____
____
____
____
____
____

Internet Resources

Read More about It Online

Directions: Read more about the topic of this selection online. You can read online *before* you read the selection to build background knowledge or *afterward* to extent your knowledge. Start with the websites below or type **"leadership styles"** in the search box of Google, Yahoo, or another search engine. When you visit any unfamiliar website, it is important to evaluate it and the information it contains. If you do not know how to conduct Internet searches or evaluate a website, see pages 24–25.

http://psychology.about.com/library/quiz/bl-leadershipquiz.htm
At About.com's psychology website, take an 18-item quiz to determine your leadership style.

www.nwlink.com/~donclark/leader/leadstl.html
The Performance Juxtaposition Site focuses on "performance, learning, leadership and knowledge." The graphics on this Web page presents leadership styles in a particularly engaging, accessible way.

Copyright © 2014 The McGraw-Hill Companies, Inc. All rights reserved.

SELECTION **4.2**

Marriage and Family

Arranged Marriages: Advantages and Changes

From *Marriages and Families*

By David Olson, John DeFrain, and Linda Skogrand

Courtship *refers to the time period when people try to gain another person's love in hopes of marrying them.* Arranged marriages *are ones in which the parents of the bride and groom select the future spouse and arrange the marriage ceremony. Some couples meet for the first time at their wedding. Others may have met only once or twice and spent a few minutes with each other. Courtship and marriage customs around the world vary widely. However, the authors of this selection write:*

> *All societies have created some system for matching individuals for marriage and parenthood. These systems range from the practice of bride purchase, to the selection of a mate by the village shaman according to astrological signs. There are also contractual systems in which a mate may serve as an indentured servant to the bride's parents—required to serve the bride's parents for a certain period to time. And, of course, there is individual choice based on personal attraction and love. In some cultures, couples are matched while they are still infants. In others, the bride and groom must prove their fertility by producing children before they are eligible for marriage. Although the customs of mate selection vary widely, all perform the necessary function of matching a couple for marriage and eventual parenthood.*

To most American young adults, the idea of having your parents pick your future spouse is shocking. But it could be argued that it might be better and safer than using an Internet matchmaking site! Read the rest of the selection below to learn more about courtship patterns and arranged marriages.

Parent-Arranged Marriages

1 Throughout much of world history, courtships were generally brief. In most cultures, the parents of the bride and groom selected the future spouse. They also made most of the arrangements for the marriage ceremony. If the prospective couple were granted any freedom of choice, they were expected to complete their arrangements in a few days. The pattern common in modern industrialized nations, in which a couple spends months or even years dating and choosing a mate, developed largely over the past century. Parent-arranged marriages, however, still occur throughout much of the non-industrialized world. Up to three-quarters of marriages in some cultures may be arranged. Although young adults in the United States today might view the practice as archaic and uncivilized, many people worldwide prefer parent-arranged marriages.

2 *Parent-arranged marriages* are based on the principle that the elders in a community have the wisdom to select the appropriate spouse. Parents or elders are likely to base their decision on economic, political, and social status considerations. They can enhance the family's status and position with their choice. In these prescribed marriages, lineage and family status are

Annotation Practice Exercises

Directions: For each exercise below, write the topic and main idea of the paragraph on the lines beside the paragraph. Then locate the stated main idea sentence of the paragraph and underline or highlight it.

Practice Exercise

Topic of paragraph 2:

____

____

Determine the *stated main idea* and underline or highlight it.

generally more important than love or affection. However, the parents may take the couple's preferences into account to some extent. Arranged marriages thus serve to extend existing family units rather than to create new units. They reinforce ties with other families in the community, which strengthens the community's order and organization.

Advantages of Arranged Marriages

3 An advantage of arranged marriages is that they are usually very stable. For one thing, it is the duty of the whole family to help the new couple get established in life. Divorce is almost unheard of—except for the reason of infertility. Divorce would bring disapproval from the parents and members of the community who made the selection. Although love between the couple before marriage is relatively unimportant, affection and respect usually grow through the years. Arranged marriages are often quite harmonious. Because there is not really a courtship period, premarital intimacy is minimal or nonexistent.

4 With arranged marriages, there is no risk of being rejected or of losing one's true love. Moreover, the person does not have to determine whether the partner is committed to the relationship. Although these may not seem like advantages, they effectively ensure a stable marriage. In short, couples in arranged marriages avoid many of the problems of American-style dating.

Patterns of Change

5 The world, in general, appears to be moving toward couple-arranged marriage (freedom of choice in marriage). This approach is sometimes referred to as the love match, though love is not always the goal of marriage in Western industrial societies.

6 As countries shift from more rural to urban industrial societies, love marriages become more common. Data from Africa, India, Israel, and Malaysia indicate that love marriages are more likely among people who marry at a later age, have a higher level of education, have a higher socioeconomic status (or the promise of a higher status), and live in an urban setting. A woman who can support herself financially is more likely to want to decide for herself whom she will marry. It is clear that the shift away from arranged marriage appears to be related to industrialization.

Cultural Variations

7 The ways people find marriage partners vary from culture to culture. In developing countries that are moving away from arranged marriages, the influence of cultural tradition may be combined with modern influences. In India, for example, it is commonly believed that there is one predestined mate who will share life with the spouse through reincarnation. Therefore parents believe they should supervise their children's marriage choices to avoid mistakes. But many young people are unhappy with this approach, and a compromise is often reached. Semi-arranged marriages, in which parental approval is obtained before the marriage, are becoming more common.

Practice Exercise

Topic of paragraph 3:

____

____

Determine the *stated main idea* and underline or highlight it.

Practice Exercise

Topic of paragraph 4:

____

____

Determine the *stated main idea* and underline or highlight it.

Practice Exercise

Topic of paragraph 5:

____

____

Determine the *stated main idea* and underline or highlight it.

Practice Exercise

Topic of paragraph 6:

____

____

Determine the *stated main idea* and underline or highlight it.

Parent-arranged marriages are usually very stable, because it is the duty of the whole family to help the new couple get established in life. Divorce is almost unheard of—except for the reason of infertility—because of the potential disapproval a couple would receive from the parent and members of the community who were responsible for the selection.

8 In China, there has been a dramatic change in mate selection from parent-arranged marriage to love-based marriage, as in the United States. Love-based mate selection happens more often in the larger cities than in the small towns and rural areas. A common problem is that many of the young Chinese people do not know how to date or select a mate. This makes dating a challenging adventure for Chinese couples. But China, like many places in the world, is changing rapidly.

9 Japan has generally moved from arranged marriages to love-based marriages. As more women have entered the labor force and gained financial independence, they have moved away from parent-arranged marriages. Japanese young people can find dating very awkward and uncomfortable because they often do not have much social contact with members of the other sex.

10 The Scandinavian countries are perhaps the most liberal in regard to marriage customs. Parent-arranged marriages disappeared decades ago, and cohabitation has become the most common type of relationship until after the birth of a child. Research in Sweden indicates a steep drop in the marriage rate. There has also been an increase in cohabitation (couples living together unmarried). In addition, there has been an increase in state and parental support for children born outside of matrimony.

Practice Exercise

Topic of paragraph 8:

____

____

Determine the *stated main idea* and underline or highlight it.

Source: Adapted from David Olson, John DeFrain, and Linda Skogrand, *Marriages and Families: Intimacy, Diversity, and Strengths,* 7th ed., pp. 278–81.
Copyright © 2011 by The McGraw-Hill Companies, Inc. Reprinted by permission of The McGraw-Hill Companies, Inc.

SELECTION **4.2**

Marriage and Family

(continued)

Comprehension and Vocabulary Quiz

This quiz has several parts. Your instructor may assign some or all of them.

Comprehension

Directions: Items 1–5 test your understanding of the selection. They are the types of questions a content-area instructor (such as a marriage and family professor) might ask on a test. You may refer to the selection as you answer the questions. Write your answer choice in the space provided.

_______ **1.** Parent-arranged marriages still occur throughout much of the:

a. industrialized world.

b. non-industrialized world.

c. United States.

d. all of the above

_______ **2.** Arranged marriages:

a. extend existing family units.

b. create new units.

c. break up large families into smaller ones.

d. tend to keep families the same size.

_______ **3.** The one likely reason for divorce in an arranged marriage is:

a. disappointment with the new spouse.

b. infertility.

c. infidelity.

d. the inability to get along with the spouse's family.

_______ **4.** A woman is more likely to want to decide for herself whom she will marry if she:

a. is able to support herself financially.

b. does not have a good relationship with her parents.

c. has been married before.

d. has very little dating experience.

_______ **5.** A country in which there has been a dramatic shift from arranged marriages to love-based marriages is:

a. Malaysia.

b. Sweden.

c. China.

d. all of the above

Vocabulary in Context

Directions: Items 6–10 test your ability to determine a word's meaning by using context clues. *Context clues* are words in a sentence that allow readers to deduce (reason out) the meaning of an unfamiliar word. They also help readers determine the meaning an author intends when a word has more than one meaning. Each item below consists of a sentence from the selection, with the vocabulary word *italicized*.

It is followed by another sentence that uses the same word in the same way. Use context clues to deduce the meaning of the *italicized* word. Be sure the meaning you choose makes sense in *both* sentences. Write each answer in the space provided. (Chapter 2 presented the skill of using context clues.)

_______ **6.** Although young adults in the United States today might view the practice as *archaic* and uncivilized, many people worldwide prefer parent-arranged marriages.

An *archaic* law in Farmington, Connecticut, stated that cows have the same rights on the roads as motorists do.

archaic (är kā′ ĭk) means:

a. wise or intelligent
b. belonging to a much earlier period of time
c. reasonable; sensible
d. decided by voters

_______ **7.** In these prescribed marriages, *lineage* and family status are generally more important than love or affection.

His family has lived in Hawaii for many generations, and he is very proud of his *lineage*.

lineage (lī′ nĭj) means:

a. ancestry
b. a group of people
c. history
d. personal appearance

_______ **8.** In India, for example, it is commonly believed that there is one *predestined* mate who will share life with the spouse through reincarnation.

Because Audrey and Michael ran into each other on a street corner ten years to the day when they had last seen each other, they concluded that it was *predestined*.

predestined (prē dĕs′ tind) means:

a. accidental or unintended
b. determined by fate beforehand
c. shocking
d. embarrassing

_______ **9.** In India, for example, it is commonly believed that there is one predestined mate who will share life with the spouse through *reincarnation*.

People who believe in *reincarnation* believe that what you do in this life will affect you in the next life.

reincarnation (rē ĭn kär nā′ shən) means:

a. a form of magical thinking
b. going from human form to animal form
c. a fantasy world
d. rebirth of the soul in another body

Copyright © 2014 The McGraw-Hill Companies, Inc. All rights reserved.

_______ **10.** The Scandinavian countries are perhaps the most *liberal* in regard to marriage customs.

With regard to appropriate clothing, most young adults are more *liberal* than their parents and grandparents.

liberal (lĭb′ ər əl) means:

a. rigid

b. enthusiastic

c. confused; unclear

d. open to new ideas

Word Structure

Directions: Items 11–15 test your ability to use word-structure clues to help determine a word's meaning. *Word-structure clues* consist of roots, prefixes, and suffixes. In this exercise, you will learn the meaning of a root and use it to determine the meaning of several words that contain it. If you need to use a dictionary to confirm your answer choice, do so. Write your answers in the spaces provided.

In paragraph 2 you encountered the word **prescribed.** It contains the root ***scrib,*** which means "to write" or "to record." The word *prescribed* describes something that is set forth in a definite manner. Use the meaning of ***scrib*** and the list of prefixes on pages 72–73 to determine the meaning of each of the following words.

_______ **11.** If a court reporter **transcribes** the proceedings recorded during a trial, the court reporter:

a. stores information on a computer disk.

b. writes out the information in complete form.

c. alters the information by shortening it.

d. checks the notes for errors in spelling and punctuation.

_______ **12.** When you **subscribe** to a magazine, you:

a. sign an agreement to pay for a specific number of issues.

b. read it every month.

c. recycle the issue after you have read it.

d. remove your name from the mailing list.

_______ **13.** In the Middle Ages, a **scribe's** job was to:

a. read documents and manuscripts to illiterate peasants.

b. translate documents written in other languages.

c. record information and make copies of documents and manuscripts.

d. memorize and recite important documents.

_______ **14.** When children **scribble,** they:

a. draw pictures.

b. paint with finger paints.

c. cut out shapes from colored paper.

d. make meaningless marks or lines.

_______ **15.** If the names of military heroes are **inscribed** on a marble monument, their names are:

a. printed in block letters.
b. written in gold.
c. chiseled in the stone.
d. crossed out.

Reading Skills Application

Directions: Items 16–20 test your ability to *apply* certain reading skills. You may not be familiar with all the skills yet, so some items will serve as a preview. As you work through *New Worlds,* you will practice and develop these skills. These are important skills, which is why they are included on the state-mandated basic skills tests that some students must take. Write each answer in the space provided.

_______ **16.** As used in paragraph 1, the word *prospective* means:

a. unhappy and unwilling.
b. future; expected to become.
c. young; immature.
d. forced.

_______ **17.** In paragraph 9 it says, "Japanese young people can find dating very awkward and uncomfortable because they often do not have much social contact with members of the other sex." What is the relationship between the parts of that sentence?

a. The second part presents a contrast to something mentioned in the first part.
b. The second part continues a sequence started in the first part.
c. The second part gives the reason for something mentioned in the first part.
d. The second part gives an example of something mentioned in the first part.

_______ **18.** The authors' primary purpose in writing this selection is to:

a. persuade readers that arranged marriage should be more widely used.
b. instruct readers how to determine if they are selecting an appropriate spouse for their child.
c. persuade parents to consider arranging their children's marriages.
d. inform readers about the advantages of, changes in, and cultural variations in arranged marriages.

_______ **19.** In paragraph 1 it says, "In most cultures, the parents of the bride and groom selected the future spouse. They also made most of the arrangements for the marriage ceremony." What is the relationship between the two sentences?

a. The second sentence changes the meaning of first sentence.
b. The second sentence clarifies the first sentence.
c. The second sentence adds information to the information in the first sentence.
d. The second sentence gives a specific example of what is stated in the first sentence.

_______ **20.** Based on information in the passage, it is logical to conclude that the custom of Americans taking months or years to date and find a mate of their own choosing would:

a. seem unreasonable to those in countries with a tradition of arranged marriages.

b. appeal greatly to parents in countries with a tradition of arranged marriages.

c. be immediately adopted by young adults in countries with a tradition of arranged marriages.

d. create resentment in young adults already in arranged marriages in other countries.

SELECTION **4.2**

Marriage and Family

(continued)

Respond in Writing

Directions: Refer to the selection as needed to answer the essay-type questions below. (Your instructor may direct you to work collaboratively with other students on one or more items. Each group member should be able to explain *all* of the group's answers.)

1. Reacting to What You Have Read: What, in your opinion, are the top two or three things that are necessary for a marriage to be successful? Explain your choices.

____

____

____

____

____

2. Comprehending the Selection Further: The authors mention several advantages of arranged marriages. List at least three of them.

____

____

____

____

____

____

____

____

3. Overall Main Idea of the Selection: In one sentence, tell what the authors want readers to understand about arranged marriages. (Be sure to include "arranged marriages" in your overall main idea sentence.)

____

____

____

____

____

____

Internet Resources

Read More about It Online

Directions: Read more about the topic of this selection online. You can read online *before* you read the selection to build background knowledge or *afterward* to extent you knowledge. Start with the websites below or type **"arranged marriage"** in the search box of Google, Yahoo, or another search engine. When you visit any unfamiliar website, it is important to evaluate it and the information it contains. If you do not know how to conduct Internet searches or evaluate a website, see pages 24–25.

www.startribune.com/templates/Print_This_Story?sid=15439136
Read these myths and facts about arranged marriages.

www.ehow.com/about_6137264_arranged-marriage-information.html
At this eHow page, read information about arranged marriages.

Copyright © 2014 The McGraw-Hill Companies, Inc. All rights reserved.

SELECTION **4.3** **Health**

Concussions: Don't Shrug Them Off!

From *The Dana Foundation and the Sports Concussion Institute websites*
Compiled by Janet Elder

Motor vehicle accidents are the primary cause of traumatic brain injuries, and falls also account for a large number. Brain injuries can happen at any age, but young adults between the ages of 15 and 24 are at greatest risk.

Traumatic brain injuries are a leading cause of death and disability. It is estimated that a head injury occurs every seven seconds. In light of that, it is no surprise that each year hospital emergency rooms treat one million people for head injuries. Any brain injury is a potential threat, and anyone who experiences a head injury should see a doctor—even if the person feels fine.[1]

Concussions are often described as "mild" brain injuries, but many experts believe it is a mistake to describe any brain injury as mild. During the last few years, public awareness of the seriousness of concussions has increased. The reason is research on the growing number of former pro football players whose lives have been forever altered by their multiple concussions.

1 According to the Sports Concussion Institute, the term **concussion** refers to a brain injury that can be caused by a direct blow to the head, or by an indirect blow to the body. It is a misconception that the person always loses consciousness. In fact, only a small percent lose consciousness, and when this does happen, it is usually brief—perhaps only a few seconds. There may be no symptoms, but the symptoms can be so subtle that they go unrecognized. For example, the person may be temporarily confused, disoriented, have difficulty concentrating, or experience memory problems. Physical symptoms can include nausea, vomiting, and headaches. There can be sleep disturbances. There may be changes in energy levels or appetite. The person may also show changes in moods, such as sadness or irritability.[2]

2 The human brain weighs about three pounds. It has a custard-like texture, and this delicate organ floats in fluid inside the skull. The fluid inside the skull is designed to cushion the brain, but when there is an impact or a whiplash, a concussion can result. It occurs when the brain moves too quickly inside the skull. Upon impact, the brain receives two jolts: the initial one, which sets the brain in motion, and a second one when it hits the opposite side of the inner skull. In a case in which the brain rotates too rapidly from one side to the other, its tissue can be strained or even torn.[3]

3 Many concussion victims do not see a doctor because after a short period of time, they feel fine. Feeling fine, however, does not mean that an injury hasn't occurred. Other victims go undiagnosed because their symptoms are subtle, or they do not associate their symptoms with a head injury. It is no wonder concussions have been described as a "hidden epidemic."[4]

4 A concussion can be dangerous at any age, but it poses a special threat to developing brains. They are more vulnerable. Recovery takes longer. Moreover, many youngsters and young

Annotation Practice Exercises

Directions: For each exercise below, write the topic of the paragraph on the lines beside the paragraph. Then locate the stated main idea of the paragraph and underline or highlight it.

Practice Exercise

Topic of paragraph 1:

____

____

Determine the *stated main idea* and underline or highlight it.

Practice Exercise

Topic of paragraph 2:

____

____

Determine the *stated main idea* and underline or highlight it.

Practice Exercise

Topic of paragraph 3:

____

____

Determine the *stated main idea* and underline or highlight it.

Copyright © 2014 The McGraw-Hill Companies, Inc. All rights reserved.

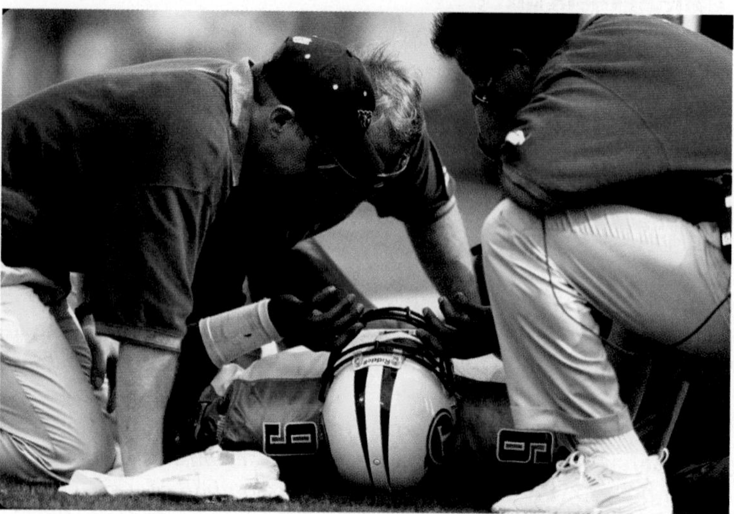

With a 75 percent chance for concussion, football is the most common sport with concussion risk for males. A professional football player will receive an estimated 900 to 1,500 blows to the head during a season.

adults play sports. One estimate is that slightly more than half of all high school athletes have sustained a concussion *prior to* their participation in high school sports. More than a third of college athletes have had multiple concussions.[5]

5 These statistics are alarming for two reasons. First, the brain's frontal lobes (sections behind the forehead) continue to develop until age 25. This area of the brain is associated with a variety of functions. Among others, they include judgment, problem solving, planning, attention, impulse control, predicting future outcomes, and motivation. Second, multiple concussions can lead to a greater likelihood of depression, dementia, and other neurological problems in later life.[6]

6 Research indicates that a person who sustains a concussion is 1–2 times more likely to have a second one. A person who has had two concussions is 2–4 times more likely to have a third one, and a person who has had three concussions is 3–9 times more likely to sustain a fourth concussion. These statistics indicate how important it is for a person to recover completely from a concussion before risking another one. Otherwise, there can be additional neurologic damage.[7]

7 The Sports Concussion Institute also cites these surprising and sometimes startling facts and figures:

- "The CDC [Centers for Disease Control] estimates reveal that 1.6 million to 3.8 million concussions occur each year.
- 5–10% of athletes will experience a concussion in any given sport season.
- Fewer than 10% of sport-related concussions involve a loss of consciousness (e.g., blacking out, seeing stars).
- Football is the most common sport with concussion risk for males (75% chance for concussion).
- Soccer is the most common sport with concussion risk for females (50% chance for concussion).

- 78% of concussions occur during games (as opposed to practices).
- Some studies suggest that females are twice as likely to sustain a concussion as males.
- Headache (85%) and dizziness (70–80%) are most commonly reported symptoms immediately following concussions for injured athletes.
- An estimated 47% of athletes do not report feeling any symptoms after a concussive blow.
- A professional football player will receive an estimated 900 to 1,500 blows to the head during a season.
- The impact speed of a professional boxer's punch is 20 mph.
- The impact speed of a football player tackling a stationary player is 25 mph.
- The impact speed of a soccer ball being headed by a player is 70 mph."[8]

8 There are several reasons youngsters are more vulnerable to head injuries than adults are. Besides the fact that their brains are still developing, children's necks are weaker, so a blow has more effect. (Female athletes also have weaker necks than male athletes.) Moreover, compared with adults, youngsters have heads that are proportionally larger relative to their bodies. Finally, their brains take up more space inside the skull than adult brains do.[9]

Practice Exercise

Topic of paragraph 8:

____

____

____

Determine the *stated main idea* and underline or highlight it.

9 Student athletes often view a head "ding" or "bell ringer" as "no big deal." Most of them are eager to get back in the game and resume play. If they go back in without realizing they are injured, they risk additional damage.[10] Moreover, since the injuries cannot be seen, concussions can be difficult to detect or diagnose. Brain imaging and X-rays are helpful only in the rare cases in which bleeding has occurred. In addition, the effects of a concussion may not become apparent for days or even weeks.[11] Approximately 300,000 sports-related concussions are reported each year. However, a vast number of them go unreported, so the CDC believes that is a gross underestimate. One CDC epidemiologist believes 750,000 to 2.25 million is more accurate.[12]

10 With regard to the brain, Guy McKhann, M.D., advocates proper protection and care. "You have only one brain," he says. "Be kind to it."[13]

Sources:

1 Patricio C. Gargollo and Adam C. Lipson, "Brain Trauma, Concussion and Coma—The Dana Guide," March 2007; The Dana Foundation, www.dana.org/news/brainhealth/detail.aspx?id=9790. Accessed 28 February 2012.

2–8 Sports Concussion Institute, www.concussiontreatment.com/concussionfacts.html. Accessed 28 February 2012.

9–10 Ann Whitman and Johanna Goldberg, Briefing Paper of Brenda Patoine's "Sports Concussions and the Immature Brain," The Dana Foundation, www.dana.org/media/detail.aspx?id=25076. Accessed 28 February 2012.

11 www.dana.org/media/detail.aspx?id=25076. Accessed 28 February 2012.

12 Ann Whitman and Johanna Goldberg, Briefing Paper of Brenda Patoine's "Sports Concussions and the Immature Brain," The Dana Foundation, www.dana.org/media/detail.aspx?id=25076. Accessed 28 February 2012.

13 Guy McKhann, "You Have Only One Brain—Be Kind to It"; The Dana Foundation, www.dana.org/news/braininthenews/detail.aspx?id=33772. Accessed 28 February 2012.

SELECTION **4.3**

Health

(continued)

Comprehension and Vocabulary Quiz

This quiz has four parts. Your instructor may assign some or all of them.

Comprehension

Directions: Items 1–5 test your understanding of the selection. They are the types of questions a content-area instructor (such as a biology or health professor) might ask on a test. You may refer to the selection as you answer the questions. Write your answer choice in the space provided.

_______ **1.** Concussions can be caused by:
a. blows to the head.
b. an indirect blow to the body.
c. blows to the head or the body.
d. none of the above

_______ **2.** With regard to losing consciousness when a concussion occurs, most victims:
a. do not lose consciousness.
b. lose consciousness for several seconds.
c. lose consciousness for a few minutes.
d. go into a coma.

_______ **3.** Youngsters are more vulnerable to concussions than adults because their:
a. brains are still developing.
b. necks are weaker and heads are proportionally larger.
c. brains take up more space inside the skull.
d. all of the above

_______ **4.** The most common symptoms injured athletes report immediately after a concussion are headaches and:
a. nausea.
b. dizziness.
c. sleep disturbances.
d. memory problems.

_______ **5.** A person who has had a concussion:
a. is at greater risk of having another one.
b. has the same odds as anyone else for having another one.
c. is unlikely to have another one.
d. develops immunity after the first one.

Vocabulary in Context

Directions: Items 6–10 test your ability to determine a word's meaning by using context clues. *Context clues* are words in a sentence that allow readers to deduce (reason out) the meaning of an unfamiliar word. They also help readers determine the meaning an author intends when a word has more than one meaning. Each item below consists of a sentence from the selection, with the vocabulary word *italicized*. It is followed by another sentence that uses the same word in the same way. Use context clues to deduce the meaning of the *italicized* word. Be sure the meaning you choose makes sense in *both* sentences. Write each answer in the space provided. (Chapter 2 presented the skill of using context clues.)

_______ **6.** It is a *misconception* that the person always loses consciousness.

Until the 17th century there was a *misconception* that the Earth was the center of the universe.

misconception (mĭs kən sĕp′ shən) means:

a. a proven concept

b. a mistaken idea

c. an understanding

d. an insight

_______ **7.** There may be no symptoms, but the symptoms can be so *subtle* that they go unrecognized.

Although my boss did not say I was going to receive a promotion, he gave some *subtle* hints.

subtle (sŭt′l) means:

a. obvious; apparent

b. so slight as to be difficult to detect

c. severe

d. easily seen

_______ **8.** Upon impact, the brain receives two *jolts*: the initial one, which sets the brain in motion, and a second one when it hits the opposite side of the inner skull.

When Tom rode his bicycle down the steps of the porch, he received a series of *jolts*.

jolts (jōltz) means:

a. sudden, violent contact between two things

b. electrical impulses

c. exciting occurrences

d. flashes

_______ **9.** They are more *vulnerable*.

People who use ATMs after dark are more *vulnerable* to robbers.

vulnerable (vŭl′nər ə bəl) means:

a. likely to be physically injured

b. highly impressionable

c. sensitive

d. likely to be affected by someone or something

_______ **10.** One estimate is that slightly more than half of all high school athletes have *sustained* a concussion prior to their participation in high school sports.

The drivers of both cars *sustained* life-threatening injuries in the head-on collision.

sustained (sə stānd′) means:

a. confirmed

b. maintained

c. died from

d. experienced

Word Structure

Directions: Items 11–15 test your ability to use word-structure clues to help determine a word's meaning. *Word-structure clues* consist of roots, prefixes, and suffixes. In this exercise, you will learn the meaning of a root and use it to determine the meaning of several words that contain it. If you need to use a dictionary to confirm your answer choice, do so. Write your answers in the spaces provided.

In paragraph 10 of the selection, you encountered the word **advocates.** It contains the root ***voc,*** which means "to say" or "to call." The word *advocates* means to *speak* out, plead, or argue in favor of someone or something. Use the meaning of the root ***voc*** and the list of prefixes on pages 72–73 to help you determine the meaning of each of the following words.

_______ **11.** If someone is described as a **vocal** person, he or she is:

a. difficult to understand.

b. outspoken; inclined to speak often and freely.

c. quiet and shy.

d. confused.

_______ **12.** Your **vocabulary** consists of:

a. the words you can spell correctly.

b. a group of words borrowed from other languages.

c. words you understand and can use when you speak and write.

d. specialized definitions that you have memorized.

_______ **13.** When you discover your **vocation,** you find:

a. your calling or occupation.

b. a solution.

c. a place to relax and renew yourself.

d. your family history or genealogy.

_______ **14.** If a crowd makes a **vociferous** protest, they are:

a. serious; solemn.

b. joyful.

c. loud and noisy.

d. silent.

_____ **15.** An **avocation,** such as coin collecting or stamp collecting, is:

a. a difficult assignment.

b. the search for something; a mystery.

c. an enormous project; a challenge.

d. a calling away from one's regular work; a hobby.

Reading Skills Application

Directions: Items 16–20 test your ability to *apply* certain reading skills. You may not be familiar with all the skills yet, so some items will serve as a preview. As you work through *New Worlds,* you will practice and develop these skills. These are important skills, which is why they are included on the state-mandated basic skills tests that some students must take. Write each answer in the space provided.

_____ **16.** What is the author's purpose for writing the selection?

a. to explain how to prevent concussions

b. to inform readers about the seriousness of concussions

c. to present the symptoms of concussions

d. to persuade coaches to learn about concussions

_____ **17.** In paragraph 9 it says, "If they go back in without realizing they are injured, they risk additional damage." What is the relationship between the parts of that sentence?

a. addition

b. sequence

c. cause-effect

d. summary

_____ **18.** The information in paragraph 1 is organized by which writing pattern?

a. list

b. sequence

c. definition

d. comparison-contrast

_____ **19.** In paragraph 9 it says, "Approximately 300,000 sports-related concussions are reported each year. However, a vast number of them go unreported, so the CDC believes that is a gross underestimate." What is the relationship between the two sentences?

a. The second sentence gives a specific example of what is stated in the first sentence.

b. The second sentence tells more about information given the first sentence.

c. The second sentence changes the meaning of first sentence.

d. The second sentence presents a contrast to information in the first sentence.

_______ **20.** The author would likely agree that parents of student athletes should:

a. inform themselves and their children about concussions.

b. not allow their children to play contact sports.

c. demand protective head gear for all sports.

d. hold coaches responsible for student athletes' concussions.

Respond in Writing

Directions: Refer to the selection as needed to answer the essay-type questions below. (Your instructor may direct you to work collaboratively with other students on one or more items. Each group member should be able to explain *all* of the group's answers.)

1. **Reacting to What You Have Read:** Have you or someone you know (or have read about) had a concussion? What caused it? What were the symptoms? Was it properly diagnosed? What were the effects?

2. **Comprehending the Selection Further:** According to the selection, there are several reasons that concussions are likely to go unrecognized, unreported, or undiagnosed. List three or four reasons why this is happening.

3. **Overall Main Idea of the Selection:** In one sentence, tell what the authors want readers to understand about concussions. (Be sure to include "concussions" in your overall main idea sentence.)

____

____

____

____

____

____

____

____

Internet Resources

Read More about It Online

Directions: Read more about the topic of this selection online. You can read online *before* you read the selection to build background knowledge or *afterward* to extend your knowledge. Start with the websites below or type **"concussions"** or **"student athletes and concussions"** in the search box of Google, Yahoo, or another search engine. When you visit any unfamiliar website, it is important to evaluate it and the information it contains. If you do not know how to conduct Internet searches or evaluate a website, see pages 72–73.

www.cdc.gov/concussion/sports/index.html
The Centers for Desease Control (CDC) offers fast facts on concussions in sports, along with many helpful links to related webpages.

http://espn.go.com/nfl/topics//page/concussions
ESPN page provides information about concussions, NLF players' lawsuit against the NFL for its failure to warn them adequately about concussions, and a list of players with career-ending concussions.

http://topics.nytimes.com/top/reference/timestopics/subjects/f/football/head_injuries/index.html
This brief *New York Times* article makes it clear that even in 2000, it was known that 60 percent of NFL players had suffered at least one concussion, and nearly a third had suffered three or more. Today, scores of former players who have suffered concussions have filed a suit against the league.

Copyright © 2014 The McGraw-Hill Companies, Inc. All rights reserved.

CHAPTER 5

Formulating an Implied Main Idea

LEARNING OBJECTIVES

In this chapter you will learn the answers to these questions:

- What is an implied main idea sentence?
- Why is it important to be able to formulate an implied main idea?
- What are three formulas for using information in a paragraph to formulate the implied main idea?

NEW INFORMATION AND SKILLS

WHAT IS AN IMPLIED MAIN IDEA, AND WHY IS IT IMPORTANT?

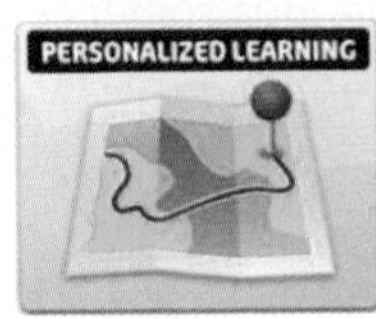

You know that every paragraph has a main idea. However, authors sometimes *suggest* the most important point, rather than state it directly as a sentence in the paragraph. In other words, the author *implies* the main point.

When authors do not state the main idea directly, it is your job to infer it (reason it out) and write a sentence that expresses it. An **implied main idea** is a sentence formulated by the reader that expresses an author's main point about the topic. (In this book the terms *implied main idea sentence* and *formulated main idea sentence* are used interchangeably to refer to the same thing.)

implied main idea

A sentence formulated by the reader that expresses the author's main point about the topic.

An implied main idea is also known as an *unstated main idea,* an *indirectly stated main idea,* and a *formulated main idea.*

Why is it important for you to formulate an implied main idea sentence whenever the author does not state the main idea? There are several reasons: First, you limit your comprehension unless you can formulate main ideas that are implied. Also, when you formulate main ideas, it helps you remember material better. Finally, college instructors assume that you will read carefully enough to understand both stated and implied main ideas. Test items are just as likely to be based on implied main ideas as on stated main ideas.

In this chapter, you will learn three "formulas" that you can use to "formulate" an implied main idea. The formula you use will depend on the type of information the author gives you in the paragraph. Sometimes the only thing you need to do is add an essential word or phrase to a sentence in the paragraph. In other cases, all you need to do is combine two or more sentences in the paragraph into one sentence. In still other cases, you will have to summarize ideas from several sentences or make a general inference based on the details. When a paragraph consists only of facts, descriptions, explanations, or examples that merely suggest the author's main point, it will be up to you to infer it and then formulate a main idea sentence. Remember, the main idea sentence you formulate must always be *based on* what is presented in the paragraph.

To be an effective reader, then, you must be able to formulate the main idea sentence when the author implies it, just as you must be able to locate the main idea when the author states it directly.

THREE FORMULAS FOR USING INFORMATION IN A PARAGRAPH TO FORMULATE AN IMPLIED MAIN IDEA

As always, you must begin by reading the paragraph and determining its topic. If you cannot locate a stated main idea sentence, ask yourself this comprehension monitoring question: "What is the most important point the author wants me to *infer* about the topic of this paragraph?" Then use one of the three "formulas" to create the "formulated" main idea sentence. Here is an explanation of each formula, along with a simple example and one from an actual college textbook.

Comprehension Monitoring Question for Implied Main Idea

"What is the most important point the author wants me to *infer* about the topic of this paragraph?"

Formula 1: Add an Essential Word or Phrase to a Sentence in the Paragraph That Almost States the Main Idea

Sometimes an author expresses *most* of the main idea in one sentence of the paragraph, yet that sentence lacks an essential piece of information. You must add that essential information to make the sentence express the *complete* main idea. Often the sentence merely needs to have the topic (a word, name, or phrase) inserted to make it express the main idea completely.

When you read a paragraph that has a sentence that almost states the main idea yet lacks essential information, use **Formula 1** to create the complete main idea sentence:

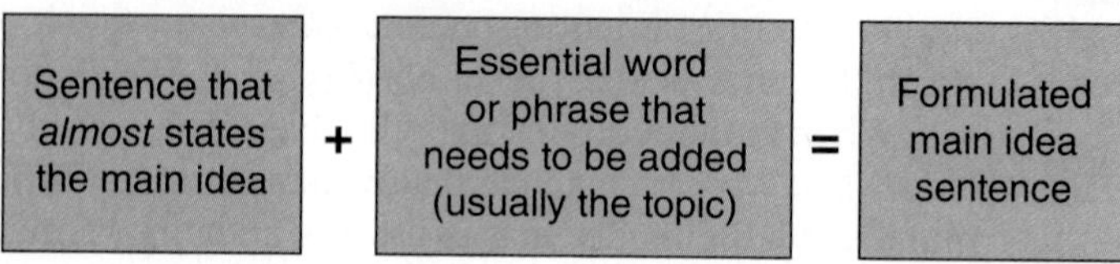

The simple paragraph below illustrates how this formula can be applied. Read it and determine the topic by asking yourself, "Who or what is this about?" Notice that there is a sentence that *almost* states the main idea yet lacks an essential piece of information. Find that sentence.

Tom is excellent with customers. He is knowledgeable about his company's products. Moreover, he is a hard worker who always exceeds his sales goals. He is the best salesperson in his company.

Here is Formula 1 with the appropriate information from the paragraph:

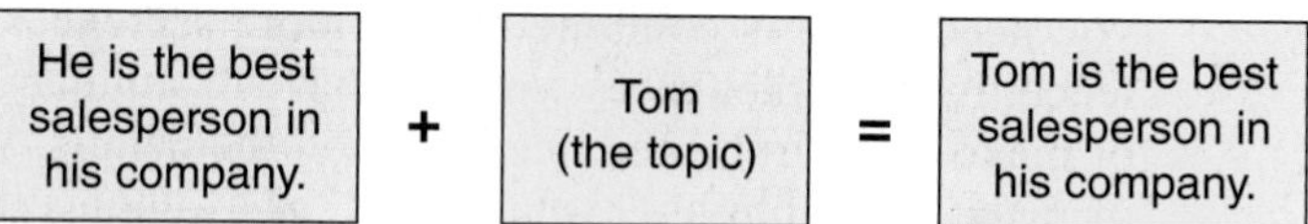

The last sentence almost states the main idea ("He is the best salesperson in his company"), but it lacks the topic (Tom). When that essential information is added, you have the complete formulated main idea sentence: *Tom is the best salesperson in his company.*

Here is a paragraph from a management textbook. Its main idea can be formulated using Formula 1. The topic is *job sharing.*

Perhaps you have heard the term **job sharing**. It occurs when two people do one job, and it can benefit both the employees and the company. One person may work from 8:00 a.m. to 12:30 p.m.; the second person comes in at 12:30 p.m. and works until 5:00 p.m. Job sharing gives both people the opportunity to work as well as time to fulfill other obligations, such as parenting or school. With job sharing, the company has the benefit of two people for one job, often at a lower total cost for salaries and benefits than one person working eight hours a day would be paid.

Formulated Main Idea Sentence

____

____

____

____

____

____

Source: O. C. Ferrell, Geoffrey Hirt, and Linda Ferrell, *Business: A Changing World,* 8th ed., p. 286. Copyright © 2011 by The McGraw-Hill Companies, Inc. Reprinted by permission of The McGraw-Hill Companies.

Stop and Annotate

Go back to the textbook excerpt on page 246. Write the formulated main idea sentence in the space provided by adding essential information to the sentence that almost states the main idea.

The second sentence of this paragraph *almost* states the authors' most important point, but it lacks an essential piece of information: the topic. A complete main idea sentence can be formulated by adding the topic, *job sharing,* to the second sentence: *Job sharing occurs when two people do one job, and it can benefit both the employees and the company.*

EXERCISE 1

This paragraph comes from a psychology textbook.

What is meditation? It is a learned technique for refocusing attention that brings about an altered state of consciousness. Meditation typically consists of the repetition of a *mantra*—a sound, word, or syllable—over and over. In other forms of meditation, the focus is on a picture, flame, or specific part of the body. The procedure involves concentrating on something so thoroughly that the person who is meditating becomes unaware of any outside stimulation. He or she reaches a different state of consciousness.

Source: Adapted from Robert S. Feldman, *Understanding Psychology,* 8th ed., p. 163. Copyright © 2008 by The McGraw-Hill Companies, Inc. Reprinted by permission of The McGraw-Hill Companies.

Write the topic: ______________________________

Formulate a main idea sentence: ______________________________

____

____

____

Formula 2: Combine Two Sentences from the Paragraph into a Single Sentence

Sometimes a paragraph contains two sentences that each give *part* of the main idea. Each sentence contains important information, yet neither sentence by itself expresses the complete main idea. Therefore, you must *combine* these two sentences into *one* sentence that expresses the complete main idea. (You already know that any main idea must be written as a single sentence.) Often you will be able to use words such as *and, but,* or *however* to join the two sentences. The two sentences you combine may follow each other in the paragraph (for example, the first two sentences of the paragraph), or they may be separated (for example, the first sentence of the paragraph and the last sentence of the paragraph).

When you realize that two sentences in a paragraph each state *part* of the main idea, use **Formula 2** to create a complete main idea that is a single sentence:

Sentence that expresses *part* of the main idea	+	Sentence that expresses *rest* of the main idea	=	Formulated main idea sentence

Here is a simple paragraph that shows how this formula can be applied. Read the paragraph and notice that there are two sentences that each give part of the main idea but that must be combined into a single sentence to formulate the complete main idea.

Copyright © 2014 The McGraw-Hill Companies, Inc. All rights reserved.

Maria is taking a full academic load this semester. She is taking history, psychology, computer science, math, and a writing course. She has classes five days a week. But she still finds time to do volunteer work. On Saturday mornings she is a volunteer at the library. On Sunday afternoons she does volunteer work at the hospital.

Here is Formula 2 with the appropriate information from the paragraph:

Maria is taking a full academic load this semester.	+	But she still finds time to do volunteer work.	=	Maria is taking a full academic load this semester, but she still finds time to do volunteer work.

The first sentence and the fourth sentence express the important information, so they must be combined into one sentence. Therefore, the formulated main idea sentence is: *Maria is taking a full academic load this semester, but she still finds time to do volunteer work.*

Here is a business communication textbook paragraph whose main idea can be formulated using Formula 2. The topic of this paragraph is *individualism and the group.*

Many people in the United States value individualism. Other countries may value the group. In traditional classrooms, U.S. students are expected to complete assignments alone; if they get much help from anyone else, they're "cheating." In Japan, in contrast, groups routinely work together to solve problems. In the dominant U.S. culture, quiet is a sign that people are working. In Japan, people talk to get things done.

Formulated Main Idea Sentence

____

Source: Kitty Locker and Stephen Kyo Kaczmarek, *Business Communication: Building Critical Skills*, 5th ed., p. 239. Copyright © 2011 by The McGraw-Hill Companies, Inc. Reprinted by permission of The McGraw-Hill Companies.

Stop and Annotate

Go back to the textbook excerpt above. Write the formulated main idea sentence in the space provided by combining the two sentences in the paragraph that together express the complete main idea.

Because the first two sentences each tell half of the main idea, the main idea sentence is formulated by combining them into a single sentence. The first sentence explains what Americans value; the second sentence explains what may be important to other countries. When these two sentences are combined, you have a complete main idea sentence: *Many people in the United States value individualism; other countries may value the group.*

Remember that there is more than one correct way to combine sentences to express an implied main idea. What is important is that the main idea is correct and complete. For example, the main idea of the excerpt could also be expressed this way: *Many people in the United States value individualism, whereas other countries may value the group.*

EXERCISE 2

This paragraph comes from an information technology textbook.

How would you feel if someone obtained a driver's license and credit cards in your name? What if that person then assumed your identity to buy clothes, cars, and a house? **Identity theft** is the illegal assumption of someone's identity for the purposes of economic gain. Every year, nearly 10 million people are victimized in this way.

Source: Adapted from Timothy O'Leary and Linda O'Leary, *Computing Essentials 2013*, p. 297. Copyright © 2013 by The McGraw-Hill Companies, Inc. Reprinted by permission of The McGraw-Hill Companies.

Write the topic: ______________________________

Formulate a main idea sentence: ______________________________

____

____

Formula 3: Summarize Important Ideas into One Sentence or Write One Sentence That Gives a General Inference Based on the Details

With some paragraphs, you will have to either formulate a main idea sentence that *summarizes* the important information in the paragraph or formulate a sentence that gives a *general inference* based on the details. Which of these you do will depend upon the type of information you are given in the paragraph. When you create this kind of formulated main idea sentence, you will often have to use some of your own words along with certain important words from the paragraph.

When a paragraph has important ideas included in several sentences or the paragraph consists only of details, **Formula 3** should be used to formulate the main idea.

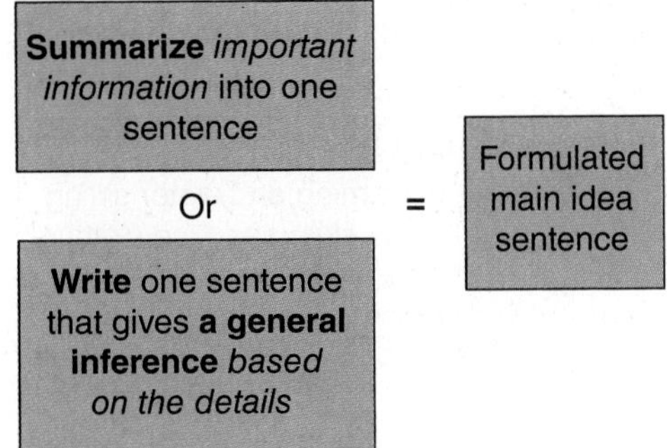
Summarize important information into one sentence
Or
Write one sentence that gives a general inference based on the details
=
Formulated main idea sentence

The simple paragraph below shows how you can summarize important ideas to create the formulated main idea. Read the paragraph and notice which ideas have been summarized to create the formulated main idea.

Johnny doesn't trust strangers. He does not trust his neighbors, nor does he trust his coworkers. He does, however, trust members of his family. And he trusts his best friend, Ramón.

Copyright © 2014 The McGraw-Hill Companies, Inc. All rights reserved.

Here is Formula 3 with the appropriate information from the paragraph.

Johnny – does not trust strangers – does not trust his neighbors – does not trust his coworkers – trusts members of his family – trusts his best friend, Ramón	=	Johnny does not trust many people, but he does trust family members and his best friend, Ramón.

A formulated main idea sentence that summarizes the important information into one sentence is *Johnny does not trust many people, but he does trust family members and his best friend, Ramón.* Of course, this could also be expressed in shorter ways: *Johnny trusts only family members and his best friend,* or *Family members and his best friend are the only people Johnny trusts.*

A word of caution: Do create one long sentence in which you merely restate all of the information, such as *Johnny doesn't trust strangers and he does not trust his neighbors and he does not trust his coworkers, but he does, however, trust members of his family and his best friend, Ramón.* Instead, summarize the information using some of your own words.

Now consider a paragraph that consists only of details. In this case, you must infer the general point the author wants to make. Then formulate a main idea sentence that expresses that point. Although none of the actual details appear in the main idea sentence, the main idea is *based* on them. For example,

> Tia likes to swim and water ski. She also enjoys snow skiing and ice skating. She has loved basketball since elementary school. She is captain of the tennis team this year. And she is very excited about her upcoming soccer season.

Here is Formula 3 with the appropriate information from the paragraph:

Tia likes – swimming and water skiing – snow skiing and ice skating – basketball – tennis – soccer	=	Tia likes many sports.

The formulated main idea sentence gives a general inference *based* on the details: *Tia likes many sports.* Notice that although the word *sports* does not appear in the paragraph, it can be used as a general term to describe the activities mentioned in the details. Of course, the main idea sentence could also be expressed in any of these ways: *Tia loves several sports; Tia enjoys many sports;* or even *Tia participates in a variety of sports.*

Here is a study skills textbook paragraph whose implied main idea can be formulated using Formula 3. The topic is *being more successful on future tests.* The implied main idea can be formulated by writing a sentence that summarizes the important information into one sentence.

When you do poorly on a test, don't blame your teacher. And don't blame your textbook. Don't blame your job that kept you from studying. Analyze the situation. See what you can change to be more successful in the future.

Formulated Main Idea Sentence

____

____

____

____

Source: Adapted from Robert S. Feldman, *P.O.W.E.R. Learning: Strategies for Success in College and Life,* p. 14. Copyright © 2005 by The McGraw-Hill Companies, Inc. Reprinted by permission of The McGraw-Hill Companies.

Stop and Annotate

Go back to the textbook excerpt above. Formulate a sentence that *summarizes* the important information from several sentences into a single sentence and write it in the space provided.

To create a main idea for this paragraph, examine the details, think about them, and ask yourself, "What is the important point the author wants me to *infer* about being more successful on future tests?" The formulated main idea is *When you do poorly on a test, analyze the situation to see what you can change to be more successful in the future.*

Here is another paragraph from the same study skills textbook that also has an implied main idea that can be formulated using Formula 3. The topic is *strategies for answering specific kinds of test questions.* The implied main idea can be formulated by writing a sentence that gives a general inference based on the details.

Are there specific strategies for answering various kinds of test questions? For essay questions, be sure to understand each question and each of its parts, interpret action words correctly, write concisely, organize the essay logically, and include examples. For multiple-choice questions, read the questions very carefully and then read all response choices. Educated guessing based on eliminating incorrect response choices is usually a reasonable strategy. For true-false and matching questions, quickly answer all the items that you are sure of and then go back to the remaining items. The best strategy for short-answer and fill-in questions is to be very sure what is being asked. Keep answers complete but brief.

Formulated Main Idea Sentence

____

____

____

____

____

Source: Adapted from Robert S. Feldman, *P.O.W.E.R., Learning: Strategies for Success in College and Life,* p. 141. Copyright © 2005 by The McGraw-Hill Companies, Inc. Reprinted by permission of The McGraw-Hill Companies.

Stop and Annotate

Go back to the textbook excerpt above. Formulate a sentence by making a *general inference* based on the details and write it in the space provided.

To create a main idea, examine the details, think about them, and ask yourself, "What is the most general point the author wants me to *infer* about strategies for answering specific kinds of test questions?" A logical formulated main idea is *There are specific strategies for answering various kinds of test questions.*

Copyright © 2014 The McGraw-Hill Companies, Inc. All rights reserved.

EXERCISE 3

This paragraph comes from a health textbook.

Are fast food "meal deals" a good deal? Burger King's King Value Meal and Wendy's Classic Triple with Cheese plus Great Biggie Fries and a Biggie Cola supply more than an entire day's worth of calories and sodium and two days of saturated and trans fats. The Meat Lover's breakfast at Denny's, which comes with three pancakes, two eggs, two strips of bacon, and two sausage links, has 1,250 calories and 86 grams of fat, according to Denny's website. The Fabulous French Toast Platter—with three slices of French toast, two bacon strips, and two sausage links—contains 1,261 calories and 79 grams of fat. Hardee's has a Monster Thickburger, with 1,400 calories and 107 grams of fat.

Source: Adapted from Wayne Payne, Dale Hahn, and Ellen Lucas, *Understanding Your Health,* 10th ed., p. 154. Copyright © 2009 by The McGraw-Hill Companies, Inc. Reprinted by permission of The McGraw-Hill Companies.

Write the topic: ______________________________

Formulate a main idea sentence: ______________________________

____

____

____

____

____

When you read a paragraph that does not have a stated main idea, use one of the formulas to create a sentence that tells the author's implied main idea. The chart below summarizes the three ways to formulate implied main idea sentences.

THREE WAYS TO FORMULATE IMPLIED MAIN IDEA SENTENCES

What the Author Presents in the Paragraph	What You Must Do with the Information to Formulate the Implied Main Idea
A sentence that *almost* states the main idea but lacks some essential piece of information (usually the topic)	*Use Formula 1.* *Add* the essential piece of information that is missing to that sentence. *How to apply the formula:* Use the sentence from the paragraph and simply add the essential piece of information to that sentence. *or* You can write the main idea in your own words as long as the meaning is the same.

What the Author Presents in the Paragraph	What You Must Do with the Information to Formulate the Implied Main Idea
Two sentences in the paragraph that each present *part* of the main idea	*Use Formula 2.* *Combine* them into one sentence (because the main idea must always be written as a single sentence). *How to apply the formula:* You will probably have to add a word or two in order to connect the two sentences (usually words such as *and, but,* and *although*). *or* You can write the main idea in your own words, as long as the meaning is the same.
Important information in several sentences	*Use Formula 3.* Summarize important information into one sentence.
Details only	*Use Formula 3.* *Write* a *general sentence* that sums up the details or gives a general inference that tells the point the author is making. *How to apply the formula:* The sentence you write will contain several of your own words.

OTHER THINGS TO KEEP IN MIND WHEN FORMULATING AN IMPLIED MAIN IDEA SENTENCE

There are three helpful things you should know about when formulating main idea sentences that have been implied:

1. **You must always use a sentence—not just a phrase—to express a formulated main idea. This means you must know the difference between a sentence and a phrase.**

The main idea must be expressed as a complete sentence that has a subject and a verb and expresses a complete thought. A phrase, on the other hand, is a group of words that does not express a complete thought, even if it is a long group of words. Use sentences, not phrases, to express main ideas.

The left column (on page 254) gives examples of phrases that could be used as topics. None of the items in this column could be used as main ideas because they are not complete sentences. The right column contains sentences that *could* be used to express main ideas because they are complete sentences. (Notice that in each case, the topic is part of the complete sentence.)

(continued on next page)

Could *Not* Be Used as a Formulated Main Idea (because it is a phrase)	Could Be Used as a Formulated Main Idea (because it is a complete sentence)
my cell phone	My cell phone was stolen.
my new cell phone	My new cell phone was stolen.
my new cell phone with a touch screen	My new cell phone with a touch screen was stolen.
my new cell phone with a touch screen and video camera	My new cell phone with a touch screen and video camera was stolen.
traveling by plane	Traveling by plane is the fastest way to travel to distant foreign countries.
fatality rates for passengers traveling by plane	Fatality rates for passengers traveling by plane are lower than fatality rates for passengers traveling by car.
why traveling by plane is the best way to go	There are several reasons why traveling by plane is the best way to go.
how to overcome fear of traveling by plane	Psychologists have several methods to teach people how to overcome fear of traveling by plane.

2. All formulated (implied) main idea sentences have certain characteristics. A formulated main idea must:

- Be a *complete sentence* that includes the *topic* of the paragraph.
- Express the *author's most important general point about the topic.* (In other words, if the formulated main idea sentence were placed at the beginning of the paragraph, the other sentences would explain, prove, or tell more about it.)
- *Make complete sense by itself* without the reader having to read the rest of the paragraph.

Here is an example of a sentence that would not be meaningful by itself, since the reader would not know whom "her" refers to: *Most historians consistently rank her among the most effective leaders of the 20th century.* Therefore, that sentence could not be a correctly formulated main idea sentence. On the other hand, this sentence could be a main idea sentence because it makes sense by itself: *Most historians consistently rank former British Prime Minister Margaret Thatcher among the most effective leaders of the 20th century.*

Remember also that an implied main idea sentence can be worded in various ways, as long as it meets the three requirements.

3. A longer passage often has an implied overall main idea that you must formulate, too.

Sometimes the reader must formulate an *overall* implied main idea that gives the general point of an entire selection. (A longer passage might consist of a section of a textbook chapter, a short reading selection, or an essay, for example.) The overall formulated main idea is a general statement or inference that is *based on* the main ideas of the selection. That is, the formulated overall main idea sentence summarizes or sums up the main ideas of the individual paragraphs in the selection, just as the main idea of each paragraph sums up the individual details in the paragraph. To be correct, a formulated overall main idea sentence must meet the same requirements as the formulated main idea of a paragraph.

EXERCISE 4

Could This Be a Formulated Main Idea Sentence?

The main idea must always be a *sentence;* it must also contain a *topic* and must make *complete sense* by itself. For example,

- There is no greater influence on children than their parents. *(Yes, this could be a main idea because the sentence makes complete sense by itself.)*
- There is no greater influence on children. *(No, this could not be a main idea sentence because we don't know what the influence is. The sentence does not make complete sense by itself.)*
- The greatest influence on children. *(No; this could not be a main idea sentence because it isn't a sentence.)*

Directions: For the items below, decide whether each could be a formulated main idea sentence. (All of them end with periods, although not all of them are sentences.) If an item contains a topic and makes complete sense by itself, write Y for Yes. If it does not, write N for No.

______ **1.** The benefits of a healthy diet.
______ **2.** There are several reasons HIV has not yet been eradicated.
______ **3.** It was the biggest scare New York City ever experienced.
______ **4.** The importance of art and music in children's lives.
______ **5.** It is the best treatment available for preventing a heart attack.
______ **6.** There are three major types.
______ **7.** Cell phones can be dangerous if people use them while driving.
______ **8.** They can be dangerous if people use them while driving.
______ **9.** Most of them are sleep deprived.
______ **10.** It was a crowning moment in Olympic history.
______ **11.** Whether the new plan will work.
______ **12.** Using a study schedule has several benefits.
______ **13.** The government should not adopt this policy.
______ **14.** How working too many hours affects college students' academic success.
______ **15.** Working too many hours affects college students' academic success.
______ **16.** He moved from Guatemala to the United States.
______ **17.** Gustavo moved from Guatemala to the United States.
______ **18.** It was the turning point of his life.
______ **19.** It was the turning point of Gustavo's life.
______ **20.** Gustavo's move from Guatemala was the turning point of his life.

Copyright © 2014 The McGraw-Hill Companies, Inc. All rights reserved.

CHAPTER 5 CHECKPOINT
Formulating an Implied Main Idea

Directions: Read each paragraph. Determine the topic and write it in the space provided. Then formulate its implied main idea and write it in the space beneath the paragraph.

1. This paragraph comes from a biology textbook.

Veins are thin-walled tubes divided into many separate chambers by vein valves. Excessive stretching occurs if veins are overfilled with blood. For example, if a person stands in one place for a long time, leg veins can't drain properly and blood pools in them. As the vein expands, vein valves become distended and fail to function. These two mechanisms cause *varicose veins*. The veins begin to bulge and become visible on the skin's surface.

Source: Adapted from Silvia Mader and Michael Windelspecht, *Human Biology*, 12th ed., p. 102. Copyright © 2012 by The McGraw-Hill Companies, Inc. Reprinted by permission of The McGraw-Hill Companies.

Topic: ______________________________

Implied main idea sentence: ______________________________

____

____

____

2. This paragraph comes from a geography textbook.

In hundreds and perhaps thousands of cases, police have used GPS (Global Positioning System) technology to catch killers, car thieves, drug dealers, sexual predators, burglars, and robbers, often without obtaining a warrant or court order. Does the covert use of GPS technology to track suspects violate the Fourth Amendment rights of protection against unreasonable searches and seizures? Should the government be required to obtain a search warrant by showing probable cause for connecting a cell phone user to a criminal activity? Existing laws do not provide clear or uniform guidelines. Some jurisdictions allow law enforcement agencies to track the location of cell phone users without search warrants; others do not.

Source: Adapted from Arthur Getis, Judith Getis, Mark Bjelland, and Jerome Fellmann, *Introduction to Geography*, 13th ed., p. 44. Copyright © 2011 by The McGraw-Hill Companies, Inc. Reprinted by permission of The McGraw-Hill Companies.

Topic: ______________________________

____

Implied main idea sentence: ______________________________

____

____

____

____

3. This paragraph comes from a textbook on adolescence.

Cliques are small groups of between 2 and 12 individuals—the average is about 5 or 6—generally of the same sex and, of course, the same age. A clique can be defined by common activities or simply by friendship. The importance of it, whatever its basis, is that it provides the main social context in which adolescents interact with one another. It is the social setting in which adolescents hang out, talk to each other, and form close friendships. The members feel they know each other well and appreciate each other more than people outside the clique do.

Source: Adapted from Laurence Steinberg, *Adolescence*, 9th ed., p. 157. Copyright © 2011 by The McGraw-Hill Companies, Inc. Reprinted by permission of The McGraw-Hill Companies.

Topic: ______________________________

____

____

Implied main idea sentence: ______________________________

____

____

4. This paragraph comes from a computing textbook.

How would you like to be turned down for a home loan because of an error in your credit history in an online database? This is much more common than you might expect. What if you could not find a job or were fired from a job because of an error in an electronic database giving you a serious criminal history? This can and has happened due to simple clerical errors. In one case, an arresting officer, while completing an arrest warrant, incorrectly recorded the Social Security number of a criminal. From that time forward, this arrest and the subsequent conviction became part of another person's electronic profile. This is an example of mistaken identity in which the electronic profile of one person is switched with another.

Source: Adapted from Timothy O'Leary and Linda O'Leary, *Computing Essentials 2013*, pp. 297–98. Copyright © 2013 by The McGraw-Hill Companies, Inc. Reprinted by permission of The McGraw-Hill Companies.

Topic: ______________________________

Implied main idea sentence: ______________________________

____

____

____

5. This paragraph is based on information in an American history textbook.

Nearly everyone has heard the phrase "a Horatio Alger story," but what does it mean? It is often used to describe someone who started with nothing but achieved great success and respect through virtue and hard work. In the last half of the

19th century, Alger wrote more than 100 inspirational adventure stories that featured impoverished boys in rags-to-riches tales. For example, a young boy, who might be an orphan, survives perilous life on the street by selling newspapers. Because of his energy and determination, he catches the eye of a wealthy man who gives him a chance to improve himself. Through honesty, charm, hard work, and aggressiveness, the boy rises in the world to become a successful man.

Source: Based on information in Alan Brinkley, *The Unfinished Nation: A Concise History of the American People*, 5th ed., p. 464. Copyright © 2008 by The McGraw-Hill Companies, Inc. Reprinted by permission of The McGraw-Hill Companies.

Topic: ______________________________

Implied main idea sentence: ______________________________

____

____

____

____

____

CHAPTER REVIEW CARDS

Directions: Complete the chapter review cards for Chapter 5 by answering the questions or following the directions on each card.

Implied Main Idea Sentences

1. What is the definition of an *implied main idea*? (See page 245.)

2. List three reasons it is important to understand and formulate the implied main idea of a paragraph. (See page 245.)

3. What question should you ask yourself in order to formulate the implied main idea of a paragraph? Be sure you write a *question.* (See page 245.)

Card 1 Chapter 5: Formulating an Implied Main Idea

Three Ways to Formulate an Implied Main Idea Sentence

Write out the three formulas for creating implied main idea sentences. (See pages 245–252.)

Formula 1:

Formula 2:

Formula 3:

What determines the formula you will use? (See page 245.)

Card 2 Chapter 5: Formulating an Implied Main Idea

When Formulating the Implied Main Idea, Keep in Mind . . .

What are the three requirements for a correctly formulated implied main idea sentence? (See page 254.)

1.

2.

3.

Card 3 Chapter 5: Formulating an Implied Main Idea

Review: An **implied main idea** is a sentence formulated by the reader that expresses the author's main point about the topic. *Formulated main ideas are always expressed as complete sentences.* As you learned in this chapter, there are three ways to formulate a main idea that has been implied:

- *Add an essential word or phrase to a sentence* in the paragraph that almost states the main idea.
- *Combine two sentences from the paragraph* into a single sentence that tells the complete main idea.
- *Summarize important ideas into one sentence* or *write one sentence that gives a general inference based on the details.*

EXAMPLE

This excerpt comes from a health textbook. Its topic is *walking.* To determine the implied main idea, read the paragraph and ask yourself, "What is the most important point the author wants me to *infer* about walking?"

Walking

Taking a long walk can help decrease anxiety and blood pressure. A brisk 10-minute walk can leave you feeling more relaxed and energetic for up to 2 hours. In a study, people who took three brisk 45-minute walks each week for 3 months reported fewer daily hassles and an increased sense of wellness.

Source: Adapted from Paul Insel and Walton Roth, *Connect Core Concepts in Health,* 12th ed., Brief, p. 36. Copyright © 2012 by McGraw-Hill, Inc. Reprinted by permission of The McGraw-Hill Companies.

The topic of this paragraph is *walking.*

b ______ What is the implied main idea of this paragraph?

a. Taking a long walk can help decrease anxiety and blood pressure.
b. Walking can make you feel better physically and mentally.
c. A brisk 10-minute walk can leave you feeling more relaxed and energetic.
d. The benefits of walking.

The correct answer is b. This formulated main idea sentence is a general sentence that tells the authors' most important point about walking: that it has several physical and mental benefits. Formula 3 was used, since it was necessary to write a general sentence that sums up the three details. Choices *a* and *c* are not correct because they are details. Also, they are stated in the paragraph, so neither can be the implied main idea. Choice *d* is incorrect: It is not a sentence; it does not tell the authors' most important point about walking and benefits—that it provides both physical and mental benefits.

Directions: Read each paragraph carefully. Then determine the implied main idea by asking yourself, "What is the most important point the author wants me to *infer* about the topic of this paragraph?" (Notice that you are told the topic of each paragraph.) Then select the answer choice that expresses the formulated main idea and write the letter in the space provided.

Copyright © 2014 The McGraw-Hill Companies, Inc. All rights reserved.

1. This paragraph comes from a biology textbook.

Fossils Tell a Story

Fossils are at least 10,000 years old. They include such items as pieces of bone and impressions of plants pressed into shale. Fossils also include insects trapped in tree resin (which we know as amber). They give a record of the history of life as recorded by remains from the past, and, over the last two centuries, paleontologists have studied them all over the world and have pieced together the story of past life.

Source: Adapted from Sylvia S. Mader, *Biology,* 8th ed., p. 292. Copyright © 2004 by The McGraw-Hill Companies, Inc. Reprinted by permission of The McGraw-Hill Companies.

The topic of this paragraph is *fossils.*

______ What is the implied main idea of this paragraph?

a. Fossils are at least 10,000 years old.

b. Fossils include such items as pieces of bone, impressions of plants pressed into shale, and insects trapped in tree resin.

c. Fossils give a record of the history of life as recorded by remains from the past, and, over the last two centuries, paleontologists have studied them all over the world and have pieced together the story of past life.

d. Fossils are at least 10,000 years old, and they include insects trapped in tree resin (amber).

2. This paragraph comes from an information technology textbook.

A typical email message has a *header*. It includes the address of the persons sending and receiving, and, optionally, anyone else who is to receive copies. The subject is a one-line description, used to present the topic of the message. There may be attachments, such as documents or image files. The *message,* the second basic element, comes next. Finally, the *signature* provides additional information about the sender. This information might include the sender's name, address, and telephone number.

Source: Adapted from Timothy O'Leary and Linda O'Leary, *Computing Essentials 2012: Making IT Work for You,* pp. 38–39. Copyright © 2012 by The McGraw-Hill Companies, Inc. Reprinted by permission of The McGraw-Hill Companies.

The topic of this paragraph is *basic elements of an e-mail message.*

______ What is the implied main idea of the paragraph?

a. There are three basic elements of an e-mail message: the header, the message, and the signature.

b. There may be attachments, such as documents or image files.

c. The *signature* provides additional information about the sender, and this information might include the sender's name, address, and telephone number.

d. A typical e-mail message has a *header* that includes the names of those sending and receiving, as well as a subject line.

3. This paragraph comes from an art appreciation textbook.

Conservation aims to slow the inevitable effects of time by keeping works of art in the safest possible conditions. It is one of the most important tasks of museums, where it is the job of highly trained specialists. Museums take many steps to prolong the life of objects in their care. Vulnerable objects are displayed in glass cases, where temperature and humidity can be carefully controlled. Works on paper are exhibited at low light-levels, and paintings are kept away from direct sunlight (and camera flashes). Each object is examined regularly for signs of deterioration.

Source: Mark Getlein, *Living with Art,* 9th ed., p. 105. Copyright © 2010 by The McGraw-Hill Companies, Inc. Reprinted by permission of The McGraw-Hill Companies.

The topic of this paragraph is *conservation.*

What is the implied main idea of the paragraph?

a. Conservation aims to slow the inevitable effects of time.

b. To protect paintings, museums must prevent visitors from using cameras with flashes.

c. Conservation aims to slow the inevitable effects of time by keeping works of art in the safest possible conditions, and it is one of the most important tasks of museums, where it is the job of highly trained specialists.

d. Museums take many steps to prolong the life of objects in their care.

4. This paragraph comes from an information technology textbook.

Nearly everyone has heard the term **wiki**, but exactly what is this strange sounding thing? It is a website specially designed to allow visitors to fill in missing information and correct inaccuracies. "Wiki" comes from the Hawaiian word for fast, which describes the simplicity of editing and publishing through wiki software. Wikis support collaborative writing in which there isn't a single expert author, but rather a community of interested people that builds knowledge over time. Perhaps the most famous example is *Wikipedia*, an online encyclopedia, written and edited by anyone who wants to contribute. It has millions of entries in more than 20 languages.

Source: Adapted from Timothy O'Leary and Linda O'Leary, *Computing Essentials 2012: Making IT Work for You*, p. 43. Copyright © 2012 by The McGraw-Hill Companies, Inc. Reprinted by permission of The McGraw-Hill Companies.

The topic of this paragraph is a *wiki.*

What is the implied main idea of the paragraph?

a. *Wikipedia* is an online encyclopedia that is written and edited by anyone who wants to contribute, and it has millions of entries in more than 20 languages.

b. Nearly everyone has heard the term wiki, but exactly what is this strange sounding thing?

c. A wiki is a website specially designed to allow visitors to fill in missing information and correct inaccuracies.

d. "Wiki" comes from the Hawaiian word for fast, which describes the simplicity of editing and publishing through wiki software.

5. This paragraph comes from a human development textbook.

Some children are more prosocial than others, but why is this so? Part of the explanation is their parenting and their environment. Children voluntarily engage in activities intended to help others because they have prosocial parents who model the behavior. The parents also show affection and follow positive discipline strategies. Another reason is siblings, peers, and teachers who model and reinforce prosocial behavior. Finally, traditional cultures in which people live in extended family groups and share work seem to instill prosocial values more than cultures that stress individual achievement.

Source: Adapted from Diane Papalia, Sally Olds, and Ruth Feldman, *Human Development*, 11th ed., pp. 274–75. Copyright © 2009 by The McGraw-Hill Companies, Inc. Reprinted by permission of The McGraw-Hill Companies.

The topic of this paragraph is *prosocial behavior in children.*

What is the implied main idea of the paragraph?

a. Some children are more prosocial than others, but why is this so?

b. There are several reasons some children are more prosocial than others.

c. Children voluntarily engage in activities intended to help others because they have prosocial parents.

d. Siblings, peers and teachers often model and reinforce prosocial behavior.

TEST YOUR UNDERSTANDING
Formulating Implied Main Ideas, Part 2

Review: An **implied main idea** is a sentence formulated by the reader that expresses the author's main point about the topic. *Formulated main ideas are always expressed as complete sentences.* Three ways to formulate the implied main idea are to:

- *Add an essential word or phrase to a sentence* in the paragraph that almost states the main idea.
- *Combine two sentences from the paragraph* into a single sentence that tells the complete main idea.
- *Summarize important ideas into one sentence* or *write one sentence that gives a general inference based on the details.*

EXAMPLE

This excerpt comes from a finance textbook. As you will see, its topic is *costs associated with renting.* To determine the implied main idea, read the paragraph and ask yourself, "What is the most important point the authors want me to *infer* about costs associated with renting?"

Costs Associated with Renting

As a renter, you will pay the monthly amount agreed to in your lease. However, there are other costs associated with renting. For many apartments, water is covered in the rent, but other utilities may not be covered. If you rent a house, the related living expenses are likely to include heat, electricity, water, and telephone.

Source: Adapted from Jack Kapoor, Les Dlabay, and Robert Hughes, *Personal Finance,* 10th ed., p. 290. Copyright © 2012 by The McGraw-Hill Companies, Inc. Reprinted by permission of The McGraw-Hill Companies.

Topic: costs of renting

Formulated main idea sentence: As a renter, you will pay the monthly amount agreed to in your lease; however, there are other costs associated with renting.

Explanation: The topic, *costs associated with renting,* appears in the second sentence. In the first sentence, the authors explain one expense (the monthly rent). In the second sentence, they mention that there are other costs as well. The complete main idea of this paragraph can be formulated by combining the first two sentences into a single sentence (Formula 2).

Directions: Read each paragraph and determine the topic by asking yourself, "Who or what is this paragraph about?" In the space provided, write the *word, name,* or *phrase* that tells the topic. Then determine the implied main idea by asking yourself, "What is the most important point the authors want me to *infer* about the topic?" Write the main idea by using one of the three formulas. (Remember that every paragraph has an implied main idea—there is no single sentence in the paragraph that is the main idea.) Your formulated main idea must:

- Be a complete sentence that includes the topic of the paragraph.
- Express the author's most important point about the topic.
- Make complete sense by itself without the reader's having to read the rest of the paragraph.

1. This paragraph comes from a health textbook.

Bias and Hate Crimes

One sad aspect of any society is how some segments of the majority treat certain people in the minority. Nowhere is this more violently pronounced than in **bias and hate crimes**. They are criminal acts directed at a person or group solely because of a specific characteristic, such as race, religion, sexual orientation, ethnic background, or some other difference. These crimes account for just 3 percent of all violent crimes, but increasingly, state and federal laws have been enacted to make bias and hate crimes serious offenses.

Source: Adapted from Wayne Payne, Dale Hahn, and Ellen Lucas, *Understanding Your Health,* 10th ed., pp. 540–41. Copyright © 2009 by The McGraw-Hill Companies, Inc. Reprinted by permission of The McGraw-Hill Companies.

Topic: ____

Formulated main idea sentence: ______________________________

____

____

____

2. This paragraph comes from a business textbook.

To stay competitive in today's global market, U.S. manufacturing companies maintain close relationships with suppliers. These companies practice continuous improvement, and they focus on quality. They save on costs through site selection and use of the Internet. They adopt new production processes, such as computer-integrated manufacturing (computer-aided design and computer-aided manufacturing).

Source: Adapted from William Nickels, James McHugh, and Susan McHugh, *Understanding Business,* 9th ed., pp. 252–53. Copyright © 2010 by The McGraw-Hill Companies, Inc. Reprinted by permission of The McGraw-Hill Companies.

Topic: ____

____

Formulated main idea sentence: ______________________________

____

____

3. This paragraph comes from a business textbook.

Google employees enjoy an energizing, creative work environment. The Googleplex is as vibrant on the inside as it is on the outside. Some Google employees use scooters or bicycles to travel to and from their workspaces, some accompanied by their dogs. "Googlers" share offices with up to four other people, working on couches and beanbag chairs, and bouncing ideas off one another. Upper managers work in the same environment as everyone else. There's also a "20% time initiative," which sets aside one day a week for Googlers to explore their passions and work on projects of their own choice. And don't forget about the gym, volleyball court, massage room, and pool tables, or the many styles of gourmet cuisine available at the Google Café. And all of these amenities are free to employees. It is no wonder they are so motivated and innovative.

Source: Adapted from William Nickels, James McHugh, and Susan McHugh, *Understanding Business,* 9th ed., pp. 254–55. Copyright © 2010 by The McGraw-Hill Companies, Inc. Reprinted by permission of The McGraw-Hill Companies.

Topic: ______________________________

Formulated main idea sentence: ______________________________

____

____

4. This paragraph comes from a music textbook.

Most people have heard of Frédéric Chopin. Called "the poet of the piano," no composer made the piano sound as beautiful as he did. He was the only great composer who wrote almost exclusively for the piano. Most of his pieces are short. Compared with other great composers, he wrote few works, but almost all of them remain in the pianist's repertoire. His music evokes a variety of moods, but his music is always elegant and graceful.

Source: Adapted from Roger Kamien, *Music: An Appreciation,* 10th ed., pp. 277–79. Copyright © 2011 by The McGraw-Hill Companies, Inc. Reprinted by permission of The McGraw-Hill Companies.

Topic: ______________________________

Formulated main idea sentence: ______________________________

____

____

5. This paragraph comes from a textbook on adolescence.

What has research discovered about *cyberbullying* among teens? One is that adolescents who engage in traditional bullying also engage in cyberbullying. Similarly, adolescents who are frequent victims of traditional bullying are also victims of electronic harassment over the Internet or via cell phones. Moreover, researchers have discovered that contrary to popular belief, most of the cyberbullying is not anonymous.

Source: Adapted from Laurence Steinberg, *Adolescence,* 9th ed., p. 176. Copyright © 2011 by The McGraw-Hill Companies, Inc. Reprinted by permission of The McGraw-Hill Companies.

Topic ______________________________

Formulated main idea sentence: ______________________________

____

____

SELECTION **5.1** **Art Appreciation**

Two Artistic Tributes: The Vietnam Memorial and the AIDS Quilt

From *Living with Art*
By Rita Gilbert

This classic selection is from Rita Gilbert's iconic art appreciation textbook. It explains why the Vietnam Memorial and the AIDS Quilt, despite their obvious differences, are two works of art that have a great deal in common.

The Vietnam Veterans Memorial, designed by an undergraduate student at Yale, draws more than 4 million visitors annually. It consists of two angled walls, each nearly 247 feet long. The tips of The Wall point toward the Washington Monument in one direction and the Lincoln Memorial on the other. The names of those who died in the Vietnam War are inscribed on the wall in chronological order, according to the date of the casualty within each day. It ranks number 10 on the American Institute of Architects' list of "America's Favorite Architecture." Visitors often leave notes and personal remembrances at The Wall. These are collected and catalogued.

The AIDS Quilt was first displayed in Washington, D.C., in 1987. It consisted of 1,920 panels and covered a space larger than a football field. The full quilt was displayed again in Washington four more times, the last being in 1996. Since then, sections continue to be lent to schools, libraries, and museums throughout the world to raise public awareness of AIDS and its impact on millions of lives.

A short section has been added at the end of the original selection. It provides additional and updated information about these two works of art.

1 There are two particular works of art that have much in common. Both commemorate death on a hideously large scale. Both are memorials to *unexpected* death—not the anticipated rest after a long life, but death coming prematurely, striking mostly the young. And both are meant to personalize each death among the many, to celebrate the individual life that was amid a mass tragedy.

2 The Vietnam Memorial in Washington, D.C., is the most-visited spot in the nation's capital. Completed in 1982, the memorial was designed by Maya Ying Lin, who was just twenty-two years old when her entry was selected from more than 1,400 submitted for this government commission.

3 When it was first unveiled to the public, its design was highly controversial. It is, after all, nothing more than two long walls of polished black granite, set into the earth so as to form a V. Many viewers felt "The Wall," as it has come to be called, flouted tradition, that it was not sufficiently respectful of those who fought the bloody Vietnam War. Many thought a statue of a heroic soldier marching off to battle would be more appropriate.

4 But public opinion changes. In time the American public came to accept this memorial—with its 58,000 names carved into the stark granite walls—as the most fitting tribute to those who died. Visitors who had no connection with the war, even young people who cannot remember the war, stand quietly before the roster of names—names on a mass tombstone. Many come to find a particular name, the name of a dead relative chiseled forever into the rock and not to be forgotten. They leave

Annotation Practice Exercises

Directions: For each exercise below, write the topic of the paragraph on the lines beside the paragraph. Then formulate a main idea sentence for the paragraph and write it on the lines provided. (Remember that you cannot use any sentence exactly as it appears in the paragraph: The annotation exercise paragraphs do not have stated main ideas.)

Practice Exercise

Topic of paragraph 3:

____

____

____

Formulate the *implied main idea* of this paragraph and write your sentence here:

____

____

Copyright © 2014 The McGraw-Hill Companies, Inc. All rights reserved.

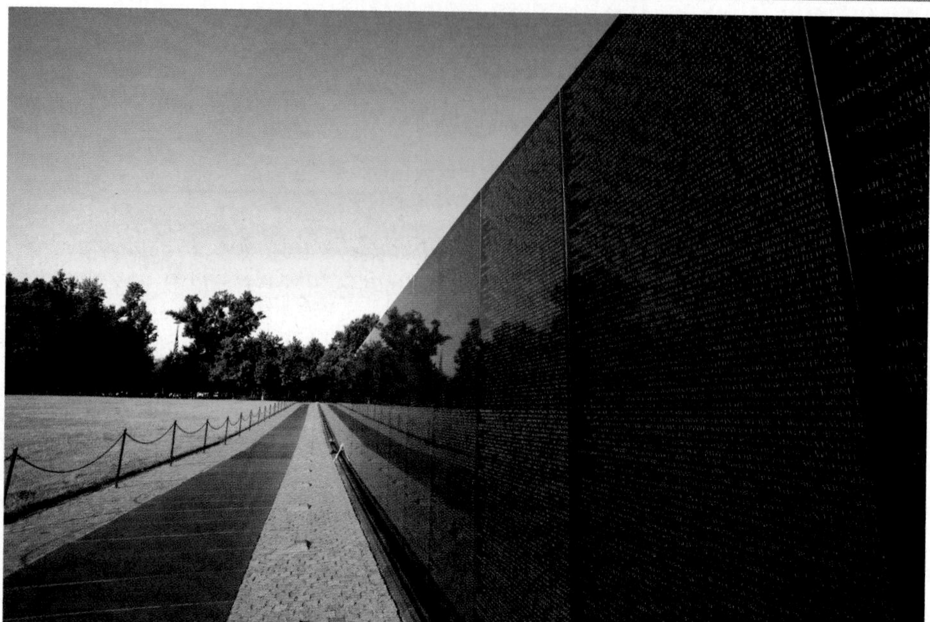

Maya Ying Lin, Vietnam Memorial, Washington, D.C., 1982. Black granite, length 492'.

flowers and poems, teddy bears and ribbons, photographs and letters, reminders of the past. Mostly the relatives touch The Wall, running fingers over the carved letters as though to touch once again the life that is gone.

5 The Vietnam War is long over; no more names will be added to the Wall. But another wave of unexpected death has swept the nation and the world, also striking primarily the young, and it will not pass soon. In the United States, San Francisco has been especially hard-hit by the epidemic, and it was there that the Names Project began. The purpose of the Names Project is simple: to memorialize as *individuals* those who have died from AIDS, to remember that each was a unique human being, though all are bound together by a common death. No better means could have been chosen than the AIDS Quilt.

6 The AIDS Quilt consists of hand-sewn panels. Each commemorates one person who has died from AIDS. Some of the 3 by 6 feet panels have a name and a photograph, others just initials or forms symbolizing that person's interests, abilities, and achievements. Each panel tells a story, a story ended too soon, therefore all the more precious in the telling.

7 The choice of a quilt format is especially meaningful. Historically, quilts have often told lifetime stories, incorporating bits of fabric from important life events. Quilts make us think of warmth and protection and nurturing. And quilting has traditionally been a community activity, so it is natural that a community should form among those grieving death from common illness.

8 Unlike the Vietnam Memorial, the AIDS Quilt cannot possibly remember all who have died. Only those whose friends or families chose to be involved in the Names Project are represented. Tragically, that number has already created a work of horrific scope. The illustration here shows The Quilt spread out in Washington, D.C., in October of 1996. By that time the quilt

Practice Exercise

Topic of paragraph 6:

Formulate the *implied main idea* of this paragraph:

The Names Project, Atlanta. *AIDS Memorial Quilt*. Displayed on the Mall; Washington, D.C., October 1996.

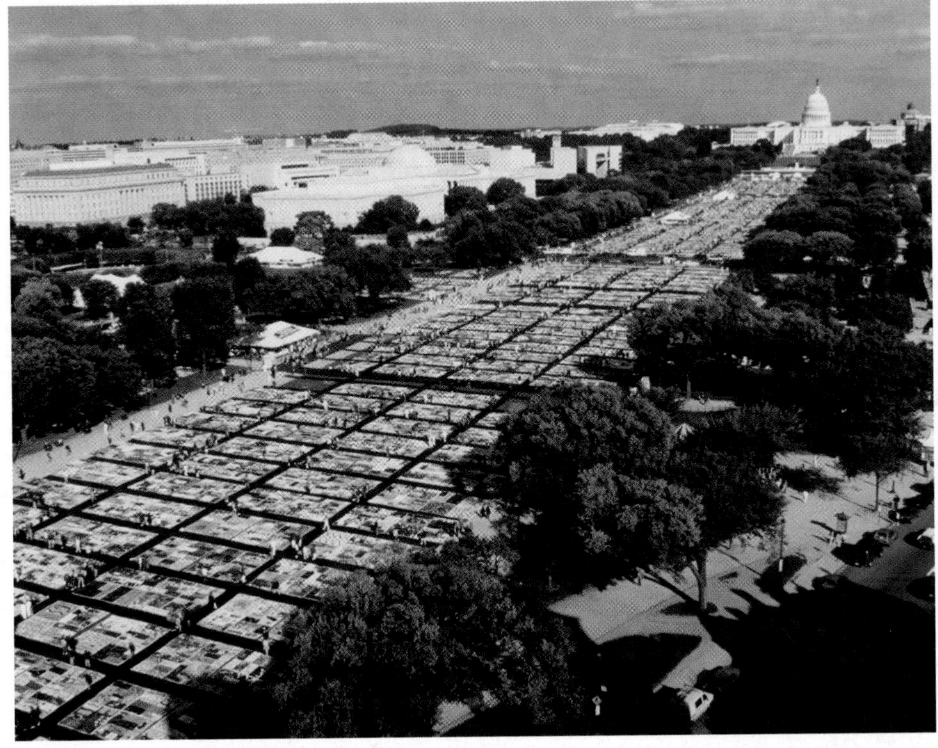

had grown to more than 37,000 panels and spread out on the Mall for nearly a mile from the U.S. Capitol to the Washington Monument.

9 As a work of art, the AIDS Quilt presents many contradictions. Few of its panels, individually, might be considered great art, yet the whole makes a powerful artistic statement. In its entirety, as we watch it grow, the work is incomparably sad, yet each panel is the celebration of a single life. Inevitably, The Quilt is a work in progress; it cannot be finished until the plague has been stopped. It is art for the dead—trying to make life bearable for the living.

Additional and Updated Information

10 Today there are 58,272 names inscribed on The Wall. The dedication on Panel 1 East of the Vietnam Memorial reads, "In honor of the men and women of the armed forces of the United States who served in the Vietnam War. The names of those who gave their lives and of those who remain missing are inscribed in the order they were taken from us." The dedication on panel 1 West reads, "Our nation honors the courage, sacrifice, and devotion to duty and country of its Vietnam veterans. This memorial was built with private contributions from the American people. November 11, 1982."[1]

11 Today, the AIDS Quilt has grown to more than 47,000 panels and contains more than 91,000 names. Because of its ever-increasing size, its last full display was in 1996. It is now so large

Practice Exercise

Topic of paragraph 11:

____

____

____

Copyright © 2014 The McGraw-Hill Companies, Inc. All rights reserved.

that if a viewer spent only one minute per panel, it would take more than 33 days to see the entire quilt! Laid end to end, the panels would extend more than 50 miles; placed next to each other, they would cover an area equivalent to 174 NCAA basketball courts. The weight of the quilt is more than 54 tons.[2]

12 Many people mistakenly believe the AIDS crisis is over or under control. Of all the sexually transmitted infections, HIV/AIDS poses the greatest health threat to the world. Currently, more than 56,000 people in the U.S. are infected each year, with a total of more than 1.1 million already infected. Worldwide, more than 33 million people are living with HIV. Infections among women and minorities are increasing disproportionately. There is no cure for AIDS, but treatments have improved. Early detection and treatment drastically reduces death rates. Most importantly, AIDS can be prevented.[3]

Formulate the *implied main idea sentence* of this paragraph:

____

____

____

____

____

____

____

Sources: Paragraphs 1–9: Adapted from Rita Gilbert, *Living with Art,* 5th ed., pp. 79–81. Copyright © 1998 by the McGraw-Hill Companies, Inc. Reprinted by permission of The McGraw-Hill Companies.

[1] http://thevirtualwall.org/VietnamVeteransMemorial; accessed 02 May 2012.

[2] www.aidsquilt.org; accessed 01 May 2012.

[3] Charles Corbin, Greg Welk, William Corbin, and Karen Welk, *Concepts of Fitness and Wellness,* 9th ed., pp. 441–43. Copyright © 2011 by The McGraw-Hill Companies, Inc. Reprinted by permission of The McGraw-Hill Companies.

Comprehension and Vocabulary Quiz

This quiz has four parts. Your instructor may assign some or all of them.

Comprehension

Directions: Use the information in the selection to answer each item below.

_____ **1.** The most significant difference between the Vietnam Memorial and the AIDS Quilt is that:

a. one is stationary and the other can be moved.
b. one memorial is complete and the other is not.
c. one is black and the other is in color.
d. an individual person designed one memorial and thousands of people designed the other.

_____ **2.** The Vietnam Memorial was:

a. completed in 1982 and has 1,400 names carved into its walls.
b. originally a statue of a heroic soldier marching off to battle.
c. completed in 1982 with 58,000 names carved on its granite walls.
d. constructed in 1996 and includes 37,000 panels.

_____ **3.** Each panel of the AIDS Quilt:

a. represents one person who has died from AIDS.
b. contains a name and a photograph.
c. gives the initials and achievements of a person who died from AIDS.
d. can be considered great art.

_____ **4.** The choice of a quilt format for the Names Project is especially meaningful because quilts:

a. remind us of death.
b. are like the stark granite walls of a memorial.
c. make us think of warmth, protection, and nurturing.
d. are powerful artistic statements that make life bearable.

_____ **5.** Both the AIDS Quilt and the Vietnam Memorial are meant to:

a. memorialize the lives of individuals.
b. record the names of everyone who died in the Vietnam War or who died from AIDS.
c. grow as the names of those who have died are added.
d. memorialize a tragic war and a terrible disease.

Vocabulary in Context

Directions: For each item below, use context clues to deduce the meaning of the *italicized* word.

_____ **6.** Both works of art *commemorate* death on a hideously large scale.

On Veterans Day, our city holds a ceremony to *commemorate* the sacrifices of those in the armed services who gave their lives for their country.

commemorate (kə mĕm′ ə rāt) means:

a. to serve as a remembrance of

b. to celebrate the victory of

c. to comment negatively upon

d. to announce prematurely

_______ **7.** Many viewers felt "The Wall," as it has come to be called, *flouted* tradition, that it was not sufficiently respectful of those who fought the bloody Vietnam War.

The man refused to put out his cigarette and was asked to leave because he *flouted* the restaurant's no-smoking rule.

flouted (flou′ təd) means:

a. established; created

b. showed disrespect; had contempt for

c. improved upon; made better

d. followed; abided by

_______ **8.** In time the American public came to accept this memorial—with its 58,000 names carved into the *stark* granite walls—as the most fitting tribute to those who had died.

The prison cell was *stark* and uncomfortable; the only furniture in it was a metal cot.

stark (stärk) means:

a. elaborate; ornate

b. colorful; cheerful

c. bare; plain

d. lonely

_______ **9.** In time the American public came to accept this memorial—with its 58,000 names carved into the stark granite walls—as the most *fitting* tribute to those who had died.

It is only *fitting* that those who work the hardest receive the greatest rewards.

fitting (fĭt′ ĭng) means:

a. proper; right

b. adjusted correctly

c. logical; reasonable

d. pertaining to luck

_______ **10.** In its entirety, as we watch it grow, the work is *incomparably* sad, yet each panel of the AIDS Quilt is the celebration of a single life.

Monet produced *incomparably* beautiful impressionistic paintings; no other painter can equal his handling of light.

incomparably (ĭn kŏm′ pər ə blē) means:

a. confusingly

b. incompletely

c. immeasurably

d. slightly

Word Structure

Directions: In the selection, you encountered the words **commemorate, memorial,** and **memorialize.** They contain the root ***mem,*** meaning "memory." In paragraph 1, *commemorate* means "to honor the memory (of a person or an event)." In paragraph 4, *memorial* refers to "a monument that hones the memory of a person or an event." In paragraph 5, *memorialize* means to "provide a memorial for" or "to commemorate." Use the meaning of ***mem*** and the list of prefixes on pages 72–73 to determine the meaning of each of the following words.

_____ **11.** Which of these would be a likely **remembrance** of a date you had with someone special?

a. a shoe
b. an embrace
c. a concert ticket stub
d. a book

_____ **12.** To **memorize** a poem means:

a. to commit it to memory.
b. to write it several times.
c. to say it aloud.
d. to interpret it correctly.

_____ **13.** If your boss sends you a **memorandum,** he or she sends you:

a. a certificate of achievement.
b. a financial report.
c. a written reminder.
d. computer software.

_____ **14.** If a former U.S. president writes his **memoir,** he writes:

a. a set of recommendations for the current president.
b. the history of the country.
c. an article on his political views.
d. recollections of his personal experiences.

_____ **15.** If your trip to Paris was **memorable,** it was:

a. taken within the last five years; recent.
b. highly unpleasant in some significant way.
c. won as a prize in a contest.
d. worth being remembered; remarkable.

Reading Skills Application

Directions: These items test your ability to *apply* certain reading skills. You may not have studied all the skills yet, so some items will serve as a preview.

_____ **16.** According to information in the selection, "The Wall":

a. will have no more names added to it.
b. is a memorial to a single life.
c. includes both names and photographs.
d. cannot be touched by visitors.

Copyright © 2014 The McGraw-Hill Companies, Inc. All rights reserved.

_______ **17.** The organization of the overall selection is a:

a. list.

b. cause-effect.

c. sequence.

d. comparison-contrast.

_______ **18.** Which of the following represents an opinion rather than a fact?

a. The AIDS Quilt consists of hand-sewn panels.

b. Each panel commemorates one person who has died from AIDS.

c. Some of the 3 by 6 feet panels have a name and a photograph, others just initials or forms symbolizing that person's interests, abilities, and achievements.

d. Each panel tells a story, a story of a life ended too soon, and therefore all the more precious in the telling.

_______ **19.** What is the meaning of *bound* as it is used in paragraph 5?

a. tied with a rope

b. linked

c. stitched together

d. forced

_______ **20.** Which of the following is the main idea of paragraph 7?

a. The choice of a quilt format is especially meaningful.

b. Historically, quilts have often told lifetime stories, incorporating bits of fabric from lifetime events.

c. Quilts make us think of warmth and protection and nurturing.

d. And quilting has traditionally been a community activity, so it is natural that a community should form among those grieving death from common illness.

SELECTION **5.1**

Art Appreciation

(continued)

Respond in Writing

Directions: Refer to the selection as needed to answer the essay-type questions below.

1. **Reacting to What You Have Read:** Have you or someone you know ever visited the Vietnam Memorial or seen panels of the AIDS Quilt displayed? Perhaps you have seen one or both on TV. Describe your reactions or those of the person you know who has seen either of these memorials. If you have not seen either in person, what is your reaction to the photos of them in the selection?

____

____

____

____

2. **Comprehending the Selection Further:** Of the two memorials you read about, which of them produces a stronger emotional response in you? Explain why.

3. **Overall Main Idea of the Selection:** In one sentence, tell what the author wants readers to understand about the Vietnam Memorial and the AIDS Quilt. (Be sure to include "Vietnam Memorial" and "the AIDS Quilt" in your overall main idea sentence.)

Internet Resources

Read More about It Online

Directions: To learn more about the topic of this selection, see the websites below or use the keywords **"Vietnam Memorial"** or **"AIDS Quilt"** with a search engine.

http://thevirtualwall.org
This site is sponsored by the Vietnam Veterans Memorial Fund and includes a "Virtual Wall" honoring Americans who lost their lives in the Vietnam War. You can post a remembrance, search for one, and view all past remembrances (approximately 270,000 as of May, 2012). You can also create and print a name rubbing of any name on The Wall. The site is in the process of trying to collect photos of all 58,272 veterans listed on The Wall.

www.encyclopedia.com/topic/Vietnam_Veterans_Memorial.aspx
Encyclopedia.com's website presents an excellent overview, interesting information, and links to YouTube videos related to The Wall. In addition, there are links to information about Maya Lin and a map of Vietnam.

www.aidsquilt.org
This website is sponsored by The Names Project Foundation, caretaker of the AIDS Memorial Quilt. Visitors to this site can view The Quilt and search for names of those memorialized on it.

SELECTION **5.2**

Management Information Systems

Companies Struggle with "Inside Jobs" and Outside Threats

From *Management Information Systems for the Information Age*

By Stephen Haag and Maeve Cummings

Everyone worries about the security of information stored on computers, especially businesses. So what can put this important information resource in jeopardy? Well, countless things. Hard disks can crash, computer parts can fail, hackers and crackers can gain access and do mischief, thieves engaged in industrial espionage can steal information, and disgruntled employees or associates can cause damage. The FBI estimates that computer sabotage costs businesses somewhere close to $10 billion every year. Companies are increasing their spending on Internet security software, a fact that Symantec Corporation can attest to. It is the largest exclusive developer of computer security software and has a market value of $19 billion, making it one of the most valuable software companies in the world. The excerpt that follows tells about computer security dangers that companies face, both from within their companies and from the outside.

Inside Jobs

1 Most press reports are about outside attacks on companies' computer systems. Actually, though, companies are in far more danger of losing money from employee misconduct than they are from outsiders. It's estimated that 75 percent of computer crime is perpetrated by insiders, although this is not a problem that's restricted to computer misuse. A 300-restaurant chain with 30 employees in each location loses, on average, $218 per employee.

2 But white-collar crime is where the big bucks are lost (see Figure 1). White-collar crime in general, from Fortune 100 firms to video stores to construction companies, accounts for about $400 billion in losses every year—$400 billion is $108 billion more than the whole federal defense budget—and information technology makes it much easier to accomplish and conceal the crime. Of all white-collar fraud, the biggest losses are those incurred by management misconduct. Manager theft of various kinds is about four times that of other employees. Take embezzlement, for example. The average cost of a non-managerial employee's theft is $60,000. When managerial employees are involved, it jumps to $250,000. The most astonishing aspect of this is that most insider fraud (up to two-thirds) is never reported to the legal authorities.

3 Computer-aided fraud includes the old standby crimes. These include vendor fraud (sending payment to a nonexistent vendor or payment for goods not delivered), writing payroll checks to fictitious employees, claiming expense reimbursements for costs never incurred, and so on. In addition, there are newer types of crimes. For example, these include stealing security codes, credit card numbers, and proprietary files. Intellectual property is one of the favorite targets of theft by insiders. In fact, the companies that make surveillance software say that employers are buying and installing the software not so much

Annotation Practice Exercises

Directions: For each exercise below, write the topic and the main idea of the paragraph on the lines beside the paragraph. Then formulate a main idea sentence for the paragraph and write it on the lines provided. (Remember that you cannot use a sentence exactly as it appears in the paragraph as your main idea sentence.)

Practice Exercise

Topic of paragraph 1:

____

____

Formulate the *implied main idea sentence* of this paragraph:

____

____

____

____

____

____

____

____

____

FIGURE 1
FIGURES ON FRAUD

Who's Committing Fraud

61%	Fraud committed by men
39%	Fraud committed by women
$250,000	Median loss from fraud committed by men
$102,000	Median loss from fraud committed by women
41%	Fraud committed by managers
39.5%	Fraud committed by employees
19.3%	Fraud committed by owners/executives

Source: 2006 ACFE Report to the Nation on Occupational Fraud

to monitor employees as to track how intellectual property, like product design sketches, schematics, and so on, is moving around the network.

4 Fraud examiners have a rule of thumb that in any group of employees, about 10 percent are completely honest, 10 percent will steal, and, for the remaining 80 percent, it will depend on circumstances. Most theft is committed by people who are strapped for cash, have access to funds that are poorly protected, and perceive a low risk of getting caught.

Outside Threats

5 In 2006, companies spent, on average, $5 million each to recover corporate data that was lost or stolen. That's 30 percent more than in 2005. The losses are the result of main problems such as someone breaking into their systems, malicious insider activity, malware like spyware and viruses, and the theft of USB devices, notebook computers, and flash memory cards. The average cost per record that was compromised was $140.

6 What do we know about threats from the outside? They are many and varied. Competitors could try to get your customer lists or the prototype for your new project. Cyber vandals could be joyriding in cyberspace looking for something interesting to see, steal, or destroy. You could become the victim of a generalized attack from a virus or worm, or could suffer a targeted attack like a denial-of-service attack. If you have something worth stealing or manipulating on your system, there could be people after that, too. For example, the online gambling industry is plagued by attacks where hackers have illicitly gained access to the servers that control the gambling, corrupting games to win millions of dollars. Exploiting well-known system weaknesses accounts for a large part of hacker damage, while only 5 percent results from breaking into systems in new ways.

7 The people who break into the computer systems of others are "hackers" (see Figure 2). Hackers are generally knowledgeable computer users who use their knowledge to invade other people's computers.

Practice Exercise

Topic of paragraph 3:

____

____

____

Formulate the *implied main idea sentence* of this paragraph:

____

____

____

____

____

____

Practice Exercise

Topic of paragraph 6:

____

____

Formulate the *implied main idea sentence* of this paragraph:

____

____

____

____

FIGURE 2
HACKER TYPES

- **White-hat hackers** find vulnerabilities in systems and plug the holes. They work at the request of the owners of the computer systems.
- **Black-hat hackers** break into other people's computer systems and may just took around, or they may steal credit card numbers or destroy information, or otherwise do damage.
- **Hacktivists** have philosophical and political reasons for breaking into systems. They often deface a Web site as a protest.
- **Script kiddies,** or script bunnies, find hacking code on the Internet and click-and-point their way into systems, to cause damage or spread viruses.
- **Crackers** are hackers for hire and are the hackers who engage in corporate espionage.
- **Cyberterrorists** are those who seek to cause harm to people or to destroy critical systems or information. They try to use the Internet as a weapon of mass destruction.

8 Some hackers do it for the fun of it. Others (called hacktivists) are motivated by a philosophical or political message they want to share. Still others (called crackers) are motivated by money: they are hired guns who illegally break in, usually to steal information, for a fee. The latter can be a very lucrative undertaking. Some highly skilled crackers charge up to $1 million per job. There are also "good guys," called white-hat hackers, who test the vulnerability of systems so that protective measures may be taken.

Practice Exercise

Topic of paragraph 8:

____

____

Formulate the *implied main idea sentence* of this paragraph:

____

____

____

____

Source: Adapted from Stephen Haag and Maeve Cummings, *Management Information Systems for the Information Age*, 8th ed., pp. 244–46. Copyright 2012 © by the McGraw-Hill Companies, Inc. Reprinted by permission of The McGraw-Hill Companies.

Copyright © 2014 The McGraw-Hill Companies, Inc. All rights reserved.

SELECTION 5.2

Management Information Systems

(continued)

Comprehension and Vocabulary Quiz

This quiz has several parts. Your instructor may assign some or all of them.

Comprehension

Directions: Use the information in the selection to answer each item below.

_______ **1.** The percent of computer crimes committed by employees is thought to be:

a. 10 percent.
b. 30 percent.
c. 75 percent.
d. 100 percent.

_______ **2.** Manager theft is:

a. half of that of employees.
b. twice that of employees.
c. three times that of employees.
d. four times that of employees.

_______ **3.** A favorite target of theft by insiders is:

a. nonexistent vendors.
b. fictitious employees.
c. security codes.
d. intellectual property.

_______ **4.** Which of the following is an example of a threat from the "outside"?

a. a customer list being stolen
b. a virus or worm
c. a denial-of-service attack
d. all of the above

_______ **5.** Hacktivists seek to:

a. exploit well-known system weaknesses.
b. share a philosophical or political message.
c. steal information for a fee.
d. test the vulnerability of systems.

Vocabulary in Context

Directions: For each item below, use context clues to deduce the meaning of the *italicized* word.

_______ **6.** It's estimated that 75 percent of computer crime is *perpetrated* by insiders, although this is not a problem that's restricted to computer misuse.

Wall Street money manager Bernie Madoff *perpetrated* the biggest financial scam in history, cheating investors out of billions of dollars.

perpetrated (pûr′pĭ trāt′əd) means:

a. ignored
b. committed
c. prevented
d. observed

_______ **7.** *White-collar crime* in general, from Fortune 100 firms to video stores to construction companies, accounts for about $400 billion in losses every year.

Commercial fraud, cheating consumers, insider stock trading, and embezzlement are examples of *white-collar crime.*

white-collar crime (hwīt′ kŏl′ ər krīm) means:

a. crime committed by people who do manual labor

b. crime committed by people who perform professional, managerial, or administrative work

c. crime committed by unemployed people

d. crime committed by people who work in the men's fashion industry

_______ **8.** These include vendor fraud (sending payment to a nonexistent *vendor* or payment for goods not delivered).

Mario bought a hot dog cart and became a successful street *vendor.*

vendor (vĕn′ dər) means:

a. customer

b. performer

c. company or person who sells something

d. company or person who buys something

_______ **9.** These include vendor fraud (sending payment to a nonexistent vendor or payment for goods not delivered), writing payroll checks to *fictitious* employees, claiming expense reimbursements for costs never incurred, and so on.

He tried to avoid arrest by giving the police officer a *fictitious* name.

fictitious (fĭk tĭsh′ əs) means:

a. imaginary; made-up

b. former; previous

c. unreliable

d. accurate

_______ **10.** There are also "good guys," called white-hat hackers, who test the *vulnerability* of systems so that protective measures may be taken.

The Secret Service's job is to minimize the president's *vulnerability* to those who would harm him.

vulnerability (vŭl′ nər ə bĭl′ ĭ tē) means:

a. ability to be attacked

b. concern about

c. interest in

d. strength against

Word Structure

Directions: In paragraph 2 of the selection, you encountered the word **involved.** It contains the root ***volv***, which means "to roll, twist, or turn." The word *involved* literally means to be "rolled up" in something—that is, to participate in it. Use the meaning of ***vol (volu)*** and the list of prefixes on pages 72–73 to determine the meaning of each of the following words.

Copyright © 2014 The McGraw-Hill Companies, Inc. All rights reserved.

_______ **11.** The Earth **revolves** around the sun. In other words, the Earth:

a. turns on its axis.
b. rolls around the sun.
c. moves uncontrollably.
d. rolls at an increasingly fast rate.

_______ **12.** If the role of president **devolves** to the vice president:

a. those two people argue over who will be president.
b. those two people share the power equally.
c. the duty or responsibility shifts to the vice president.
d. the president refuses to give the vice president any power.

_______ **13.** If an idea eventually **evolves** into a complete plan, it:

a. unrolls or develops gradually.
b. gets all twisted and confused.
c. rolls around in someone's head.
d. turns out to be a bad idea.

_______ **14.** A **convoluted** seashell has:

a. straight lines on it.
b. a strong outer layer.
c. overlapping coils.
d. sharp edges.

_______ **15.** To **revolt** against a government means to:

a. refuse to vote for it.
b. feel disgusted with it.
c. write negative articles about it.
d. turn against it and rebel.

Reading Skills Application

Directions: These items test your ability to *apply* certain reading skills. You may not have studied all the skills yet, so some items will serve as a preview.

_______ **16.** According to Figure 1, the greatest fraud losses are due to:

a. managers.
b. employees.
c. executives.
d. owners.

_______ **17.** Identify the relationship between these two sentences in paragraph 8: "Some hackers do it for the fun of it. Others (called hacktivists) are motivated by a philosophical or political message they want to share."

a. example
b. sequence
c. contrast
d. summary

_____ **18.** In paragraph 2 it says, "The most astonishing aspect of this is that most insider fraud (up to two-thirds) is never reported to the legal authorities." Does the statement represent a fact or an opinion?

a. fact

b. opinion

_____ **19.** In paragraph 3 it says, "Computer-aided fraud includes the old standby crimes. These include vendor fraud (sending payment to a nonexistent vendor or payment for goods not delivered), writing payroll checks to fictitious employees, claiming expense reimbursements for costs never incurred, and so on." What is the relationship between the two sentences?

a. The second sentence presents a contrast with something mentioned in the first sentence.

b. The second sentence presents a comparison with something in the first sentence.

c. The second sentence gives examples of something that is mentioned in the first sentence.

d. The second sentence continues a sequence begun in the first sentence.

_____ **20.** In paragraph 4 the phrase "strapped for cash" means:

a. robbery victims.

b. careful with their money.

c. short of money.

d. greedy.

SELECTION **5.2**

Management Information Systems

(continued)

Respond in Writing

Directions: Refer to the selection as needed to answer the essay-type questions below.

1. **Reacting to What You Have Read:** Do you think businesses and companies should be more concerned with security threats from insiders (employees) or with outside threats? Why?

____

____

____

____

____

____

____

2. **Comprehending the Selection Further:** The authors note several types of "inside crimes" and several types of "outsider threats." List at least four of each type.

____

____

3. **Overall Main Idea of the Selection:** In one sentence, tell what the authors want readers to understand about threats to companies. (Be sure to include "computer security threats" in your overall main idea sentence.)

Internet Resources

Read More about It Online

Directions: To learn more about the topic of this selection, see the websites below or use the keywords **"security threats from employees"** or **"hackers"** with a search engine.

www.eweek.com/c/a/Security/10-Ways-Your-Employees-Pose-a-Security-Risk-for-Your-Organization/
This brief, to-the-point slide show presents "10 Ways Your Employees Pose a Security Risk for Your Organization."

www.thecollaredsheep.com/a-security-threat-related-to-employee-behavior
In the article "A Security Threat Related to Employee Behavior," the author speaks specifically about threats from young employees and lists 11 things that can be done to manage security threats.

SELECTION **5.3** **Biology**

Avian Flu: A Coming Pandemic?

From *Biology*
By Sylvia Mader

"Avian" means "pertaining to birds." "Flu" is short for "influenza," an acute contagious viral infection that causes inflammation of the respiratory tract, fever, chills, muscular pain, weakness, exhaustion, and even collapse. "Avian flu" is another name for "bird flu."

According to the National Library of Medicine, "Birds, just like people, get the flu. Bird flu viruses infect birds, including chickens, other poultry, and wild birds such as ducks. Most bird flu viruses can only infect other birds. However, bird flu can pose health risks to people. Human infection is still very rare, but the virus that causes the infection in birds might change, or mutate, to more easily infect humans. This could lead to a pandemic, or a worldwide outbreak of the illness" (www.nlm.nih.gov/medlineplus/birdflu.html; accessed 27 April 2008).

That was in 2008. Where do things stand now? Medical Xpress reports: "Since late 2003, the H5N1 viruses have infected at least 600 humans, mostly in Asia, and killed more than half of the people infected. But the virus, which can be acquired through close contact with domestic fowl, does not easily transmit from human-to-human, a phenomenon that led some scientists to believe H5N1 posed little threat as a potential agent for a global flu pandemic." It goes on to say that new research indicates that the virus could acquire the ability to spread among humans at any time and become a pandemic.

Medical Xpress cites a report published in the journal Nature *(May 3, 2012). It gives the findings of University of Wisconsin at Madison flu researcher Yoshihiro Kawaoka: "H1N1 viruses remain a significant threat for humans as a potential pandemic flu strain. We have found [in laboratory research] that relatively few mutations enable this virus to transmit in mammals. These same mutations have the potential to occur in nature." Whether or not the H5N1 viruses currently circulating in the world can easily acquire the additional mutations needed to cause a pandemic is an open question, according to Kawaoka. "It is hard to predict," he says. "The additional mutations may emerge as the virus continues to circulate" (http://medicalxpress.com/news/2012-05-epic-debate-avian-flu-day.html; accessed 2 May 2012).*

In 2011, cases of avian flu in humans were reported in Egypt, Cambodia, Indonesia, and Bangladesh. Between January 1 and March 12, 2012, cases were reported in China, Egypt, Indonesia, Cambodia, Vietnam, and Bangladesh. The following selection explains more about this continuing global threat.

1 Imagine waking up one morning with a sore throat, slight fever, and achy muscles. After going to the doctor, you are diagnosed with a case of the flu. As you sit at home resting, you notice the latest news about the avian bird flu and you begin to worry, thinking it might be avian flu.

Jumping the Species Barrier

2 Birds can become infected by coming into contact with the saliva, feces, or mucus of another infected bird. Many forms of avian flu will cause mild or no symptoms in infected birds. However, some strains are producing a highly contagious and rapidly fatal disease.

3 Since 1997, a deadly strain of avian flu (H5N1) has been showing up in Asia. Vietnam, Cambodia, China, and several other Asian countries have experienced serious outbreaks of avian flu among their domesticated poultry (chicken, geese, and ducks).

Annotation Practice Exercises

Directions: For each exercise below, write the topic of the paragraph on the lines beside the paragraph. Then formulate a main idea sentence for the paragraph and write it on the lines provided. (Remember that you cannot use any sentence exactly as it appears in the paragraph: the annotation exercise paragraphs do not have stated main ideas.)

Practice Exercise

Topic of paragraph 2:

____

____

4 The ability of a virus to "jump the species" and infect humans is what concerns the scientific community. In Hong Kong, in 1997, the virus was discovered in several people who had been in close contact with infected birds. Six of the infected people died. In early February 2006, the confirmed death toll as a result of avian flu was 103 people. The lethal strain of bird flu has killed approximately one-third of the people that have been infected.

Formulate the *implied main idea* of this paragraph:

Possibility of a Pandemic

5 There is a growing concern among the scientific community that the bird flu could merge with a human flu virus to create a new hybrid virus. This new virus could be highly infectious, fatal, and easily transmitted from person to person. Rapid travel between countries would enable people to spread the flu virus across the globe at an unprecedented rate, triggering a global pandemic (a disease that occurs worldwide).

6 There are two possibilities for the avian flu virus and human flu virus to merge and become a hybrid virus. The first possibility is when a human is infected with the human flu and then comes into contact with the avian flu. The two viruses could meet in the person's body and swap genes with each other. If the new hybrid virus has the avian flu gene for lethality and the human flu genes that allow it to be passed from person to person, a pandemic could be the result. The second possibility is if the two viruses infect a different host species and swap their genes in that host species. Pigs are seen as the potential alternate host species because they are susceptible to both the avian and human flu virus. If a new hybrid virus forms in the pigs, it could easily be passed back to human farmers who come in contact with infected pigs.

7 In January 2005, the first case of human-to-human transmission of avian flu was recorded. The woman contracted the virus from her sick daughter, and both women died from the avian flu. Every time it jumps from a bird to a person, the risk of a hybrid virus increases.

Practice Exercise

Topic of paragraph 3:

Formulate the *implied main idea* of this paragraph:

Practice Exercise

Topic of paragraph 7:

Formulate the *implied main idea* of this paragraph:

Actions Taken

8 Currently, there are no known vaccinations that work against the bird flu. Several drugs are being trialed and have produced mixed results. Scientists are racing to find a potential vaccination. However, they face the challenge of dealing with a virus that is constantly evolving.

9 In countries that have been affected by the avian flu, governments have begun programs to remove the infected and potentially infected birds. In Asia, farmers were compelled to kill millions of domesticated birds in an attempt to control the spread of the virus. It is hoped that eliminating the birds will contain the virus and decrease the potential of spreading. The containment efforts by the infected Asian countries have been somewhat successful at keeping the virus from spreading among domesticated livestock.

10 Preventing the spread of the avian flu virus among wild waterfowl as they migrate across the globe is a major problem. As of February 2006, confirmations of the deadly strain of avian flu in waterfowl have been reported in Asia, Africa, the Middle East, and Europe. It is only a matter of time before it reaches the United States and Central and South America.

Practice Exercise

Topic of paragraph 8:

____

____

Formulate the *implied main idea* of this paragraph:

____

____

____

____

____

____

____

____

____

____

____

____

Practice Exercise

Topic of paragraph 10:

____

____

Formulate the *implied main idea* of this paragraph:

____

____

____

____

____

____

____

____

____

____

Source: Adapted from Sylvia Mader, *Human Biology*, 10th ed., p. 125. Copyright © 2008 by The McGraw-Hill Companies, Inc. Reprinted by permission of The McGraw-Hill Companies.

Copyright © 2014 The McGraw-Hill Companies, Inc. All rights reserved.

SELECTION **5.3**

Biology

(continued)

Comprehension and Vocabulary Quiz

This quiz has four parts. Your instructor may assign some or all of them.

Comprehension

Directions: Use the information in the selection to answer each item below.

_______ **1.** Since 1997, birds infected with avian flu have been showing up in:

a. the United States.
b. Asia.
c. Europe.
d. South and Central America.

_______ **2.** Infected migratory waterfowl pose a special problem in the spread of avian flu because:

a. humans often consume them for food and become infected.
b. they migrate across the globe.
c. other animals can eat them for food and become infected.
d. all of the above

_______ **3.** One reason scientists are finding it difficult to develop a vaccine against avian flu is:

a. governments of some countries refuse to participate.
b. there is no way to track where the cases are likely to occur.
c. the avian flu virus has a hybrid nature.
d. the virus keeps changing.

_______ **4.** Pigs are a potential host species for a hybrid virus because:

a. they can contract both avian flu virus and the human flu virus.
b. H5N1 is a fatal virus.
c. other animals could eat infected pigs.
d. farmers often come in contact with pigs.

_______ **5.** Human-to-human transmission of the avian virus:

a. is predicted not to occur.
b. has not yet occurred.
c. has not yet occurred, but it is only a matter of time until it occurs.
d. has already occurred.

Vocabulary in Context

Directions: For each item below, use context clues to deduce the meaning of the *italicized* word.

_______ **6.** The ability of a virus to "jump the *species*" and infect humans is what concerns the scientific community.

Zoologists believe they may have discovered a new *species* of lizards that is similar to one that disappeared a few years ago.

species (spē′ shēz) means:

a. a group of organisms that has become extinct

b. a high barrier or obstruction

c. a group of organisms that resemble one another and are capable of breeding with one another

d. a group of organisms capable of moving from one group to another

_______ **7.** The *lethal* strain of bird flu has killed approximately one-third of the people that have been infected.

Because many household cleaning products contain *lethal* chemicals, parents should keep them away from young children.

lethal (lē′ thəl) means:

a. unusual

b. colorful

c. tempting

d. deadly

_______ **8.** The lethal *strain* of bird flu has killed approximately one-third of the people that have been infected.

The scientists announced that they had developed a superior *strain* of corn that resists insects and disease.

strain (strān) means:

a. a physical injury resulting from excessive tension, effort, or use

b. organisms of the same species that have distinctive characteristics but are not considered a separate variety

c. extreme effort or work

d. the act of pulling or stretching tight

_______ **9.** Rapid travel between countries would enable people to spread the flu virus across the globe at an *unprecedented* rate, triggering a global pandemic (a disease that occurs worldwide).

The hospital was delighted with the *unprecedented* donation; it has never before received such a large donation.

unprecedented (ŭn prĕs′ ĭ dĕn tĭd) means:

a. having no earlier equivalent; unmatched

b. unacceptable; undesirable

c. gradually increasing

d. not capable of being understood; confusing

_______ **10.** It is hoped that eliminating the birds will *contain* the virus and decrease the potential of spreading.

To *contain* the measles outbreak, the elementary school canceled classes for a week.

contain (kən tān′) means:

a. to halt the spread or development of

b. to enclose within a larger object

c. to increase the scope of
d. to monitor by observing closely

Word Structure

Directions: In paragraph 9 of the selection, you encountered the word **compelled.** It contains the root ***pel***, which means to "to push," "drive," or "thrust." The word *compelled* literally means pushed to do something, or in other words, forced to do it. Use the meaning of ***pel*** and the list of prefixes on pages 72–73 to determine the meaning of each of the following words.

_______ **11.** A **propeller** is a device that:
a. thrusts a vehicle backward.
b. thrusts airplanes and boats forward.
c. brings an airplane or a boat to a gradual halt.
d. pushes a vehicle faster and faster.

_______ **12.** If the wind **dispels** the clouds, it:
a. drives or scatters them away.
b. causes them to form unusual shapes.
c. makes them look fluffy.
d. gives them a pink tinge.

_______ **13.** If a student is **expelled** from school, he or she is:
a. asked to wait outside.
b. driven out or forced to leave.
c. given a serious warning
d. recognized for excellence.

_______ **14.** If your conscience **impels** you to tell the truth, it:
a. prevents you from being truthful.
b. makes you unable to distinguish the truth.
c. blurs the truth.
d. drives you to tell the truth.

_______ **15.** A spray that **repels** mosquitoes:
a. has a pleasant scent.
b. prevents mosquitoes from breeding.
c. kills mosquitoes.
d. drives mosquitoes away.

Reading Skills Application

Directions: These items test your ability to *apply* certain reading skills. You may not have studied all the skills yet, so some items will serve as a preview.

_______ **16.** Which of the following is the meaning of *triggering* as it is used in paragraph 5?
a. preventing
b. causing
c. slowing
d. stopping

_______ **17.** Which pattern is used to organize the information in paragraph 6?

a. list

b. sequence

c. definition

d. comparison

_______ **18.** The author's primary purpose in writing this selection is to:

a. persuade readers to pressure the government to deal with avian flu.

b. instruct readers how they can avoid getting avian flu.

c. inform readers about avian flu and the threat it poses.

d. convince readers that avian flu is a serious problem in the United States today.

_______ **19.** Which of the following represents the main idea of paragraph 6?

a. There are two possibilities for the avian flu virus and human flu virus to merge and become a hybrid virus.

b. The two viruses could meet in the person's body and swap genes with each other.

c. The second possibility is if the two viruses infect a different host species and swap their genes in that host species.

d. Pigs are seen as the potential alternate host species because they are susceptible to both the avian and human flu virus.

_______ **20.** Which of the following represents an opinion rather than a fact?

a. In countries that have been affected by the avian flu, governments have begun programs to remove the infected and potentially infected birds.

b. In Asia, millions of domesticated birds have been killed in an attempt to control the spread of the virus.

c. It is hoped that eliminating the birds will contain the virus and decrease the potential of spreading.

d. The containment efforts by the infected Asian countries have been somewhat successful at keeping the virus from spreading among domesticated livestock.

Copyright © 2014 The McGraw-Hill Companies, Inc. All rights reserved.

Respond in Writing

Directions: Refer to the selection as needed to answer the essay-type questions below.

1. **Reacting to What You Have Read:** How much did you know about the avian flu before reading this selection? What steps do you think the government should take to deal with the threat of avian flu in this country?

2. **Comprehending the Selection Further:** The author notes several reasons avian flu presents an unusually dangerous, worldwide threat. List at least five reasons this disease is so potentially devastating.

3. **Overall Main Idea of the Selection:** In one sentence, tell what the authors want readers to understand about the avian flu. (Be sure to include "avian flu" in your overall main idea sentence.)

____

____

____

____

____

____

____

Read More about It Online

Internet Resources

Directions: To learn more about the topic of this selection, see the website below or use the keywords **"avian flu"** or **"bird flu"** with a search engine.

www.cdc.gov/flu/avianflu
The government's Centers for Disease Control website has facts about avian flu, infection in humans, and the current situation, as well as information about the virus, its spread, and its prevention.

Copyright © 2014 The McGraw-Hill Companies, Inc. All rights reserved.

CHAPTER 6

Identifying Supporting Details

LEARNING OBJECTIVES

In this chapter you will learn the answers to these questions:

- What are supporting details, and why is it important to be able to identify them?
- What is the method for identifying supporting details?
- What is the difference between major and minor details?

CHAPTER CONTENTS

NEW INFORMATION AND SKILLS

WHAT ARE SUPPORTING DETAILS, AND WHY ARE THEY IMPORTANT?

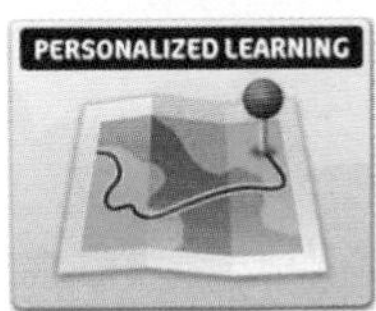

supporting details

Additional information in the paragraph that helps you understand the main idea completely.

Supporting details are also known simply as *support* or *details*.

A paragraph consists of a topic, a main idea, and supporting details. The topic and the main idea are essential to understanding the paragraph, of course, but it is the ***supporting details*** that provide the additional information that helps you understand the main idea *completely*.

Do not confuse a paragraph's supporting details with its main idea. Supporting details are *related* to the main idea, but they are not the same thing. Supporting details provide *specific* information (such as examples, descriptions, and explanations), whereas the main idea expresses the author's most important *general* point. Supporting details consist of names, dates, places, statistics, results of research studies, and other information that explains the main idea further or illustrates it by giving examples.

Every detail in a paragraph supports the main idea. However, some details are more important than others. The more important details are referred to as "primary details" because they relate *directly* to (support or explain) the main idea. Some details explain other details or give less important examples. These less important details are referred to as "minor details" or "secondary details." Read the following paragraph. The main idea is the first sentence. The three primary details are italicized. The other details are secondary details that explain these more important details.

> Older workers and younger workers tend to have very different attitudes toward their jobs. *Older workers are more committed to their jobs than younger workers.* For example, older workers will more often go beyond the job requirements when a situation requires it. They will stay later or carry out extra responsibilities. *Older workers also tend to exhibit less job turnover than younger workers.* It is not unusual to find older workers who have had the same job all of their adult lives. *Finally, older workers report a higher degree of job satisfaction than younger workers.* This may be due to the fact that they are more experienced and, hence, competent; that they have the respect that goes with seniority; and are paid better wages than younger employees who are just starting out.

Why is it important to identify supporting details? There are three reasons. First, the *details* explain or tell more about the main idea. When a paragraph has an implied main idea, the details help you formulate the main idea because the main idea is *based on* supporting details.

Second, listing the details after you read a textbook assignment can help you study more efficiently. There will be many instances when you will want to list details in order to learn and remember them. This is why you should include important details on the chapter review cards you prepare. Instructors often base test questions on supporting details—names, dates, places, and other pertinent information. Noting the details that explain, illustrate, or support the main idea of the paragraph makes it easier for you to:

- Mark your textbooks effectively.
- Make study notes or create review cards.
- Remember the material.

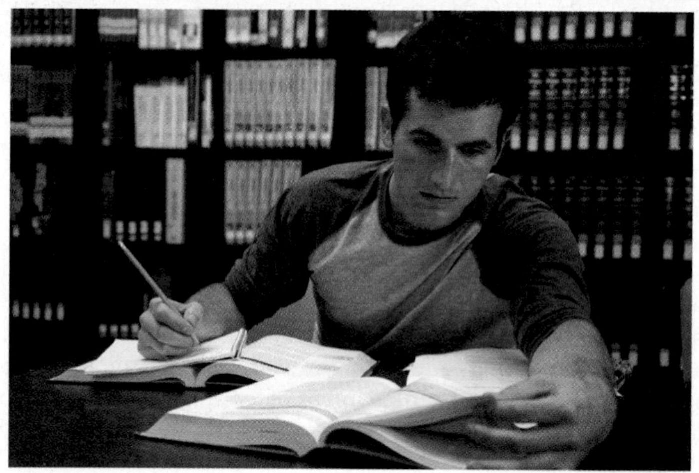

Identifying supporting details that explain, illustrate, or support the main idea of a paragraph makes it easier for you to mark your textbooks effectively, take notes as you read, and remember the material you are studying.

And third, identifying the details helps you grasp the pattern of organization of a paragraph. For example, authors may organize details as simple lists, as steps in a process (a sequence), as similarities and differences (comparisons and contrasts), or as reasons and results (causes and effects). (These patterns of organization will be discussed in Chapter 7.)

Along with determining the topic and the main idea, then, identifying supporting details helps you become a more successful reader and student.

WHAT IS THE METHOD FOR IDENTIFYING SUPPORTING DETAILS?

Comprehension Monitoring Question for Identifying Supporting Details

"What additional information does the author provide to help me understand the main idea completely?"

Once you have determined the stated main idea of a paragraph, you have also identified the supporting details: all the rest of the sentences in the paragraph! You can also ask yourself this comprehension monitoring question: "What additional information does the author provide to help me understand the main idea completely?" To determine the additional information you need to know, turn the main idea sentence into a question by using the word *who, what, where, when, why,* or *how.* For example, suppose the main idea is *In any club or organization, the treasurer has several important responsibilities.* You could change that into the question "*What are* the important responsibilities of the treasurer?" This question would lead you to the details that describe those responsibilities and, therefore, help you understand the main idea completely.

From time to time, you may need to turn a main idea sentence into a two-part question. For example, suppose you read a paragraph with the main idea "Spreadsheets can serve small-business owners many ways." This could be changed into the two-part question: "What are spreadsheets, and how can they serve small-business owners?"

Sometimes when you read a paragraph, it will become obvious that a list of details is about to be presented. For example, you would expect a list of details after phrases such as *There are many types of . . . , There are five reasons that . . . , Two kinds of . . . , There are several ways . . . ,* or *Some symptoms include . . . .*

Details are often introduced by signal words such as *for example, first, second, next, and, also, in addition,* and *moreover.* Authors also use clues such as numbers (1, 2, 3), letters *(a, b, c),* and bullets (• • •) when they present details in the form of a list. Be aware, however, that not every detail is introduced by a signal word or some other clue.

Here is an excerpt from a health textbook. Its topic is *date rape and post-traumatic stress syndrome.* The first sentence is the main idea: *Nearly all survivors of date rape seem to suffer from the effects of post-traumatic stress syndrome.* This main idea can be turned into the question "*What* are the effects of post-traumatic stress syndrome that date-rape survivors suffer?" Now read the paragraph to identify the details that answer this question.

> Nearly all survivors of date rape seem to suffer from post-traumatic stress syndrome. They can have anxiety, sleeplessness, eating disorders, and nightmares. Moreover, they can experience guilt concerning their own behavior, poor self-esteem, and the negative judgment of others. In addition, some individuals may require professional counseling.
>
> *Source:* Adapted from Wayne Payne, Dale Hahn, and Ellen Lucas, *Understanding Your Health,* 10th ed., p. 540. Copyright © 2009 by The McGraw-Hill Companies, Inc. Reprinted by permission of The McGraw-Hill Companies.

There are eight details that answer the question "What are the effects of post-traumatic stress syndrome that date-rape survivors suffer?" Notice that the details help you understand more about the main idea by explaining what the effects are. You can also see from the second and third sentences that a single sentence can contain more than one supporting detail. Here is a list of the effects of post-traumatic stress syndrome, the eight details in this paragraph:

- anxiety
- sleeplessness
- eating disorders
- nightmares
- guilt
- poor self-esteem
- negative judgment of others
- may require professional counseling

Stop and Annotate

Go back to the previous textbook excerpt. Locate the eight supporting details and number them with a small ①, ②, ③, ④, etc.

Underline or highlight the signal words *and, Moreover,* and *In addition.*

Notice how clearly the details stand out when they are listed on separate lines and identified with bullets. Since you are responsible for understanding the details in textbooks, you may find it helpful to list them this way in your notes and on review cards.

Or you may prefer, after you have read a paragraph, to go back and insert a number next to each detail. Numbering the details is helpful for at least three reasons. First, it helps you locate all the details. Second, it helps you remember how many details there were. Third, it prevents you from overmarking the paragraph by underlining or highlighting too much.

Here is another example. Its topic is *a person's religion.* The first sentence states the main idea: *Religion can influence a person's thinking on many matters.* To identify

Copyright © 2014 The McGraw-Hill Companies, Inc. All rights reserved.

the details, turn this main idea sentence into the question "*How* does religion influence a person's thinking on many matters?" Now read the paragraph to find the answer to this question.

> Religion can influence a person's thinking on many matters. Mormons are committed to self-reliance, church and family. To them, church and family, not the government, should aid those who are experiencing financial difficulties. For this reason, they tend not to favor the existing welfare system. For thousands of years, Jews have valued learning and education, and therefore are more likely to support tax increases that benefit colleges and universities. Catholics generally oppose abortion and most forms of birth control. Hindus believe in reincarnation, and for that reason are least likely to rush into any decision. And Quakers are pacifists who favor human rights and oppose violence of all types.
>
> *Source:* Larry Samovar and Jack Mills, *Oral Communication: Speaking across Cultures,* 10th ed. (Boston: McGraw-Hill, 1998), p. 256. Reprinted by permission of Oxford University Press, Inc.

Stop and Annotate

Go back to the textbook excerpt. Locate the five supporting details and number them with a small ①, ②, ③, ④, and ⑤.

Underline or highlight the signal word *And* that helped you identify the last detail.

The details of this paragraph are examples that answer the question "How does religion influence a person's thinking on many matters?" Notice that even though there are five details in this paragraph, only one signal word is used (the word *And* is used to introduce this last detail). Here is a list of the five details (the examples) in this paragraph:

- Mormons—committed to self-reliance, church and family
- Jews—value learning and education; likely to support taxes for education
- Catholics—oppose abortion and most birth control
- Hindus—believe in reincarnation, so least likely to rush into any decision
- Quakers—pacifists who favor human rights and oppose violence of all types

paraphrasing

Restating an author's material in your own words.

In the list above, the details are not written exactly as they appear in the paragraph. When you list details, it is not necessary to use the exact words of the paragraph or write complete sentences. Rather, you will want to restate them briefly in your own words. Restating someone else's material in your own words is called **paraphrasing.** For example, you could paraphrase the items above in this even briefer way and list them on a study card with a question like this:

How can religion influence a person's thinking?
• Mormons—committed to self-reliance, church and family
• Jews—value learning and education; likely to support taxes for it
• Catholics—oppose abortion and most birth control
• Hindus—believe in reincarnation; least likely to rush into decisions
• Quakers—favor human rights; against all violence

EXERCISE 1

This paragraph comes from a science textbook.

The primary goal of a sustainable community is to protect and enhance the environment. Sustainable communities achieve this by using energy, water, and other natural resources efficiently and with care. Sustainable communities also minimize waste, then reuse or recover it through recycling, composting, or energy production. Another characteristic of a sustainable community is that it limits pollution to levels that do not damage natural systems. A sustainable community values and protects the diversity of nature.

Source: Adapted from Eldon Enger and Bradley Smith, *Environmental Science: A Study of Interrelationships*, 12th ed., p. 282. Copyright © 2010 by The McGraw-Hill Companies, Inc. Reprinted by permission of The McGraw-Hill Companies.

List the four supporting details about sustainable communities. Use a bullet for each detail and start each detail on a new line.

____

____

____

____

____

____

____

____

____

____

____

____

There are other ways to organize details besides listing them. Sometimes it is more helpful to organize them as numbered steps in a process (a sequence), in a table or chart that shows similarities and differences (comparisons and contrasts) or reasons and results (causes and effects). These patterns of organization are presented in Chapter 7. Also, you may discover that in some cases you prefer to include details in your study notes in the form of an outline or a study map. These techniques are presented in Chapter 11.

MAJOR AND MINOR DETAILS

major details

Details that directly support the main idea.

Major details are also known as *primary details.*

All the details in a paragraph ultimately support the main idea by explaining, illustrating, or proving it. In each example presented earlier, all the details *directly* supported (explained) the main idea. Details that directly support the main idea are called **major details** (or *primary details*). However, there are also paragraphs in which some details support or explain *other details.* These are called **minor details** (or *secondary details*).

Copyright © 2014 The McGraw-Hill Companies, Inc. All rights reserved.

The following diagram shows the relationship between the main idea, major details, and minor details.

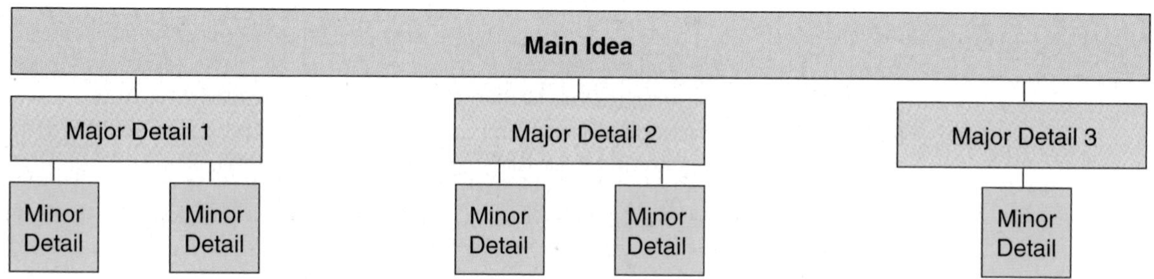

minor details

Details that support other details.

Minor details are also known as *secondary details.*

The simple paragraph below illustrates major and minor details. Its topic is *uses of pepper.* Its stated main idea is the first sentence, *Throughout history, pepper has been used many different ways besides as a way to season food.* There are three major details that explain important uses of pepper. The other sentences are minor details that explain the major details.

> Throughout history, pepper has had many other uses besides as a way to season food. Pepper was also one of the first ways of preserving meat. During the Crusades pepper was used to preserve sausages. Pepper is still used to preserve meat today. Pepper has also been used as a medicine. In medieval times peppercorns were prescribed to cure aches and pains. Native Americans today use pepper to cure toothaches. Today, pepper is also used to control insects. For example, the French and Dutch use pepper to kill moths and to repel other insects.

The following diagram shows the relationship between the main idea and the major and minor details for this paragraph.

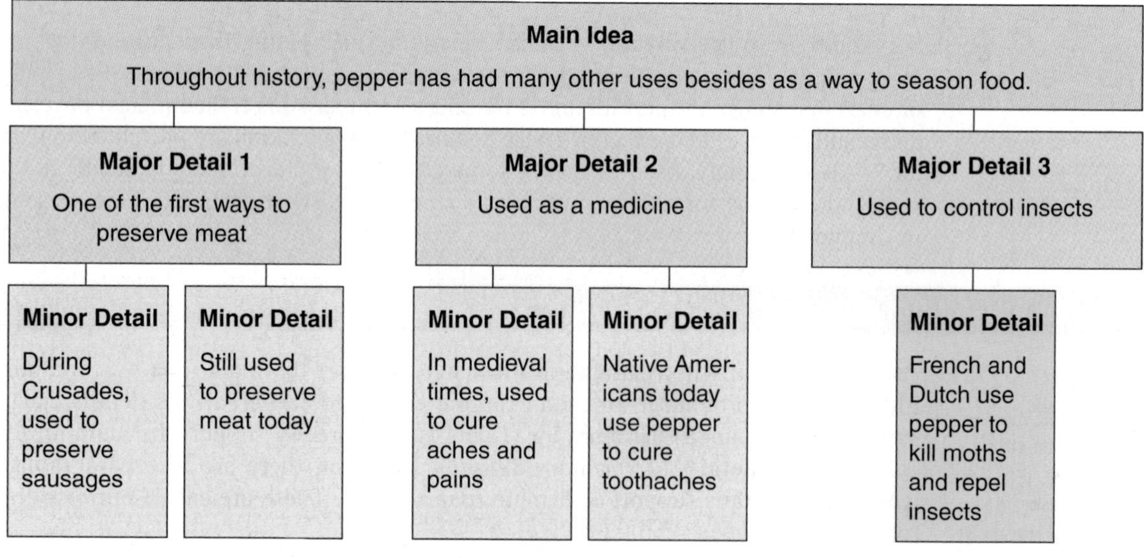

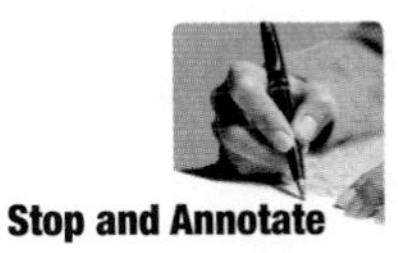

Stop and Annotate

Go back to the excerpt on page 304. Locate the three major details and number them with a small ①, ②, and ③.

Again, notice that only three details directly answer the main idea question, "How has pepper been used in different ways throughout history besides as a way to season food?" Therefore, those three are major details. The passage would make sense with only the main idea and those details. However, the author explains even more fully by giving examples of the three ways pepper is used. Therefore, those details, which explain other details, are minor details.

Remember, to identify the supporting details of a paragraph, ask yourself, "What *additional information* does the author provide to help me understand the main idea completely?" Change the main idea into a question; then look for the major details that answer the question. Be aware that the author may also include minor details. Don't spend too much time worrying about whether a detail is major or minor. The important thing is simply that you distinguish between the main idea and the details.

EXERCISE 2

This paragraph comes from a psychology textbook.

Parenting Styles and Social Development. Parents' child-rearing practices are critical in shaping their children's social competence, and—according to classic research by developmental psychologist Diana Baumrind—four main categories describe different parenting styles. Rigid and punitive, authoritarian parents value unquestioning obedience from their children. They have strict standards and discourage expressions of disagreement. Permissive parents give their children relaxed or inconsistent direction and, although warm, require little of them. In contrast, authoritative parents are firm, setting limits for their children. As the children get older, these parents try to reason and explain things to them. They also give clear goals and encourage their children's independence. Finally, uninvolved parents show little interest in their children. Emotionally detached, they view parenting as nothing more than providing food, clothing, and shelter for children. At their most extreme, uninvolved parents are guilty of neglect, a form of child abuse.

Source: Adapted from Robert S. Feldman, *Understanding Psychology*, 8th ed., pp. 419–20. Copyright © 2008 by The McGraw-Hill Companies, Inc. Reprinted by permission of The McGraw-Hill Companies.

Describe each of the four major supporting details.

- authoritarian parents: ______________________________

____

____

- permissive parents: ______________________________

____

____

- authoritative parents: ______________________________

____

____

- uninvolved parents: ______________________________

____

____

Copyright © 2014 The McGraw-Hill Companies, Inc. All rights reserved.

EXERCISE 3

This paragraph comes from an information technology textbook.

Microcomputers

Microcomputers are the most widely used and fastest-growing type of computer. There are several kinds of microcomputers. **Desktop computers** are small enough to fit on top of or alongside a desk yet are too big to carry around. An Apple iMac is a popular example of a desktop computer. **Notebook computers,** also known as *laptop computers*, are portable, lightweight, and fit into most briefcases. The Dell Inspiron and Sony Vaio are examples of notebook computers. A **tablet PC** is a type of notebook that accepts your handwriting. This input is digitized and converted to standardized text that can be further processed by programs such as word processors. Apple iPad, Motorola Zoom, and Samsung Galaxy are widely used tablet PCs. **Handheld computers** are the smallest kind of microcomputer and are designed to fit into the palm of one hand. Also known as *palm computers* or *personal digital assistants* (*PDAs*), these systems typically combine pen input, writing recognition, personal organizational tools, and communications abilities in a very small package. The Blackberry and the HP iPAQ are examples of handheld computers.

Source: Adapted from Timothy O'Leary and Linda O'Leary, *Computing Essentials 2013*, p. 11. Copyright © 2013 by The McGraw-Hill Companies, Inc. Reprinted by permission of The McGraw-Hill Companies.

List the four *major* supporting details, using a bullet for each *major* detail. Below each, list one or two *minor* details that give examples of it. Use a separate line for each major and minor detail.

____

____

____

____

____

____

____

____

____

____

____

____

____

____

____

OTHER THINGS TO KEEP IN MIND WHEN IDENTIFYING SUPPORTING DETAILS

Here are three other helpful things you should know about identifying supporting details:

1. **Watch for clues that indicate a list of details will follow. These include:**
   - Phrases such as *There are many types of . . . , Five reasons that . . . , Two kinds of . . . , There are several ways . . . ,* and *Some symptoms include . . . .*
   - Signal words such as *for example, first, second, next, and, also, in addition,* and *moreover.*
   - Items identified with numbers (1, 2, 3) and letters *(a, b, c).*
   - Lists with items identified with bullets (• • •).

   Remember, though, that not every detail will be introduced by signal words or other clues.
2. **Avoid overmarking your textbook by numbering the supporting details in a paragraph rather than highlighting or underlining them.**

   Numbering the details will make it easier for you to locate and recall them when you study. Of course, when the details are already presented as bulleted or numbered lists, you will not need to do anything more.
3. **Listing the details on separate lines in your study notes or on review cards can help you learn the information more efficiently.**

   Writing the details in your study notes or on review cards is one way to rehearse the material and transfer it into your long-term memory. It is especially helpful to write each detail *on a separate line.* That way, each detail stands out, making it easy to see how many there are. Listing paraphrased details below a question is an ideal format for study cards.

Copyright © 2014 The McGraw-Hill Companies, Inc. All rights reserved.

CHAPTER 6 CHECKPOINT
Identifying Supporting Details

Directions: Read each paragraph to determine the topic and the main idea. Then answer the question about the supporting details. Read the questions carefully. Sometimes you will be asked to distinguish the main idea from the details. Sometimes you will be asked to identify the *major supporting details* or the *mino*r supporting details.

1. This paragraph comes from an economics textbook.

A **patent** is the exclusive right of an inventor to use, or to allow another to use, her or his invention. Patents and patent laws aim to protect the inventor from rivals who would use the invention without having shared in the effort and expense of developing it. At the same time, patents provide the inventor with a monopoly position for the life of the patent. The world's nations have agreed on a uniform patent length of 20 years from the time of application. Patents have figured prominently in the growth of modern-day giants such as IBM, Pfizer, Kodak, Xerox, Intel, General Electric, and DuPont.

Source: Stanley Brue, Campbell McConnell, and Sean Flynn, *Essentials of Economics,* 2nd ed., pp. 182–83. Copyright © 2010 by The McGraw-Hill Companies, Inc. Reprinted by permission of The McGraw-Hill Companies.

_______ Which of the following are *supporting details*? Choose all that apply.

a. A *patent* is the exclusive right of an inventor to use, or to allow another to use, her or his invention.

b. Patents and patent laws aim to protect the inventor from rivals who would use the invention without having shared in the effort and expense of developing it.

c. At the same time, patents provide the inventor with a monopoly position for the life of the patent.

d. The world's nations have agreed on a uniform patent length of 20 years from the time of application.

e. Patents have figured prominently in the growth of modern-day giants such as IBM, Pfizer, Kodak, Xerox, Intel, General Electric, and DuPont.

2. This paragraph comes from a biology textbook.

Proteins have several important functions. Perhaps the most important proteins are enzymes, which have the key role in cells of lowering the energy required to initiate particular chemical reactions. Other proteins play structural roles. Cartilage, bones, and tendons all contain a structural protein called collagen. Keratin, another structural protein, forms hair, the horns of a rhinoceros, and feathers. Still other proteins act as chemical messengers within the brain and throughout the body.

Source: Adapted from George Johnson, *The Living World,* 7th ed., p. 149. Copyright © 2012 by The McGraw-Hill Companies, Inc. Reprinted by permission of The McGraw-Hill Companies.

_______ Which of the following are *major supporting details*? Choose all that apply.

a. Proteins have several important functions.

b. Perhaps the most important proteins are enzymes, which have the key role in cells of lowering the energy required to initiate particular chemical reactions.

c. Other proteins play structural roles.

d. Cartilage, bones, and tendons all contain a structural protein called collagen.

e. Keratin, another structural protein, forms hair, the horns of a rhinoceros, and feathers.

f. Still other proteins act as chemical messengers within the brain and throughout the body.

3. This paragraph comes from an information technology textbook.

Posting your résumé online for prospective employers to view is attractive because of its low (or zero) cost and wide reach, but it has some disadvantages. Certainly it might be a disadvantage if the employer who sees your posting happens to be the one you're currently working for. In addition, you have to be aware that you lose control over anything broadcast into cyberspace. You're putting your credentials out there for the whole world to see, and you need to be somewhat concerned about who might gain access to them.

Source: Brian Williams and Stacey Sawyer, *Using Information Technology*, Complete Version, 9th ed., pp. 12–13. Copyright © 2011 by The McGraw-Hill Companies, Inc. Reprinted by permission of The McGraw-Hill Companies.

______ Which of the following are *major supporting details*? Choose all that apply.

a. Posting your résumé online for prospective employers to view is attractive because of its low (or zero) cost and wide reach, but it has some disadvantages.

b. Certainly it might be a disadvantage if the employer who sees your posting happens to be the one you're currently working for.

c. In addition, you have to be aware that you lose control over anything broadcast into cyberspace.

d. You're putting your credentials out there for the whole world to see, and you need to be somewhat concerned about who might gain access to them.

4. This paragraph comes from a personal finance textbook.

Younger investors tend to invest a large percentage of their nest egg in growth-oriented investments. If their investments take a nosedive they have time to recover. On the other hand, older investors tend to be more conservative. They typically invest in government bonds, high quality corporate bonds, and very safe corporate stocks or mutual funds. In short, your age is a factor to consider when choosing an investment.

Source: Adapted from Jack Kapoor, Les Dlabay, and Robert Hughes, *Personal Finance*, 10th ed., p. 439. Copyright © 2012 by The McGraw-Hill Companies, Inc. Reprinted by permission of The McGraw-Hill Companies.

______ Which of the following are *minor supporting details*? Choose all that apply.

a. Younger investors tend to invest a large percentage of their nest egg in growth-oriented investments.

b. If their investments take a nosedive they have time to recover.

Copyright © 2014 The McGraw-Hill Companies, Inc. All rights reserved.

c. On the other hand, older investors tend to be more conservative.

d. They typically invest in government bonds, high quality corporate bonds, and very safe corporate stocks or mutual funds.

e. In short, your age is a factor to consider when choosing an investment.

5. This paragraph comes from an American history textbook.

Cities of the late–nineteenth century exhibited a ringed pattern. The poor, some immigrants, African Americans, and lower-class laborers moved into the slums of the central city. Curled around the slums was the "zone of emergence," an income-graded band of those "emerging" from poverty. It contained second-generation city dwellers, factory workers, skilled laborers, and professional mechanics. They lived in progressively better tenements and neater row houses as the distance from the center city increased. Farther out was the suburban fringe, home to the new class of white-collar managers and executives. They lived in larger houses with individual lots on neat, tree-lined streets.

Source: James Davidson, Brian DeLay, Christine Heyrman, Mark Lytle, and Mark Stoff, *Nation of Nations, Volume II: Since 1865*, 6th ed., p. 574. Copyright © 2008 by The McGraw-Hill Companies, Inc. Reprinted by permission of The McGraw-Hill Companies.

_______ Which of the following are *minor supporting details*? Choose all that apply.

a. Cities of the late–nineteenth century exhibited a ringed pattern.

b. The poor, some immigrants, African Americans, and lower-class laborers moved into the slums of the central city.

c. Curled around the slums was the "zone of emergence," an income-graded band of those "emerging" from poverty.

d. It contained second-generation city dwellers, factory workers, skilled laborers, and professional mechanics.

e. They lived in progressively better tenements and neater row houses as the distance from the center city increased.

f. Farther out was the suburban fringe, home to the new class of white-collar managers and executives.

g. They lived in larger houses with individual lots on neat, tree-lined streets.

Directions: Complete the chapter review cards for Chapter 6 by answering the questions or following the directions on each card.

Supporting Details

1. What is the definition of *supporting details*?

2. List three reasons why it is important to identify supporting details.

3. What question should you ask yourself to identify supporting details? Be sure you write a *question.*

Card 1 Chapter 6: Identifying Supporting Details

The Method for Identifying Supporting Details

1. What can be done to a main idea sentence of a paragraph to help you identify details that support it?

2. List some signal words and other clues an author may provide to help you identify a list of supporting details.

3. What is the difference between major and minor details?

Card 2 Chapter 6: Identifying Supporting Details

When Identifying Supporting Details, Keep in Mind . . .

Write the three things you should remember about identifying supporting details.

1.

2.

3.

Card 3 Chapter 6: Identifying Supporting Details

TEST YOUR UNDERSTANDING
Identifying Supporting Details, Part 1

Review: **Supporting details** provide additional information in the paragraph that helps you understand the main idea completely. They *explain, illustrate,* or *prove the main idea* of a paragraph. Supporting details can be written in your notes as short phrases, paraphrased, or written as complete sentences—whichever works best for you.

EXAMPLE

This excerpt comes from a health textbook. Its topic is *coping with speech anxiety.* Read the paragraph. Then determine the main idea by asking yourself, "What is the most important point the authors want me to understand about speech anxiety?" To identify supporting details, ask yourself, "What additional information do the authors provide to help me understand more about coping with speech anxiety?"

Do you feel anxious when you have to give a speech? Speech anxiety, or fear of public speaking, is common. Since students are frequently required to give oral presentations, this can present a problem for some. Along with basic stress-management techniques, certain strategies can help students cope with speech anxiety. Volunteer to go first so that pressure and expectations don't mount, and you won't be comparing your presentation to anyone else's. Second, practice in front of a mirror and for your friends. Solicit feedback: do you need to slow down or speak louder? Engage in positive visualization. Take deep, comfortable breaths and imagine giving your speech with confidence and positive feedback. Vary your presentation style and format. Use visuals and engage your audience so they are an active part of your presentation. This takes some of the focus and pressure away from you.

Source: Abridged from Wayne Payne, Dale Hahn, and Ellen Lucas, *Understanding Your Health,* 10th ed., p. 74. Copyright © 2009 by The McGraw-Hill Companies, Inc. Reprinted by permission of The McGraw-Hill Companies.

The topic of this paragraph is *coping with speech anxiety.*

__c__ What is the main idea of this paragraph?

a. Do you feel anxious when you have to give a speech?

b. Speech anxiety, or fear of public speaking, is common.

c. Along with basic stress-management techniques, certain strategies can help students cope with speech anxiety.

d. Volunteer to go first so that pressure and expectations don't mount, and you won't be comparing your presentation to anyone else's.

The correct answer is c. The fourth sentence is the stated main idea because it tells the authors' most important point about speech anxiety. Answer choice *a* is a question; the main idea is never a question. The next two sentences are introductory sentences that lead up to the main idea.

__c__ Which of the following is a supporting detail?

a. There are some strategies students can use to help them cope with speech anxiety.

b. Do you feel anxious when you have to give a speech?

c. Engage in positive visualization.

d. Coping with speech anxiety.

The correct answer is c. "Engage in positive visualization" is a strategy for coping with speech anxiety. Choice *a* is a restatement of the main idea. Choice *b* is an introductory question. Choice *d* is the topic.

Copyright © 2014 The McGraw-Hill Companies, Inc. All rights reserved.

Directions: Read each paragraph and determine its main idea by asking yourself, "What is the most important point the author wants me to *understand* about the topic of this paragraph?" (You are told the topic of each paragraph.) Write your answer choice in the space provided. Then identify the supporting details by asking yourself, "What additional information does the author provide to help me understand the main idea completely?" Remember that main ideas are *general* and supporting details are *specific.*

1. This paragraph comes from a health textbook.

Our response to stress involves many physiological changes collectively called the *fight or flight response.* Sometimes you may be in a situation in which you must react immediately to danger. In that case, it is advisable to either fight off the danger or flee. For example, you are walking back from a class at night, thinking about all the studying you need to do and you begin to cross the street. Suddenly, out of nowhere, a car's headlights are coming right at you. Since your best response is probably not to fight the car, you run as fast as you can to the other side of the road.

Source: Adapted from Wayne Payne, Dale Hahn, and Ellen Lucas, *Understanding Your Health,* 10th ed., p. 65. Copyright © 2009 by The McGraw-Hill Companies, Inc. Reprinted by permission of The McGraw-Hill Companies.

The topic of this paragraph is the *flight or flight response.*

______ What is the main idea of this paragraph?

a. Our response to stress involves many physiological changes collectively called the *fight or flight response.*

b. Sometimes you may be in a situation in which you must react immediately to danger.

c. In that case, it is advisable to either fight off the danger or flee.

d. Suddenly, out of nowhere, a car's headlights are coming right at you.

______ Which of the following is a supporting detail?

a. Fight and flight are physiological responses to stress.

b. Sometimes you may be in a situation in which you must react immediately to danger.

c. All stress involves danger.

d. Walking back from a class at night.

2. This paragraph comes from a business textbook.

What to Wear for a Job Interview

If you are interviewing for a management or office job, wear a business suit. What kind of suit? If you've got good taste and a good eye for color, follow your instincts. If fashion isn't your strong point, read John Molloy's *New Dress for Success* (men's clothes) and *The New Woman's Dress for Success Book.* Perhaps the best suggestion in the books is his advice to visit expensive stores, noting details—the exact shade of blue in a suit, the number of buttons on the sleeve, the placement of pockets, the width of lapels. Then go to stores in your price range and buy a suit that has the details found on more expensive clothes.

Source: Kitty Locker and Stephen Kyo Kaczmarek, *Business Communication: Building Critical Skills,* 5th ed., p. 519. Copyright © 2011 by The McGraw-Hill Companies, Inc. Reprinted by permission of The McGraw-Hill Companies.

The topic of this paragraph is *what to wear for a job interview.*

______ What is the main idea of this paragraph?

a. If you are interviewing for a management or office job, wear a business suit.

b. What kind of suit?

c. If you've got good taste and a good eye for color, follow your instincts.

d. Then go to stores in your price range and buy a suit that has the details found on more expensive clothes.

_______ Which of the following is a supporting detail?

a. What to wear for a job interview.

b. If you've got good taste and a good eye for color, follow your instincts.

c. What kind of suit?

d. If you are interviewing for a management or office job, wear a business suit.

3. This paragraph comes from a health textbook.

The information, values, traditions, and messages you receive from your family have a significant impact on your dietary habits. If an infant's cries for food are immediately responded to, that child will likely learn what the sensation of hunger is and what the appropriate response is. If crying unrelated to hunger is responded to by the offer of a cookie or candy, the child will learn to soothe himself or herself with food. Children become confused about what hunger is and how to satisfy it if their hunger needs are neglected in infancy. The same is true if they are overindulged in infancy.

Source: Adapted from Wayne Payne, Dale Hahn, and Ellen Lucas, *Understanding Your Health,* 10th ed., p. 180. Copyright © 2009 by The McGraw-Hill Companies, Inc. Reprinted by permission of The McGraw-Hill Companies.

The topic of this paragraph is *the impact of family on dietary habits.*

_______ What is the main idea of this paragraph?

a. The information, values, traditions, and messages you receive from your family have a significant impact on your dietary habits.

b. If an infant's cries for food are immediately responded to, that child will likely learn what the sensation of hunger is and what the appropriate response is.

c. If crying unrelated to hunger is responded to by the offer of a cookie or candy, the child will learn to soothe himself or herself with food.

d. Children become confused about what hunger is and how to satisfy it if their hunger needs are neglected in infancy.

_______ Which of the following is a supporting detail?

a. The information, values, traditions, and messages you receive from your family have a significant impact on your dietary habits.

b. If an infant's cries for food are immediately responded to, that child will likely learn what the sensation of hunger is and what the appropriate response is.

c. Offering children cookies or candy.

d. Children who are overindulged in infancy are confused.

4. This paragraph comes from a health textbook.

A Realistic Perspective on Stress and Life

Stress is actually normal and healthy at a certain level. However, you need to understand how you uniquely deal with stress and what helps you cope. The development of a realistic approach to today's fast-paced, stressful lifestyle may best be achieved by fostering certain perspectives.

- *Anticipate problems and see yourself as a problem solver.* Although each specific problem is unique, it is most likely similar to past ones. Use these past experiences to quickly recognize ways of resolving new problems.

Copyright © 2014 The McGraw-Hill Companies, Inc. All rights reserved.

- *Search for solutions.* Act on a partial solution, even when a complete solution seems distant.
- *Take control of your own future.* Set out to accomplish your goals. Do not view yourself as a victim.
- *Be aware of self-fulfilling prophecies.* Do not extend or generalize difficulties from one area into another.
- *Visualize success.* Focus on those things that are possible to ensure success.
- *Accept the unchangeable.* Focus on taking control of what you can and letting go of the rest.
- *Live each day well.* Celebrate special occasions. Undertake new experiences. Learn from your mistakes.
- *Act on your capacity for growth.* Undertake new experiences and then extract from them new information about your own interests and capacities.
- *Allow for renewal.* Make time for yourself, and take advantage of opportunities to pursue new and fulfilling relationships.
- *Accept mistakes.* Carefully evaluated, mistakes can serve as the basis for even greater knowledge and more likely success in those activities not yet undertaken.
- *Keep life simple.* Keep the demands of life as orderly and manageable as you can. Learning to prioritize and postpone activities is key to building a productive and enjoyable life.

Source: Abridged from Wayne Payne, Dale Hahn, and Ellen Lucas, *Understanding Your Health,* 10th ed., pp. 65, 89–90. Copyright © 2009 by The McGraw-Hill Companies, Inc. Reprinted by permission of The McGraw-Hill Companies.

The topic of this paragraph is *a realistic perspective on stress and life.*

________ What is the main idea of this paragraph?

a. Stress is actually normal and healthy at a certain level.

b. However, you need to understand how you uniquely deal with stress and what helps you cope.

c. The development of a realistic approach to today's fast-paced, stressful lifestyle may best be achieved by fostering certain perspectives.

d. A realistic perspective on stress and life.

________ Which of the following is a supporting detail?

a. The development of a realistic approach to today's fast-paced, stressful lifestyle may best be achieved by fostering certain perspectives.

b. Take control of your own future.

c. A realistic perspective on stress and life.

d. Stress makes life much harder than it otherwise would be.

5. This paragraph comes from a business textbook.

When you go to a job interview, bring extra copies of your résumé. It is also a good idea to bring something to write on and something to write with. Bring copies of your work or portfolio: an engineering design, a copy of a memo you wrote on a job or in a business writing class, an article you wrote for the campus paper. In addition, you should bring the names, addresses, and phone numbers of references if you didn't put them on your résumé. Bring complete details about your work history and education, including dates and street addresses, in case you're asked to fill out an application form. If you can afford it, buy a briefcase to carry these items.

Source: Kitty Locker and Stephen Kyo Kaczmarek, *Business Communication: Building Critical Skills,* 5th ed., p. 520. Copyright © 2011 by The McGraw-Hill Companies, Inc. Reprinted by permission of The McGraw-Hill Companies.

The topic of this paragraph is *what to bring to a job interview.*

______ What is the main idea of this paragraph?

a. When you go to a job interview, bring extra copies of your résumé.

b. A job interview.

c. Bring complete details about your work history and education, including dates and street addresses, in case you're asked to fill out an application form.

d. There are things you should bring with you to a job interview.

______ Which of the following is a supporting detail?

a. When you go to a job interview, bring extra copies of your résumé.

b. Preparing for a job interview.

c. What to bring to a job interview.

d. There are things you should bring with you to a job interview.

Copyright © 2014 The McGraw-Hill Companies, Inc. All rights reserved.

Review: **Supporting details** provide additional information in the paragraph that helps you understand the main idea completely. *They explain, illustrate, or prove the main idea of a paragraph.* Supporting details can be listed in notes as short phrases, paraphrased, or written as complete sentences.

EXAMPLE

This excerpt comes from a sociology textbook. Its topic is *professional criminals.* Read the paragraph. Then determine the main idea by asking yourself, "What is the most important point the authors want me to understand about professional criminals?" To identify supporting details, ask yourself, "What additional information do the authors provide to help me understand more about professional criminals?"

Professional Criminals

Many people make a career of illegal activities. A **professional criminal**, or *career criminal*, is a person who pursues crime as a day-to-day occupation, developing skilled techniques and enjoying a certain degree of status among other criminals. Some professional criminals①specialize in burglary, safecracking, hijacking of cargo, pickpocketing, and shoplifting. Such people have②acquired skills that reduce the likelihood of arrest, conviction, and imprisonment. As a result, they③may have long careers in their chosen profession.

Source: Adapted from Richard Schaefer, *Sociology: A Brief Introduction*, 9th ed., p. 176. Copyright © 2011 by The McGraw-Hill Companies, Inc. Reprinted by permission of The McGraw-Hill Companies.

The topic of this paragraph is *professional criminals.*

Write the main idea sentence: A professional criminal, or career criminal, is a person who pursues crime as a day-to-day occupation, developing skilled techniques and enjoying a certain degree of status among other criminals.

List the supporting details on separate lines:

- may specialize: burglary, safecracking, hijacking of cargo, pickpocketing, shoplifting
- may have acquired skills to reduce likelihood of arrest, conviction, and imprisonment
- may have long careers

Explanation: The first sentence is an introductory sentence. The second sentence is the main idea sentence. It presents the author's most important point, the definition of a professional (career) criminal. The remaining sentences present three details that tell more about professional criminals: their specific types of crimes; their skill in avoiding arrest, conviction, and imprisonment; and that they may have long careers.

Directions: Read each paragraph. (You are told the topic of each paragraph.) Determine the main idea. If it is stated, write it in the space provided. If it is implied, formulate a main idea sentence and write the sentence in the space provided. Last, identify the supporting details and *list each one on a separate line in the space provided.* You may find it helpful to number the details in the paragraph first or mark clue words that signal the details.

1. This paragraph comes from a criminal investigation textbook.

When investigating threats of violence in schools, ask the right questions, and then listen carefully to witnesses in order to correctly identify the level of threat and take appropriate action. Key questions include:

- Who made the threat?
- To whom was the threat made?
- Under what circumstances was the threat made?
- Exactly what words were said?
- How often were threats made?

Source: Adapted from Charles Swanson, Neil Chamelin, Leonard Territo, and Robert Taylor, *Criminal Investigation,* 11th ed., p. 337. Copyright © 2012 by The McGraw-Hill Companies, Inc. Reprinted by permission of The McGraw-Hill Companies.

The topic of this paragraph is *investigating threats of school violence.*

Write the main idea sentence:

____

____

____

List the supporting details on separate lines:

____

____

____

____

____

2. This paragraph comes from a government textbook.

If you want to get involved with politics, become a delegate to your party's state or national political convention. If you are eighteen and registered to vote, you probably qualify. Contact your precinct leader or your party's local office. In some states, you can become a delegate by working directly for a candidate if he or she wins the primary election. In others, delegates have to file their own nominating petitions and are elected directly by voters. In most states, you can also work closely with your local party to be considered as a delegate from your district.

Source: Adapted from Joseph Losco and Ralph Baker, *Am Gov, 2011,* p. 213. Copyright © 2011 by The McGraw-Hill Companies, Inc. Reprinted by permission of The McGraw-Hill Companies.

The topic of this paragraph is *becoming a political party convention delegate.*

Write the main idea sentence: ______________________________

____

List the supporting details on separate lines:

____

3. This paragraph comes from a business textbook.

What exactly does a corporation's board of directors do? For one thing, it oversees the corporation's general operations. Second, it sets the corporation's long-range objectives and ensures they are achieved on schedule. The board also makes sure funds are spent appropriately. Another important duty is to hire corporate officers, such as the president and the chief executive officer.

Source: Adapted from O. C. Ferrell, Geoffrey Hirt, and Linda Ferrell, *Business: A Changing World,* 8th ed., pp. 133–34. Copyright © 2011 by The McGraw-Hill Companies, Inc. Reprinted by permission of The McGraw-Hill Companies.

The topic of this paragraph is *a corporation's board of directors.*

Write the main idea sentence: ______________________

List the supporting details on separate lines:

4. This paragraph comes from a textbook on adolescence.

Adolescents who do not go to college face increasing economic challenges. As manufacturing jobs began to be replaced by minimum-wage service jobs, the chances of making a decent living without at least two years of college have worsened appreciably. Today, young adults without college experience often must try to make ends meet on minimum-wage jobs. These are jobs that offer little in the way of promotion or advancement. Moreover, non-college-bound-youth must also deal with the rising costs of essentials such as housing and healthcare.

Source: Adapted from Laurence Steinberg, *Adolescence,* 9th ed., p. 207. Copyright © 2011 by The McGraw-Hill Companies, Inc. Reprinted by permission of The McGraw-Hill Companies.

The topic of this paragraph is *adolescents who do not go to college.*

Write the main idea sentence: ______________________

List the supporting details on separate lines:

____

____

____

____

____

____

5. This paragraph comes from a career-planning textbook.

A professionally prepared résumé is essential to any job search. Next to the interview, it is the tool most widely used by employers to evaluate the qualifications of job applicants. Choose a résumé style that best portrays your qualifications. You can create a résumé that stands out from others by taking time to target your résumé to a specific job or company. When used appropriately, power words and keywords can help you tailor your résumé to match keywords in job postings or on the website for the company you are interested in. Have your résumé reviewed by an instructor or another person who knows you and can provide input.

Source: Adapted from Donna Yena, *Career Directions: The Path to an Ideal Career,* 5th ed., p. 191. Copyright © 2011 by the McGraw-Hill Companies, Inc. Reprinted by permission of The McGraw-Hill Companies.

The topic of this paragraph is the *résumé.*

Write the main idea sentence: ______________________________

____

List the supporting details on separate lines:

____

____

____

____

____

____

____

____

SELECTION **6.1**

Environmental Science

"Hold It! You Can Recycle That!" Recycling: A Twenty-First Century Necessity

From *Environmental Science: A Study of Interrelationships*

By Eldon Enger and Bradley Smith

What do plastic water bottles, glass containers, plastic milk jugs, newspapers, magazines, aluminum cans, plastic soft-drink bottles, cardboard boxes, steel cans, tires, and automobile batteries have in common? The answer is that all of them can be re-processed—if consumers will simply make the effort to recycle them. Recycling conserves resources. It benefits the environment. It saves consumers money. It can create jobs. It is a great way to "go green." In short, recycling makes sense.

All of us should get into the habit of recycling. This passage from an environmental science textbook explains why. It presents examples of recycling efforts, along with related data. Recycling is becoming a necessity in today's world, and a growing number of colleges and universities are joining in the effort.

Recycling

1 **Recycling** is one of the best environmental success stories of the late twentieth century. (See Figure 1.) In the United States, recycling, including composting, diverted about 30 percent of the solid waste stream from landfills and incinerators in 2007, up from about 16 percent in 1990. Several kinds of programs have contributed to the increase in the recycling rate. Some benefits of recycling are resource conservation, pollutant reduction, energy savings, job creation, and reduced need for landfills and incinerators. However, incentives are needed to encourage people to participate in recycling programs.

2 Three types of incentives have made recycling efforts more successful. *Container laws* provide an economic incentive to recycle. In October 1972, Oregon became the first state to enact a "bottle bill." The law required a deposit of two to five cents on all beverage containers that could be reused. It banned the sale of one-time-use beverage bottles and cans. One of the primary goals of the law was to reduce the amount of litter, and it worked. Within two years of when it went into effect, beverage-container litter decreased by about 49 percent. Many argue that a national bottle bill is long overdue. *Mandatory recycling laws* provide a statutory incentive to recycle. Many states and cities have passed mandatory recycling laws. (See Figure 1.) Some require residents to separate their recyclables from other trash. Other laws require particular products such as beverage containers be recycled. Some require businesses to recycle certain kinds of materials such as cardboard or batteries. Finally, some laws forbid the disposal of certain kinds of materials in landfills. States and cities with mandatory recycling laws understandably have high recycling rates. *Curbside recycling* provides a convenient way for people to recycle. In 1990, a thousand U.S. cities had curbside recycling programs. By 2008, the number had grown to about 11,000 cities. By 1999, mandatory recycling laws for all materials had

Annotation Practice Exercises

Directions: For each exercise below, write the topic and the main idea on the lines beside the paragraph. (You may need to formulate the main idea.) Then identify the supporting details and list them *separately* on the lines provided.

Practice Exercise

Topic of paragraph 1:

____

Main idea sentence of paragraph 1:

____

____

____

____

____

____

____

List the *supporting details* on separate lines:

____

____

____

Copyright © 2014 The McGraw-Hill Companies, Inc. All rights reserved.

FIGURE 1

RECYCLING RATES FROM 1960–2007 AND RECYCLING PERCENTAGE FOR SELECTED MATERIALS (2005)

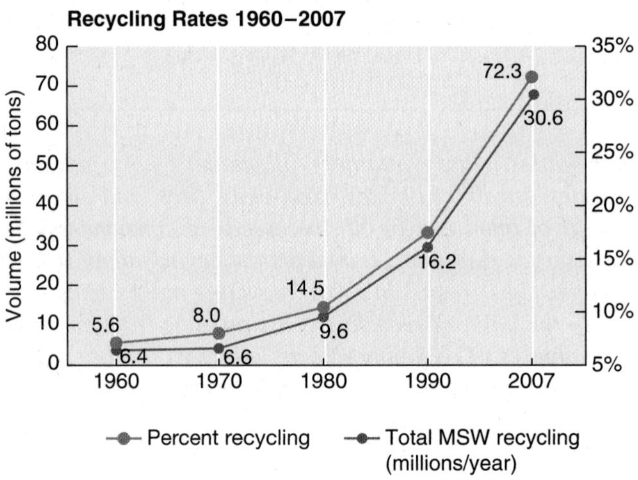

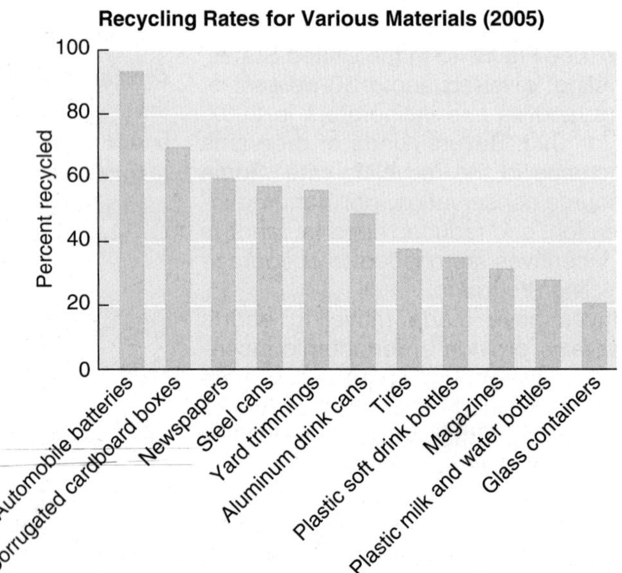

Recycling rates for materials that have high value such as automobile batteries are extremely high. Other materials are more difficult to market. But recycling rates today are much higher than in the past as technology and markets have found uses for materials that once were considered valueless.

Source: Data from the U.S. Environmental Protection Agency, *Characterization of Municipal Solid Waste in the United States,* 2007.

been passed in 15 states. Some large cities—such as Portland, Oregon; San Jose, California; Los Angeles, California; and Minneapolis, Minnesota—have achieved recycling rates of 50 percent or more. In general, these cities have curbside recycling and accept a wide variety of materials, including junk mail and cereal boxes. By contrast, cities that do not provide curbside recycling have recycling rates of less than 10 percent.

Recycling Concerns

3 Although recycling programs have successfully reduced the amount of material that needs to be trucked to a landfill or incinerated, there are many technical and economic problems associated with recycling. Technical questions are of particular concern when recycling plastics. While the plastics used in packaging are recyclable, the recycling technology differs from plastic to plastic. There are many different types of plastic polymers. Since each type has its own chemical makeup, different plastics cannot be recycled together. A milk container, an egg container, and a soft-drink bottle are each made from different types of plastics. Until a new technology is developed, it will be necessary to separate different plastics before reprocessing them.

4 The economics of recycling are also a primary area of concern. The stepped-up commitment to recycling in many developed nations has produced a glut of certain materials on the market. Markets for collected materials fill up just like landfills. Unless the demand for recycled products keep space with the growing supply, recycling programs will face an uncertain future.

5 The long-term success of recycling programs is also tied to other economic incentives, such as taxing issues and the development of and demand for products manufactured from recycled material. Government policies need to be readjusted to encourage recycling efforts. In addition, on an individual level, we can have an impact by purchasing products made from recycled materials. The demand for recycled products must grow if recycling is to succeed on a large scale.

Beverage Container Waste

6 In 2008, consumers in the United States failed to recycle an estimated 155 billion aluminum, glass, and plastic beverage containers. This is 33 percent more containers than were disposed of a decade ago. Disposal of them continues to be a significant problem. First, aluminum, glass, and plastic beverage containers disposed of in landfills and incinerators represent a loss of valuable resources and reduce employment opportunities in the domestic recycling industry. Second, disposal of these containers leads to increased greenhouse gas emissions and other forms of pollution when replacement containers are manufactured. Third, manufacturing aluminum cans from used cans requires only 4 percent of the energy required to make new cans. Fourth, beverage containers account for 40 percent of the total volume of litter on our roads and highways.

Practice Exercise

Topic of paragraph 2:

____

Main idea sentence of paragraph 2:

____

____

____

____

List the *supporting details* on separate lines:

____

____

____

Practice Exercise

Topic of paragraph 6:

____

Main idea sentence of paragraph 6:

____

____

____

List the *supporting details* on separate lines:

____

____

____

____

____

____

____

Copyright © 2014 The McGraw-Hill Companies, Inc. All rights reserved.

Paper or Plastic or Plastax?

7 Before 2002, Ireland's 3.9 million people were using 1.2 billion plastic bags per year. These bags were generally nonrecyclable. They took 20 to 1,000 years to break down in the environment. They were littering the countryside, clogging storm drains, and adding to the burden on the country's landfill sites.

8 The innovative idea of the "plastax" or tax on plastic bags was first announced in 1999. In 2002, Ireland's environment minister launched the program, one of the first of its kind in the world. For every bag used at the checkout counter of the supermarket, a 15 euro cents (about 25 U.S. cents) surcharge was added. The revenue raised from this tax would be put toward a "green fund" for environmental projects such as recycling refrigerators and other large appliances.

9 In 2008, China banned free plastic bags from shops, supermarkets, and all public transportation and scenic locations. The Chinese were using 3 billion plastic bags every day. In the U.S., which has less than one-quarter of China's 1.3 billion people, almost 100 billion plastic bags are thrown out each year, only a fraction make it to the recycling bin. It is estimated that if every one of New York City's 8 million people used one less grocery bag per year, it would reduce waste by about 220,000 pounds.

What You Can Do

10 You can make a difference. The following suggestions will not only reduce waste and help the environment, they will also save you money. Buy things that last, keep them as long as possible, and have them repaired, if possible. Buy things that are reusable and recyclable, and be sure to reuse or recycle them. Buy beverages in refillable glass containers instead of cans or throwaway bottles. Use rechargeable batteries. Skip the bag when you buy a single item or anything you can carry in your hands. Recycle all newspaper, glass, and aluminum, and any other items accepted for recycling in your community.

Source: Adapted from Eldon Enger and Bradley Smith, *Environmental Science: A Study of Interrelationships,* 12th ed., pp. 402–6. Copyright © 2012 by The McGraw-Hill Companies, Inc.

SELECTION 6.1
Environmental Science
(continued)

Comprehension and Vocabulary Quiz

This quiz has four parts. Your instructor may assign some or all of them.

Comprehension

Directions: Use the information in the selection to answer each question below.

_______ **1.** In 1990 the recycling rate for solid waste in the United States was about 16 percent, but by 2007 our nation's recycling rate had increased to about:

a. 30 percent.
b. 49 percent.
c. 50 percent.
d. 90 percent.

_______ **2.** Some large cities such as Portland, Oregon, and San Jose, California, have achieved recycling rates of 50 percent or more as a result of their:

a. mandatory recycling law.
b. curbside recycling program.
c. "plastax."
d. all of the above

_______ **3.** By 2008 the number of city curbside recycling programs in the United States increased to approximately:

a. 750.
b. 1,500.
c. 11,000.
d. 25,000.

_______ **4.** There are technical and economic problems associated with recycling plastics because:

a. not all plastics can be recycled.
b. different plastics cannot be recycled together and must be separated before re-processing.
c. plastics are becoming too expensive to recycle.
d. there is already an oversupply of recycled plastics.

_______ **5.** Ireland's "plastax" is a:

a. surcharge paid by citizens for plastic recycling.
b. deposit of two to five cents on all beverage bottles.
c. tax on plastic bags.
d. government regulation prohibiting the use of plastic bags.

SELECTION 6.1

Copyright © 2014 The McGraw-Hill Companies, Inc. All rights reserved.

Vocabulary in Context

Directions: For each item below, use context clues to deduce the meaning of the *italicized* word.

_______ **6.** However, *incentives* are needed to encourage people to participate in recycling programs.

The increased likelihood of an interesting career, a good salary, and opportunities for advancement are *incentives* for earning a college degree.

incentives (ĭn sĕn′ tĭvz) means:

a. government regulations
b. guaranteed outcomes
c. rewards that motivate action
d. requirements for success

_______ **7.** The Oregon "bottle bill" *banned* the sale of one-time-use beverage bottles and cans.

The use of cell phones while driving has been *banned* in many countries.

banned (bănd) means:

a. removed
b. prohibited
c. allowed
d. discouraged

_______ **8.** States and cities with *mandatory* recycling laws understandably have higher recycling rates.

For international travel, possession of a valid passport is *mandatory.*

mandatory (măn′ də tôr ē) means:

a. complimentary
b. optional
c. recommended
d. required

_______ **9.** The stepped-up commitment to recycling in many developed nations has produced a *glut* of certain materials on the market.

The *glut* of new college graduates with majors in psychology made it extremely difficult for them to find jobs in their field.

glut (glŭt) means:

a. number
b. shortage
c. oversupply
d. problem

_______ **10.** For every bag used at the checkout counter of the supermarket, a 15 euro cents (about 25 U.S. cents) *surcharge* was added.

Airline passengers whose luggage exceeds the weight limit must pay a *surcharge*.

surcharge (sûr′ chärj′) means:

a. a sum added to the usual cost

b. ten percent increase

c. unfair charge

d. fee charged by the government

Word Structure

Directions: In paragraph 8 of the selection, you encountered the word **innovative.** It contains the root ***nov***, which means "new." The word *innovative* describes something that is newly introduced. Use the meaning of ***nov*** and the list of prefixes on pages 72–73 to determine the meaning of each of the following words.

_______ **11.** If you are a **novice** at skiing, you are:

a. learning very quickly.

b. a beginner.

c. not interested in the sport.

d. looking for an outdoor sport.

_______ **12.** At the beginning of the twentieth century, the automobile was still a **novel** invention. In other words, it was still:

a. extremely expensive.

b. inefficient and unreliable.

c. strikingly new or different.

d. unsafe to the point of dangerous.

_______ **13.** If you **renovate** your kitchen, you:

a. make it larger.

b. repair it.

c. replace the appliances.

d. make it "like new" again.

_______ **14.** Once the **novelty** of a toy wears off, children tend to:

a. put it in a safe place to save it for later.

b. play with it often because they have grown very fond of it.

c. become bored with it because it no longer seems new.

d. break it because they are frustrated with it.

_______ **15.** A **nova** is a variable star that suddenly increases to several times its original brightness, but eventually returns to its original appearance. Astronomers call this a **nova** because:

a. it is a phenomenon that does not occur very often.

b. it temporarily looks like a new or different star.

c. it breaks into several different stars.

d. they do not know why this phenomenon happens.

Copyright © 2014 The McGraw-Hill Companies, Inc. All rights reserved.

Reading Skills Application

Directions: These items test your ability to *apply* certain reading skills. You may not have studied all the skills yet, so some items will serve as a preview.

_______ **16.** According to information in this selection, one of the primary goals of Oregon's "bottle bill" was to:

a. reduce the amount of litter in the state.

b. discourage consumers from buying glass containers.

c. raise money for resource conservation.

d. encourage soft-drink manufacturers to use plastic bottles that could be recycled.

_______ **17.** According to the bar graph of "Recycling Rates for Various Materials" in Figure 1, which of the following materials have a higher recycling rate than plastic soft-drink bottles?

a. glass containers

b. magazines

c. aluminum drink cans

d. plastic milk and water bottles

_______ **18.** The information in paragraph 9 of the selection is organized by which of the following patterns?

a. list

b. definition

c. comparison-contrast

d. sequence

_______ **19.** Which of the following describes the authors' primary purpose for writing this selection?

a. to explain why people do not participate in recycling programs

b. to show that there are many technical and economic difficulties associated with recycling

c. to persuade everyone to participate in recycling programs regularly and to convince readers that recycling is a global necessity today

d. to persuade consumers to buy products made from recycled materials

_______ **20.** What is the relationship between the parts of this sentence? "Although recycling programs have successfully reduced the amount of material that needs to be trucked to a landfill or incinerated, there are many technical and economic problems associated with recycling." (The second part begins after the comma.)

a. The second part defines something that is mentioned in the first part.

b. The second part presents a similarity with something in the first part.

c. The second part presents a contrast with something in the first part.

d. The second part presents an example of something in the first part.

Respond in Writing

Directions: Refer to the selection as needed to answer the essay-type questions below.

1. **Reacting to What You Have Read:** Do you think your community would support a "plastax" on plastic bags like the program in Ireland? Who would be opposed to such a program? How would a complete ban on plastic bags alter your lifestyle?

2. **Comprehending the Selection Further:** The final section of the selection lists suggestions for reducing waste, helping the environment, and saving money in the process. List the two suggestions that in your opinion are most important. *Add at least two suggestions of your own that go beyond what is mentioned in the selection.*

3. **Overall Main Idea of the Selection:** In one sentence, tell what the authors want readers to understand about recycling. (Be sure to include "recycling" in your overall main idea sentence.)

Internet Resources

Read More about It Online

Directions: To learn more about the topic of this selection, see the websites below or use the keyword **"recycling"** with a search engine.

www.kab.org/site/PageServer?pagename=index
This is the website for Keep America Beautiful. The largest community improvement organization in the United States, this environmental organization was founded in 1953 with the goal of involving all Americans in preventing litter, reducing waste, and beautifying communities.

www.reuseit.com
A commercial website, this award-winning company offers "reusables" in an array of categories, with the goal of helping people eliminate disposables from every part of their lives. The website contains links to many helpful resources and lifestyles guides.

http://en.wikipedia.org/wiki/Recycling
This website discusses multiple aspects of recycling both in the United States and in other countries.

SELECTION **6.2**
History

The Life of Buddha: The Path to Nirvana

From *The 100: A Ranking of the Most Influential Persons in History*
By Michael Hart

Gautama Buddha lived approximately 2,500 years ago (563 to 483 B.C.E.*). He founded Buddhism, a worldwide religion that has influenced millions of people over the centuries. Currently, there are about 300 million Buddhists. Historian Michael Hart ranks Buddha among the top five most influential persons in the history of the world. In this selection he tells about Buddha's 80-year life and his beliefs, and he explains why he considers Buddha so influential.*

Seated Buddha (Siddhartha Gautama).

1 Gautama Buddha, whose original name was Prince Siddhartha, was the founder of Buddhism, one of the world's great religions. Siddhartha was the son of a king ruling in Kapilavastu, a city in northeast India, near the borders of Nepal. Siddhartha himself (of the clan of Gautama and the tribe of Sakya) was purportedly born in 563 B.C., in Lumbini, within the present borders of Nepal. He was married at sixteen to a cousin of the same age. Brought up in the luxurious royal palace, Prince Siddhartha did not want for material comforts.

2 Nevertheless, Siddhartha was profoundly dissatisfied. He observed that most human beings were poor and continually suffered from want. Even those who were wealthy were frequently frustrated and unhappy, and all humans were subject to disease and ultimately succumbed to death. Surely, Siddhartha

Annotation Practice Exercises

Directions: For each exercise below, write the topic and the main idea of the paragraph on the lines beside the paragraph. Then identify the supporting details and list them *separately* on the lines provided.

Practice Exercise

Topic of paragraph 1:

____

____

Main idea sentence:

____

____

____

____

____

List the *supporting details* on separate lines:

____

____

____

____

____

____

____

____

thought, there must be more to life than transitory pleasures, which were all too soon obliterated by suffering and death.

3 When he was twenty-nine, just after the birth of his first son, Gautama decided that he must abandon the life he was living and devote himself wholeheartedly to the search for truth. He departed from the palace, leaving behind his wife, his infant son, and all his worldly possessions, and became a penniless wanderer. For a while he studied with some of the famed holy men of the day, but after mastering their teachings, he found their solutions to the problems of the human situation unsatisfactory. It was widely believed that extreme asceticism was the pathway to true wisdom. Gautama therefore attempted to become an ascetic by engaging in extreme fasts and self-mortification for several years. Eventually, however, he realized that tormenting his body only clouded his brain, without leading him any closer to true wisdom. He therefore resumed eating normally and abandoned asceticism.

4 In solitude, he grappled with the problems of human existence. Finally, one evening, as he sat beneath a giant fig tree, all the pieces of the puzzle seemed to fall into place. Siddhartha spent the whole night in deep reflection, and when the morning came, he was convinced that he had found the solution and that he was now a Buddha, an "enlightened one."

5 At this time, he was thirty-five years old. For the remaining forty-five years of his life, he traveled throughout northern India, preaching his new philosophy to all who were willing to listen. By the time he died, in 483 B.C., he had made thousands of converts. Though his words had not been written down, his disciples had memorized many of his teachings, and they were passed to succeeding generations by word of mouth.

6 The principal teachings of the Buddha can be summarized in what Buddhists call the "Four Noble Truths." These are first, that human life is intrinsically unhappy; second, that the cause of this unhappiness is human selfishness and desire; third, that individual selfishness and desire can be brought to an end—the resulting state, when all desire and cravings have been eliminated, is termed *nirvana* (literally "blowing out" or "extinction"); fourth, that the method of escape from selfishness and desire is what is called the "Eightfold Path": right views, right thought, right speech, right action, right livelihood, right effort, right mindfulness, and right meditation.

7 Buddha, as the founder of one of the world's major religions, clearly deserves a place among the most influential people in history. Since there are only about 400 million Buddhists in the world, compared with over 1.5 billion Moslems and about 2.2 billion Christians, it would seem evident that Buddha has influenced fewer people than either Muhammad or Jesus. However, the difference in numbers can be misleading. One reason that Buddhism died out in India is that Hinduism absorbed many of its ideas and principles. In China, too, large numbers of persons who do not call themselves Buddhists have been strongly influenced by Buddhist philosophy.

8 Buddhism, far more than Christianity or Islam, has a very strong pacifist element. This orientation toward nonviolence has played a significant role in the political history of Buddhist countries.

Practice Exercise

Topic of paragraph 6:

____

____

Main idea sentence:

____

____

____

____

____

____

List the *supporting details* on separate lines:

____

____

____

____

____

____

____

____

____

____

____

Source: Adapted from Michael Hart, *The 100: A Ranking of the Most Influential Persons in History.* Copyright © 1978, 1992 Michael H. Hart, Inc. All rights reserved. Reprinted by arrangement with Kensington Publishing Corporation. www.kensingtonbooks.com.

Comprehension and Vocabulary Quiz

This quiz has four parts. Your instructor may assign some or all of them.

Comprehension

Directions: Use the information in the selection to answer the questions below.

______ **1.** Gautama Buddha spent the first 29 years of his life:
a. as a penniless wanderer.
b. as a prince in a royal palace.
c. training to become a holy man.
d. as an ascetic.

______ **2.** The term "Buddha" means:
a. enlightened one.
b. royal prince.
c. ascetic.
d. one whose teachings are passed to succeeding generations.

______ **3.** The teachings of Buddha were memorized by his disciples and then:
a. written down in a holy book called *The Four Noble Truths.*
b. passed on by word of mouth.
c. developed into the "Eightfold Path."
d. adopted by Hinduism and Christianity.

______ **4.** One of the four principal teachings of the Buddha is that:
a. Buddhism is open to all.
b. individual selfishness and desire can be brought to an end.
c. happiness is the natural state of human life.
d. human beings are intrinsically happy.

______ **5.** Buddhism has a strong orientation toward:
a. peace and nonviolence.
b. other religions such as Hinduism and Islam.
c. the teachings of Muhammad and Jesus.
d. asceticism and self-mortification.

Vocabulary in Context

Directions: For each item below, use context clues to deduce the meaning of the *italicized* word.

______ **6.** Brought up in the luxurious royal palace, Prince Siddhartha did not want for *material* comforts.

Many people complain that American society places too much emphasis on clothes, cars, electronic devices, and other *material* goods.

Copyright © 2014 The McGraw-Hill Companies, Inc. All rights reserved.

material (mə tĭr′ ē əl) means:

a. pertaining to cloth
b. pertaining to a humble lifestyle
c. pertaining to physical well-being
d. pertaining to things that are inexpensive

______ **7.** Gautama therefore attempted to become an *ascetic,* for several years engaging in extreme fasts and self-mortification.

Because Jake is an *ascetic,* he chooses to live alone in a small mountain cabin with no electricity, no running water, and no telephone.

ascetic (ə sĕt′ ĭk) means:

a. extremely religious person
b. person who leads a life of self-discipline and without comforts
c. person who plans things in a careful, detailed manner
d. extremely unfriendly

______ **8.** Siddhartha spent the whole night in deep reflection, and when the morning came, he was convinced that he had found the solution and that he was now a Buddha, an "*enlightened* one."

We all suddenly felt *enlightened* after hearing our math professor explain the difficult concepts in a way we could understand.

enlightened (ĕn līt′ nd) means:

a. made lighter
b. relieved; free from worry
c. having spiritual or intellectual insight
d. confused and frustrated

______ **9.** The principal teachings of the Buddha can be summarized in what Buddhists call the "Four Noble Truths": first, that human life is *intrinsically* unhappy.

Because the judge is *intrinsically* fair, she is effective and highly respected.

intrinsically (ĭn trĭn′ zĭk lē) means:

a. inherently or naturally
b. from time to time
c. partially or incompletely
d. never

______ **10.** Buddhism, far more than Christianity or Islam, has a very strong *pacifist* element.

Last week, antiwar demonstrators and other *pacifist* groups held protests in the nation's capital.

pacifist (păs′ ə fĭst) means:

a. opposed to war or violence as a means of settling disputes
b. from the Pacific coast region

c. well-organized politically
d. pertaining to religion

Word Structure

In paragraph 3 of the selection, you encountered the word **self-mortification.** This word contains the root ***mort,*** which means "death." The word *mortification* means "to discipline (one's body and physical appetites) by self-denial or self-inflicted privation." You can see the connection with the meaning of the root because if one "disciplined" and "denied" one's body to an extreme, it would result in death. (*Mortify* also has come to mean "to humiliate" and "to feel shame or wounded pride.") Use the meaning of ***mort*** and the list of prefixes on pages 72–73 to help you determine the meaning of each of the following words.

_______ **11.** A **mortuary** is a:
a. funeral home.
b. sacred shrine.
c. public area.
d. type of wreath.

_______ **12.** An autopsy, or **post mortem** examination, is conducted:
a. on weekdays only.
b. only after employees complete their routine duties.
c. on the body after a person has died.
d. by a person involved in criminal investigation.

_______ **13.** A **mortician** is a person who:
a. knows emergency procedures.
b. counsels families.
c. presides at a religious service.
d. is a funeral director or undertaker.

_______ **14.** If a hospital patient is **moribund,** the person is:
a. ill.
b. dying.
c. in intensive care.
d. on a heart monitor.

_______ **15.** If a solider receives a **mortal** wound, it is:
a. a serious injury.
b. a head wound.
c. an injury that causes extensive blood loss.
d. a fatal wound.

Reading Skills Application

Directions: These items test your ability to *apply* certain reading skills. You may not have studied all the skills at this point, so some items will serve as a helpful preview.

Copyright © 2014 The McGraw-Hill Companies, Inc. All rights reserved.

_______ **16** Based on information in the selection, which of the following represents a logical inference about Buddha and his "search for truth"?

a. Buddha regretted his decision to leave his home and family to "search for truth."

b. If Buddha had grown up in poverty, he might never have begun a "search for truth."

c. Buddha's family and friends thought his decision to "search for truth" was foolish.

d. Buddha failed in his "search for truth" and died bitter and frustrated.

_______ **17.** Which of the following represents an opinion about Buddha rather than a fact?

a. He was married at 16 to a cousin the same age.

b. He therefore resumed eating normally and abandoned asceticism.

c. By the time he died, in 483 B.C., he had made thousands of converts.

d. Buddha, as the founder of one of the world's major religions, clearly deserves a place among the most influential people in history.

_______ **18.** Which of the following is the meaning of *clouded* as it is used in paragraph 3?

a. refreshed

b. strengthened

c. confused

d. destroyed

_______ **19.** In paragraph 4 the author says "all the pieces of the puzzle seemed to fall into place" for Siddhartha, to mean that Siddhartha:

a. finally achieved the insight into human existence that he had sought for so long.

b. gave up because none of the solutions he found had worked.

c. continued to be puzzled and perplexed about the human condition.

d. became puzzled by the challenges that seemed to befall him.

_______ **20.** The pattern of organization in paragraphs 1–5 can best be described as a:

a. list.

b. sequence.

c. cause and an effect.

d. comparison.

SELECTION **6.2**
History
(continued)

Respond in Writing

Directions: Refer to the selection as needed to answer the essay-type questions below.

1. Reacting to What You Have Read: Many people today buy more things than they can afford, and although they have more possessions, they complain that they are still not truly happy. Why do you think this is so?

____

____

____

____

____

2. **Comprehending the Selection Further:** Do you agree with Buddha's first "Noble Truth" that human life is intrinsically unhappy? Explain why you agree or disagree.

3. **Overall Main Idea of the Selection:** In one sentence, tell what the author wants readers to understand about Buddha. (Be sure to include the name "Buddha" in your overall main idea sentence.)

Internet Resources

Read More about It Online

Directions: To learn more about the topic of the selection, visit the website below or use the keyword "Buddha" or "Buddhism" with a search engine.

www.buddhanet.net/e-learning/5minbud.htm
"BuddhaNet Basic Buddhism Guide: A Five-Minute Introduction"

SELECTION **6.3**

History

The New Immigrants: Asian Americans and Latinos

From *Nation of Nations: A Narrative History of the American Republic*
By James Davidson et al.

Between 1990 and 2005, immigration to the United States changed dramatically. Never before had our nation experienced such ethnic and racial diversity among our immigrant newcomers. Today the country's 50.5 million Latinos make up 16.3% of the population: One in every six individuals and one in every four children are Latino. Approximately 65 percent are of Mexican descent. Latinos represent more than $1 trillion in buying power. In 2010 the nation's 17.3 million Asian Americans made up 5.6 percent of the population: 14.7 million identified themselves as Asian alone; 2.6 million identified themselves as Asian combined with one or more other races. Their buying power is the fastest growing of any ethnic group; in 2009 it was $528 billion. As these figures indicate, the groups are having a profound impact on the nation and will increasingly do so in the future.

The U.S. Census Bureau projects that by 2050 the nation's population will be 438 million, and that 82 percent of the increase will be due to immigrants arriving from 2005 to 2050 and their descendants. The ethnic mix will be 46 percent Anglo/Non-Hispanic whites (down from 67 percent in 2005), 29 percent Latino (up from 14 percent in 2005), 13 percent African American (roughly the same as in 2005), and 9 percent Asian (up from 5 percent in 2005). This U.S. history textbook selection explains the background and nature of this dramatic shift.

1 The Immigration Act of 1965 altered the face of American life. The lawmakers who passed the act did not expect such far-reaching consequences, because they assumed that Europeans would continue to predominate among newcomers. Yet reform of the old quota system opened the way for a wave of immigrants unequaled since the beginning of the century.

Economic and Political Causes of Immigration

2 Turmoil abroad pushed many immigrants toward the United States, beginning in the 1960s with Fidel Castro's revolution in Cuba and unrest in the Dominican Republic. The war in Vietnam and its aftermath produced more than 500,000 refugees in the 15 years after 1975. Revolutionary conflicts in Central America during the 1980s launched new streams. Yet economic factors played as great a role as the terrors of war. Although some Filipinos fled the repressive regime of Ferdinand Marcos, many more came to the United States in a more straightforward search for economic prosperity. When Mexico suffered an economic downturn in the 1980s, emigration there rose sharply.

3 In all, about 13 million immigrants arrived in the United States between 1990 and 2005. The nation's foreign-born population rose to 11.7 percent, the highest proportion since World War II. In the 1990s, the Latino population increased by over 35 percent to about 30.3 million. The Asian American population grew at an even faster rate, to about 10.8 million. Through the decade a steadily expanding economy made immigrants a welcome source of new labor. Prosperity, in turn, reduced—though it did not eliminate—conflict among long-standing residents, new immigrants, and people on the margin of the labor market.

Annotation Practice Exercises

Directions: For each exercise below, write the topic and the main idea on the lines beside the paragraph. (You may need to formulate the main idea.) Then identify the supporting details and list them *separately* on the lines provided.

Practice Exercise

Topic of paragraph 2:

____

____

Main idea sentence of paragraph 2:

____

____

____

____

List the *supporting details* on separate lines:

____

____

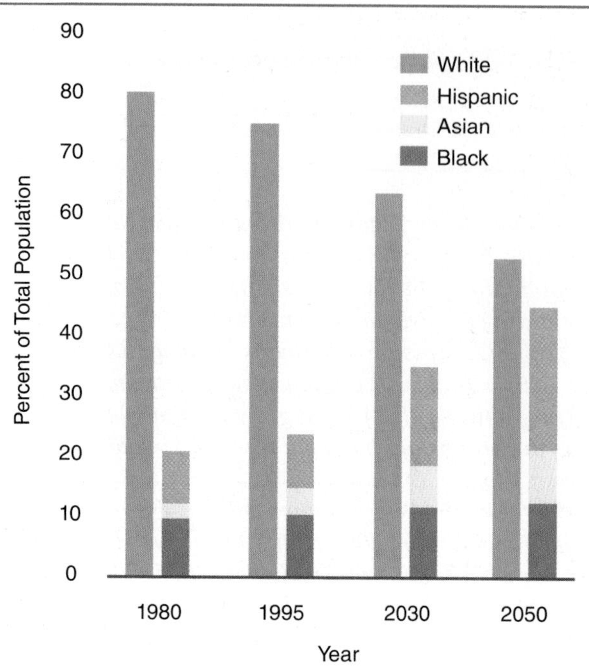

Projected Population Shifts, 1980–2050
The 6.5 million immigrants who arrived between 1990 and 1998 accounted for 32 percent of the increase in the total U.S. population. Census figures project an increasing racial and ethnic diversity. White population is projected to drop from 80 percent in 1980 to about 53 percent in 2050, with the nation's Latino population rising most sharply.

The New Look of America—Asian Americans

4 In 1970, 96 percent of Asian Americans were Japanese, Chinese, or Filipino. By the year 2000, those same three groups constituted only about half of all Asian Americans. As the diversity of Asian immigration increased, Asian Indians, Koreans, and Vietnamese came to outnumber Japanese Americans. The newcomers also varied dramatically in economic background, crowding both ends of the economic spectrum.

Prosperous Newcomers

5 The higher end included many Chinese students who, beginning in the 1960s, sought out the United States for a college education, then found a job and stayed, eventually bringing in their families. "My brother-in-law left his wife in Taiwan and came here as a student to get his Ph.D. in engineering," explained Subi Lin Felipe. "After he received his degree, he got a job in San Jose. Then he brought in a sister and his wife, who brought over one of her brothers and me. And my brother's wife then came."

6 Asian Indians were even more acculturated upon arrival because about two-thirds entered the United States already speaking English and with college degrees already in hand. Indian engineers played a vital role in the computer and software industries. Similarly, Korean and Filipino professionals took skilled jobs, particularly in medical fields.

Blue-Collar Asians

7 Yet Asian immigrants also included those on the lower rungs of the economic ladder. Among the new wave of Chinese immigrants, many blue-collar workers settled in the nation's

Chinatowns, where they worked in restaurants or sewed in sweatshops. Without education and language skills, often in debt to labor contractors, most remained trapped in Chinatown's ethnic economy. Refugees from war and revolution in Southeast Asia often made harrowing journeys. Vietnamese families crowded into barely seaworthy boats, sometimes only to be terrorized by pirates, other times nearly drowned in storms before reaching poorly equipped Thai refugee camps. By 1990 almost a million war refugees had arrived in the United States, three-quarters of them from Vietnam, most of the others from Laos or Cambodia.

8 Thus the profile of Asian immigration resembled an hourglass, with the most newcomers either relatively affluent or extremely poor. Even so, such statistics could be misleading. More than half of all Asian American families lived in just five metropolitan areas—Honolulu, Los Angeles, San Francisco, Chicago, and New York—where the cost of living ranked among the nation's highest. High prices meant real earnings were lower. With professions like dentistry, nursing, and health technology where Asians found work, they often held lower-paying positions. Those Asians who worked in sales were more often retail clerks than insurance agents or stockbrokers.

Asian Downward Mobility

9 Asian American immigrants experienced two forms of downward mobility. First, highly educated Asian immigrants often found it difficult or impossible to land jobs in their professions. To

Practice Exercise

Topic of paragraph 9:

____

____

Main idea sentence of paragraph 9:

____

____

____

List the *supporting details* on separate lines:

____

____

____

____

____

____

____

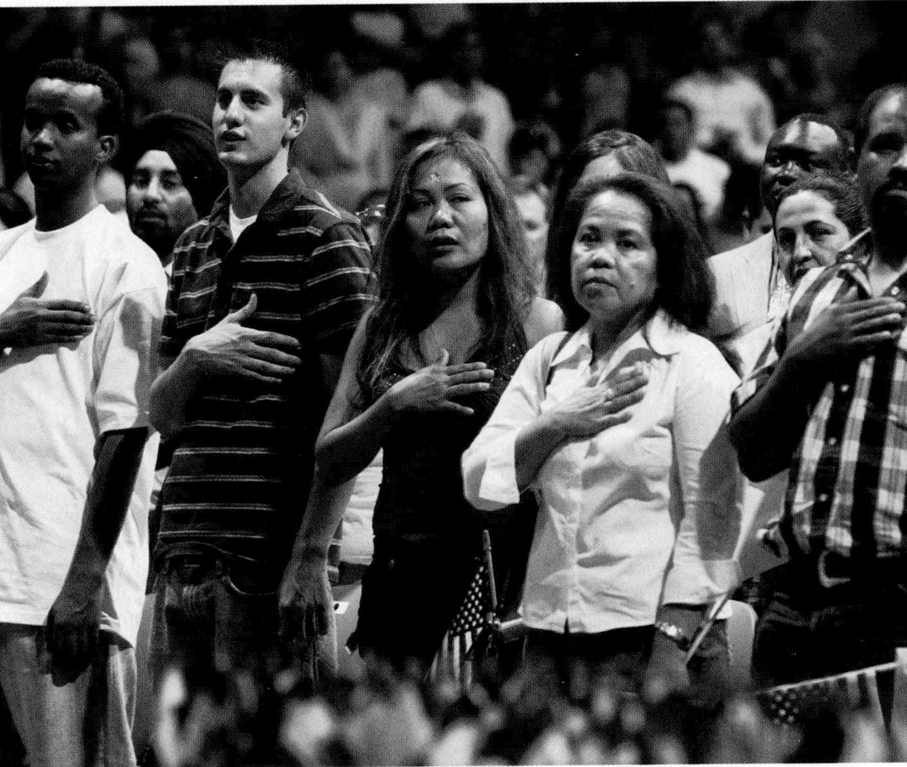

Today's immigrants represent a broad range of nationalities and cultures. These immigrants are at a ceremony that officially makes them U.S. citizens.

Copyright © 2014 The McGraw-Hill Companies, Inc. All rights reserved.

American observers, Korean shopkeepers seemed examples of success, when in fact such owners often enough had been former professionals in their native countries. Here they were forced into the risky small-business world. Second, schools reported significant numbers of Asian American students who were failing. This "lost generation" were most often the children of families who entered the United States with little education and few job skills.

The New Look of America—Latinos

10 Like Asian Americans, Latinos in the United States constituted a diverse group, reflecting dozens of immigrant streams. Although the groups shared a language, they usually settled in distinct urban and suburban barrios across the United States. Such enclave communities provided support to newcomers and an economic foothold for newly established businesses. Money circulated within a community; the workers and owners of an ethnic grocery, for example, spent their wages at neighboring stores, whose profits fueled other immigrant businesses in a chain reaction.

11 Washington Heights, at the northern tip of New York City, followed that path as nearly a quarter of a million Dominicans settled there during the 1970s and 1980s. A hundred blocks to the south, Manhattan's skyscrapers seemed distant; shopkeepers' stereos along the major thoroughfares boomed music of trumpets and congas, while peddlers pushed heavily loaded shopping carts through busy streets, crying "*¡A peso! ¡A peso!*" (*"For a dollar!"*). In addition, Dominican social clubs planned dances or hosted political discussions. Sports clubs competed actively. Similarly, in Miami and elsewhere in South Florida, Cuban Americans created their own self-sustaining enclaves. A large professional class and strong community leadership brought them prosperity and political influence.

12 Along the West Coast, Los Angeles was the urban magnet for many Latino (and Asian) immigrants. Mexican immigrants had long flocked to East Los Angeles, which in the 1990s continued to allow access to the jobs in factories, warehouses, and railroad yards across the river. Many Mexican Americans now owned their own businesses and homes. But beginning in the mid-1980s and 1990s the Los Angeles neighborhood of MacArthur Park became the focal point for the newest immigrants from Mexico and Central America. MacArthur Park was less developed as a community, and many of its residents were transient, passing quickly to other neighborhoods or jobs.

13 More factories and service industries became decentralized locating themselves beyond urban downtowns; the barrios followed as well. Las Americas near Houston was one example; but suburban barrios could be found dotted all across the nation, from Rockville, Maryland, to Pacoima, California, near Burbank. Pacoima's well-kept bungalows housed working-class Mexican Americans who had lived in California for decades. But the front lawns of many houses were often paved over to hold the cars of additional workers or families, and the garages were converted to dormitories with a sink and toilet, where four or five newcomers from Central America could rent a spot to lay a bedroll on the cement floor.

Changes in the Patterns of Global Immigration

14 By the end of the twentieth century, immigration patterns had changed in important ways. Although cities remained the mecca of most immigrants, many newcomers of the 1980s and 1990s settled in suburban areas, particularly in the West and Southwest. Industrial factories provided the lion's share in the 1890s, but a century later the service industries—grocery stores, fast-food chains, janitorial companies—absorbed many more of the new arrivals. Even the faces had changed, as European immigrants found themselves outnumbered by Latinos and Asians, not to mention increasing numbers of Arabs from the Middle East and Africans.

15 This broad geographic range reflected perhaps the most important shift in immigration today: its truly global character.

Practice Exercise

Topic of paragraph 14:

______

______

Main idea sentence of paragraph 14:

______

______

______

______

______

List the *supporting details* on separate lines:

______

______

______

______

______

______

______

______

______

Source: Adapted from James Davidson et al., *Nation of Nations: A Narrative History of the American Republic, Vol. II: Since 1865,* 6th ed., pp. 958–61.

Copyright © 2008 by The McGraw-Hill Companies, Inc. Reprinted by permission of The McGraw-Hill Companies.

Copyright © 2014 The McGraw-Hill Companies, Inc. All rights reserved.

SELECTION **6.3**

History

(continued)

Comprehension and Vocabulary Quiz

This quiz has four parts. Your instructor may assign some or all of them.

Comprehension

Directions: Use the information in the selection to answer each item below.

_______ **1.** Immigration from Mexico rose sharply in the 1980s due to:
a. political unrest.
b. revolutionary conflicts in neighboring countries.
c. downturn in the Mexican economy.
d. all of the above

_______ **2.** The population group in the United States that is projected to have the sharpest increase during the next 50 years is:
a. Hispanics.
b. Asians.
c. Blacks.
d. Whites.

_______ **3.** By 1990, almost three-quarters of a million war refugees had arrived in the United States from:
a. China.
b. Thailand.
c. Vietnam.
d. Cambodia.

_______ **4.** By the end of the twentieth century, more immigrants:
a. had settled in suburban areas.
b. had found work in the service industries.
c. were non-Europeans.
d. all of the above

_______ **5.** The population group in the United States that is projected to remain about the same size during the next 50 years is:
a. Hispanic.
b. Asian.
c. Black.
d. White.

Vocabulary in Context

Directions: For each item below, use context clues to deduce the meaning of the *italicized* word.

_______ **6.** *Turmoil* abroad pushed many immigrants toward the United States, beginning in the 1960s with Fidel Castro's revolution in Cuba and unrest in the Dominican Republic.

European countries have often experienced *turmoil* from massive labor strikes.

turmoil (tûr′ moil) means:

a. arguments

b. agitation; disturbance

c. economic problems

d. revolution

_______ **7.** When Mexico suffered an economic downturn in the 1980s, *emigration* there rose sharply.

After the Nazis came to power, there was a large *emigration* of scientists from Germany to the United States.

emigration (ĕm ĭ grā′ shən) means:

a. problems caused by a poor economy

b. change in a population

c. entering or settling in a country or a region

d. leaving a country or region to settle in another

_______ **8.** Thus the profile of Asian immigration resembled an *hourglass,* with the most newcomers relatively affluent or extremely poor.

The children liked the *hourglass* on display at the museum; they were fascinated that sand trickling through it was once a way to tell time.

hourglass (our′ glăs) means:

a. a large, fragile clock

b. a piece of children's play equipment that consisted of loops and twists

c. an instrument for measuring time, consisting of two glass chambers connected by a narrow neck

d. an instrument of lenses and mirrors that functions as a small telescope

_______ **9.** More than half of all Asian American families lived in five *metropolitan* areas—Honolulu, Los Angeles, San Francisco, Chicago, and New York—where the cost of living ranked among the nation's highest.

The New York Times and *The Washington Post* are two of the best-known *metropolitan* newspapers.

metropolitan (mĕt rə pŏl′ ĭ tən) means:

a. highly interesting; intriguing

b. extremely competitive

c. related to the coast of the United States

d. related to a major city or urbanized area

_______ **10.** MacArthur Park was less developed as a community, and many of its residents were *transient,* passing quickly to other neighborhoods or jobs.

At harvest time, *transient* farm laborers go from farm to farm to pick crops.

transient (trăn′ zē ənt) means:

a. coming from another country

b. remaining in a place only a brief time

c. new to an area

d. homeless

Copyright © 2014 The McGraw-Hill Companies, Inc. All rights reserved.

Word Structure

Directions: In paragraph 9 of the selection, you encountered the word ***generation.*** This word contains the root ***gen,*** which means "birth" or "origin." The word *generation* describes the children, grandchildren, and great-grandchildren of people, the offspring of a family through time. Use the meaning of the root ***gen*** and the list of prefixes on pages 72–73 to help you determine the meaning of each of the following words that contain the same root.

_______ **11.** The science of **genetics** focuses on:

a. the origins of inherited characteristics; heredity.
b. disease and illness.
c. the science of life; biology.
d. nutrition and exercise.

_______ **12.** When a family records their **genealogy,** they:

a. maintain a health record.
b. write a family history.
c. document their descent from their ancestors and their origins.
d. collect heirlooms and memorabilia from relatives.

_______ **13.** To **generate** ideas means:

a. to explain them to others.
b. to produce or give birth to them.
c. to examine or inspect them.
d. to accept them.

_______ **14.** If a person is **ingenious**, he or she:

a. is unskilled.
b. has many relatives.
c. cannot learn new things quickly.
d. has inborn talent.

_______ **15.** Your **progeny** are your:

a. ancestors.
b. enemies.
c. offspring or descendants.
d. friends and neighbors.

Reading Skills Application

Directions: These items test your ability to *apply* certain reading skills. You may not have studied all the skills yet, so some items will serve as a preview.

_______ **16.** Which of the following is the meaning of the term *economic spectrum* as it is used in paragraph 4?

a. variety of backgrounds
b. range of incomes

c. economic specialties
d. wealthy newcomers

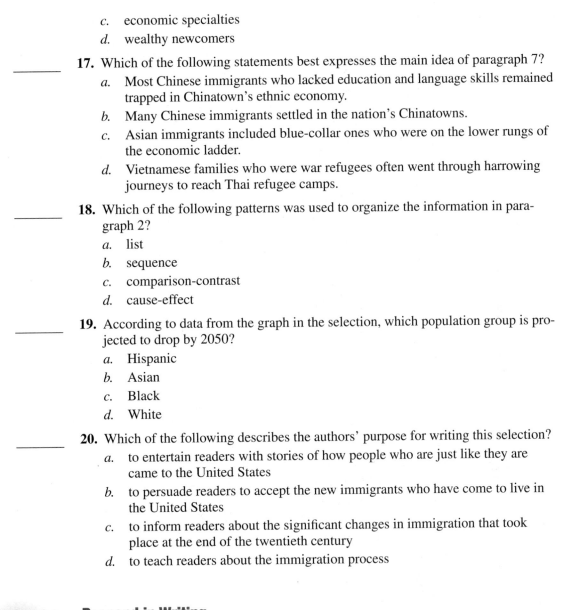

_______ **17.** Which of the following statements best expresses the main idea of paragraph 7?

a. Most Chinese immigrants who lacked education and language skills remained trapped in Chinatown's ethnic economy.
b. Many Chinese immigrants settled in the nation's Chinatowns.
c. Asian immigrants included blue-collar ones who were on the lower rungs of the economic ladder.
d. Vietnamese families who were war refugees often went through harrowing journeys to reach Thai refugee camps.

_______ **18.** Which of the following patterns was used to organize the information in paragraph 2?

a. list
b. sequence
c. comparison-contrast
d. cause-effect

_______ **19.** According to data from the graph in the selection, which population group is projected to drop by 2050?

a. Hispanic
b. Asian
c. Black
d. White

_______ **20.** Which of the following describes the authors' purpose for writing this selection?

a. to entertain readers with stories of how people who are just like they are came to the United States
b. to persuade readers to accept the new immigrants who have come to live in the United States
c. to inform readers about the significant changes in immigration that took place at the end of the twentieth century
d. to teach readers about the immigration process

SELECTION **6.3**
History
(continued)

Respond in Writing

Directions: Refer to the selection as needed to answer the essay-type questions below.

1. **Reacting to What You Have Read:** Most U.S. states and cities have experienced notable immigration trends during the last 20 years. Name the immigrant groups that have settled recently in your city or region of the country. Have any population groups grown? Have any population groups declined?

____

____

____

Copyright © 2014 The McGraw-Hill Companies, Inc. All rights reserved.

2. **Comprehending the Selection Further:** The authors of this selection discuss how immigration has become truly global, with immigrants coming to the United States from every part of the world. In what ways do immigrants who settle in the United States enrich our culture and economy? List at least 4 ways.

3. **Overall Main Idea of the Selection:** In one sentence, tell what the authors want readers to understand about the recent changes in immigration to the United States. (Be sure to include "immigration," "Asian American," and "Latino" in your overall main idea sentence.)

Internet Resources

Read More about It Online

Directions: To learn more about the topic of this selection, see the websites below or use the keywords **"U.S. immigration," "Asian Americans,"** or **"U.S. Latinos"** with a search engine.

http://en.wikipedia.org/wiki/Immigration_to_the_United_States
At this Wikipedia entry, see the sections on "Contemporary Immigration," "Demography," and "Origin."

www.census.gov/newsroom/releases/archives/facts_for_features_special_editions/cb11-ff06.html
U.S. Census Bureau website's "Profile American: Facts for Features"; posted for Asian/Pacific Heritage Month. Facts about the Asian American population and other aspects of their lives and culture; explains why May was chosen as Asian/Pacific Heritage Month.

www.census.gov/newsroom/releases/archives/facts_for_features_special_editions/cb11-ff18.html
U.S. Census Bureau website's "Profile American: Facts for Features"; posted for Hispanic Heritage Month, September 15–October 15, 2011. Data about this group of Americans; explains why September 15–October was chosen as Hispanic Heritage Month.

www.usimmigrationsupport.org
This is the United States Government Immigration Support site. It contains information about obtaining U.S. citizenship, green cards, and U.S. visas.

Copyright © 2014 The McGraw-Hill Companies, Inc. All rights reserved.

CHAPTER 7

Recognizing Authors' Writing Patterns

LEARNING OBJECTIVES

In this chapter you will learn the answers to these questions:

- What are authors' writing patterns, and why are they important?
- How are transition words used to indicate the relationship of ideas within and between sentences?
- What is the method for recognizing authors' writing patterns?

CHAPTER CONTENTS

NEW INFORMATION AND SKILLS

WHAT ARE AUTHORS' WRITING PATTERNS, AND WHY ARE THEY IMPORTANT?

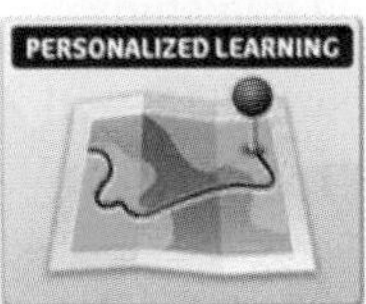

In the first part of this chapter, you will learn how authors use transition words to show the relationship of ideas within sentences and the relationship of ideas between sentences.

Next, you will be introduced to five common writing patterns textbook authors frequently use to organize paragraphs and longer selections they write:

- Definition pattern
- List pattern
- Sequence pattern
- Comparison-contrast pattern
- Cause-effect pattern

Finally, you will be introduced to other patterns you are likely to encounter in college textbooks and other materials:

- Definition-and-example pattern
- Generalization-and-example pattern
- Location or spatial order pattern
- Summary pattern
- Classification pattern
- Addition pattern
- Statement-and-clarification pattern

writing patterns

Ways authors organize the information they present.

Writing patterns are also known as *organizational patterns, patterns of development,* and *thinking patterns.*

Writing patterns are ways authors organize the information they present. You may hear writing patterns referred to as *patterns of organization, patterns of development,* or *thinking patterns.* These are all names for the same thing.

We all use patterns to organize our thoughts in ways that seem logical to us. The patterns authors use are the same thinking patterns that you use every day. If you can identify the pattern an author is using and "think along" with the author as you read, you will find it easier to comprehend what he or she is saying.

The specific transition words or pattern an author uses depends on the important relationship among the ideas, the relationship he or she wants to emphasize. The author chooses the most logical pattern that will accomplish this.

Just as textbook authors use patterns to organize their thoughts, so do you and all college students. Here are everyday examples of how college students use patterns to organize their thoughts. Notice how the content of their comments matches the pattern of organization being used.

"My art professor asked me to prepare a portfolio, a representative collection of my work." *(definition)*

"I'm taking four courses this semester: history, psychology, reading, and math." *(list pattern)*

"I have my history class first, then psychology class. On alternate days, I have my reading class first, then my math class." *(sequence pattern)*

"I have weekly quizzes in history and math, but not in reading or psychology." *(comparison-contrast pattern)*

"If I maintain at least a B average this semester, my scholarship will be renewed." *(cause-effect pattern)*

Copyright © 2014 The McGraw-Hill Companies, Inc. All rights reserved.

Although you use patterns when you speak or write, you may not be in the habit of recognizing them when you read and study your textbooks. This chapter will show you how to recognize the patterns when you are reading.

Why is it important to be able to recognize authors' writing patterns? There are four advantages to recognizing authors' writing patterns when you read and study:

- *Your comprehension will improve.* You will comprehend more because you will be able to follow and understand the writers' ideas more accurately and more efficiently.
- *You will be able to predict what is coming next.* As soon as you identify the pattern, you can make predictions about what is likely to come next in a paragraph. As you learned in Chapter 1, effective readers are active readers who make logical predictions as they read.
- *It will be easier to memorize information when you study.* You can memorize information more efficiently when you understand the way it is organized. Consequently, you will also be able to recall it more effectively.
- *Your writing will improve.* Using these patterns when you write will enable you to write paragraphs that are clearer and better organized. This also means you can write better answers on essay tests simply by using appropriate patterns to organize information.

TRANSITION WORDS THAT SIGNAL THE RELATIONSHIP OF IDEAS WITHIN SENTENCES AND BETWEEN SENTENCES

Did you realize that within each sample sentence on page 355 there was a relationship among the ideas it contained? These relationships are so common that we barely notice them when we read them or use them when we speak or write.We understand them and their importance, however. For example, you would have one expectation if your sister begins a sentence, "I was hoping my boyfriend would propose, *and*. . . ." You would have a different expectation if she said, "I was hoping my boyfriend would propose, *but*. . . ." The words *and* and *but* suggest two very different endings to the sentence—and outcomes!

Like everyone else, authors use certain words to show the relationship of ideas within sentences and between sentences. Words and phrases that show relationships among ideas in sentences, paragraphs, and longer selections are called **transition words.** (You will learn later in the chapter that they use these same words to signal the organization of paragraphs and longer selections, as well.) You can improve your comprehension of college textbooks if you pay attention to transition words. Now read about the types of relationships below and the transition words that signal them. In the examples, the transition words are italicized.

transition words

Words and phrases that show relationships among ideas in sentences, paragraphs, and longer selections.

Addition The transition words signal that the author is giving additional information. The order of the information or facts is not important. Transition words that signal addition include *moreover, another, in addition, also, first, second,* and *next*.

- *Within-sentence example:* "Swimmer Michael Phelps has won 22 Olympic medals, 18 of them gold; *moreover,* he received a special award at the 2012 Olympics declaring him the greatest Olympic athlete of all time."
- *Between-sentences example:* "At the opening ceremonies of the Olympics, the Olympic torch is ignited. *Another* tradition is the releasing of doves. *In addition,* each country's athletes parade around the stadium track."

Sequence The transition words signal that the author is presenting things in the order in which they happened or will happen. Watch for words that indicate time, such as *first, then, later, previous, before, earlier, during, next, last,* and *finally*. Some of the same words used for the addition relationship can also indicate a time relationship if the order matters.

- *Within-sentence example:* "In December 1787, the *first* state to enter the United States was Delaware, *followed by* Pennsylvania, and *then* New Jersey."
- *Between-sentences example:* "*During* 1959, the final two states joined the Union. In August, Hawaii became the *last* state to join. Alaska joined eight months *earlier,* in January."

Contrast The transition words signal that the author is presenting a difference, an opposing view, or an exception. These words include *in contrast, but, on the other hand, on the contrary, unlike,* and *although*.

- *Within-sentence examples:* "*Although* presidential conventions used to be lively events, today they are duller, made-for-television affairs" and "There is still no cure for AIDS, *but* there are effective drugs."
- *Between-sentences examples:* "Crossword puzzles have always been popular. *However,* sudoku math puzzles are gaining widespread popularity" and "Halley's comet appears every 75 years. *In contrast,* the Hale-Bopp comet appears every 2,400 years."

Comparison The transition words signal that the author is presenting one or more ways that things are alike (makes a comparison). Transition words such as *similarly, like, likewise, in the same way, along the same lines, in the same manner,* and *both* indicate that a comparison is being made.

- *Within-sentence example*: "The Olympics is a competition among the world's best athletes; *similarly,* the Paralympics is a world competition among people with physical disabilities who have top-level athletic ability."
- *Between-sentences example:* "Facebook is a top social media website. *Similarly*, Twitter is highly popular."

Cause-Effect The transition words signal that the author is presenting causes (reasons things happen) or effects (results or outcomes). Watch for transitions such as *resulted in, as a result, led to, caused, due to, because, caused by, so, consequently, therefore,* and *thus*.

- *Within-sentence example:* "*Because* the Senate of ancient Rome wanted to honor Julius Caesar, it named the month of July in his honor." (*cause:* Senate wanted to honor Julius Caesar; *effect/result:* it named the month of July after him.)
- *Between-sentences example:* "The Roman Senate also wanted to honor Emperor Augustus Caesar. *Consequently,* it named the month of August after him." (*cause:* Senate wanted to honor Emperor Augustus Caesar; *effect/result:* it named the month of August after him.)

Example The transition words signal that the author is presenting an example that will help clarify or explain something. Transition words that announce examples are *to illustrate, such as, for instance,* and *for example*.

- *Within-sentence example:* "Florida boasts some unique national parks, *such as* the Everglades."

Copyright © 2014 The McGraw-Hill Companies, Inc. All rights reserved.

- *Between-sentences example:* "California has many famous national parks. *Examples* include Yosemite National Park, Redwood National Park, and Sequoia National Park."

Conclusion The transition words signal that the author is presenting a conclusion, an outcome based on facts that preceded it. Signal words include *in conclusion, thus, therefore,* and *consequently.*

- *Within-sentence example:* "The chairman of the board was accused of wrongdoing, and *thus* he was forced to resign."
- *Between-sentences example:* "Bogus U.S. paper currency has become a massive problem. *Consequently,* the government is introducing paper currency that is much more difficult to counterfeit."

Summary The transition words signal that the author is presenting a summary, a restatement of the most important point or points. Signal words include *to summarize, in summary, in brief,* and *in short.*

- *Within-sentence example:* "*In short,* world population increase and environmental damage go hand in hand."
- *Between-sentences example:* "Behavioral, genetic, hormonal, environmental, and cultural factors contribute to obesity. It can be said, *in summary,* that there are multiple causes of obesity."

Authors do not always use transition words to signal the relationship of ideas within sentences and between sentences. Even when there are no transition words, you still need to figure out the relationship among the ideas. Go back through the material and think about how it is organized. Seeing the relationship among ideas will help you understand and remember the material. And, as writing and English instructors will tell you, the correct use of transition words will make your own writing clearer and more effective.

Here is a short selection with the transition words italicized. Notice how they guide you through the material from one thought to the next:

> A cup of coffee is harmless, right? Perhaps, but people who drink too much coffee can experience undesirable changes in their heart rate, breathing rate, and blood pressure. *Moreover,* those who are allergic to caffeine can experience severe reactions, *such as* excruciating migraine headaches. Even those who do not have severe reactions may still experience irritation to their stomach lining when they drink coffee on an empty stomach. *And,* of course, everyone knows that coffee can make you jumpy and jittery. *On the other hand,* for those who are about to exercise, a small amount of caffeine can actually improve athletic performance. *The point is,* you must know your own body and respect its tolerance for coffee.

Here is the same passage, but explanations of the transitions have been inserted [*in italics, in brackets, and highlighted, like this*]. Notice how the author uses the transitions to steer or guide readers through the ideas.

A cup of coffee is harmless, right? [*Introductory question designed to get the reader's attention.*] Perhaps, but people who drink too much coffee can experience undesirable changes in their heart rate, breathing rate, and blood pressure. [*Answers the introductory question by listing some possible negative effects.*] *Moreover,* [*the explanation of undesirable effects is going to be continued*] those who are allergic to caffeine can experience severe reactions, *such as* [*an example is being introduced*] excruciating migraine headaches. Even those who do not have severe reactions may still experience irritation to their stomach lining when they drink coffee on an empty stomach. *And,* [*more negative effects will be presented*] of course, everyone knows that coffee can make you jumpy and jittery. *On the other hand,* [*a change; something positive about coffee will be presented*] for those who are about to exercise, a small amount of caffeine can actually improve athletic performance. *The point is,* [*announces the main idea*] you must know your own body and respect its tolerance for coffee.

As you read, be alert for transition words that show the relationship of ideas within and between sentences. They also provide clues to the author's pattern of organization. Recognizing the pattern or "big picture" is a skill that will make you a more effective, efficient reader.

EXERCISE 1

Relationships of Ideas within and between Sentences

Directions: Read the following paragraph. Decide which transition word belongs in each sentence and write it in the blank.

later	and	as a result of	consequently	because	however

Mount Rushmore is South Dakota's most famous attraction. Sculptor Gutzon Borglum created it ______________ he wished to commemorate four great American presidents. In 1927, he began carving 60-foot-tall faces of Washington, Jefferson, Lincoln, ______________ Theodore Roosevelt on the side of the mountain. He died in 1941, ______________. ______________, his son, Lincoln, completed the project ______________ that year. ______________ Borglum's vision, dedication, and artistry, America gained a unique landmark.

Directions: Read the sentences of the following paragraph. Then circle the letter that answers each question about the relationships of ideas within and between sentences. The sentences in the paragraph are numbered for convenience.

(1) Thomas Edison is one of the most brilliant, hardworking, and prolific inventors in American history. (2) However, he had only three months of formal schooling. (3) Edison's teacher thought he was "addled," so Nancy Edison home-schooled her son. (4) Besides having limited formal education, young Edison developed hearing problems that worsened throughout his life. (5) Despite these challenges, he ultimately held more

(continued on the next page)

than 1,300 U.S. and foreign patents for inventions he developed. (6) In short, Edison was remarkable both as a person and as an inventor.

1. What is the relationship between sentence 1 and sentence 2?
a. contrast
b. conclusion
c. example
d. cause-effect

2. What is the relationship of the ideas within sentence 3?
a. addition
b. example
c. summary
d. cause-effect

3. What is the relationship between the two ideas in sentence 4?
a. addition
b. contrast
c. summary
d. cause-effect

4. What is the relationship between the two ideas in sentence 5?
a. addition
b. contrast
c. summary
d. cause-effect

5. How does sentence 6 relate to the previous sentences?
a. Sentence 6 adds information to the previous sentences.
b. Sentence 6 presents a comparison with the previous sentences.
c. Sentence 6 presents a cause-effect relationship with the previous sentences.
d. Sentence 6 summarizes information in the previous sentences.

FIVE COMMON WRITING PATTERNS

Comprehension Monitoring Question for Recognizing Authors' Writing Patterns

"What pattern did the author use to organize the main idea and the supporting details?"

Five common writing patterns are described in this section, along with textbook excerpts that illustrate each pattern. You will be pleased to learn that every pattern has certain words and phrases that serve as signals or clues to the pattern that is being used. These signal words for a pattern will be the same regardless of what the material is about. For example, the words *In contrast* will still signal a contrast, or difference, regardless of whether the topic is types of trees or parenting styles. Keep in mind that the pattern will be determined by the organization of the ideas in the entire paragraph or selection, not by the presence of a single signal word or clue. In other words, seeing a word that can be used as a signal for a pattern does not automatically mean that the entire paragraph has that pattern. For example, a paragraph might contain the word *because* in one of its sentences, yet the entire paragraph could be a comparison and contrast pattern, not a cause-effect pattern.

After you read a textbook paragraph, ask yourself the comprehension monitoring question, "What pattern did the author use to organize the main idea and the supporting details?"

Definition Pattern

Every college textbook contains important terms that will be new to students. To help you understand these key terms, authors typically define them. The sentence that gives the definition is usually the stated main idea. The rest of the paragraph will consist of additional information about the meaning of the term. When authors present the meaning of an important term that is discussed throughout the passage, they are using the **definition pattern.** Key terms and their definitions are important. Learn them, and learn to spell them. Expect to be asked them on tests.

definition pattern

Pattern presenting the meaning of an important term discussed throughout the paragraph.

The definition can occur anywhere in a paragraph. Signal words that announce definitions are *this term, means, is known as, is called, refers to,* and *is defined as.* In addition, the key term may appear in **bold,** *italics,* or **color.** Sometimes the definition follows a colon (:) or a comma (,), is set off in parentheses ( ) or in brackets [], or appears after a dash (—) or between dashes. (See "Other Things to Keep in Mind When Developing a College-Level Vocabulary," page 79, for examples of definitions set off with punctuation.) The author may use a synonym (word or phrase with a similar meaning) to define the term. Synonyms are introduced by words such as *or, in other words,* and *that is.* A definition pattern paragraph is typically organized like this:

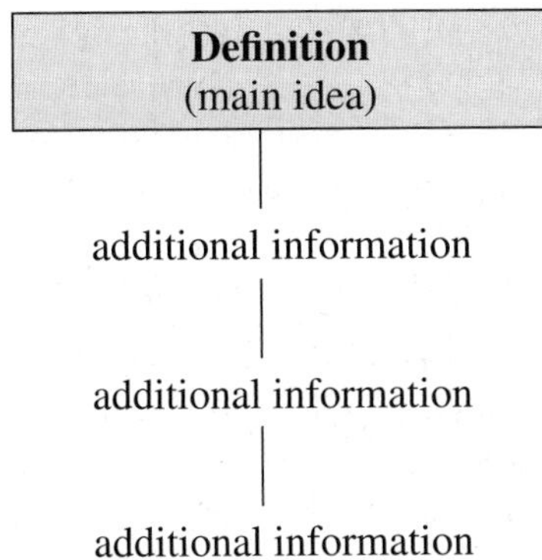

Here is a sample definition pattern paragraph from a business textbook. The topic is *productivity.* The first sentence presents the definition. Notice that it is also the main idea and that the other sentence is a detail that supplies additional information.

> **Productivity** refers to the amount of output you generate given the amount of input. The more you can produce in any given period of time, the more money you are worth to companies.
>
> *Source:* Adapted from William Nickels, James McHugh, and Susan McHugh, *Understanding Business*, 9th ed., p. 14. Copyright © 2010 by The McGraw-Hill Companies, Inc. Reprinted by permission of The McGraw-Hill Companies.

Stop and Annotate

Go back to the textbook excerpt. Underline or highlight the signal words *refers to* that announce the definition.

The phrase *refers to* introduces the definition: "the amount of output you generate given the amount of input."

EXERCISE 2

Directions: In each sentence, underline the clues and signal words that indicate a definition, and then highlight the definition.

Example: *Inductive reasoning* is defined as the process of arriving at a general conclusion based on specific facts or instances. (Clues: term in italics, is defined as)

1. Sociologists use the term **exogamy** to describe the custom of marrying outside the tribe, family, clan, or other social unit.
2. You may hear a compassionate person who unselfishly helps others referred to as a "good Samaritan."
3. Some infomercials sell nostrums—quack medicines that contain "secret" ingredients and whose effectiveness is unproved.
4. Writer Samuel Clemens used "Mark Twain" as his pseudonym, or pen name.
5. When authors write under a ***pseudonym,*** it means they write under a fictitious rather than their own name.

EXERCISE 3

This paragraph comes from a science textbook.

The concept of an **ecological footprint** has been developed to help people measure their environmental impact on the earth. One's ecological footprint is defined as "the area of Earth's productive land and water required to supply the resources that an individual demands, as well as to absorb the wastes that the individual produces." Websites exist that allow you to estimate your ecological footprint and compare it to the footprint of others by answering a few questions about your lifestyle. Running through one of these exercises is a good way to gain a sense of personal responsibility for your own environmental impact.

Source: Eldon Enger and Bradley Smith, *Environmental Science: A Study of Interrelationships*, 12th ed., p. 29. Copyright © 2010 by The McGraw-Hill Companies, Inc. Reprinted by permission of The McGraw-Hill Companies.

Which writing pattern did the author use to organize the main idea and the supporting details?

____

Write the clues that caused you to choose this pattern.

____

____

____

EXERCISE 4

This paragraph comes from a psychology textbook.

The scientific study of behavior and mental processes is known as **psychology**. The phrase *behavior and mental processes* in the definition of psychology must be understood to mean many things: It encompasses not just people's

Stop and Annotate

Go back to the preceding textbook excerpt. Underline or highlight the words five rules and the colon that signals a list. Then write a small ①, ②, ③, ④, and ⑤ beside the five items on the list.

The five details (the rules of courtesy) are in no specific order and are in a list that is set off from the rest of the paragraph. It is announced by the phrase "The following five rules . . ." and also by a colon (:). Each of the five guidelines is bulleted so that it stands out clearly. Writing a small number beside each item will help you remember that there are five rules.

EXERCISE 5

Directions: In each sentence, underline or highlight the clues and signal words that indicate a list.

Example: Clouds are generally divided into <u>two categories:</u> convective and layered.

1. Be sure to see these tourist attractions in Philadelphia's Independence National Historical Park: Congress Hall, Independence Hall, and the Liberty Bell Pavilion.
2. Primary colors that can be combined to create a range of other colors are
   - red
   - blue
   - yellow
3. The governor will be at the fundraiser. In addition, both state senators, as well as four representatives, will be there.
4. Clouds are categorized according to their height above the earth. High clouds include (1) cirrus clouds, (2) cirrocumulus clouds, and (3) cirrostratus clouds.
5. In the Four Corners area of the southwestern United States, the corners of Colorado, New Mexico, Arizona, and Utah come together at right angles.

EXERCISE 6

This paragraph comes from a health textbook.

The Millennial Generation

"Millennial generation" is the name given to today's young adults, 18 to 28 years old. Persons born between 1982 and 2000 are referred to collectively by sociologists as "millennials." Studies have found that millennials are more inclined to drop out of college for a period of time, and take longer to finish college even if they have not dropped out. Also, millennials are more likely to change colleges, and to change residences while attending the same college. In addition, they are more likely to share a residence with friends from college than to live alone or to return to home. Individuals within this generation are more likely to fill leisure time with technology-based media. Another characteristic of millennials is that they are more likely to have a diverse group of friends, in terms of both gender and race. Millennials are more likely to return home to live after completing college—the "boomerang" phenomenon.

Source: Adapted from Wayne Payne, Dale Hahn, and Ellen Lucas. *Understanding Your Health,* 10th ed., p. 2. Copyright © 2009 by The McGraw-Hill Companies, Inc. Reprinted by permission of The McGraw-Hill Companies.

Copyright © 2014 The McGraw-Hill Companies, Inc. All rights reserved.

Which writing pattern did the author use to organize the main idea and the supporting details?

____

Write the clues that caused you to choose this pattern.

____

____

Sequence Pattern

sequence pattern

A list of items presented in a specific order because the order is important.

The sequence pattern is also known as *time order, chronological order, a process,* or *a series.*

In the **sequence pattern** a list of items is presented *in a specific order* because the order is important. A sequence is a type of list, but it differs from a list because the order of the items matters. A common type of sequence is a series of events presented in the order in which they happened. For this reason, the sequence pattern is sometimes called *time order, chronological order, a process,* or *a series.* Sets of directions (such as recipes, instructions for changing a tire or for loading a software program on a computer) are sequences you encounter daily. Examples of processes include life cycles described in a biology textbook or a description in a government textbook about how legislation is created.

To emphasize or set off separate items in a sequence pattern, authors often use:

- Words such as *first, second, third, then, next, finally.*
- Words and phrases that refer to time, such as dates, days of the week, names of months or phrases such as *during the 20th century* or *in the previous decade.*
- Enumeration (*1, 2, 3,* etc.).
- Letters (*a, b, c,* etc.).
- Signal words such as *steps, stages, phases, progression, process, series,* and even the word *sequence.* (These often occur in the main idea sentence.)

Paragraphs with the sequence pattern are typically structured like this:

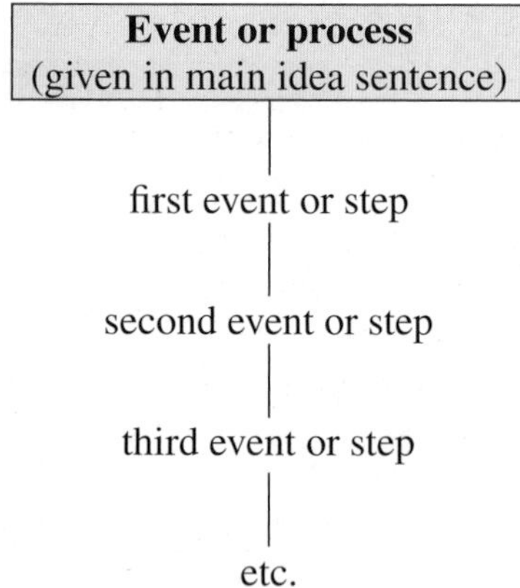

Here is an excerpt from a music appreciation textbook. In it, the author uses a sequence pattern to present some events of *Louis Armstrong's life* (the topic). The stated main idea is the first sentence *From humble beginnings, trumpeter and singer Louis "Satchmo" Armstrong went on to have a long career and a worldwide impact on jazz.* Read the paragraph and notice the dates that indicate the events that are being presented in chronological order.

From humble beginnings, trumpeter and singer Louis "Satchmo" Armstrong went on to have a long career and a worldwide impact on jazz. Born in 1901 in a poor black section of New Orleans, he learned to play the cornet in a reformatory, where he was sent at the age of thirteen for shooting a gun in the air during a New Year's celebration. On his release after one year of confinement, Armstrong was soon playing in honky-tonks at night. In 1918 he joined the famous Kid Ory Band. Four years later, he went to Chicago to join King Oliver's Creole Band. In 1925 he started to make a series of recordings that established his reputation as a leading jazz trumpeter. After 1930 he appeared with a wide variety of groups, made many tours, and was featured in many films. In the 1950s and 1960s he served as a "goodwill ambassador" for the United States. In 1964, at the age of 64, he had his greatest popular success, the hit recording *Hello, Dolly!* When Armstrong died in 1971, jazz lost one of its greats.

Source: Adapted from Roger Kamien, *Music: An Appreciation,* 10th ed., p. 478. Copyright © 2011 by The McGraw-Hill Companies, Inc. Reprinted by permission of The McGraw-Hill Companies.

Stop and Annotate

Go back to the textbook excerpt. Underline or highlight the dates and the references to Armstrong at different ages. Then write a ① beside *In 1901*, a ② beside *at the age of thirteen*, a ③ beside *after one year*, a ④ beside *soon*, a ⑤ beside *In 1918*, and so forth.

The supporting details in this sequence tell some key events in his life in the order they occurred. The order of the information is important because the sequence tells steps in Armstrong's career in the order they occurred.

EXERCISE 7

Directions: For each sentence, write on the line provided the event that happened first. Remember that you need to identify the event that came first in reality, which may or may not be the event mentioned first in the sentence. Underline the signal word or words in each sentence.

	Event That Happens or Happened First
Example: Paul addressed the postcard and then mailed it.	Paul addressed the postcard
1. A tadpole uses its front legs to crawl onto land after it reaches a certain stage of development.	
2. It took until 5 o'clock to finish the project, even though we started at noon.	
3. Information must enter short-term memory before it can move into long-term memory.	
4. She did remember me, although I had to tell her my name first.	
5. We went to the aquarium and later we went to the zoo.	

EXERCISE 8

This paragraph comes from a psychology textbook.

The SQ3R method consists of five steps, designated by the initials S-Q-R-R-R. The first step is to *survey,* in which you give yourself an overview of the major points of the material. The next step is to *question.* Formulate questions about the material—either aloud or in writing—prior to actually reading a section of the text. In the next step, *read* the material carefully and, even more important, actively and critically. The *recite* step involves describing and explaining to yourself the material you have just read and answering the questions you posed earlier. Finally, *review* the material, looking it over, reading end-of-chapter summaries, and answering the in-text review questions.

Source: Adapted from Robert Feldman, *P.O.W.E.R. Learning: Strategies for Success in College and Life,* 5th ed., pp. 158–59. Copyright © 2011 by The McGraw-Hill Companies, Inc. Reprinted by permission of The McGraw-Hill Companies.

Which writing pattern did the author use to organize the main idea and the supporting details?

____

Write the clues that caused you to choose this pattern.

____

____

EXERCISE 9

This paragraph comes from a government textbook.

Early Colonization

The first permanent British colony in North America was Jamestown, founded in 1607 by the Virginia Company of London for the purpose of developing trade and mining gold. By 1619, colonists realized that there was no gold, and harsh conditions coupled with conflicts with native populations hampered trade. The Crown took control of the failing colony in 1624, replacing the colony's president with a royal governor.

Source: Adapted from Joseph Losco and Ralph Baker, *AM GOV 2011,* p. 19. Copyright © 2011 by The McGraw-Hill Companies, Inc. Reprinted by permission of The McGraw-Hill Companies.

Which writing pattern did the authors use to organize the main idea and the supporting details?

____

Write the clues that caused you to choose this pattern.

____

____

comparison-contrast pattern

Similarities (comparisons) between two or more things are presented, differences (contrasts) between two or more things are presented, or both similarities and differences are presented.

The comparison-contrast pattern is also known as *ideas in opposition.*

Comparison-Contrast Pattern

Often writers want to emphasize comparisons and contrasts. A *comparison* shows how two or more things are similar (alike). A *contrast* points out the differences between them. In the **comparison-contrast pattern,** similarities (comparisons) between two or more things are presented, differences (contrasts) between two or more things are presented, or both similarities and differences are presented.

To signal comparisons, authors use words such as *similarly, likewise, both, same,* and *also.* To signal contrasts, authors use clues such as *on the other hand, in contrast, however, while, whereas, although, nevertheless, different, unlike,* and *some . . . others.* Contrasts are also signaled by words in a paragraph that have opposite meanings, such as *liberals and conservatives, Internet users and non-Internet users,* and *people who attended college and people who never attended college.*

Paragraphs organized to show comparisons and/or contrasts are typically structured like this:

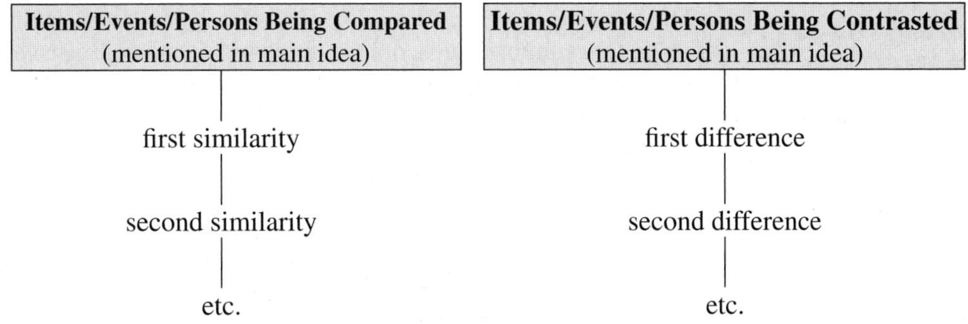

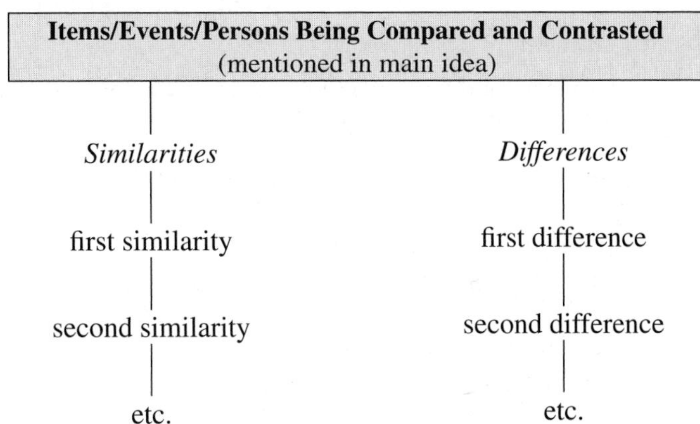

As the heading suggests, the following excerpt from a business textbook has as its topic *mediation and arbitration.* The first sentence is the stated main idea: *Rather than go to court, many businesspeople are turning to mediation and arbitration, two alternative methods of settling business arguments.* As you read the paragraph, ask yourself, "What are mediation and arbitration, and how are they alike and different?"

Mediation and Arbitration

Rather than go to court, many businesspeople are turning to mediation and arbitration, two alternative methods of settling business arguments. Two of these are mediation and arbitration. *Mediation* is a type of negotiation in which one or more third-party mediators, usually chosen by the disputing parties, help to reach a settlement. The mediator suggests ways to solve the problem. The participants do not have to accept the mediator's suggestions. In *arbitration,* the dispute is submitted to arbitrators. As with mediators, the arbitrators are usually chosen by the disputing parties. However, arbitration differs from mediation in that an arbitrator's decision must be followed, whereas a mediator merely offers suggestions and facilitates negotiations.

Source: O.C. Ferrell, Geoffrey Hirt, and Linda Ferrell, *Business: A Changing World,* 8th ed., p. 70. Copyright © 2011 by The McGraw-Hill Companies, Inc. Reprinted by permission of The McGraw-Hill Companies.

Stop and Annotate

Go back to the textbook excerpt. Underline or highlight the clues that signal a comparison-contrast pattern: *Rather than, As with, However, differs from,* and *whereas.*

The words *Rather than, As with, However, differs from,* and *whereas* are clues or signals that the author is presenting a comparison and contrast. Mediation and arbitration are being compared and contrasted. Both are ways to resolve business disputes. Both involve bringing in outside help that the disputing parties agree on. The difference is that mediators recommend solutions but the disputing parties do not have to accept them, whereas an arbitrator's solution must be accepted.

EXERCISE 10

Directions: Decide whether each sentence presents a comparison or a contrast. On the line provided, write the items that are being compared or contrasted. Underline the signal word or words in each sentence that help you distinguish whether a comparison is being made or a contrast is being presented.

	Comparison or Contrast	Items Compared or Contrasted
Example: Bob likes baseball, although he likes football even more.	contrast	baseball, football (how much Bob likes each)
1. June is hot, but July is hotter.	________	________
2. Both Juan and Maria serve as Red Cross volunteers.	________	________
3. We thought the test items would be multiple-choice; however, they consisted of only three essay questions.	________	________
4. Beth is very easygoing, and her sister has a similar temperament.	________	________
5. Some students choose liberal arts majors; others choose majors in science or technical fields.	________	________

EXERCISE 11

This paragraph comes from a psychology textbook.

How to appropriately and effectively teach the increasing number of children who do not speak English is not always clear. Many educators maintain that *bilingual education* is best. With a bilingual approach, students learn some subjects in their native language while simultaneously learning English. Proponents of bilingualism believe that students must develop a sound footing in basic subject areas and that, initially at least, teaching those subjects in their native language is the only way to provide them with that foundation. In contrast, other educators insist that all instruction ought to be in English from the moment students, including those who speak no English at all, enroll in school. In *immersion programs*, students are immediately plunged into English instruction in all subjects. The reasoning is that teaching students in a language other than English simply hinders nonnative English speakers' integration into society and ultimately does them a disservice.

Source: Adapted from Robert S. Feldman, *Understanding Psychology*, 8th ed., pp. 281–82. Copyright © 2008 by The McGraw-Hill Companies, Inc. Reprinted by permission of The McGraw-Hill Companies.

Which writing pattern did the author use to organize the main idea and the supporting details?

____

Write the clues that caused you to choose this pattern.

____

____

Cause-Effect Pattern

cause-effect pattern

Reasons (causes) and results (effects) of events or conditions are presented.

The **cause-effect pattern** presents reasons (causes) of events or conditions and results (effects) of events or conditions. Authors often use these words to indicate a cause: *because, the reasons, causes, is due to,* and *is caused by.* These words are often used to indicate an effect: *therefore, consequently, thus, as a consequence, led to, the result, as a result, the effect was,* and *this resulted in.*

In reality, causes always precede effects, and authors typically present causes first and then their effects. However, authors sometimes present an effect and *then* state its cause. Read these two sentences: *The extreme changes in the weather are due to global warming* and *Global warming has caused extreme changes in the weather.* Both sentences have the same message. And, in both cases, *global warming* is the cause and *the extreme changes in weather* is the effect. The order that the cause and effect are presented *in the sentence* does not change which one is the cause and which one is the effect. Do not assume that whatever is mentioned first *in a sentence* is always the cause! You must determine which event occurred first *in reality.*

Paragraphs organized to show causes and/or effects are typically structured in one of the following ways:

Copyright © 2014 The McGraw-Hill Companies, Inc. All rights reserved.

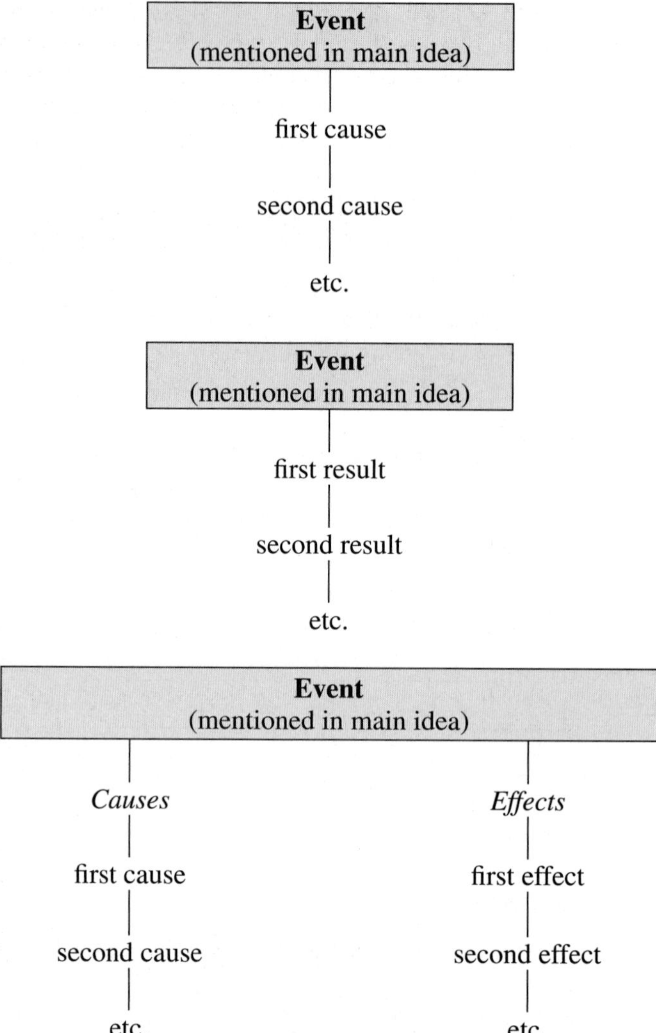

The following excerpt from a marriage and family textbook uses the cause-effect pattern. Its topic is the *effects of deployment*. The first sentence is the stated main idea, *For families in the military, deployment, the time when a military person leaves his or her family and engages in training or combat, affects many aspects of life.* As you read the paragraph, ask yourself, "How does deployment affect military families?"

For families in the military, **deployment**, the time when a military person leaves his or her family and engages in training or combat, affects many aspects of life. Because the couple and family have no control over where or when the family member will be deployed, it produces uncertainty. Those who are deployed may experience the lasting effects of trauma from their war experience. The family members remaining at home experience the effects of separation, reunion, and other difficulties. Sleep disorders, anxiety, depression, and other mental health issues can also result.

Source: Adapted from David Olson, John DeFrain, and Linda Skogrand, *Marriages and Families: Intimacy, Diversity, and Strengths,* 7th ed., pp. 411, 413. Copyright © 2011 by The McGraw-Hill Companies, Inc. Reprinted by permission of The McGraw-Hill Companies.

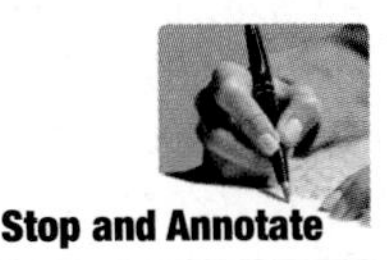

Stop and Annotate

Go back to the preceding textbook excerpt. Underline or highlight the clue words that signal a cause-effect pattern: *affects, Because, produces, effects,* and *result.*

The words *affects, Because, produces, effects,* and *result* signal a cause-effect pattern. The paragraph mentions the effects of deployment on military families: the uncertainty, the possible trauma to the military person during deployment, the effects on family members of separation, reunion, and other difficulties, and sleep disorders, anxiety, depression, and other mental health issues.

EXERCISE 12

Directions: On the lines provided, write the cause and the effect presented in each sentence. Underline the signal word or words in each sentence that helped you distinguish the cause from the effect.

	Cause	Effect
Example: He came in second; thus, he won the silver medal.	*he came in second*	*he won the silver medal*
1. Because of the rainstorm, the streets were flooded.	__________	__________
2. Banks are closed today due to the national holiday.	__________	__________
3. Carla's medication resulted in a weight gain.	__________	__________
4. The reason he left was that he was mad.	__________	__________
5. The cause of the accident was faulty brakes.	__________	__________

EXERCISE 13

This paragraph comes from a psychology textbook.

Caffeine produces several reactions. One major behavioral effect is an increase in attentiveness. Another major behavioral effect is a decrease in reaction time. Caffeine can also bring about an improvement in mood, most likely by mimicking the effects of a natural brain chemical, adenosine. Too much caffeine, however, can result in nervousness and insomnia. People can build up a biological dependence on the drug. Regular users who suddenly stop drinking coffee may experience headache or depression. Many people who drink large amounts of coffee on weekdays have headaches on weekends because of the sudden drop in the amount of caffeine they are consuming.

Source: Adapted from Robert S. Feldman, *Understanding Psychology,* 8th ed., pp. 169–70. Copyright © 2008 by The McGraw-Hill Companies, Inc. Reprinted by permission of The McGraw-Hill Companies.

Which writing pattern did the author use to organize the main idea and the supporting details?

____

Write the clues that caused you to choose this pattern.

____

____

You have now met five common writing patterns that authors often use. You may have noticed the main idea sentence itself often contains important clues about which pattern is being used. Focus on the primary relationship between the main idea and the details that support it by asking yourself, "What pattern did the author use to organize the main idea and the supporting details?"

SUMMARY OF FIVE COMMON PARAGRAPH PATTERN SIGNALS AND CLUE WORDS

1. Definition Pattern

words in bold
words in italics
words in color
means
the term
is, is known as
in other words
that is (also abbreviated *i.e*, for *id est*, Latin for "that is")
is defined as
refers to, is referred to as
is called
by this we mean
punctuation that sets off a definition or synonym , : ( ) [ ] —

2. List Pattern

and
also
another
moreover
in addition
first, second, third
finally
1, 2, 3 . . .
a, b, c . . .
bullets (•)
asterisks (*)
words that announce lists
(such as *categories, kinds, types, ways, classes, groups, parts, elements, characteristics, features*)

3. Sequence Pattern

first, second, third
now, then, next, finally
dates
1, 2, 3 . . .
a, b, c . . .
steps
phases
progression
words that refer to time
series
stages
when
before, during, after
at last
process, spectrum, continuum
hierarchy
instructions and directions

4. Comparison-Contrast Pattern

Comparisons:
similarly
likewise
both
same
also
resembles
parallels
in the same manner
in the same way
words that compare
(adjectives that describe comparisons, such as *safer, slower, lighter, more valuable, less toxic*)

Contrasts:
in contrast
however
on the other hand
whereas
while
although
nevertheless
instead (of)
different
unlike
conversely
rather than
as opposed to
some . . . others
opposite words

5. Cause-Effect Pattern

Causes:
the reason(s)
the causes(s)
because
is due to (cause)
was caused by (cause)
(cause) *led to*
resulted from (cause)
since

Effects:
the result(s)
the effect(s)
the outcome
the final product
therefore
thus
consequently
as a consequence
hence
on that account
resulted in, results in (effect)
(effect) *was caused by*
(effect) *is due to*
led to (effect)
(effect) *resulted from*

Copyright © 2014 The McGraw-Hill Companies, Inc. All rights reserved.

EXERCISE 14

Directions: Read each paragraph. Underline any signals and transition words. Then circle the letter of the pattern the author has used to organize the information in the paragraph.

1. Why is stress so damaging to the immune system? One reason is that stress may overstimulate the immune system, causing it to attack the body itself and damage healthy tissue instead of fighting invading bacteria, viruses, and other foreign invaders. When that happens, it can lead to disorders such as arthritis and an allergic reaction.

Source: Adapted from Robert S. Feldman, *Understanding Psychology,* 8th ed., p. 493. Copyright © 2008 by The McGraw-Hill Companies, Inc. Reprinted by permission of The McGraw-Hill Companies.

a. list pattern
b. sequence pattern
c. comparison-contrast pattern
d. cause-effect pattern

2. For male members of the Awa tribe in New Guinea, the transition *from childhood to adulthood* is a painful process. First come whippings with sticks and prickly branches, both for the boys' own past misdeeds and in honor of those tribesmen who were killed in warfare. In the next phase of the ritual, adults jab sharpened sticks into the boys' nostrils. Then they force a five-foot length of vine into the boys' throats, until they gag and vomit. Finally, tribesmen cut the boys' genitals, causing severe bleeding.

Source: Adapted from Robert S. Feldman, *Understanding Psychology,* 8th ed., p. 437. Copyright © 2008 by The McGraw-Hill Companies, Inc. Reprinted by permission of The McGraw-Hill Companies.

a. list pattern
b. sequence pattern
c. comparison-contrast pattern
d. cause-effect pattern

3. Smoking has both psychological and biological components, and few habits are as difficult to break. Long-term successful treatment typically occurs in just 15 percent of those who try to stop smoking, and once smoking becomes a habit, it is as hard to stop as an addiction to cocaine or heroin. In fact, some of the biochemical reactions to nicotine are similar to those to cocaine, amphetamines, and morphine.

Source: Adapted from Robert S. Feldman, *Understanding Psychology,* 8th ed., p. 504. Copyright © 2008 by The McGraw-Hill Companies, Inc. Reprinted by permission of The McGraw-Hill Companies.

a. list pattern
b. sequence pattern
c. comparison-contrast pattern
d. cause-effect pattern

4. There are several things patients can do to improve communication with doctors and other health care providers. Here are some tips provided by one physician:

1. Make a list of health-related concerns before you visit a health care provider.
2. Before a visit, write down the names and dosages of every drug you are currently taking.
3. Determine if your provider will communicate with you via e-mail and has your correct e-mail address.
4. If you find yourself intimidated, take along an advocate—friend or relative—who can help you communicate more effectively.
5. Take notes during the visit.

Source: Adapted from Robert S. Feldman, *Understanding Psychology,* 8th ed., p. 509. Copyright © 2008 by The McGraw-Hill Companies, Inc. Reprinted by permission of The McGraw-Hill Companies.

a. list pattern
b. sequence pattern
c. comparison-contrast pattern
d. cause-effect pattern

5. A transcript is an official record of a student's courses and grades at a college or university. You can obtain one from the registrar's office (and perhaps online). If you transfer to a different school, you will be asked for a copy of your transcript. Many employers often ask job applicants for a transcript.

a. list pattern
b. sequence pattern
c. definition pattern
d. cause-effect pattern

ADDITIONAL PARAGRAPH PATTERNS

In this chapter so far, you have already learned about five very common patterns: definition, list, sequence (time order), cause-effect, and comparison-contrast. Besides these, there are additional patterns you will encounter in college textbooks and other material you read.

Definition-and-Example Pattern

Along with a definition, authors often include one or more examples. The main idea sentence usually states the definition. The examples (details) in the paragraph help explain or illustrate that definition. For that reason, the pattern is also known as the "definition-and-example" pattern. A definition-and-example paragraph is typically organized like this:

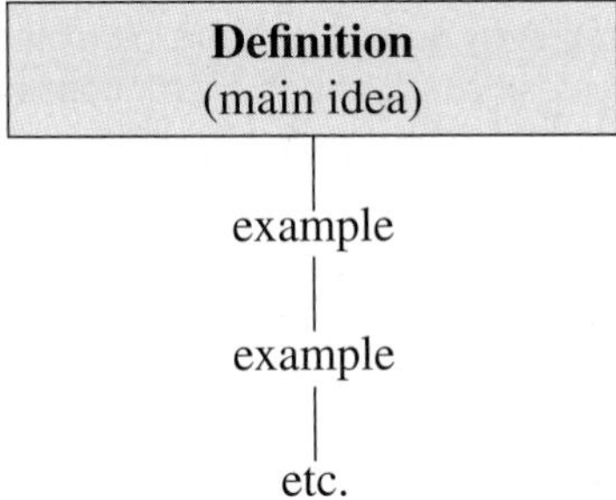

- Watch for signal words such as *this term, means, is known as, is called, refers to, is defined as,* and so forth, for the definition. In addition, the key term may appear in bold, italics, or color. Watch for *such as, to illustrate*, and *for example* to introduce the examples.
- *Example:* A biology text paragraph presents a definition in the first sentence (the main idea) along with examples (supporting details):

> An **organ** is a group of tissues that perform a specific function or set of functions. There are several organs in the human body, such as the brain, eyes, heart, and lungs. Other examples are the stomach, liver, kidneys, and bone. The largest organ is the skin.

Generalization-and-Example Pattern

This pattern is similar to the definition-and-example pattern, but instead of a definition and examples of a key term, the author presents an important general concept, rule, or principle, followed by examples. (You learned the difference between general and specific when you learned about topic. *A generalization* is a statement, idea, or principle that applies broadly; that is, it applies to many people or things, or in many circumstances.) The structure of a generalization-and-example paragraph is typically like this:

Copyright © 2014 The McGraw-Hill Companies, Inc. All rights reserved.

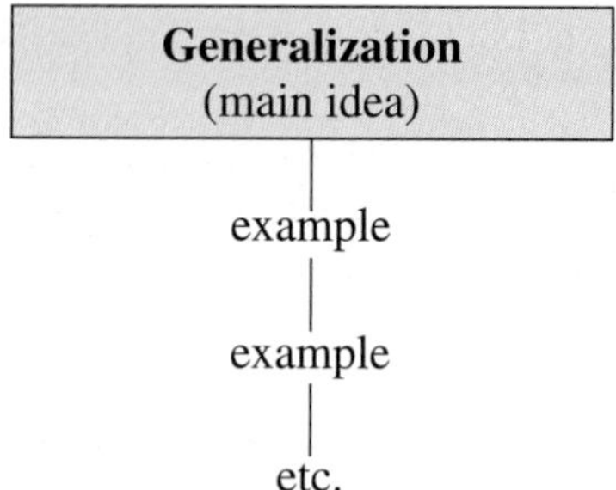

- Watch for signal words that introduce examples, such as *to illustrate, for example, for instance,* and *that is.*
- *Example:* A biology text paragraph opens with a generalization, followed by one or more specific examples:

> Life comes only from life; every living thing reproduces. For example, at the simplest level, even one-cell organisms multiply by dividing in two. In more complex organisms, such as human beings, reproduction occurs by a sperm fertilizing an egg, followed by innumerable cell divisions and differentiations.

Location or Spatial Order Pattern

This pattern is similar to time order, but it describes objects' *position* or *location* in space rather than events' place in time. (An art history textbook author might describe the floor plan of medieval cathedrals; an astronomy textbook author might describe the way the planets are arranged in the solar system.) A location or spatial order paragraph is usually organized this way:

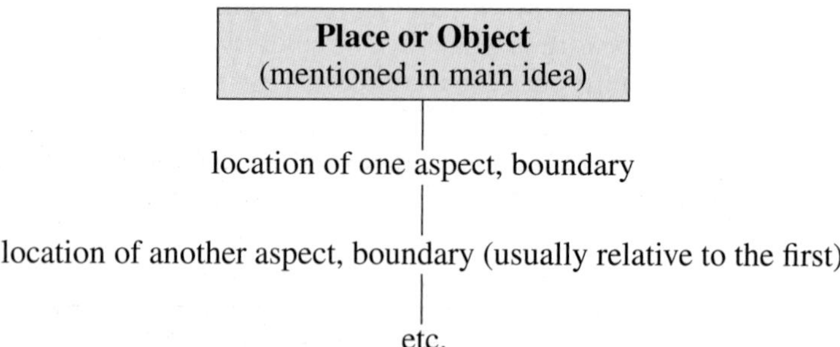

- Watch for signal words such as *above, below, behind, beside, near, farther from, within, facing, opposite, north/south/east/west of, to the left/right, outside of,* and other words that indicate the position of one object relative to another.
- *Example:* A sociology textbook presents a paragraph such as this one:

> According to the concentric zone theory of urban growth, cities develop outward in expanding rings or zones. At the center is the central business district. Expanding outward from it are the manufacturing district, low-class, middle-class, and high-class residential areas. Even farther out are the heavy manufacturing and outlying business district. The most distant zones are the residential suburb, industrial suburb, and the commuters' zone.

Summary Pattern

At the end of a section, an author may present a concluding paragraph that summarizes the section. (You were introduced to this concept in Chapter 4 on stated main ideas. Chapter 11 presents summarizing in depth.) The structure of a summary paragraph is typically like this:

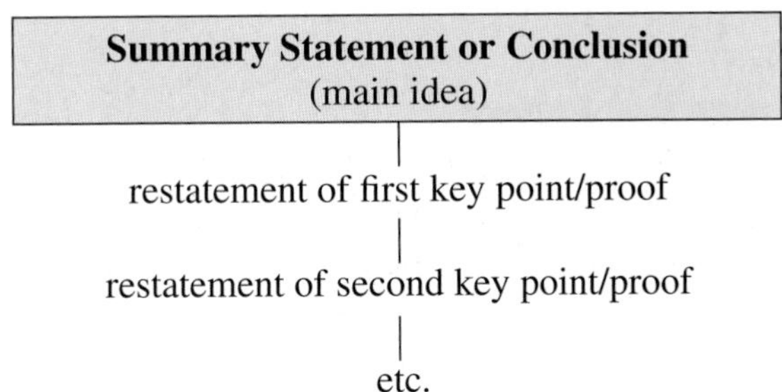

- Watch for signal words such as *In summary, In short, To sum up, In a nutshell, In brief, The point is, Thus,* and *Therefore.*
- *Example:* An author ends a section in a political science textbook with this paragraph:

> The point is, computer technology has made it increasingly easier for any business, government agency, or individual to retrieve information about individual citizens. Inappropriate access to personal information violates privacy rights. An important public policy issue today is how much the government should restrict access to electronic information.

Classification Pattern

This is simply a variation of the list pattern, but the items that are listed are put into groups or categories. The structure of a classification paragraph is typically like this:

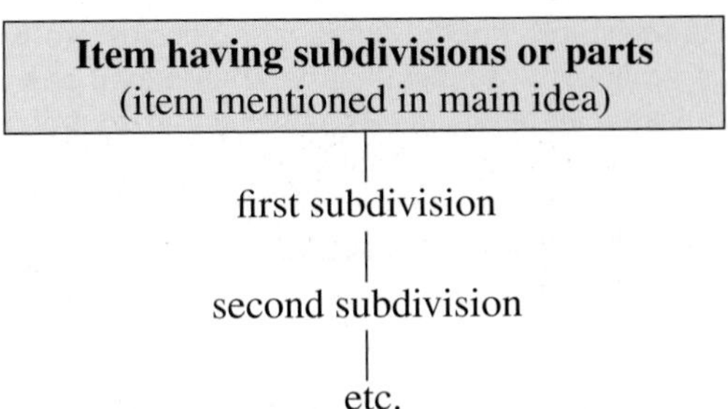

- Watch for signal words such as *groups, categories, ways, types, elements, factors,* and *classes.*
- *Example:* A biology text paragraph discusses the two layers of the skin:

Copyright © 2014 The McGraw-Hill Companies, Inc. All rights reserved.

> Skin has two layers: the epidermis and the dermis. The outer layer is the *epidermis*. It consists of epithelial cells. New cells come from basal cells that flatten and harden as they push to the surface. The *dermis,* the other layer, is a region of fibrous connective tissue beneath the epidermis. The dermis contains collagen and elastic fibers, as well as blood vessels that feed the skin.

Addition Pattern

The author simply adds information. It could mean adding items to a list, or it could be that the author is adding causes, effects, similarities, differences, categories, or examples. It is sometimes called the *elaboration* pattern since information is presented in greater detail. The structure of an addition paragraph is typically like this:

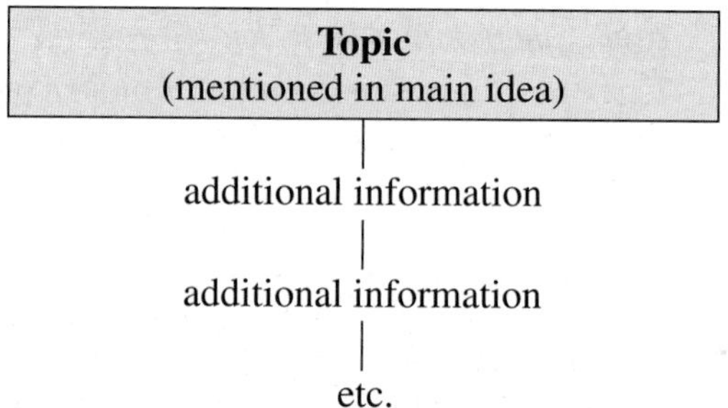

- Watch for signal words such as *also, besides, in addition, furthermore, and, further,* and *moreover.*
- *Example:* A music text tells facts about woodwind instruments:

> Most woodwind instruments produce vibrations of air within a tube made of wood, although modern flutes and piccolos are made of metal. In addition, woodwind instruments have holes that can be opened and closed when players place their fingers over them or press on mechanisms that control pads that cover the holes. Furthermore, some woodwind instruments, such as clarinets and oboes, have reeds that vibrate when the player blows into the mouthpiece.

Statement-and-Clarification Pattern

The passage consists of a general statement followed by additional information that clarifies the information in the general statement. (An education textbook might say that home-schooled children do not have as many opportunities to interact with others their same age during the school day. The rest of the paragraph might explain ways parents can compensate for this.) The structure of a statement-and-clarification paragraph is typically like this:

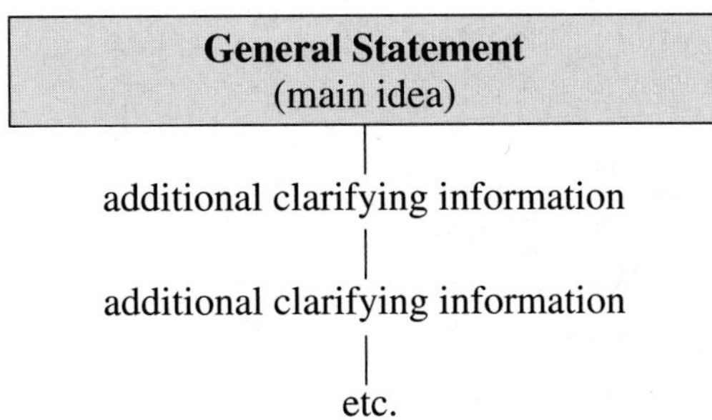

- Watch for signal words such as *in other words, in fact, obviously, as a matter of fact, evidently, clearly,* and *of course.*
- *Example:* An art history text paragraph opens with a general statement about "certain types of ancient vessels," clarifies what "ancient" means, and tells more about those "certain types" of vessels:

> Certain types of ancient ceramic jars and bowls are known today as Mimbres vessels. They are considered ancient artifacts because they date from the 3rd to the 12th centuries C.E. and most were recovered from ancient graves in what is now New Mexico. Evidently, these pottery vessels were used for household purposes. Painted with black-on-white designs, they are decorated with stylized animal or human figures or with geometric designs.

SUMMARY OF ADDITIONAL PARAGRAPH PATTERN CLUES AND SIGNAL WORDS

1. Definition-and-Example Pattern

Definition:		Examples:	
this term is called	*is referred to as*	*for example*	*for instance*
means	*refers to*	*to illustrate*	*such as*
is known as	*is defined as*		

2. Generalization-and-Example Pattern

General concept, rule, or principle, followed by examples introduced by

for example *for instance* *to illustrate* *such as*

(continued on next page)

Copyright © 2014 The McGraw-Hill Companies, Inc. All rights reserved.

3. Location or Spatial Order Pattern

above	*north/south/east/west of*
below	*facing*
behind	*opposite to*
beside	*to the left/right of*
near	*outside*
farther	*adjacent to*
from	*close by*
within	*inside*

4. Summary Pattern

In summary	*The point is*
In short	*On the whole*
To sum up	*Thus*
In a nutshell	*Therefore*
In brief	*In conclusion*
To summarize	

5. Classification Pattern

groups	*elements*
categories	*factors*
ways	*classes*
types	*kinds*

6. Addition Pattern

also	*and*
besides	*moreover*
in addition	*further*
furthermore	*equally important*

7. Statement-and-Clarification Pattern

clearly	*in other words*
in fact	*as a matter of fact*
of course	*obviously*
evidently	

EXERCISE 15

Directions: Circle the answer choice of the letter that tells the pattern used in each paragraph.

1. In short, expect to see many changes in the banking system in coming years. Banks will increase their range of services: you will be able to buy insurance, real estate, stocks, and other securities through them. You will be able to get foreign currency, tickets to events, and music downloads from ATMs. Increasing use of online banking and electronic funds transfer may also change banking dramatically.

a. spatial pattern
b. definition-and-example pattern
c. summary pattern
d. classification pattern

2. Caffeine is a stimulant, a drug that affects the central nervous system by causing a rise in heart rate, blood pressure, and muscular tension. Coffee is the best-known example of a beverage that contains caffeine. Other examples of caffeine-containing foods and beverages are tea, soft drinks, energy drinks, and chocolate. Some maximun strength nonprescription drugs, such as Excedrin, Anacin, NoDoz tablets, and Dexatrim, also contain caffeine.

a. spatial pattern
b. definition-and-example pattern
c. summary pattern
d. classification pattern

3. The gastrocnemius, the largest muscle in the calf, is located on the backside of the leg. The heel raise is a good exercise for strengthening it. The correct position for this simple exercise is to stand with your feet pointed forward, shoulder-width apart. Rest the bar on the back of the shoulders, holding it in place with hands facing forward. Press down with your toes as you move your heels away from the floor. Return to the starting position.

a. spatial pattern
b. generalization-and-example pattern
c. addition pattern
d. classification pattern

4. Muscles, bones, connective tissues, and organ tissues are categorized as *fat-free mass.* The second type of body mass is *body fat.* There are two kinds of body fat: essential and nonessential.

a. spatial pattern
b. definition-and-example pattern
c. summary pattern
d. classification pattern

5. Spot reducing, trying to lose body fat in specific parts of the body by doing exercises for that part, is not effective. As a matter of fact, spot-reducing exercises aid fat loss only to the extent they burn calories. In other words, reducing fat in any specific area can be accomplished only by burning up more calories through metabolism and exercise than are consumed through food.

a. spatial pattern
b. statement-and-clarification pattern
c. summary pattern
d. classification pattern

6. Bustling New York City is located at the mouth of the Hudson River on the Eastern Atlantic coast of the United States. It's also the nation's largest city, with the 2000 census showing more than eight million inhabitants. In addition, it boasts the Statue of Liberty, Empire State Building, Central Park, Brooklyn Bridge, and Times Square. Known as "The Big Apple," the city is comprised of the five boroughs: Brooklyn, Queens, Manhattan, Staten Island, and the Bronx.

a. spatial pattern
b. statement-and-clarification pattern
c. addition pattern
d. classification pattern

7. The rule for planning weekly study time is to allot two hours of studying for every one hour you spend in class. To illustrate, if you take four three-hour courses, you spend 12 hours a week in class. That means you should allow twice that many hours—24 hours—of study time in your weekly schedule (since $2 \times 12 = 24$).

a. spatial pattern
b. generalization-and-example pattern
c. addition pattern
d. classification pattern

Copyright © 2014 The McGraw-Hill Companies, Inc. All rights reserved.

OTHER THINGS TO KEEP IN MIND WHEN RECOGNIZING AUTHORS' WRITING PATTERNS

Here are four helpful things to keep in mind about authors' writing patterns:

1. Lists and sequences differ in an important way.

Items in a list appear in no specific order; however, items in a sequence are presented in a specific order because the order is important. On a shopping list, for example, it makes no difference what order the items are in: "eggs, bread, milk" is the same as "milk, bread, eggs." In a recipe, though, the steps occur in a specific order because the sequence is important: "Add eggs and milk to the mixture, stir well, and then bake" is obviously not the same as "Bake, stir well, and then add eggs and milk to the mixture."

2. Avoid identifying every paragraph as having a list pattern.

At first, it may seem as if every paragraph uses a list pattern. Whenever you encounter what appears to be a list, be cautious and ask yourself this additional question, "a list of *what*?" Your answer should help you recognize when the author is using one of the other patterns instead. For instance, if your answer is "a list of *events in a particular order,*" then the paragraph has a sequence pattern. If your answer is "a list of *similarities or differences,*" the paragraph has a comparison-contrast pattern. If your answer is "a list of *causes, reasons, or results,*" then the paragraph has a cause-effect pattern. View a paragraph as having a list pattern only when you are certain that no other pattern can be used to describe the way the ideas are organized.

Sometimes the same clue words may be used in more than one pattern. For example, words such as *first, second,* and *third* are used for items in a sequence, but they can also be used to indicate items in a list (even though the order is not important).

3. Authors often mix patterns in the same paragraph.

Each of the textbook excerpts in this chapter was used to illustrate a single pattern. However, authors often use a combination of two or more patterns in the same paragraph. This is called a *mixed pattern.* For example, a paragraph might present a series of events (sequence pattern) that led to a certain result (cause-effect pattern). Or an author could present causes and effects (cause-effect pattern), but describe some effects that were positive and other effects that were negative (comparison-contrast pattern). Remember, authors use the patterns or a combination of patterns that they believe organizes and presents their material in the most logical way.

4. A longer selection may contain several patterns and have an overall pattern as well.

In addition to individual paragraphs, longer selections are often organized by an overall pattern. An entire selection may be organized as a list, a sequence, a comparison-contrast, or a cause-effect pattern. For example, you already know that a biography, the story of a person's life, usually follows a sequence pattern. Science textbooks often present information as steps in a process (sequence) and history textbooks often present information as causes and effects. Other subjects frequently use the comparison-contrast pattern to organize the information being presented.

Remember, a longer textbook selection can consist of paragraphs with different patterns and have an overall pattern as well. For example, a section in a history textbook might discuss several events (causes) leading up to World War II, yet have a sequence as the overall pattern.

Directions: Read each paragraph. Determine its main idea and then identify the writing pattern the author uses to organize the supporting details.

1. This paragraph comes from a music appreciation textbook.

Wolfgang Amadeus Mozart, a musical prodigy born in Salzburg, Austria, in 1756, had an astonishing early history. By the time he was six, he could play the harpsichord and violin, improvise fugues, write minuets, and read music perfectly at first sight. At the age of eight, he wrote a symphony; at eleven, an oratorio; at twelve, an opera. By his early teens, Mozart had behind him many works that would have brought credit to a composer three times his age.

Source: Adapted from Roger Kamien, *Music: An Appreciation,* 10th ed., p. 212. Copyright © 2011 by The McGraw-Hill Companies, Inc. Reprinted by permission of The McGraw-Hill Companies.

_______ What is the *main idea* of this paragraph?

a. Wolfgang Amadeus Mozart, a musical prodigy born in Salzburg, Austria, in 1756, had an astonishing early history.

b. By the time he was six, he could play the harpsichord and violin, improvise fugues, write minuets, and read music perfectly at first sight.

c. At the age of eight, he wrote a symphony; at eleven, an oratorio; at twelve, an opera.

d. By his early teens, Mozart had behind him many works that would have brought credit to a composer three times his age.

_______ Which writing *pattern* did the author use to organize the supporting details?

a. definition

b. list

c. sequence

d. comparison-contrast

2. This paragraph comes from a business communication textbook.

What is the difference between **monochronic** cultures and **polychronic** ones? According to American anthropoloist and cross-cultural researcher Edward T. Hall, monochronic cultures treat time as a resource, whereas in polychronic ones, relationships are emphasized. When U.S. managers feel offended because a Latin American manager also sees other people during "their" appointment, the two kinds of time are in conflict.

Source: Adapted from Kitty Locker and Stephen Kaczmarek, *Business Communication,* 5th ed., p. 46. Copyright © 2012 by The McGraw-Hill Companies, Inc. Reprinted by permission of The McGraw-Hill Companies.

_______ What is the *main idea* of this paragraph?

a. What is the difference between monochronic cultures and polychronic ones?

b. According to American anthropologist and cross-cultural researcher Edward T. Hall, monochronic cultures treat time as a resource, whereas in polychronic ones, relationships are emphasized.

Copyright © 2014 The McGraw-Hill Companies, Inc. All rights reserved.

c. When U.S. managers feel offended because a Latin American manager also sees other people during "their" appointment, the two kinds of time are in conflict.

_______ Which writing *pattern* did the authors use to organize the supporting details?

a. list

b. sequence

c. comparison-contrast

d. cause-effect

3. This paragraph comes from an art history textbook.

In his painting *The Madonna of the Meadows*, Raphael has grouped the figures of Mary, the young John the Baptist, and the young Jesus so that we perceive them as a single, triangular whole. Mary's head defines the apex (top), and John the Baptist the lower left corner. Defining the lower right corner is Mary's exposed foot, which draws our eyes because of the way the pale flesh contrasts with the darker tones around it.

Source: Mark Getlein, *Living with Art,* 9th ed., p. 84. Copyright © 2010 by The McGraw-Hill Companies, Inc. Reprinted by permission of The McGraw-Hill Companies.

_______ What is the *main idea* of this paragraph?

a. In his painting *The Madonna of the Meadows,* Raphael has grouped the figures of Mary, the young John the Baptist, and the young Jesus so that we perceive them as a single, triangular whole.

b. Mary's head defines the apex (top), and John the Baptist the lower left corner.

c. Defining the lower right corner is Mary's exposed foot, which draws our eyes because of the way the pale flesh contrasts with the darker tones around it.

_______ Which writing *pattern* did the author use to organize the supporting details?

a. definition

b. list

c. sequence

d. spatial

4. This paragraph comes from a sociology textbook.

Gender, in most sociological writing, refers to the social and cultural characteristics that distinguish women from men. In our society, such characteristics include the different clothing that men and women wear. Another example is the expectation that boys shouldn't cry when they are hurt. Gender is said to be a social creation, not a biological one.

Source: Adapted from Andrew Cherlin, *Public and Private Families: An Introduction,* 6th ed., p. 574. Copyright © 2010 by The McGraw-Hill Companies, Inc. Reprinted by permission of The McGraw-Hill Companies.

_______ What is the *main idea* of this paragraph?

a. Gender, in most sociological writing, refers to the social and cultural characteristics that distinguish women from men, and it is said to be a social creation, not a biological one.

b. In our society, such characteristics include the different clothing that men and women wear or the expectation that boys shouldn't cry when they are hurt.

c. Another example is the expectation that boys shouldn't cry when they are hurt.

d. Gender is said to be a social creation, not a biological one.

_______ Which writing *pattern* did the author use to organize the supporting details?

a. definition

b. list

c. comparison-contrast

d. cause-effect

5. This paragraph comes from a criminology textbook.

A rash of school shootings during the 1998–1999 academic year caused great concern across the nation. Criminologists, police, educators, lawmakers, and parents struggled to figure out why these young men and boys decided to pick up firearms and destroy the lives of their teachers and classmates. Many blamed the easy access to guns; others pointed to the social isolation these students experienced; still others looked to broader sociological explanations.

Source: Fred Adler, Gerhard Mueller, and William Laufer, *Criminal Justice: An Introduction,* 5th ed., p. 105. Copyright © 2009 by The McGraw-Hill Companies, Inc. Reprinted by permission of The McGraw-Hill Companies.

_______ What is the *main idea* of this paragraph?

a. A rash of school shootings during the 1998–1999 academic year caused great concern across the nation.

b. Criminologists, police, educators, lawmakers, and parents struggled to figure out why these young men and boys decided to pick up firearms and destroy the lives of their teachers and classmates.

c. Many blamed the easy access to guns; others pointed to the social isolation these students experienced; still others looked to broader sociological explanations.

_______ Which *writing* pattern did the authors use to organize the supporting details?

a. definition

b. sequence

c. comparison-contrast

d. cause-effect

Copyright © 2014 The McGraw-Hill Companies, Inc. All rights reserved.

CHAPTER REVIEW CARDS

Review cards or *summary cards* are a way to select, organize, and summarize the important information in a textbook chapter. Preparing review cards helps you organize the information so that you can learn and memorize it more easily. In other words, chapter review cards are effective study tools.

Preparing chapter review cards for each chapter of *New Worlds* will give you practice in creating these valuable study tools. Once you have learned how to make chapter review cards, you can use actual index cards to create them for textbook material in any of your other courses and use them when you study for tests.

Directions: Complete the chapter review cards for Chapter 7 by answering the questions or following the directions on each card.

Authors' Writing Patterns

1. What is the definition of a *writing pattern*?

2. What are five common writing patterns textbook authors use?

3. What are four advantages to recognizing authors' writing patterns?

4. What comprehension monitoring question should you ask yourself in order to recognize an author's writing pattern?

Card 1 Chapter 7: Recognizing Authors' Writing Patterns

Copyright © 2014 The McGraw-Hill Companies, Inc. All rights reserved.

Transition Words That Signal the Relationship of Ideas within Sentences and between Sentences

1. What is the definition of *transition words?*

2. What is the *addition* relationship, and what are some transition words that signal it?

3. What is the *sequence* relationship, and what are some transition words that signal it?

Card 2 Chapter 7: Recognizing Authors' Writing Patterns

Transition Words That Signal the Relationship of Ideas within Sentences and between Sentences *(Continued)*

1. What is the *contrast* relationship, and what are some transition words that signal it?

2. What is the *comparison* relationship, and what are some transition words that signal it?

3. What is the *cause-effect* relationship, and what are some transition words that signal it?

Card 3 Chapter 7: Recognizing Authors' Writing Patterns

Transition Words That Signal the Relationship of Ideas within Sentences and between Sentences *(Continued)*

1. What is the *example* relationship, and what are some transition words that signal it?

2. What is the *conclusion* relationship, and what are some transition words that signal it?

3. What is the *summary* relationship, and what are some transition words that signal it?

Card 4 Chapter 7: Recognizing Authors' Writing Patterns

Authors' Writing Patterns

Define these five writing patterns commonly used by textbook authors.

1. Definition:

2. List:

3. Sequence:

4. Comparison-Contrast:

5. Cause-Effect:

Card 5 Chapter 7: Recognizing Authors' Writing Patterns

Copyright © 2014 The McGraw-Hill Companies, Inc. All rights reserved.

Signal Words and Other Clues to Authors' Writing Patterns

Write the signal words and other clues that identify each of the five writing patterns.

1. Definition:

2. List:

3. Sequence:

4. Comparison-Contrast:

5. Cause-Effect:

Card 6 Chapter 7: Recognizing Authors' Writing Patterns

Additional Paragraph Patterns

Tell the purpose of each pattern, and then list some transition words that signal it.

1. Definition-and-Example Pattern:

2. Generalization-and-Example Pattern:

3. Location or Spatial Order Pattern:

4. Summary Pattern:

Card 7 Chapter 7: Recognizing Authors' Writing Patterns

Additional Paragraph Patterns *(continued)*

Tell the purpose of each pattern, and then list some transition words that signal it.

5. Classification Pattern:

6. Addition Pattern:

7. Statement-and-Clarification Pattern:

Card 8 Chapter 7: Recognizing Authors' Writing Patterns

As You Recognize Authors' Writing Patterns, Keep in Mind . . .

1. What is the difference between the list pattern and the sequence pattern?

2. What additional question should you ask yourself to avoid identifying every paragraph as having a list pattern?

3. What is a mixed pattern?

4. What is an overall pattern?

Card 9 Chapter 7: Recognizing Authors' Writing Patterns

TEST YOUR UNDERSTANDING
Recognizing Authors' Writing Patterns, Part 1

Review: **Writing patterns** are ways that authors organize the information they present. Five writing patterns commonly used by textbook authors are:

- **definition**—presents the meaning of an important term discussed throughout the paragraph
- **list**—a group of items presented in no specific order, since the order is not important
- **sequence**—a list of items presented in a certain order because the order is important
- **comparison-contrast**—similarities and differences between two or more things are presented
- **cause-effect**—reasons and results of events and conditions are presented

EXAMPLE

This excerpt comes from a health textbook.

> Students often wonder, "What causes a person to be gay?" This question has no simple answer. Some research has pointed to differences in the sizes of certain brain structures as a possible basis. Other research proposes causes that have a possible genetic, environmental, hormonal element. Research has produced no single theory regarding the cause of sexual orientation in general. The consensus of scientific opinion is that people do not choose their sexual orientation. Thus, being straight or being gay is something that "just happens." Most gays and lesbians report that no specific event "triggered" them into being gay. In short, the cause is not yet known.
>
> *Source:* Adapted from Wayne Payne, Dale Hahn, and Ellen Lucas, *Understanding Your Health,* 10th ed.; p. 440. Copyright © 2009 by The McGraw-Hill Companies, Inc. Reprinted by permission of The McGraw-Hill Companies.

The topic of this paragraph is *what causes a person to be gay.*

___c___ What is the main idea of this paragraph?

a. What causes a person to be gay?
b. This question has no simple answer.
c. What causes a person to be gay is not yet known.
d. Most gays and lesbians report that no specific event "triggered" them into being gay.

Explanation: The correct answer is c. This sentence sums up the important general point of the paragraph. Choice *a* is a question, not a sentence. Choice *b* does not contain the topic. Choice *d* is a detail.

___d___ Which writing pattern did the authors use to organize the supporting details?

a. list
b. sequence
c. comparison-contrast
d. cause-effect

Explanation: The correct answer is d. The words *causes, produced,* and *Thus* indicate that this is a cause-effect pattern. The effect is *being gay*. The cause is *not yet known.*

Directions: Read each paragraph and determine its main idea by asking yourself, "What is the most important point the author wants me to *understand* about the topic of this paragraph?" (You are told the topic.) Write the answer in the space provided. Then determine the writing pattern by asking yourself, "Which pattern did the author use to organize the main idea and the supporting details?" Write your answer in the space provided. Remember that the main idea sentence often gives a clue to the pattern. Refer to the list of signals and clue words on pages 374–375 as you complete the exercises.

1. This paragraph comes from a health textbook.

Cigarette, cigar, and pipe smoke can be described on the basis of two phases: a particulate phase and a gaseous phase. The *particulate* phase includes nicotine, water, and a variety of powerful chemicals known collectively as tar. A pack-a-day smoker will collect four ounces of tar in the lungs in a year. The *gaseous* phase of tobacco smoke is composed of a variety of physiologically active compounds, at least 60 of which are capable of stimulating the development of cancer.

Source: Adapted from Wayne Payne, Dale Hahn, and Ellen Lucas, *Understanding Your Health,* 10th ed., pp. 270–71. Copyright © 2009 by The McGraw-Hill Companies, Inc. Reprinted by permission of The McGraw-Hill Companies.

The topic of this paragraph is *cigarette, cigar, and pipe smoke (or tobacco smoke).*

_______ What is the main idea of this paragraph?

a. Cigarette, cigar, and pipe smoke can be described on the basis of two phases: a particulate phase and a gaseous phase.

b. The particulate phase includes nicotine, water, and a variety of powerful chemicals known collectively as tar.

c. A pack-a-day smoker will collect four ounces of tar in the lungs in a year.

d. The gaseous phase of tobacco smoke is composed of a variety of physiologically active compounds, at least 60 of which are capable of stimulating the development of cancer.

_______ Which writing pattern did the authors use to organize the supporting details?

a. list

b. sequence

c. comparison-contrast

d. cause-effect

2. This paragraph comes from a health textbook.

Television, magazines, billboards, movies, and a variety of other sources constantly bombard us with messages about how we should look. How realistic are these images? While the average woman's measurements are 37-29-40, (chest, waist, hips), store mannequins measure 38-18-28. The average American woman is 5 feet 4 inches tall, weighs 140 pounds, and wears size 12–14. Contrast this with the average American female model, who is 5 feet 11 inches tall, weighs 117 pounds and wears a size 2.

Source: Wayne Payne, Dale Hahn, and Ellen Lucas, *Understanding Your Health,* 10th ed., p. 170. Copyright © 2009 by The McGraw-Hill Companies, Inc. Reprinted by permission of The McGraw-Hill Companies.

The topic of this paragraph is *media's messages of how American women should look.*

_______ What is the main idea of this paragraph?

a. American women need to get in better shape to match the proper way they should look.

b. Media let American women know the correct way they should look.

c. Media's messages of how American women should look does not match reality.

d. Models are considerably taller than the average American woman.

______ Which writing pattern did the authors use to organize the supporting details?

a. list

b. sequence

c. comparison-contrast

d. cause-effect

3. This paragraph comes from a business textbook.

The Increase in the Number of Older Americans

People ages 45 to 54 are currently the richest group in U.S. society. They have a median income of $55,917. They thus represent a lucrative market for companies involved with food service, transportation, entertainment, education, lodging and so on. What do such demographic changes mean for you and for businesses in the future? Think of the products the middle-aged and elderly will need—travel, medicine, nursing homes, assisted-living facilities, adult day care, home health care, recreation, and the like—and you'll see opportunities for successful businesses of the 21st century. Consequently, businesses that cater to them will have the opportunity for exceptional growth in the near future.

Source: William Nickels, James McHugh, and Susan McHugh, *Understanding Business,* 9th ed., pp. 17–18. Copyright © 2010 by The McGraw-Hill Companies, Inc. Reprinted by permission of The McGraw-Hill Companies.

The topic of this paragraph is *older Americans and their effect on business.*

______ What is the main idea of this paragraph?

a. People ages 45 to 54 are currently the richest group in U.S. society.

b. Businesses that cater to older Americans will have exceptional growth opportunities in the near future.

c. Those with money will demand more and better health care, more recreation and travel, and new and different products and services of all kinds.

d. By 2030, the baby boomers will be senior citizens.

4. This paragraph comes from the U.S. Department of Education, National Center for Education Statistics.

For young adults ages 25–34 who worked full time (35 or more hours per week) throughout a full year (50 or more weeks of employment), higher educational attainment was associated with higher median earnings. This was consistent for each year between 1995 and 2009. For example, young adults with a bachelor's degree consistently had higher median earnings than those with less education. In 2009, the median of the earnings for young adults with a bachelor's degree was $45,000, while the median was $21,000 for those without a high school diploma or its equivalent, $30,00 for those with a high school diploma or its equivalent, and $36,000 for those with an associate's degree. In other words, in 2009, those with a bachelor's degree earned more than twice as much as those without a high school diploma or its equivalent.

Source: U.S. Department of Education, National Center for Education Statistics, *The Condition of Education 2011* (NCES 2011-033, indicator 17). http://nces.ed.gov/fastfacts/display.asp?id=770; accessed 14 May 2012.

The topic of this paragraph is *young adults' education level and median earnings.*

______ What is the main idea of this paragraph?

a. For young adults ages 25–34 who worked full time throughout a full year, higher educational attainment was associated with higher median earnings

Copyright © 2014 The McGraw-Hill Companies, Inc. All rights reserved.

b. For young adults ages 25–34 who worked full time throughout a full year, higher educational attainment was associated with higher median earnings, and this was consistent for each year between 1995 and 2009.

c. For example, young adults with a bachelor's degree consistently had higher median earnings than those with less education.

d. In 2009, the median of the earnings for young adults with a bachelor's degree was $45,000, which was twice as much as those without a high school diploma or its equivalent.

_______ Which writing pattern did the authors use to organize the supporting details?

a. definition

b. list

c. sequence

d. comparison-contrast

5. This paragraph comes from a health textbook.

Much can be done in early childhood to prevent children from smoking when they reach adolescence. For children in kindergarten through third grade, new skills and insights need to be developed to deal with drugs, including tobacco products. Adults should attempt to:

- Help the child recognize and understand family rules.
- Discuss how television advertisements try to persuade people to buy their products.
- Practice ways in which a child can say no to other people.
- Develop a "helper" file made up of names and phone numbers of people the child can turn to when confronted by others who want them to try smoking or smokeless tobacco.

Source: Adapted from Wayne Payne, Dale Hahn, and Ellen Lucas, *Understanding Your Health,* 10th ed., p. 270. Copyright © 2009 by The McGraw-Hill Companies, Inc. Reprinted by permission of The McGraw-Hill Companies.

The topic of this paragraph is *preventing children from smoking when they reach adolescence.*

_______ What is the main idea of this paragraph?

a. Much can be done in early childhood to prevent children from smoking or using drugs when they reach adolescence.

b. Children need to recognize and understand family rules.

c. Adults should help children in kindergarten through third grade say no to tobacco and drugs.

d. Develop a "helper" file made up of names and phone numbers of people the child can turn to when confronted by others who want them to try smoking or smokeless tobacco.

_______ Which writing pattern did the authors use to organize the supporting details?

a. definition

b. comparison-contrast

c. sequence

d. list

Review: **Writing patterns** are ways that authors organize the information they present. Five writing patterns commonly used by textbook authors are:

- **definition**—presents the meaning of an important term discussed throughout the paragraph
- **list**—a group of items presented in no specific order, since the order is not important
- **sequence**—a list of items presented in a certain order because the order is important
- **comparison-contrast**—similarities and differences between two or more things are presented
- **cause-effect**—reasons and results of events and conditions are presented

EXAMPLE

This excerpt comes from a government textbook.

Incarceration Rates

Although the states are required under the Constitution to uphold defendants' rights, their criminal justice systems differ markedly in other respects. Sentencing laws are an example. States differ substantially in the proportion of their residents who are in prison. Louisiana has the highest incarceration rate, with 865 inmates for every 100,000 residents. Mississippi, Texas, Oklahoma and Alabama are the other top five. Maine has the lowest incarceration rate—159 inmates per 100,000 residents. On a per capita basis, Louisiana imprisons five times as many of its residents as does Maine. Minnesota, North Dakota, Rhode Island, and Utah are the other states that rank in the lowest five in terms of number of inmates.

Source: Adapted from Thomas E. Patterson, *We the People: A Concise Introduction to American Politics*, 9th ed., pp. 135–36. Copyright © 2011 by The McGraw-Hill Companies, Inc. Reprinted by permission of The McGraw-Hill Companies.

The topic of this paragraph is *states' incarceration rates.*

Write the main idea sentence: Although the states are required under the Constitution to uphold defendants' rights, they differ markedly in their sentencing laws (in the proportion of their residents they sentence to prison).

Which writing pattern did the author use to organize the supporting details?

comparison-contrast

Write the clue(s) that caused you to choose this pattern.

Although, differ, highest, other top five, lowest, five times as many, and in the lowest five

Explanation: The main idea is formulated by combining the important point in the paragraph into a single sentence. The words *Although, differ, highest, other top five, lowest, five times as many,* and *in the lowest five* indicate contrasts (differences).

Directions: Read each paragraph and determine its main idea by asking yourself, "What is the most important point the author wants me to *understand* about the topic of this paragraph?" (You are told the topic.) If the main idea is stated, write the complete sentence in the space

Copyright © 2014 The McGraw-Hill Companies, Inc. All rights reserved.

provided. If it is implied, formulate the implied main idea and write it in the space provided. Next, determine the writing pattern in the paragraph by asking yourself, "Which pattern did the author use to organize the main idea and the supporting details?" Write the pattern name in the space provided. Finally, list the clues or signals that indicate the pattern. Refer to the list of signals and clue words on pages 374–375 as you complete the exercises.

1. This paragraph is the type that might be found in a business or career exploration textbook.

The Résumé

Any résumé you submit should look polished and professional. Even if you create it yourself, it should meet these criteria. A professional looking résumé is:

- accurate and error free.
- easy to be read because the information is organized and uncrowded.
- printed on heavyweight paper that is white or a light neutral color.
- printed on a high-quality printer or copier so that the print is sharp and clear.

The topic of this paragraph is *the résumé.*

Write the main idea sentence:

____

____

Which writing pattern did the author use to organize the supporting details?

____

Write the clue(s) that caused you to choose this pattern.

____

____

2. This paragraph comes from a health textbook.

What's the difference between acquisitions and mergers? A **merger** is the result of two firms joining to form one company. It is similar to a marriage, joining two individuals as one family. On the other hand, an **acquisition** is one company's purchase of the property and obligations of another company. It is more like buying a house than entering a marriage.

Source: Adapted from William Nickels, James McHugh, and Susan McHugh, *Understanding Business,* 9th ed., p. 129. Copyright © 2010 by The McGraw-Hill Companies, Inc. Reprinted by permission of The McGraw-Hill Companies.

The topic of this paragraph is *mergers and acquisitions.*

Write the main idea sentence:

____

____

____

Which writing pattern did the author use to organize the supporting details?

____

Write the clue(s) that caused you to choose this pattern.

____

____

3. This paragraph comes from an advertising textbook.

Motivation refers to the underlying forces (or motives) that contribute to our purchasing actions. These motives stem from the conscious and unconscious goal of satisfying our needs and wants. Motivation cannot be directly observed. When we see people eat, we assume they are hungry, but we may be wrong. People eat for a variety of reasons besides hunger: They want to be sociable, it's time to eat, or maybe they're nervous or bored.

Source: Adapted from William Arens, Michael Weigold, and Christian Arens, *Contemporary Advertising,* 13th ed., p. 168. Copyright © 2011 by The McGraw-Hill Companies. Reprinted by permission of The McGraw-Hill Companies.

The topic of this paragraph is *motivation.*

Write the main idea sentence:

____

____

Which writing pattern did the author use to organize the supporting details?

____

Write the clue(s) that caused you to choose this pattern.

____

4. This paragraph is the type that might be found in human development textbook.

A Person's Twenties: The Defining Decade

According to University of Virginia clinical psychologist Meg Jay, the twenties are the "defining decade"—the most important time—in a young person's life. She says this is true for college grads and non-college grads. Why does she think this? For one thing, our personalities change more during this time period than at any other time in life. Our brains complete their last growth spurt. Another reason is that by age 30, the majority of Americans are married, living or dating their future partner. Also, during his or her twenties, a person's fertility peaks. Yet another reason the twenties are such a crucial decade is because 70 percent of lifetime wage growth occurs during the first decade of a career. Poor decisions during the twenties can cause people to pay a high price later in life—romantically, reproductively, professionally, and economically. In short, our twenties matter. To a large extent, the decisions we make then set the course for the rest of our lives.

The topic of this paragraph is *a person's twenties, the defining decade.*

Write the main idea sentence:

____

____

____

Which writing pattern did the author use to organize the supporting details?

____

Copyright © 2014 The McGraw-Hill Companies, Inc. All rights reserved.

Write the clue(s) that caused you to choose this pattern.

___

5. This paragraph is from a human development textbook.

In 1969, Elisabeth Kübler-Ross brought the subject of death into the open with her observation that those facing impending death tend to move through five broad stages. These stages are:

1. *Denial.* In this stage, people resist the idea that they are dying. Even if they are told that their chances for survival are small, they refuse to admit they are facing death.
2. *Anger.* After moving beyond the denial stage, dying people become angry—at people around them who are in good health, at medical professionals for being ineffective, at God.
3. *Bargaining.* Anger leads to bargaining, in which the dying try to think of ways to postpone death. They may dedicate their lives to religion if God saves them; they may say, "If only I can live to see my son married, I will accept death."
4. *Depression.* When dying people come to feel that bargaining is of no use, they move to the next stage: depression. They realize that their lives really are coming to an end, leading up to what Kübler-Ross calls "preparatory grief" for their own impending deaths.
5. *Acceptance.* In this stage, people accept impending death. Usually they are unemotional and uncommunicative; it is as if they have made peace with themselves and are accepting death with no bitterness.

Source: Robert Feldman, *Understanding Psychology*, 8th ed., p. 447. Copyright © 2008 by The McGraw-Hill Companies, Inc. Reprinted by permission of The McGraw-Hill Companies.

The topic of this paragraph is *stages of those facing impending death.*

Write the main idea sentence:

___

___

___

___

Which writing pattern did the author use to organize the supporting details?

___

Write the clue(s) that caused you to choose this pattern.

___

___

___

SELECTION **7.1** **Health**

Viruses: Easily Spread and Ever Evolving

From *Connect Core Concepts in Health*
By Paul Insel and Walton Roth

Everyone has had colds and flu, common ailments that are caused by viruses. Throughout history, though, hundreds of millions of people have been killed by viruses. Two examples are the 1918 influenza epidemic and the 2009 outbreak of swine flu. The worldwide influenza pandemic of 1918 infected more than one-fifth of the world's population, including more than one-fourth of the U.S. population. Worldwide, the "Spanish flu," as it was called, killed an estimated 50 million people. The reality was that the virus killed more people than died in World War I.

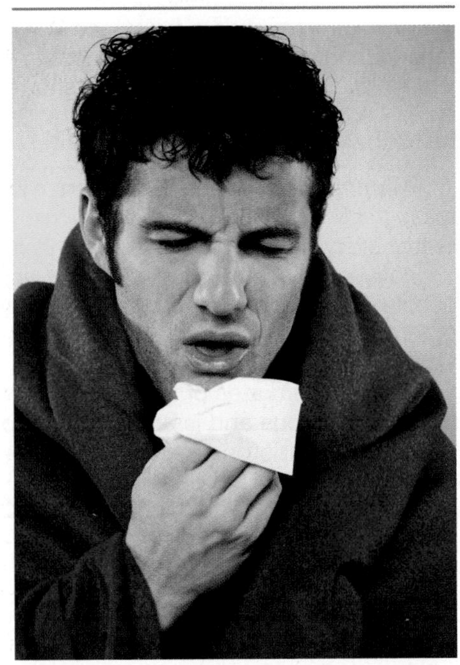

In 2009, there was another outbreak of the same H1N1 influenza virus, this time called "swine flu." The outbreaks began in North America in April, and within two months, flu was reported in 74 countries. The World Health Organization declared that a pandemic was under way. By October, the Centers for Disease Control estimated that there were between 14 million and 34 million cases. By the following February, the number of cases had reached an estimated 42 million to 86 million. It was usually severe and deadly. This flu outbreak was unusual in two ways: First, it was a summer flu; second, it mainly struck down healthy young adults. Although H1N1 vaccine was unavailable at the outset of the pandemic, it is now available. The CDC recommends immunization for everyone over the age of 6 months.

As the above examples make clear, viruses must be taken seriously for a variety of reasons. In this selection you will learn more about viruses, about several common illnesses caused by them, whether these illnesses can be treated or prevented, and if so, how.

Viruses

1 Viruses cannot grow by themselves. Instead, they are parasites: they take what they need for growth and reproduction from the cells they invade. Once a virus is inside the host cell, it takes control of the cell and manufactures more viruses like itself. Viruses can be spread several different ways, and illnesses caused by them are the most common forms of contagious disease.

Annotation Practice Exercises

Directions: For each exercise below, write the topic and the main idea of the paragraph on the lines beside the paragraph. Then identify the writing pattern the authors used to organize the supporting details.

The Common Cold

2 Although generally brief, lasting only 1–2 weeks, colds are nonetheless irritating and often interfere temporarily with one's normal activities. A cold may be caused by any of more than 200 different viruses that attack the lining of the nasal passages.

3 There are two ways to lessen your risk of cold viruses, which are almost always transmitted by hand-to-hand contact. First, wash your hands frequently. Second, if you touch someone else, avoid touching your face until after you've washed your hands.

Practice Exercise

Topic of paragraph 3:

____

____

Copyright © 2014 The McGraw-Hill Companies, Inc. All rights reserved.

4 If you catch a cold, over-the-counter cold remedies may help treat your symptoms but they cannot directly attack the viral cause. Avoid multi-symptom cold remedies. Because these products include drugs to treat symptoms you may not have, you risk suffering from side effects of medications you don't need. It's better to treat each symptom separately.

5 Antibiotics will not help a cold unless a bacterial infection such as strep throat is also present. Also, overuse of antibiotics leads to the development of drug resistance.The jury is still out on whether other remedies, including zinc gluconate lozenges, echinacea, and vitamin C, will relieve symptoms or shorten the duration of a cold.

Influenza

6 Commonly called the flu, **influenza** is an infection of the respiratory tract caused by the influenza virus. The form changes so easily that every year new strains arise. This makes treatment difficult.

7 Influenza usually includes a fever and extreme fatigue. Most people who get the flu recover within 1–2 weeks, but some develop potentially life-threatening complications, such as pneumonia. Compared to the common cold, influenza is a more serious illness.

8 The highest rates of infection occur in children. Influenza is highly contagious and is spread via respiratory droplets. Vaccination can be appropriate for anyone age 6 months or older who wants to reduce his or her risk of the flu.

Chicken Pox, Cold Sores, and Other Herpesvirus Infections

9 The **herpesviruses** are a large group of viruses. Once infected, the host is never free of the virus. The virus lies latent within certain cells and becomes active periodically, producing symptoms.

10 The family of herpesviruses includes varicella-zoster virus, which causes chicken pox and shingles. Other forms of the herpesviruses are the herpes simplex virus (HSV) types 1 and 2, which cause cold sores and genital herpes. Herpesviruses also include Epstein-Barr virus (EBV), which causes infectious mononucleosis.

Viral Hepatitis

11 Viral **hepatitis** is a term used to describe several different infections that cause inflammation of the liver. Hepatitis A virus (HAV), caused by food or water contaminated by sewage or by an infected person, is the mildest form of the disease. Hepatitis B (HBV) is usually transmitted sexually. Hepatitis C (HCV) can also be transmitted sexually, but it is much more commonly passed through direct contact with infected blood via injection drug use or, prior to the development of screening tests, blood transfusions. HBV and, to a lesser extent, HCV can also be passed from a pregnant woman to her child. There are effective vaccines for hepatitis A and B.

12 Symptoms of acute hepatitis infection can include fatigue and jaundice (characterized by yellowing of the skin and the whites of the eyes). There can also be abdominal pain, loss of appetite, nausea and diarrhea.

13 Most people recover from hepatitis A within a month or so. However, 5–10% of people infected with HBV and 85–90% of people infected with HCV become chronic carriers of the virus.

Main idea sentence:

____

____

____

____

____

Writing pattern:

____

____

____

Practice Exercise

Topic of paragraph 6:

____

____

Main idea sentence:

____

____

____

____

____

Writing pattern:

____

Practice Exercise

Topic of paragraph 7:

____

____

Main idea sentence:

____

____

____

Writing pattern:

____

____

____

____

____

This means they are capable of infecting others for the rest of their lives. Some chronic carriers remain asymptomatic, while others slowly develop chronic liver disease, cirrhosis, or liver cancer. An estimated 4 million Americans and 500 million people worldwide may be chronic carriers of hepatitis.

14 The extent of HCV infection has only recently been recognized. Moreover, most infected people are unaware of their condition. To ensure proper treatment and prevention, testing for HCV may be recommended for people at risk. These include people who have never injected drugs (even once) who received a blood transfusion or a donated organ prior to July 1992. They include those who have engaged in high-risk sexual behavior or who have had body piercing, tattoos, or acupuncture involving unsterile equipment. If you are considering getting a tattoo or body piercing, choose the artist carefully and follow aftercare directions.

Human Papillomavirus (HPV)

15 The more than 100 different types of HPV cause a variety of warts, including common warts on the hands, plantar warts on the soles of the feet, and genital warts. Depending on their location,warts may be removed using over-the-counter preparations or by a doctor. Because HPV infection is chronic, warts can reappear despite treatment. HPV causes the majority of cases of cervical cancer; a vaccine is available and recommended for girls and women age 9–26. Experts now advise that boys receive HPV vaccine to protect them against genital warts and to prevent certain cancers later in life.

16 HPV is especially common in young people, with some of the highest rates among college students. People can be infected with the virus and capable of transmitting it to their sex partners without having any symptoms at all. The vast majority of people with HPV have no visible warts or symptoms of any kind. Although 80% of sexually active people become infected with HPV by age 50, most show no symptoms at all.

Treating Viral Illnesses

17 Antibiotics are not effective against viral illnesses. Antiviral drugs typically work by interfering with some part of the viral life cycle. For example, they may prevent a virus from entering body cells or from successfully reproducing within cells. Antivirals are currently available to fight infections caused by HIV, influenza, herpes simplex, varicella-zoster, HBV and HCV. Most other viral diseases must simply run their course.

Practice Exercise

Topic of paragraph 15:

____

____

Main idea sentence:

____

____

____

____

____

____

Writing pattern:

____

____

____

____

Source: Adapted from Paul Insel and Walton Roth, *Connect Core Concepts in Health,* 12th ed., Brief, pp. 525–26, 538–39. Copyright © 2012 by the McGraw-Hill Companies. Reprinted by permission of The McGraw-Hill Companies.

SELECTION 7.1
Health
(continued)

Comprehension and Vocabulary Quiz

This quiz has four parts. Your instructor may assign some or all of them.

Comprehension

Directions: Use the information in the selection to answer each item below.

_______ **1.** Over-the-counter cold remedies:
- *a.* may help treat symptoms.
- *b.* do not directly treat the viral cause of the cold.
- *c.* can include drugs for symptoms the person does not have.
- *d.* all of the above

_______ **2.** A person with influenza usually has:
- *a.* cold sores.
- *b.* fever and extreme fatigue.
- *c.* life-threatening complications.
- *d.* pneumonia.

_______ **3.** Cold sores are caused by the type of herpesvirus known as:
- *a.* varicella-zoster virus.
- *b.* herpes simplex (HSV).
- *c.* Epstein-Barr virus (EBV).
- *d.* human papillomavirus (HPV).

_______ **4.** Unsterile tattooing and body-piercing equipment can cause:
- *a.* influenza.
- *b.* herpesvirus infections.
- *c.* hepatitis C.
- *d.* human papillomavirus (HPV) infections.

_______ **5.** Which two of the following viruses may eventually result in cancer?
- *a.* cold and influenza viruses
- *b.* influenza virus and herpesviruses
- *c.* herpesviruses and hepatitis B virus (HBV)
- *d.* hepatitis C virus (HCV) and human papillomavirus (HPV)

Vocabulary in Context

Directions: For each item below, use context clues to deduce the meaning of the *italicized* word.

_______ **6.** Once infected, the *host* is never free of the virus.

Many species of animals act as a *host* for tapeworms that live in their digestive system.

host (hōst) means:
- *a.* one who entertains guests
- *b.* a person who manages a hotel

c. an emcee or interviewer on a radio or television program

d. an animal in which another organism lives

______ **7.** The virus lies *latent* within certain cells and becomes active periodically, producing symptoms.

His allergies are *latent* until grass and tree pollens trigger them every spring.

latent (lāt′ nt) means:

a. unable to be diagnosed

b. present but not active

c. severe

d. out of control

______ **8.** Symptoms of *acute* hepatitis infection can include fatigue and jaundice (characterized by yellowing of the skin and the whites of the eyes).

Because of *acute* appendicitis, she had emergency surgery.

acute (ə kyo͞ot′) means:

a. coming on quickly and following a short, severe course

b. involving unusually high fever and chills

c. non-life-threatening

d. mild, but persistently annoying

______ **9.** However, 5–10% of people infected with HBV and 85–90% of people infected with HCV become *chronic* carriers of the virus.

Some construction workers develop *chronic* back pain that leaves them unable to work.

chronic (krŏn′ ĭc) means:

a. recurring

b. related to one's occupation

c. minor

d. caused by stress

______ **10.** Depending on their location, warts may be removed using *over-the-counter* preparations or by a doctor.

Aspirin, eye drops, first-aid cream, and decongestants are examples of *over-the-counter* products.

over-the-counter (ō′ vər-thə-koun′ tər) means:

a. highly advertised

b. inexpensive

c. can be sold legally without a doctor's prescription

d. having a long shelf life

Word Structure

Directions: In paragraph 2 of the selection, you encountered the word **temporarily.** It contains the root ***tempor***, which means "time." The word *temporarily* literally means "lasting for a limited time." Use the meaning of the root ***tempor*** and the list of prefixes on pages 72–73 to help you determine the meaning of the following words.

_______ **11.** If you give an **extemporaneous** toast at a friend's wedding reception, you:

a. are very fond of your friend.

b. have had too much to drink.

c. speak without taking time to prepare formal remarks.

d. are a member of the wedding party.

_______ **12.** My grandfather likes to spend time with his *contemporaries* at the senior citizens' center. **Contemporaries** means people who:

a. are about the same age.

b. get along well.

c. enjoy social activities.

d. like to play cards.

_______ **13.** If a child's **temporal** fantasy is to be a superhero, the fantasy:

a. endures into adolescence.

b. disappears as soon as it occurs.

c. lasts a lifetime.

d. lasts for only a limited time.

_______ **14.** The *tempo* of life is slower in Latin American countries than in European countries. **Tempo** means:

a. enjoyment or pleasure.

b. pace.

c. length or duration.

d. destruction or extinction.

_______ **15.** A **contemporary** art museum is a museum that:

a. contains primarily art works that have been donated to it.

b. displays only sculptures and large-scale works of art.

c. focuses on paintings from other countries.

d. features modern art or art from the present time.

Reading Skills Application

Directions: These items test your ability to *apply* certain reading skills. You may not have studied all the skills yet, so some items will serve as a preview.

_______ **16.** Based on its word parts, the word *antiviral* in paragraph 17 means:

a. promoting growth and reproduction in viruses.

b. destroying or restricting the growth and reproduction of viruses.

c. before a virus occurs.

d. within viruses.

_______ **17.** In paragraph 15 it says, "Because HPV infection is chronic, warts can reappear despite treatment." What is the relationship between the parts of that sentence?

a. addition

b. sequence

c. cause-effect

d. summary

_____ **18.** The authors' primary purpose in writing this selection is to:

a. persuade readers to be immunized against viruses.

b. instruct readers how to recognize certain viruses.

c. inform readers about viruses, illnesses they cause, and their prevention or treatment.

d. persuade readers to protect themselves against exposure to viruses.

_____ **19.** In paragraph 9 it says, "Once infected, the host is never free of the virus.The virus lies latent within certain cells and becomes active periodically, producing symptoms." What is the relationship between the two sentences?

a. The second sentence continues a list begun in the first sentence.

b. The second sentence presents a comparison with something in the first sentence.

c. The second sentence gives an example of something mentioned in the first sentence.

d. The second sentence clarifies the first sentence.

_____ **20.** Based on information in the passage, it is logical to conclude that:

a. all viral illnesses should be left to run their course.

b. antibiotics can be used to treat most viral diseases.

c. immunizations could reduce the number of cases of some viral illnesses.

d. researchers do not understand viruses.

Respond in Writing

Directions: Refer to the selection as needed to answer the essay-type questions below.

1. **Reacting to What You Have Read:** Which viruses mentioned in the selection were you already aware of? What were some misconceptions you had about viruses that the selection cleared up? What one piece of new information did you find most surprising or helpful?

____

____

____

____

____

____

____

2. **Comprehending the Selection Further:** The authors note several reasons viruses are difficult to deal with. List at least four of them.

____

____

____

Copyright © 2014 The McGraw-Hill Companies, Inc. All rights reserved.

3. **Overall Main Idea of the Selection:** In one sentence, tell what the authors want readers to understand about viruses. (Be sure to include "viruses" in your overall main idea sentence.)

Internet Resources

Read More about It Online

Directions: To learn more about the topic of this selection, see the websites below or use the keyword **"human viruses"** (or the names of any specific viral infection mentioned in the selection) with a search engine.

http://science.howstuffworks.com/environmental/life/cellular-microscopic/virus-human
This article, "How Viruses Work," presents helpful information in an understandable way. Includes links to related topics.

www.livescience.com/topics/virus
Launched in 2004, this website covers science, health, and technology news and presents it in an engaging way.

SELECTION **7.2**

Government

The Right to Vote: Valued but Underutilized

From *We the People: A Concise Introduction to American Politics*

By Thomas E. Patterson

Historically, young adults have been much less likely to vote than middle-aged and senior citizens. The 2008 election, however, was historic in that between 22 and 24 million Americans aged 18–29 voted. This means an estimated 49.3 to 54.5 percent of eligible young adults voted, an increase of 1 to 6 percentage points over the estimated youth turnout in 2004. (The only election in which turnout was higher in this group was in 1972, the first presidential election in which 18-year-olds could vote.) Because 66 percent of young adult voters voted for one candidate, Barack Obama, they made a crucial difference in the outcome of the election. Declare Yourself is a nonpartisan initiative dedicated to youth voters. In a survey it conducted, 61 percent of young adult voters said they will be more active in politics in the future, while only 2 percent said they would be less active; 37 percent said they will participate the same amount.

Along with age, economic class and education affect voter turnout. Americans at the bottom of the economic ladder are much less likely to vote than those at the top. In presidential elections, for example, the turnout rate of low-income citizens is only about half that of high-income citizens. Persons with a college education are about 40 percent more likely to vote than persons with a grade school education. Education, in fact, is the best predictor of voter turnout.

If you were qualified to vote in the last presidential election, did you vote? Most Americans recognize that voting is a form of political participation, a way they can exert influence on public policy and leadership. In light of that, do you think that the majority of Americans vote in most elections? Do Americans who do not vote still value their right to vote? How does voter turnout in this country compare with voter turnout in other democracies? These questions and many more are answered in this excerpt from a government textbook.

Suffrage: The Right to Vote

1 At the nation's founding, **suffrage**—the right to vote—was limited to property-owning males. Thomas Paine ridiculed this restriction in *Common Sense*. Observing that a man whose only item of property was a jackass would lose his right to vote if the jackass died, Paine asked, "Now tell me, which was the voter, the man or the jackass?" Fifty years elapsed before the property restriction was lifted in all the states.

2 Women did not secure the vote until 1920, with the ratification of the Nineteenth Amendment. Decades earlier, Susan B. Anthony had tried to vote in her hometown of Rochester, New York, asserting that it was her right as a U.S. citizen. She was arrested for "illegal voting" and told that her proper place was in the home. By 1920, men had run out of excuses for denying the vote to women. As Senator Wendell Phillips observed, "One of two things is true: either woman is like man—and if she is, then a ballot based on brains belongs to her as well as to him. Or she is different, and then man does not know how to vote for her as she herself does."

3 African Americans had to wait nearly fifty years longer than women to secure their right to vote. Blacks seemed to have gained that right after the Civil War with passage of the Fifteenth

Annotation Practice Exercises

Directions: For each exercise below, write the topic and the main idea of the paragraph on the lines beside the paragraph. Then identify the writing pattern the author used to organize the supporting details.

Copyright © 2014 The McGraw-Hill Companies, Inc. All rights reserved.

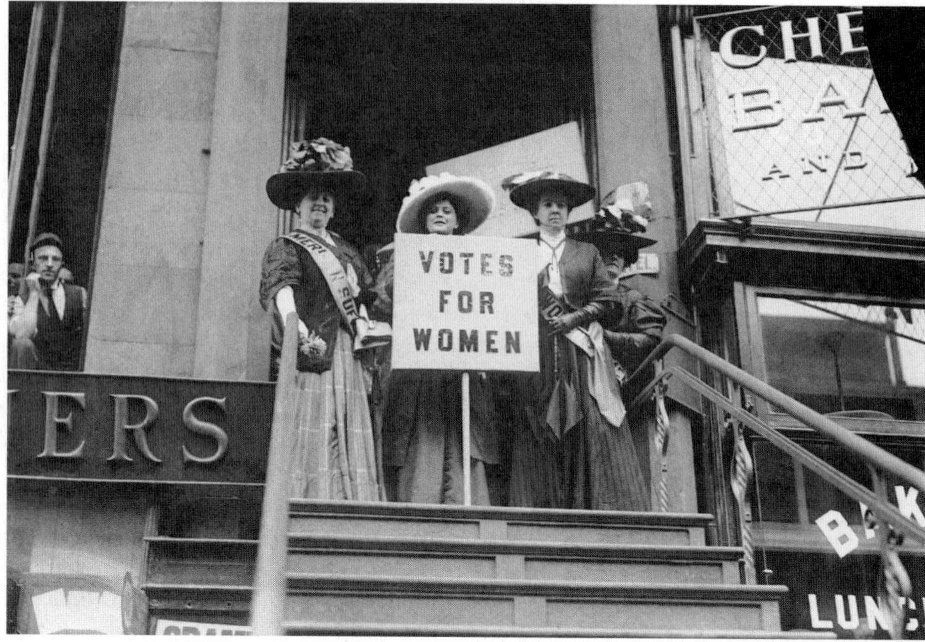

After a hard-fought, decades-long campaign, American women finally won the right to vote in 1920.

Amendment, but they were disenfranchised in the South by intimidation and electoral trickery, including whites-only primaries, rigged literacy tests, and poll taxes. Not until the 1960s were the last legal barriers to equal suffrage for African Americans swept away through congressional and court action.

Factors in Voter Turnout: The United States in Comparative Perspective

4 In 1971, the Twenty-sixth Amendment extended voting rights to include citizens eighteen years of age or older. Previously, nearly all states had restricted voting to those twenty-one years of age or older.

5 Today nearly any American adult—rich or poor, man or woman, black or white—who is determined to vote can legally and actually do so. Nearly all Americans embrace the symbolism of the vote, saying that they have a duty to vote in elections. Nevertheless, many Americans shirk their duty. Millions choose not to vote regularly.

6 Since the 1960s, **voter turnout**—the proportion of adult citizens who actually vote in a given election—has averaged about 55 percent in presidential elections (see Figure 1). Turnout is even lower in the midterm congressional elections that take place between presidential elections. Midterm election turnout has not reached 50 percent since 1920 and has hovered around 40 percent in recent decades. Turnout in local elections is even lower. In many places, less than 20 percent of eligible voters participate.

7 There is, however, an upward trend in presidential election voting. Turnout rebounded sharply in the presidential elections of 2004 and 2008 when compared to those of 1996 and 2000. In fact, turnout in 2008 was the highest since the 1960s. Turnout

Practice Exercise

Topic of paragraph 5:

___

Main idea sentence:

___

___

___

___

___

___

___

Writing pattern:

___

___

___

___

___

FIGURE 1: VOTER TURNOUT IN PRESIDENTIAL ELECTIONS, 1960–2008

After 1960, as indicated by the proportion of eligible voters who voted, turnout declined steadily. In the past two decades, turnout has fluctuated, depending on the issues at stake in the particular election. *Source:* U.S. Census Bureau.

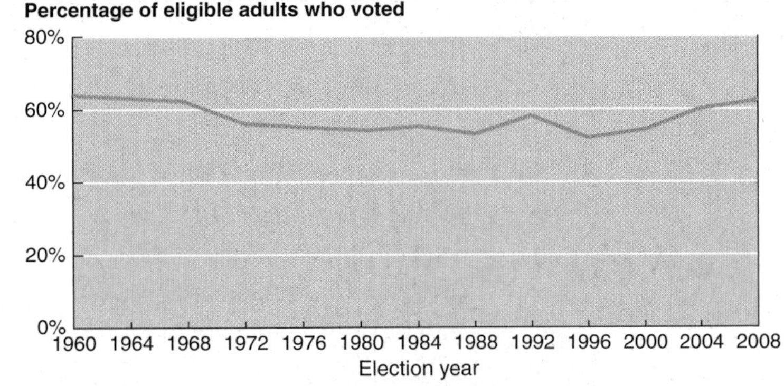

was also up in the 2008 presidential primaries, driven mainly by participation in the close Democratic race between Barack Obama and Hillary Clinton. Although only a third of eligible adults participated in the 2008 primaries, the voting rate was the highest since the 1970s. African Americans and young adults were among the groups with the sharpest increases in turnout.

8 Voter participation is lower in the United States than in other democracies. In recent decades, turnout in national elections has averaged more than 90 percent in Belgium and more than 80 percent in France, Germany, and Denmark.

9 America's lower turnout is largely the result of registration requirements and the frequency of elections. Individual Americans are responsible for registering to vote, whereas in most other democracies, voters are registered automatically by government officials. In addition, unlike some other democracies, the United States does not encourage voting by holding elections on the weekend or by imposing penalties, such as fines, on those who do not participate. Another factor is the absence of a major labor or socialist party, which would serve to bring lower-income citizens to the polls. America's individualist culture and its electoral system have inhibited the establishment of a major labor or socialist party. In democracies where such parties exist, the turnout difference between upper- and lower-income groups is relatively small. In the United States, the gap in the turnout levels of lower- and upper-income persons is substantial.

Practice Exercise

Topic of paragraph 8:

____

Main idea sentence:

____

____

____

____

Writing pattern:

____

____

____

Practice Exercise

Topic of paragraph 9:

____

Main idea sentence:

____

____

____

____

Writing pattern:

____

____

____

____

____

Source: Adapted from Thomas E. Patterson, *We the People: A Concise Introduction to American Politics,* 9th ed., pp. 224–28. Copyright © 2011, by The McGraw-Hill Companies, Inc. Reprinted by permission of The McGraw-Hill Companies.

Copyright © 2014 The McGraw-Hill Companies, Inc. All rights reserved.

SELECTION **7.2**
Government
(continued)

Comprehension and Vocabulary Quiz

This quiz has several parts. Your instructor may assign some or all of them.

Comprehension

Directions: Use the information in the selection to answer each item below.

_______ **1.** Suffrage for women in the United States was attained with the ratification of the:
a. Fifteenth Amendment after the Civil War.
b. Nineteenth Amendment in 1920.
c. Twenty-fourth Amendment in 1964.
d. Twenty-sixth Amendment in 1971.

_______ **2.** African Americans overcame the last legal barriers to suffrage through:
a. increased voter turnout.
b. congressional and court action.
c. midterm congressional elections.
d. all of the above

_______ **3.** Between the 1984 presidential election and the 2000 one, which year had the highest voter turnout?
a. 1980
b. 1992
c. 1996
d. 2000

_______ **4.** In the 2008 presidential election, the greatest increase in voter turnout was among
a. women.
b. women and college students.
c. middle-class citizens.
d. African Americans and young adults.

_______ **5.** Voting rights were extended to include those 18 years of age or older in:
a. 1920.
b. 1964.
c. 1971.
d. 2000.

Vocabulary in Context

Directions: For each item below, use context clues to deduce the meaning of the *italicized* word.

_______ **6.** Women did not secure the vote until 1920, with the *ratification* of the Nineteenth Amendment.

Officials from both countries met last week for a ceremony celebrating the *ratification* of their new trade agreement.

ratification (răt ə fĭ cā′ shən) means:

a. open discussion
b. complete dissolution
c. quick reversal
d. formal approval

7. Blacks seemed to have gained that right after the Civil War with passage of the Fifteenth Amendment, but they were *disenfranchised* in the South by intimidation and electoral trickery, including whites-only primaries, rigged literacy tests, and poll taxes.

Many women continue to feel *disenfranchised* because in certain jobs they are still not paid the same wages that men are for doing the same work.

disenfranchised (dĭs ĕn frăn′ chīzd) means:

a. hostile; angry
b. deprived of a legal right
c. offended
d. unwilling to cooperate

8. Nevertheless, many Americans *shirk* their duty.

Children may *shirk* their household chores if there is something more interesting to do.

shirk (shûrk) means:

a. complete or finish
b. respect or honor
c. avoid or neglect
d. celebrate

9. Midterm election turnout has not reached 50 percent since 1920 and has *hovered* around 40 percent in recent decades.

All summer long the daytime temperature *hovered* around 95 degrees.

hovered (hŭv′ ərd) means:

a. remained near
b. exceeded
c. came near to
d. fell below

10. Turnout *rebounded* sharply in the presidential elections of 2004 and 2008 when compared to those of 1996 and 2000.

The company's stock price had dropped to $32 per share, but it *rebounded* when the company announced higher than expected earnings.

rebounded (rē′ bound′ əd) means:

a. bounced back
b. sank
c. stayed the same
d. decreased

Copyright © 2014 The McGraw-Hill Companies, Inc. All rights reserved.

Word Structure

Directions: In paragraph 4 of the selection, you encountered the word **include.** It contains the root ***clude,*** which means "to close," or "to shut." *Include* literally means "to close in" or "to contain (something) within as part of the whole." Use the meaning of ***clude*** and the list of prefixes on pages 72–73 to help you determine the meaning of each of the following words.

_______ **11.** If a sign at an amusement park says, "Children under age 5 are **excluded** from this ride," it means these children:

a. must be accompanied by a parent or an adult.
b. are not permitted to ride.
c. are required to have a ticket.
d. are restricted in the number of times they may ride.

_______ **12.** If a person's coronary artery is **occluded,** the artery is:

a. torn through.
b. blocked.
c. weak.
d. punctured.

_______ **13.** If you seek a **secluded** spot for a picnic, you are looking for a place that is:

a. far enough away to shut out other people and noise.
b. green and grassy.
c. situated in an open area.
d. in a field or meadow.

_______ **14.** If a broken arm **precludes** you from participating in a tennis tournament, your broken arm:

a. limits your participation.
b. increases your participation.
c. prevents your participation.
d. delays your participation.

_______ **15.** If diplomats **conclude** negotiations between their countries, they:

a. begin or enter into them.
b. continue or maintain them.
c. close out or finish them.
d. break off or terminate them.

Reading Skills Application

Directions: These items test your ability to *apply* certain reading skills. You may not have studied all the skills yet, so some items will serve as a preview.

_______ **16.** Which of the following best describes the author's tone in this selection?

a. humorous
b. factual
c. sentimental
d. compassionate

_______ **17.** In paragraph 9 it says, "America's lower turnout is largely the result of registration requirements and the frequency of elections." What is the relationship between the parts of that sentence?

a. addition

b. sequence

c. cause-effect

d. summary

_______ **18.** The author's primary purpose in writing this selection is to:

a. persuade readers to vote in midterm elections.

b. instruct readers how to register to vote.

c. inform readers about the history of voting rights and voter participation in the United States.

d. inform readers about several constitutional amendments.

_______ **19.** In paragraph 6 it says, "Turnout in local elections is even lower. In many places, less than 20 percent of eligible voters participate." What is the relationship between the two sentences?

a. The second sentence changes the meaning of first sentence.

b. The second sentence categorizes information given in the first sentence.

c. The second sentence gives a specific example of what is stated in the first sentence.

d. The second sentence clarifies the first sentence.

_______ **20.** Does the following statement from paragraph 9 represent a fact or an opinion? "Individual Americans are responsible for registering to vote, whereas in most other democracies, voters are registered automatically by government officials."

a. fact

b. opinion

SELECTION **7.2**
Government
(continued)

Respond in Writing

Directions: Refer to the selection as needed to answer the essay-type questions below.

1. **Reacting to What You Have Read:** If you are qualified to vote, do you? Why or why not? If you are qualified to vote but have not registered or do not vote, do you think you will start exercising this right? Why or why not?

____

____

____

____

____

____

____

Copyright © 2014 The McGraw-Hill Companies, Inc. All rights reserved.

2. **Comprehending the Selection Further:** List the reasons the author gives as to why American voter turnout is less than that of citizens in other democracies. Then list at least three reasons why, in your opinion, Americans *should* vote in elections.

Reasons U.S. citizens do not vote:

Reasons U.S. citizens *should* vote:

3. **Overall Main Idea of the Selection:** In one sentence, tell what the author wants readers to understand about our right to vote. (Be sure to include "right to vote" in your overall main idea sentence.)

Internet Resources

Read More about It Online

Directions: To learn more about the topic of the selection, see the websites below or use the keywords **"U.S. voter turnout"** with a search engine.

www.infoplease.com/ipa/A0781450.htm
This fact sheet shows U.S. presidential election results from 1789 to 2004.

www.lwv.org
This is the official website for the League of Women Voters. It contains information about voter registration, voter turnout, candidates, and national, state, and local elections.

SELECTION **7.3** **Personal Finance**

Are You Shopping Smart?

From *Personal Finance*
By Jack Kapoor, Les Dlabay, and Robert Hughes

Do you like to shop? Do you spend a lot of time shopping? The authors of this personal finance textbook excerpt report, "In times of economic and financial difficulty, the number of unwise buying decisions often increases. People are tempted into scams that promise they will 'earn easy money' or 'get out of debt fast.' Unplanned and careless buying will reduce your potential for long-term financial security. Impulse buying activities of a few dollars a week can cost you thousands in just a couple of years. Many wise buying strategies are available to avoid poor purchasing choices." The selection below discusses those "wise buying strategies."

By the way, the authors say that the answers to the following questions can reveal whether you have a problem with compulsive shopping: Do you have an overwhelming desire to buy things? Do you buy to change your mood? Do your shopping habits hurt your relationships? Does overshopping damage your finances?

Financial Implications of Consumer Decisions

1 Every person making personal financial decisions is a consumer. Regardless of age, income, or household situation, we all use goods and services. Daily buying decisions involve a trade-off between current spending and saving for the future.

2 Various economic, social, and personal factors affect daily buying habits. These factors are the basis for spending, saving, investing, and achieving personal financial goals. In very simple terms, the only way you can have long-term financial security is to not spend all of your current income. In addition, overspending leads to misuse of credit and financial difficulties.

3 Throughout your life, your buying decisions reflect many influences. You should consider opportunity costs to maximize the satisfaction you obtain from available financial resources. Commonly overlooked trade-offs when buying include

- Paying a higher price over time by using credit to buy items that you need now.
- Buying unknown, possibly poor-quality brands that are less expensive.
- Selecting brands that may be difficult to service or repair.
- Ordering by mail or online, which saves time and money but may make it harder to return, replace, or repair purchases.
- Taking time and effort to comparison-shop to save money and obtain better after-sale service.

4 Your buying decisions reflect many aspects of your personality, life situation, values, and goals. Combine this fact with the complexity of the marketplace, and you can see that most purchase decisions require analysis.

Annotation Practice Exercises

Directions: For each exercise below, write the topic and the main idea of the paragraph on the lines beside the paragraph. Then identify the writing pattern the authors used to organize the supporting details.

Practice Exercise

Topic of paragraph 2:

____

____

Main idea sentence:

____

____

____

____

____

____

Writing pattern:

____

____

____

____

Practical Purchasing Strategies

5 ***Comparison shopping*** is the process of considering alternative stores, brands, and prices. In contrast, ***impulse buying*** is unplanned purchasing, which can result in financial problems. Several buying techniques are commonly suggested to help manage finances through wise buying.

6 **Timing Purchases** Certain types or categories of items go on sale the same time each year. You can obtain bargains by buying winter clothing in mid- or late winter, or summer clothing in mid- or late summer. Many people save by buying holiday items and other products at reduced prices in late December and early January.

7 Weather reports and other news can also help you plan your purchasing. A crop failure can quickly results in higher prices for certain food products. Changing economic conditions and political difficulties around the world may result in higher prices and reduced supplies of certain products. Awareness of such situations can help you buy when prices are relatively low.

8 **Store Selection** Your decision to use a particular retailer is probably influenced by location, price, product selection, and services available. Competition and technology have changed retailing with superstores, specialty shops, and online buying. This expanded shopping environment provides consumers with greater choice, potentially lower prices, and the need to carefully consider buying alternatives.

9 One alternative is the ***cooperative***, a nonprofit organization whose member-owners may save money on certain products or services. A credit union is an example of a financial services cooperative. Food cooperatives, usually based in a community group or church, buy grocery items in large quantities. The savings on these bulk purchases are passed on to the co-op's members in the form of lower food prices. Cooperatives have also been organized to provide less expensive childcare, recreational equipment, health care, cable television, and burial services.

10 **Brand Comparison** Food and other products come in various brands. *National-brand* products are highly advertised items available in many stores. You are probably familiar with brands such as Green Giant, Nabisco, Del Monte, Kellogg's, Kraft, Sony, Kodak, Tylenol, and Gap. Brand-name products are usually more expensive than nonbrand products, but they offer consistency of quality for which people are willing to pay.

11 *Store-brand* and *private-label* products, sold by one chain of stores, are low-cost alternatives to famous-name products. These products have labels that identify them with a specific retail chain, such as Safeway, Kroger, Osco, Walgreen's, and Walmart. Since store-brand products are frequently manufactured by the same companies that produce brand-name counterparts, these lower-cost alternatives allow consumers to save money. Private-label and store-brand items can result in extensive savings over time.

12 **Label Information** Certain label information is helpful; however, other information is nothing more than advertising. Federal law requires that food labels contain information. Product labeling for appliances includes information about operating costs, to assist you in selecting the most energy-efficient models.

Consumers face an endless variety of buying decisions.

Practice Exercise

Topic of paragraph 5:

___

Main idea sentence:

___

Writing pattern:

___

Practice Exercise

Topic of paragraph 9:

___

Open dating describes the freshness or shelf life of a perishable product. Phrases such as "Use before May 2013" or "Not to be sold after October 8" appear on most grocery items.

13 **Price Comparison** ***Unit pricing*** uses a standard unit of measurement to compare the prices of packages of different sizes. To calculate the unit price, divide the price by the number of units of measurement, such as ounces, pounds, gallons, or number of sheets (for items such as paper towels and facial tissues). Then, compare the unit prices for various sizes, brands, and stores.

14 Coupons and rebates also provide better pricing for wise consumers. A family saving about $8 a week on their groceries by using coupons will save $416 over a year and $2,080 over five years (not counting interest). A ***rebate*** is a partial refund of the price of a product.

15 When comparing prices, remember that

- More store convenience (location, hours, sales staff) usually means higher prices.
- Ready-to-use products have higher prices.
- Large packages are usually the best buy; however, compare using unit pricing.
- "Sale" may not always mean saving money.

Main idea sentence:

Writing pattern:

Practice Exercise

Topic of paragraph 15:

Main idea sentence:

Writing pattern:

SELECTION 7.3

Source: Jack Kapoor, Les Dlabay, and Robert Hughes, *Personal Finance*, 10th ed., pp. 252–57. Copyright © 2012 by The McGraw-Hill Companies, Inc. Reprinted by permission of The McGraw-Hill Companies.

Copyright © 2014 The McGraw-Hill Companies, Inc. All rights reserved.

SELECTION 7.3
Personal Finance
(continued)

Comprehension and Vocabulary Quiz

This quiz has several parts. Your instructor may assign some or all of them.

Comprehension

Directions: Use the information in the selection to answer each item below.

_______ **1.** The types of factors that influence daily buying habits are:

a. economic.
b. social.
c. personal.
d. all of the above

_______ **2.** A partial refund of the price of a product is called:

a. unit pricing.
b. a cooperative.
c. a rebate.
d. open dating.

_______ **3.** Certain types or categories of items go on sale:

a. in mid- or late winter.
b. in mid- or late summer.
c. during December and early January.
d. at the same time each year.

_______ **4.** Kraft, Sony, and Gap are examples of:

a. national brands.
b. store brands.
c. private-label brands.
d. none of the above

_______ **5.** Federal law requires that:

a. food labels contain information.
b. all products have open dating.
c. items be put on sale at least once a year.
d. food prices be increased with there is a crop failure.

Vocabulary in Context

Directions: For each item below, use context clues to deduce the meaning of the *italicized* word.

_______ **6.** Your buying decisions *reflect* many aspects of your personality, life situation, values, and goals.

Bill and Melinda Gates's charitable contributions *reflect* their commitment to improving education and world health.

reflect (rĭ flĕkt′) means:

a. express; make apparent
b. limit; restrict

c. show as an image
d. go against

_______ **7.** Awareness of such situations can help you buy when prices are *relatively* low.

Losing my job made all my other problems seem *relatively* minor.

relatively (rĕl′ ə tĭv lē) means:
a. related as a family member
b. barely
c. in comparison with something else
d. surprisingly

_______ **8.** Your decision to use a particular *retailer* is probably influenced by location, price, product selection, and services available.

Each *retailer* in the shopping mall took out an ad in the Sunday newspaper.

retailer (rē′ tāl′ ər) means:
a. one who repeats gossip or stories to others
b. one who sells good directly to consumers
c. one who purchases good or services
d. one who advertises

_______ **9.** The savings on these *bulk* purchases are passed on to the co-op's members in the form of lower food prices.

Companies that send out thousands of catalogs pay a *bulk* mail rate.

bulk (bŭlk) means:
a. expanded
b. related to the post office
c. expensive
d. pertaining to a large quantity

_______ **10.** Open dating describes the freshness or shelf life of a *perishable* product.

Because bananas are *perishable*, they should be used within a few days of purchase.

perishable (pĕr′ ĭ shə bəl) means:
a. unfairly priced
b. liable to rot or spoil
c. organically grown
d. damaged

Word Structure

Directions: In paragraph 5 of the selection, you encountered the word **manage.** It contains the root ***manu***, which means "hand." The word *manage* literally means "to take in hand," or in other words, to direct or control. Use the meaning of ***manu*** and the list of prefixes on pages 72–73 to determine the meaning of the following words.

Copyright © 2014 The McGraw-Hill Companies, Inc. All rights reserved.

_______ **11. Manual** labor is:

a. performed by men only.
b. done by hand.
c. performed by machines.
d. completed quickly.

_______ **12.** Ancient **manuscripts** were:

a. written in code.
b. rare.
c. written by hand.
d. difficult to read.

_______ **13.** If a pilot **manipulates** the controls of a jetliner, she

a. shuts them off.
b. scans them constantly.
c. turns them over to the co-pilot.
d. operates them with her hands.

_______ **14.** A prisoner in **manacles** is wearing:

a. a striped prison uniform.
b. a number.
c. prison-issued shoes.
d. thick metal hand restraints.

_______ **15.** When you **maneuver** your car in traffic, you:

a. proceed as fast as possible.
b. stop immediately.
c. maintain control as you handle your way through.
d. discover a shorter route to your destination.

Reading Skills Application

Directions: These items test your ability to *apply* certain reading skills. You may not have studied all the skills yet, so some items will serve as a preview.

_______ **16.** Does the following statement from paragraph 8 represent a fact or an opinion? "Your decision to use a particular retailer is probably influenced by location, price, product selection, and services available."

a. fact
b. opinion

_______ **17.** To calculate the unit price, the price is divided by the:

a. ounces.
b. rebate price.
c. number of units of measurement.
d. bulk price.

_______ **18.** The authors' primary purpose in writing this selection is to:

a. persuade readers to buy items only when they are on sale.
b. instruct readers about practical purchasing strategies.
c. inform readers about the factors that cause them to make impulse buys.
d. persuade readers to join cooperatives.

_______ **19.** In paragraph 12 it says, "Certain label information is helpful; however, other information is nothing more than advertising." What is the relationship between the parts of that sentence? (The second part starts after the semicolon.)

a. list
b. sequence
c. cause-effect
d. comparison-contrast

_______ **20.** Based on information in the passage, it is logical to conclude that:

a. unit pricing is too complicated for most consumers to understand.
b. the government should sponsor cooperatives.
c. most consumers could become smarter shoppers.
d. private-label products are of inferior quality.

Respond in Writing

Directions: Refer to the selection as needed to answer the essay-type questions below.

1. **Reacting to What You Have Read:** What one piece of new information did you find most surprising or helpful?

____
____
____
____
____
____
____

2. **Comprehending the Selection Further:** To help consumers shop smarter, the authors present information in five areas. List them. Then tell which one was most valuable to you and why.

____
____
____
____
____
____
____
____

Copyright © 2014 The McGraw-Hill Companies, Inc. All rights reserved.

3. **Overall Main Idea of the Selection:** In one sentence, tell what the authors want readers to understand about consumer decisions. (Be sure to include "consumer decisions" in your overall main idea sentence.)

____

____

____

____

____

____

Internet Resources

Read More about It Online

Directions: To learn more about the topic of this selection, see the websites below or use the keywords **"consumer buying tips"** with a search engine.

www.usa.gov/topics/consumer/smart-shopping/tips.shtml
USA.gov is the U.S. government's official web portal. This webpage presents "Tips for Being a Savvy Consumer." It includes links to information on local consumer affairs offices and Better Business Bureau offices, as well as information about disputing a charge made on your credit card. There is also a link for ordering a free Consumer Action Handbook.

www.consumerworld.org/pages/buyadv.htm
With more than 2,000 links, Consumer World bills itself as a resource for "everything 'consumer' on the Internet," including general consumer information, buying advice, product reviews, recalls, and scam alerts.

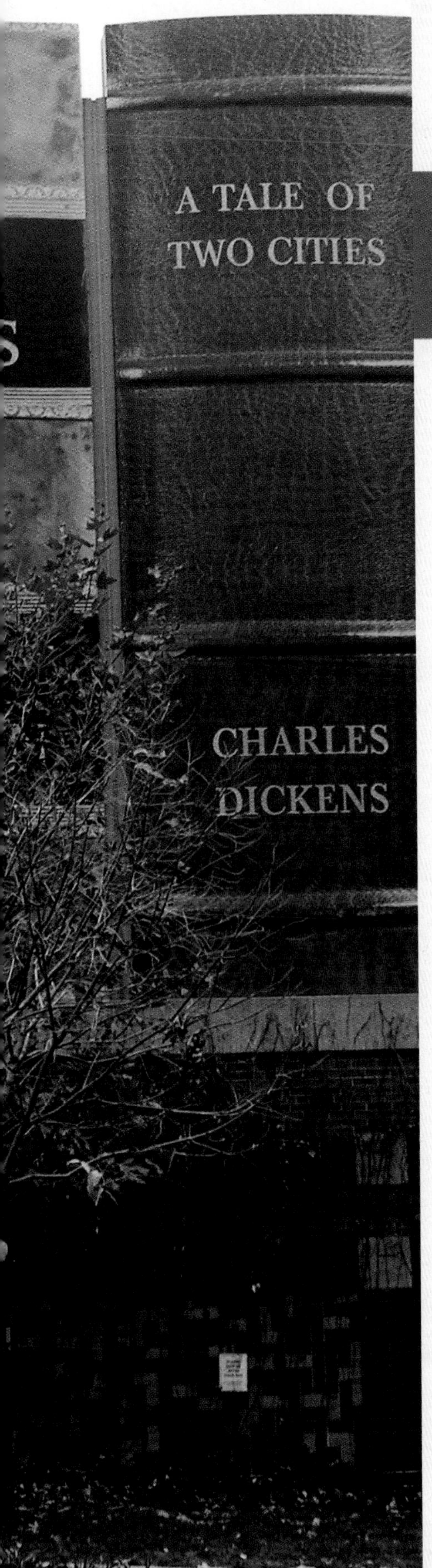

PART 3

A New World of Reading and Thinking Critically

CHAPTERS IN PART THREE

CHAPTER 8

Reading Critically

LEARNING OBJECTIVES

In this chapter you will learn the answers to these questions:

- What is critical reading, and why is it important?
- How can I determine an author's point of view?
- How can I determine an author's purpose?
- How can I determine an author's intended audience?
- How can I determine an author's tone?

CHAPTER CONTENTS

NEW INFORMATION AND SKILLS

What Is Critical Reading, and Why Is It Important?

What Is Author's Point of View, and How Can You Determine It?

What Is Author's Purpose, and How Can You Determine It?

What Is Author's Intended Audience, and How Can You Determine It?

What Is Author's Tone, and How Can You Determine It?

Other Things to Keep in Mind When Reading Critically:

- You should avoid seeing the purpose of everything you read as *to inform*.
- If the author's purpose is to persuade you to adopt his or her point of view, you should determine which side of an issue he or she favors.
- Understanding the author's tone will enable you to grasp the true or intended meaning, even when the author's words may appear to be saying something different.
- There are two forms of irony: irony in tone and irony in situations.
- Sarcasm and irony are not the same thing.

CHECKPOINT: READING CRITICALLY

CHAPTER REVIEW CARDS

TEST YOUR UNDERSTANDING

Reading Critically, Part 1

Reading Critically, Part 2

READINGS

Selection 8.1 "Excerpt"
from *For One More Day*
by Mitch Albom (Literature)

Selection 8.2 "I Never Made It to the NFL"
from *The Last Lecture*
by Randy Pausch with Jeffrey Zaslow (Literature)

Selection 8.3 "You? A Millionaire? Yes!"
from *Understanding Business*
by William Nickels, James McHugh, and Susan McHugh (Business)

NEW INFORMATION AND SKILLS

WHAT IS CRITICAL READING, AND WHY IS IT IMPORTANT?

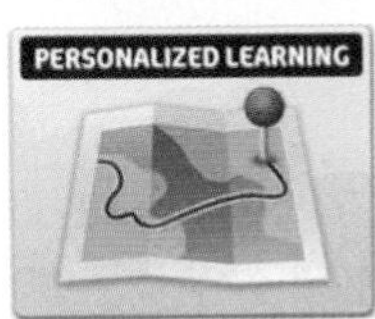

When you read, you should always identify the basic information of topic, main idea, and supporting details. You should also note the author's organizational pattern, especially if you are reading a textbook. However, you often need to understand more than those basic elements and read critically. **Critical reading** means going *beyond* comprehending the topic, main idea, and supporting details to gain additional insights and understanding.

To understand an author's message accurately and completely, you must often read critically. Your professors expect you to be able to do this.

critical reading

Gaining additional insights and understanding that go beyond comprehending the topic, main idea, and supporting details.

Critical reading is also referred to as *critical reasoning* or *critical thinking.*

In this chapter, you will be introduced to these critical reading skills:

- Determining an author's point of view (the author's position on an issue)
- Determining an author's purpose (the author's reason for writing)
- Determining an author's intended audience (whom the author had in mind as his or her readers)
- Determining an author's tone (a way the author reveals his or her attitude toward the topic)

Reading critically involves asking certain comprehension monitoring questions after you read a passage. Once you have asked yourself these questions, you must take time to reread and reconsider the author's message in depth. This enables you to make more intelligent judgments about what you are reading and to gain additional insights and greater understanding.

Let's take a closer look at the four critical reading skills listed above and the comprehension monitoring questions that will guide you toward reading critically.

WHAT IS AUTHOR'S POINT OF VIEW, AND HOW CAN YOU DETERMINE IT?

point of view

An author's position (opinion) on an issue.

Point of view is also known as the *author's argument* or the *author's bias.*

There is always more than one side to any issue. An author may be in *favor* of an issue (support it) or he or she may be *opposed* to it (is against it). For example, one author may have this point of view on state lotteries: "State lotteries encourage gambling and should be prohibited." Another author may have the opposite point of view: "State lotteries are harmless entertainment and should be allowed." **Point of view** refers to an author's position on an issue. It is his or her opinion on an issue. Point of view is also known as the *author's argument* (the overall main idea the author is "arguing" for) and the *author's bias* (the side of an issue the author favors). If you do not determine an author's point of view correctly, you will not understand which side of an issue the author supports.

Comprehension Monitoring Question for Determining an Author's Point of View

"What is the author's position on this issue?"

To determine the author's point of view, critical readers ask themselves this comprehension monitoring question: "What is the author's position on this issue?" To answer this question, look for words that reveal the author's support of or opposition to something. Here are examples of wording that reflect a point of view in *favor* of having a state lottery:

- *Supporting* state lotteries is *essential* because...
- The proposed lottery will *benefit* all the citizens of our state because...

Copyright © 2014 The McGraw-Hill Companies, Inc. All rights reserved.

Here are examples of wording that reflect a point of view in *opposition* to the same issue:

- It is *not in the best interest of* the state to have a lottery because...
- Voters should *oppose* the creation of a state lottery because...
- Concerned citizens should *speak out against* the proposed lottery because...

Now read the following paragraph. Its topic is *quitting smoking*. The formulated main idea is *Even if it takes several attempts, smokers will benefit from quitting because it quickly decreases the risk of heart disease*. As you read the paragraph, ask yourself, "What is the author's point of view on quitting smoking?"

It's Never Too Late to Quit

Perhaps you're a longtime smoker who feels that it is useless to try to quit. Perhaps you've tried in the past to quit, but were unsuccessful. Don't give up! The American Heart Association indicates that if you quit smoking, your risk of heart disease quickly decreases—even if you are a heavy smoker or have smoked for a long time. Within three years of quitting, those who smoke a pack a day or less will have virtually the same risk as those who never smoked. The good news is that since the damage can be reversed, smokers will benefit from quitting. Smoking is highly addictive, so if you have just started to smoke, quit now before you are hooked and there is damage to undo. It takes most smokers several attempts to quit before they ultimately succeed. Be patient. Stay with it. You *can* break the habit.

What Is the Author's Point of View?

____

____

____

____

____

____

Stop and Annotate

Go back to the textbook excerpt above. Write the author's point of view in the space provided.

In this passage, the author expresses a point of view (position) on smoking: Everyone who smokes should quit. The details explain that the damage from smoking can be reversed by quitting, and that both longtime and new smokers will benefit. The author indicates a strong bias against smoking and urges readers to stay with it until they succeed in quitting.

Here is another passage. Its topic is *raising children in marriage-absent homes*. The formulated main idea is *Children raised in marriage-absent homes are at greater risk, and for the sake of children, parents need to be committed, caring, and married.* Read the passage. Then determine the author's point of view by asking yourself, "What is the author's point of view regarding marriage-absent homes and children's well-being?"

Today, one-third of all U.S. children—24 million of them—live in marriage-absent homes. Marriage-absent means the children live with one parent or live with parents who cohabit, but are unmarried. Living in a marriage-absent home puts children at increased risk for all sorts of difficulties. They are more likely to

- have asthma
- be hurt in home accidents
- be abused physically and/or sexually
- become obese
- start to smoke
- abuse alcohol and/or drugs
- not do well in school
- drop out of school
- become delinquent
- be in jail by the time they are young adults
- earn less as adults
- if female, to become pregnant as a teenager and become a single parent.

What Is the Author's Point of View?

____

____

____

____

____

____

Nothing enhances children's well-being more than knowing their parents are in a committed, loving relationship. Wake up, America! For the sake of children, it's time we insist that couples who plan to have children be committed, caring—and married.

Source: Based on John Rosemond's *Living with Children* (column), "Dad's Role as Husband Vital in Raising Kids," *The Santa Fe New Mexican*, April 23, 2012, p. A-9.

Stop and Annotate

Go back to the textbook excerpt above. Write the author's point of view in the space provided.

In this passage, the author's point of view (position) is expressed in the last sentence: For the sake of children, it's time we insist that couples who plan to have children be committed, caring—and married. To indicate that he feels strongly about the issue, the author says, "Wake up!" and uses the word "insist." The details explain the reasons for this point of view: the increased risks to children of living in marriage-absent homes.

EXERCISE 1

This paragraph comes from a personal finance textbook. Read the paragraph and determine the authors' point of view by asking yourself. "What is the authors' position on this issue?"

Should You Cosign a Loan?

What would you do if a relative or friend asked you to cosign a loan? It may not sound like much to ask, but they are asking you to guarantee that *you* will pay their debt if they are unable to. Even if they have every intention of repaying the loan, all kinds of things can go wrong. Could you afford to pay off their debt if you had to? Even if you could afford it, do you really want to accept that responsibility? Some studies of certain types of lenders show that *as many as three of four cosigners are asked to wholly or partially repay the loan.* That statistic should not surprise you. After all, you are being asked to take a risk that a professional lender will not take. Think about it for a minute: the lender would not require a cosigner if the borrower met the lender's criteria for making a loan. An even more

(continued on next page)

Copyright © 2014 The McGraw-Hill Companies, Inc. All rights reserved.

frightening fact is that in most states, if your relative or friend misses a payment, *the lender can collect the entire debt from you immediately without first pursuing the borrower.* Moreover, the creditor can sue you or garnish your wages to collect. If you can't pay immediately, you could be charged penalties and late fees in addition to the amount of the debt. If the matter goes to court, you could get stuck with legal fees, and if the lender wins, it may be able to take your wages and property. If you default on the loan, it may become part of your credit record and damage your credit rating or your ability to get a loan. And if these potential problems aren't enough to dissuade you, agreeing to cosign a loan can permanently ruin a relationship if the borrower defaults. You'd better think twice before signing on the dotted line! The potential trouble that can result from cosigning a loan should make you reluctant to be a cosigner—ever.

Source: Based on Jack Kapoor, Les Dlabay, and Robert Hughes, *Personal Finance,* 10th ed., p. 185. Copyright © 2012 by The McGraw-Hill Companies, Inc. Reprinted by permission of The McGraw-Hill Companies.

What is the *authors' point of view* about cosigning a loan?____________________

____

____

WHAT IS AUTHOR'S PURPOSE, AND HOW CAN YOU DETERMINE IT?

purpose

An author's reason for writing.

Comprehension Monitoring Question for Determining an Author's Purpose

"Why did the author write this?"

A second critical reading skill is determining the author's purpose. Whenever authors write, they write for specific purposes. For that matter, so do you. An author's **purpose** is simply his or her reason for writing. The author's purpose may be *to inform, to instruct, to entertain,* or *to persuade* the reader to believe something or to take a certain action.

Most textbook authors write for the purpose of informing (giving information or explaining something) or instructing (teaching the reader how to do something). However, some authors, such as scientists, historians, newspaper editors, political writers, movie critics, and other experts in their fields, write to give their opinion or to persuade. Finally, other writers, such as humorists or certain newspaper columnists, write for the purpose of entertaining. They may write humorous stories or enjoyable descriptions. It is important to understand an author's purpose for writing. If you are aware of his or her motive for writing, you will have greater insight into what is important in the message.

To determine an author's purpose, critical readers ask themselves this comprehension monitoring question: "Why did the author write this?" Fortunately, authors often state their purpose directly. For example, the author of a biology textbook might write, "The purpose of this section is to define and explain the types of root systems in plants" (to inform). Or the author of a newspaper editorial might state, "The citizens of our city should vote 'yes' on funding a new municipal sports arena" (to persuade). Sometimes, authors do not directly state their purposes for writing because they feel the purpose is obvious, and they assume the reader can infer it.

To determine an author's purpose, notice the words the author uses and the way the information is presented:

- When the author's purpose is *to inform (give information,* or *explain),* he or she will use phrases such as *It is interesting to know that . . .* or *There are different types of. . . .*

- When the author's purpose is *to instruct*, he or she will typically give a set of directions *(instructions)* or a sequence of steps to follow.
- When the author's purpose is *to persuade*, he or she will use emotional language or choose words that are designed to influence your thinking and persuade you to respond a certain way. *Any reasonable person will agree that . . . , Only an uninformed student would believe that . . . ,* and *The only intelligent choice, then, is . . .* are examples of such language.
- When the author's purpose is *to entertain*, he or she may tell a funny story, use wild exaggeration (hyperbole), or simply describe a pleasant event or place. For example, writers might begin, *A funny thing happened to me on the way to . . .* or *Vermont is perhaps the loveliest place to be in autumn.*

Here is an excerpt from a U.S. history textbook. Its topic is *the first people to come to America.* The formulated main idea is *The first people probably came from Asia to America by walking across a land bridge that existed thousands of years ago.* Read this passage; then determine the authors' purpose by asking yourself, "Why did the authors write this?"

People probably first came from Asia to America during a prehistoric glacial period—either before 35,000 B.C. or about 10,000 years later—when huge amounts of the world's water froze into sheets of ice. Sea levels dropped so drastically that the Bering Strait became a broad, grassy plain. Across that land bridge between the two continents both humans and animals escaped icebound Siberia for ice-free Alaska. Whenever the first migration took place, the movement of Asians to America continued, even after 8000 B.C. when world temperatures rose again and the water from melting glaciers flooded back into the ocean, submerging the Bering Strait.

What Is the Authors' Purpose?

____

____

____

____

____

____

Source: Adapted from James Davidson et al., *Nation of Nations: A Narrative History of the American Republic, Vol I: to 1877,* 5th ed. Copyright © 2005 by The McGraw-Hill Companies, Inc. Reprinted by permission of The McGraw-Hill Companies.

Stop and Annotate

Go back to the textbook excerpt above. Write the authors' purpose in the space provided.

The authors' purpose for writing this passage is *to inform* the reader about a particular event: the way people probably first came from Asia to America. The passage consists of historical information the authors want you to know. (People from Asia came on foot to America over a land bridge that existed thousands of years ago.) Notice that the authors are not trying to instruct the reader how to do anything, nor are they trying to persuade you to accept their ideas or to entertain you.

Here is a passage from a health textbook. Its topic is given in the heading: *minimizing the risk of rape.* The stated main idea is *There are commonsense things you can do to reduce your risk of being raped.* Now read the passage and determine the authors' purpose by asking yourself, "Why did the authors write this?"

Copyright © 2014 The McGraw-Hill Companies, Inc. All rights reserved.

Minimizing the Risk of Rape

As violence in our society increases, the incidence of rape and other sexual assault correspondingly increases. We are all potential victims, and self-protection is critical. There are commonsense things you can do to reduce your risk of being raped. They include:

- Think carefully about your patterns of movement to and from class or work. Alter your routes frequently.
- Walk briskly with a sense of purpose. Try not to walk alone at night.
- Dress so that the clothes you wear do not unnecessarily restrict your movement or make you vulnerable.
- Always be aware of your surroundings. Look over your shoulder occasionally. Know where you are so that you won't get lost.
- If you think you are being followed, look for a safe retreat. This might be a store, a fire or police station, or a group of people.
- Let trusted friends know where you are and when you plan to return.
- Keep your car in good working order. Think beforehand how you would handle the situation should your car break down.
- Limit, or even avoid, alcohol to minimize the risk of rape.
- Trust your instincts if you are assaulted. Each situation is different. Do what you can to protect your life.

What Is the Authors' Purpose?

____

____

____

____

____

Source: Adapted from Wayne Payne, Dale Hahn, and Ellen Lucas, *Understanding Your Health*, 10th ed., pp. 538, 540. Copyright © 2009 by The McGraw-Hill Companies, Inc. Reprinted by permission of The McGraw-Hill Companies.

Stop and Annotate

Go back to the textbook excerpt above. Write the authors' purpose in the space provided.

The authors' purpose for writing this passage is *to instruct* readers in what to do to minimize their risk of being raped. They say, "There are commonsense things you can do," and then they list the things you can do to reduce the risk. They are doing more than merely informing you: They are instructing you about specific actions you can take. They are not writing primarily to persuade you, although they undoubtedly are hoping you will follow their recommendations. And they certainly did not write the passage to entertain you.

As the heading of the next paragraph indicates, its topic is *energy-wise computer use.* The formulated main idea is *For energy-wise computer use, turn it off after work hours or use an energy-efficient laptop.* Now read the passage and determine the authors' purpose by asking yourself, "Why did the authors write this?"

Energy-Wise Computer Use

Make a point of turning off your computer after work hours. Leaving it on needlessly wastes energy. Or use an energy-efficient laptop. For example, a laptop with up to seven hours of battery life costs about $2,000, but the savings mount up over time. Both solutions are simple. There's just no excuse for not being energy wise with your computer!

What Is the Authors' Purpose?

____

____

____

____

Source: Based on Wayne Payne, Dale Hahn, and Ellen Lucas, *Understanding Your Heath*, 10th ed., p. B-14. Copyright © 2009 by The McGraw-Hill Companies, Inc. Reprinted by permission of The McGraw-Hill Companies.

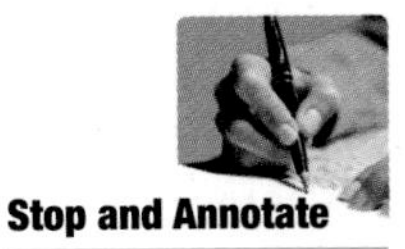

Stop and Annotate

Go back to the textbook excerpt above. Write the authors' purpose in the space provided.

The authors' purpose for writing this passage is *to persuade* computer users to turn their computers off after work hours or to use energy-efficient laptops. They explain why: Leaving computers on after work wastes energy; laptops use far less energy. Notice the exclamation point at the end of the final sentence. It is the authors' way of urging readers to do what they recommend, another indication their purpose is to persuade readers to accept their advice. Their purpose is more than just giving information, and they clearly are not writing to entertain readers.

EXERCISE 2

This paragraph about cosigning a loan appeared earlier in this chapter. Reread the paragraph and determine the authors' purpose by asking yourself, "Why did the authors write this?"

Should You Cosign a Loan?

What would you do if a relative or friend asked you to cosign a loan? It may not sound like much to ask, but they are asking you to guarantee that *you* will pay their debt if they are unable to. Even if they have every intention of repaying the loan, all kinds of things can go wrong. Could you afford to pay off their debt if you had to? Even if you could afford it, do you really want to accept that responsibility? Some studies of certain types of lenders show that *as many as three of four cosigners are asked to wholly or partially repay the loan.* That statistic should not surprise you. After all, you are being asked to take a risk that a professional lender will not take. Think about it for a minute: the lender would not require a cosigner if the borrower met the lender's criteria for making a loan. An even more frightening fact is that in most states, if your relative or friend misses a payment, *the lender can collect the entire debt from you immediately without first pursuing the borrower.* Moreover, the creditor can sue you or garnish your wages to collect. If you can't pay immediately, you could be charged penalties and late fees in addition to the amount of the debt. If the matter goes to court, you could get stuck with legal fees, and if the lender wins, it may be able to take your wages and property. If you default on the loan, it may become part of your credit record and damage your credit rating or your ability to get a loan. And if these potential problems aren't enough to dissuade you, agreeing to cosign a loan can permanently ruin a relationship if the borrower defaults. You'd better think twice before signing on the dotted line! The potential trouble that can result from cosigning a loan should make you reluctant to be a cosigner—ever.

Source: Based on Jack Kapoor, Les Dlabay, and Robert Hughes, *Personal Finance,* 10th ed., p. 185. Copyright © 2012 by The McGraw-Hill Companies, Inc. Reprinted by permission of the McGraw-Hill Companies.

What is the *authors' purpose* in writing this selection? _______________

____

____

WHAT IS AUTHOR'S INTENDED AUDIENCE, AND HOW CAN YOU DETERMINE IT?

When speakers make a presentation, they have an audience, and they adjust their presentation to the type of people in the audience. Suppose a doctor is asked to give a presentation on alcoholism. If her audience is other doctors, her speech will probably be very technical and contain specialized medical terms. If, however, her audience is students in a high school biology class, then her presentation will be quite different.

Intended audience

People an author has in mind as his or her readers.

When authors write, they also have specific "audiences" in mind. Their audiences are the people they anticipate will be reading what they have written. An author's **intended audience** is the people the author has in mind as his or her readers. For instance, a computer scientist may write an introductory-level textbook for students who have no knowledge of computer programming. Having this particular audience in mind will influence the material the computer scientist includes, how he or she presents it, and how simple or sophisticated an approach he or she chooses. However, if that same computer scientist were writing an article for other computer scientists, the level of the material and how it is presented would be very different.

Why is it important to determine an author's audience? There are several reasons. First, if you are not among those in the intended audience (people knowledgeable about computer programming, for example), you may need to do extra work to understand the material. Second, if you are doing research, you can decide whether material on the topic is written for the audience you are part of (for example, those who know little or nothing about computer programming). Third, knowing who the audience is gives you insight into the author's purpose, his or her reason for writing. This, in turn, allows you to evaluate whether or not that purpose was accomplished. Perhaps the most important reason for becoming aware of audience is that it can make you a better writer: Writing instructors can help you learn to shape your message to your intended audience, and this will enable you to communicate your message more effectively.

Comprehension Monitoring Question for Determining an Author's Intended Audience

"Who did the author intend to read this?"

Critical readers ask themselves the comprehension monitoring question "Who did the author intend to read this?" Sometimes an author will state who the intended audience is, but if the author does not, you can determine the audience by considering these three things:

- *the topic* (Is it a common topic? Or is it an unusual or specialized one?)
- *the level of language used* (Is it simple? Sophisticated? Specialized?)
- *the author's purpose for writing* (Is it to inform? To instruct? To persuade?)

This is the excerpt you read earlier on quitting smoking. Reread it and then determine the author's audience by asking yourself, "Who did the author intend to read this?"

It's Never Too Late to Quit

Perhaps you're a longtime smoker who feels that it is useless to try to quit. Perhaps you've tried in the past to quit, but were unsuccessful. Don't give up! The American Heart Association indicates that if you quit smoking, your risk of heart disease quickly decreases—even if you are a heavy smoker or have smoked for a long time. Within three years of quitting, those who smoke a pack a day or less will have virtually the same risk as those who never smoked. The good news is that since the damage can be reversed, smokers will benefit from quitting. Smoking is highly addictive, so if you have just started to smoke, quit now before you are hooked and there is damage to undo. It takes most smokers several attempts to quit before they ultimately succeed. Be patient. Stay with it. You *can* break the habit.

Who Is the Author's Intended Audience?

____

____

____

____

____

Stop and Annotate

Go back to the textbook excerpt above. Write the author's intended audience in the space provided.

The author's intended audience is *everyone who smokes, both those who have smoked for a long time and those who have just begun.* Throughout the paragraph, the author uses the word "you" to indicate that he or she is speaking directly to readers who smoke.

Here is the passage you read earlier about energy-wise computer use. Reread it and then determine the authors' intended audience. Ask yourself, "Who did the authors intend to read this?"

Energy-Wise Computer Use

Make a point of turning off your computer after work hours. Leaving it on needlessly wastes energy. Or use an energy-efficient laptop. For example, a laptop with up to seven hours of battery life costs about $2,000, but the savings mount up over time. Both solutions are simple. There's just no excuse for not being energy wise with your computer!

Who Is the Author's Intended Audience?

____

____

____

____

Source: Based on Wayne Payne, Dale Hahn, and Ellen Lucas, *Understanding Your Health*, 10th ed., p. B-14. Copyright © 2009 by The McGraw-Hill Companies, Inc. Reprinted by permission of The McGraw-Hill Companies.

Stop and Annotate

Go back to the textbook excerpt above. Write the authors' intended audience in the space provided.

The authors' intended audience is *everyone who uses computers.* "Work hours" could mean working at a job or just the hours a person spends working at a computer.

Copyright © 2014 The McGraw-Hill Companies, Inc. All rights reserved.

EXERCISE 3

Determine the authors' intended audience for this paragraph by asking yourself, "Who did the authors intend to read this?"

Should You Cosign a Loan?

What would you do if a relative or friend asked you to cosign a loan? It may not sound like much to ask, but they are asking you to guarantee that *you* will pay their debt if they are unable to. Even if they have every intention of repaying the loan, all kinds of things can go wrong. Could you afford to pay off their debt if you had to? Even if you could afford it, do you really want to accept that responsibility? Some studies of certain types of lenders show that *as many as three of four cosigners are asked to wholly or partially repay the loan.* That statistic should not surprise you. After all, you are being asked to take a risk that a professional lender will not take. Think about it for a minute: the lender would not require a cosigner if the borrower met the lender's criteria for making a loan. An even more frightening fact is that in most states, if your relative or friend misses a payment, *the lender can collect the entire debt from you immediately without first pursuing the borrower.* Moreover, the creditor can sue you or garnish your wages to collect. If you can't pay immediately, you could be charged penalties and late fees in addition to the amount of the debt. If the matter goes to court, you could get stuck with legal fees, and if the lender wins, it may be able to take your wages and property. If you default on the loan, it may become part of your credit record and damage your credit rating or your ability to get a loan. And if these potential problems aren't enough to dissuade you, agreeing to cosign a loan can permanently ruin a relationship if the borrower defaults. You'd better think twice before signing on the dotted line! The potential trouble that can result from cosigning a loan should make you reluctant to be a cosigner—ever.

Source: Based on Jack Kapoor, Les Dlabay, and Robert Hughes, *Personal Finance,* 10th ed., p. 185. Copyright © 2012 by The McGraw-Hill Companies, Inc. Reprinted by permission of The McGraw-Hill Companies.

Who is the *authors' intended audience*? ______________________________

____

WHAT IS AUTHOR'S TONE, AND HOW CAN YOU DETERMINE IT?

When people speak, their tone of voice often reveals their attitude toward whatever they are speaking about. To convey a tone, speakers rely on pitch, volume, and inflection, along with their choice of words. You can usually tell by people's tone, for example, if they are serious, joking, happy, upset, or angry. If a friend said, "I made a C on my history test!" you would know by his or her tone whether your friend was thrilled, relieved, or disappointed.

tone

Manner of writing (choice of words and writing style) that reveals an author's attitude toward a topic.

Authors use tone just as speakers do. An author's **tone** is a manner of writing that reveals the author's attitude toward a topic. Authors' tone helps convey their point of view and purpose. Authors may, for example, use tones that are factual, humorous, urgent, encouraging, angry, or sarcastic. You can determine an author's tone by examining his or her word choice and writing style. It may also help you to think about what the author's tone of voice would sound like if he or she were saying something rather than writing it.

Comprehension Monitoring Question for Determining an Author's Tone

"What do the author's choice of words and style of writing reveal about his or her attitude toward the topic?"

It is important to determine an author's tone because if you misunderstand the tone, you may misinterpret the message. To illustrate, you might think the author was being sincere when he was actually joking or being sarcastic. To determine an author's tone, ask yourself, "What do the author's choice of words and style of writing reveal about his or her attitude toward the topic?"

As noted above, *word choice* is one way authors reveal their tone. For example, when describing an angry athlete's behavior, one sportswriter might use "temper tantrum" to convey a disapproving tone. Another sportswriter, who thinks the athlete's behavior was justified, might describe it with the milder words "outburst" or "incident" to convey a more sympathetic tone.

Now consider how an author's *writing style* can be used to convey tone. Each of these sentences contains the same message, but the writing style makes their tone quite different:

- The most successful college graduates of tomorrow will be those who can use a wide range of computer applications effectively.
- Unless you want to flip burgers all your life, you'd better learn how to use that laptop!

Both sentences suggest that it is important to educate yourself about the use of computers, but the first sentence has a formal, serious tone. It is the type of sentence you might find in a business or computer science textbook. The second sentence, however, has a much more informal tone. The phrase *unless you want to flip burgers all your life* reveals this tone. This sentence might appear in a flyer advertising computer training, but it would not be appropriate for a college textbook.

There are many words that can describe an author's tone, but 48 common ones are listed and defined in the chart that follows. You should familiarize yourself with any of these words that are new to you.

WORDS THAT DESCRIBE TONE

There are many words that can be used to describe tone, and you already know lots of them, such as *happy, sad,* and *angry.* There are many others, however, that you may not be familiar with. Here is a list of several. (They are also valuable words to have in your own vocabulary.) To make it easier for you to learn the words, they are grouped into general categories.

Words That Describe a *Neutral* Tone

(typically used in textbooks, reference material, sets of directions, instructional manuals, most newspaper and magazine articles, and other factual, objective material that is presented in a straightforward manner)

unemotional	involving little or no emotion or feeling
dispassionate	devoid of or unaffected by passion, emotion, or bias
indifferent	appearing to have no preference or concern

Words That Describe a *Serious* Tone

(typically used in important formal announcements and obituaries, for example)

solemn	deeply earnest, serious, and sober
serious	grave, earnest, not trifling or jesting; deeply interested or involved
reserved	marked by self-restraint and reticence

Words That Describe an *Emotional* Tone

(typically found in personal articles, political writing, and some persuasive writing, such as editorials)

compassionate	showing kindness, mercy, or compassion; sympathetic
concerned	caring deeply about a person or issue
impassioned	characterized by passion or zeal
nostalgic	feeling bittersweet longing for things, persons, or situations in the past
sentimental	based on emotion rather than reason
remorseful	feeling regret
self-pitying	feeling sorry for oneself
urgent	calling for immediate attention; instantly important
defiant	intentionally contemptuous; resisting authority or force

(continued on next page)

Copyright © 2014 The McGraw-Hill Companies, Inc. All rights reserved.

Words That Describe a *Critical, Disapproving* Tone

(typically found in movie and book reviews, editorials, some magazine articles)

critical	inclined to criticize or find fault
disapproving	passing unfavorable judgment upon; condemning
pessimistic	expecting the worst; having a negative attitude or gloomy outlook
intolerant	not allowing a difference of opinion or sentiment
indignant	angered by something unjust, mean, or unworthy; irate

Words That Describe a *Humorous, Sarcastic, Ironic,* or *Satiric* Tone

(can appear in writing of many sorts, including literature and social criticism and some newspaper and magazine columns and articles)

lighthearted	not being burdened by trouble, worry, or care; happy and carefree
irreverent	disrespectful; critical of what is generally accepted or respected; showing a lack of reverence
cynical	scornful of the motives, virtue, or integrity of others; expressing scorn and bitter mockery
scornful	treating someone or something as despicable or unworthy; showing utter contempt
contemptuous	showing open disrespect or haughty disdain
mocking	treating with scorn or contempt
malicious	intended to cause harm or suffering; having wicked or mischievous intentions or motives
ironic	humorously sarcastic or mocking
sarcastic	characterized by the desire to show scorn or contempt
bitter	characterized by sharpness, severity, or cruelty
skeptical	reluctant to believe; doubting or questioning everything
disbelieving	not believing; refusing to believe

Words That Describe a *Supportive* Tone

(found in writing of many types, such as certain textbooks, inspirational writing, some magazine articles, and personal correspondence)

encouraging	showing support
supportive	showing support or assistance
enthusiastic	showing excitement
optimistic	expecting the best; having a positive outlook
approving	expressing approval or agreement
positive	being in favor of; supportive; optimistic
sympathetic	inclined to sympathy; showing pity
tolerant	showing respect for the rights or opinions or practices of others

Some *Other* Words That Can Describe Tone

authoritative	speaking in a definite and confident manner
ambivalent	having opposite feelings or attitudes at the same time
conciliatory	willing to give in on some matters
cautious	careful; not wanting to take chances; wary
arrogant	giving oneself an undue degree of importance; haughty
grim	gloomy; dismal; forbidding
humble	marked by meekness or modesty; not arrogant or prideful
apologetic	self-deprecating; humble; offering or expressing an apology or excuse

Here is the passage about minimizing the risk of rape that you read earlier. To determine the tone the authors use, reread this passage and then ask yourself, "What do the authors' choice of words and style of writing reveal about their attitude about reducing the risk of rape?"

Minimizing the Risk of Rape

As violence in our society increases, the incidence of rape and other sexual assault correspondingly increases. We are all potential victims, and self-protection is critical. There are commonsense things you can do to reduce your risk of being raped. They include:

- Think carefully about your patterns of movement to and from class or work. Alter your routes frequently.
- Walk briskly with a sense of purpose. Try not to walk alone at night.
- Dress so that the clothes you wear do not unnecessarily restrict your movement or make you vulnerable.
- Always be aware of your surroundings. Look over your shoulder occasionally. Know where you are so that you won't get lost.
- If you think you are being followed, look for a safe retreat. This might be a store, a fire or police station, or a group of people.
- Let trusted friends know where you are and when you plan to return.
- Keep your car in good working order. Think beforehand how you would handle the situation should your car break down.
- Limit, or even avoid, alcohol to minimize the risk of rape.
- Trust your instincts if you are assaulted. Each situation is different. Do what you can to protect your life.

What Is the Authors' Tone?

____

____

____

____

Source: Adapted from Wayne Payne, Dale Hahn, and Ellen Lucas, *Understanding Your Health*, 10th ed., pp. 538, 540. Copyright © 2009 by The McGraw-Hill Companies, Inc. Reprinted by permission of The McGraw-Hill Companies.

Stop and Annotate

Go back to the textbook excerpt above. Write the authors' tone in the space provided.

The authors' tone is *serious* and *unemotional.* Even though rape can be an emotional issue, the authors do not use an emotional tone. Their tone is not upset or alarmed. They calmly suggest some "commonsense" things you can do to minimize the risk of rape. They do not use any alarming words.

Here is the excerpt on quitting smoking. Reread it and then determine the author's tone by asking yourself, "What do the author's choice of words and style of writing reveal about his or her attitude toward quitting smoking?"

Copyright © 2014 The McGraw-Hill Companies, Inc. All rights reserved.

It's Never Too Late to Quit

Perhaps you're a longtime smoker who feels that it is useless to try to quit. Perhaps you've tried in the past to quit, but were unsuccessful. Don't give up! The American Heart Association indicates that if you quit smoking, your risk of heart disease quickly decreases—even if you are a heavy smoker or have smoked for a long time. Within three years of quitting, those who smoke a pack a day or less will have virtually the same risk as those who never smoked. The good news is that since the damage can be reversed, smokers will benefit from quitting. Smoking is highly addictive, so if you have just started to smoke, quit now before you are hooked and there is damage to undo. It takes most smokers several attempts to quit before they ultimately succeed. Be patient. Stay with it. You *can* break the habit.

What Is the Author's Tone?

____

____

____

____

Stop and Annotate

Go back to the textbook excerpt above. Write the author's tone in the space provided.

The author's tone is encouraging and supportive. The author says, "Don't give up!", encourages smokers to "be patient," talks about the "good news," and in the last sentence of the paragraph italicizes the word *can* for emphasis.

EXERCISE 4

Determine the authors' tone for this paragraph by asking yourself, "What do the authors' choice of words and style of writing reveal about their attitude toward the topic?"

Should You Cosign a Loan?

What would you do if a relative or friend asked you to cosign a loan? It may not sound like much to ask, but they are asking you to guarantee that *you* will pay their debt if they are unable to. Even if they have every intention of repaying the loan, all kinds of things can go wrong. Could you afford to pay off their debt if you had to? Even if you could afford it, do you really want to accept that responsibility? Some studies of certain types of lenders show that *as many as three of four cosigners are asked to wholly or partially repay the loan.* That statistic should not surprise you. After all, you are being asked to take a risk that a professional lender will not take. Think about it for a minute: the lender would not require a cosigner if the borrower met the lender's criteria for making a loan. An even more frightening fact is that in most states, if your relative or friend misses a payment, *the lender can collect the entire debt from you immediately without first pursuing the borrower.* Moreover, the creditor can sue you or garnish your wages to collect. If you can't pay immediately, you could be charged penalties and late fees in additions to the amount of the debt. If the matter goes to court, you could get stuck with legal fees, and if the lender wins, it may be able to take your wages and property. If you default on the loan, it my become part of your credit record and damage your credit rating or your ability to get a loan. And if these potential problems aren't enough to dissuade you, agreeing to cosign a loan can permanently ruin a relationship if the borrower defaults. You'd better think twice before signing on the dotted line! The potential trouble that can result from cosigning a loan should make you reluctant to be a cosigner—ever.

Source: Based on Jack Kapoor, Les Dlabay, and Robert Hughes, *Personal Finance,* 10th ed., p. 185. Copyright © 2012 by The McGraw-Hill Companies, Inc. Reprinted by permission of The McGraw-Hill Companies.

What is the *authors' tone* in this selection? ______________________________

____

____

As you may have noticed, author's purpose, tone, point of view, and intended audience are related to one another. The chart below shows *interrelationship* among author's purpose, tone, point of view, and intended audience.

HOW THE CRITICAL READING SKILLS ARE INTERRELATED

The author's purpose causes him or her to use a certain tone to convey a point of view to an intended audience.

- The author decides on a *purpose* (reason) for writing:

  to inform   to instruct   to persuade   to entertain

- To accomplish his or her purpose, the author uses an appropriate *tone,* such as:

serious	formal	sincere	enthusiastic
disapproving	sympathetic	informal	humorous
ironic	lighthearted	ambivalent	encouraging

- To convey his or her main idea or *point of view* (position on an issue):

  expresses *support* for an issue or *opposition* to an issue.

- To an *intended audience:*

  the general public   a specific group   a particular person

The chart below illustrates the application of critical reading skills to a piece of writing, a music critic's review of an imaginary album. It is also designed to show that critical reading skills are often part of everyday reading.

EXAMPLE OF CRITICAL READING APPLIED TO A MUSIC CRITIC'S REVIEW OF A NEW ALBUM

The controversial group The Gate Crashers has just released its first album, *The Gate Crashers—Live!* Is it worth buying? That depends: Are you put off by vulgar lyrics that glorify violence? Do you mind listening to painfully bad hip-hop musicians? Do you have any problem sitting through twelve tracks (47 excruciating minutes!) of mind-numbing noise? If not, then you'll surely want to add *The Gate Crashers—Live!* to your collection.

Questions	**Answers**
What is the author's purpose?	To persuade readers not to buy this new album
Who is the author's intended audience?	People who buy music albums
What is the author's point of view?	*The Gate Crashers—Live!* album is awful.*
What is the author's tone?	Sarcastic

*Notice that this is also the author's main idea, or "argument."

OTHER THINGS TO KEEP IN MIND WHEN READING CRITICALLY

Here are five helpful things you should keep in mind about critical reading:

1. **You should avoid seeing the purpose of everything you read as *to inform.***

   When you are determining the author's purpose, use *inform* as a last choice. Instead of really thinking about the author's purpose, you may be tempted to label the purpose of every passage as "to inform." If the author is explaining how to do something, then the purpose is *to instruct.* If the author is trying to convince readers of something, then the purpose is *to persuade.* If the author is presenting material that is simply amusing or pleasant to read, then the purpose is *to entertain.* Only when the author is just providing information is the purpose to inform.

2. **If the author's purpose is to persuade you, you should determine his or her point of view (which side of an issue he or she favors).**

   One way you can determine which side of an issue an author favors is by examining whether or not the author presents both sides of an issue, or whether the author presents good things about only one side (the side he or she favors). You can check to see if the author has left out important information that might weaken his or her position. Or perhaps the author presents only negative things about the side or position he opposes.

   There are times, of course, when an author does present both sides of an issue and, rather than taking a position, allows readers to make up their own minds. If the author presents both sides fairly, we say that the author is *objective* or *unbiased.* When an author favors one side of an issue, we say the author is *biased.*

3. **Understanding the author's tone will enable you to grasp the true or intended meaning, even when the author's words may appear to be saying something different.**

   Although an author's tone is often obvious, there may be times when the tone is less clear and requires careful thought on your part. If you misunderstand an author's tone, you may misinterpret the message. You may think she is saying something different from what she really means. For example, if you read a short story and you miss the author's ironic tone, you will mistakenly think her meaning is the opposite of what it actually is. Or if you overlook irony, you may think authors are being serious when they are actually joking; you may think that they are calm when, in fact, they are angry, or that they are in favor of something when, in reality, they oppose it.

4. **There are two forms of irony: irony in tone and irony in situations.**

   When authors are being ironic, they create a deliberate contrast between their apparent meaning and their intended meaning; they say one thing but mean the opposite. That is, the words are intended to express something different from their literal meaning. You use irony every day in conversation. For example, you might say, "Well, that test was a breeze!" but your ironic tone makes it clear how difficult the test actually was.

   Another form of irony occurs when there is incongruity or difference between what is expected and what actually occurs. For example, it would be ironic if you made a surprise visit to a friend in another city, and your friend was not there because he was making a trip to pay a surprise visit to you in your city!

5. **Sarcasm and irony are not the same thing.**

   Students sometimes confuse sarcasm with irony. *Sarcasm* is a cutting, often ironic remark that is intended to convey contempt or ridicule. Sarcasm is always meant to hurt; irony is not. An example of a hurtful, sarcastic remark is "That college must have bought its band uniforms at a thrift shop sale!" An example of an ironic remark is "This winter makes last winter seem like a day at the beach" (meaning this winter is much colder than last winter).

Directions: Read each paragraph and then answer the critical reading questions that follow.

1. This paragraph comes from a health issues textbook.

Males who are involved in weight-oriented sports such as wrestling, gymnastics, and track are at an increased risk of developing an eating disorder such as anorexia or bulimia nervosa. The pressure to win, excel, and be competitive combined with any nonathletic pressures in their lives can contribute to the development of eating disorders. Men who suffer from an eating disorder may also experience problems with alcohol and/or substance abuse concurrently. In addition, as with women, there may also be a correlation between ADHD in male sufferers of anorexia and bulimia nervosa. More research is needed in this area.

Source: "Postscript: Do Ultrathin Models and Actresses Influence the Onset of Eating Disorders?" in *Taking Sides: Clashing Views in Health and Society*, 10th ed., Eileen Daniel, Ed. p. 251. Copyright © 2012 by The McGraw-Hill Companies, Inc. Reprinted by permission of The McGraw-Hill Companies.

_______ What is the author's *point of view* regarding the causes of eating disorders in males?

a. ADHD in males is likely to cause them to develop eating disorders.

b. Eating disorders are more likely if males participate in certain sports and also experience other pressures in life.

c. Eating disorders in men are likely to be caused by alcohol abuse and/or substance abuse.

d. More research is needed as to the causes of eating disorders in males.

_______ What is the author's *purpose*?

a. to inform readers about eating disorders

b. to inform readers about differences in causes of eating disorders in men and women

c. to inform readers about the signs of eating disorders in males

d. to inform readers about eating disorders in males

2. This paragraph comes from a critical thinking textbook.

Many college students assume that their online social networking profiles and posts are private. By not thinking critically before posting a message, these students may place obstacles in the way of achieving their life goals. You need to do your research about social networking sites and how to use them. You also need to think twice before making a posting. What may seem like a joke or just having fun can end up getting a person expelled from college or denied a coveted job interview.

Source: Adapted from Judith Boss, *Think: Critical Thinking and Logic Skills for Everyday Life,* 2nd ed., p. 353. Copyright © 2012 by The McGraw-Hill Companies, Inc. Reprinted by permission of The McGraw-Hill Companies.

_______ Who is the author's *intended audience*?

a. users of social networking websites

b. college students who use social networking websites

Copyright © 2014 The McGraw-Hill Companies, Inc. All rights reserved.

c. college students

d. employers who check job applicants' profiles and postings on social networking websites

______ What is the author's *tone*?

a. angry

b. optimistic

c. serious and authoritative

d. lighthearted and irreverent

3. This paragraph comes from a critical thinking textbook.

Have you wondered why credit-card companies are so keen on signing up college students? According to *USA Today* (July 26, 2005), people between the ages of 18 and 29 have the poorest credit ratings of all age groups. In fact, credit-card companies make most of their money from people who don't pay off their balance each month, which is the case with 80 percent of college students. Many students regard credit cards as a convenient way to pay for tuition. Over time, however, it could cost you several thousand dollars more in interest than a student loan for the same amount.

Source: Adapted from Judith Boss, *Think: Critical Thinking and Logic Skills for Everyday Life,* 2nd ed., p. 245. Copyright © 2012 by The McGraw-Hill Companies, Inc. Reprinted by permission of The McGraw-Hill Companies.

______ Who is the author's *intended audience*?

a. college students who pay back their student loans with credit cards

b. college students who sign up for a large number of credit cards

c. college students who use credit cards but cannot pay off the balance each month

d. college students between the ages of 18 and 29 who have poor credit ratings

______ What is the author's *point of view* regarding the use of credit cards to pay tuition?

a. Paying tuition with credit cards can help students establish credit, which will be helpful when they finish college.

b. Paying tuition with credit cards is convenient and can save students money in the long run.

c. Paying tuition with credit cards should not be allowed by colleges and universities.

d. Paying tuition with credit cards may prove not to be a good idea in the long run.

4. This paragraph comes from a critical thinking textbook.

Should food advertising aimed at children be regulated more strongly? The average American child is exposed to over 100 advertisements each day. Almost half of television advertising for children ages 6 through 11 is for what is commonly known as "junk food." Research suggests that by promoting nutritionally deficient and high-calorie foods, these ads may be contributing to the increase in childhood obesity. This, in turn, has led to calls for limits on junk food advertising to children.

A Yale University poll found that 73 percent of Americans favor restrictions on children's food advertising. Several countries, including Sweden, Norway, Canada, and Greece, have adopted strict measures limiting advertising to children. In the United States, broadcasters are obligated to limit the amount of advertising during children's programs.

Source: Adapted from Judith Boss, *Think: Critical Thinking and Logic Skills for Everyday Life,* 2nd ed., p. 332. Copyright © 2012 by The McGraw-Hill Companies, Inc. Reprinted by permission of The McGraw-Hill Companies.

_______ Who is the author's *intended audience*?

a. junk food manufacturers who advertise on television

b. television executives responsible for their corporations' advertising policies

c. children who watch a great deal of television

d. adults concerned about childhood obesity

_______ The author is likely to have which *point of view* regarding children and television advertising?

a. It is the parents' responsibility to limit the amount of television, and therefore advertisements, they allow their children to watch.

b. Junk food advertising during children's television programs should be reduced.

c. Nothing can be done to control the number of junk food ads on television.

d. Nothing should be done to restrict the number of junk food ads children see on television.

_______ What is the author's *purpose*?

a. to persuade junk food manufacturers not to advertise during children's television programs

b. to instruct parents about how to limit their children's exposure to junk food television ads

c. to persuade readers that junk food television ads aimed at children are a problem

d. to inform readers what various countries have done about junk food ads aimed at children

5. This paragraph comes from a health issues textbook.

When we think of the drug war, it's the heavy-duty narcotics like heroin and cocaine that get most of the attention. And why not? That's where the action is. It's not marijuana that is sustaining the Taliban in Afghanistan, after all. When Crips and Bloods descend into gun battles in the streets of Los Angeles, they're not usually fighting over pot. The junkie who breaks into your house and steals your Blu-ray player isn't doing it so he can score a couple of spliffs.

Source: Kevin Drum, "The Patriot's Guide to Legalization," in *Taking Sides: Clashing Views in Health and Society*, 10th ed., Eileen Daniel, Ed. p. 84. Copyright © 2012 by The McGraw-Hill Companies, Inc. Reprinted by permission of The McGraw-Hill Companies.

Copyright © 2014 The McGraw-Hill Companies, Inc. All rights reserved.

_______ Who is the author's *intended audience*?

a. gang members and junkies who deal in marijuana
b. people who are concerned about home burglaries
c. people interested in the issue of marijuana legalization
d. lawmakers who create drug legislation

_______ What is the author's *tone*?

a. supportive
b. sentimental
c. informal
d. pessimistic

CHAPTER REVIEW CARDS

Complete the chapter review cards for Chapter 8 by answering the questions or following the directions on each card.

Reading Critically

1. Define *critical reading.*

2. Why is it important to be able to read critically?

Card 1 Chapter 8: Reading Critically

Author's Point of View

1. What is meant by *author's point of view*?

2. Why is it important to determine an author's point of view?

3. What comprehension monitoring question should you ask yourself in order to determine an author's point of view?

Card 2 Chapter 8: Reading Critically

Author's Purpose

1. Define *author's purpose*.

2. List four common purposes that authors have:

   1)

   2)

   3)

   4)

3. What comprehension monitoring question should you ask yourself in order to determine an author's purpose?

Card 3 Chapter 8: Reading Critically

Author's Intended Audience

1. Define *author's intended audience.*

2. List three factors that can help you determine the author's intended audience:

1)

2)

3)

3. What comprehension monitoring question should you ask yourself in order to determine an author's audience?

Card 4 Chapter 8: Reading Critically

Author's Tone

1. Define *author's tone.*

2. List two factors that can help you determine the author's tone:

1)

2)

3. What comprehension monitoring question should you ask yourself in order to determine an author's tone?

Card 5 Chapter 8: Reading Critically

Copyright © 2014 The McGraw-Hill Companies, Inc. All rights reserved.

TEST YOUR UNDERSTANDING
Reading Critically, Part 1

Review: **Critical reading** involves gaining insights and going beyond comprehending the topic, main idea, and supporting details. Reading critically requires you to ask certain questions after you read a passage and to think carefully about what you have read. The four critical reading skills presented in this chapter are *interrelated.* An author's *purpose* causes him or her to present certain facts and opinions, and to use a certain *tone* to convey a *point of view* to an *intended audience.*

- **Author's point of view**—an author's *position* (opinion) on an issue. To identify an author's point of view, ask yourself, "What is the author's position on this issue?"
- **Author's purpose**—an author's *reason* for writing. To identify an author's purpose, ask yourself, "Why did the author write this?"
- **Author's intended audience**—people an author has in mind as his or her *readers.* To identify an author's intended audience, ask yourself, "Who did the author intend to read this?"
- **Author's tone**—manner of writing that reveals an author's *attitude* toward a topic. To identify an author's tone, ask yourself, "What do the author's choice of words and style of writing reveal about his or her attitude toward the topic?"

EXAMPLE

This passage comes from a critical thinking textbook. Its topic is *the error of automatic rejection.* Read the paragraph. Notice that its main idea is given below it. Then determine the author's purpose and tone by asking yourself these comprehension monitoring questions: "Why did the author write this?" and "What does the author's choice of words and style reveal about his attitude?"

The Error of Automatic Rejection

It is easy to reject information of ideas because it conflicts with what we already believe. It is just as easy to readily accept it if it fits with what we already believe. As critical thinkers we need a reasonable basis for accepting or rejecting any argument or claim, including ones that challenge our ideas. The only way to establish that basis is to evaluate the challenge and make an honest determination of its worth. Liking or disliking it, feeling pleased or displeased with it, is not enough. To reject criticism without giving it a fair hearing is to commit the error of *automatic rejection.*

Source: Adapted from Vincent Ruggiero, *Beyond Feelings: A Guide to Critical Thinking,* 9th ed., p. 137. Copyright © 2009 by The McGraw-Hill Companies, Inc. Reprinted by permission of The McGraw-Hill Companies.

Main idea: *To reject criticism without giving it a fair hearing is to commit the error of automatic rejection.*

__a__ What is the author's purpose?

a. to inform

b. to instruct

c. to persuade

d. to entertain

(continued on next page)

b What is the author's tone?

a. disapproving and bitter

b. unemotional and straightforward

c. nostalgic

d. indifferent

Explanation: The correct answer to the first question is a. The author's purpose is to inform readers about the error of automatic rejection (what it is). *The correct answer to the second question is b.* The tone is unemotional and straightforward, which we would expect, since the purpose is to give information.

Directions: Read each paragraph. (Notice that you are told the main idea. It tells the author's point of view.) Then answer the questions about the author's purpose, intended audience, and tone. Write your answers in the spaces provided.

1. This passage comes from a psychology of success textbook.

Are some personality traits "better" than others? No, although some traits may help us succeed in a particular setting or profession. For example, a sociable, talkative person would do better in a sales career than someone who is more reserved and quiet. An inquisitive, unconventional student might have trouble relating to a teacher who is close-minded.

Source: Dennis Waitley, *Psychology of Success: Finding Meaning in Work and Life,* 5th ed., p. 142. Copyright © 2010 by The McGraw-Hill Companies, Inc. Reprinted by permission of The McGraw-Hill Companies.

Main idea: *No personality traits are better than others, although some traits may help us succeed in a particular setting or profession.*

_______ What is the author's purpose?

a. to inform readers about whether some personality traits are better than others

b. to instruct readers how to develop their personality traits

c. to persuade readers to evaluate their personality traits

d. to persuade readers to pursue a sales career if they are sociable and talkative

_______ What is the author's tone?

a. compassionate

b. disbelieving

c. humorous

d. neutral

_______ Who is the author's intended audience?

a. recruiters who interview job applicants

b. teachers

c. students seeking a career in sales

d. general public

2. This passage comes from a psychology of success textbook.

The best way to stay out of driving conflicts is not to be an aggressive driver. What can drivers do to reduce stress and thus reduce the tendency toward aggression behind the wheel? First, we can allow enough travel time. We often fail to allow enough time to get where we are going. Worse, we don't allow extra time for traffic, road repairs, weather, and other likely delays. Second, we can listen to calming music rather than, say, frenetic music or politically-charged talk shows. Third, we can make our vehicles more comfortable. Last, and most important, we can accept the fact that we can't control traffic or other drivers: all we can do is control our reactions to them.

Main idea: *The best way to stay out of driving conflicts is to reduce your stress and not to be an aggressive driver.*

_______ What is the author's purpose?

a. to inform readers about aggressive driving

b. to instruct readers how to reduce their stress when driving

c. to persuade readers not to drive when they are stressed

d. to persuade readers to turn off the radio in the car

_______ What is the author's tone?

a. sentimental

b. teasing

c. disgusted; annoyed

d. polite; supportive

_______ Who is the author's intended audience?

a. drivers who listen to frenetic music

b. drivers who have been arrested for road rage

c. drivers whose stress causes them to become aggressive

d. general public

3. This passage is the type that might appear in a blog.

Unfortunately, big companies generally ignore the needs of us employees who are working parents. These corporations make millions of dollars as a result of our efforts. It's disgusting that they do so little to help us mesh our jobs and family responsibilities. How hard would it be for a multi-million-dollar company to provide parental leave following the birth of a baby or to provide caregiver leave, with the assurance that our jobs will be waiting for us when we return? What about offering us more flexible hours or job-sharing options? On-premise childcare? If our stress is reduced, we can concentrate on our jobs more fully and be even more productive. To all corporate boards of directors and CEOs: The time for you to step up and do the right thing is long overdue!

Main idea: *Many big companies ignore the needs of employees who are working parents, and they need to do more to help those employees mesh their jobs and family responsibilities.*

_______ What is the author's purpose?

a. to inform readers about problems working parents face

b. to instruct employees how to get corporate employers to address their needs

c. to persuade corporations to address the needs of employees who are working parents

d. to persuade corporations to hire parents as employees

_______ What is the author's tone?

a. reluctant; cautious

b. disapproving; frustrated

c. ironic

d. supportive; encouraging

Copyright © 2014 The McGraw-Hill Companies, Inc. All rights reserved.

_______ What is the author's point of view?

a. Corporations need to do more to help employees who are working parents.

b. Working parents need to join together to confront big corporations.

c. Employees are never satisfied.

d. Working parents need to learn to reduce their stress.

_______ Who is the author's intended audience?

a. working parents who are employed by big companies

b. working parents

c. working parents who have lost their jobs

d. corporate boards of directors and CEOs

4. This passage is the type that might appear in a psychology textbook.

You are walking across campus. You pass a classmate who is in your biology class, saying hello on your way by. She walks right past you without returning your greeting or even glancing in your direction. You might be tempted to think, "What a snob!" Not so fast. Consider another possibility—she may be very shy. Shyness is anxiety in social situations that comes from worrying about what others think of us. Extreme shyness can lead to such anxiety that it becomes difficult just to say hello to others or make eye contact. Before you decide someone is a cold, aloof person, remember that there may be another explanation: shyness.

Main idea: *Before you decide someone is a cold, aloof person, remember that there may be another explanation: shyness.*

_______ What is the author's point of view?

a. People who do not speak are rude.

b. Don't make hasty judgments about someone's seemingly rude behavior.

c. Shy people should explain to others what their problem is.

d. If you are a shy person, get help to overcome it.

_______ Who is the author's intended audience?

a. students

b. shy people

c. people who are snobs

d. people who seem cold and aloof

5. This passage is from a textbook on marriages and families.

The beatings that many women in shelters have endured from their husbands and live-in boyfriends would fit anyone's definition of family violence. As a sociology student, you may wonder how far in the other direction the concept of domestic violence should go. Is a slap in the face domestic violence, or should the term be reserved for more serious acts of aggression? There is disagreement among the public and academic researchers about exactly what constitutes domestic violence. It is not even clear how to define the term "domestic." Most early studies of adult domestic violence focused on married and cohabiting couples, but many recent studies have focused on the broader concept of "intimate partners," or boyfriends and girlfriends.

Source: Adapted from Andrew Cherlin, *Public and Private Families*, 6th ed., p. 347. Copyright © 2010 by the McGraw-Hill Companies. Reprinted by permission of The McGraw-Hill Companies.

Main idea: *There is disagreement among the public and academic researchers about exactly what constitutes domestic violence, and it is not even clear how to define the term "domestic."*

______ What is the author's purpose?

a. to inform readers about the causes of domestic violence

b. to inform readers about the lack of agreement about the definition of "domestic violence"

c. to instruct readers in how to recognize domestic violence

d. to persuade readers to report domestic violence immediately

______ What is the author's tone?

a. tolerant

b. sarcastic

c. unemotional

d. approving

______ Who is the author's intended audience?

a. adults involved in domestic violence

b. women in shelters

c. intimate partners

d. sociology students

TEST YOUR UNDERSTANDING
Reading Critically, Part 2

Review: **Critical reading** involves gaining insights and going beyond comprehending the topic, main idea, and supporting details. Reading critically requires you to ask certain questions after you read a passage and to think carefully about what you have read. The four critical reading skills presented in this chapter are *interrelated.* An author's *purpose* causes him or her to present certain facts and opinions, and to use a certain *tone* to convey a *point of view* to an *intended audience.*

- **Author's point of view**—an author's *position* (opinion) on an issue. To identify an author's point of view, ask yourself, "What is the author's position on this issue?"
- **Author's purpose**—an author's *reason* for writing. To identify an author's purpose, ask yourself, "Why did the author write this?"
- **Author's intended audience**—people an author has in mind as his or her *readers.* To identify an author's intended audience, ask yourself, "Who did the author intend to read this?"
- **Author's tone**—manner of writing that reveals an author's *attitude* toward a topic. To identify an author's tone, ask yourself, "What do the author's choice of words and style of writing reveal about his or her attitude toward the topic?"

EXAMPLE

This passage is the sort that might appear in an academic publication. Its topic is *learning styles.* Read the paragraph. Notice that its main idea is given below it. Then determine the author's purpose and intended audience by asking yourself these comprehension monitoring questions: "Why did the author write this?" and "Who did the author intend to read this?"

For years, everyone heard the term "learning styles," but do they really exist? Today, many neuroscientists, psychologists, sociologists, and educators criticize the term. They cite the lack of research proving that learning styles exist. Even if they exist, there is no proof or agreement as to what they are. These professionals say that labeling students as specific types of learners—especially learners from different cultures—is problematic and could actually interfere with learning. In addition, they point out that the same person learns differently in different contexts. The term "learning preference" is a more accurate term since learners do, in fact, have preferences. The important implications for us as teachers are (1) not to label students as one type of learner or another, and (2) to encourage students to use as wide a variety of styles as possible.

Main idea: *For several reasons, many professionals now reject the notion of "learning styles" and believe that "learning preference" is more accurate; this has important implications for teachers.*

What is the author's purpose?

to inform

Explanation: The purpose is *to inform* readers about the terms "learning styles" and "learning preference."

Who is the intended audience?

teachers

Explanation: The last sentence ("for us as teachers") makes it clear that teachers are the intended audience.

Copyright © 2014 The McGraw-Hill Companies, Inc. All rights reserved.

Directions: Read each paragraph and locate or formulate its main idea. Write the main idea sentence in the space provided. Then answer the questions about the author's point of view, purpose, intended audience, and tone and write your answers in the spaces provided.

- For author's point of view, *write a sentence that gives the author's position or opinion.*
- For author's purpose, *determine if the author wants to inform, instruct, persuade,* or *entertain.*
- For author's intended audience, *tell who the author had in mind to read the paragraph.*
- For author's tone, *select tone words that tell the author's attitude toward the topic.*

1. This passage comes from a psychology of success textbook.

One way college students can assess their strengths and weaknesses is to take a personal inventory. A *personal inventory* is a list of your plusses and minuses in the key areas of your life, such as appearance, intimate relationships, social skills, school performance, as well as more accurate and compassionate views of your flaws. When you make your inventory, be objective, accurate, specific, and look for strengths. Keep your self-inventory and go over it every day for a month. It is sometimes difficult to overcome patterns of negative self-thought, but using this new inventory will help you teach your mind to accept your flaws, affirm your positive qualities, and move on.

Source: Dennis Waitley, *Psychology of Success: Finding Meaning in Work and Life,* 5th ed., pp. 143, 146. Copyright © 2010 by The McGraw-Hill Companies, Inc. Reprinted by permission of The McGraw-Hill Companies.

What is the author's point of view? (Write the main idea sentence.)

____

____

____

What is the author's purpose?

____

What is the author's tone?

____

Who is the author's intended audience?

____

2. This passage comes from a career success textbook.

Communication skills are at the top of the list of most employer surveys conducted by professional associations each year. Employers require good communication skills because they are the foundation for most levels of job functions. Good communication skills are necessary for dealing with the public. You will need communication skills to work in teams and to mentor and lead others. In the workplace you will be judged by the impression you make with how you communicate. College is the perfect time for you to improve these skills. Every effort you make to improve your communication skills will pay big dividends in your future career.

Source: Adapted from Donna Yena, *Career Directions: The Path to an Ideal Career,* 5th ed., p. 52. Copyright © 2011 by the McGraw-Hill Companies, Inc. Reprinted by permission of The McGraw-Hill Companies.

What is the author's point of view? (Write the main idea sentence.)

____

____

What is the author's purpose?

____

____

What is the author's tone?

____

Who is the author's intended audience?

____

3. This passage comes from a critical thinking textbook.

Sadly, public figures often change the subject to avoid answering an interviewer's question. Clever individuals will manage to mention the subject of the question and talk about something else, thus giving us citizens the impression they are being forthright when in fact they are not. For example, a candidate who is asked the question "What is your position on abortion?" might answer something like this: "The issue of abortion has divided our nation more than any other issue of the twentieth century. What disturbs me most is that the tone of the discussion has become so harsh and distrustful that meaningful debate is all but impossible. If I am elected, I pledge to do my part to create the conditions that will make a meaningful, respectful debate possible." This is an eloquent, moving answer to a question that *wasn't* asked! Meanwhile, the question that *was* asked is left unanswered. The public needs to be alert for this deceptive tactic: politicians use it all the time.

Source: Adapted from Vincent Ruggiero, *Beyond Feelings: A Guide to Critical Thinking,* 9th ed., p. 138. Copyright © 2009 by The McGraw-Hill Companies, Inc. Reprinted by permission of The McGraw-Hill Companies.

What is the author's point of view? (Write the main idea sentence.)

____

____

What is the author's purpose?

____

What is the author's tone?

____

Who is the author's intended audience?

____

4. This passage comes from a psychology of success textbook.

Is a negative self-image holding you back? If so, it's time to take a new look at yourself—objectively—and assess your strengths and weaknesses. Knowing your strengths can help you set challenging goals, overcome obstacles, and take advantage of opportunities. Knowing your weaknesses helps you see they aren't as bad as you thought! Are you really a "slob," or are you just not as tidy as you could be? Are you really "ugly," or do you have a nose you wish was a bit smaller?

Source: Dennis Waitley, *Psychology of Success: Finding Meaning in Work and Life,* 5th ed., p. 142. Copyright © 2010 by The McGraw-Hill Companies, Inc. Reprinted by permission of The McGraw-Hill Companies.

What is the author's point of view? (Write the main idea sentence.)

____

____

What is the author's purpose?

____

What is the author's tone?

____

Who is the author's intended audience?

____

5. This passage comes from the same psychology of success textbook.

Logic is the process of reasoning correctly and drawing the correct conclusions from the facts. Being logical also involves providing valid explanations for your conclusions. Instead of taking ideas for granted, make sure solid evidence supports them. To determine whether your reasoning is logical, ask yourself:

- Do I have evidence for this statement?
- Is there any evidence that contradicts this statement?
- Is this really true, or am I just taking it for granted?
- Is there any other possible conclusion?
- Do any of my ideas contradict each other?

Source: Dennis Waitley, *Psychology of Success: Finding Meaning in Work and Life,* 5th ed., p. 238. Copyright © 2010 by The McGraw-Hill Companies, Inc. Reprinted by permission of The McGraw-Hill Companies.

What is the author's point of view? (Write the main idea sentence.)

____

____

____

What is the author's purpose?

____

What is the author's tone?

____

Who is the author's intended audience?

____

SELECTION **8.1**
Fiction

From *For One More Day*

By Mitch Albom

Mitch Albom, who began as a sportswriter, first gained public acclaim in 1997 for his book Tuesdays with Morrie. *The book, which chronicles the days he spent with a beloved, dying college professor of his, stayed on the* New York Times *bestseller list for four straight years. Albom's novels* The Five People You Meet in Heaven *and* For One More Day *have also become bestsellers, and all three have been made into successful TV movies. His 2009 nonfiction work* Have a Little Faith *was also a number-one* New York Times *bestseller and is now a Hallmark Hall of Fame movie. His latest book is* The Time Keeper, *which was released in the fall of 2012.*

*On his website, Albom explains, "*For One More Day *is a story about a former baseball player named Charley 'Chick' Benetto who receives the gift—or is it a hallucination—of spending 'one more day' with his mother, Posey, who has been deceased for several years. In* For One More Day, *the love between a mother and her child is shown to be strong enough to save that child, now a grown man, from the clutches of death. By spending 'one more day' with his mother, Charley learns that even a life replete with errors is worth living. 'Never give up' is the message that Posey gives her son Charley as she returns him to the world of the living." Albom continues, "The inspiration for* For One More Day *came, again, from a real person, my mother, who stood up for me all my life, even when I didn't always stand up for her. I have imagined what life will be like when she is no longer here, and I know I will want another day with her." In this selection, Charley tells about the day his mother took him to college for the first time.*

1 I would guess the day I went to college was one of the happiest of my mother's life. At least it started out that way. The university had offered to pay half my tuition with a baseball scholarship, although, when my mother told her friends, she just said "scholarship," her love of that word eclipsing any possibility that I was admitted to hit the ball, not the books.

2 I remember the morning we drove up for my freshman year. She'd been awake before sunrise, and there was a full breakfast waiting for me when I stumbled down the stairs: pancakes, bacon, eggs—six people couldn't have finished that much food. My sister Roberta had wanted to come with us, but I said no way—what I meant was, it was bad enough that I had to go with my mother—so she consoled herself with a plateful of syrup-covered French toast. We dropped her at a neighbor's house and began our four-hour trek.

3 Because, to my mother, this was a big occasion, she wore one of her "outfits"—a purple pantsuit, a scarf, high heels, and sunglasses, and she insisted that I wear a white shirt and a necktie. "You're starting college, not going fishing," she said. Together we would have stood out badly enough in Pepperville Beach, but remember, this was college in the mid-60s, where the less correctly you were dressed, the more you were dressed correctly. So when we finally got to campus and stepped out of our Chevy station wagon, we were surrounded by young women in sandals and peasant skirts, and young men in tank tops and shorts, their hair worn long over their ears. And there we were, a necktie and a purple pantsuit, and I felt, once more, that my mother was shining a ridiculous light on me.

Annotation Practice Exercises

Directions: After you have read the selection, answer the critical reading questions below. This will help you gain additional insights about what you have read.

Practice Exercise

Who is the *author's intended audience*?

____

____

Practice Exercise

What is the *author's purpose* in writing this?

____

____

____

4 She wanted to know where the library was, and she found someone to give us directions. "Charley, look at all the books," she marveled as we walked around the ground floor. "You could stay in here all four years and never make a dent."

5 Everywhere we went she kept pointing. "Look! That cubicle—you could study there." And, "Look, that cafeteria table, you could eat there." I tolerated it because I knew she would be leaving soon. But as we walked across the lawn, a good looking girl—gum-chewing, white lipstick, bangs on her forehead—caught my eye and I caught hers and I flexed my arm muscles and I thought, my first college girl, who knows? And at that very moment my mother said, "Did we pack your toiletry kit?"

6 How do you answer that? A yes? A no? A "Gee, Mom!" It's all bad. The girl continued past us and she sort of guffawed, or maybe I just imagined that. Anyhow, we didn't exist in her universe. I watched her sashay over to two bearded guys sprawled under a tree. She kissed one on the lips and she fell in alongside them, and here I was with my mother asking about my toiletry kit.

7 An hour later, I hoisted my trunk to the stairwell of my dorm. My mother was carrying my two "lucky" baseball bats with which I had led the Pepperville County Conference in home runs.

8 "Here," I said, holding out my hand, "I'll take the bats."

9 "I'll go up with you."

10 "No, it's all right."

11 "But I want to see your room."

12 "Mom."

13 "What?"

14 "Come on."

15 "You know. Come on."

16 I couldn't think of anything else that wouldn't hurt her feelings, so I just pushed my hand out farther. Her face sank. I was six inches taller than her now. She handed me the bats. I balanced them atop the trunk.

17 "Charley," she said. Her voice was softer now, and it sounded different. "Give your mother a kiss."

18 I put the trunk down with a small thud. I leaned toward her. Just then two older students came bounding down the stairs, feet thumping, voices loud and laughing. I instinctively jerked away from my mother.

19 "Scuse please," one of them said as they maneuvered around us.

20 Once they were gone, I leaned forward, only intending a peck on the cheek, but she threw her arms around my neck and she drew me close. I could smell her perfume, her hair spray, her skin moisturizer, all the assorted potions and lotions she had doused herself with for this special day.

21 I pulled away, lifted the trunk, and began my climb, leaving my mother in the stairwell of a dormitory, as close as she would ever get to a college education.

Practice Exercise

This fictional story is told by Charley, the main character. Rather than the *author's tone* in this selection, what is the tone of Charley, the narrator?

____

____

____

Practice Exercise

Rather than the *author's point of view,* what is Charley's point of view regarding his mother's taking him to college?

____

____

____

____

____

Source: From *For One More Day* by Mitch Albom. Copyright © 2006 by Mitch Albom, Inc. Reprinted by permission of Hyperion and Little, Brown Book Group Limited. All rights reserved.

SELECTION 8.1
Fiction
(continued)

Comprehension and Vocabulary Quiz

This quiz has four parts. Your instructor may assign some or all of them.

Comprehension

Directions: Use the information in the selection to answer the questions below.

_____ **1.** Regarding a college education, Charley's mother:
- *a.* believes a college education should be only for those who have scholarships.
- *b.* respects a college education, but never had an opportunity for one herself.
- *c.* sees a college education as a way to meet people who can help you later in life.
- *d.* feels a true college education comes from reading the books in the college's library.

_____ **2.** Charley doesn't want his mother to come up to his dorm room because:
- *a.* it is up several flights of stairs.
- *b.* it would be embarrassing to have her accompany him.
- *c.* she would try to arrange and decorate it.
- *d.* women are not allowed in dorm rooms.

_____ **3.** It is clear that taking Charley to college is important to his mother because she:
- *a.* awoke before sunrise that day.
- *b.* fixed him an unusually large breakfast.
- *c.* wore one of her special outfits.
- *d.* all of the above

_____ **4.** The university gave Charley:
- *a.* an academic scholarship.
- *b.* a baseball scholarship.
- *c.* a combined academic and baseball scholarship.
- *d.* no scholarship money.

_____ **5.** The university is located:
- *a.* several hours from Charley's home.
- *b.* in the next state.
- *c.* in Charley's hometown.
- *d.* Pepperville.

Vocabulary in Context

Directions: For each item below, use context clues to deduce the meaning of the *italicized* word.

_____ **6.** The university had offered to pay half my tuition with a baseball scholarship, although, when my mother told her friends, she just said "scholarship," her love of that word *eclipsing* any possibility that I was admitted to hit the ball, not the books.

The actress complained that in important scenes, the presence of a child actor kept *eclipsing* her own role.

Copyright © 2014 The McGraw-Hill Companies, Inc. All rights reserved.

eclipsing (ē klĭp′ sĭng) means:

a. circling
b. diminishing in importance
c. causing disgrace or humiliation
d. removing from sight

_______ **7.** The girl continued past us and she sort of *guffawed,* or maybe I just imagined that.

The children squealed, clapped, and *guffawed* whenever they watched cartoons.

guffawed (gə fôd′) means:

a. acted in an unkind manner
b. laughed loudly
c. paid no attention
d. rolled the eyes upward

_______ **8.** I watched her *sashay* over to two bearded guys sprawled under a tree.

At parties, she likes to *sashay* around so that everyone will see her trendy clothes and jewelry.

sashay (să shā′) means:

a. move quickly and directly
b. strut in a showy, self-important manner
c. wait for others to approach
d. twirl, spin

_______ **9.** An hour later, I *hoisted* my trunk to the stairwell of my dorm.

The divers hooked cables to the sunken ship and *hoisted* it from the bottom of the sea.

hoisted (hoist′ əd) means:

a. lifted; hauled up
b. did not disturb; left in place
c. tilted; angled
d. returned

_______ **10.** I could smell her perfume, her hair spray, her skin moisturizer, and all the assorted potions and lotions she had *doused* herself with for this special day.

The arsonist *doused* the car with gasoline and then set it on fire.

doused (dousd) means:

a. cleaned
b. refreshed
c. wet thoroughly; drenched
d. decorated; adorned

Word Structure

Directions: In paragraph 20 of the selection, you encountered the word **intending.** This word contains the root ***ten,*** which means "to stretch" or "to hold or grasp." The word *intending* literally means "stretching toward something," or, in other words, having a specific purpose or plan in mind. Use the meaning of ***ten*** and the list of prefixes on pages 72–73 to help you determine the meaning of each of the following words.

______ **11.** If a professor **extends** the deadline for turning in an assignment, it means that:
a. the assignment is due immediately.
b. students can decide the point at which they turn in the assignment.
c. the deadline has been canceled, so there is no deadline.
d. the time until it is due has been lengthened or stretched out.

______ **12.** If you are a **tenacious** person, it means you:
a. like to shake hands with other people.
b. have a birthday on the tenth day of the month.
c. hang on and do not give up.
d. are a kind, gentle person.

______ **13.** If a scientific theory turns out to be **untenable,** the theory:
a. is unpopular with the general public.
b. does not hold up when tested or examined logically.
c. cannot be understood by anyone other than scientists.
d. does not conflict with other theories.

______ **14.** If a dog eats tainted food that **distends** its stomach, the dog's stomach is:
a. upset.
b. empty.
c. swollen.
d. ruptured.

______ **15.** When you pay **attention** to something, you:
a. concentrate or hold your focus on it.
b. display it proudly.
c. disregard it.
d. try to make sense of it.

Reading Skills Application

Directions: These items test your ability to *apply* certain skills. You may not have studied all the skills yet, so some items will serve as a preview.

______ **16.** Which of the following is the meaning of *"shining a ridiculous light on me"* as it is used in paragraph 3?
a. making me look foolish
b. pointing a funny-looking light at me
c. showing me how to do something
d. making me appear clever

______ **17.** Which pattern is used to organize the information in paragraph 18?
a. list
b. definition

Copyright © 2014 The McGraw-Hill Companies, Inc. All rights reserved.

c. cause-effect
d. comparison-contrast

_______ **18.** Which of the following represents the main idea of paragraph 3?
a. Charley was embarrassed by the way he and his mother were dressed.
b. Charley was much better dressed than the other students.
c. Clothing styles in the mid-60s were very casual.
d. Charley's mother had poor taste in clothes.

_______ **19.** Based on the selection, it can be inferred that Charley:
a. was angry with his mother and didn't care if he hurt her feelings.
b. did care about his mother and did not want to hurt her feelings any more than necessary.
c. was very pleased that his mother was so interested in him and his first day of college.
d. wished he had decided not to attend college.

_______ **20.** In paragraph 3, the details about the other students' dress and appearance are used to illustrate:
a. how badly college students dress.
b. the styles that were popular among college students during the mid-60s.
c. the need for a campus dress code for students.
d. what was popular and how different it was from what Charley and his mother were wearing.

SELECTION **8.1**
Fiction
(continued)

Respond in Writing

Directions: Refer to the selection as needed to answer the questions below.

1. **Reacting to What You Have Read:** What was your first day of college like? Did you come by yourself? If not, who came with you? Did you feel that you fit in with the other students? Explain your answers to these questions.

____

____

____

____

____

2. **Comprehending the Selection Further:** The author provides ample evidence that Charley's mother loves him. List at least three bits of evidence from the selection that show this.

____

____

____

____

3. **Overall Main Idea of the Selection:** In one sentence, tell what the author wants readers to understand about Charley's first day of college. (Be sure to include "Charley," "first day," and "college" in your overall main idea sentence.)

Internet Resources

Read More about It Online

Directions: To learn more about the topic of this selection, see the websites below or use the keywords **"Mitch Albom"** with a search engine.

www.mitchalbom.com
This site is the official online resource for information about Mitch Albom, his books, his charitable work, and his sports blog.

Copyright © 2014 The McGraw-Hill Companies, Inc. All rights reserved.

SELECTION **8.2**

Memoir

I Never Made It to the NFL

From *The Last Lecture*

By Randy Pausch with Jeffrey Zaslow

Professors are sometimes asked what they would say in a "last lecture." In other words, what wisdom and important life lessons would they share, if they knew it was their last chance? When Carnegie-Mellon computer science professor Randy Pausch was asked to participate in his university's "last lecture" series, he was in a unique situation: He had recently been diagnosed with terminal pancreatic cancer. On September 18, 2007, he gave what would indeed be his last lecture. Pausch, a married father of three young children, was only 46 at the time. Since then, ten million people have watched the video of his lecture, "Really Achieving Your Childhood Dreams" (www.thelastlecture.com). In April 2008, the book The Last Lecture *was published. It contained the information in the lecture, as well as additional insights Pausch wanted to share. The book immediately became a number-one bestseller. The following selection is an excerpt from that book. Although Pausch reports in the book that he "never made it to the NFL" (National Football League), a few months after his lecture, he was invited to participate in a Pittsburgh Steelers practice. So in a different way from what he had envisioned as a boy, Pausch did achieve his childhood dream of "making it to the NFL."*

An award-winning teacher and researcher, Pausch also led the Alice Project (www.alice.org), which uses storytelling and interactive game playing in a 3-D environment to introduce young people to computer programming. The software makes it easy for users to create animation. Professor Pausch has also worked with Google, Adobe, Electronic Arts, and Walt Disney Imagineering—achieving many of his childhood dreams along the way.

---

1 I love football. *Tackle* football. I started playing when I was nine years old, and football got me through. It helped make me who I am today. And even though I did not reach the National Football League, I sometimes think I got more from pursuing that dream, and not accomplishing it, than I did from many of the ones I did accomplish.

2 My romance with football started when my dad dragged me, kicking and screaming, to join a league. I had no desire to be there. I was naturally wimpy, and the smallest kid by far. Fear turned to awe when I met my coach, Jim Graham, a hulking, six-foot-four wall-of-a-guy. He had been a linebacker at Penn State, and was seriously old-school. I mean, really old-school; like he thought the forward pass was a trick play.

3 On the first day of practice, we were all scared to death. Plus he hadn't brought along any footballs.

4 One kid finally spoke up for all of us. "Excuse me, Coach. There are no footballs."

5 And Coach Graham responded, "We don't need any footballs."

6 There was a silence, while we thought about that . . .

7 "How many men are on the football field at a time?" he asked us.

8 Eleven on a team, we answered. So that makes twenty-two.

9 "And how many people are touching the football at any given time?"

10 One of them.

Annotation Practice Exercises

Directions: After you have read the selection, answer the critical reading questions below. This will help you gain additional insights about what you have read.

Practice Exercise

Who is the *author's intended audience*?

____

____

____

Copyright © 2014 The McGraw-Hill Companies, Inc. All rights reserved.

11 "Right!" he said. "So we're going to work on what those other twenty-one guys are doing."

12 Fundamentals. That was a great gift Coach Graham gave us. Fundamentals, fundamentals, fundamentals. As a college professor, I've seen this as one lesson so many kids ignore, always to their detriment: You've got to get the fundamentals down, because otherwise the fancy stuff is not going to work.

* * *

13 Coach Graham used to ride me hard. I remember one practice in particular. "You're doing it all wrong, Pausch. Go back! Do it again!" I tried to do what he wanted. It wasn't enough. "You owe me, Pausch! You're doing push-ups after practice."

14 When I was finally dismissed, one of the assistant coaches came over to reassure me. "Coach Graham rode you pretty hard, didn't he?" he said.

15 I could barely muster a "yeah."

16 "That's a good thing," the assistant told me. "When you're screwing up and nobody says anything to you anymore, that means they've given up on you."

17 That lesson has stuck with me my whole life. When you see yourself doing something badly and nobody's bothering to tell you anymore, that's a bad place to be. You may not want to hear it, but your critics are often the ones telling you they still love you and care about you, and want to make you better.

18 There's a lot of talk these days about giving children self-esteem. It's not something you can give; it's something they have to build. Coach Graham worked in a no-coddling zone. Self-esteem? He knew there was really only one way to teach kids how to develop it. You give them something they can't do, they work hard until they find they can do it, and you just keep repeating the process.

19 When Coach Graham first got hold of me, I was this wimpy kid with no skills, no physical strength, and no conditioning. But he made me realize that if I work hard enough, there will be things I can do tomorrow that I can't do today. Even now, having just turned forty-seven, I can give you a three-point stance that any NFL lineman would be proud of.

20 I realize that, these days, a guy like Coach Graham might get thrown out of a youth sports league. He'd be too tough. Parents would complain.

21 I haven't seen Coach Graham since I was a teen, but he just keeps showing up in my head, forcing me to work harder whenever I feel like quitting, forcing me to be better. He gave me a feedback loop for life.

* * *

22 When we send our kids to play organized sports—football, soccer, swimming, whatever—for most of us, it's not because we're desperate for them to learn the intricacies of the sport.

23 What we really want them to learn is far more important: teamwork, perseverance, sportsmanship, the value of hard work, an ability to deal with adversity. This kind of indirect learning is what some of us like to call a "head fake."

Practice Exercise

What is the *author's purpose* in writing this?

____

____

____

____

Practice Exercise

What is the *author's tone* in this selection?

____

____

____

Practice Exercise

What is the *author's point of view* about "fundamentals"?

____

____

____

____

____

____

Practice Exercise

What is the *author's point of view* regarding organized sports for kids?

____

____

____

____

____

____

____

____

24 There are two kinds of head fakes. The first is literal. On a football field, a player will move his head one way so you'll think he's going in that direction. Then he goes the opposite way. It's like a magician using misdirection. Coach Graham used to tell us to watch a player's waist. "Where his belly button goes, his body goes," he'd say.

25 The second kind of head fake is the really important one—the one that teaches people things they don't realize they're learning until well into the process. If you're a head-fake specialist, your hidden objective is to get them to learn something you want them to learn.

26 This kind of head-fake learning is absolutely vital. And Coach Graham was the master.

Professor Randy Pausch with his wife Jai (pronounced "Jay") and their children.

Source: From *The Last Lecture* by Randy Pausch, with Jeffrey Zaslow. Copyright © 2008 by Randy Pausch. Reprinted by permission of Hyperion. All rights reserved.

Copyright © 2014 The McGraw-Hill Companies, Inc. All rights reserved.

Comprehension and Vocabulary Quiz

This quiz has four parts. Your instructor may assign some or all of them.

Comprehension

Directions: Use the information in the selection to answer the questions below.

_______ **1.** With regard to his childhood dream of playing football in the NFL, Randy Pausch believed that:

a. he was treated unfairly.
b. he obtained a great deal merely from pursuing the dream.
c. it was the greatest disappointment of his life.
d. he would still have a chance to play.

_______ **2.** According to the author, people develop self-esteem by:

a. playing organized sports, such as football.
b. achieving increasingly difficult goals by working hard.
c. receiving criticism.
d. experiencing "head-fakes."

_______ **3.** "Head-fake learning" refers to:

a. a football player learning how to move his head in one direction to mislead the opposition.
b. a trick learned by magicians.
c. football players guessing the direction the ball is actually going to be thrown.
d. learning things without realizing it at first because they are being taught to you indirectly.

_______ **4.** Coach Graham was hard on Pausch because the coach:

a. cared about Pausch and believed he could become a better football player.
b. didn't like Pausch's quitter attitude.
c. was a difficult man who demanded too much of every player.
d. was frustrated that as a former Penn State linebacker, he was now having to coach a boys' team.

_______ **5.** According to the author, Coach Graham:

a. emphasized fundamentals.
b. helped players develop self-esteem.
c. forced him to work harder when he felt like quitting.
d. all of the above

Vocabulary in Context

Directions: For each item below, use context clues to deduce the meaning of the *italicized* word.

_______ **6.** As a college professor, I've seen this as one lesson so many kids ignore, always to their *detriment:* You've got to get the fundamentals down, because otherwise the fancy stuff is not going to work.

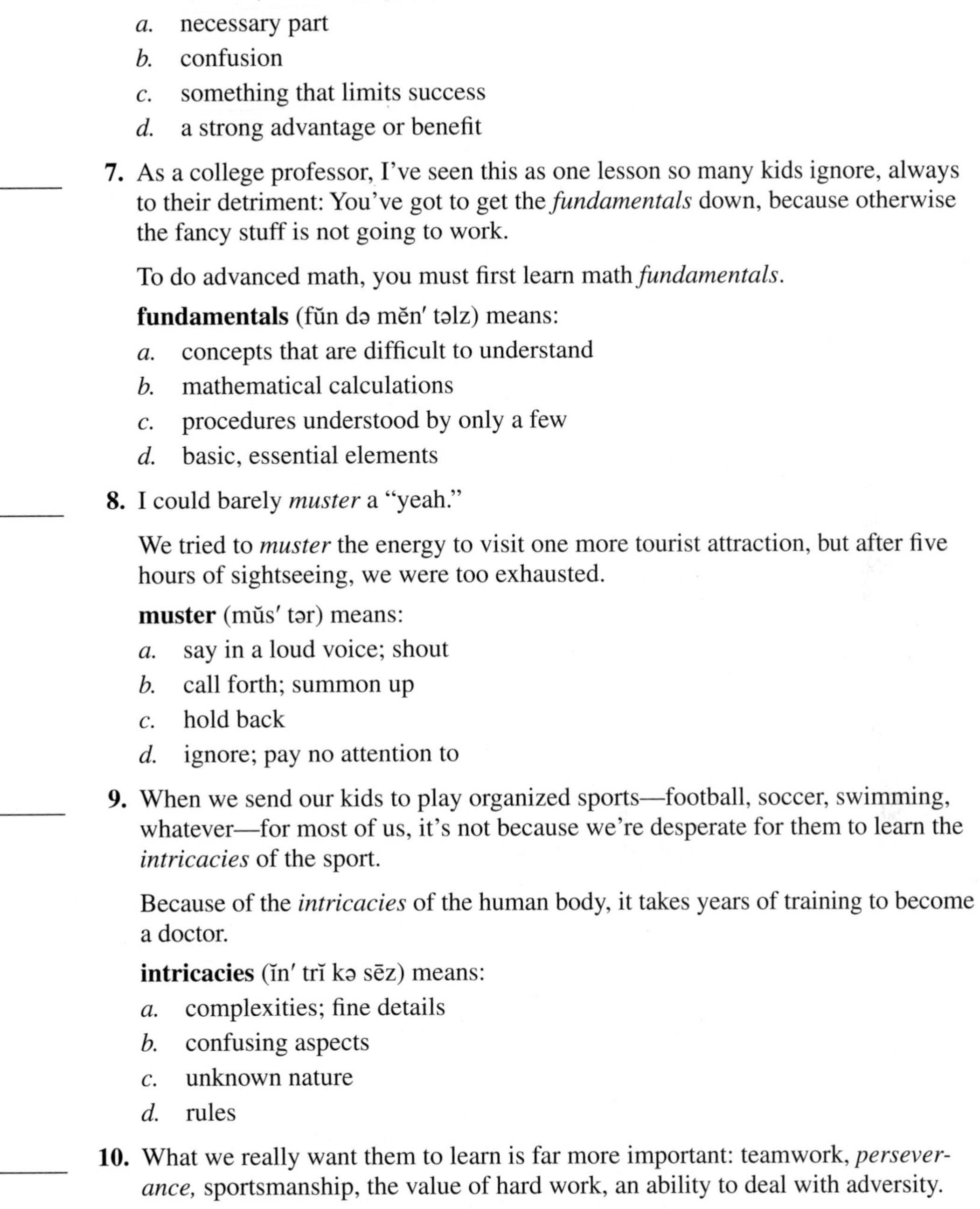

Working too many hours a week at a job can be a *detriment* to a student's success.

detriment (dĕt′ rə mənt) means:

a. necessary part
b. confusion
c. something that limits success
d. a strong advantage or benefit

_______ **7.** As a college professor, I've seen this as one lesson so many kids ignore, always to their detriment: You've got to get the *fundamentals* down, because otherwise the fancy stuff is not going to work.

To do advanced math, you must first learn math *fundamentals*.

fundamentals (fŭn də mĕn′ təlz) means:

a. concepts that are difficult to understand
b. mathematical calculations
c. procedures understood by only a few
d. basic, essential elements

_______ **8.** I could barely *muster* a "yeah."

We tried to *muster* the energy to visit one more tourist attraction, but after five hours of sightseeing, we were too exhausted.

muster (mŭs′ tər) means:

a. say in a loud voice; shout
b. call forth; summon up
c. hold back
d. ignore; pay no attention to

_______ **9.** When we send our kids to play organized sports—football, soccer, swimming, whatever—for most of us, it's not because we're desperate for them to learn the *intricacies* of the sport.

Because of the *intricacies* of the human body, it takes years of training to become a doctor.

intricacies (ĭn′ trĭ kə sēz) means:

a. complexities; fine details
b. confusing aspects
c. unknown nature
d. rules

_______ **10.** What we really want them to learn is far more important: teamwork, *perseverance,* sportsmanship, the value of hard work, an ability to deal with adversity.

Through *perseverance* and hard work, the Ortegas were able to expand their business from a single restaurant into a highly successful chain.

perseverance (pûr sə vîr′ əns) means:

a. not giving up
b. luck; good fortune
c. working as a team
d. networking

SELECTION 8.2

Copyright © 2014 The McGraw-Hill Companies, Inc. All rights reserved.

Word Structure

Directions: In paragraph 14 of the selection, you encountered the word ***dismissed.*** This word contains the root ***miss,*** which means "to send" or "to let go." (Another form of the root is ***mit.***) The word *dismissed* literally means "sent away." When elementary school students are dismissed at the end of the day, they are "sent away" (free to leave). Use the meaning of ***miss*** and the list of prefixes on pages 72–73 to help you determine the meaning of each of the following words.

_______ **11.** **Transmission** of information via the Internet occurs very rapidly. This means the information is:

a. lost.
b. sent out.
c. rejected.
d. verified.

_______ **12.** The **emission** of radioactive particles from isotopes is sometimes used in treating cancer. This means the radioactive particles are:

a. destroyed.
b. collected from the isotopes.
c. sent out from the isotopes.
d. isolated from the isotopes.

_______ **13.** If a diplomat is given a **mission,** it means the person:

a. is sent to accomplish a specific task.
b. is asked to resign.
c. receives an award or recognition.
d. is given a dangerous job.

_______ **14.** If there is an **omission** of important information in a report, it means the information is:

a. given at the beginning.
b. included at the end.
c. missing.
d. highlighted throughout.

_______ **15.** If a disease is in **remission,** it means the patient's symptoms have:

a. increased slightly.
b. triggered another illness.
c. returned stronger than before.
d. been sent back to lower levels; lessened.

Reading Skills Application

Directions: These items test your ability to *apply* certain skills. You may not have studied all of the skills at this point, so some items will serve as a helpful preview.

_______ **16.** Which of the following is the meaning of *no-coddling* as it is used in paragraph 18?

a. referring to the section of the football field near the goal posts
b. not pampering or treating gently
c. relating to defense rather than offense
d. not asking or demanding much

_______ **17.** Which pattern is used to organize the information in paragraph 12?

a. cause-effect
b. list
c. sequence
d. definition

_______ **18.** Based on information in the selection, the author would be likely to agree with which of the following statements?

a. Every child should be required to play an organized sport.
b. Coaches should be kinder and more patient with the youngsters they coach.
c. People from our childhood can have a positive influence on us that lasts the rest of our lives.
d. Every learning experience includes both types of head-fakes.

_______ **19.** Which of the following represents the main idea of paragraph 17?

a. That lesson has stuck with me my whole life.
b. When you see yourself doing something badly and nobody's bothering to tell you anymore, that's a bad place to be.
c. You may not want to hear it, but your critics are often the ones telling you they still love you and care about you, and want to make you better.
d. When people criticize you, it means they have given up on you.

_______ **20.** Which of the following represents an opinion rather than a fact?

a. On the first day of practice, we were all scared to death.
b. Plus he hadn't brought along any footballs.
c. One kid finally spoke up for all of us.
d. "Excuse me, Coach. There are no footballs."

SELECTION **8.2**
Memoir
(continued)

Respond in Writing

Directions: Refer to the selection as needed to answer the questions below.

1. **Reacting to What You Have Read:** Randy Pausch describes the impact that Coach Graham had on his life. Think of someone, other than your relatives, who has had a significant impact on your life. Who were they (you do not have to give a name; you can simply say, "a coach," "a neighbor," "a teacher," etc.)? In what way did they help you learn to see yourself or the world differently?

____

____

____

____

Copyright © 2014 The McGraw-Hill Companies, Inc. All rights reserved.

2. **Comprehending the Selection Further:** The author mentions several things he gained from participating in football as a boy. List at least three of those.

3. **Overall Main Idea of the Selection:** In one sentence, tell what the author wants readers to understand about dreams we pursue but do not achieve. (Be sure to include "dreams" in your overall main idea sentence.)

Read More about It Online

Internet Resources

Directions: To learn more about the topic of this selection, see the website below or use the keywords "Randy Pausch" or "the last lecture" with a search engine.

www.thelastlecture.com
You can watch Randy Pausch's "last lecture" at this website, which also has information about the book, several "online extras," and links to his website, his time management lecture, and media coverage of Professor Pausch.

SELECTION **8.3** **Business**

You? A Millionaire? Yes!

From *Understanding Business*
By William Nickels, James McHugh, and Susan McHugh

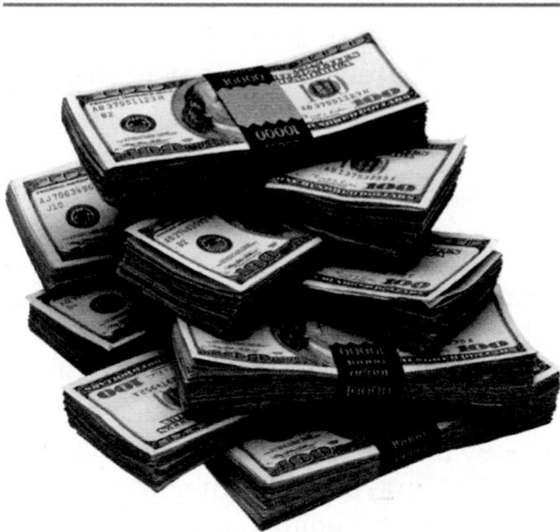

The Wall Street Journal *reported that the number of U.S. millionaires in 2010 was 3.1 million, a record. (A "millionaire" is defined as a person with $1 million or more in investable assets, not including their primary home, collectibles, consumables, and durable consumer goods.) Experts say millionaires are doing much better than everyone else because of the improvement in the financial markets (stock market). U.S. male millionaires far outnumber female millionaires: 63 percent are men; 37 percent are women. (CNN reported that the number of U.S.* households *worth at least $1 million rose to 8.4 million in 2010.)*

States with the most millionaires tend to be small states with large concentrations of highly educated professionals and business owners. In 2010 the states with the most millionaires were (in order): Hawaii, Maryland, New Jersey, Connecticut, Massachusetts, Alaska, Virginia, New Hampshire. California, and Delaware. The District of Columbia ranked between California and Delaware.

Who do you think is the "typical" millionaire in this country? How do most new millionaires acquire their wealth? It is possible that you could join the ranks of millionaires? Read this selection and see if your thinking changes. You may be surprised at some of what you discover.

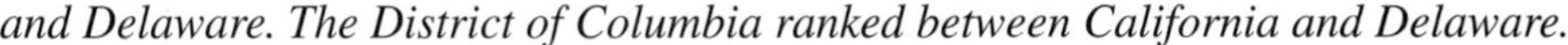

Think You Could Never Become a Millionaire? Think Again!

1 No matter how many articles you may read about how the world economy is struggling, also making the news is the large number of millionaires in the United States and throughout the world. There's no reason you couldn't be one of them if you want to. One of the best ways to learn how to become a millionaire is to do what companies do: copy those who are successful. Find out what all those millionaires did to make their money.

2 Thomas Stanley and William Danko have been studying millionaires for years. Their research is available in a book called *The Millionaire Next Door: The Surprising Secrets of America's Wealthy.* Stanley and Danko found that the majority are entrepreneurs who own one or more small businesses. Self-employed people are about five times as likely to be millionaires as people who earn a paycheck working for others. Yet the average income of U.S. millionaires is only about $131,000 a year. So how did they get to be millionaires? They didn't win their money on a game show. They saved it! To become a millionaire by the time you are 50 or so, you have to save about 15 percent of your income every year—starting when you are in your 20s. If you start later, you have to save an even larger percentage. The secret is to put your money in a place where it will grow without your having to pay taxes on it.

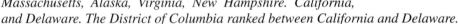

Annotation Practice Exercises

Directions: After you have read the selection, answer the critical reading questions below. This will help you gain additional insight about what you have read.

Practice Exercise

What is the *authors' purpose* in paragraph 1?

____

____

____

____

____

____

Copyright © 2014 The McGraw-Hill Companies, Inc. All rights reserved.

3 To save that 15 percent a year, you have to spend less than you earn. That is getting more and more difficult as the cost of living rises. Discipline in spending must begin with your first job and stay with you all your life. The millionaires Stanley studied tended to own modest homes and buy used cars. In short, becoming a millionaire has as much or more to do with thrift as with how much you earn. Want to go for more? In 2008 *Forbes* magazine found over 1,000 billionaires around the world. Believe it or not, Russia has 87 of them! There were fewer billionaires in 2009 as a result of the recession. To become a millionaire, get an education, work hard, save your money, and make purchases carefully.

Practice Exercise

Who is the authors' *intended audience?*

____

____

____

____

____

____

The Need for Personal Financial Planning

4 The United States is largely a capitalist country. It follows, then, that the secret to success in such a country is to have capital, or money. With capital, you can take nice vacations, raise a family, invest in stocks and bonds, buy the goods and services you want, give generously to others, and retire with enough money to see you through. Money management, however, is not easy. You have to earn the money in the first place. Your chances of becoming wealthy are much greater if you choose to become an entrepreneur. Of course, there are risks in starting a business, but the best time to take risks is when you are young.

5 After you earn the money, you have to learn to spend some wisely, save the rest, and insure yourself against the risks of serious accidents, illness, or death. With a little bit of luck, you may be one of the millionaires Stanley and Danko interview for their next book.

6 You'll likely need some help. Recently high school seniors averaged a grade of 48.3 percent on questions having to do with financial concepts. Another report found that college students are also poorly educated about financial matters such as IRAs and 401(k) plans. The sections that follow will give you some of the basics so that you'll be ahead of the game. Financial management is so important to your fiscal health that you may enjoy taking an entire course on it.

Practice Exercise

What is the *authors' tone*?

____

____

____

____

____

____

____

____

____

Complete College: Financial Planning Begins with Making Money

7 You already know one of the secrets to finding a good-paying job is having a good education. Throughout history, an investment in education has paid off regardless of the state of the economy or political ups and downs. Benjamin Franklin said, "If a man empties his purse into his head, no one can take it away from him. An investment in knowledge always pays the best interest." Education has become even more important since we entered the information age. A typical full-time worker in the United States with a four-year college degree earns about $50,000—62 percent more than one with only a high school diploma. The lifetime income of families headed by individuals with a bachelor's degree will be about $1.6 million more than the incomes of families headed by those with a high school diploma. One way to start to become a millionaire, therefore, is to finish college. The government is eager for you to go to college and

Practice Exercise

What is the *authors' point of view* as to whether it is easy or difficult to become a millionaire?

____

____

____

____

is willing to help you with tax breaks like tax-free education savings accounts. Make sure you investigate all the financial help available to you.

8 Making money is one thing; saving, investing, and spending it wisely is something else. The following six steps will help you become one of those with enough to live in comfort throughout your life.

Six Steps to Controlling Your Assets

9 The only way to save enough money to do all the things you want to do in life is to spend less than you make. Although you may find it hard to save today, it is not only possible but imperative if you want to accumulate enough to be financially secure. Fewer than 1 in 10 U.S. adults has accumulated enough money by retirement age to live comfortably, and 36 percent of U.S. households don't have a retirement account. Don't become one of them. Here are steps you can take today to get control of your finances:

Step 1: Take an inventory of your financial assets. Develop a balance sheet that shows your assets (such as a computer, a car, and savings account) and liabilities (such as credit card debt and a car loan). Create an income statement. To get your *net income*, subtract your costs and expenses (rent, credit card, etc.) from your revenue (income).

Step 2: Keep track of all of your expenses. The only way to trace where your money is going is to keep track of every cent you spend. Recording your expenses is tedious but necessary if you want to learn self-discipline—and it could turn out to be enjoyable because it gives you such a feeling of control and confidence. You won't believe how much you fritter way on miscellaneous items unless you keep a *detailed* record for at least a couple of months. Cutting back from five $4.25 venti mocha frappuccinos a week to one a week would save you more than $850 a year. Over 10 years, that could mean an extra $12,000 for retirement, if you invest the money wisely.

Step 3: Prepare a budget. Budgets are financial plans. A household budget includes mortgage or rent, utilities, food, clothing, vehicles, furniture, life insurance, car insurance and medical insurance. Running a household is similar to running a small business. Check out Mint.com for help with your budgeting needs.

Step 4: Pay off your debts. The first thing to do with the money remaining after you pay your monthly bills is to pay off your debts, starting with those carrying the highest interest rates. Check your credit card statements to find the interest rates.

Step 5: Start a savings plan. It's important to save some money each month in a separate account for large purchases you'd like to make (such as a car or house). The best way to save money is to *pay yourself first.* When you get your paycheck, first take out the money for savings and then plan what to do with the rest. Some banks will do an automatic monthly deduction for savings. You'll be pleasantly surprised when the money starts accumulating and earning interest over time. With some discipline, you can

Practice Exercise

What is the *authors' purpose* in giving the six steps in paragraph 9?

____

____

____

____

____

SELECTION 8.3

Copyright © 2014 The McGraw-Hill Companies, Inc. All rights reserved.

eventually reach your goal of becoming a millionaire. It's not as difficult as you may think.

Step 6: Borrow only to buy assets that increase in value or generate income. Don't borrow money for ordinary expenses; you'll only get more into debt that way. If you have budgeted for emergencies, such as car repairs or health care, you should be able to stay financially secure. Most financial experts advise saving about six months of earnings for contingencies. Only the most unexpected of expense should cause you to borrow.

10 If you follow these six steps, not only will you have the money for investment, but you'll have developed most of the financial techniques needed to become financially secure. If you find it hard to live within a budget at first, remember the payoff is well worth the effort.

Sources: Section 1, as cited in William Nickels, James McHugh, and Susan McHugh, *Understanding Business,* 9th ed., pp. D–D1; Mary Beth Franklin, "6 Simple Ways to Retire Rich," *Kiplinger's Personal Finance,* February 2008; Jessica Chen, Lindsay Holloway, Amanda C. Kooser, Kim Orr, James Park, Nichole L. Torres, and Sara Wilson, "Young Millionaires," *Entrepreneur*, October 2007; "Billionaires 2008," *Forbes*, March 24, 2008; Sarah Wilson, "How to Make a Million," *Entrepreneur*, October 2008; and Duncan Greenberg and Tatiana Serafin, "Up in Smoke," *Forbes*, March 30, 2009. Sections 2–4: Adapted from William Nickels, James McHugh, and Susan McHugh, *Understanding Business,* 9th ed., pp. D2–D6. Copyright © 2010 by The McGraw-Hill Companies, Inc.

SELECTION 8.3
Business
(continued)

Comprehension and Vocabulary Quiz

This quiz has several parts. Your instructor may assign some or all of them.

Comprehension

Directions: Use the information in the selection to answer each item below.

_____ **1.** In general, to become a millionaire by age 50, people in their 20s should start saving what percent of their income?
- *a.* 10
- *b.* 15
- *c.* 20
- *d.* 25

_____ **2.** The self-made millionaires Thomas Stanley reports on in *The Millionaire Next Door* tended to:
- *a.* live in apartments and use public transportation.
- *b.* live in modest homes and buy used cars.
- *c.* live in moderate homes and drive mid-level sedans.
- *d.* live in expensive homes and drive luxury automobiles.

_____ **3.** In general, most college students:
- *a.* enroll in a personal finance or financial planning course.
- *b.* know little about financial matters.
- *c.* start saving while they are still in college.
- *d.* begin saving as soon as they graduate and get their first job.

_____ **4.** The percentage of U.S. adults who have enough money for a comfortable retirement is:
- *a.* less than 10 percent.
- *b.* approximately 15 percent.
- *c.* 36 percent.
- *d.* 48.3 percent.

_____ **5.** The majority of self-made millionaires surveyed in *The Millionaire Next Door:*
- *a.* work for small companies.
- *b.* work for large corporations.
- *c.* are self-employed.
- *d.* are unemployed.

Vocabulary in Context

Directions: For each item below, use context clues to deduce the meaning of the *italicized* word.

_____ **6.** With *capital*, you can take nice vacations, raise a family, invest in stocks and bonds, buy the goods and services you want, give generously to others, and retire with enough money to see you through.

SELECTION 8.3

Copyright © 2014 The McGraw-Hill Companies, Inc. All rights reserved.

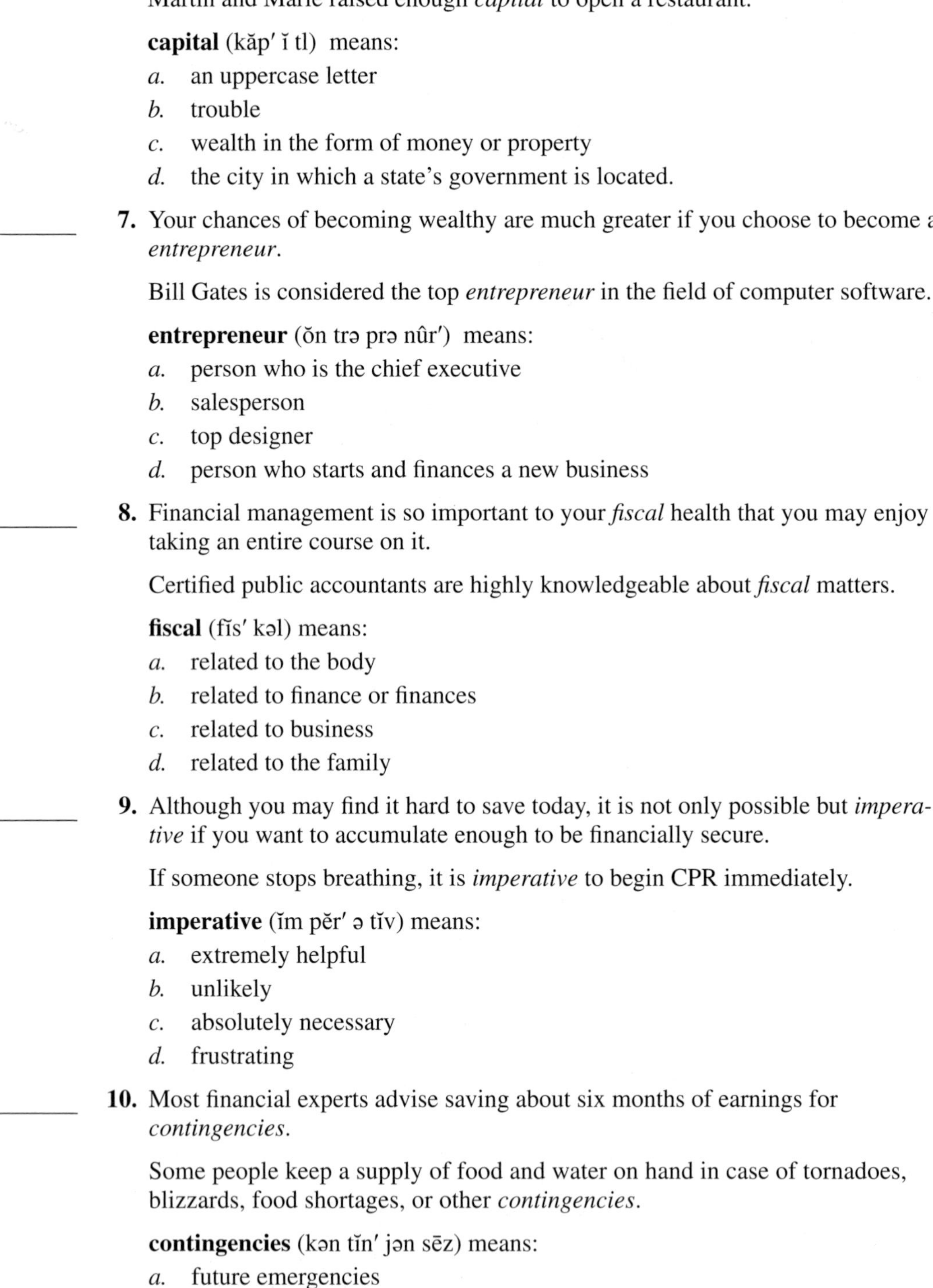

Martin and Marie raised enough *capital* to open a restaurant.

capital (kăp′ ĭ tl) means:

a. an uppercase letter
b. trouble
c. wealth in the form of money or property
d. the city in which a state's government is located.

_______ **7.** Your chances of becoming wealthy are much greater if you choose to become an *entrepreneur*.

Bill Gates is considered the top *entrepreneur* in the field of computer software.

entrepreneur (ŏn trə prə nûr′) means:

a. person who is the chief executive
b. salesperson
c. top designer
d. person who starts and finances a new business

_______ **8.** Financial management is so important to your *fiscal* health that you may enjoy taking an entire course on it.

Certified public accountants are highly knowledgeable about *fiscal* matters.

fiscal (fĭs′ kəl) means:

a. related to the body
b. related to finance or finances
c. related to business
d. related to the family

_______ **9.** Although you may find it hard to save today, it is not only possible but *imperative* if you want to accumulate enough to be financially secure.

If someone stops breathing, it is *imperative* to begin CPR immediately.

imperative (ĭm pĕr′ ə tĭv) means:

a. extremely helpful
b. unlikely
c. absolutely necessary
d. frustrating

_______ **10.** Most financial experts advise saving about six months of earnings for *contingencies*.

Some people keep a supply of food and water on hand in case of tornadoes, blizzards, food shortages, or other *contingencies*.

contingencies (kən tĭn′ jən sēz) means:

a. future emergencies
b. weather events
c. retirement
d. luxury items

Word Structure

Directions: In paragraph 9, Step 2, of the selection, you encountered the word **confidence.** This word contains the root ***fid,*** which means "faith" or "trust." The word *confidence* means "having *faith* or *trust* in someone or something." Use the meaning of ***fid*** and the list of prefixes on pages 72–73 to help you determine the meaning of each of the following words.

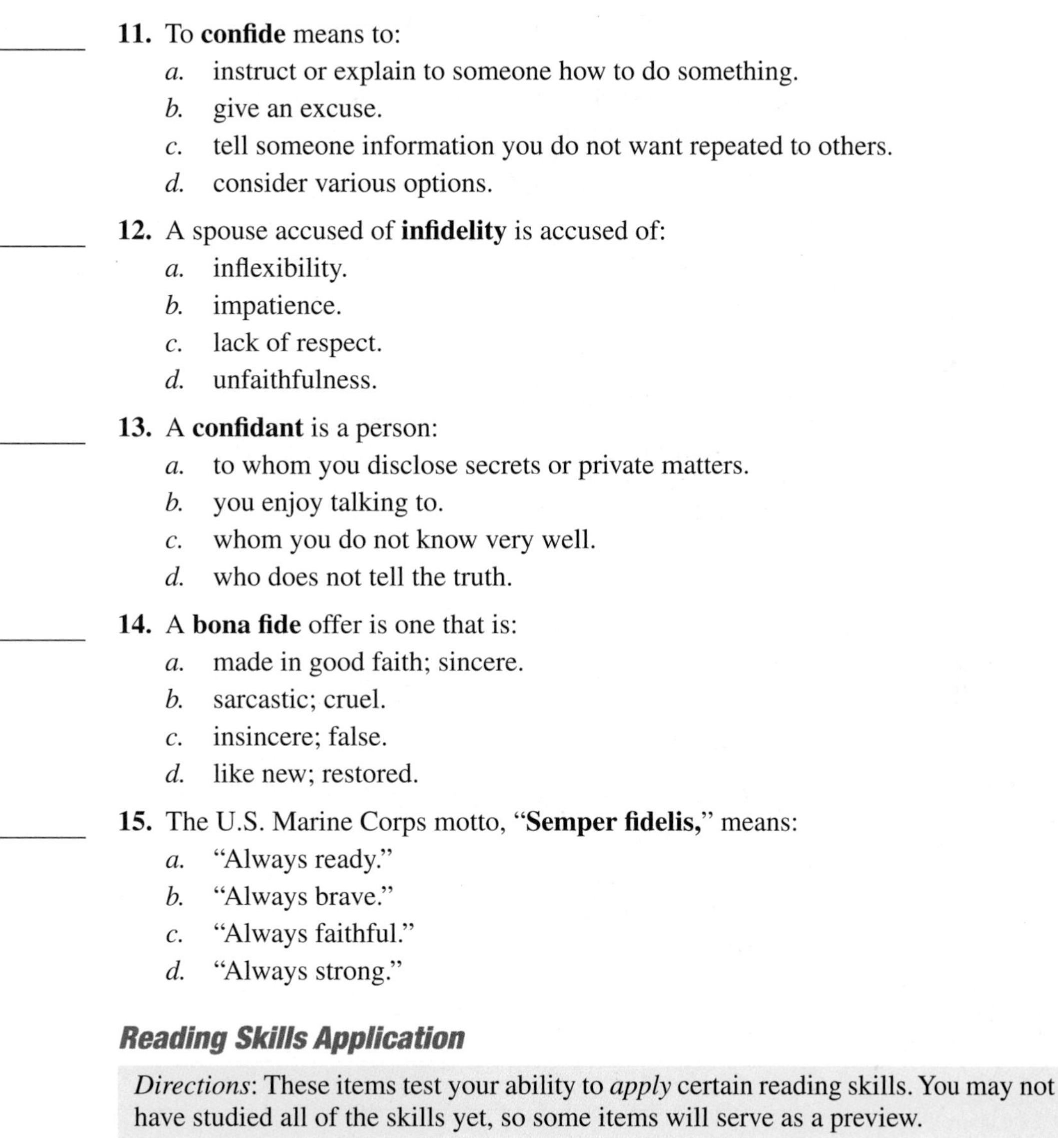

11. To **confide** means to:
- *a.* instruct or explain to someone how to do something.
- *b.* give an excuse.
- *c.* tell someone information you do not want repeated to others.
- *d.* consider various options.

12. A spouse accused of **infidelity** is accused of:
- *a.* inflexibility.
- *b.* impatience.
- *c.* lack of respect.
- *d.* unfaithfulness.

13. A **confidant** is a person:
- *a.* to whom you disclose secrets or private matters.
- *b.* you enjoy talking to.
- *c.* whom you do not know very well.
- *d.* who does not tell the truth.

14. A **bona fide** offer is one that is:
- *a.* made in good faith; sincere.
- *b.* sarcastic; cruel.
- *c.* insincere; false.
- *d.* like new; restored.

15. The U.S. Marine Corps motto, "**Semper fidelis,**" means:
- *a.* "Always ready."
- *b.* "Always brave."
- *c.* "Always faithful."
- *d.* "Always strong."

Reading Skills Application

Directions: These items test your ability to *apply* certain reading skills. You may not have studied all of the skills yet, so some items will serve as a preview.

16. According to the selection, the best way to save money is to:
- *a.* prepare a budget.
- *b.* set up an automatic monthly deduction.
- *c.* borrow only to buy assets to increase in value or generate income.
- *d.* pay yourself first.

_______ **17.** In paragraph 6 it says, "Financial management is so important to your fiscal health that you may enjoy taking an entire course on it." Does that statement express a fact or an opinion?

a. fact

b. opinion

_______ **18.** Paragraph 7 says, "Benjamin Franklin said, 'If a man empties his purse into his head, no one can take it away from him. An investment in knowledge always pays the best interest.'" The phrase "empties his purse into his head" means:

a. spends without thinking.

b. puts his money into his education.

c. borrows money to buy books.

d. lends money to students.

_______ **19.** As used in paragraph 9, Step 2, the word *fritter* means to

a. save.

b. squander little by little.

c. give.

d. spend all at once.

_______ **20.** The information in paragraph 10 of the selection is organized using which of the following patterns?

a. cause-effect

b. list

c. sequence

d. comparison-contrast

SELECTION **8.3**

Business

(continued)

Respond in Writing

Directions: Refer to the selection as needed to answer the essay-type questions below.

1. What difference do you think it would make (or would have made) in your life if you were a millionaire by the age of 50?

____

____

____

____

____

____

____

____

____

2. **Comprehending the Selection Further:** Which of the six guidelines for achieving wealth (given in paragraph 9) do you currently follow? If you do not currently follow any of them, which two do you think would help you most? Why?

3. **Overall Main Idea of the Selection:** In one sentence, tell what the authors want readers to understand about U.S. millionaires. (Be sure to include "U.S. millionaires" in your overall main idea sentence.)

Read More about It Online

Internet Resources

Directions: To learn more about the topic of this selection, see the websites below or use the keyword **"becoming a millionaire"** or **"U.S. millionaires"** with a search engine.

www.mint.com
Mint.com automatically pulls all your financial information into one place, so you can finally get the entire picture. It lets you set a budget, track your goals and do more with your money. This award-winning website is free, and information is secure.

http://genxfinance.com/the-top-5-ways-to-become-a-millionaire
Generation X Finance (genxfinance.com) was created in late 2006 by Jeremy Vohwinkle as a means for discussing financial issues that are important to this unique generation. Vohwinkle, who specializes in retirement planning, also writes on the topic of financial planning for About.com.

Copyright © 2014 The McGraw-Hill Companies, Inc. All rights reserved.

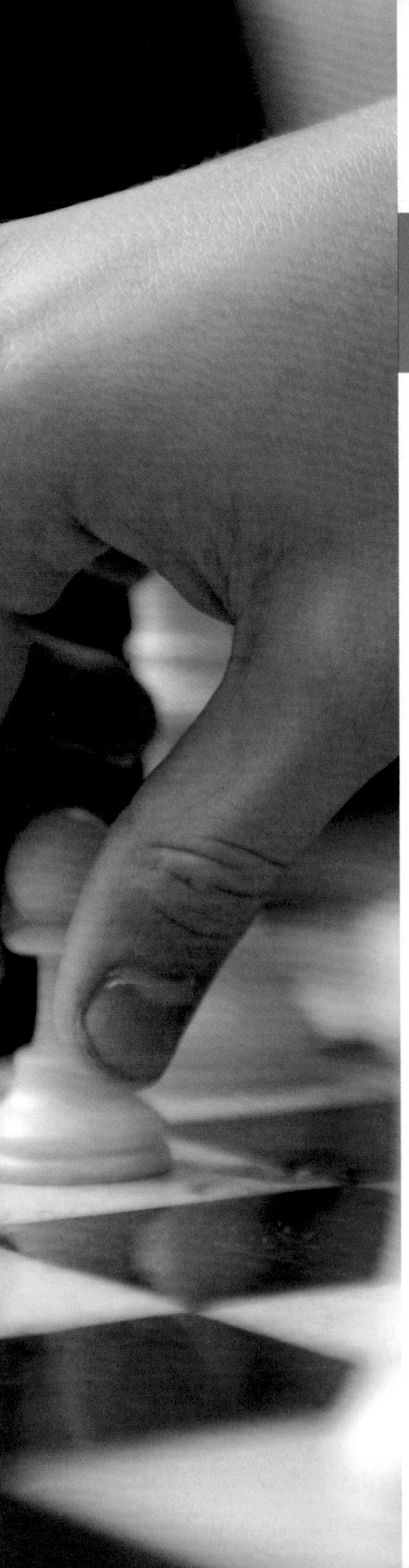

CHAPTER 9

Thinking Critically

LEARNING OBJECTIVES

In this chapter you will learn the answers to these questions:

- What is thinking critically, and why is it important?
- What are facts and opinions, and why is it important to be able to distinguish between them?
- What are logical inferences, and why is it important to make them?

CHAPTER CONTENTS

NEW INFORMATION AND SKILLS

What Is Thinking Critically, and Why Is It Important?

What Are Facts and Opinions, and Why Is It Important to Be Able to Distinguish between Them?

What Are Inferences, and Why Is It Important to Make Them?

Other Things to Keep in Mind When Thinking Critically:

- Facts and opinions may or may not appear together.
- Authors sometimes present opinions in such a way that they *appear* to be facts.
- Other critical thinking skills, such as *recognizing propaganda devices* and *recognizing fallacies,* can also be used to evaluate written material.

CHECKPOINT: THINKING CRITICALLY

CHAPTER REVIEW CARDS

TEST YOUR UNDERSTANDING

Thinking Critically: Fact and Opinion

Thinking Critically: Making Logical Inferences

READINGS

Selection 9.1 "Taboos and Myths about Conflict and Anger"
from *Marriages and Families: Intimacy, Diversity, and Strengths*
by David Olson, John DeFrain, and Linda Skogrand (Marriage and Family)

Selection 9.2 "Planet Under Stress: Curbing Population Growth"
from *The Living World: Basic Concepts*
by George B. Johnson (Biology)

Selection 9.3 "For Better or Worse: Divorce"
from *Human Development*
by Diane Papalia, Sally Olds, and Ruth Feldman (Human Development)

NEW INFORMATION AND SKILLS

WHAT IS THINKING CRITICALLY, AND WHY IS IT IMPORTANT?

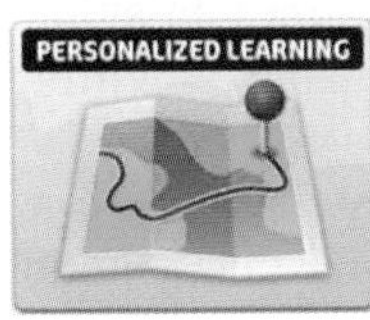

As you learned in Chapter 8, critical reading means going beyond basic comprehension (such as identifying the topic, main idea, and supporting details) by determining point of view, purpose, intended audience, and tone. This requires rereading and reconsidering the author's message. Sometimes, though, you must go one step further and include **thinking critically:** thinking in an organized way about material in order to evaluate it accurately. To think critically, you can use the skills of:

thinking critically
Thinking in an organized way about material in order to evaluate it accurately.

- Distinguishing between facts and opinions.
- Making inferences and drawing logical conclusions.

WHAT ARE FACTS AND OPINIONS, AND WHY IS IT IMPORTANT TO BE ABLE TO DISTINGUISH BETWEEN THEM?

fact
Something that can be proved to exist or to have happened.

What is the difference between a fact and an opinion? A **fact** is something that can be proved to exist or to have happened. For example, these are facts because the information can be verified: *Alexander the Great, a fourth-century B.C.E. ruler of Greece, conquered most of the ancient world,* and *As a boy, Alexander had as his teacher the philosopher Aristotle.* Proving that something is a fact (that it is true) can be accomplished through research, direct observation or experience, or conducting an experiment. Through research, a person could prove or verify that the statements about Alexander are factual.

opinion
Something that cannot be proved or disproved; a judgment or belief.

An **opinion** is a judgment or belief that cannot be proved *or disproved.* For example, the following statements represent opinions because there is no way to prove or disprove them: *Alexander the Great was the most successful military leader who ever lived,* and *Alexander would never have become an outstanding ruler and military leader if he had not studied with the philosopher Aristotle.* Moreover, these statements contain words that represent judgments ("successful" and "outstanding"). Everyone has a slightly different idea of what words such as "successful" and "outstanding" mean, and people would not agree exactly on their meaning. For this reason, these two statements about Alexander the Great are opinions.

Most statements that refer to events that might happen in the future are opinions. For example, consider the statement "Computer software manufacturing will be the world's largest industry throughout the 21st century." Because this event is a future event and cannot be proved before it happens, this statement represents an opinion. It would remain an opinion until it has happened (or not). That is, it would remain an opinion until it is proved to be a fact or disproved as incorrect information.

When an author includes opinions, it is important for you to evaluate them because not all opinions are valid or useful. It is also important to realize that although opinions cannot be proved, they can nevertheless be supported by valid reasons and reasonable evidence. An opinion is valuable if it is *well supported.* "Well supported" means that the author presents facts and logical reasons for the opinion that he or she holds. Well-supported opinions are based on facts or on the ideas of knowledgeable people. Consequently, well-supported opinions can be as important and useful as facts. Opinions in textbooks typically represent valuable opinions because they are the well-reasoned beliefs of the author or other experts. Scientific theories are also examples of "expert

Copyright © 2014 The McGraw-Hill Companies, Inc. All rights reserved.

opinions." (Incidentally, if a theory could be proved, it would no longer be a theory. It would become a fact.) Of course, poorly supported or unsupported opinions are not useful, but do not make the mistake of thinking that all opinions are valueless.

Needless to say, an opinion is of little value if it is poorly supported (that is, if the author does not give good reasons for believing it). A warning: Sometimes an author might try to make a poorly supported opinion *seem* believable and valuable by writing very persuasively or emotionally.

To see the difference between a well-supported opinion and a poorly supported one, consider the example below. It presents two sets of reasons (support) for this opinion: *City College makes an excellent, affordable education available to almost everyone.* (This statement is an opinion, of course, because of the judgment words "excellent" and "affordable.") Note the difference between the two sets of support for this opinion, and decide which would more likely cause someone to accept the opinion as valid.

Opinion: *City College makes an excellent, affordable education available to almost everyone.*

Examples of well-reasoned support

City College makes an excellent, affordable education available to almost everyone because . . .

- It offers more than 80 programs and majors. *(fact)*
- Its tuition is the lowest in the state. *(fact)*
- Its financial aid office offers information about more than 200 scholarships, grants, and loans. *(fact)*
- Classes are offered days, evenings, weekends, and online. *(fact)*
- The computer labs are equipped with more than 500 computers. *(fact)*
- The faculty is friendly and supportive. *(opinion)*
- More than half of the faculty have earned doctoral degrees. *(fact)*

Examples of poorly reasoned support

City College makes an excellent, affordable education available to almost everyone because . . .

- It is located less than a mile from the beach. *(fact)*
- The campus has beautiful architecture. *(opinion)*
- The buildings are attractive and well maintained. *(opinion)*
- It has a swimming pool, tennis courts, and a jogging path. *(fact)*
- There is plenty of free, convenient parking. *(opinion)*
- The food in the cafeteria is good. *(opinion)*
- There are a dozen different video games in the student center. *(fact)*
- One of its former students is now a major league baseball star. *(fact)*

Clearly, the first set of reasons is stronger than the second. If someone gave you the first set of reasons to explain why he or she believes City College makes an excellent, affordable education available to almost everyone, you would probably agree that it does. However, if someone presented only the second set of reasons, that person probably would not convince you of his or her opinion about City College.

As you now know, opinions represent judgments, beliefs, or interpretations. Authors often use the following words and phrases to indicate that they are presenting an opinion. They typically appear at the beginning of a sentence, although many of them can appear within a sentence as well. They include:

Perhaps	In our opinion
Apparently	It could be that
It seems	It may be that

It appears	It seems likely
Presumably	This suggests
One possibility is	In our view
One interpretation is	In the opinion of

Now look at the following examples and notice the use of those words in these opinions:

> Most Americans, *in our opinion,* do not eat a balanced, nutritious diet.
>
> *Apparently,* more and more people feel comfortable investing in the stock market.
>
> Improving one's study habits, *it appears,* can dramatically improve one's self-esteem.
>
> *It seems likely* that the majority of consumer products companies will eventually sell their products directly over the Internet as well.

In addition, words that indicate someone's *value judgments* can signal opinions. A value judgment is represented by a word that reflects someone's personal evaluation of something or someone. These words signal opinions because they can be interpreted in different ways by different people. Examples of words that signal value judgments are:

greatest	wealthy
best	successful
worst	fascinating
excellent	effective
interesting	humorous
beautiful	pleasant

These words can signal opinions because different people rarely use these words to mean exactly the same thing. For example, people will disagree about what is considered "successful," "fascinating," "beautiful," and so on. Consider the sentence *Students who finish college will be more successful.* The word "successful" could mean successful financially, personally, socially, or in all those ways. Because there are many interpretations of what "successful" means, it would be impossible to prove this statement (although it could be supported with certain facts about college graduates). Also, many students who do not complete college are "successful" in some or all those ways. Consequently, this statement expresses the writer's opinion about college graduates. (Even though this may be a widely held opinion, it is still an opinion; *it cannot be proved.*) As you read, then, watch for judgment words that can be interpreted in different ways. They are clues that you are reading an opinion.

Students sometimes confuse incorrect information with opinions because they assume that if something is not a fact, it must automatically be an opinion. However, this is not so. There are three possibilities: (1) Information can be a fact (it is correct information), or (2) it can be an opinion (it represents someone's belief), or (3) it can simply be incorrect information. The statements *Alaska has a higher average temperature than Hawaii* and *Water boils at 32°F* are examples of incorrect information. The statement *There have been forty-three U.S. presidents* is an example of out-of-date information. Even though these statements are written without judgment words and may seem factual, they can be proved *incorrect.* Therefore, they are not facts. They are not opinions either. They are simply statements of incorrect information. (Provable facts, of course, are *Hawaii is warmer than Alaska* and *Water freezes—not boils—at 32°F.*)

Comprehension Monitoring Question for Thinking Critically to Evaluate Whether Statements in Written Material Are Facts or Opinions

"Can the information the author presents be proved or disproved, or does it represent a judgment?"

Finally, do not make the mistake that many students make: They assume that everything that appears in print, especially in textbooks, is a fact. This is incorrect. College textbooks contain countless facts, but they typically include a wealth of valuable expert opinions as well.

To distinguish between facts and opinions when reading critically, ask yourself these questions in this order:

- Can the information in the statement be *proved*? If so, it is correct information and, therefore, a *fact.*
- Can the information in the statement be *disproved*? If so, it is simply *incorrect information.*
- Is the information in the statement something that *cannot be proved or disproved*? If so, it is an *opinion.* (If it is an opinion, consider how well supported it is.)

The chart below summarizes this process for evaluating whether statements are facts or opinions. Use this process to distinguish between facts and well-supported opinions (which are valuable), and incorrect information and unsupported or poorly supported opinions (which are of no value).

To distinguish facts from opinions and, therefore, think critically, you should ask yourself, "Can the information the author presents be proved or disproved, or does it represent a judgment?" If the information can be proved, it represents a fact. If it cannot be proved or disproved, it represents an opinion.

DETERMINING WHETHER A STATEMENT REPRESENTS A FACT, INCORRECT INFORMATION, OR AN OPINION

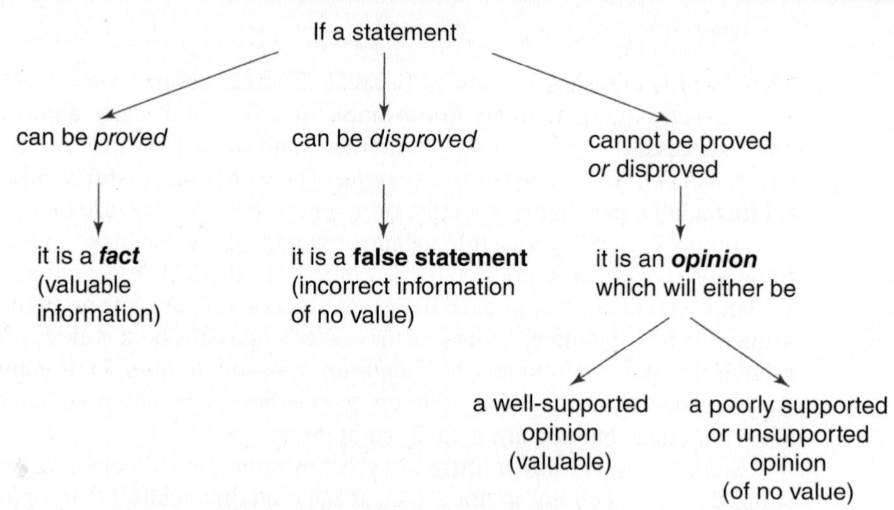

To distinguish between facts and opinions, ask yourself these questions in this order:

1. Can the information in the statement be proved? If so, it is a ***fact*** (correct information).
2. Can the information in the statement be disproved? If so, it is a ***false statement*** (incorrect information).
3. Is the information in the statement something that cannot be proved or disproved? If so, it is an ***opinion***. When the statement is an opinion, ask yourself these additional questions:

- Is the opinion *well supported*? (That is, is it based on valid reasons and plausible evidence?) If so, it is a valuable opinion.
- Is the opinion *poorly supported or unsupported*? If so, it is of little or no value.

Let's apply these steps to a sample passage. The following excerpt is from a health textbook. Its topic is *the health benefits of regular physical activity.* Its stated main idea sentence is *There are so many health benefits of regular physical exercise that it is surprising not everyone engages in it.* All the sentences except the last two are facts.

> Regular physical activity that is performed on most days of the week reduces the risk of developing or dying from some of the leading causes of death in the U.S. It reduces the risk of dying prematurely. It reduces the risk of dying from heart disease. It reduces the risk of developing diabetes, high blood pressure, and colon cancer. It helps reduce blood pressure in people who already have high blood pressure. It helps control weight, and builds and maintains healthy bones, muscles, and joints. It helps older adults become stronger and better able to move about without falling. It promotes psychological well-being, and reduces feelings of depression and anxiety. There are so many health benefits of regular physical exercise that it is surprising not everyone engages in it. If you start exercising, you'll be hooked in no time.
>
> *Source:* USDDHS 2008 Physical Activity Guidelines for Americans, as cited in Richard Blonna, *Coping with Stress in a Changing World,* 5th ed., p. 308. Copyright © 2012 by The McGraw-Hill Companies, Inc. Reprinted by permission of The McGraw-Hill Companies.

Now look at some sentences and the explanations of why each is a fact or an opinion.

Facts

- Regular physical activity that is performed on most days of the week reduces the risk of developing or dying from some of the leading causes of death in the U.S.
- It reduces the risk of dying prematurely. It reduces the risk of dying from heart disease.
- It reduces the risk of developing diabetes, high blood pressure, and colon cancer.
- It helps reduce blood pressure in people who already have high blood pressure.
- It helps control weight, and builds and maintains healthy bones, muscles, and joints.
- It helps older adults become stronger and better able to move about without falling.
- It promotes psychological well-being, and reduces feelings of depression and anxiety.

These statements represent facts because they can be confirmed by research.

Opinions

- There are so many health benefits of regular physical exercise that it is surprising not everyone engages in it.
- If you start exercising, you'll be hooked in no time.

These statements represent opinions. The first sentence includes the value word "surprising," which signals an opinion. The second sentence is an opinion because it talks about something that might happen in the future. Future events cannot be proved; therefore, they represent opinions.

EXERCISE 1

This paragraph comes from a computer science textbook. After you have read the paragraph, decide whether each statement that follows represents a fact or an opinion.

Imagine if you could store every conversation you ever had on a single disk. What if you could capture your entire life on video stored in just a few disks? What if you could hold in your pocket the contents of the Library of Congress? Innovations in secondary storage capacity using molecular storage seem to promise all this and more. Currently, information is stored on magnetic or optical disks. In the future, the electron state of atoms in a molecule will hold information at a much greater density. The capability to store vast amounts of data offers a future both tantalizing and problematic. How could you sort through so much material? Fortunately, computer scientists are developing computer programs that can rapidly sort through material.

Source: Adapted from Timothy O'Leary and Linda O'Leary, *Computing Essentials 2012: Making IT Work for You,* p. 45.
Copyright © 2012 by The McGraw-Hill Companies, Inc Reprinted by permission of The McGraw-Hill Companies.

Identify each of these statements from the excerpt as either a fact or an opinion. Write your answer in the space provided.

1. Innovations in secondary storage capacity using molecular storage seem to promise all this and more.

____

2. Currently, information is stored on magnetic or optical disks.

____

3. In the future, the electron state of atoms in a molecule will hold information at a much greater density.

____

4. The capability to store vast amounts of data offers a future both tantalizing and problematic.

____

5. Fortunately, computer scientists are developing computer programs that can rapidly sort through material.

____

____

WHAT ARE INFERENCES, AND WHY IS IT IMPORTANT TO MAKE THEM?

inference

A logical conclusion based on what an author has stated.

Comprehension Monitoring Question for Critically Evaluating Written Material by Going Beyond What Is Stated

What logical inference (conclusion) can I make based on what the author has stated?

In addition to distinguishing between facts and opinions, it is the responsibility of critical thinkers to make inferences about what they have read. An **inference** is a logical conclusion based on what an author has stated. In other words, a critical thinker understands not only what an author states directly but also what the author *suggests* or *implies.* Inferences go *beyond* what the author states, but they are always *based* on what the author has said. A logical *conclusion* is a decision that is reached after thoughtful consideration of information the author presents.

Because inferences go beyond what an author has stated directly, you cannot use as an inference information stated by the author. This is logical: If the author has already *stated* something, you cannot infer it. If the author has already stated something, you do not *need* to infer it.

Nor are you making an inference if you merely restate (paraphrase) information in the paragraph: You would simply be retelling information. For example, if the author states, "Superstorm Sandy was the largest, most destructive storm ever to hit the U.S.

East Coast," you cannot make the inference "It was a large, destructive storm." You *could,* however, make the inference "Superstorm Sandy caused billions of dollars of damage." This is a logical inference because Superstorm Sandy was so extremely large and destructive.

If you think critically as you read, you will ask yourself, "What logical inference or conclusion can I make based on what the author has stated?" Often, an author believes that the conclusion is obvious and does not state it directly. The author expects you to make the appropriate inference, that is, draw the logical conclusion.

To make an inference, the reader must *deduce,* or reason out, the author's meaning. You must use the evidence and information the author presents in order to arrive at the inference the author wants you to make. You must make the leap from what an author says to what the author wants you to conclude. Sometimes you conclude that the author wants you to believe or do something. For example, a writer might describe the benefits of regular exercise, yet not state directly, "You should exercise regularly." The author expects *you* to make the inference (draw the conclusion) that you should exercise regularly.

In Chapter 5 you learned to formulate implied main ideas. To formulate an implied main idea, you must make a logical inference. When authors *suggest* a main idea but do not state it directly, they are *implying* it. When readers correctly comprehend an implied main idea, they are *inferring* it. The writer implies the main idea; the reader infers it. Sometimes, formulating an implied main idea is the only inference you need to make about a passage.

Thinking critically, however, may involve making additional inferences. You can make inferences on the basis of longer passages as well as single paragraphs. And sometimes, of course, there are no inferences to be made about the material in a textbook passage. In this case, you need only to understand the topic, stated main idea, and supporting details.

Making inferences is actually something you do every day. In fact, you make them continually. Your ability to understand jokes and cartoons depends on your ability to make correct inferences. Sometimes, when a joke or a cartoon does not seem funny, it is because you did not make the right inference. (Look at the two cartoons on pages 500–501 and think about the inferences you must make to get each joke.) Every day you draw conclusions on the basis of descriptions, facts, opinions, experiences, and observations. Assume, for example, that another student in your class arrives late. Although he always brings his books to class, he does not have his book bag with him. He seems upset and frustrated, even angry. It would be a logical inference that something has happened to his book bag. He may have accidentally locked it in his car, left it on the bus, or even had it stolen when he momentarily left it unattended. These inferences are logical because they are based on your observations and the fact that he has always brought his book bag in the past. Therefore, it would *not* be logical to assume that he is upset and frustrated today because he broke up with his girlfriend or lost his job.

You also make inferences when you read. For instance, suppose that you wake up and find that your roommate has left you a note saying, "Hope you don't need your car this morning. I have to meet my history study group in the library at 8:00 A.M. I'll be back in time for you to make your 10 o'clock class." After reading the note, you would infer that your roommate is using your car. "I borrowed your car" is your roommate's *intended (implied) meaning,* even though this information is not stated in the note.

You can learn to make logical inferences by studying examples of correct inferences, such as the ones that follow. Here is an excerpt from a U.S. history textbook. It presents several details upon which certain inferences can be based. Its topic

MAKING INFERENCES
What inferences must you make to understand this cartoon and the one on the next page? In other words, what logical conclusions can you draw about what happened or what is going to happen?

THE FAR SIDE® By GARY LARSON

© 1980 FarWorks, Inc. All Rights Reserved/Dist. by Creators Syndicate

The Far Side® by Gary Larson, "Shark Attack"

is *witchcraft in colonial America.* Its main idea is the first sentence: *Colonial communities sometimes responded to assertive women with accusations of witchcraft.* After reading this excerpt, study the details in the paragraph and the logical inferences that are based on them.

Colonial communities sometimes responded to assertive women with accusations of witchcraft. Like most early Europeans during the late 1600s, New Englanders believed in wizards and witches, men and women who were said to acquire supernatural powers by signing a compact with Satan. A total of 344 New Englanders were charged with witchcraft during the first century of settlement. The notorious Salem village episode of 1692 produced the largest outpouring of accusations and 20 executions. More than three-quarters of all accused witches were women. These women were usually middle-aged and older, and most of those accused were regarded as unduly independent. Before they were charged with witchcraft, many had been suspected of heretical religious beliefs. Others were suspected of sexual impropriety. Still others had inherited property or stood to inherit property.

Source: James Davidson, William Geinapp, Christine Heyrman, Mark Lytle, and Michael Stoff, *Nation of Nations,* Vol. 1, 6th ed., p. 98. Copyright © 2008 by The McGraw-Hill Companies, Inc. Reprinted by permission of The McGraw-Hill Companies.

THE FAR SIDE® By GARY LARSON

© 1983 FarWorks, Inc. All Rights Reserved/Dist. by Creators Syndicate

The Far Side® by Gary Larson, "Missile Joke"

Reread these two supporting details from this paragraph:

- "More than three-quarters of all accused witches were women."
- "These women were usually middle-aged and older, and most of those accused were regarded as unduly independent."

Here are some logical inferences that are based on these two details:

- Men were not as likely to be accused of witchcraft.
- Girls and younger women were not as likely to be accused of witchcraft.
- Nonassertive, nonindependent women were not as likely to be accused of witchcraft.

Notice that none of these things is stated in the details, but they are logical conclusions based on what was stated.

Reread these other supporting details from this paragraph:

- "Before they were charged with witchcraft, many women had been suspected of heretical religious beliefs."
- "Others were suspected of sexual impropriety."
- "Still others had inherited property or stood to inherit property."

Here are some logical inferences that are based on these three details:

- Some of the women accused of witchcraft were really being persecuted for other, unrelated reasons.
- Some women were accused of witchcraft because someone wanted to gain control of property they had inherited or were about to inherit.

Again, notice that although these things are not stated in the paragraph, they are logical conclusions.

EXERCISE 2

This paragraph comes from an American history textbook. After you have read the paragraph, study the details listed below it so that you can make logical inferences based on them.

> Colonial women suffered legal disadvantages. In 1690, English common law and colonial legal codes allowed married women no control over property. Wives could not sue or be sued. They could not make contracts. They surrendered to their husbands any property they possessed before marriage. Divorce was almost impossible to obtain until the late eighteenth century. Only widows and a few single women had the same property rights as men, but they could not vote in colony elections.
>
> *Source:* Adapted from James Davidson, William Geinapp, Christine Heyrman, Mark Lytle, and Michael Stoff, *Nation of Nations, Vol. 1,* 6th ed., p. 96. Copyright © 2008 by The McGraw-Hill Companies, Inc. Reprinted by permission of The McGraw-Hill Companies.

Here are the six supporting details that are presented in the passage. Reread them, then make logical inferences based on them.

- "English common law and colonial legal codes allowed married women no control over property."
- "Wives could not sue or be sued."
- "They could not make contracts."
- "They surrendered to their husbands any property they possessed before marriage."
- "Divorce was almost impossible to obtain until the late eighteenth century."
- "Only widows and a few single women had the same property rights as men, but they could not vote in colony elections."

1. Write one logical inference about the legal rights and property rights of colonial *men:*

____

____

____

____

2. Write one logical inference about the *number* of colonial women who owned property:

____

____

____

____

3. Write one logical inference about the legal rights of colonial women compared with the legal rights of American women *today:*

___

___

___

___

___

When you read, ask yourself, "Based on what the author has stated, what inference (logical conclusion) can I make?"

The skills of identifying facts and opinions, as well as making inferences (drawing logical conclusions), complement the critical reading skills you learned in the previous chapter. The box below contains the same review of an imaginary album that you read in Chapter 8. Notice, however, that the critical thinking skills presented in this chapter have been added.

EXAMPLE OF CRITICAL READING AND THINKING SKILLS APPLIED TO A CRITIC'S REVIEW OF AN ALBUM

The controversial group The Gate Crashers has just released its first album, *The Gate Crashers—Live!* Is it worth buying? That depends: Are you put off by vulgar lyrics that glorify violence? Do you mind listening to painfully bad hip-hop musicians? Do you have any problem sitting through twelve tracks (47 excruciating minutes!) of mind-numbing noise? If not, then you'll surely want to add *The Gate Crashers—Live!* to your collection.

Questions	Answers
What is the author's purpose?	To persuade readers not to buy this new album
Who is the author's intended audience?	People who buy music albums
What is the author's point of view?	*The Gate Crashers —Live!* album is awful.*
What is the author's tone?	Sarcastic
Does the author include facts, opinions, or both?	Both facts and opinions
What inference (logical conclusion) does the author expect you to make?	Buying this album would be a waste of money because you would not like it.

*Notice that this is also the author's main idea, or "argument."

By distinguishing facts from opinions, and by making logical inferences about what you have read, you will be a more critical reader and will evaluate written material more skillfully.

Copyright © 2014 The McGraw-Hill Companies, Inc. All rights reserved.

OTHER THINGS TO KEEP IN MIND WHEN THINKING CRITICALLY

Here are three helpful things you should keep in mind about thinking critically:

1. **Facts and opinions may or may not appear together.**
   - Some paragraphs contain facts *only* or opinions *only*.
   - Some paragraphs consist of *both* facts and opinions.
   - Sometimes facts and opinions are presented in the *same sentence*. For example, consider the sentence "Sidney Smith would make an excellent senator because he has eight years' experience in the House of Representatives." The first part of the sentence presents an opinion: "Sidney Smith would make an excellent senator." The last part presents a fact: "He has eight years' experience in the House of Representatives."
2. **Authors sometimes present opinions in such a way that they *appear* to be facts.**

   An author may intentionally present opinions in ways that make them *appear* to be facts. For example, a writer might introduce an opinion by stating, "*The fact is . . .* " ("The fact is, you need a college degree to get a job in the computer industry.") Stating that something is a fact, however, does not make it a fact. (There are many different jobs in the computer industry. Not all of them require a college degree.)

   Ideally, of course, authors would always express opinions in ways that make it clear that they are opinions. ("In this writer's opinion, you need a college degree to get a job in the computer industry.") But authors do not always do this, and it is your job to think critically and distinguish between facts and opinions. Remember, when you identify an opinion, you should always determine whether or not it is well supported.
3. **Other critical thinking skills, such as *recognizing propaganda devices* and *recognizing fallacies,* can also be used to evaluate written material.**

   You should be aware that, although a full discussion of them is beyond the scope of this textbook, there are additional critical thinking skills that can be used to evaluate written material. These include:
   - Recognizing *propaganda* techniques (such as appeals to emotions, "bandwagoning," presenting either-or false choices, overgeneralizations, appeals to authority, testimonials and endorsements, and "stacking the deck").
   - Recognizing *fallacies* (implausible arguments using false or invalid inferences).

   Here is a brief overview of propaganda devices along with an exercise.

Propaganda Devices

Writers want readers to believe what they say, and sometimes they resort to propaganda devices to try to accomplish this. **Propaganda devices** are techniques authors use to unfairly influence the reader to accept their point of view. "Unfairly" means that propaganda techniques are intended to mislead readers, obscure the truth, or dodge the issue.

Propaganda is designed to manipulate. Some propaganda devices appeal to emotion. Other types rely on flawed reasoning to mislead and manipulate readers. These techniques are often used in advertisements, editorials, and political campaigns.

Columnist and author William Vaughan once observed, "There's a mighty big difference between good, sound reasons and reasons that sound good." If you become aware of these techniques and read critically, you can avoid falling for "reasons that sound good." When you are reading, ask yourself, "Has the author tried to unfairly influence me to accept his or her point of view?"

Now read about these types of propaganda devices, with examples of each.

Circular reasoning. The author restates the argument or conclusion as the truth without ever presenting any evidence or real support. This is also called *circular thinking* or *begging the question* because the author, like a beggar, asks for something (that you accept his or her point of view), but gives nothing (in this case, no proof) in return. The author's premises include the claim that the conclusion is already true (so there is no need to provide proof or support for it).

Examples

- "City College is the best place to start college because there's no place better to begin."
- "You can improve your health by making healthier lifestyle choices."
- "If he were not an effective manager, he would not have been promoted to manager."

Either-or. The author puts everything in one of two mutually exclusive categories and acts as if there are no other possibilities besides one or the other. In other words, the author acts as if there are only two choices when in reality there are other possibilities.

Examples

- "America: Love it or leave it."
- "Either get an education or have an unfulfilling life."
- "Are you among the sophisticated people who drink Bubblemore Champagne or simply an ordinary beer drinker?"

Non sequitur. The author links two ideas or events that are not related; one does not follow from the other.

Examples

- "You should turn your TV off when it rains. This morning it rained, and after that my TV stopped working."
- "Maria is wonderful at creative writing and tennis. She'll probably own her own company someday."

Hasty generalization. The author jumps to a conclusion that is based on insufficient proof or evidence.

Examples

- "Forty students polled at the university believe current gun control laws are insufficient. It's clear that today's college students believe the country needs stronger gun control legislation."
- "Yesterday I was nearly run off the road by a truck driver. Truck drivers are reckless."

Appeals to emotion. The author appeals to readers' emotions (such as fear, guilt, sympathy, pity, hate) rather than to reason.

Examples

- "Don't risk your family's life! Install an XYZ Burglar Alarm System today!" (*fear*)
- "Now that you're working, you're embarrassed by your tattoos. Ask your dermatologist about the Laser-Rite tattoo removal procedure." (*embarrassment*)
- "Think how smart you'll look when you drive up in your new hybrid Prius!" (*pride; vanity*)
- "Hundreds of abandoned, neglected, and unwanted pets are waiting for loving homes. Call your local animal shelter and adopt a pet today." (*sympathy; pity*)

Red herring. The author presents an irrelevant issue to draw the reader's attention away from the central issue. The name comes from a trick used to throw hunting dogs off the scent of the track: drag a red herring (a strong-smelling fish) across his tracks.

Examples

- "This issue isn't about homeowners' rights; it's actually about whether we're going to allow the city council to tell us how to run our lives."

(continued on next page)

Copyright © 2014 The McGraw-Hill Companies, Inc. All rights reserved.

- "It is often said that many mathematicians and scientists do not write very well, but think about how hard they had to work to become trained in their fields."

Post hoc. The author implies that because one event happened before another, it caused the second event.

Examples

- "After I took Cold-Away tablets, I began to feel better. Cold-Away really works!" (*Maybe it was because time went by or the person got more rest, or perhaps there was some other reason.*)
- "If the troops hadn't ignored the omen of the comet the night before, they would have won the battle." (*The outcome of the battle was not determined by the appearance of a comet.*)

Ad hominem. The author attacks the person rather than the arguments, views, or ideas the person presents.

Examples

- "How can we expect the candidate to be an effective senator when he's had two failed marriages?"
- "The mayor is a liar. How can we believe anything she promises about improving our public schools?"

Bandwagon. The author says that "everyone" believes, accepts, or does what he is describing, and therefore, the reader should also "get on the bandwagon." This is similar to peer pressure; it appeals to people's desire to be part of the crowd and like everyone else. The fact that something is widely accepted does not means it is true.

Examples

- "Join the thousands of Americans who have tripled their income with this simple at-home business. Call today for information about how you, too, can become a successful business owner."
- "All true patriots will urge their government representatives to support the new reform bill."
- "He's the best player in the NFL. Everyone knows that."

Hypostatization. The author treats an abstract concept as if it is a concrete reality.

Examples

- "History has taught us that as long as there are people there will be wars."
- "Government pokes its nose into every aspect of our lives. We have to protect our privacy from this intrusive monster."

False analogy. The author makes a comparison that is either inaccurate or inappropriate. Also called *faulty analogy.*

Examples

- "If the city can prohibit us from talking on cell phones while driving, they are just as likely to prohibit us from listening to the radio while driving."
- "You can't make an omelet without breaking some eggs, and we can't reduce the crime rate without coming down hard on criminals."
- "It's obvious that movie stars are nothing more than spoiled, self-centered children."

Transfer. The author transfers the good or bad qualities of one person or thing to another to influence the reader's perception of that person or thing.

Examples

- "He has Jay Leno's sense of humor."
- "This is the kind of project Mother Teresa would have supported."

Plain folks. The author appeals to readers by presenting himself or herself as someone who is just like the readers.

Examples

- "Wealthy people may spend their weekends at their country homes. For the rest of us, there's our back yard. Call Lawn Delight for a consultation about how to transform your back yard into your own little piece of heaven."
- "Crunch-It cereal: No fancy packaging. No exotic ingredients you can't pronounce. No inflated prices. Just plain, good food from a hometown company that takes pride in its products."

Sweeping generalization. The author presents a broad (general) statement that goes far beyond the evidence. (*Stereotyping* is one form of sweeping generalization.)

Examples

- "Student athletes do not excel in academics."
- "Women are too emotional to make good decisions."
- "Men would rather sit and watch television than do anything else."

Straw man. The author misrepresents what an opponent believes, and then attacks that belief.

Examples

- "The senator says that he favors a tax cut, but he has supported numerous spending bills. During these times of economic stress, it's wrong for members of Congress to keep spending money so freely."
- "My professor counts off for late homework. Obviously, he doesn't care about whether or not students are learning. He should be fired and replaced with a faculty member who cares about student success."

Appeal to authority. The author tries to influence the reader to accept his or her argument or point of view by citing some authority who believes it.

Examples

- "To treat occasional heartburn, eight out of ten doctors recommend Acid-Stop."
- "Dr. Milton Vosky, a researcher at Crumpfield University, believes that text messaging and tweeting cause deterioration in students' ability to spell English words properly."

Testimonial. A famous person endorses an idea or a project in order to influence others to believe or buy it. The person's endorsement may mean nothing, since he or she may have no special knowledge about it or even any experience with it. Also called *endorsement.*

Examples

- "As a model, I'm often in front of the camera. Soft Touch soap leaves my skin looking younger than ever. It'll do the same for you. Try it and see the difference in just two weeks."
- "Top athletes like Michael Jordan depend on Nike shoes to help make them winners."

Copyright © 2014 The McGraw-Hill Companies, Inc. All rights reserved.

EXERCISE 3

Propaganda Devices

Directions: Read each sentence and circle the letter that answers the question.

1. Talking on the cell phone while driving endangers your life and the lives of others.

In the sentence above, is the author's argument logically valid or invalid?
a. valid
b. invalid

2. More women than men develop breast cancer. If either of my parents develops this form of cancer, my mother is more likely to develop it than my father is.

In the sentence above, is the author's argument logically valid or invalid?
a. valid
b. invalid

3. Some college athletes become professional athletes who are paid millions of dollars a year. Because they grew up in poverty, they will not be able to manage their financial affairs wisely once they become wealthy.

In the sentence above, is the author's argument logically valid or invalid?
a. valid
b. invalid

4. The pond is covered with ice. All ice melts when warmed sufficiently. When the weather becomes warm enough, the ice on the pond will melt.

In the sentence above, is the author's argument logically valid or invalid?
a. valid
b. invalid

5. My sister has been coughing since last night. Either she has allergies or she's coming down with the flu.

Which of the following fallacies does the author use in an effort to support the argument?
a. circular thinking
b. either-or
c. non sequitur
d. hasty generalization

6. Four of my teenage son's friends have gotten speeding tickets or been involved in traffic accidents. The high school's driver education course is not doing a good job of preparing young people to drive.

Which of the following fallacies does the author use in an effort to support the argument?
a. circular thinking
b. either-or
c. non sequitur
d. hasty generalization

7. Astrological horoscopes are scientifically based. After all, most major newspapers and popular magazines publish horoscopes. They wouldn't publish horoscopes if astrology weren't an accurate, reliable way of predicting people's futures.

Which of the following fallacies does the author use in an effort to support the argument?

a. circular thinking
b. either-or
c. non sequitur
d. hasty generalization

8. Bob majored in computer science. That must be why he has such a high-paying job.

Which of the following fallacies does the author use in an effort to support the argument?

a. circular thinking
b. either-or
c. non sequitur
d. hasty generalization

Copyright © 2014 The McGraw-Hill Companies, Inc. All rights reserved.

CHAPTER 9 CHECKPOINT
Thinking Critically

Directions: Read each paragraph and then answer the critical thinking questions that follow.

Many Americans have been seduced by fad diets, investing hope only to harvest frustration. The Atkins diet is the fad diet most have tried—*Dr. Atkins' Diet Revolution* is one of the 10 top-selling books in history, and was (and is) prominently displayed in bookstores. The reason this diet doesn't deliver on its promise of pain-free weight loss is well understood by science, but not the general public. Only hope and hype make it a perpetual bestseller.

_______ **1.** Is the last sentence of the paragraph ("Only hope and hype make it a perpetual bestseller") a *fact* or an *opinion*?

a. fact

b. opinion

_______ **2.** Which of the following is a logical *inference* about sales of *Dr. Atkins' Diet Revolution*?

a. Sales began declining a decade ago.

b. Booksellers push the book because they receive kickbacks from the publisher.

c. Sales are likely to continue until the public understands the diet is not based on scientific information.

d. In the United States, diet books are the all-time best-selling category of books.

The secret of the Atkins diet, simply stated, is to avoid carbohydrates. Those who try the Atkins diet often lose weight in two or three weeks. In three months it's all back, and then some. So what happened? The temporary weight loss turns out to have a simple explanation. Carbohydrates act as water sponges in your body, and so forcing your body to become depleted of carbohydrates causes your body to lose water. The 10 pounds lost on this diet was not fat weight but water weight, quickly regained with the first starchy foods eaten.

_______ **3.** Is the second sentence of the paragraph ("Those who try the Atkins diet often lose weight in two or three weeks") a *fact* or an *opinion*?

a. fact

b. opinion

_______ **4.** Based on information in the paragraph, which of the following is a reasonable *conclusion*?

a. Eliminating carbohydrates is not an effective way to lose weight permanently.

b. The Atkins diet is a good choice for people who want to lose weight quickly and permanently.

c. People on the Atkins diet should limit the amount of water they drink.

d. Fat-weight loss and water-weight loss are equally good ways to lose weight.

The Atkins diet is the sort of diet the American Heart Association tells us to avoid because of all those saturated fats and cholesterol. It is also difficult to stay on. If you do hang in there, you will lose weight, simply because you eat less. Other popular diets these days, *The Zone* diet of Dr. Barry Sears and *The South Beach Diet* of Dr. Arthur Agatston, are also low-carbohydrate diets, although not as extreme as the Atkins diet. Like the Atkins diet, they work not for the bizarre reasons claimed by the promoters, but simply because they are low-calorie diets.

_______ **5.** Is the first sentence of the paragraph ("The Atkins diet is the sort of diet the American Heart Association tells us to avoid because of all those saturated fats and cholesterol") a *fact* or an *opinion*?

a. fact

b. opinion

_______ **6.** Based on information in the paragraph, which of the following is a reasonable *conclusion*?

a. The Atkins, Zone, and South Beach diets are all effective approaches to losing weight.

b. All low-carbohydrate diets are created by doctors.

c. Regarding weight loss, doctors know best.

d. The Zone and South Beach diets may be easier to stay on than the Atkins diet.

Even when you try to lose weight by exercising and eating less, your body will attempt to compensate by metabolizing more efficiently. It has a fixed weight, what researchers call a "set point," a weight to which it will keep trying to return. A few years ago, a group of researchers at Rockefeller University in New York, in a landmark study, found that if you lose weight, your metabolism slows down and becomes more efficient, burning fewer calories to do the same work. In short, your body will do everything it can to gain the weight back. Similarly, if you gain weight, your metabolism speeds up. In this way your body uses its own natural weight control system to keep your weight at its set point. No wonder it's hard to lose weight!

_______ **7.** Is the last sentence of the paragraph ("No wonder it's hard to lose weight!") a *fact* or an *opinion*?

a. fact

b. opinion

_______ **8.** Based on information in the paragraph, which of the following is a logical *inference*?

a. Weight and metabolism are unrelated.

b. The body's set point makes it difficult to change the body's weight permanently.

c. It is harder for an overweight person to lose weight than for an underweight person to gain weight.

d. Rockefeller University researchers are the most respected researchers in the country.

Copyright © 2014 The McGraw-Hill Companies, Inc. All rights reserved.

This doesn't mean that we should give up and learn to love our fat. Rather, now that we are beginning to understand the biology of weight gain, we must recognize that we cannot beat the requirements of the two diet laws: eat less and exercise more. The real trick is not to give up. Eat less and exercise more, and keep at it. In one year, or two, or three, your body will readjust its set point to reflect the new reality you have imposed by constant struggle. There simply isn't any easy way to lose weight.

______ **9.** Is the second sentence of the paragraph ("Rather, now that we are beginning to understand the biology of weight gain, we must recognize that we cannot beat the requirements of the two diet laws: exercise more and eat less") a *fact* or an *opinion*?

a. fact

b. opinion

______ **10.** Based on information in the paragraph, which of the following is a reasonable *conclusion*?

a. Learning to love our fat would reduce our frustration with dieting.

b. Realistically, the average person might as well give up trying to lose weight: it's simply too difficult and frustrating.

c. Weight loss is possible, but it takes time, effort, and commitment.

d. Science has made progress in understanding the biology of weight gain.

Source: George Johnson, "Fad Diets and Impossible Dreams," *The Living World,* 7th ed., p. 149. Copyright © 2012 by The McGraw-Hill Companies, Inc. Reprinted by permission of The McGraw-Hill Companies.

CHAPTER REVIEW CARDS

Directions: Complete the chapter review cards for Chapter 9 by answering the questions or following the directions on each card.

Thinking Critically to Evaluate Written Material

1. What is the definition of *thinking critically*?

2. Why is it important to be able to think critically?

Card 1 Chapter 9: Thinking Critically

Copyright © 2014 The McGraw-Hill Companies, Inc. All rights reserved.

Facts and Opinions

1. What is the definition of a *fact*?

2. What is the definition of an *opinion*?

3. List in order the three questions you should ask yourself to distinguish between facts and opinions.

Card 2 Chapter 9: Thinking Critically

Opinions

1. List at least five *words or phrases* that authors use to indicate that they are presenting an opinion.

2. List at least five *value judgment words* that indicate an opinion is being presented.

Card 3 Chapter 9: Thinking Critically

Making Logical Inferences

1. What is an *inference*?

2. Why is it not an inference if a reader simply copies or paraphrases information that the author states?

Card 4 Chapter 9: Thinking Critically

Things to Keep in Mind When Thinking Critically

List the three additional things you should keep in mind when thinking critically.

1.

2.

3.

Define propaganda devices and fallacies.

Card 5 Chapter 9: Thinking Critically

Copyright © 2014 The McGraw-Hill Companies, Inc. All rights reserved.

TEST YOUR UNDERSTANDING
Thinking Critically: Fact and Opinion

Review: **Critical thinking** means thinking in an organized way about material that you have read in order to evaluate it accurately. Critical thinking simply means applying certain reading and thinking skills in a systematic, thorough way. In other words, critical thinking means consistently asking certain additional questions and applying logic when you read. Like critical reading skills, critical thinking skills are *interrelated.* An author's purpose causes him or her to present certain *facts or opinions.*

- **Distinguishing facts from opinions:** A **fact** is something that can be proved to exist or have happened. An **opinion** is a judgment or belief that cannot be proved or disproved. To determine whether statements in written material are facts or opinions, ask yourself, "Can the information the author presents be proved, or does it represent a judgment?"

EXAMPLE

The excerpt below is from a government textbook. Its topic is *Constitution and Citizenship Day,* or *celebrating our Constitution.* The main idea is *Although Congress passed legislation for Constitution and Citizenship Day for public institutions that receive federal funds, Americans don't need a special day to remind them of their Constitutional heritage: Millions practice it every day.* Read the paragraph below to see how the information you learned in this chapter can be used to think critically. Read the explanation that is given for the correct answers. Then distinguish between facts and opinions by asking yourself, "Can the information the author presents be proved, or does it represent a judgment?"

In 2004, Congress passed legislation requiring public institutions that receive federal funds to set aside September 17, the anniversary of the signing of the Constitution, as Constitution and Citizenship Day. On this day, educators are required to conduct programs designed to commemorate the legacy of our founding document. Americans, however, don't need a special day to remind them of their Constitutional heritage. Millions practice it every day. We celebrate our Constitution every time we write our senators and representatives about some important issue, read press accounts of current events, attend religious services, donate money to a political cause or candidate, engage in political debate in the classroom or make a donation to an interest group. All of these activities are enshrined in our Constitution.

Source: Joseph Losco and Ralph Baker, *Am Gov 2011,* p. 36. Copyright © 2011 by The McGraw-Hill Companies, Inc. Reprinted by permission of The McGraw-Hill Companies.

__c__ Which of the following statements represents an opinion?

a. In 2004, Congress passed legislation requiring public institutions that receive federal funds to set aside September 17, the anniversary of the signing of the Constitution, as Constitution and Citizenship Day.

b. On this day, educators are required to conduct programs designed to commemorate the legacy of our founding document.

c. Americans, however, don't need a special day to remind them of their Constitutional heritage.

d. All of these activities are enshrined in our Constitution.

Explanation: The correct answer is c. Research could confirm the information in answers *a, b,* and *d.* Answer *c* represents an opinion. There is no way to prove it. Also, the word "special" indicates it is an opinion: People would disagree as to what "special" means.

Copyright © 2014 The McGraw-Hill Companies, Inc. All rights reserved.

Directions: Read each paragraph carefully. Then answer the question, "Which of the following statements is an *opinion*?" or "Which of the following statements is a *fact*?" (Refer to the chart on page 496 as you evaluate the answer choices.)

1. This paragraph comes from a human development textbook.

On the average, a full-term newborn is between 19 and 22 inches long and weighs 5½ to 9½ pounds. Many newborns give the appearance of a defeated prizefighter. They often have a puffy bluish-red face, a broad, flat nose, swollen eyelids, and ears skewed at odd angles. Their heads are often misshapen and elongated. In most infants the chin recedes and the lower jaw is underdeveloped. Bowleggedness is the rule, and the feet might be pigeon-toed.

Source: Adapted from James Vander Zanden, revised by Thomas Crandell and Corinne Crandell, *Human Development.* Updated 7th ed., p. 115. Copyright © 2003 by The McGraw-Hill Companies, Inc. Reprinted by permission of The McGraw-Hill Companies.

________ Which of the following statements is an *opinion*?

a. On the average, a full-term newborn is between 19 and 22 inches long and weighs 5½ to 9½ pounds.

b. Many newborns give the appearance of a defeated prizefighter.

c. Their heads are often misshapen and elongated.

d. In most infants, the chin recedes and the lower jaw is underdeveloped.

2. This paragraph comes from a public speaking textbook.

Global plagiarism is stealing your speech entirely from another source and passing it off as your own. The most blatant—and unforgivable—kind of plagiarism, it is grossly unethical. Global plagiarism in a college classroom usually occurs because a student puts off the assignment until the last minute. Then, in an act of desperation, the student downloads a speech from the Internet or gets one written by a friend and delivers it as his or her own. The best way to avoid this, of course, is not to leave your speech until the last minute. If, for some reason, you fail to get your speech ready on time, do not succumb to the lure of plagiarism. Whatever the penalty you suffer from being late will pale in comparison with the consequences if you are caught plagiarizing.

Source: Adapted from Stephen Lucas, *The Art of Public Speaking,* 10th ed., p. 38. Copyright © 2009 by The McGraw-Hill Companies, Inc. Reprinted by permission of The McGraw-Hill Companies.

________ Which of the following statements is a *fact*?

a. Global plagiarism is stealing your speech entirely from another source and passing it off as your own.

b. The most blatant—and unforgivable—kind of plagiarism, it is grossly unethical.

c. If, for some reason, you fail to get your speech ready on time, do not succumb to the lure of plagiarism.

d. Whatever the penalty you suffer from being late will pale in comparison with the consequences if you are caught plagiarizing.

3. This paragraph comes from a political science textbook.

Media has undergone an interesting change. Traditional news outlets such as newspapers, magazines, radio, and television, aimed to broadcast the news to large numbers of people at once. Today's abundance of media sources has led to "narrowcasting"—that is, targeting news to individuals who choose only programming that really interests them. Today's media are characterized by declining interest in traditional news sources. This worries some observers, who wonder how the young can fulfill their citizenship responsibilities without getting the news in the same way as their parents and grandparents.

Source: Adapted from Joseph Losco and Ralph Baker, *Am Gov 2011,* p. 233. Copyright © 2011 by The McGraw-Hill Companies, Inc. Reprinted by permission of The McGraw-Hill Companies.

_______ Which of the following statements is an *opinion*?

a. Media has undergone an interesting change.

b. Traditional news outlets such as newspapers, magazines, radio, and television, aimed to broadcast the news to large numbers of people at once.

c. Today's abundance of media sources has led to "narrowcasting"—that is, targeting news to individuals who choose only programming that really interests them.

d. This worries some observers, who wonder how the young can fulfill their citizenship responsibilities without getting the news in the same way as their parents and grandparents.

4. This paragraph comes from an information technology textbook.

E-mail is the transmission of electronic messages over the Internet. All you need to send and receive e-mail is a computer with an Internet connection and an e-mail account. There are two basic types of e-mail accounts: client based and Web based. For individual use, Webmail is more widely used because you can access your e-mail from any computer anywhere that has Internet access. E-mail can be a convenient asset in your personal and professional life.

_______ Which of the following statements is an *opinion*?

a. E-mail is the transmission of electronic messages over the Internet.

b. All you need to send and receive e-mail is a computer with an Internet connection and an e-mail account.

c. There are two basic types of e-mail accounts: client based and Web based.

d. E-mail can be a convenient asset in your personal and professional life.

5. This paragraph comes from an information technology textbook.

It is important that you learn how computer technology is being used within your profession. Every field has trade journals, whether the field is interior design, personnel management, or advertising. Most such journals regularly present articles about the uses of computers. It's important that you also belong to a trade or industry association and go to its meetings. Many associations sponsor seminars and conferences that describe the latest information and techniques.

Source: Adapted from Timothy O'Leary and Linda O'Leary, *Computing Essentials 2012: Making IT Work for You*, pp. 334–35. Copyright © 2012 by The McGraw-Hill Companies, Inc. Reprinted by permission of The McGraw-Hill Companies.

_______ Which of the following statements is an *opinion*?

a. It is important that you learn how computer technology is being used within your profession.

b. Every field has trade journals, whether the field is interior design, personnel management, or advertising.

c. Most such journals regularly present articles about the uses of computers.

d. Many associations sponsor seminars and conferences that describe the latest information and techniques.

Copyright © 2014 The McGraw-Hill Companies, Inc. All rights reserved.

Review: **Critical thinking** means thinking in an organized way about material that you have read in order to evaluate it accurately. Critical thinking simply means applying certain reading and thinking skills in a systematic, thorough way. In other words, critical thinking means consistently asking certain additional questions and applying logic when you read. Like critical reading skills, critical thinking skills are *interrelated.* An author's purpose causes him or her to present certain *facts or opinions.* This allows readers to *make logical inferences* based on what the author has stated.

- **Making logical inferences:** An **inference** is a logical conclusion that is based on what an author has stated. A **conclusion** is a decision that is reached after thoughtful consideration of information the author presents. After you read, you should ask yourself, "What logical inference can I make, based on what the author has stated?"

EXAMPLE

The excerpt below is from a business textbook. Its topic is *flextime.* The main idea is *Flextime is a program that allows employees to choose their starting and ending times, as long as they are at work during a specified core period.* As you read the paragraph, ask yourself the comprehension monitoring question "Based on what the authors have stated, what logical inference can I make?"

> **Flextime** is a program that allows employees to choose their starting and ending times, as long as they are at work during a specified core period. It does not reduce the total number of hours that employees work. Instead, it gives employees more flexibility in choosing which hours they work. A firm may specify that employees must be present from 10:00 A.M. to 3:00 P.M. One employee may choose to come in at 7:00 A.M. and leave at the end of the core time.
>
> *Source:* O. C. Ferrell, Geoffrey Hirt, and Linda Ferrell, *Business: A Changing World,* 8th ed., p. 286. Copyright © 2011 by The McGraw-Hill Companies, Inc. Reprinted by permission of The McGraw-Hill Companies.

Even though an employee's eight-hour shift must include the company's core period, *who can you infer might appreciate having flexibility in choosing his or her own starting and quitting times?*

- An employee who wants to be home with children in the morning and be able to drop them at day care or at school
- A parent who wants to be home when children get out of school
- A "morning person" who prefers an early start
- A person who is working two jobs
- A person who wants to leave at the end of the core time to take classes at a nearby college

Explanation: These inferences are logical: They are based on information given in the paragraph, but they go beyond what is stated in it.

Directions: Read each paragraph and make a logical inference. The italicized words tell what your inference should be about. Remember that you cannot use a sentence from the paragraph (or a restatement of it) as your inference. Your inference must be a logical conclusion

Copyright © 2011 The McGraw-Hill Companies, Inc. All rights reserved.

based on information stated in the paragraph, however. Write your answers in the spaces provided.

1. The excerpt below is from a business textbook.

The Malcolm Baldrige National Quality Awards set the standard for quality in manufacturing, services, small business, education, and health care. Applying organizations must show quality in seven key areas. The focus is not only on quality, but also on providing top quality customer services in all respects. In 2005, Richland College, in Dallas, Texas, was the first community college to receive a Baldrige Award. With over 20,000 students, Richland reduced its operational costs while improving services and implementing stakeholder listening services to measure satisfaction. Seven years later, it remains the only community college to attain this prestigious award.

Source: Adapted from William Nickels, James McHugh, and Susan McHugh, *Understanding Business*, 9th ed., p. 245. Copyright © 2010 by The McGraw-Hill Companies, Inc. Reprinted by permission of The McGraw-Hill Companies.

What can you infer about *how difficult it is for a college to attain the Baldrige Award*?

____

____

2. This is the type of passage that might appear in a textbook on child development.

Most smokers begin using cigarettes during early adolescence. Repeatedly seeing smokers in movies can be particularly influential in adolescents' decisions. Filmmakers put a disproportional emphasis on smoking. Young adolescents often favor white male antagonists in the movies—the characters most likely to smoke. Moreover, these preteens see many attractive film characters who smoke.

Based on information in the passage, what can you infer about *what filmmakers could do to help prevent adolescents from starting to smoke*?

____

____

3. This is the type of passage that might appear in a marketing textbook.

For obvious reasons, a brand name should be simple, such as Tide detergent or Puffs tissues, and emotional, such as Joy dishwashing detergent or Passion perfume. When companies develop product names for international use, it is often helpful to have a nonmeaningful brand name. For example, a name such as Exxon does not have any undesirable associations in any country or language. One company learned this the hard way. The soft drink 7Up translated in the local dialect of Shanghai, China, as "death through drinking"—hardly a help to sales!

Based on information in the passage, what can you infer about *choosing a brand name for a product*?

____

____

4. This is the type of passage that might appear in a marketing textbook.

Duke University has installed 5000 low-water-flow showerheads for faculty, staff, and off-campus students (who shower after P.E. classes or after bicycling or walking to campus) and 1000 of these showerheads in residence halls. It is estimated these showerheads will save Duke 7300 gallons of water annually. At Princeton, older toilets are being replaced with dual-flush ones that use less water for liquid waste and more for solid waste. By 2020, Princeton aims to decrease per capita water usage up to 25 percent of its current levels. Cuyamaca College is promoting water conservation in the southern California landscape through exhibits and programs that educate and inspire the public. Their five-acre garden showcases water-conservation, as well as how-to displays, such as mulch and irrigation exhibits.

Source: Adapted from Eldon Enger and Bradley Smith, *Environmental Science: A Study of Interrelationships,* 12th ed., p. 282. Copyright © 2010 by The McGraw-Hill Companies. Reprinted by permission of The McGraw-Hill Companies.

Based on information in the passage, what can you infer about *water conservation efforts at colleges and universities*?

____

____

5. This passage is from a government textbook.

Today, survey research is everywhere. Hardly a day goes by when we do not hear about one survey or another regarding almost every aspect of life, from health care to fashion to politics. Survey research can aid in making life more enjoyable and interesting. However, it can also be used to manipulate consumer and voter preferences and behavior.

Source: Joseph Losco and Ralph Baker, *Am Gov 2011,* p. 129. Copyright © 2011 by The McGraw-Hill Companies, Inc. Reprinted by permission of The McGraw-Hill Companies.

Based on information in the passage, what can you infer about *consumers, voters, and survey research*?

____

____

SELECTION **9.1**

Marriage and Family

Taboos and Myths about Conflict and Anger

From *Marriages and Families: Intimacy, Diversity, and Strengths*
By David Olson, John DeFrain, and Linda Skogrand

The authors of this selection point out that, "In life, intimacy and conflict are bound together. There is the difficult balance between love and anger, the dance of anger that couples and families perform, and the sources of conflict in intimate relationships. This is only natural: the more a person knows about another person, the more possibilities there are for disagreement and dislike. If a relationship is to survive and thrive, each of these differences has to be worked out in some way. Folk wisdom tells us that 'you always hurt the ones you love.'" Perhaps, but understanding conflict and anger can minimize this.

Do you and someone you are close to—a family member or your best friend, for example—ever get angry with each other? Have you ever had a truly heated, angry exchange with that person? Does it happen very often? How did you feel about the fact that you became angry? How did you feel afterward? What was the effect on the relationship?

A taboo *is something that is avoided (or even forbidden) by social custom or because it is intensely disliked for emotional reasons. As used in the following selection, a* myth *is a popular belief. This marriage and family textbook excerpt discusses taboos and myths related to anger and conflict. Read it to see if you perhaps have some of these attitudes and beliefs, and to learn some facts about the true nature of anger.*

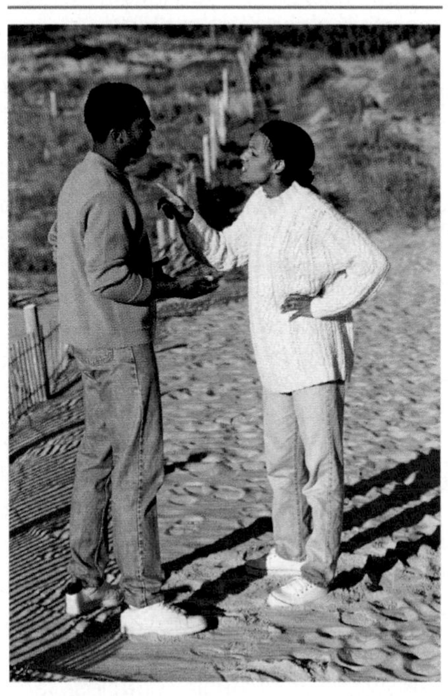

Anger and Conflict Taboos

1 Most couples are afraid of negative emotions—anger, resentment, jealousy, bitterness, hurt, disgust, and hatred—and have a difficult time learning how to deal with them. A common tactic is to suppress negative emotions, hoping they will disappear with time. There are two predominant reasons for suppressing negative emotions. One is sociological in nature; the other is psychological.

2 Our culture and many others have a taboo against the expression of anger. This message, transmitted verbally and nonverbally from generation to generation, says that nice and competent people do not show anger, that anger is wrong, and that anger indicates that something is terribly wrong in a relationship. This message requires individuals to deny their genuine feelings and keeps them from being in touch with their true emotions. Repressed anger can lead to high levels of stress for individuals and their relationships.

3 The psychological reason for suppressing negative emotions has to do with human insecurity. Individuals think, "If I let other people know what I am really thinking and who

Annotation Practice Exercises

Directions: For each exercise below, read critically to answer the questions.

Practice Exercise

Does paragraph 2 contain facts, opinions, or both?

Copyright © 2014 The McGraw-Hill Companies, Inc. All rights reserved.

I really am, they won't love me and I will be abandoned." In intimate relationships, partners struggle to find a delicate balance between dependence on each other and independence from each other. Some observers call that balance interdependence. In families, too, children and adolescents struggle to differentiate themselves from their parents and their siblings, to stake out territory and beliefs that are their own. People search for individuality while at the same time trying to maintain close relationships.

4 Some have been socialized to believe that all disagreements in a relationship are wrong, falsely assuming that the essence of marriage is harmony at any price. Such beliefs can be devastating to a relationship in the long run.

5 People tend to have negative attitudes toward conflict because of the popular assumption that love is the opposite of hate. Both love and hate are intense feelings. Rather than being opposites, however, they are more like two sides of the same coin. The line between the two is a fine one, with feelings of love often preceding those of hate. Nevertheless, when negative feelings are stifled, positive feelings also die. People often say, "I don't feel anything toward my spouse anymore. Not love or hate. I'm just indifferent." Indifference—lack of feeling—is the opposite of anger and love and hate. In the words of one loving father about his children, "If I didn't give a damn, I wouldn't get mad." Anger and love are connected; we often are angriest with the ones we love.

Practice Exercise

Based on the information in paragraph 4, what *inference* could be drawn about an adult whose parents believed that a married couple should never have any arguments?

____

____

____

____

____

____

____

Myths and Facts about Anger

6 One expert maintains, "Of all the human emotions, anger has created the most harm and caused the greatest destruction within individuals, couples, families, and between social groups and nations." Anger is a double-edged sword: just as it is directed at others, so it becomes internalized by the angry individual. In short, it is impossible to hate, despise, or resent somebody without suffering oneself. Although anger can sometimes make people feel good, it can also make them feel guilty and less positive about themselves.

7 Anger can also produce a feeling of strength and power. It deludes people into thinking that they are doing something constructive about the problems they face, when actually they are only making things worse. Anger lets people substitute feelings of superiority for those of hurt and rejection. It also allows them to think anything they want about another person without fear of retaliation.

8 Four common but false beliefs about anger are that it is externally caused, that it is best to express anger openly and directly, that it can be a helpful and beneficial emotion, and that it will prevent other people from taking advantage of you. Let's take a closer look at these beliefs.

- *Anger is caused by others.* Many people believe that "somebody or something outside of you magically gets into your gut and makes you angry or gets you upset." One's happiness or unhappiness, however, is not externally caused. Anger, like any other human emotion, is self-created, usually when someone else does something we don't like.

Practice Exercise

Based on the information in paragraph 6, what *inference* could be made about people who come to understand that their internalized anger causes *them* to suffer?

____

____

____

____

____

Practice Exercise

Based on the information in paragraph 8, what *inference* could be drawn about people who believe that the four myths are facts rather than mistaken ideas?

____

____

____

____

- *The best way to deal with anger is to let it all out.* Although venting anger may make people feel better for the moment, it won't help them get any better. Letting it all out does not resolve the underlying issues. In fact, it tends to bring out those same feelings in others, increasing both people's anger.
- *Anger is a beneficial emotion.* This is simply not true. Individuals may find in the short run that they get their way by getting angry, but in the long run they will push others away from them or provoke them to get even.
- *You're a wimp if you don't get angry.* Some people believe that if they don't get angry, others will take advantage of them or consider them weak and inferior. People must *decide* how they want to feel, rather than let someone else determine how they are going to feel. Firm and assertive statements, such as "I disagree" or "I don't like that," let us take more control of situations. We do not have to get angry; we choose to get angry—and we can therefore choose a different approach. We can divert our emotion into more constructive ways of dealing with conflict.

Box 1 presents additional facts and common myths about anger.

Box 1: Putting It Together

Anger: Myths and Facts

When it comes to anger, the ability to distinguish fact from myth helps to provide the insight needed to manage anger, promoting both emotional health and a positive and nurturing couple relationship. Below are some common facts and myths about anger to keep in mind:

Facts

- Anger is a feeling, with psychological components.
- Anger is universal among human beings.
- The nonexpression of anger leads to an increased risk of coronary disease.
- The venting of anger—"catharsis"—is of value only when it sets the stage for resolution.
- Aggression leads to further aggression, not resolution.
- Most anger is directed toward those close to us, not toward strangers.
- Depression, shyness, and suicide are expressions of anger at oneself.

Myths

- Venting (by yelling or pounding pillows) "releases" anger and therefore "deals with" it.
- Women get less angry than men.
- Some people never get angry.
- Anger always results from frustration.
- Aggressive behavior is a sure sign of an "angry person."
- TV violence, active sports, and/or competitive work "release" anger.

Source: Adapted from Robert E. Alberti and Michael Emmons, *Your Perfect Right: Assertiveness and Equality in Your Life and Relationships, Ninth Edition.* Copyright © 2008 by Robert E. Alberti and Michael Emmons. Reproduced with the permission of Impact Publishers, Inc., P.O. Box 1094, Atascadero, CA 93423.

Source: Adapted from David Olson, John DeFrain, and Linda Skogrand, *Marriages and Families: Intimacy, Diversity, and Strengths,* 7th ed., pp. 134–37. Copyright © 2011 by The McGraw-Hill Companies, Inc. Reprinted by permission of The McGraw-Hill Companies.

Comprehension and Vocabulary Quiz

This quiz has several parts. Your instructor may assign some or all of them.

Comprehension

Directions: Use the information in the selection to answer each item below.

_______ **1.** The opposite of anger, love, and hate is:
a. aggression.
b. individuality.
c. harmony.
d. indifference.

_______ **2.** The psychological reason for suppressing anger is that we fear others will:
a. get angry at us in return.
b. feel superior to us.
c. abandon us if we tell them what we are really feeling.
d. become more assertive.

_______ **3.** Believing that there should never be any disagreements in a close relationship:
a. leads to a harmonious, frustration-free relationship.
b. enables those in the relationship to differentiate themselves.
c. creates interdependence.
d. can ultimately devastate the relationship.

_______ **4.** Anger is:
a. caused by other people.
b. caused by frustrating events.
c. self-created.
d. all of the above

_______ **5.** Anger typically causes suffering in:
a. the person at whom it is directed.
b. the person who expresses it.
c. both *a* and *b*
d. neither *a* nor *b*

Vocabulary in Context

Directions: For each item below, use context clues to deduce the meaning of the *italicized* word.

_______ **6.** A common tactic is to *suppress* negative emotions, hoping they will disappear with time.

When Bob walked with his T-shirt on backwards, we tried to *suppress* our laughter, but we ended up laughing anyway.

suppress (sə prĕs′) means:

a. ignore; pay no attention to

b. hold back; inhibit

c. reduce

d. express openly

_______ **7.** There are two *predominant* reasons for suppressing negative emotions.

The *predominant* color in her house is blue, her favorite color.

predominant (prĭ dŏm′ ə nənt) means:

a. extremely interesting

b. main; most important

c. well understood

d. shocking

_______ **8.** In families, too, children and adolescents struggle to *differentiate* themselves from their parents and their siblings, to stake out territory and beliefs that are their own.

To *differentiate* her fashions from those of other designers, Marla decided she would use only fabrics with brightly colored bold prints.

differentiate (dĭf′ ə rĕn′ shē āt′) means:

a. remove

b. protect

c. make or become different from

d. limit or restrict

_______ **9.** Nevertheless, when negative feelings are *stifled,* positive feelings also die.

Not wanting to be impolite, I *stifled* a yawn and continued to listen to Joe tell about his vacation.

stifled (stī′ fəld) means:

a. kept in; held back

b. interrupted

c. enjoyed the benefit of

d. expressed fully

_______ **10.** Anger *deludes* people into thinking that they are doing something constructive about the problems they face, when actually they are only making things worse.

One Internet scam *deludes* victims into thinking they will receive money from a deceased relative if they send in money to "process" the claim.

deludes (dĭ lo͞od′ z) means:

a. leads into a false belief

b. prevents

c. pushes or prods

d. forces

Word Structure

Directions: In paragraph 8, bullet 4, of the selection, you encountered the word **divert.** It contains the root ***ver,*** which means "to turn." The word *divert* literally means "to turn aside" or "to turn in a different direction." Use the meaning of ***ver*** and the list of prefixes on pages 72–73 to determine the meaning of the following words.

_______ **11.** When a person **converts** to a different religion, he or she:

a. changes religions.

b. stops attending religious services

c. takes vows to join a religious order.

d. becomes a religious leader.

_______ **12.** If you travel in the **reverse** direction, you:

a. go north.

b. turn around and go in the opposite direction.

c. turn right.

d. travel more slowly than you did when you started out.

_______ **13.** If you **avert** your eyes when you see a scary scene in a horror movie, you:

a. close your eyes.

b. stare in disbelief at the screen.

c. blink repeatedly.

d. turn your eyes away from the screen.

_______ **14.** If a person exhibits **perverted** behavior, the person:

a. possesses an unusual sense of humor.

b. socializes with eccentric individuals.

c. deviates greatly from what is considered right or correct.

d. achieves popularity and fame.

_______ **15.** People who are **extroverts** are:

a. interested in things and people around them.

b. focused in their own thoughts and feelings.

c. preoccupied with learning new information.

d. intensely interested in current events.

Reading Skills Application

Directions: These items test your ability to *apply* certain reading skills. You may not have studied all the skills yet, so some items will serve as a preview.

_______ **16.** Based on its use in paragraph 6, the phrase *double-edged sword* refers to:

a. words that are sharp and cutting.

b. something that hurts both parties in a situation.

c. something that has both positive and negative outcomes.

d. a knife fight between two people.

_______ **17.** The organizational pattern used in paragraph 4 is

a. addition.

b. sequence.

c. cause-effect.

d. summary.

_______ **18.** The authors' primary purpose in writing this selection is to:

a. persuade readers to not to get angry.

b. instruct readers how to avoid getting angry.

c. present readers with correct information about anger.

d. persuade readers to seek help if they are unable to control their anger.

_______ **19.** In paragraph 1 it says, "There are two predominant reasons for suppressing negative emotions. One is sociological in nature; the other is psychological." What is the relationship between the two sentences?

a. The second sentence changes the meaning of the first sentence.

b. The second sentence categorizes information given in the first sentence.

c. The second sentence gives a specific example of what is stated in the first sentence.

d. The second sentence clarifies something in the first sentence.

_______ **20.** Which of the following is the main idea of paragraph 8?

a. Four common but false beliefs about anger are that it is externally caused, that it is best to express anger openly and directly, that it can be a helpful and beneficial emotion, and that it will prevent other people from taking advantage of you.

b. Let's take a closer look at these beliefs.

c. Although venting anger may make people feel better for the moment, it won't help them get any better.

d. People must decide how they want to feel, rather than let someone else determine how they are going to feel.

SELECTION **9.1**

Marriage and Family

(continued)

Respond in Writing

Directions: Refer to the selection as needed to answer the essay-type questions below.

1. **Reacting to What You Have Read:** When you were growing up, what was your parents' attitude toward getting angry? Was anger acceptable or unacceptable? How did members of your family typically deal with anger?

____

____

____

____

____

____

____

Copyright © 2014 The McGraw-Hill Companies, Inc. All rights reserved.

2. **Comprehending the Selection Further:** The authors list four myths about anger. List them and tell which one would be most helpful to you in dealing with conflicts that arise. Explain why you chose that one.

____

____

____

____

____

____

____

____

3. **Overall Main Idea of the Selection:** In one sentence, tell what the authors want readers to understand about conflict and anger. (Be sure to include "conflict" and "anger" in your overall main idea sentence.)

____

____

____

____

____

____

____

____

____

Internet Resources

Read More about It Online

Directions: To learn more about the topic of this selection, see the websites below or use the keywords **"anger"** or **"anger management"** with a search engine.

www.mayoclinic.com/health/anger-management/MH00102
The respected Mayo Clinic offers "10 Tips to Tame Your Temper."

http://psychologytoday.tests.psychtests.com/take_test.php?idRegTest=1298
Take a 10-item 5-minute Anger Management Test at the *Psychology Today* website. After finishing the test, you will receive a brief personalized interpretation of your score that includes a graph and information on the test topic.

READING

SELECTION **9.2**

Biology

Planet Under Stress: Curbing Population Growth

From *The Living World: Basic Concepts*

By George B. Johnson

World population *is the sum total of all human beings on Earth. How many people do you think inhabit this planet? A million? A billion? A trillion? It is estimated that world population now exceeds 7 billion! If we were to solve the world's environmental problems caused by pollution, the greenhouse effect, waste disposal, and the loss of biodiversity, we would merely buy time to address the planet's fundamental problem: There are getting to be too many of us.*

The rapidly growing human population is at the core of many environmental issues. This selection from a biology textbook presents an overview of the world's population growth and then focuses on solutions—on what can be done to prevent the severe problems that will result from unrestrained population growth. It contains numerous facts about the world's population and invites readers to draw logical conclusions based on the facts that are presented. After reading the selection, you can make some inferences about what must be done to reduce the stress on our planet. What can be done to curb, or restrain, population growth?

1 Humans first reached North America at least 12,000 to 13,000 years ago, crossing the narrow straits between Siberia and Alaska and moving swiftly to the southern tip of South America. By 10,000 years ago, when the continental ice sheets withdrew and agriculture first developed, about 5 million people lived on earth, distributed over all the continents except Antarctica. With the new and much more dependable sources of food that became available through agriculture, the human population began to grow more rapidly. By the time of Christ, 2,000 years ago, an estimated 130 million people lived on earth. By the year 1650, the world's population reached 500 million.

2 The human population has grown explosively for the last 300 years. (See Figure 1.) The average human **birthrate** has

Annotation Practice Exercises

Directions: For each exercise below, read critically to answer the question.

FIGURE 1

GROWTH CURVE OF HUMAN POPULATION

Currently, there are over 7 billion people on Earth.

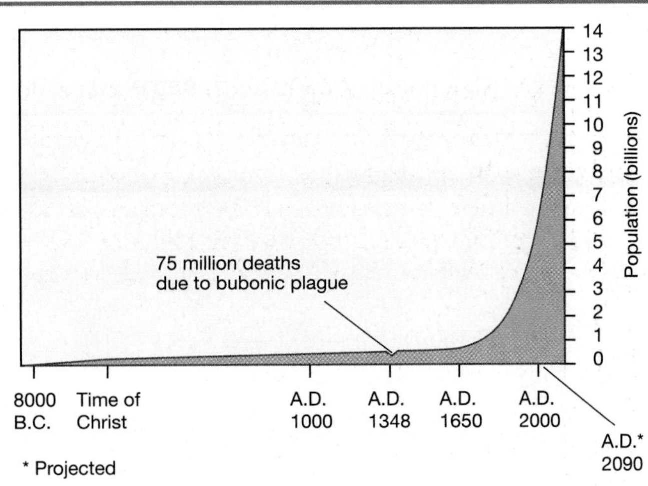

SELECTION 9.2

stabilized at about 22 births per year per 1,000 people worldwide. However, with the spread of better sanitation and improved medical techniques, the **death rate** has fallen steadily, to its present level of 9 per 1,000 per year. The difference between birth and death rates amounts to a population **growth rate** of 1.3% per year, which seems like a small number, but it is not, given the large size of the world's population.

3 The world population reached 6.3 billion people in 2003, and the annual increase now amounts to about 80 million people, which leads to a doubling of the world population in about 53 years. Put another way, more than 216,000 people are added to the world population each day, or more than 150 people every minute. At this rate the world's population will continue to grow to well over 6.3 billion, and perhaps stabilize at a figure between 8.5 billion and 20 billion, creating a tortuous situation for humanity. Such growth cannot continue, because our world cannot support it. Just as a cancer cannot grow unabated in your body without eventually killing you, so humanity cannot continue to grow unchecked in the biosphere without killing it.

4 One of the most alarming trends taking place in developing countries is the massive movement to urban centers. For example, Mexico City, one of the largest cities in the world, is plagued by smog, traffic, inadequate waste disposal, and other problems; it has a population of nearly 21 million people. (See Figure 2.) The prospects of supplying adequate food, water, and sanitation to this city's people are almost unimaginable.

5 In view of the limited resources available to the human population, and the need to learn how to manage those resources well, the first and most necessary step toward global prosperity is to stabilize the human population. One of the surest signs of the pressure being placed on the environment is human use of about 40% of the total food-producing productivity of land. Given that statistic, a doubling of the human population in 53 years poses extraordinarily severe problems. The facts virtually demand that we restrain population growth. If and when technology is developed that would allow greater

Practice Exercise

Does paragraph 3 contain *facts, opinions,* or *both*?

____

Practice Exercise

Does paragraph 5 contain *facts, opinions,* or *both*?

____

FIGURE 2

THE WORLD'S POPULATION IS CENTERED IN MEGA-CITIES

Mexico City, one of the world's largest cities, has more than 20 million inhabitants.

numbers of people to inhabit the earth in a stable condition, the human population can be increased to whatever level might be appropriate.

6 A key element in the world's population growth is its uneven distribution among countries. Of the billion people added to the world's population in the 1990s, 80% to 90% live in developing countries and of that number, about 60% of the people in the world live in countries that are at least partly tropical or subtropical. An additional 20% live in China. The remaining 20% live in the so-called developed, or industrialized, countries: Europe, Russia, Japan, the United States, Canada, Australia, and New Zealand. Whereas the populations of the developed countries are growing at an annual rate of only about 0.1%, those of the less developed countries are growing at an annual rate estimated to be about 1.9%.

7 Most countries are devoting considerable attention to slowing the growth rate of their populations, and there are genuine signs of progress. If it continues, the United Nations estimates that the world's population may stabilize at the 2100 level of 13 to 15 billion people. No one knows whether the world can support so many people indefinitely. Finding a way to do so is the greatest task facing humanity. The quality of life that will be available for your children and grandchildren in the next century will depend to a large extent on our success.

Population Growth Rate Has Been Declining

8 The world population growth rate has been declining, from a high of 2.0% in the period 1965–1970 to 1.3% in 2003. Nonetheless, because of the larger population, this amounts to an increase of 80 million people per year to the world population, compared to 53 million per year in the 1960s.

9 The United Nations attributes this decline in the population growth rate to family planning efforts and the increased economic power and social status of women. Although the United Nations applauds the United States for leading the world in funding family planning programs abroad, some oppose spending money on international family planning. The opposition states that money is better spent on improving education and the economy in other countries, leading to an increased awareness and lowered fertility rates. The United Nations certainly supports the improvement of education programs in developing countries, but, interestingly, it has reported increased education levels following a decrease in family size as a result of family planning.

10 Slowing population growth will help sustain the world's resources, but per capita consumption is also important. Even though the vast majority of the world's population is in developing countries, the vast majority of the resource consumption occurs in the developed world. The wealthiest 20% of the world's population accounts for 80% of the world's consumption of resources, whereas the poorest 20% is responsible for only 1.3% of consumption. The developed world must lessen the impact each of us makes.

11 It is easy to become discouraged when considering the world's environmental problems, such as pollution, wasting resources, and population growth, but do not lose track of the fact

Practice Exercise

Based on the information in paragraph 6, what *inference* can you make about restraining population growth in less developed countries?

____

____

____

____

____

____

Practice Exercise

Does paragraph 7 contain *facts, opinions,* or *both*?

____

Practice Exercise

Does paragraph 8 contain *facts, opinions,* or *both*?

____

Practice Exercise

Based on the information in paragraph 9, what *inference* can you make about why a decrease in family size would result in increased education levels?

____

____

____

____

____

____

Copyright © 2014 The McGraw-Hill Companies, Inc. All rights reserved.

that each problem is solvable. A polluted lake can be cleaned; a dirty smokestack can be altered to remove noxious gas; waste of key resources can be stopped; population growth can be restrained. What is required is a clear understanding of the problem and a commitment to doing something about it.

Source: Adapted from George B. Johnson, *The Living World: Basic Concepts,* 4th ed., pp. 753, 764–65, 770. Copyright © 2006 by The McGraw-Hill Companies, Inc. Reprinted by permission of The McGraw-Hill Companies.

SELECTION 9.2
Biology
(continued)

Comprehension and Vocabulary Quiz

This quiz has four parts. Your instructor may assign some or all of them.

Comprehension

Directions: Use the information in the selection to answer the questions below.

_______ **1.** The current world population:
a. is about 80 million people.
b. will double in about 53 years.
c. is declining because of the decline in the growth rate.
d. increases by more than 150 people every day.

_______ **2.** An alarming and troublesome trend taking place in developing countries is the:
a. decline in the growth rate.
b. increased movement of people from rural areas to urban centers.
c. stabilization of the birth rate.
d. inadequate waste disposal and increases in smog and traffic.

_______ **3.** According to the information in the selection, the decline in the worldwide growth rate is caused by:
a. family planning efforts.
b. the increased social status of women.
c. women's increased economic power.
d. all of the above

_______ **4.** How much of the total world's resources does the wealthiest 20% of the world population consume?
a. 2%
b. 20%
c. 50%
d. 80%

_______ **5.** The author states that the problem of restraining population growth is:
a. dependent on the development of technology for food production.
b. the responsibility of the developing countries.
c. the responsibility of the developed, or industrialized, countries.
d. solvable.

Vocabulary in Context

Directions: For each item below, use context clues to determine the meaning of the *italicized* word.

_______ **6.** The human population has grown *explosively* for the last 300 years.

The sale of personal computers increased *explosively* in the 1980s.

SELECTION 9.2

Copyright © 2014 The McGraw-Hill Companies, Inc. All rights reserved.

explosively (ĭk splō′ sĭv lē) means:

a. violently

b. suddenly and dramatically

c. unexpectedly

d. for reasons that are not known

_______ **7.** Just as a cancer cannot grow *unabated* in your body without eventually killing you, so humanity cannot continue to grow unchecked in the biosphere without killing it.

Jasmine's *unabated* use of credit cards eventually forced her to file for bankruptcy.

unabated (ŭn ə bā′ tĭd) means:

a. uncontrolled

b. unseen

c. unaided

d. unplanned

_______ **8.** For example, Mexico City, one of the largest cities in the world, is *plagued* by smog, traffic, inadequate waste disposal, and other problems; it has a population of about 21 million people.

We are often *plagued* by telemarketers who call during the dinner hour.

plagued (plāgd) means:

a. interrupted

b. caused considerable trouble

c. helped

d. covered

_______ **9.** The facts virtually demand that we *restrain* population growth.

To *restrain* the protestors, the police officers formed a line.

restrain (rĭ strān′) means:

a. prevent; avoid

b. maximize; enlarge

c. maintain; preserve

d. restrict; hold back

_______ **10.** The United Nations *attributes* this decline in the population growth rate to family planning efforts and the increased economic power and social status of women.

James *attributes* his love for sports to his father and his older brother, both of whom were professional athletes.

attributes (ə trĭb′ yo͞ots) means:

a. regards as the cause of

b. shows an interest in

c. takes advantage of

d. understands the meaning of

Word Structure

Directions: In paragraph 3 of the selection, you encountered the word **tortuous.** This word contains the root ***tort,*** which means "to twist" or "to bend." A *tortuous* mountain road is one that winds, one with many twists and turns. A *tortuous* situation is one that is complex and intricate. Use the meaning of ***tort*** and the list of prefixes on pages 72–73 to help you determine the meaning of each of the following words.

_______ **11.** If someone **distorts** the truth, that person:

a. states the facts.
b. twists the facts.
c. distinguishes fact from opinion.
d. presents a personal opinion.

_______ **12.** Clowns and other performers who are **contortionists:**

a. make audiences laugh.
b. wear bright, ridiculous costumes and wigs.
c. twist and bend their bodies in extreme ways.
d. paint on funny, exaggerated faces.

_______ **13.** The Arctic explorers endured *torturous* subzero temperatures, near starvation, and exhaustion. **Torturous** means:

a. slow and time-consuming.
b. requiring extensive, careful planning.
c. done at night.
d. inflicting severe physical and mental anguish or pain.

_______ **14.** This is an example of a famous *retort* given by British Prime Minister Winston Churchill to Lady Astor, a woman who disliked him, and whom he disliked. She said, "If I were married to you, I'd serve you poison tea." His *retort* was, "Madam, if I were married to you, I'd drink it." A **retort** is a:

a. funny comment spoken in public intended to amuse others.
b. cruel reply to a kind comment.
c. clever, quick reply that turns the first speaker's words to his or her disadvantage.
d. thoughtful comment intended to reduce the tension in a social situation.

_______ **15.** Ticket scalpers often make buyers pay four or five times the original amount for tickets, and many people view this as *extortion.* **Extortion** means:

a. a giveaway.
b. an economical service.
c. charging an excessive amount.
d. a sale.

Reading Skills Application

Directions: These items test your ability to *apply* certain reading skills. You may not have studied all the skills yet, so some will serve as a preview.

Copyright © 2014 The McGraw-Hill Companies, Inc. All rights reserved.

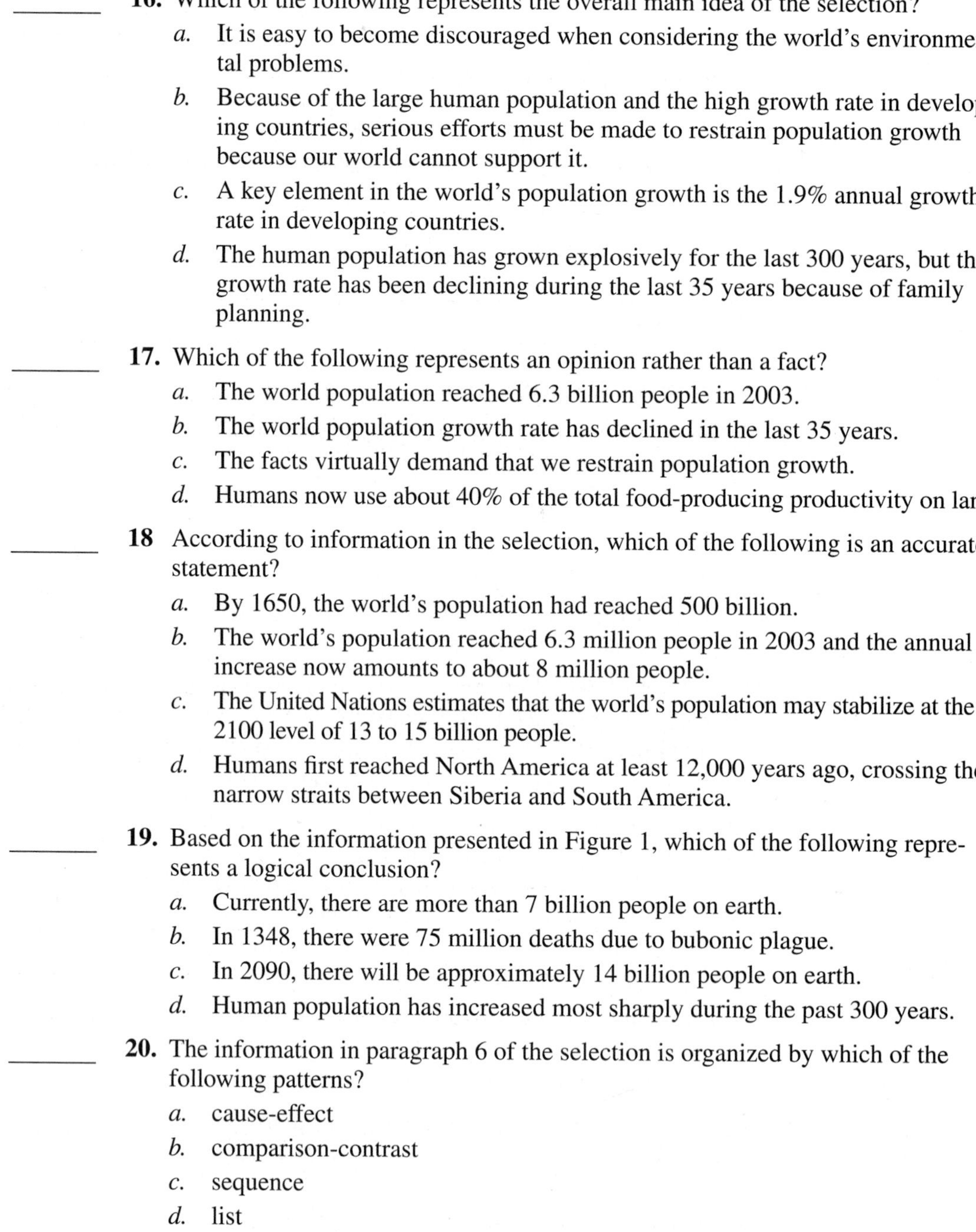

_______ **16.** Which of the following represents the overall main idea of the selection?

a. It is easy to become discouraged when considering the world's environmental problems.

b. Because of the large human population and the high growth rate in developing countries, serious efforts must be made to restrain population growth because our world cannot support it.

c. A key element in the world's population growth is the 1.9% annual growth rate in developing countries.

d. The human population has grown explosively for the last 300 years, but the growth rate has been declining during the last 35 years because of family planning.

_______ **17.** Which of the following represents an opinion rather than a fact?

a. The world population reached 6.3 billion people in 2003.

b. The world population growth rate has declined in the last 35 years.

c. The facts virtually demand that we restrain population growth.

d. Humans now use about 40% of the total food-producing productivity on land.

_______ **18** According to information in the selection, which of the following is an accurate statement?

a. By 1650, the world's population had reached 500 billion.

b. The world's population reached 6.3 million people in 2003 and the annual increase now amounts to about 8 million people.

c. The United Nations estimates that the world's population may stabilize at the 2100 level of 13 to 15 billion people.

d. Humans first reached North America at least 12,000 years ago, crossing the narrow straits between Siberia and South America.

_______ **19.** Based on the information presented in Figure 1, which of the following represents a logical conclusion?

a. Currently, there are more than 7 billion people on earth.

b. In 1348, there were 75 million deaths due to bubonic plague.

c. In 2090, there will be approximately 14 billion people on earth.

d. Human population has increased most sharply during the past 300 years.

_______ **20.** The information in paragraph 6 of the selection is organized by which of the following patterns?

a. cause-effect

b. comparison-contrast

c. sequence

d. list

SELECTION **9.2**

Biology

(continued)

Respond in Writing

Directions: Refer to the selection as needed to answer the essay-type questions below.

1. **Reacting to What You Have Read:** The author presents many facts about global population growth in this selection. List four factual statements about the world's population that were especially surprising to you.

1. ______________________________

2. ______________________________

3. ______________________________

4. ______________________________

2. **Comprehending the Selection Further:** The author explains that although the world's population is increasing, the global growth *rate* is declining. List four causes for the decline in the global growth rate suggested by the author.

   1. ______________________________
   2. ______________________________
   3. ______________________________
   4. ______________________________

3. **Overall Main Idea of the Selection:** In one sentence, tell what the authors want readers to understand about the human population growth rate. (Be sure to include "human population" and "growth rate" in your overall main idea sentence.)

Copyright © 2014 The McGraw-Hill Companies, Inc. All rights reserved.

Internet Resources

Read More about It Online

Directions: To learn more about the topic of this selection, see the websites below or use the keywords **"world population"** with a search engine.

http://en.wikipedia.org/wiki/World_population
This Wikipedia entry discusses world population growth. It presents information about the population of each continent and includes a map showing worldwide population density.

www.internetworldstats.com/stats8.htm
This site presents data about the current world population and includes a list of the ten countries with the highest population, as well as their estimated population by 2050.

www.census.gov/main/www/popclock.html
This site, sponsored by the U.S. Census Bureau, gives daily estimates of United States and world population. Click on *U.S. POPClock* or *World POPClock* links.

SELECTION **9.3** **Human Development**

For Better or Worse: Divorce

From *Human Development*

By Diane Papalia, Sally Olds, and Ruth Feldman

Someone once joked, "The major cause of divorce is marriage." No doubt, but still, divorce is hardly a joking matter: Today, half of all marriages in the United States end in divorce. According to CNBC, though, the divorce rate in America is actually declining. One reason seems to be that couples are marrying later, with the median age at first marriage being 28 for men and 26 for women. They are more mature, and they often defer marriage until they find the right person. Many marriages that might have ended in divorce simply don't occur. Another reason for the falling divorce rate, according to some, is that couples are more successfully managing the two-income life that may have created stress in marriages in the past. (www.cnbc.com/id/46797203/As_Two_Income_Family_Model_Matures_Divorce_Rate_Falls; accessed 12 May 2012).

Even if the divorce rate is starting to slow down, divorce still represents the death of a relationship and typically takes a toll on those involved. The authors of this human development textbook excerpt look at divorce, the most common reasons for it, and the adjustment it requires, and present some perhaps surprising facts about remarriage.

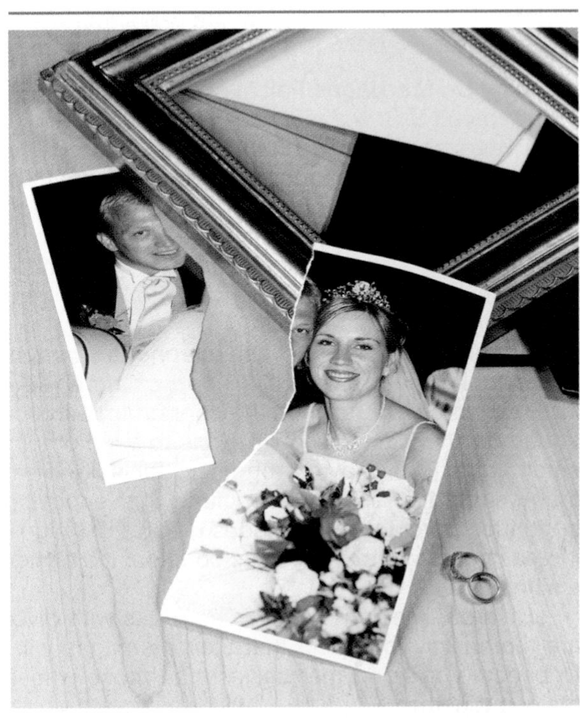

1 In the United States, the average marriage that ends in divorce does so after seven to eight years. Divorce, more often than not, leads to remarriage with a new partner and the formation of a stepfamily, which includes children born to or adopted by one or both partners before the current marriage.

Divorce

2 The U.S. divorce rate in 2006 was at its lowest point since 1970—3.6 divorces per 1,000 married women ages 15 and older, according to provisional data. This rate is about twice what it was in 1960 but has fallen gradually since its peak in 1981. About 1 in 5 U.S. adults has been divorced.

3 According to the U.S. Census Bureau, 2007, the sharpest drop in divorce has occurred among younger cohorts—those born since the mid-1950s. College-educated women,who previously had the most permissive views about divorce, have become less so, whereas women with lower educational levels have become more permissive and thus more likely to divorce.

Annotation Practice Exercises

Directions: For each exercise below, read critically to answer the questions.

Practice Exercise

Does paragraph 1 contain facts, opinions, or both?

____

Practice Exercise

Based on the information in paragraph 3, what *inference* could be drawn about the factors associated with the divorces of those born earlier (between 1900 and

Copyright © 2014 The McGraw-Hill Companies, Inc. All rights reserved.

Age at marriage is another predictor of whether a union will last. Thus, the decline in divorce may reflect higher educational levels as well as the later age of first marriages, both of which are associated with marital stability. It also may reflect the rise in cohabitation, which, if it ends, does not end in divorce. Teenagers, high school dropouts, and nonreligious persons have higher divorce rates. The rates of marital disruption for black women remain higher than for white women.

1940—the older people in the 2007 U.S. Census Bureau study)?

4 **Why Do Marriages Fail?** Looking back on their marriages, 130 divorced U.S. women who had been married an average of eight years showed remarkable agreement on the reasons for the failure of their marriages. The most frequently cited reasons were incompatibility and lack of emotional support; for more recently divorced, presumably younger, women, this included lack of career support. Spousal abuse was third, suggesting that intimate partner violence may be more frequent than is generally realized.

5 According to a randomized telephone survey of 1,704 married people, the greatest likelihood of *either* spouse's bringing up divorce exists when the economic resources are about equal and their financial obligations to each other are relatively small. Instead of staying together "for sake of the children," many embattled spouses conclude that exposing children to continued parental conflict does greater damage. And, for the increasing number of childless couples, it's easier to return to a single state.

6 Divorce breeds more divorce. Adults with divorced parents are more likely to expect that their marriages will not last and to become divorced themselves than those whose parents remained together.

7 **Adjusting to Divorce** The impact of divorce depends on several factors, and ending even an unhappy marriage can be painful for both partners, especially when there are young children in the home. Issues concerning custody and visitation often force divorced parents to maintain contact with each other, and these contacts may be stressful.

8 Divorce tends to reduce long-term well-being, especially for the partner who did not initiate the divorce or does not remarry. Especially for men, divorce can have negative effects on physical or mental health or both. Women are more likely than men to experience a sharp reduction in economic resources and living standards after separation or divorce. People who were—or thought they were—happily married tend to react more negatively and adapt more slowly to divorce. On the other hand, when a marriage was highly conflicted, its ending may improve well-being.

9 An important factor in adjustment is emotional detachment from the former spouse. People who argue with their ex-mates or who have not found a new partner or spouse experience more distress. An active social life, both at the time of divorce and afterward, helps.

Practice Exercise

Based on the information in paragraphs 7–8, what *inference* could be drawn about the long-term well-being of a divorced man who has children, who thought his marriage was happy, and who does not remarry?

Remarriage

10 Remarriage, said the essayist Samuel Johnson, "is the triumph of hope over experience." Evidence for the truth of that statement is that remarriages are more likely than first marriages to end in divorce.

11 In the United States and abroad, rates of remarriage are high and rising. More than 1 out of 3 U.S. marriages are remarriages for both bride and groom. Half of those who remarry after divorce from a first marriage do so within three to four years.

Source: Adapted from Diane Papalia, Sally Olds, and Ruth Feldman, *Human Development,* 11th ed., pp. 474, 476. Copyright © 2009 by The McGraw-Hill Companies, Inc. Reprinted by permission of The McGraw-Hill Companies.

Copyright © 2014 The McGraw-Hill Companies, Inc. All rights reserved.

SELECTION 9.3
Human Development
(continued)

Comprehension and Vocabulary Quiz

This quiz has several parts. Your instructor may assign some or all of them.

Comprehension

Directions: Use the information in the selection to answer each item below.

_______ **1.** The partner who does not initiate the divorce or remarry is more likely to:
- *a.* suffer negative effects.
- *b.* suffer financially.
- *c.* file a lawsuit against the former spouse.
- *d.* gain custody of the children.

_______ **2.** Divorce peaked in the United States in:
- *a.* 1960.
- *b.* 1970.
- *c.* 1981.
- *d.* 2006.

_______ **3.** A frequently cited reason women gave for the failure of their marriages was:
- *a.* spousal abuse.
- *b.* incompatibility.
- *c.* lack of support.
- *d.* all of the above

_______ **4.** An active social life can:
- *a.* support a couple's effort to stay married.
- *b.* cause a marriage to fail.
- *c.* help with adjustment during and after a divorce.
- *d.* none of the above

_______ **5.** Which marriage is most likely to end in divorce?
- *a.* a first marriage
- *b.* a marriage between two people who have similar economic resources
- *c.* a remarriage
- *d.* a childless marriage

Vocabulary in Context

Directions: For each item below, use context clues to deduce the meaning of the *italicized* word.

_______ **6.** The U.S. divorce rate in 2006 was at its lowest point since 1970—3.6 divorces per 1,000 married women ages 15 and older, according to *provisional* data.

Next month there will be a vote to determine whether the citizens of the island nation approve of the *provisional* government.

provisional (prə vĭzh′ ə nəl) means:

a. created from numerous and varied sources

b. incorrect; inaccurate

c. widely disputed or contested

d. temporary, pending confirmation or validation

_______ **7.** According to the U.S. Census Bureau, 2007, the sharpest drop in divorce has occurred among younger *cohorts*—those born since the mid-1950s.

The Generation Y (the "Millennials") and Generation Z (also called the "iGeneration") *cohorts* tend to be technology and computer savvy.

cohorts (kō′ hôrt′ z) means:

a. groups of people born about the same time

b. siblings; brothers and sisters

c. subjects in a research study

d. groups of students enrolled in the same school

_______ **8.** The most frequently cited reasons were *incompatibility* and lack of emotional support; for more recently divorced, presumably younger, women, this included lack of career support.

Because of the *incompatibility* of their religious views, the couple broke off their engagement.

incompatibility (ĭn′ kəm păt′ ə bəl ĭ tē) means:

a. similarity

b. discomfort

c. inability to be blended

d. inability to understand

_______ **9.** Instead of staying together "for sake of the children," many *embattled* spouses conclude that exposing children to continued parental conflict does greater damage.

The lawsuit between the *embattled* corporations dragged on for five years.

embattled (ĕm băt′ ld) means:

a. divorcing

b. fighting

c. mature

d. unhappy

_______ **10.** An important factor in adjustment is emotional *detachment* from the former spouse.

Detachment from one's co-workers can be a sign of job burnout.

detachment (dĭ tăch′ mənt) means:

a. separation

b. pressure

c. acceptance

d. closeness

Copyright © 2014 The McGraw-Hill Companies, Inc. All rights reserved.

Word Structure

Directions: In paragraph 7 of the selection, you encountered the word **depends.** It contains the root ***pend,*** which means "to hang." The word *depends* literally means that one thing "hangs" (is conditioned) on something or someone else. Use the meaning of ***pend*** and the list of prefixes on pages 72–73 to determine the meaning of the following words.

_______ **11.** In cooperative learning, students are *interdependent* on one another for success. **Interdependent** means each person:

a. operates independently.
b. distrusts the others.
c. depends on the others.
d. checks with the others weekly.

_______ **12.** A **pendulum** on a grandfather clock consists of the:

a. suspended piece that swings back and forth to regulate the clock.
b. hands that indicate the hour and minutes.
c. chimes that sound at set intervals.
d. mechanism and case of the clock.

_______ **13.** If you invent a new product and the patent is **pending,** it means the patent:

a. has not yet been applied for.
b. has been applied for but has not yet been received.
c. has been denied by the patent office.
d. has been issued.

_______ **14.** If you **suspend** a ceiling fan in your den, you:

a. remove it from the ceiling.
b. paint it to match the ceiling.
c. install it above the ceiling.
d. hang it from the ceiling.

_______ **15.** If you give your mother a **pendant** necklace, the necklace is:

a. a strand of pearl or beads.
b. a chain with something that hangs from it.
c. a double chain.
d. an antique.

Reading Skills Application

Directions: These items test your ability to *apply* certain reading skills. You may not have studied all the skills yet, so some items will serve as a preview.

_______ **16.** As used in paragraph 3, what is the meaning of *union*?

a. engagement
b. marriage
c. friendship
d. parenthood

_______ **17.** The pattern used to organize the information in paragraph 2 is:

a. list.

b. sequence.

c. cause-effect.

d. comparison-contrast.

_______ **18.** The authors' primary purpose in writing this selection is to:

a. inform readers about marriage, divorce, adjustment to divorce, and remarriage in the United States.

b. instruct readers how to avoid a marriage that is likely to fail.

c. persuade readers to complete a college education and wait until they are older to marry.

d. explain how to adjust to divorce with fewer negative effects.

_______ **19.** In paragraph 9 it says, "An important factor in adjustment is emotional detachment from the former spouse. People who argue with their ex-mates or who have not found a new partner or spouse experience more distress." What is the relationship between the two sentences?

a. The second sentence contrasts with information given in the first sentence.

b. The second sentence clarifies information given in the first sentence.

c. The second sentence gives an example of something that is mentioned in the first sentence.

d. The second sentence tells the result of something that is mentioned in the first sentence.

_______ **20.** In paragraph 10 is the sentence "Remarriage, said the essayist Samuel Johnson, 'is the triumph of hope over experience.' " What is the relationship between the parts of that sentence?

a. The second part of the sentence contrasts with information in the first part.

b. The second part of the sentence clarifies information given in the first part.

c. The second part of the sentence gives a specific example of something that is mentioned in the first part.

d. The second part of the sentence defines something that is mentioned in the first part.

SELECTION **9.3**
Human Development
(continued)

Respond in Writing

Directions: Refer to the selection as needed to answer the essay-type questions below.

1. Reacting to What You Have Read: Nearly everyone in the United States has been touched directly or indirectly by divorce. Perhaps your parents, a relative, or a friend has been through a divorce. Did that divorce comes as surprise to you or to either of the people involved? Why, or why not? What was the effect on you?

____

____

____

____

Copyright © 2014 The McGraw-Hill Companies, Inc. All rights reserved.

2. **Comprehending the Selection Further:** The authors present several trends related to divorce and remarriage in the United States. Summarize those trends. (You may write them in the form of a bulleted list.)

3. **Overall Main Idea of the Selection:** In one sentence, tell what the authors want readers to understand about divorce. (Be sure to include "divorce" in your overall main idea sentence.)

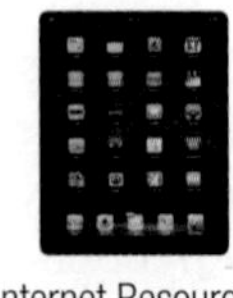
Internet Resources

Read More about It Online

Directions: To learn more about the topic of this selection, see the websites below or use the keyword **"divorce"** or **"remarriage"** with a search engine.

http://people.howstuffworks.com/divorce.htm
The article "How Divorce Works" presents factors related to divorce, "types of divorce, what the procedures are and what's involved in the final divorce agreement." It also looks at mediation and DIY (Do-It-Yourself) divorces.

www.nlm.nih.gov/medlineplus/divorce.html
This is a service of the U.S. National Library of Medicine National Institutes of Health (NIH). It gives an overview, the latest news, information on coping, and other related issues, such as financial ones.

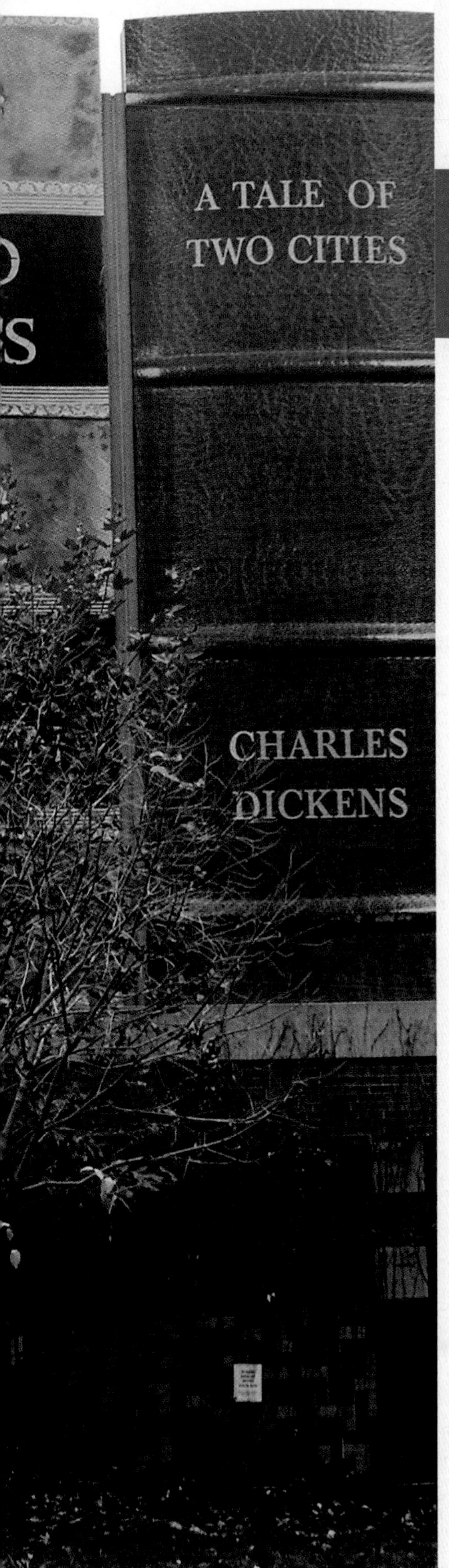

PART 4

A New World of Studying

Effective and Efficient Study Techniques

CHAPTERS IN PART FOUR

CHAPTER 10

Studying College Textbooks and Interpreting Visual and Graphic Aids

LEARNING OBJECTIVES

In this chapter you will learn the answers to these questions:

- What is the three-step process for studying college textbooks?
- What are textbook features?
- How can you interpret visual aids?
- How can you interpret graphic aids?

NEW INFORMATION AND SKILLS

What Is the Three-Step Process for Studying College Textbooks?

- Step 1: Prepare to Read
  Preview the Material
  Assess Your Prior Knowledge
  Plan Your Reading and Study Time
- Step 2: Ask and Answer Questions to Guide Your Reading
  Ask Questions as You Read
  Answer Questions as You Read
- Step 3: Review by Rehearsing Your Answers

What Are Textbook Features?

- Chapter Introductions and Chapter Objectives
- Chapter Outlines
- Vocabulary Aids and Glossaries
- Boxes
- Chapter Summaries
- Study Questions and Activities
- Other Textbook Features

How Can You Interpret Visuals and Graphic Aids?

How Can You Interpret Visual Aids?

- Photographs
- Diagrams
- Maps
- Cartoons

How Can You Interpret Graphic Aids?

- Line graphs
- Pie charts
- Bar graphs
- Flowcharts
- Tables

Other Things to Keep in Mind When Studying Textbook Material:

- You will benefit from examining the features in all of your textbooks at the beginning of the semester.

CHAPTER REVIEW CARDS

TEST YOUR UNDERSTANDING

Interpreting Graphic Aids

READING

Selection 10.1 "Living with Stress"
from *P.O.W.E.R. Learning: Strategies for Success in College and Life by Robert Feldman* (Student Success)

NEW INFORMATION AND SKILLS

WHAT IS THE THREE-STEP PROCESS FOR STUDYING COLLEGE TEXTBOOKS?

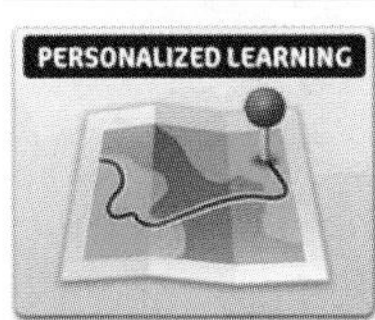

From the first day of classes, you should read and study your textbooks as if you were preparing for your final exams. If you read and study your textbooks thoroughly the first time, you will not have to start over again and cram when it is time for a test.

As you know, reading and studying textbooks takes time and effort, and your time will be more productive if you use a study *process.* An effective **study-reading process** consists of the three steps of preparing to read, asking and answering questions as you read, and reviewing by rehearsing the answers to your questions. The three steps in this process are explained in the next section and summarized in the box on pages 558–559. This study-reading process is similar to the SQ3R study system introduced in Chapter 1 (see page 9).

study-reading process
The three steps of preparing to read, asking and answering questions as you read, and reviewing by rehearsing the answers to your questions.

Step 1: Prepare to Read

The first step of the study-reading process is to prepare to read. Before you begin to read a textbook selection or a chapter, you should spend a few minutes preparing to read. **Preparing to read** involves previewing the material, assessing your prior knowledge, and planning your reading and study time. Let's take a closer look at each of these.

preparing to read
Previewing the material, assessing your prior knowledge, and planning your reading and studying time.

Preview the Material

Previewing means examining reading material before reading it to determine its topic and organization. This gives you a general idea of what it will be about, and lets you see how the material is organized. This technique is the same as the "survey" step in the SQ3R study system. Previewing not only helps you comprehend what you read but also improves your concentration, motivation, and interest in what you are about to read.

previewing
Examining reading material before reading it to determine its topic and organization.

To preview a section of a textbook or a textbook chapter:

- *First, read the title.* It usually indicates the overall topic.
- *Next, read the introduction.* An introduction (if there is one) usually presents some of the important points made in the selection, the organization, or background information that you will need.
- *Read the headings and subheadings of each section.* They tell you the specific topics the author has included, and they provide an outline of how information in the selection or chapter is organized.
- *Read words in special print.* Notice any words that appear in **color,** *italic,* or **bold print.** They are important terms you will be expected to understand and remember.
- *Look at any visuals and graphics,* such as pictures, charts, or diagrams. They provide visual representations of material.
- *Read any questions included in the chapter or the study guide.* They alert you to important information to watch for as you read. The author expects you to be able to answer them when you have finished reading.
- *Finally, read the summary.* A summary presents in brief form many of the most important ideas of the selection or chapter. Like an introduction, it is especially useful. Take advantage of it.

As you preview, you should make predictions: that is, make "educated guesses" about what is in the selection you are about to read. Ask yourself, "What topics does the author seem to be emphasizing?" and "How are the topics organized?"

Assess Your Prior Knowledge

assessing your prior knowledge

Determining what you already know about a topic.

When you lack background knowledge in a subject—and this is often the case with college textbooks—you have greater difficulty comprehending the material. **Assessing your prior knowledge** means determining what you already know about a topic. After you preview, take a moment to assess your prior knowledge: How much do you already know about the topic? If the material is largely unfamiliar to you, it is your responsibility to take steps to increase your background knowledge. Try some or all of these strategies:

- Read parts of other, perhaps easier, material on the same subject. These might be other college textbooks or more general study aids, such as an outline of American history or a supplemental book with a title such as *Biology Made Easy*.
- Consult an online encyclopedia, a dictionary, or some other reference book.
- Talk with someone who is knowledgeable about the subject.

These steps require extra effort, but *there are no shortcuts.* Going the extra mile to get necessary background information is part of being a responsible, mature learner and student. As a bonus, you may discover that it is exciting and satisfying to understand new or difficult material through your own efforts. You will also find that taking increased responsibility for your own learning makes you feel good about yourself as a student. (Remember that a *student* is someone who *studies.*)

Plan Your Reading and Study Time

By previewing the material, you can decide whether you can read the entire selection in just one session or whether you need to study the material in smaller sections over several sessions.

If you decide that you need more than one study session, divide the assignment into several shorter segments and plan to complete them at times when you know you can concentrate best. For example, you could divide a 20-page chapter into two 10-page segments and read them on separate days. Or you could divide the assignment into three one-hour study sessions on the same day, perhaps at 1, 5, and 8 P.M. You may find it helpful to paper-clip the smaller sections together or to insert stick-on notes between the sections. In any case, *plan* your study-reading session(s) and follow your plan. Then reward yourself *after* you complete your studying.

Step 2: Ask and Answer Questions to Guide Your Reading

The second step in the study-reading process is guiding your reading by asking and answering questions. To read and study effectively, you need to read and understand *each paragraph or section.* This means you must determine what is important to learn and remember in each section. To put it another way, you need to read for a specific purpose. This will increase your interest and concentration and enable you to monitor (evaluate) your comprehension while you are reading. One of the best ways to learn the material is to ask and answer questions as you read.

Ask Questions as You Read

Creating one or more questions for each section of a reading assignment can guide you to the important information and help you remember it. When you read to seek answers to questions, you are reading with a specific purpose: You are reading *selectively and purposefully.*

Turning chapter headings and subheadings into questions is the easiest way to do this. For example, if a section in a history textbook has a heading "The Civil War Ends," you could ask, "*Who* won the Civil War?" and "*Why* did it end?" You may also want to ask, "*When and where* did it end?" This technique is the same as the "Question" step in the SQ3R study system.

When a section or paragraph has no heading, create a question based on what that section or paragraph appears to be about. If you see a term or a phrase in **bold print** or *italic,* create a question about it. Create questions about names of people, places, events, and so on. You will be able to refine your questions later, when you read the material more carefully.

In addition to creating your own questions for each section, you may find that the author has included questions at the end of the chapter, at the beginning, throughout a chapter (perhaps in the margins), or in an accompanying study guide. If a chapter contains such questions, read them *before* you read the chapter. Then keep them in mind as you read. When you have finished the chapter, you should be able to answer these questions. In fact, you will probably be asked some of these same questions on tests. Chapter questions also let you monitor your comprehension. You can tell if you are getting the important information the author and your instructor expect you to know.

Finally, your instructor may provide study questions. You should be able to answer them by the time you finish reading and studying the chapter.

Answer Questions as You Read

As you read each paragraph or section, look for answers to your questions. Then, *after* you have read that paragraph or section, record the answers by writing them down. An important word of warning: Although you will be answering questions in your head as you read, do not try to write your answers *while* you are reading a section. Switching between reading and writing disrupts your comprehension and greatly slows you down. The time to write your answers is immediately after you *finish* reading a section, not while you are reading it for the first time.

There are several effective ways to record your answers. One is to write or type the questions and answers. Another is to write them in the margins of your textbook. Some techniques are described in the next chapter. Still another way is to make review cards, like the chapter review cards in this book. In addition, you may want to mark information that answers your questions by highlighting it.

What if you cannot determine the answer to one or more of your questions? In that case:

- Read ahead to see if the answer becomes apparent.
- If the question involves an important term you need to know, look the term up in the textbook's glossary or in a dictionary.
- Go back and reread the paragraph.
- Ask a classmate, a tutor, or your instructor.

If you still cannot answer all your questions after you have read an assignment, note which ones remain unanswered. Put a question mark in the margin, or make a list of the unanswered questions. One way or another, be sure to find the answers.

Copyright © 2014 The McGraw-Hill Companies, Inc. All rights reserved.

As you can see, actively seeking answers to questions encourages you to concentrate and focus on *understanding* as you read. Reading to answer specific questions can help you remember more and ultimately score higher on tests. When you are asked test questions that are identical to the ones you asked yourself, you will be especially glad you took the time to use this study technique.

Step 3: Review by Rehearsing Your Answers

Experienced college students know that to remember what they read, they must take certain steps to make this happen. They also know that it is essential to take these steps *immediately* after they finish reading, while the material is still fresh in their minds.

Forgetting occurs very rapidly, so you need to rehearse material immediately to transfer it into permanent, or long-term, memory. The shocking fact is that unless you take some special action beyond simply reading a textbook assignment, you will forget half of what you read by the time you finish reading it.

One highly effective way to rehearse important points is to *recite* your questions and answers about the material. Simply rereading your answers is not good enough; you must *say them aloud* until you can do so *without looking at the answers.* It is this simple: If you can't say it from memory, you don't know it. This technique is the same as the "Recite" step in the SQ3R study system.

Another highly effective way to rehearse important points is to *write them from memory.* When you give yourself a "practice test" in this way, you discover what you know and what you still need to learn. And in the process, you are transferring the material into long-term memory. When you check your answers, make corrections and add any information needed to make your answers complete. This technique is the same as the "Review" step in the SQ3R study system. Taking time to review and rehearse immediately after you finish reading a chapter not only helps you remember what you learned but also gives you a feeling of accomplishment that will encourage you to continue learning.

If you use the three-step process just outlined for studying college textbooks, you will learn more from your textbook assignments. It also provides the foundation for effective test preparation. Preparing for a test *begins* with reading textbook material effectively. Specific techniques for preparing for tests are discussed in Chapter 11. They include annotating textbooks by writing marginal study notes, outlining, mapping, and writing summaries.

SUMMARY OF THE THREE-STEP PROCESS FOR READING AND STUDYING COLLEGE TEXTBOOKS

Step 1: Prepare to Read

Preview the selection to see what it contains and how it is organized:

- Read the title.
- Read the introduction.
- Read headings and subheadings in each section.
- Read words in italics or bold print.
- Look over illustrations, charts, and diagrams.

- Read any questions that are included in the chapter or a study guide.
- Read the summary.

Ask yourself: "What topics does the author seem to be emphasizing?" and "How are the topics organized?"
Assess your prior knowledge. Ask yourself: "What do I already know about the topic?" and "How familiar am I with this topic?" *Plan your reading and study time.* Ask yourself: "How can I best allot my time for this assignment?" and "Do I need to divide the assignment into smaller units?"

Step 2: Ask and Answer Questions as You Read

Guide your reading by asking and answering questions:

- Turn chapter headings into questions.
- Create questions based on what the paragraphs or sections appear to be about.
- If the author has included questions, answer them.
- Use questions in a study guide, if there is one.
- Use questions given out by the instructor.

Read actively:

- Look for answers to your questions.

Record the answers to your questions:

- Write the answers on notebook paper or in the margins of the textbook.
- Create notes for the material.
- Emphasize the answers by highlighting or underlining them.

Step 3: Review by Rehearsing the Answers to Your Questions

Review the material and transfer it into long-term memory by rehearsing:

- Recite (say aloud) the answers to your questions.
- Try to write the important points from memory.

WHAT ARE TEXTBOOK FEATURES?

textbook feature

Any device an author uses to emphasize important material or to show how it is organized. Textbook features are also called *learning aids.*

A **textbook feature** is any device an author uses to emphasize important material or to show how it is organized. Another term for a textbook feature is a *learning aid.*

There are many kinds of textbook features, and in this section you will look at some of the most important ones. Though no single college textbook is likely to include all these features, your textbooks will have many of them.

Keep in mind that different authors may call the same feature by different names. For example, what one author may call a *Chapter Summary,* another may call *Chapter Review, Chapter Highlights, Key Points, Points to Remember, A Look Back,* or *Summing Up.*

Take advantage of textbook features as you study: They are there to help you locate, select, and organize the material you must learn.

The following sections will introduce you to common textbook features. There is a description of each, the various names by which it might be called, and an explanation of how to use it to full advantage. In addition, you will see examples of each.

Copyright © 2014 The McGraw-Hill Companies, Inc. All rights reserved.

Chapter Introductions and Chapter Objectives

chapter introduction

Textbook feature at the beginning of a chapter that describes the overall purpose and major topics.

A chapter introduction is a textbook feature at the beginning of a chapter that describes the overall purpose and major topics of the chapter. It may also describe their sequence or how the chapter is linked to preceding chapters. Or it may set the scene by giving, for instance, a case study or an anecdote. A chapter introduction may be called *Introduction* (such as the one from a computing essentials textbook in the example below), or it may be indicated by special type or a large ornamental letter at the beginning of the first word. Read chapter introductions carefully; they are a helpful guide to what lies ahead.

EXAMPLE OF A CHAPTER INTRODUCTION

INTRODUCTION

The purpose of this book is to help you become competent with computer technology. **Computer competency** refers to acquiring computer-related skills—indispensable tools for today. They include how to effectively use popular application packages and the Internet.

In this chapter, we present an overview of an information system: people, procedures, software, hardware, and data. It is essential to understand these basic parts and how connectivity through the Internet and the Web expands the role of information technology in our lives. Later, we will describe these parts of an information system in detail.

Fifteen years ago, most people had little to do with computers, at least directly. Of course, they filled out computerized forms, took computerized tests, and paid computerized bills. But the real work was handled by specialists. Then microcomputers came along and changed everything. Today it is easy for nearly everybody to use a computer.

- Microcomputers are common tools in all areas of life. Writers write, artists draw, engineers and scientists calculate—all on microcomputers. Students and businesspeople do all this, and more.
- New forms of learning have developed. People who are homebound, who work odd hours, or who travel frequently may take online courses. A college course need not fit within a quarter or a semester.
- New ways to communicate, to find people with similar interests, and to buy goods are available. People use electronic mail, electronic commerce, and the Internet to meet and to share ideas and products.

To be competent with computer technology, you need to know the five parts of an information system: people, procedures, software, hardware, and data. You also need to understand connectivity, the wireless revolution, the Internet, and the Web and to recognize the role of information technology in your personal life as well as your professional life.

Source: Timothy O'Leary and Linda O'Leary, *Computing Essentials 2013: Introductory Edition.* Copyright © 2013 by The McGraw-Hill Companies, Inc. Reprinted by permission of The McGraw-Hill Companies.

chapter objectives

Textbook feature at the beginning of a chapter telling you what you should know or be able to do after studying the chapter.

Chapter objectives at the beginning of a chapter tell you what you should know or be able to do after studying the chapter. They may also be called *Preview Questions, What You'll Learn, Goals,* and so on. In the example from a text about stress on page 561, the author states directly, "By the end of the chapter, students will . . ." and he has worded the objectives as if they were items on an essay test. Note the directions such as *describe, explain,* and *compare.*

Chapter Outlines

chapter outline

A list of chapter topics or headings in their order of appearance in the chapter.

A **chapter outline** is a list of chapter topics or headings in their order of appearance in the chapter. It provides a preliminary overview that helps you see in advance the content and organization of the entire chapter. Reading a chapter without first seeing its outline is like trying to solve a jigsaw puzzle without looking at the picture on the box: It can be done, but it takes longer and is much more difficult.

Chapter outlines may be called by names such as *Chapter Contents, Chapter Topics, Preview, Overview,* or *In This Chapter,* or may have no title at all. They may or may not actually be set up in outline style, and they may be general or detailed.

Chapter outlines in *New Worlds,* for instance, appear at the beginning of each chapter and include headings and subheadings, as well as titles of reading selections. The example from a textbook on coping with stress shown below is also in outline style. Notice that below it is the list of chapter objectives.

EXAMPLE OF CHAPTER OBJECTIVES AND OUTLINE

CHAPTER

1

WHAT IS STRESS?

OUTLINE

Four Common Ways of Describing Stress
- Stress as Response
- Stress as Stimulus
- Stress as a Transaction
- Stress as a Holistic Health Phenomenon

A New View of Stress
- A New Definition of Stress
- A Final Word about Stressors

OBJECTIVES

By the end of the chapter, students will:
- Describe the four classical ways of describing stress.
- Explain the relationship between life events and the stress response.
- Describe the three phases of Selye's General Adaptation Syndrome (GAS).
- Describe the role of threat appraisal in the stress response.
- Describe how the stress response is related to a person's level of functioning across the six dimensions of wellness.
- Compare the author's definition of stress with the classical definitions.

Source: Richard Blonna, *Coping with Stress in a Changing World,* 5th ed., p. 3. Copyright © 2012 by The McGraw-Hill Companies, Inc. Reprinted by permission of The McGraw-Hill Companies.

Copyright © 2014 The McGraw-Hill Companies, Inc. All rights reserved.

Vocabulary Aids and Glossaries

vocabulary aids

Textbook devices that identify important terms and definitions.

Among the most common and helpful textbook features are **vocabulary aids,** devices that identify important terms and definitions. Authors emphasize vocabulary in a variety of ways. Important terms may be set in **boldface,** *italic,* or **color.** They may also be printed in the margins, such as the key terms in *New Worlds* (one of which appears here). There may be a list of terms, perhaps with page numbers, at the end of a chapter (like the example shown below) or after reading a section. These lists can also appear at the beginning of a chapter or a reading. They may be called *Key Terms, Basic Terms, Terms to Know, Vocabulary, Terms to Remember,* and so forth.

EXAMPLE OF END-OF-CHAPTER LIST OF TERMS

KEY TERMS

self-esteem (p. 122)	**accomplishment (p. 136)**	**possible selves (p. 148)**
anxiety (p. 123)	**coping (p. 136)**	**self-talk (p. 151)**
unconditional positive regard (p. 129)	**avoidance (p. 136)**	**inner critic (p. 151)**
conditional positive regard (p. 130)	**self-acceptance (p. 141)**	**label (p. 152)**
social support (p. 130)	**body image (p. 143)**	**affirmation (p. 153)**
loneliness (p. 130)	**social comparison (p. 147)**	**criticism (p. 156)**
self-expectancy (p. 134)	**ideal self (p. 148)**	**probing (p. 159)**

Source: Dennis Waitley, *Psychology of Success,* 5th ed., p. 165. Copyright © 2010 by The McGraw-Hill Companies, Inc. Reprinted by permission of The McGraw-Hill Companies.

glossary

A list of important terms and definitions from the entire textbook that is located near the end of a textbook.

A list of important terms and definitions from the entire textbook may appear near the end of the book in a **glossary.** A glossary is a minidictionary for the book. (Shown on page 563 as an example is the first page of the glossary of a music appreciation textbook.) Pay attention to vocabulary aids: Instructors expect you to know important terms, and they usually include them on tests.

EXAMPLE OF A GLOSSARY

glossary

A B form See *two-part form.*

A B A form See *three-part form.*

Absolute music Instrumental music having *no* intended association with a story, poem, idea, or scene; nonprogram music.

A cappella Choral music without instrumental accompaniment.

Accelerando Becoming faster.

Accent Emphasis of a note, which may result from its being louder, longer, or higher in pitch than the notes near it.

Accompanied recitative Speechlike melody that is sung by a solo voice accompanied by the orchestra.

Accordion Instrument consisting of a bellows between two keyboards (piano-like keys played by the right hand, and buttons played by the left hand) whose sound is produced by air pressure that causes free steel reeds to vibrate.

Adagio Slow.

Aerophone Any instrument—such as a flute or trumpet—whose sound is generated by a vibrating column of air.

Affections Emotional states like joy, grief, and agitation represented in baroque music through specific musical languages.

Aleatory music See *Chance music.*

Allegretto Moderately fast.

Allegro Fast.

Alto (contralto) Female voice of low range.

Andante Moderately slow, a walking pace.

Answer Second presentation of the subject in a fugue, usually in the dominant scale.

Aria Song for solo voice with orchestral accompaniment, usually expressing an emotional state through its outpouring of melody; found in operas, oratorios, and cantatas.

Arioso Vocal solo more lyrical than a recitative and less elaborate than an aria.

Arpeggio See *broken chord.*

Ars nova (new art) A term used by musical theorists to describe the profound stylistic changes of Italian and French music in the fourteenth century.

Art song Setting of a poem for solo voice and piano, translating the poem's mood and imagery into music, common in the romantic period.

Atonality Absence of tonality, or key, characteristic of much music of the twentieth and early twenty-first centuries.

Augmentation Variation of a fugue subject in which the original time values of the subject are lengthened.

Ballata In medieval music, an Italian poetic and musical form with the structure A BB AA.

Bar Another term for *measure,* often used in jazz.

Baritone Male voice range lower than a tenor and higher than a bass.

Baritone horn Brass instrument similar in shape to the tuba, with a higher range, commonly used in bands.

Bass (1) Male voice of low range. (2) See *double bass.*

Bass clarinet Member of the clarinet family, having a low range. Its shape is curved at the end before flaring into a bell.

Bass clef Symbol on the staff indicating relatively low pitch ranges, such as those played by a pianist's left hand.

Bass drum Percussion instrument of indefinite pitch, the largest of the orchestral drums.

Bass fiddle See *double bass.*

Basso continuo Baroque accompaniment made up of a bass part usually played by two instruments: a keyboard plus a low melodic instrument. (See also *figured bass.*)

Basso ostinato See *ground bass.*

Bassoon Double-reed woodwind instrument, made of wood, having a low range.

Baton Thin stick used by many conductors to beat time and indicate pulse and tempo.

Beam Horizontal line connecting the flags of several eighth notes or sixteenth notes in succession, to facilitate reading these notes.

Beat Regular, recurrent pulsation that divides music into equal units of time.

Bebop (bop) Complex jazz style, usually for small groups, developed in the 1940s and meant for attentive listening rather than dancing.

Bitonality Approach to pitch organization using two keys at one time, often found in twentieth-century music.

Blues Term referring both to a style of performance and to a form; an early source of jazz, characterized by flatted, or "blue," notes in the scale; vocal blues consist of 3-line stanzas in the form a a′ b.

Source: Roger Kamien, *Music: An Appreciation,* 10th ed., p. 548. Copyright © 2011 by The McGraw-Hill Companies, Inc. Reprinted by permission of The McGraw-Hill Companies.

Boxes

box
Supplementary material that is separated from the regular text. A box is also known as a *sidebar.*

A **box,** or **sidebar,** is supplementary material that is separated from the regular text. It may appear at the bottom or top of a page of text (such as the example shown on page 564) or on one or more pages by itself. Boxed material may or may not be in an actual box; it may be set off with shading, in columns, in a different typeface, or by color. The example box on the next page, from a health text, presents information related to a topic in that chapter.

Copyright © 2014 The McGraw-Hill Companies, Inc. All rights reserved.

EXAMPLE OF BOXED MATERIAL

Resolving Conflict through Better Communication

Every relationship presents challenges to the individuals involved. Therapists would argue that couples who can learn to resolve conflict effectively have the best chance of maintaining long-term relationships. The hallmark of effective conflict resolution is that each person ends up feeling respected by his or her partner. Not surprisingly, this process is built on effective communication.

Here are some successful ways to communicate better to manage conflict:

- Show mutual respect. Remain calm.
- Identify and resolve the real issue.
- Be a good listener.
- Seek areas of agreement.
- Do not interrupt.
- Mutually participate in decision making.
- Be cooperative and specific.
- Focus on the present and future—not the past.
- Don't try to assign blame.
- Say what you are thinking and feeling.
- When talking, use sentences that begin with "I."
- Avoid using sentences that start with "You" or "Why."
- Set a time limit for discussing problems.
- Accept responsibility.
- Do something fun together.

Source: Wayne Payne, Dale-Hahn, and Ellen Lucas, *Understanding Your Health,* 10th ed., p. 447. Copyright © 2009 by The McGraw-Hill Companies, Inc. Reprinted by permission of The McGraw-Hill Companies.

Boxes can contain case studies, research studies, biographical sketches, interviews, excerpts from other works, controversial issues, practical applications—the possibilities are almost endless. Authors use boxes to clarify important points, provide vivid examples, and broaden and deepen your understanding of the material. They choose titles that describe the boxes' purposes: for example, *Points to Ponder, Issues and Debate, Close-Up, Speaking Out, Current Research,* and *What Do You Think?*

Chapter Summaries

chapter summary

Textbook feature in which the author consolidates most of the main ideas.

A **chapter summary** is one of the most helpful textbook features because it consolidates most of the main ideas. Many students find it useful to read a chapter summary both *before and after* studying a chapter. When you read a summary before you read the chapter, you may not understand it completely, but you will have a general idea about the important material in the chapter.

A summary may also be called *Conclusion, Recapitulation, Looking Back, Summing Up, Key Points, Key Concepts,* and so on. It may be written as paragraphs or as a list, as in the example on page 565, from a health text.

EXAMPLE OF A SUMMARY

Summary

- The cardiovascular system circulates blood throughout the body. The heart pumps blood to the lungs via the pulmonary artery and to the body via the aorta.
- The six major risk factors for CVD that can be changed are smoking, high blood pressure, unhealthy cholesterol levels, inactivity, overweight and obesity, and diabetes.
- Hypertension occurs when blood pressure exceeds normal limits most of the time. It weakens the heart, scars and hardens arteries, and can damage the eyes and kidneys.
- Physical inactivity, obesity, and diabetes are interrelated and are associated with high blood pressure and unhealthy cholesterol levels.
- Contributing risk factors that can be changed include high triglyceride levels and psychological and social factors.
- Risk factors for CVD that can't be changed include being over 65, being male, being African American, and having a family history of CVD.
- Atherosclerosis is a progressive hardening and narrowing of arteries that can lead to restricted blood flow and even complete blockage.
- Heart attacks are usually the result of a long-term disease process.
- A stroke occurs when the blood supply to the brain is cut off by a blood clot or hemorrhage.
- Congestive heart failure occurs when the heart's pumping action becomes less efficient and fluid collects in the lungs or in other parts of the body.
- CVD risk can be reduced by engaging in regular exercise, avoiding tobacco and environmental tobacco smoke, knowing and managing your blood pressure and cholesterol levels, and developing effective ways of handling stress and anger.
- A malignant tumor can invade surrounding structures and spread to distant sites via the blood and lymphatic system, producing additional tumors.
- Lung cancer kills more people than any other type of cancer. Tobacco smoke is the primary cause.
- Colon and rectal cancer is linked to age, heredity, obesity, and a diet rich in red meat and low in fruits and vegetables. Most colon cancers arise from preexisting polyps.

Source: Paul Insel and Walton Roth, *Connect Core Concepts in Health*, 12th ed., Brief, p. 313. Copyright © 2012 by The McGraw-Hill Companies, Inc. Reprinted by permission of The McGraw-Hill Companies.

Study Questions and Activities

study questions and activities

Exercises, drills, and practice sections that direct your attention to or review information you will be expected to know.

Many textbooks include **study questions and activities:** exercises, drills, and practice sections that direct your attention to or review information you will be expected to know. These can be among the most important features you use. Take time to do them. They provide valuable practice and give you a way to monitor your comprehension. Also, instructors often use these items or similar items on tests. Generally, if you are able to answer study questions and exercises, you can do well on an actual test.

Study questions and activities may appear at the beginning or end of a chapter, a reading, or other subdivisions of the text. In addition to the terms noted above, questions or activities may be called *Questions for Study and Review, Review, Ask Yourself, Self-Test,*

Check Your Mastery, Mastery Test, Learning Check, Check Your Understanding, Topics for Discussion, Problems, and so on. The examples shown below are typical.

Other Textbook Features

Here are other textbook features that can help you when you study:

Preface: Introductory section in which authors tell readers about the book.

Index: Alphabetical listing of topics and names in a textbook, with page numbers, usually appearing at the end of the book.

Appendix: Section at the end of a book that includes supplemental material or specialized information.

Bibliography: List of sources from which the author of the text has drawn information or a list of recommended reading.

EXAMPLE OF STUDY QUESTIONS AND ACTIVITIES

Review Questions

1. Shoplifting is often thought of as a "small time" crime. Is this true or false?
2. Why is so little property stolen in larceny/thefts recovered?
3. How does a three-person pickpocket operation work?
4. Give two definitions of *white-collar crime*.
5. List eight ways identity thieves can get a victim's personal information.
6. What are organized retail theft and organized retail crime?
7. After identity theft is committed, follow-on crimes occur. Identify five types of follow-on crimes.
8. What is smurfing?
9. What is shoulder surfing?
10. What are upcoding and unbundling charges used for?
11. What is the most common type of worker compensation fraud?
12. How does the swoop and squat method work?
13. Describe a viatical settlement fraud.
14. Why is it difficult to know how honest Internet gambling sites are?
15. How are bank-examiner and pigeon-drop cons run?
16. What is money laundering, and why do criminals want to do it?
17. What are pump and dump schemes?
18. How are prime bank and promissory note frauds operated?
19. Identify and discuss two telephone/pager scams.
20. The missing person fraud is cruel. How is it run?

Internet Activities

1. Visit the website for the National Association of Shoplifting Prevention (NASP) at *www.shopliftingprevention.org/main.asp*. Search through the website and learn about "shoplifting addiction." Discuss the addictive qualities of committing petty crimes, including shoplifting. What can be done to stop this vicious cycle?
2. Visit the website of the Federal Trade Commission at *www.ftc.gov* and click on the link entitled "Identity Theft." Discuss the steps that you can take to "deter, detect, and defend" against identity theft. List at least three other Internet sites that provide detailed information about what to do if you become a victim of identity theft.

Source: Charles Swanson, Neil Chamelin, Leonard Territo, and Robert Taylor, *Criminal Investigation*, 11th ed., p. 434. Copyright © 2012 by The McGraw-Hill Companies, Inc. Reprinted by permission of The McGraw-Hill Companies.

Students often remark that in college textbooks "everything seems important." They also find it hard to get a sense of how the facts and concepts add up to a coherent whole. Taking advantage of textbook features as you read can enable you to identify the essential information in a chapter and to understand its organization. Authors want to help you study and learn from their textbooks. For this reason, they put a great deal of time, effort, and thought into designing the extra textbook features. Use these helpful study tools!

HOW CAN YOU INTERPRET VISUALS AND GRAPHIC AIDS?

If you have ever read a copy of *USA Today,* you know this highly popular newspaper is filled with visuals and graphics. The reason is simple: Attention-grabbing graphics make it easier for readers to understand and remember information. A picture is indeed worth a thousand words.

Because of improved technology, today's textbooks and educational resources abound with visuals and graphics. You must be able to read, interpret, and integrate the information in them with the written explanations of the material. Visual aids include illustrations such as photographs, diagrams, maps, and cartoons. Graphic aids consist of bar graphs, pie charts, line graphs, time lines, flowcharts, and tables.

Don't skip over visuals and graphic aids. They provide visual explanations of concepts and relationships in a way that is often more concise and easier to understand than words alone. They can simplify, clarify, illustrate, and summarize information. They show how things relate to and compare with one another. They emphasize important points and reveal trends and patterns. They make the material more memorable. Sometimes a visual or graphic aid includes information that goes beyond the written explanation, for example, to offer support or proof.

When you preview a reading assignment, notice the types of visuals and graphic aids. Authors refer to them at points they believe will help readers most, so *stop and examine each one when the author first mentions it.* For example, if the author says, "As Illustration 2.3 shows," or "See Table 4.1," stop and examine it by following the steps described later in the chapter. Move back and forth between the written explanation and the visual or graphic aid as needed. For example, if you are reading about the four chambers of the heart, refer to the labeled illustration each time a new chamber is described.

Now find out more about how to use visual and graphics aids to full advantage.

HOW CAN YOU INTERPRET VISUAL AIDS?

visual aids

Photographs, diagrams, maps, and cartoons that supplement or illustrate narrative information.

In this section, you will learn how to interpret visual aids. **Visual aids** are photographs, diagrams, maps, and cartoons that supplement or illustrate narrative information. Read about each type of visual aid, look at the example, and try the sample exercise.

Photographs

Photographs, images recorded by a camera, serve many purposes.They can bring information to life, make it concrete, and help you visualize it, such as a photo of a wedding ceremony from another culture. They can show an example, such as a photo of a mosaic in an art history book. Sometimes photographs are there to help readers to

Copyright © 2014 The McGraw-Hill Companies, Inc. All rights reserved.

relate to material on an emotional level. For example, a psychology text discussion of stress might include a photo of Japanese tsunami victims standing amid the wreckage of what used to be their village. When you encounter photographs in textbooks, study them and read the accompanying captions. Ask yourself questions such as "What are the main elements (people, objects, activities) of the photograph? What does the photo illustrate or exemplify: what is its most important message? How does it fit with the written material? Is the date of the photograph given? The location at which the photograph was taken?"

The photograph below is from a music appreciation textbook. Suppose you had never seen the instrument called chimes and that you had only a written description, such as the one that accompanies the photo: "Chimes are a set of metal tubes hung from a frame. They are struck with a hammer and sound like church bells." Based only on that, would you have had an accurate idea of what chimes look like?

EXAMPLE OF A PHOTOGRAPH

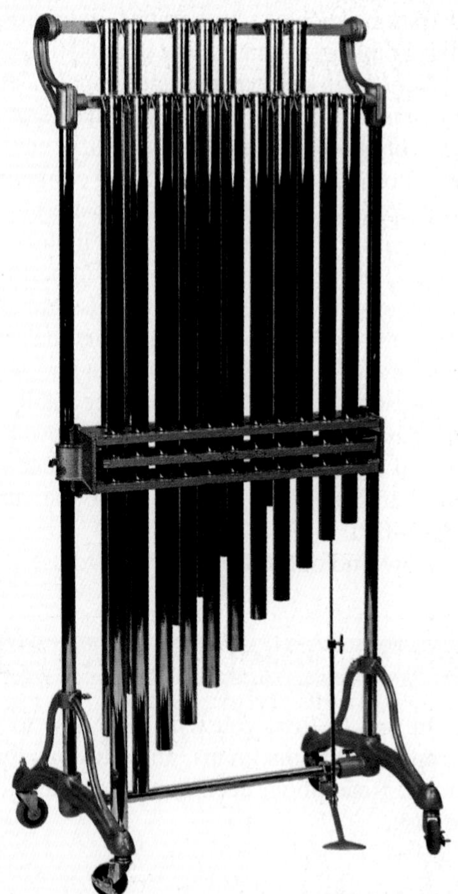

Chimes are a set of metal tubes hung from a frame. They are struck with a hammer and sound like church bells.

Source: Roger Kamien, *Music,* 9th ed., p. 36. Copyright © 2008 by The McGraw-Hill Companies, Inc. Reprinted by permission of The McGraw-Hill Companies.

EXERCISE 1

Interpreting a Photograph

Directions: Examine the following photograph and then answer the questions about it.

THE UNEMPLOYED, 1930. Thousands of unemployed men wait to be fed outside the Municipal Lodgers House in New York City. *(Library of Congress)*

Source: Alan Brinkley, *The Unfinished Nation,* 5th ed., p. 656. Copyright © 2008 by The McGraw-Hill Companies, Inc. Reprinted by permission of The McGraw-Hill Companies.

1. When was the photograph taken and why is this important? ______________________

____

2. What is happening in the photograph? ______________________

____

3. Where was the photograph taken? ______________________

4. What point does the photograph make? ______________________

____

Diagrams

Diagrams are sketches, drawings, or plans that show or explain how something works or shows the relationship between the parts of a whole. The "something" might be an object (a carburetor), a process (the evaporation/condensation cycle of water), or an idea (a proposed solution to the problem of low-cost housing). Flowcharts are a specific type of diagram that shows steps in a process. Diagrams appear in nearly every type of textbook.

Copyright © 2014 The McGraw-Hill Companies, Inc. All rights reserved.

When you study any diagram, ask yourself, "What is the purpose of this diagram? Why is it included? What does it show?" A good test preparation strategy is to photocopy any important diagram from your text. In a biology text, for example, it might be a diagram of a cell or of the lobes of the brain. Cover the labels and make one or more copies.Test yourself to see if you can correctly label the parts. You can also make diagrams or drawings of your own. Creating them is an excellent study strategy.

The environmental science textbook diagram below shows the process of photosynthesis that allows green plants to synthesize carbohydrates by using light as an energy source. For a test, you would need to be able to list the steps. A diagram with a green leaf, the sun, and sky is more effective and memorable than a flowchart of boxes with the same information.

EXAMPLE OF A DIAGRAM

FIGURE 4.9
PHOTOSYNTHESIS

This reaction is an example of one that requires an input of energy (sunlight) to combine low-energy molecules (CO_2 and H_2O) to form sugar ($C_6H_{12}O_6$) with a greater amount of chemical bond energy. Molecular oxygen (O_2) is also produced.

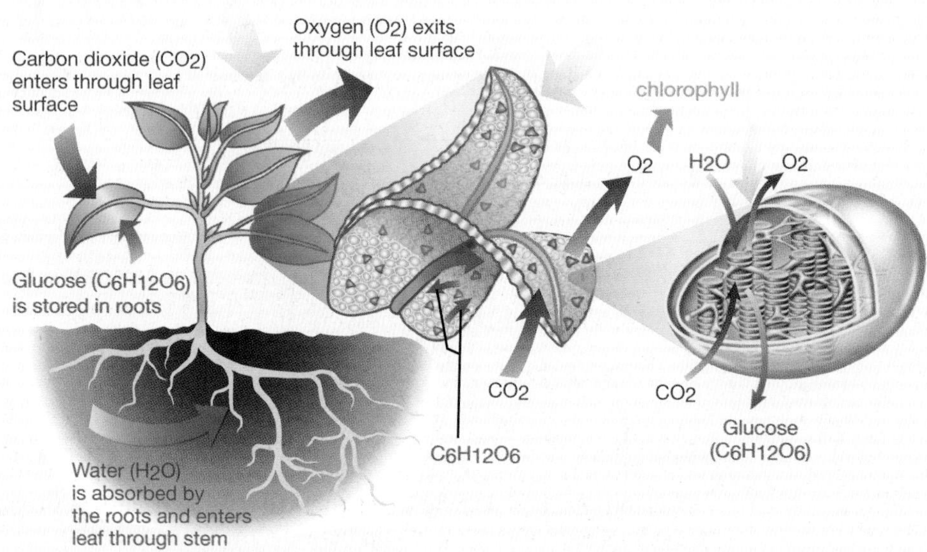

Source: Eldon Enger and Bradley Smith, *Environmental Science*, 11th ed., p. 71. Copyright © 2009 by The McGraw-Hill Companies, Inc. Reprinted by permission of The McGraw-Hill Companies.

EXERCISE 2

Interpreting a Diagram

Directions: Use the diagram of the mouth to answer the questions that follow.

FIGURE 8.3
ADULT MOUTH AND TEETH

The chisel-shaped incisors bite; the pointed canines tear; the fairly flat premolars grind; and the flattened molars crush food.

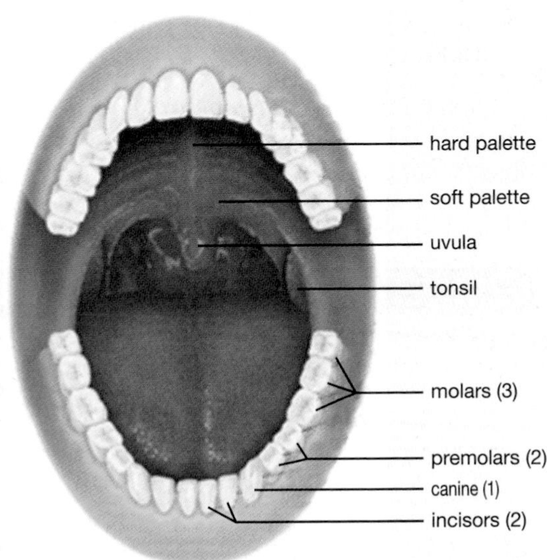

Source: Sylvia Mader, *Human Biology*, 12th ed., Fig. 8.3, p. 172. Copyright © 2012 by The McGraw-Hill Companies, Inc. Reprinted by permission of The McGraw-Hill Companies.

1. Which type of teeth occur in the greatest number? ______
2. What structure is located in the top, center of the mouth? ______
3. Which teeth are located at the front of the mouth? ______
4. What is the name for the roof (top) of the mouth? ______
5. Are the premolars located in front of or behind the molars? ______

Maps

Maps are representations of regions or other information presented on a flat surface. You've undoubtedly used a *location map:* a road map, an atlas, or even a campus map. For any map, ask yourself, "What is the purpose of this map? What important information does it show? What does the date of its creation suggest about the information it contains?"

You will encounter maps in courses such as history, geography, archaeology, anthropology, and astronomy. Some maps are designed to show the exact location of cities, states, countries, battlefields, mountain ranges, rivers, and other physical objects. Pay particular attention to each item's position relative to every other item. For

Copyright © 2014 The McGraw-Hill Companies, Inc. All rights reserved.

example, a map might indicate that vegetation decreases as regions of the world become colder. In maps such as these, note the following:

- *Title:* the subject matter of the map
- *Legend or key:* an explanatory table or list of symbols in the map and the use of color or shading (such as a star for capital cities, or various colors or shading to indicate different age categories)
- *Scale:* a ratio showing the relationship between the dimensions on the map and the object it represents, such as 1" = 100 miles; enables users to calculate the actual size of features represented on the map
- *Compass:* a symbol indicating the directions north, south, east, and west
- *Source:* the mapmaker; the person, agency, or group that created the map
- *Date:* when the map was created (for example, it might be ancient, from the 1800s, or recent)

Some maps are *thematic* or *special-purpose maps.* They present factual or statistical information for a specific region rather than showing the location of physical objects. For example, a map might use different colors to show voting patterns in parts

FIGURE 2.16

VARIATION IN MOTOR VEHICLE THEFT RATES BY STATE, 1998

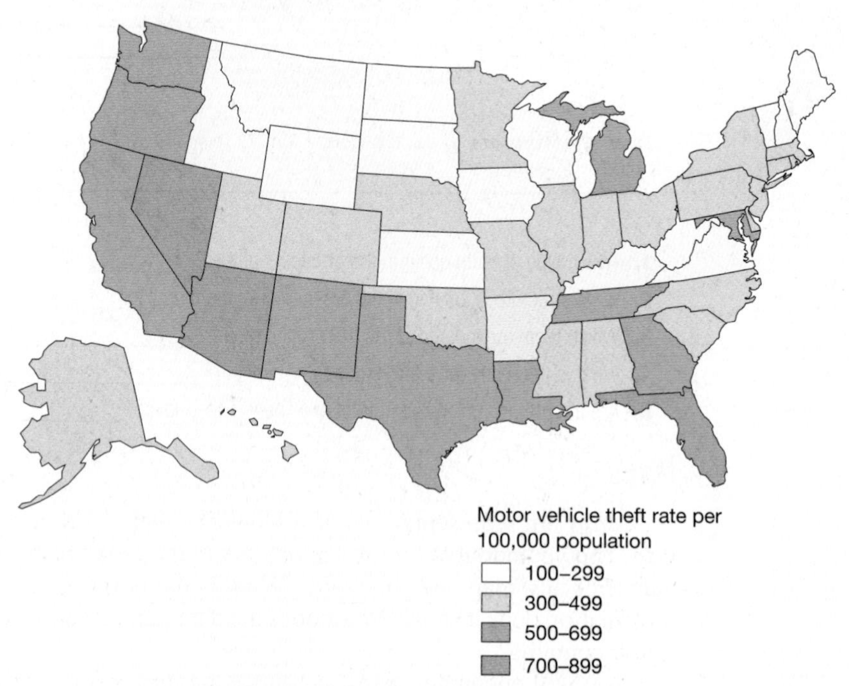

Source: Redrawn from *Crime and Justice Atlas* 2000, U.S. Department of Justice, p. 55.

Source: Arthur Getis, Judith Getis, and Jerome Fellmann, *Introduction to Geography,* 13th ed., p. 35. Copyright © 2011 by The McGraw-Hill Companies, Inc. Reprinted by permission of The McGraw-Hill Companies.

of the United States during the last presidential election. A map of a coastline might show the amount of erosion in the previous century. In such maps, look for patterns and trends, in addition to the other aspects noted above. Remember that you can create maps of your own as study aids.

The sample thematic map on page 572 uses color to show for each state the number of stolen motor vehicles per 100,000 people. Theft rates are higher in Florida, near the Great Lakes, and in the southwest and western states. One reasonable conclusion is that vehicles are more likely to be stolen in states with higher populations and/or that border on other countries or in coastal states, in which stolen vehicles can easily be moved offshore. Notice how much more easily the information is visualized in map form than if it were presented in the form of a table.

EXERCISE 3

Interpreting a Map

Directions: Study the following map and then answer the questions about it.

FIGURE 1.3

REGIONS OF NORTH AMERICA

Because of natural features of the land and the use people make of the land, different regions of North America face different kinds of environmental issues. In each region people face a large number of specific issues, but certain kinds of issues are more important in some regions than in others.

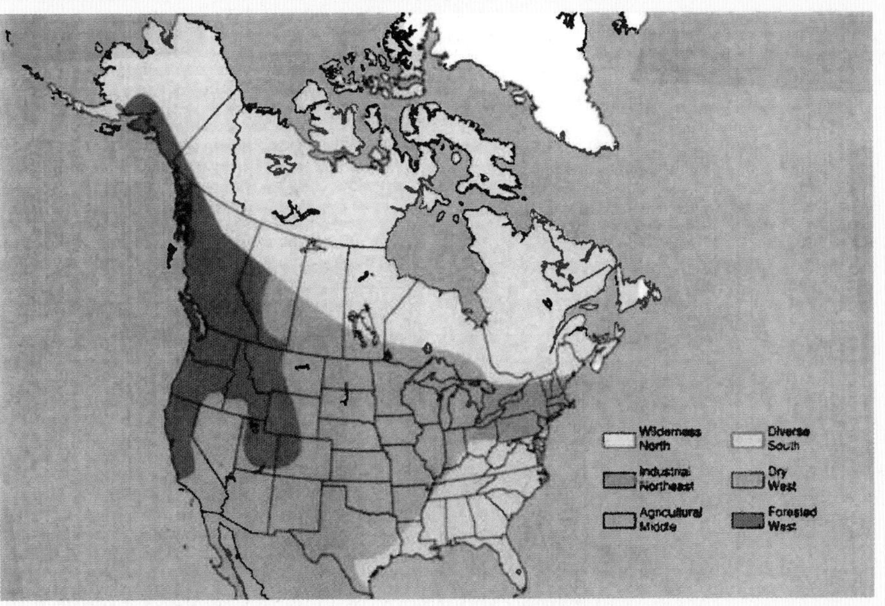

Source: Eldon Enger and Bradley Smith, *Environmental Science*, 12th ed., p. 6. Copyright © 2010 by The McGraw-Hill Companies, Inc. Reprinted by permission of The McGraw-Hill Companies.

1. How many regions of North America are there? ____________________

2. Which region covers the largest part of the United States? ____________________

3. How many regions are there in Texas? ____________________

4. What is the smallest region in the United States? ____________________

5. Where in the United States are there the most forests? ____________________

EXERCISE 4

Interpreting a Cartoon

"We lost!"

Source: © The New Yorker Collection 2006 Leo Cullum from cartoonbank.com. All Rights Reserved.

What point does the cartoon make? In other words, what is the cartoonist's point of view about children's participation in sports today?

____

____

____

Cartoons

Cartoons are humorous drawings that may or may not include a caption. Why do authors occasionally include them in textbooks? Well, a cartoon obviously lightens things up, but it can also present a point of view or illustrate a point in a memorable way. (You learned about point of view in Chapter 8.) Look at the cartoon in Exercise 4 and then answer the question that follows.

Political cartoons reflect a newspaper's or magazine's point of view on an issue, often by poking fun at a public figure or current issue. They are also called *editorial* cartoons because they appear on newspapers' editorial pages. These cartoons may contain caricatures, in which a person's distinctive features are exaggerated (such as George W. Bush's ears or Barack Obama's). Cartoonists also use visual metaphors, such as Uncle Sam to represent the United States, an elephant for the Republican Party, and a donkey for the Democrats.

Understanding cartoons depends on your prior knowledge. If a cartoon doesn't make sense, it is usually because you lack background information. For example, in Exercise 5, the cartoon on the left makes a statement about world population and world resources. The world's resources (the meat in the cartoon) are far too small for the world's population (the bun). This can be interpreted to mean that the world's resources have shrunk in relation to its population.

EXERCISE 5

Interpreting Political and Editorial Cartoons

Source: Clay Bennett, www.cartoonistgroup.com, n.d.

Source: Aislin, *The Montreal Gazette*, 2008.

What does the editorial cartoon on the right suggest?

____

____

____

____

HOW CAN YOU INTERPRET GRAPHIC AIDS?

graphic aids

Tables, diagrams, graphs, and charts that present narrative information in an alternative format.

Nearly every textbook contains line graphs, pie charts, bar graphs, flowcharts, and tables. As with visuals, stop and examine **graphic aids** when the author first mentions them. Then return to your reading.

Graphic aids contain important information, but they can appear difficult unless you know how to interpret them. The following steps will enable you to interpret graphic aids more effectively and efficiently.

Copyright © 2014 The McGraw-Hill Companies, Inc. All rights reserved.

- First, read the *title* and any *explanation* that accompany the graph. The title tells you the aspect of the topic that is being clarified or illustrated by the graph or table. The explanation may tell you the key point or points.
- Next, check the *source* of the information presented in the graphic aid to see if it is current and reliable. Read any footnotes.
- Third, read all the *headings* and *labels* to determine what is being presented or measured. These may appear at the top, bottom, and side of a table or graph. For example, in a bar graph that compares the amount of money workers earn and their educational levels, the side of a bar graph may be labeled "Annual Income in Thousands of Dollars" and the bottom may be labeled "Level of Education."
- Then, examine the *units of measurement* in a graph (for example, decades, percents, thousands of dollars, per hour, kilograms, per capita, milliseconds).
- Study the graphic aid. Try to understand how the information on the graphic clarifies, exemplifies, or proves the written explanation. See if there are *patterns* or *trends* in the data. Note any extremes, any highs and lows in the data.
- Finally, use the information provided collectively by the title and explanation, source, headings and labels, and units of measurements to determine the *important points* or *conclusions* the author is conveying.

Here are explanations and examples of five commonly used graphic aids: line graphs, pie charts, bar graphs, flowcharts, and tables. With bar graphs, line graphs, and tables, look for trends. A *trend* is important because it means there is a steady, overall increase or decrease. Along with the example of each graphic aid is a summary of its important elements as well as the important conclusions that can be drawn from it.

Line Graphs

A **line graph** is a diagram whose points are connected to show a relationship between two or more variables. There may be one line or several lines, depending on what the author wishes to convey. Watch especially for highs, lows, and trends. The example line graph on page 577 comes from a biology textbook, and it conveys the following:

Title and explanation: "Human Population Growth." (The explanation appears below the title.)

Source: Population Reference Bureau.

Headings and labels: Populations in less-developed countries and more-developed countries (in billions) and dates between 1750 and 2250 given in 50-year increments.

Units of measurement: Billions (number of people) and 50-year periods (of time).

Important points and conclusions: Starting in approximately 1950, the population began to rise dramatically in less-developed countries. This appears to slow down or level off around 2050. However, the world's population will then be approaching 12 billion, with the less-developed countries continuing to contribute overwhelmingly more to world population growth.

EXAMPLE OF A LINE GRAPH

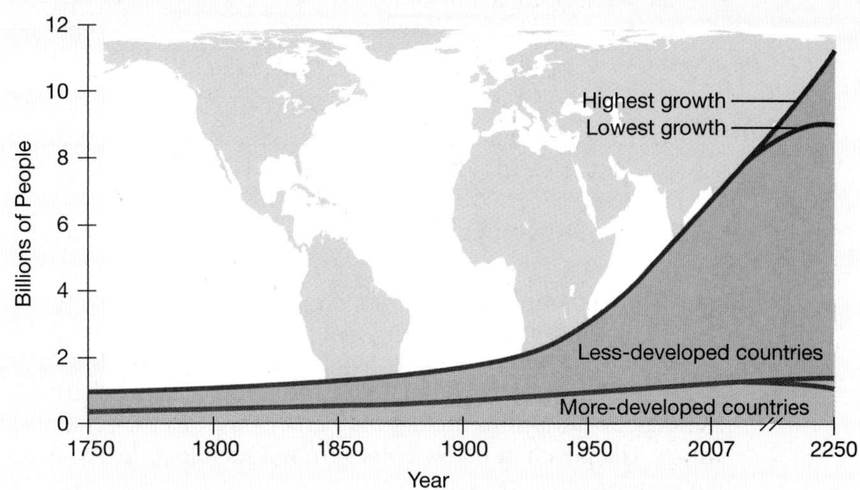

HUMAN POPULATION GROWTH

The less-developed countries will contribute most to human population growth.

Source: Population Reference Bureau.

Source: Sylvia Mader, *Human Biology*, 12th ed., p. 568. Copyright © 2012 by The McGraw-Hill Companies, Inc. Reprinted by permission of The McGraw-Hill Companies.

EXERCISE 6

Studying Line Graphs

1. The populations of which two groups are being compared on the line graph?

____

____

2. What is the *total* number of years spanned on the graph?

____

3. In approximately which year did the population of less-developed countries begin to increase sharply?

____

4. Approximately what is the population of the less-developed countries expected to be in 2050?

____

5. Approximately what is the population of the more-developed countries expected to be in 2050?

____

Copyright © 2014 The McGraw-Hill Companies, Inc. All rights reserved.

6. List at least two logical conclusions that can be drawn about *what life might be like in less-developed countries in 2250.*

____

____

____

____

Pie Charts

A **pie chart,** as its name suggests, is a circle graph in which the sizes of the "slices" represent proportional parts of the whole. Pie charts are a convenient way to show the relationships among the parts as well as the relationship of each part to the whole. The pie chart below comes from a sociology textbook and conveys the following information:

Title and explanation: "Asian American and Pacific Islander Population by Origin." No explanation is given.

Source: 2008 data from American Community Survey 2009: Tables B02006, B02007.

EXAMPLE OF A PIE CHART

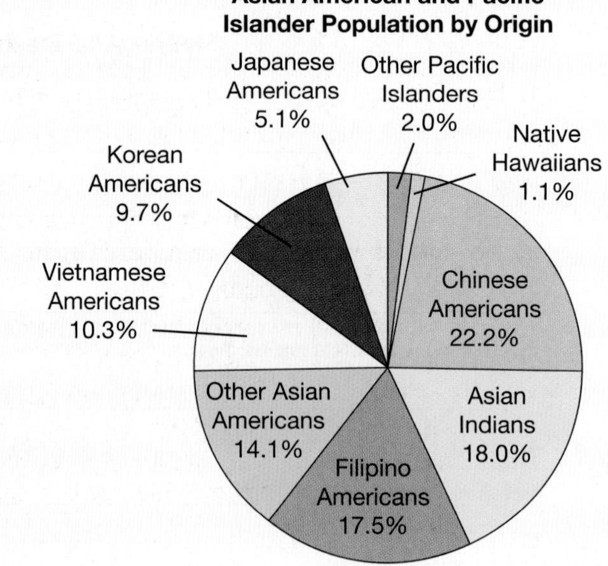

Source: Richard Schaefer, *Sociology: A Brief Introduction*, 9th ed., p. 260. Copyright © 2011 by The McGraw-Hill Companies, Inc. Reprinted by permission of The McGraw-Hill Companies.

Headings and labels: Sectors are labeled by origin (descent).

Units of measurement: Percentages.

Important points and conclusions: Asian Americans are a diverse group, with the largest representation coming from Chinese Americans, Asian Indians, and Filipino Americans.

EXERCISE 7

Interpreting Pie Charts

1. Which segment is greater in the pie chart: Korean Americans or Vietnamese Americans?

____

2. What percentage of Asian Americans are of Chinese origin?

____

3. Which group makes up the smallest percentage of Americans of Asian or Pacific Islander origin?

____

4. What conclusions can be drawn about the majority of Americans of Asian American or Pacific Islander origin?

____

____

Bar Graphs

A **bar graph** is a chart in which the length of parallel rectangular bars is used to indicate relative amounts of the items being compared. The bars in a bar graph may be vertical or horizontal. The bar graph on page 580 comes from a textbook on human development and conveys the following information:

Title and explanation: "Heart disease death rates of Americans, 2006."

Source: National Center for Health Statistics, 2010. *Health, United States, 2009.* Hyattsville, Maryland: National Center for Health Statistics.

Headings and labels: Numbers; "Males" and "Females"

Units of measurement: Numbers between 0 and 350, in increments of 50 (deaths per 100,000 people); colors: ethnic groups.

Important points and conclusions: The overall death rate for Americans who died of heart disease in 2006 was 200 people for every 100,000 people. For males, Black men have the highest rate; for women, Black women have the highest rate, yet is it still lower than that of White men.

EXAMPLE OF A BAR GRAPH

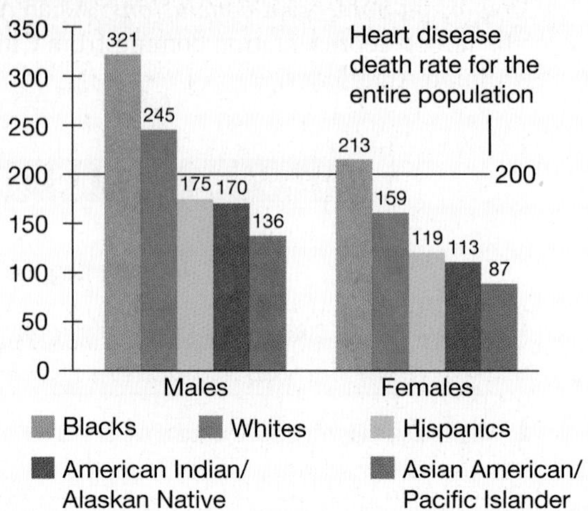

HEART DISEASE DEATH RATES OF AMERICANS, 2006

Source: National Center for Health Statistics, 2010. *Health, United States, 2009.* Hyattsville, Maryland: National Center for Health Statistics.

Source: Paul Insel and Walton Roth, *Core Concepts in Health,* 12th ed., p. 457. Copyright © 2012 by The McGraw-Hill Companies, Inc. Reprinted by permission of The McGraw-Hill Companies.

EXERCISE 8

Interpreting Bar Graphs

1. Of the genders and ethnicities represented in the graph, which group or groups had fewer than 100 heart-disease deaths per 100,000 people in 2006?

____

2. What is the overall trend across both genders?

____

____

____

3. For both males and females, which two ethnic groups have the most similar death rates for males and females?

____

4. Which ethnic group had the biggest gender differences in heart-disease-related death rates in 2006?

____

Some graphics, including diagrams and bar graphs, contain *pictograms,* in which a picture or a symbol represents numerical data or relationships. The symbols could be dollar signs, stick figures of people, flags, or bushels of grain. The greater the number of symbols, the greater the proportional quantity represented. Pictograms, or *pictographs,* make information more realistic, appealing, and memorable. For example, a bar graph that uses one cross to represent every 1,000 people killed by drunk drivers carries more emotional impact than a plain bar graph with numbers. The example pictogram below shows 2005 United Nations data on HIV/AIDS worldwide. It sharply reveals the problem Africa faces and the growing threat Asia faces from HIV/AIDS.

EXAMPLE OF A PICTOGRAM

FIGURE 3

HIV/AIDS has been a significant problem around the world for two decades. According to the United Nations AIDS program the most cases of the incurable sexually transmitted infection are found in Africa although it is a growing problem in Asia. (*Source:* UNAIDS, 2005.)

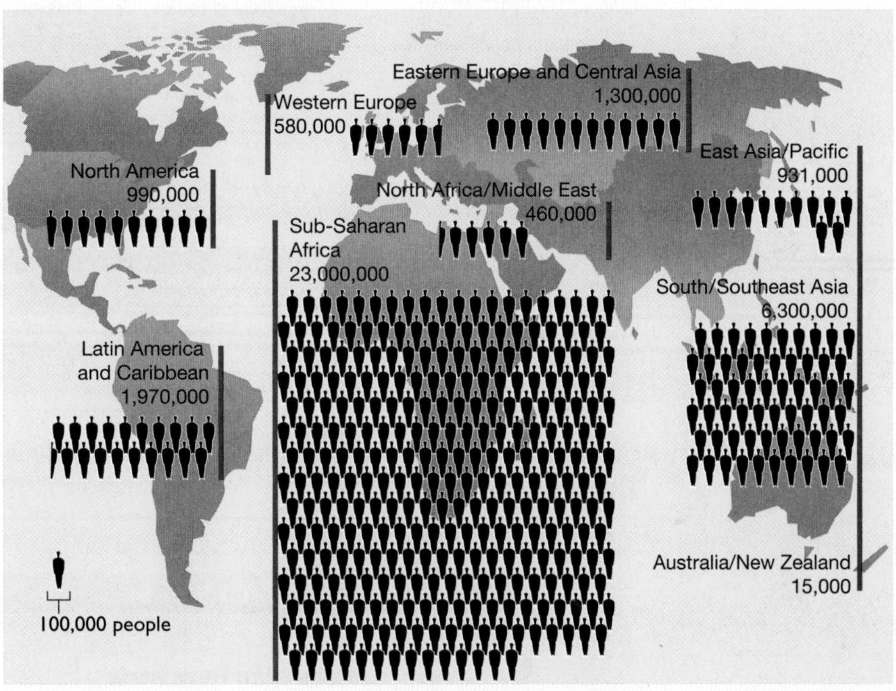

Source: Adapted from Robert S. Feldman, *Understanding Psychology,* 8th ed., p. 391. Copyright © 2008 by The McGraw-Hill Companies, Inc. Reprinted by permission of The McGraw-Hill Companies.

Flowcharts

A **flowchart** is a type of diagram that shows steps in procedures or processes by using boxes, circles, and other shapes that are connected with lines or arrows. The flowchart on page 582 is from *The New Dictionary of Cultural Literacy* and presents the legislative process of how a bill becomes a law. It conveys the following information:

Title: "How a bill becomes a law."

Source: Presumably the authors of the book, since no other source is given.

Headings and labels: Introduction, Committee action, Floor action, Enactment into law.

Copyright © 2014 The McGraw-Hill Companies, Inc. All rights reserved.

Units of measurement: None.

Important points and conclusions: Although bills can be introduced in either the House or the Senate, all bills must go through committee hearings and through floor action in both the House and the Senate before the bill is submitted to the president for enactment into law.

EXAMPLE OF A FLOWCHART

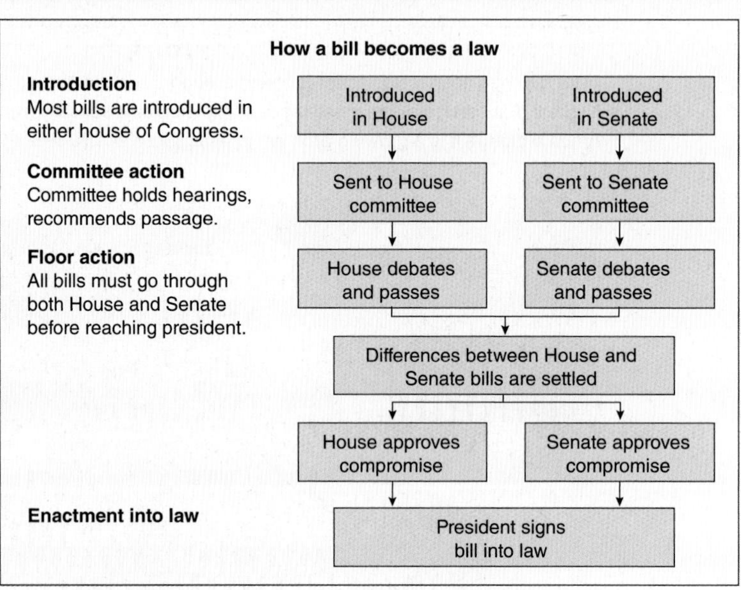

Source: E. D. Hirsch, Jr., Joseph Kett, and James Trefil, eds., *The New Dictionary of Cultural Literacy,* p. 344. Copyright © 2002 by Houghton Mifflin Company. Reprinted by permission of Houghton Mifflin Harcourt Publishing Company. All rights reserved.

EXERCISE 9

Interpreting Flowcharts

1. List the four stages a bill goes through to become a law.

____

____

____

____

2. What is the second step in a bill becoming a law? ______________________________

____

3. In which stage are differences worked out between House and Senate bills?

____

EXAMPLE OF A TABLE

TABLE 14.1
JUSTICES OF THE SUPREME COURT

Most recent appointees held an appellate court position before being nominated to the Supreme Court.

Justice	Year of Appointment	Nominating President	Position before Appointment
Antonin Scalia	1986	Reagan	Judge, D.C, Circuit Court of Appeals
Anthony Kennedy	1988	Reagan	Judge, 9th Circuit Court of Appeals
Clarence Thomas	1991	G. H. W. Bush	Judge, D.C. Circuit Court of Appeals
Ruth Bader Ginsburg	1993	Clinton	Judge, D.C. Circuit Court of Appeals
Stephen Breyer	1994	Clinton	Judge, 1st Circuit Court of Appeals
John Roberts, Jr.*	2005	G. W. Bush	Judge, D.C. Circuit Court of Appeals
Samuel Alito, Jr.	2006	G. W. Bush	Judge, 3rd Circuit Court of Appeals
Sonia Sotomayor	2009	Obama	Judge, 2nd Circuit Court of Appeals
Elena Kagan	2010	Obama	Solicitor general of the United States

*Chief justice.

Source: Thomas Patterson, *We the People: A Concise Introduction to American Politics*, 9th ed., p. 502. Copyright © 2011 by The McGraw-Hill Companies, Inc. Reprinted by permission of The McGraw-Hill Companies.

Tables

A **table** is a systematic listing of data in rows and columns. The example above, from a government textbook, presents this information on Supreme Court Justices:

Title and explanation: "Justices of the Supreme Court." Most recent appointees were former appeals court judges.

Source: Presumably the author of the book, since no other source is given.

Headings and labels: Justice, Year of Appointment, Nominating President, Position before Appointment.

Units of measurement: None.

Important points and conclusions: As shown in the table, eight of the nine justices are former U.S. Court of Appeals judges. As of 2012, three previous presidents have each appointed two justices, as has Obama. The majority of the justices were appointed in 1994 or earlier. There are three female justices.

EXERCISE 10

Studying Tables

1. Which president nominated Sonia Sotomayor? ______________________
2. What is the total number of Supreme Court Justices? ______________________
3. How many Supreme Court Justices are female? ______________________
4. Which president nominated Clarence Thomas? ______________________
5. Which justice was U.S. Solicitor General before being nominated to the Supreme Court?

   ____
6. Who is the Chief Justice? ______________________

Whenever you see graphic aids in your textbooks, be sure to take advantage of them. Read and study them: They contain valuable information that will enhance your understanding.

OTHER THINGS TO KEEP IN MIND WHEN STUDYING TEXTBOOK MATERIAL

Here is another helpful thing you should know about studying textbook material:

You will benefit from examining the features in all your textbooks at the beginning of the semester.

It has been estimated that, in college, approximately 80 percent of the material asked on tests comes directly from your textbooks. That means that it will be very important to you to use your textbooks as effectively as possible from the beginning of the semester. Take time at the beginning of every semester to familiarize yourself with the features of each of your textbooks.

Directions: Complete the chapter review cards for Chapter 10 by answering the questions or following the directions on each card.

Three-Step Process for Studying College Textbooks

List the *steps in the three-step process* of studying college textbooks.

1.

2.

3.

Card 1 Chapter 10: Studying College Textbooks and Interpreting Visual and Graphic Aids

Copyright © 2014 The McGraw-Hill Companies, Inc. All rights reserved.

Rehearsing Information

1. What is *rehearsing*?

2. When should you rehearse the answers to questions from your textbook assignments? Why is it important to do it at that time?

3. How can you tell when you have rehearsed material sufficiently?

Card 2 Chapter 10: Studying College Textbooks and Interpreting Visual and Graphic Aids

Textbook Features

1. Define the term *textbook feature.*

2. List at least four types of textbook features.

Card 3 Chapter 10: Studying College Textbooks and Interpreting Visual and Graphic Aids

Interpreting Visual Aids

1. Define *visual aids.*

2. List and define on separate lines four types of visual aids.

Card 4 Chapter 10: Studying College Textbooks and Interpreting Visual and Graphic Aids

Interpreting Graphic Aids

1. Define *graphic aids.*

2. List and define on separate lines five types of graphic aids commonly found in textbooks.

Card 5 Chapter 10: Studying College Textbooks and Interpreting Visual and Graphic Aids

Copyright © 2014 The McGraw-Hill Companies, Inc. All rights reserved.

TEST YOUR UNDERSTANDING
Interpreting Graphic Aids

Directions: Study each graphic aid and answer the questions that follow it.

EXHIBIT 7–7
U.S. Consumer Bankruptcy Filings

Source: Administrative Office of the U.S. Courts, www.uscourts.gov/bankruptcystats/bankrupt_fztable_dec2006.x/s, accessed January 22, 2009.

Line Graph

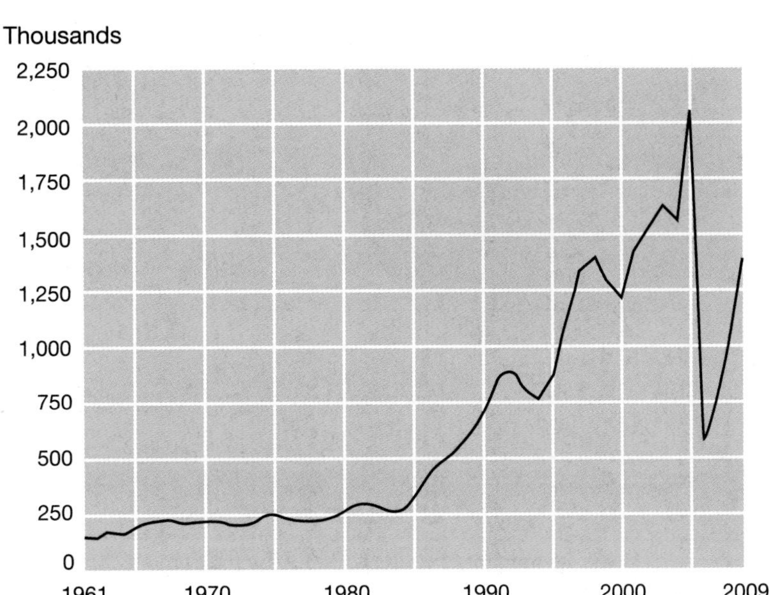

Source: Jack Kapoor, Les Dlabay, and Robert Hughes, *Personal Finance,* 10th ed., p. 241. Copyright © 2012 by The McGraw-Hill Companies, Inc. Reprinted by permission of The McGraw-Hill Companies.

1. What is the topic of the line graph? ______________________________

____

2. What is the unit of measurement? ______________________________

3. How many years are covered in the graph? ______________________________

4. How many personal bankruptcies were there in the year 2000? ______________________________

____

5. In which year was there the highest number of personal bankruptcies? ______________________________

Pie Chart

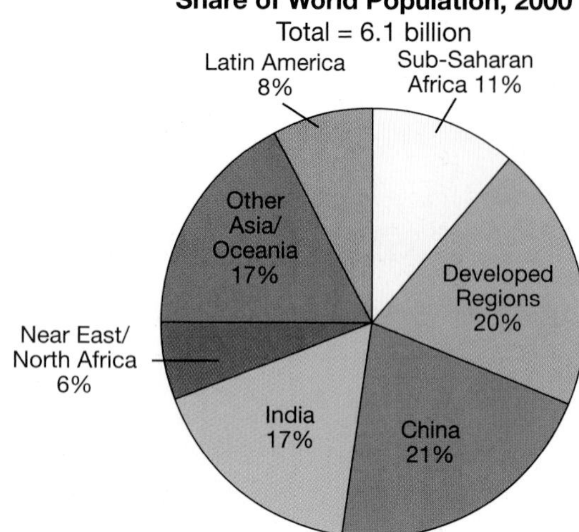

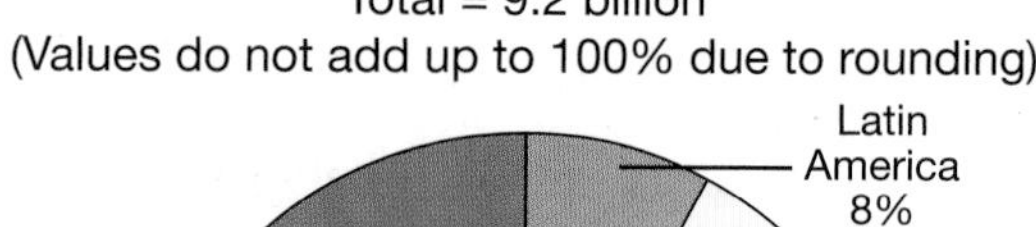

Estimated Share of World Population, 2050
Total = 9.2 billion
(Values do not add up to 100% due to rounding)

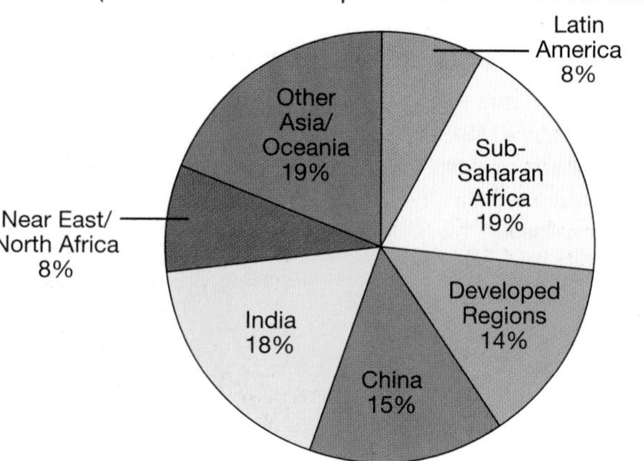

Source: Arthur Getis, Judith Getis, Mark Bjelland, and Jerome Fellmann, *Introduction to Geography,* 13th ed., p.162. Copyright © 2011 by The McGraw-Hill Companies, Inc. Reprinted by permission of The McGraw-Hill Companies.

1. What amount of time is covered by the two pie charts? ______________________

____

2. Which less-developed region of the world is projected to have the greatest increase in world population by 2050, and by what percent? ______________________

____

3. Which country and region are expected to decrease their share of world population by 2050, and by what percent? ______________________

____

4. Which region is projected to remain stable in its share of world population?

____

FIGURE 3
How much caffeine do you consume? This chart shows the range of caffeine found in common foods and drinks. (*The New York Times*, 1991). The average person in the United States consumes about 200 miligrams of caffeine each day.

Bar Graph

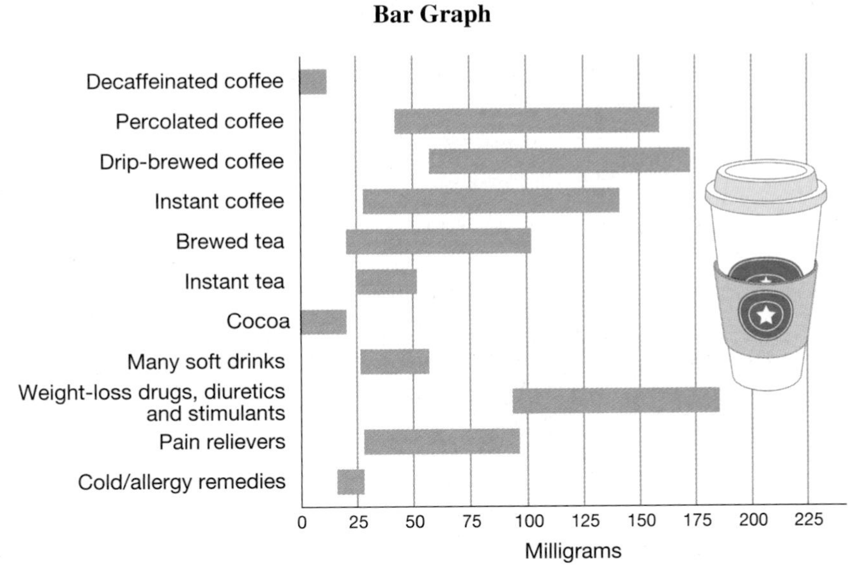

Source: Adapted from Robert Feldman, *Understanding Psychology,* 8th ed., p. 169. Copyright © 2008 by The McGraw-Hill Companies, Inc. Reprinted by permission of The McGraw-Hill Companies.

1. Which beverage contains the greatest number of milligrams of caffeine? ______________

____

____

2. How much caffeine does the average U.S. citizen consume daily? ______________

____

3. Should a person trying to limit caffeine choose a soft drink or brewed tea? ______________

4. The information in the graph is from 1991. Is that relevant? Why, or why not? ______________

____

FIGURE 4
The cycle of low self-esteem begins with an individual already having low self-esteem. As a consequence, the person will have low performance expectations and expect to fail a test, thereby producing anxiety and reduced effort. As a result, the person will actually fail, and failure in turn reinforces low self-esteem.

Flowchart

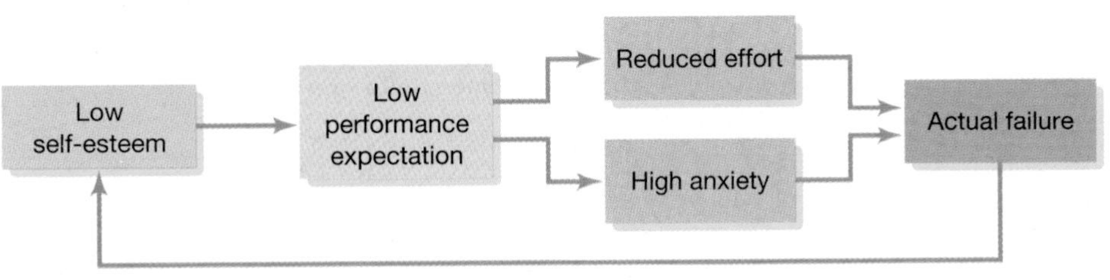

Source: Robert Feldman, *Essentials of Understanding Psychology,* 9th ed., p. 393. Copyright © 2011 by The McGraw-Hill Companies, Inc. Reprinted by permission of The McGraw-Hill Companies.

Copyright © 2014 The McGraw-Hill Companies, Inc. All rights reserved.

1. What is the topic of this flowchart? ______________________________

2. What are the immediate results of low performance expectation? ______________________________

3. What is the result of the person's actually failing the test? ______________________________

TABLE 4.1
SOURCES OF DNA EVIDENCE

Evidence	Possible Location of DNA on the Evidence	Source of DNA
Baseball bat or similar weapon	Handle, end	Sweat, skin, blood, tissue
Hat, bandanna, or mask	Inside	Sweat, hair, dandruff
Eyeglasses	Nose or ear pieces, lens	Sweat, skin
Facial tissue or cotton swab	Surface area	Mucus, blood, sweat, semen, earwax
Dirty laundry	Surface area	Blood, sweat, semen, vomit
Toothpick	Tips	Saliva
Used cigarette	Cigarette butt	Saliva
Stamp or envelope	Licked area	Saliva
Tape or ligature	Inside or outside surface	Skin, sweat
Bottle, can, or glass	Sides, mouthpiece	Saliva, sweat
Used condom	Inside or outside surface	Semen, vaginal or rectal cells
Blanket, pillow, or sheet	Surface area	Sweat, hair, semen, urine, saliva, dandruff
"Through and through" bullet	Outside surface	Blood, tissue
Bite mark	Person's skin or clothing	Saliva
Fingernail or partial fingernail	Scrapings	Blood, sweat, tissue

Source: www.dba.Gov/Basics/Evidence_Collection/Identifying, January 5, 2011.

Source: Charles Swanson, Neil Chamelin, Leonard Territo, and Robert Taylor, *Criminal Investigation,* 11th ed., p. 106. Copyright © 2012 by The McGraw-Hill Companies, Inc. Reprinted by permission of The McGraw-Hill Companies.

1. From which types of evidence could saliva be collected? ______________________________

2. Which two types of evidence have the greatest number of DNA sources? ______________________________

3. On a baseball bat or similar weapon, where are the possible locations of DNA evidence? ______________________________

SELECTION **10.1** **Student Success**

Living with Stress

From *P.O.W.E.R. Learning: Strategies for Success in College and Life*
By Robert Feldman

If you're feeling the stress of college on top of everyday living, you're not alone! The author of this selection, psychology professor Robert Feldman, reports that all students experience stress to varying degrees throughout their college careers. In fact, research indicates that almost a third of first-year students report feeling frequently overwhelmed with all they have to do. He continues: "Coping with stress is one of the challenges that college students face. The many demands on your time can make you feel that you'll never finish what needs to get done. This pressure produces wear and tear on your body and mind, and it's easy to fall prey to ill health as a result. However, stress and poor health are not inevitable outcomes of college. In fact, by following simple guidelines for managing stress and deciding to make health a conscious priority, you can maintain good physical and mental health."

The selection below explains more about stress and its effects, and offers strategies for dealing with it effectively. These strategies help you cope with stress in other areas of your life as well, and they will continue to work for you long after you have left college.

1 Stressed out? Tests, papers, reading assignments, job demands, roommate problems, volunteer activities, committee work. . . . It's no surprise that these can produce stress. But it may be a surprise to know that so can graduating from high school, starting your dream job, falling in love, getting married, and even winning the lottery.

2 Virtually *anything*—good or bad—is capable of producing stress if it presents us with a challenge. Stress is the physical and emotional response we have to events that threaten or challenge us. It is rooted in the primitive "fight or flight" response wired into all animals—human and nonhuman. You see it in cats, for instance, when confronted by a dog or other threat. Their backs go up, their hair stands on end, their eyes widen, and, ultimately, they either take off or attack. The challenge stimulating this revved-up response is called a *stressor.* For humans, stressors can range from a first date to losing our chemistry notes to facing a flash flood.

3 Because our everyday lives are filled with events that can be interpreted as threatening or challenging, stress is commonplace in most people's lives. There are three main types of stressors:

4 **1. Cataclysmic events** are events that occur suddenly and affect many people simultaneously. Tornadoes, hurricanes, and plane crashes are examples of cataclysmic events. Although they may produce powerful immediate consequences, ironically they produce less stress than other types of stressors. The reason? Cataclysmic events have a clear endpoint, which can make them more manageable. Furthermore, because they affect many people simultaneously, their consequences are shared with others, and no individual feels singled out.

5 **2. Personal stressors** are major life events that produce a negative physical and psychological reaction. Failing a course, losing a job, and ending a relationship are

Annotation Practice

Directions: As you read this selection, underline or highlight main ideas and key terms. Use the space in the margins to write out the key terms and their definitions.

Copyright © 2014 The McGraw-Hill Companies, Inc. All rights reserved.

all examples of personal stressors. Sometimes positive events—such as getting married or starting a new job—can act as personal stressors. Although the short-term impact of a personal stressor can be difficult, the long-term consequences may decline as people learn to adapt to the situation.

6 3. **Daily hassles** are the minor irritants of life that, singly, produce relatively little stress. Waiting in a traffic jam, receiving a tuition bill riddled with mistakes, and being interrupted by noises of major construction while trying to study are examples of such minor irritants. However, daily hassles add up, and cumulatively they can produce even more stress than a single larger-scale event. (Figure 1 indicates the most common daily hassles in people's lives.)

What Is Happening When We Are Stressed Out

7 Stress does more than make us feel anxious, upset, and fearful. Beneath those responses, we are experiencing many different physical reactions, each placing a high demand on our body's resources. Our hearts beat faster, our breathing becomes more rapid and shallow, and we produce more sweat. Our internal organs churn out a variety of hormones. In the long run, these physical responses wear down our immune system, our body's defense against disease. We become more susceptible to a variety of diseases, ranging from the common cold and headaches to strokes and heart disease. In fact, surveys have found that the greater the number of stressful events a person experiences over the course of a year, the more likely it is that he or she will have a major illness (see *Try It 1,* "Assess Your Susceptibility to Stress-Related Illness," pages 596–597).

FIGURE 1
DAILY HASSLES

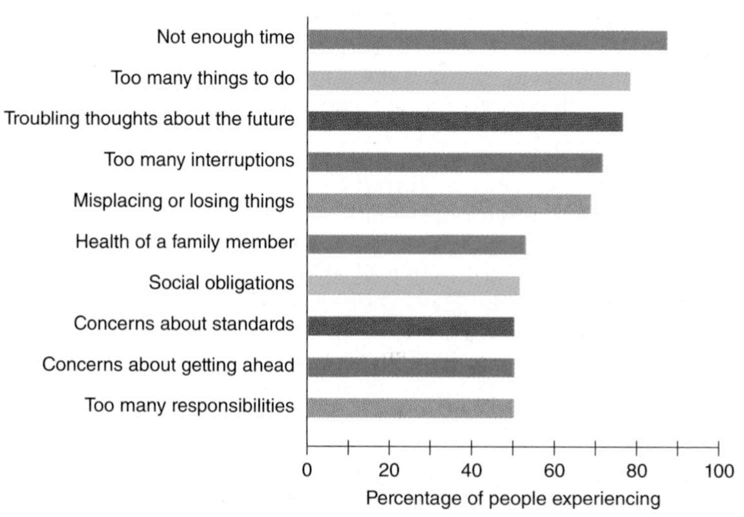

Handling Stress

8 Stress is an inevitable part of life. In fact, a life with no stress at all would be so boring, so uneventful, that you'd quickly miss the stress that had been removed. That doesn't mean, though, that we have to sit back and accept stress when it does arise. **Coping** is the effort to control, reduce, or tolerate the threats that lead to stress. Using the P.O.W.E.R. principles described below can help you ward off stress and actively deal with it. (Each letter in the word "POWER" stands for one of the steps: Prepare, Organize, Work, Evaluate, Rethink.)

Prepare: Readying Yourself Physically

9 Being in good physical condition is the primary way to prepare for future stress. Stress takes its toll on your body, so it makes sense that the stronger and fitter you are, the less negative impact stress will have on you. For example, a regular exercise program reduces heart rate, respiration rate, and blood pressure at times when the body is at rest—making us better able to withstand the negative consequences of stress. Furthermore, vigorous exercise produces endorphins, natural painkilling chemicals in the brain. Endorphins produce feelings of happiness—even euphoria—and may be responsible for the "runner's high," the positive feelings often reported by long-distance runners following long runs. Through the production of endorphins, then, exercise can help our bodies produce a natural coping response to stress.

10 If you now drink a lot of coffee or soda, a change in your diet may be enough to bring about a reduction in stress. Coffee, soda, chocolate, and a surprising number of other foods contain caffeine, which can make you feel jittery and anxious even without stress; add a stressor, and the reaction can be very intense and unpleasant.

11 Eating right can alleviate another problem: obesity. Around one-third of people in the United States are obese, defined as having body weight more than 20 percent above the average weight for a person of a given height. Obesity can bring on stress for several reasons. For one thing, being overweight drags down the functioning of the body, leading to fatigue and a reduced ability to bounce back when we encounter challenges to our well-being. In addition, feeling heavy in a society that acclaims the virtues of slimness can be stressful in and of itself.

Organize: Identifying What Is Causing You Stress

12 You can't cope effectively with stress until you know what's causing it. In some cases, it's obvious—a series of bad test grades in a course, a roommate problem that keeps getting worse, a job supervisor who seems to delight in making things difficult. In other cases, however, the causes of stress may be more subtle. Perhaps your relationship with your boyfriend or girlfriend is rocky, and you have a nagging feeling that something is wrong.

13 Whatever the source of stress, you can't deal with it unless you know what it is. To organize your assault on stress, then, take a piece of paper and list the major circumstances that are

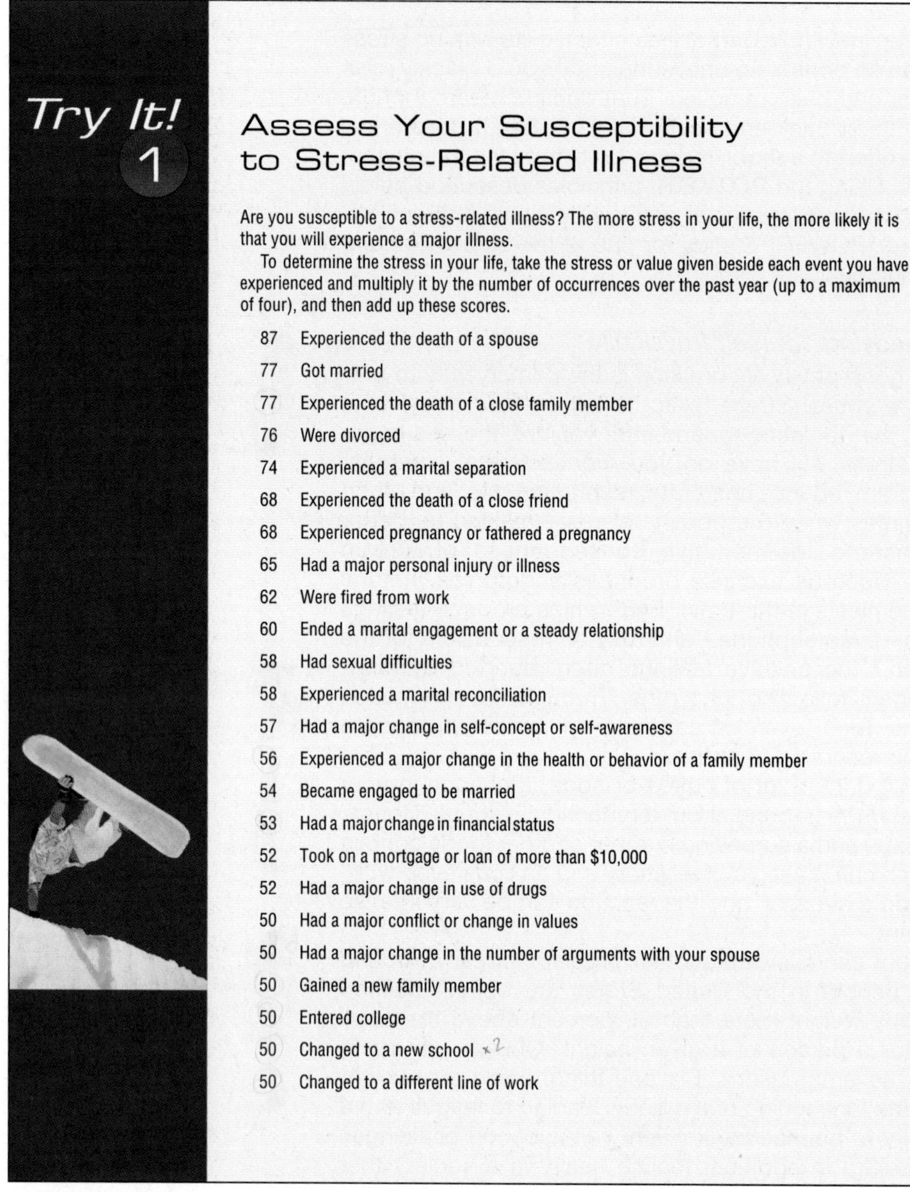

Try It! 1

Assess Your Susceptibility to Stress-Related Illness

Are you susceptible to a stress-related illness? The more stress in your life, the more likely it is that you will experience a major illness.

To determine the stress in your life, take the stress or value given beside each event you have experienced and multiply it by the number of occurrences over the past year (up to a maximum of four), and then add up these scores.

87 Experienced the death of a spouse
77 Got married
77 Experienced the death of a close family member
76 Were divorced
74 Experienced a marital separation
68 Experienced the death of a close friend
68 Experienced pregnancy or fathered a pregnancy
65 Had a major personal injury or illness
62 Were fired from work
60 Ended a marital engagement or a steady relationship
58 Had sexual difficulties
58 Experienced a marital reconciliation
57 Had a major change in self-concept or self-awareness
56 Experienced a major change in the health or behavior of a family member
54 Became engaged to be married
53 Had a major change in financial status
52 Took on a mortgage or loan of more than $10,000
52 Had a major change in use of drugs
50 Had a major conflict or change in values
50 Had a major change in the number of arguments with your spouse
50 Gained a new family member
50 Entered college
50 Changed to a new school
50 Changed to a different line of work

causing you stress. Just listing them will help put you in control, and you'll be better able to figure out strategies for coping with them.

Work: Developing Effective Coping Strategies

14 A wide variety of tactics can help you deal with stress. Among the most effective approaches to coping are these:

15 • **Take charge of the situation.** Stress is most apt to arise when we are faced with situations over which we have little or no control. If you take charge of the

49	Had a major change in amount of independence and responsibility
47	Had a major change in responsibilities at work
46	Experienced a major change in use of alcohol
45	Revised personal habits
44	Had trouble with school administration
43	Held a job while attending school
43	Had a major change in social activities
42	Had trouble with in-laws
42	Had a major change in working hours or conditions
42	Changed residence or living conditions
41	Had your spouse begin or cease work outside the home
41	Changed your choice of major field of study
41	Changed dating habits
40	Had an outstanding personal achievement
38	Had trouble with your boss
38	Had a major change in amount of participation in school activities
37	Had a major change in type and/or amount of recreation
36	Had a major change in religious activities
34	Had a major change of sleeping habits
33	Took a trip or vacation
30	Had a major change in eating habits
26	Had a major change in the number of family get-togethers
22	Were found guilty of minor violations of the law

Scoring: If your total score is above 1,435, you are in a high-stress category and therefore more at risk for experiencing a stress-related illness. A high score does *not* mean that you are sure to get sick. Many other factors determine ill health, and high stress is only one cause. Other positive factors in your life, such as getting enough sleep and exercise, may prevent illness. Still, having an unusually high amount of stress in your life is a cause for concern, and you may want to take steps to reduce it.

To Try It online, go to **www.mhhe.com/power**.

situation, you'll reduce the experience of stress. For example, if several assignments are all due on the same day, you might try negotiating with one of your instructors for a later due date.

16 • **Don't waste energy trying to change the unchangeable.** There are some situations that you simply can't control. You can't change the fact that you have come down with a case of mono, and you can't change your performance on a test you took last week. Don't hit your head against a brick wall and try to modify things that can't be changed. Use your energy to improve the situation, not to rewrite history.

17 • **Look for the silver lining.** Stress arises when we perceive a situation as negative and threatening. If we

Copyright © 2014 The McGraw-Hill Companies, Inc. All rights reserved.

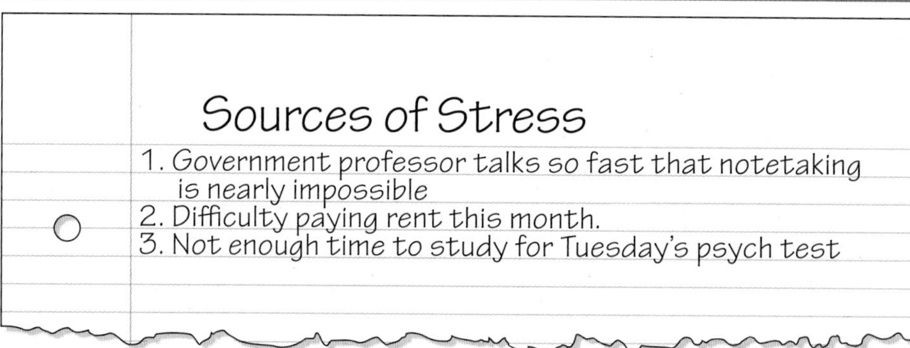

can change how we perceive that situation and find something good about it, we can change our reactions to it. For instance, if your computer science instructor requires you to learn a difficult spreadsheet program in a very short time, the saving grace is that you may be able to use the skill to your advantage in getting a high-paying temporary job during school vacation. (You can practice finding the silver lining in *Try It 2*.)

Sources of Stress
1. Government professor talks so fast that notetaking is nearly impossible
2. Difficulty paying rent this month.
3. Not enough time to study for Tuesday's psych test

18 • **Talk to your friends.** Social support assistance and comfort supplied by others can help us through stressful periods. Turning to our friends and family and simply talking about the stress we're under can help us tolerate it more effectively. Even anonymous telephone hotlines can provide us with social support (The U.S. Public Health Service maintains a master toll-free number that can provide telephone numbers and addresses of many national helplines and support groups. You can reach it by calling 800-336-4794.)

19 • **Relax.** Because stress produces constant wear and tear on the body, it seems possible that practices that lead to the relaxation of the body might lead to a reduction in stress. And that's just what happens. Using any one of several techniques for producing physical relaxation can prevent stress. Among the best relaxation techniques:

20 • **Meditation.** Though often associated with its roots in the ancient Eastern religion of Zen Buddhism, meditation, a technique for refocusing attention and producing bodily relaxation, is practiced in some form by members of virtually every major religion. Meditation reduces blood pressure, slows respiration, and in general reduces bodily tension.

21 • **How do you meditate?** The process is actually rather simple. As summarized in Table 1, it includes sitting in a quiet room with eyes closed or focused on a point about 6 feet away from you and paying attention to your breathing. Though the specifics of what you do may vary, meditation works by helping you concentrate on breathing deeply and rhythmically, sometimes murmuring a word or sound repeatedly.

Look for the Silver Lining

Consider the following list of potentially stressful situations. Try to find something positive—a silver lining—in each of them. The first two are completed to get you started.

Situation	Silver Lining
1. Your car just broke down and repairing it is more than you can afford right now.	1. This is the perfect time to begin exercising by walking and using your bicycle.
2. Your boss just yelled at you and threatened to fire you.	2. Either this is a good time to open an honest discussion with your boss about your job situation, OR this is a good time to get a more interesting job.
3. You have two papers due on Monday and there's a great concert you wanted to go to on Saturday night.	3.
4. You just failed an important test.	4.
5. You're flat broke, you have a date on Saturday, and you wanted to buy some things beforehand.	5.
6. Your last date went poorly and you think your girlfriend/boyfriend was hinting that it was time to break up.	6.
7. Your parents just told you that they can't afford to pay your tuition next semester.	7.
8. You just got cut from a sports team or club activity you loved.	8.
9. Your best friend is starting to turn weird and seems not to enjoy being with you as much as before.	9.
10. You just realized you don't really like your academic major, and you're not even sure you like your college much anymore.	10.

Working in a Group: After you have considered each of these situations individually, discuss each of them in a group. What similarities and differences in others' responses did you find? Evaluate the different responses, and consider whether—and why—some ways of reframing the situations were better than others.

To Try It online, go to **www.mhhe.com/power**.

22 • **Progressive Relaxation.** Progressive relaxation does some of the same things that meditation does, but in a more direct way. To use progressive relaxation, you systematically tense and then relax different groups of muscles. For example, you might start with your lower arm, tensing it for 5 seconds and then relaxing it for a similar amount of time. By doing the same thing throughout the parts of your body, you'll be able to learn the "feel" of bodily relaxation. You can use the technique when you feel that stress is getting the better of you. (Use *Try It 3* to experience progressive relaxation for yourself.)

23 • **Remember that wimping out doesn't work—so keep your commitments.** Suppose you've promised a friend that you'll help him move, and you've promised yourself that you'll spend more time with your children. You've also been elected to the student body governing board, and you've made a commitment to bring more speakers to campus. Now you are facing all the demands connected to these commitments and feeling stressed.

Copyright © 2014 The McGraw-Hill Companies, Inc. All rights reserved.

TABLE 1
METHODS OF MEDITATION

Step 1. Pick a focus word or short phrase that's firmly rooted in your personal belief system. For example, a nonreligious individual might choose a neutral word like *one* or *peace* or *love.* A Christian person desiring to use a prayer could pick the opening words of Psalm 23, *The Lord is my shepherd;* a Jewish person could choose *Shalom.*

Step 2. Sit quietly in a comfortable position.

Step 3. Close your eyes.

Step 4. Relax your muscles.

Step 5. Breathe slowly and naturally, repeating your focus word or phrase silently as you exhale.

Step 6. Throughout, assume a passive attitude. Don't worry about how well you're doing. When other thoughts come to mind, simply say to yourself, "Oh, well," and gently return to the repetition.

Step 7. Continue for 10 to 20 minutes. You may open your eyes to check the time, but do not use an alarm. When you finish, sit quietly for a minute or so, at first with your eyes closed and later with your eyes open. Then do not stand for 1 or 2 minutes.

Step 8. Practice the technique once or twice a day.

24 You may be tempted to cope with the feeling by breaking some or all of your commitments, thinking, "I just need to sit at home and relax in front of the television!" This is not coping. It is escaping, and it doesn't reduce stress. Ducking out of commitments, whether to yourself or to others, will make you feel guilty and anxious, and will be another source of stress—one without the satisfaction of having accomplished what you set out to do. Keep your promises.

Evaluate: Asking If Your Strategies for Dealing with Stress Are Effective

25 Just as the experience of stress depends on how we interpret circumstances, the strategies for dealing with stress also vary in effectiveness depending on who we are. So if your efforts at coping aren't working, it's time to reconsider your approach. If talking to friends hasn't helped ease your stress response, maybe you need a different approach. Maybe you need to see the silver lining or cut back on some of your commitments.

26 If one coping strategy doesn't work for you, try another. What's critical is that you not become paralyzed, unable to deal with a situation. Instead, try something different until you find the right combination of strategies to improve the situation.

Rethink: Placing Stress in Perspective

27 It's easy to think of stress as an enemy. In fact, the coping steps outlined in the P.O.W.E.R. Plan are geared to overcoming its negative consequences. But consider the following two principles, which in the end may help you more than any others in dealing with stress:

Try Progressive Relaxation

You can undertake progressive relaxation almost anywhere, including the library, a sports field, or a classroom, since tensing and relaxing muscles is quiet and unobtrusive. Although the following exercise suggests you lie down, you can use parts of it no matter where you are.

1. Lie flat on your back, get comfortable, and focus on your toes.
2. Become aware of your left toes. Bunch them up into a tight ball, then let them go. Then let them relax even further.
3. Now work on your left foot, from the toes to the heel. Without tensing your toes, tighten up the rest of your foot and then let it relax. Then relax it more.
4. Work your way up your left leg, first tensing and then relaxing each part. You may move up as slowly or as quickly as you wish, using big leaps (e.g., the entire lower leg) or small steps (e.g., the ankle, the calf, the front of the lower leg, the knee, etc.).
5. Repeat the process for the right leg.
6. Now tense and relax progressively your groin, buttocks, abdomen, lower back, ribs, upper back, and shoulders.
7. Work your way down each arm, one at a time, until you reach the fingers.
8. Return to the neck, then the jaw, cheeks, nose, eyes, ears, forehead, and skull.

By now you should be completely relaxed. In fact, you may even be asleep—this technique works well as a sleep-induction strategy.

To vary the routine, play with it. Try going from top to bottom, or from your extremities in and ending with your groin. Or target any other part of your body to end up at, and take the most circuitous route you can think of.

To Try It online, go to **www.mhhe.com/power**.

28 • **Don't sweat the small stuff . . . and it's all small stuff.** Stress expert Richard Carlson emphasizes the importance of putting the circumstances we encounter into the proper perspective. He argues that we frequently let ourselves get upset about situations that are actually minor. So what if someone cuts us off in traffic, or does less than his or her share on a group project, or unfairly criticizes us? It's hardly the end of the world, and the behavior of the other people involved in such situations reflects negatively on them, not us. One of the best ways to reduce stress, consequently, is to maintain an appropriate perspective on the events of your life.

29 • **Make peace with stress.** Think of what it would be like to have no stress—none at all—in your life. Would you really be happier, better adjusted, and more successful? The answer is "probably not." A life that presented no challenges would probably be, in a word, boring. So think about stress as an exciting, although admittedly sometimes difficult, friend. Welcome it, because its presence indicates that your life is stimulating, challenging, and exciting—and who would want it any other way?

Source: Robert Feldman, *P.O.W.E.R. Learning,* 2005 ed., pp. 364–74. Copyright © 2005 by The McGraw-Hill Companies, Inc. Reprinted by permission of The McGraw-Hill Companies.

Copyright © 2014 The McGraw-Hill Companies, Inc. All rights reserved.

SELECTION **10.1** **Student Success** *(continued)*

Comprehension and Vocabulary Quiz

This quiz has four parts. Your instructor may assign some or all of them.

Comprehension

Directions: Use the information in the selection to answer the questions below.

_______ **1.** Cataclysmic events are:

a. major life events that produce a negative physical and psychological reaction.
b. minor irritants of life that, singly, produce relatively little stress.
c. events that occur suddenly and affect many people at the same time.
d. events that lead to mental and physical problems.

_______ **2.** The greater the number of stressful events a person experiences in a year's time:

a. the more likely it is he or she will have a major illness.
b. the faster the heart beats.
c. the more hormones are produced in the body.
d. the more rapid and shallow a person's breathing becomes.

_______ **3.** Losing a job is an example of:

a. a cataclysmic stressor.
b. a personal stressor.
c. a daily hassle.
d. bad luck.

_______ **4.** Which of the following can contribute to stress?

a. drinking large amounts of coffee and soda
b. being overweight
c. lack of regular exercise
d. all of the above

_______ **5.** The strategy of looking for a silver lining refers to:

a. using your energy to improve a situation, not to rewrite history.
b. seeking assistance in the form of social support.
c. refocusing attention to produce bodily relaxation.
d. changing how you perceive a negative situation to find something good about it.

Vocabulary in Context

Directions: For each item below, use context clues to deduce the meaning of the *italicized* word.

_______ **6.** Endorphins produce feelings of happiness—even *euphoria*—and may be responsible for the "runner's high," the positive feelings often reported by long-distance runners following long runs.

The wrestler's *euphoria* over winning disappeared when he was later disqualified for an illegal move.

euphoria (yōō fôr′ ē ə) means:

a. the "runner's high"

b. feeling of great disappointment

c. feeling of great happiness or well-being

d. feeling of deep anger or hostility

_______ **7.** Eating right can *alleviate* another problem: obesity.

There are many over-the-counter medications designed to *alleviate* cold symptoms.

alleviate (ə lē′ vē āt) means:

a. to make less severe

b. to become increasingly unpleasant

c. to assist or aid

d. to intensify

_______ **8.** In addition, feeling heavy in a society that *acclaims* the virtues of slimness can be stressful in and of itself.

The series of ads *acclaims* the candidate's achievements without revealing his previous bankruptcies.

acclaims (ə klāmz′) means:

a. mentions or refers to incidentally

b. praises enthusiastically and often publicly

c. directs to a source of help or information

d. pertains to, concerns

_______ **9.** Though the specifics of what you do may vary, meditation works by helping you concentrate on breathing deeply and rhythmically, sometimes *murmuring* a word or sound repeatedly.

The breeze was *murmuring* through the trees and made a comforting, soothing sound.

murmuring (mûr′ mər ĭng) means:

a. making a high-pitched sound

b. making a buzzing sound

c. making a low, continuous, indistinct sound

d. making a loud, short sound

_______ **10.** To use *progressive* relaxation, you systematically tense and then relax different groups of muscles.

Rather than make sudden, drastic changes in the company, the new owner made *progressive* changes over the course of two years.

progressive (prə grĕs′ ĭv) means:

a. promoting new ideas and better conditions

b. decreasing, diminishing

Copyright © 2014 The McGraw-Hill Companies, Inc. All rights reserved.

c. proceeding in steps

d. changing from one position to another

Word Structure

Directions: In paragraph 18 of the selection, you encountered the word **anonymous.** It contains the root ***nym,*** which means "name." The word *anonymous* means having an unknown or unacknowledged name (such as an anonymous author or an anonymous donor). Use the meaning of ***nym*** and the list of prefixes on pages 72–73 to help you determine the meaning of each of the following words.

_______ **11.** If you know that the word part *pseudo* means "false," then a **pseudonym** would be:

a. an author's actual name.

b. a fictitious name an author uses instead of his or her actual name.

c. a nickname.

d. the name of a famous person.

_______ **12.** "Little" and "small" are examples of synonyms. **Synonyms** are words that:

a. have 5 letters.

b. refer to something that is tiny.

c. appear in the English language.

d. have the same or nearly the same meaning.

_______ **13.** "Big" and "little" are examples of antonyms. **Antonyms** are words that:

a. have opposite meanings.

b. have the same spelling.

c. mean the same thing.

d. have the same sound.

_______ **14.** The words *row* (verb; to propel a boat with oars) and *row* (noun: a straight line) are examples of homonyms. **Homonyms** are words that:

a. look alike.

b. sound alike.

c. mean the same thing

d. have the same sound and spelling, but different meanings.

_______ **15.** *Bow* (noun: a knot with loops) and *bow* (verb: to bend the upper body forward) are examples of heteronyms. **Heteronyms** are words that:

a. sound alike.

b. have the same spelling and pronunciation.

c. mean the same thing.

d. have the same spelling, but different sound and meaning.

Reading Skills Application

Directions: These items test your ability to *apply* certain reading skills to information in the selection.

_______ **16.** The information in the section "Handling Stress" is organized using which overall pattern?

a. list

b. sequence

c. comparison

d. contrast

_______ **17.** In the "Rethink" section, the author's tone is:

a. emotional and opinionated.

b. angry and bitter.

c. apologetic.

d. encouraging and supportive.

_______ **18.** What is the author's attitude toward stress?

a. Stress is inevitable and can be difficult, but being in good physical health can help you cope effectively with it.

b. Stress is inevitable, and it has harmful mental and physical effects.

c. Stress is inevitable and can be difficult, but it also makes life stimulating, challenging, and exciting.

d. Stress is inevitable, but it also makes life bearable.

_______ **19.** The author's intended audience for this selection is:

a. business professionals.

b. people who are coping with health problems.

c. college students.

d. the general public.

_______ **20.** Which of the following assumptions does the author make?

a. College students experience a greater number of cataclysmic events than other people.

b. College students should take whatever steps are necessary to avoid experiencing any stress.

c. College students are not capable of recognizing and dealing with stress.

d. College students experience a great deal of stress, but if they are made aware of coping strategies, they will use them.

SELECTION **10.1**
Student Success
(continued)

Respond in Writing

Directions: Refer to the selection as needed to answer the essay-type questions below.

1. **Reacting to What You Have Read:** Which of the strategies in the "Work" section (paragraphs 14–24) do you currently use? If you do not currently use any of them, which ones do you think might work for you? Explain how you use them or how you might use them. In which types of circumstances would they be especially helpful?

____

____

Copyright © 2014 The McGraw-Hill Companies, Inc. All rights reserved.

____

____

____

____

____

____

2. **Comprehending the Selection Further:** Based on information in the selection about stress, decide which category each of the following stressors represents. For each stressor, place a check mark in the appropriate column.

	Cataclysmic Event	Personal Stressor	Daily Hassle
1. house fire	_____	_____	_____
2. flash flooding of region	_____	_____	_____
3. flu epidemic in a city	_____	_____	_____
4. losing a computer file	_____	_____	_____
5. becoming engaged	_____	_____	_____
6. car is stolen	_____	_____	_____
7. massive hailstorm	_____	_____	_____
8. misplaced keys	_____	_____	_____
9. flat tire	_____	_____	_____
10. final interview for an important job	_____	_____	_____

3. **Overall Main Idea of the Selection:** In one sentence, tell what the author wants readers to understand about stress. (Be sure to include "stress" in your overall main idea sentence.)

____

____

____

____

Read More about It Online

Internet Resources

Directions: To learn more about the topic of this selection, see the website below or use the keywords **"coping with stress"** with a search engine.

www.usu.edu/arc/StudySmart/resources.cfm
This site is sponsored by the Utah Academic Resource Center. It presents valuable information and videos about managing stress. (Other information on time management, procrastination, test-taking, public speaking, etc., can also reduce stress!)

CHAPTER 11

Preparing for Tests: Study-Reading, Rehearsal, and Memory

LEARNING OBJECTIVES

In this chapter you will learn the answers to these questions:

- What is rehearsal, and how does it pertain to memory?
- How can you underline, highlight, and annotate your textbooks?
- How can you take notes from a textbook by outlining, mapping, and summarizing?
- How can you follow written directions?

CHAPTER CONTENTS

NEW INFORMATION AND SKILLS

How Are Rehearsal and Memory Related?

How Can You Underline, Highlight, and Annotate Your Textbooks?

How Can You Take Notes from Textbooks?

- Guidelines for Outlining
- Guidelines for Mapping
- Guidelines for Summarizing

How Can You Follow Directions?

Other Things to Keep in Mind As You Prepare for Tests by Applying Core Comprehension Skills

- When you study, choose the appropriate study techniques.
- Learn how to handle outline, summary, and mapped notes questions on standardized reading tests.

CHAPTER REVIEW CARDS

READING (available through the Online Learning Center)

Selection 11.1 "Information Technology, the Internet, and You"
from *Computing Essentials*
by Timothy O'Leary and Linda O'Leary (Information Technology)

NEW INFORMATION AND SKILLS

HOW ARE REHEARSAL AND MEMORY RELATED?

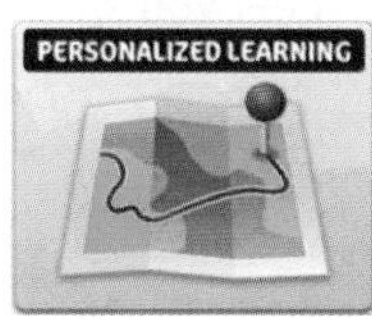

As you may have discovered, it is difficult to memorize information you do not understand. This is why you must focus on understanding material before attempting to memorize it. Thorough comprehension allows you to memorize more efficiently.

Even when you understand material, however, you should not underestimate the time or effort needed to memorize it. To do well on tests, you must study information effectively enough to store it in **long-term memory** (permanent memory). One serious mistake students make is leaving too little time before the test to transfer material into long-term memory. Instead, they try to rely on **short-term memory.** However, material stays in short-term memory only briefly. If you rely on short-term memory only (this is called *cramming*), most of the information will not be there when you try to recall it on the test.

long-term memory
Permanent memory.

short-term memory
Temporary memory.

To understand the difference between long-term and short-term memory, consider a telephone number you have just heard on the radio. The number is only in your short-term memory and will be forgotten in a matter of seconds *unless you do something to transfer it into long-term memory*. In other words, you will forget the number unless you "rehearse" it in some way.

rehearsal
Steps taken to transfer information into long-term memory.

Rehearsal refers to taking specific steps to transfer information into long-term memory. Typical steps include writing information down or repeatedly reciting it aloud. In the example above, for instance, rehearsing the telephone number would probably involve writing it, saying it aloud several times, or both.

In Chapter 1, you read about visual, auditory, and tactile/kinesthetic learning preferences and about their particular importance to students. It is obvious that rehearsing information by writing and reciting involves all the senses and addresses all the learning preferences. Rehearsing by writing and reciting involves speaking, hearing, writing, and reading. Writing the information has the added benefit of helping you learn to spell important terms and names that you may need to know for essay tests.

Consider how much information you already have stored in long-term memory: the alphabet; the multiplication tables; the names of countless people, places, and things; and the meanings and spellings of thousands of words. How did these items make it into your long-term memory? You successfully stored them in long-term memory because you rehearsed them again and again.

Perhaps the greatest mistake students make when trying to memorize information for a test is that they spend their time merely rereading it. You can reread endlessly, but you will not remember the information. Rereading is not the same as rehearsing.

As noted in Chapter 10, rehearsal is the third key to effective studying. When you prepare for a test, spread your studying over several days, enough days to allow you to transfer information into long-term memory. Both sufficient time and ample repetition are needed to accomplish this transfer.

Before you can rehearse textbook information efficiently, you need to *organize* it. The better you organize it, the more efficiently you will be able to memorize it. If you organize the material as you study, right from the beginning of the semester, you will be prepared to rehearse and memorize it for each test. You can organize material by using any of these techniques (which are presented later in this chapter):

- Underlining and annotating textbook material
- Outlining or mapping information

- Preparing summaries
- Making review or summary cards (like the ones in each chapter of *New Worlds*)

Review cards, which you have been working with throughout *New Worlds,* are another important study tool. The very act of preparing these study tools helps you store information in long-term memory.

After you have organized material, rehearse by doing one or more of the following:

- Reciting from your notes
- Writing out the information again from memory
- Reciting from chapter review cards or test review sheets

As noted earlier, students too often review for a test simply by reading through their notes and their textbook several times. But this time-consuming process does not automatically result in remembering. About 80 percent of the time spent studying for a test should be used for memorizing, that is, for transferring information into long-term memory. Here is an example of how you could apply this "80 percent rule." If you need five hours to study for a test, you would spend the first hour organizing the material and getting help with things you do not understand. The remaining four hours would be spent rehearsing the material to memorize it.

You may be wondering, "How can I tell when I have successfully transferred information into long-term memory?" The answer is simple: Test yourself. Try to write the information from memory on a blank sheet of paper. If the material is in your long-term memory, you will be able to recall it and write it down. If you cannot write it, or can write only a part of it, then you need to rehearse it further. Until you can write or say the material aloud without looking at your notes, book, or review cards, you haven't mastered it, and you need to keep rehearsing. Isn't it better, though, to make that discovery while there's still time to learn it than to make that discovery when you are taking the test?

These steps may sound like a lot of work, but they are necessary if you want to lock information into long-term memory. It is precisely this type of study effort that leads to mastery.

HOW CAN YOU UNDERLINE, HIGHLIGHT, AND ANNOTATE YOUR TEXTBOOKS?

It has been estimated that more than three-quarters of the material on college tests comes from the textbooks. For this reason alone, you need to be able to underline, highlight, and annotate the important information in them.

underlining and highlighting

Techniques for marking topics, main ideas, and definitions.

annotating

Writing explanatory notes in the margins of your textbook to organize and remember important information.

Underlining and **highlighting** are techniques for marking topics, main ideas, and important definitions in textbooks. **Annotating** refers to writing explanatory notes in the margins of your textbook to organize and remember important information. Taking a moment to annotate information (write it down) also helps you concentrate and stay focused on your studying. When you are reading a difficult textbook, you may need to concentrate on it paragraph by paragraph. Effective students combine underlining or highlighting with annotating.

Underlining and highlighting textbook material is a selective process. This means you need to avoid the most common mistake students make in marking textbooks: *overmarking*—underlining or highlighting too much. They generally make this mistake because they underline or highlight while they are reading a paragraph for the first time instead of *after* they have read it. You cannot know what is important until you have *finished* reading. The main idea sometimes does not appear until the end of a paragraph. Also, you may not be able to understand some paragraphs until you have read an entire section. The rule, then, is this: *Read first, and underline only after you have identified the important ideas.* A word of caution: Some students substitute underlining and highlighting for *thinking*. They mistakenly believe that if they have marked a lot in a chapter, they must have read it carefully, have found the important information, and understand it. To avoid this error, follow these steps: Read and *think; then* underline or highlight *selectively*.

Second, you need to know the kinds of things you *should* underline or highlight. As mentioned above, underline or highlight the *topic* of a paragraph and the *main idea* of a paragraph if it is stated directly. Keep in mind that you won't always need to underline every word of a main idea sentence to capture the idea it is expressing. Underline or highlight important *terms* and *definitions*.

Third, you need to know the kinds of things you should *not* underline or highlight. Do not underline or highlight examples or other supporting details because this results in overmarking. (As you will learn below, annotation can be used effectively for supporting details.)

Once you have underlined and highlighted topics, main ideas, and important terms, you will want to *annotate:* that is, write explanatory notes and symbols in the margins. If a textbook has narrow margins, you may prefer to use notebook paper or even stick-on notes. You may be wondering what types of annotations are helpful and why it is necessary to annotate as well as to underline or highlight. Of course, you can jot the *topic* in the margin beside each paragraph. This is especially helpful with complex material and with passages on standardized reading tests. In addition, writing out an important *term* and its *definition* in the margin helps you remember it. When your instructor uses those terms in class, you will recognize them and be able to use them in your lecture notes. And, of course, you will need to know terms for tests.

Also, you may choose to list essential *supporting details* in shortened (paraphrased) form in the margin. Annotating is an effective, convenient, concise way to organize details, and jotting details in the margin helps you connect them with the main ideas they support.

Formulated main ideas are another type of helpful annotation. Write them in the margin next to the paragraph.

Symbols and *abbreviations* are still another helpful type of annotation. They enable you to locate important material quickly and find passages that need further study. Here are examples of abbreviations and symbols you can use in the margins:

def	*Definition.* Use *def* when an important term is defined.
1, 2, 3 . . .	*Numbers.* Use numbers when an author gives items in a list or series, or when you want to make the primary supporting details stand out.
*	Use an *asterisk* to mark important information, such as information the instructor has indicated will be on a test.
?	*Question mark.* Use this when you do not understand something and need to come back to it for further study or get help with it.
ex	Use *ex* to identify helpful examples.

The box on page 612 shows how a passage from a human development textbook (about different forms of marriage) could be underlined and annotated. Notice how helpful these markings would be when reviewing for a test on the material.

Copyright © 2014 The McGraw-Hill Companies, Inc. All rights reserved.

AN EXAMPLE OF UNDERLINING AND ANNOTATION

Marriage

A lifestyle practice that appears to exist in all contemporary societies is marriage—a socially, legally, and/or religiously sanctioned union between a woman and a man with the expectation that they will perform the mutually supportive roles of wife and husband. In cultures around the world, marriages serve basic social functions that include creating stable unions to ① regulate mating and reproduction, ② provide for a division of labor, ③ have children, and ④ provide for the material, psychological, and emotional needs of a couple and any young children.

Societies differ in how they structure the social institution of marriage through laws, values, and traditions that convey how the spouses relate to one another, what marriage means, and what it is intended to do. Four main patterns of relationships are found: *monogamy* (one husband and one wife) and forms of polygamy: *polygyny* (one husband and two or more wives), *polyandry* (two or more husbands and one wife), and *group marriage* (two or more husbands and two or more wives). Although in the United States we use polygamy to refer to polygyny, it also includes polyandry. Monogamy is so prevalent in the United States that it is hard to imagine other practices.

Polygyny has been widely practiced throughout the world. It is still a preferred form of marriage in many cultures in Africa, Asia, and the Middle East. Usually only the rich men in a society can afford to support more than one family.

In contrast with polygyny, polyandry is rare among the world's societies. And in practice, women in polyandrous societies are not free to choose their mates; often polyandry simply means that younger brothers have sexual access to the wife of an older brother. Tibetan serfs practice polyandry as a way to cope with a land shortage. If brothers can marry the same women, the family can keep the family land intact rather than splitting it up among the brothers in separate monogamous unions.

Anthropologists disagree about whether group marriage genuinely exists in any society as a normatively encouraged lifestyle. There is some evidence that it might take place among the Marquesans of the South Pacific, the Chukchee of Asia (men make wife-lending contracts with each other), the Kaingang of Brazil, and the Todas and Dahari of India.

def marriage: socially, legally, and/or religiously sanctioned union btwn a woman and a man with expectation they will perform mutually supportive roles of wife and husband

4 patterns of marriage:
— monogamy: 1 husband/1 wife (U.S.)
— polygyny: 1 husband/2+ wives
— polyandry: 2+ husbands/1 wife
— group marriage: 2+ husbands/2+ wives

Polygyny
— has been widely practiced worldwide
— still the preferred form in many cultures in Africa, Asia, Middle East
— usually only rich men polygynous

Polyandry
— women not free to choose their mates
— often just means younger brothers have sexual access to wife of older brother

Group marriage
Disagreement about its existence

tribes?

Source: Thomas Crandell, Corinne Crandell, and James Vander Zanden, *Human Development*, 9th ed., pp. 461–62. Copyright © 2009 by The McGraw-Hill Companies, Inc. Reprinted by permission of The McGraw-Hill Companies.

HOW CAN YOU TAKE NOTES FROM TEXTBOOKS?

In addition to underlining, highlighting, and marginal annotations, *taking notes from textbooks* is another important study skill. Three very useful forms of textbook note-taking are outlining, mapping, and summarizing.

Guidelines for Outlining

outlining

Formal way of organizing main ideas and supporting details to show the relationships among them.

Outlining is a formal way of organizing main ideas and supporting details to show the relationships among them. Even if you underline main ideas in your textbook and annotate the details in the margin, there will be times when it is helpful to outline a section or a chapter. Outlines are especially useful for organizing complex material. Outlining is best done on separate paper rather than written in the textbook.

Obviously, you will not need to outline every assignment, so when should you outline? Besides organizing complex material, outlining lets you condense a lengthy section or chapter so you can get an overview. Seeing how an entire section or chapter is organized makes the material easier to study and remember.

How do you create an outline of textbook material? To outline a paragraph, you first write its main idea. Then, on separate, indented lines below the main idea, write each supporting detail that goes with it, like this:

I. Main idea sentence
    A. Supporting detail
    B. Supporting detail
    C. Supporting detail
    D. Supporting detail

For longer passages consisting of several paragraphs, continue your outline in the same way:

I. First main idea sentence
    A. Supporting detail for main idea I
    B. Supporting detail for main idea I
    C. Supporting detail for main idea I
    D. Supporting detail for main idea I

II. Second main idea sentence
    A. Supporting detail for main idea II
    B. Supporting detail for main idea II

III. Third main idea sentence
    A. Supporting detail for main idea III
    B. Supporting detail for main idea III
    C. Supporting detail for main idea III

The purpose of your study outline is to show how the ideas are related. Making your outline look perfect is not as important as making sure that the relationships are clear to *you*. Main ideas should stand out, however, and it should be obvious which details go with each main idea. Roman numerals (I, II, III, etc.) are often used for main ideas, and uppercase letters (A, B, C, D, etc.) are used for the major supporting details below them. Arabic numerals (1, 2, 3, etc.) are used for minor supporting details. The indentation also shows how ideas are related: The farther an item is indented (to the right), the less important it is. When the information you are writing is longer than a single line, indent the second line below the first word in the line above it. Do not go any farther to the left: The goal is to make the numbers and letters stand out clearly.

An outline can consist of phrases or sentences. (An outline that consists of phrases is called a *topic outline*.) When you have complex material, a sentence outline works well because it gives complete thoughts.

Use the same title for your outline as the one that appears in the original material. Do not title your outline "Outline." It will be obvious from the way the information is organized on the page that it is an outline. The box on this page and the next shows a sentence outline of the passage "Who's the Boss? Leaders, Managers, and Leadership Styles," which appears as Selection 4.1. Notice that the actual outline has the same title as the selection itself.

SAMPLE OUTLINE

Who's the Boss? Leaders, Managers, and Leadership Styles

I. Leaders and managers have different roles and responsibilities, and a person who is good at one may not be good at the other.
  A. Managers strive to produce order and stability, whereas leaders embrace and manage change.
  B. Leadership is creating a vision for others to follow, establishing corporate values and ethics, and transforming the way the organization does business in order to improve its effectiveness and efficiency.
  C. Good leaders motivate workers and create the environment for them to motivate themselves; management is carrying out the leader's vision.

II. Leaders must do five things.
  A. Communicate a vision and rally others around that vision.
    1. The leader should be openly sensitive to the concerns of followers, give them responsibility, and win their trust.
    2. A successful leader must influence the actions of others.
  B. Establish corporate values.
    1. These include concern for employees, for customers, for the environment, and for the quality of the company's products.
    2. When companies set their business goals, they're defining the company's values as well.
      a. The number-one trait that others look for in a leader is honesty.
      b. The second requirement is that the leader be forward looking.
  C. Promote corporate ethics.
    1. Ethical behavior includes an unfailing demand for honesty and an insistence that everyone in the company gets treated fairly.
    2. Many businesspeople have made the news by giving away huge amounts to charity, thus setting a model of social concern for their employees and others.
  D. Embrace change.
    1. A leader's most important job may be to transform the way the company does business so that it's more effective and more efficient.
  E. Stress accountability and responsibility.
    1. Leaders need to be held accountable and need to feel responsible for their actions.
    2. Transparency is the presentation of a company's facts and figures in a way that is clear and apparent to all stakeholders.

III. All organizations need leaders, and all employees can help lead.
  A. You don't have to be a manager to perform a leadership function.
  B. Any employee can motivate others to work well, add to a company's ethical environment, and report ethical lapses when they occur.

IV. Management researchers have found that leadership traits are hard to pin down, and very different types of people can be equally effective.

V. No one set of traits describes a leader, and no one style of leadership works best in all situations, but there are three commonly recognized leadership styles, each of which can be effective in certain situations.

A. Autocratic leadership means making managerial decisions without consulting others.
   1. This style is effective in emergencies and when absolute followership is needed.
   2. It is also effective sometimes with new, relatively unskilled workers who need clear direction and guidance.
B. Participative (democratic) leadership involves managers and employees working together to make decisions.
   1. This style may not always increase effectiveness, but it usually does increase job satisfaction.
   2. Many large organizations and most smaller firms have been highly successful using this style of leadership: It values traits such as flexibility, good listening skills, and empathy.
   3. Employees meet to discuss and resolve management issues by giving everyone some opportunity to contribute to decisions.
C. In free-rein leadership managers set objectives and employees are free to do whatever is appropriate to accomplish those objectives.
   1. It is often the most successful in certain organizations, such as those in which managers supervise professionals.
   2. The traits managers need in such organizations include warmth, friendliness, and understanding.
   3. More and more firms are adopting this style of leadership with at least some of their employees.

VI. Individual leaders rarely fit neatly into just one of these categories, so we can think of leadership as a continuum. Along this continuum, employee participation varies, from purely boss-centered leadership to subordinate-centered leadership.

VII. Research tells us that the leadership style that works best depends largely on what the goals and values of the firm are, who's being led, and in what situations.
   A. A manager may be autocratic but friendly with a new trainee, democratic with an experienced employee, and free-rein with a trusted long-term supervisor.

VIII. There's no such thing as a leadership trait that is effective in all situations, or a leadership style that always works best: A truly successful leader has the ability to adopt the leadership style most appropriate to the situation and the employees.

Source: Adapted from William Nickels, James McHugh, and Susan McHugh, *Understanding Business*, 9th ed., pp. 189–92. Copyright © 2010 by The McGraw-Hill Companies, Inc. Reprinted by permission of The McGraw-Hill Companies.

Guidelines for Mapping

mapping

Informal way of organizing main ideas and supporting details by using boxes, circles, lines, arrows, etc.

Another form of textbook note-taking is mapping. **Mapping** is an informal way of organizing main ideas and supporting details by using boxes, circles, lines, arrows, and the like. The idea is to show information in a way that clarifies relationships among ideas. Like outlining, mapping is done on a separate sheet of paper rather than in the textbook. With some maps, it works better to turn the page sideways. If you prefer to work on a computer, consider using mapping software. Commercial, shareware, and freeware mapping software are available. Google "free mind mapping software for students," "mind mapping software for students," or "concept mapping software for students." See www.bubbl.us for an example of free, easy-to-use mapping software.

One simple type of map consists of the topic in a circle or box in the middle of the sheet of paper, with main ideas written on lines radiating out from it, or with the main idea in the center with the supporting details radiating out. Another type has the main idea in a box at the top of the page, with the supporting ideas in smaller boxes below it and connected to it by arrows or leader lines. If the information is sequential (for instance, significant events in World War I), a map can take the form of a flowchart. Samples of these kinds of maps are shown on next page.

A study map for paragraph 5 of Selection 4.1, "Who's the Boss? Leaders, Managers, and Leadership Styles," is shown on page 617. It condenses the important information into a single diagram.

THREE EXAMPLES OF MAPPING

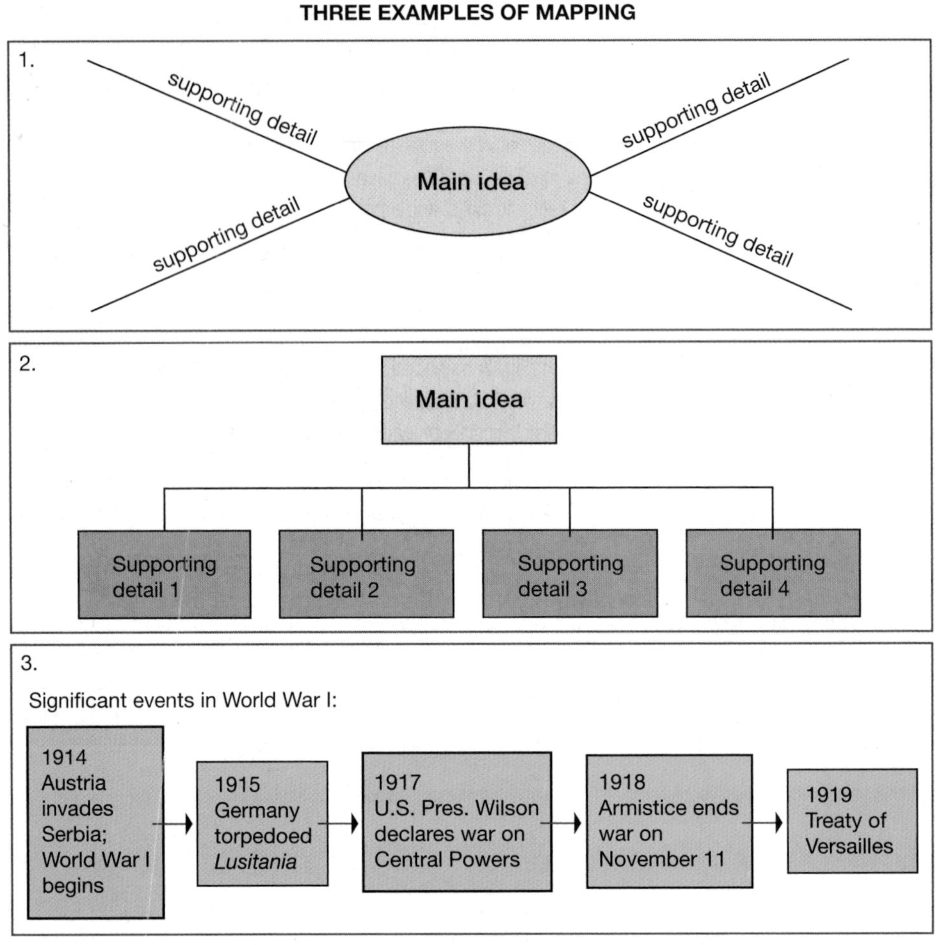

It is obvious that a study map takes thought and effort. The very process of *creating* a map, however, helps you understand and transfer the information into your long-term memory. And, of course, you have created a valuable study aid to refer to when you prepare for a test.

Since outlines and study maps both show relationships among important ideas in a passage, how can you decide when to use each? Your decision will depend on how familiar you are with each technique, how the passage itself is written, and your own personal preference. Keep in mind that mapping is an informal study technique, whereas outlining can be formal or informal. When you are asked to prepare a formal outline in a college course, do not assume that you can substitute an informal outline or a study map.

Guidelines for Summarizing

summary
Single-paragraph condensation of all the main ideas presented in a longer passage.

A third technique of textbook note-taking is summarizing. A **summary** condenses into one paragraph all the main ideas in a longer selection (such as an essay or an article) or a section of a chapter. When you have identified the main ideas in a passage, you have identified the information for the summary.

SAMPLE MAP

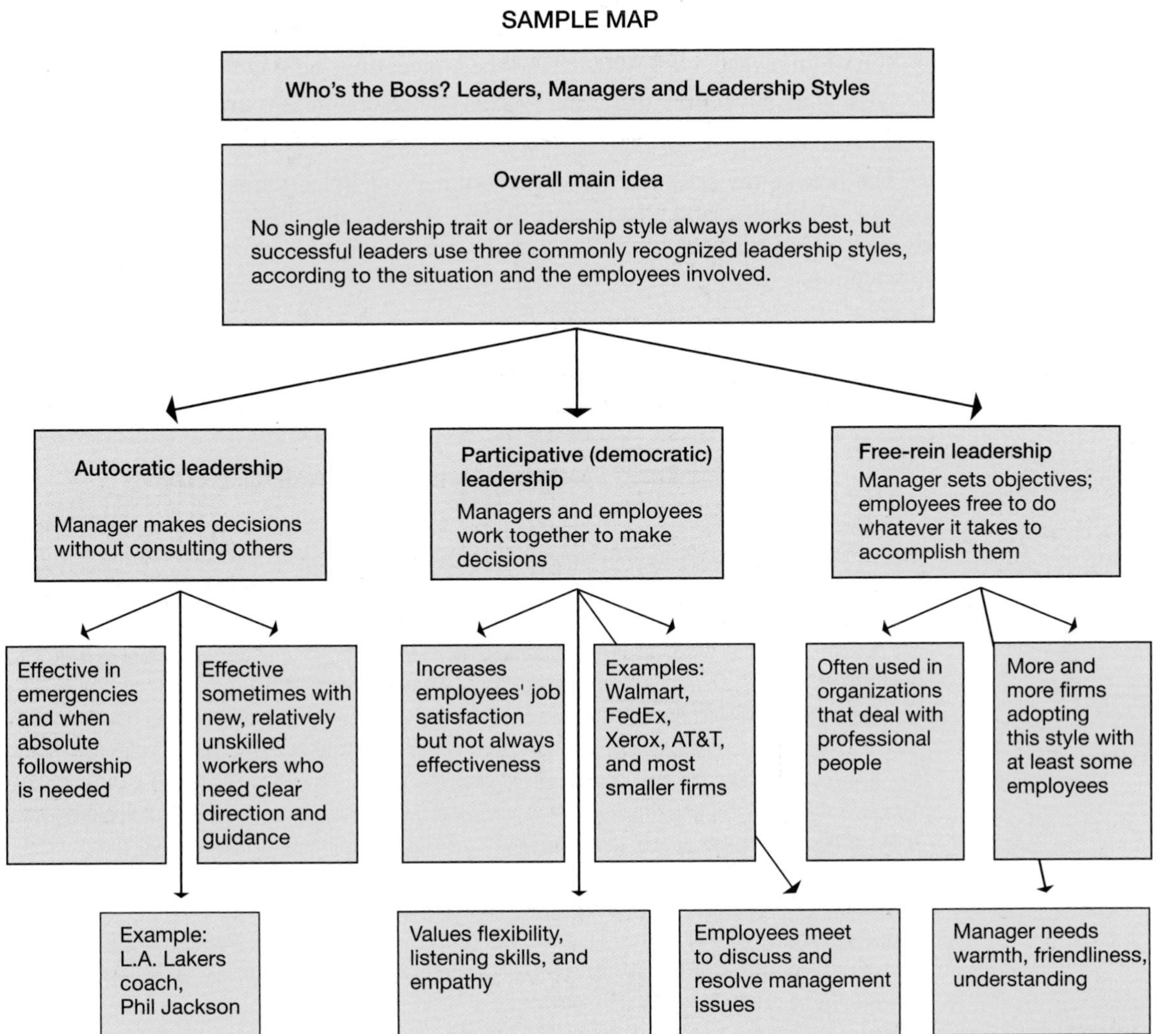

Summarizing is an effective way to check your comprehension. Writing a summary also helps you transfer the material into your long-term memory. You learn key terms and how to spell them correctly. Summarizing is particularly helpful when you will be asked essay questions on a test: Summarizing allows you to "rehearse" answers you are likely to have to write on a test.

Here are guidelines for writing a summary:

- **Include all the main ideas.** Include a supporting detail only if a main idea cannot be understood without it.
- **Do not add anything beyond what appears in the selection itself.** Do not add your own opinions, other information you know about the subject, or anything else that is not one of the author's ideas.
- **Keep the author's original sequence of ideas.** Present the ideas in your summary in the same order that the author presents them. Do not rearrange them.

- **Reword as necessary, providing transitions between main points.** You can paraphrase (reword) the main ideas if you like. Include clear transitions so that you or your reader will understand the connections among the author's ideas.
- **Give your summary the same title as the selection you are summarizing.** Do not title your summary "Summary."

The box below contains a sample summary of Selection 4.1, "Who's the Boss? Leaders, Managers, and Leadership Styles." Notice that it has the same title as the original selection. It contains all the main ideas in the same order as they appeared in the selection.

SAMPLE SUMMARY

Who's the Boss? Leaders, Managers, and Leadership Styles

Leaders and managers' roles and responsibilities are different roles, and a person is not necessarily good at both. While managers try to create order and stability, leaders welcome and manage change. Leaders have five main responsibilities: (1) to convey a vision and motivate others to support it; (2) to establish company values; (3) to promote company ethics; (4) to be open to change; and (5) to emphasize accountability and responsibility. Every organization needs leaders, and every employee can help lead. Research indicates that leadership traits are difficult to pinpoint, and very different types of people can be equally effective. Leaders possess no one set of traits, and no single style of leadership works best in all situations. However, there are three commonly recognized leadership styles, each of which can work well in certain circumstances. They are (1) autocratic leadership (making managerial decisions without consulting others), (2) participative or democratic leadership (in which managers and employees make decisions together), and (3) free-rein leadership (although managers set objectives, employees can do whatever they think is required to accomplish them). A leader rarely fits precisely into just one of these categories. Consequently, it is more helpful to view leadership as a continuum. The leadership style that works best hinges mainly on the company's goals and values, who's being led, and in what situations. Moreover, no leadership trait is effective in all situations, nor is there one leadership style that always works best. Leaders who are truly successful choose the leadership style best suited to the situation and the employees.

Source: Adapted from William Nickels, James McHugh, and Susan McHugh, *Understanding Business*, 9th ed., pp. 189–92. Copyright © 2010 by The McGraw-Hill Companies. Reprinted by permission of The McGraw-Hill Companies.

PRACTICE EXERCISES

Creating an Outline, a Summary, and a Study Map

1. On notebook paper, write a topic *outline* of paragraphs 8–29 of Selection 10.1, "Living with Stress." Be sure to give your outline the correct title.
2. Use the information in your outline to write a *summary* of paragraphs 2–6 of Selection 10.1, "Living with Stress." Write your summary on notebook paper. Be sure to give your summary the correct title.
3. On notebook paper, create a *study map* for paragraphs 6–18 of Selection 11.1, "Information Technology, the Internet, and You" (available through the Online Learning Center). Be sure to label your map with the correct title.

HOW CAN YOU FOLLOW DIRECTIONS?

An important part of college reading is following written directions. You need to understand directions in order to do assignments correctly, carry out procedures in classes and labs, and earn high grades on tests.

You know from experience that problems arise from misunderstanding or failing to follow directions. Perhaps you once answered an entire set of test questions instead of the specific number stated in the directions ("Answer any *five* of the following seven essay questions"). Or perhaps you lost points on a report because you did not follow the correct format ("Double-space your paper and number the pages"). When you do not follow directions, you waste time and may lower your grade.

Guidelines for Following Directions

There are a few simple points to remember about following written directions:

- **Read the entire set of directions carefully before doing any of the steps.** It is tempting to assume you know what to do and to plunge in without reading the directions. That's a mistake. This is one time when you should slow down and pay attention to every word.
- **Make sure you understand all the words in the directions.** Although directions may include words you see often, you may still not know precisely what some words mean. For example, on an essay test you might be asked to *compare* two poems or *contrast* two pieces of music. Do you know the difference between *compare* and *contrast*? Unless you do, you cannot answer the question correctly. Words in test questions, such as *enumerate, justify, explain,* and *illustrate,* each have a specific meaning. General direction words include *above, below, consecutive, preceding, succeeding, former,* and *latter*. Directions in textbooks and assignments often include specialized terms that you must understand. For example, in a set of directions for a biology lab experiment, you might be instructed to "stain a tissue sample on a slide." The words *stain, tissue,* and *slide* have specific meanings in biology.
- **Circle signal words that announce steps in directions and underline key words.** Not every step in a set of directions will have a signal word, but steps in sets of directions frequently are introduced by letters or numbers (*a, b, c,* or *1, 2, 3,* etc.) or words such as *first, second, third, next, then, finally,* and *last* to indicate the order of the steps.
- **Mark directions before you begin following them, since you must understand what you are to do before you try to do it.** Find and number steps if they are not already numbered. A single sentence sometimes contains more than one step (for example, "Type your name, enter your I.D. number, and press the Enter key"). When you are working on a test or an assignment, it is easy to become distracted and leave a step out or do the steps in the wrong order. Another reason to number the steps is that even though the steps may not include signal words, you are still responsible for finding each step. Especially on tests, then, you should number each step and mark key words in directions.

Look at the box on page 620 that shows a set of directions from a computer textbook. The directions explain how to create and share a document online using Google docs. Notice that the steps are not numbered. If you were actually following these directions, you would read the entire set first, number each step, then mark keywords.

Copyright © 2014 The McGraw-Hill Companies, Inc. All rights reserved.

CREATING AND SHARING A DOCUMENT ONLINE IN GOOGLE DOCS

Sometimes you need to collaborate with others on a document, a presentation, or a spreadsheet. Or perhaps you need access to a document from both home and school. *Google Docs* is a free online resource that can address these needs. It is an online office suite that allows you to create and edit documents directly through a Web page with no additional software to install on your computer. (*Office suites* contain professional-grade word processing, spreadsheets, and more. Microsoft Office is an example.) Here is the procedure for creating and sharing a document online in Google docs.

Visit http://docs.google.com. Follow the on-screen instructions to create a free Google account if you do not already have one.

Click the *Create new* button.

Select the type of document you want to create, such as a word processing document, presentation or spreadsheet. The new document is displayed and can be edited directly through the Web page.

To give others access to view and edit your document, click the *Share* button. Select *Share . . .*

Enter the e-mail addresses of the people to invite. Optionally enter a brief message to the people you are inviting.

Click the *Share* button. The people you invited will receive an e-mail with instructions for accessing the document. You will be able to see any changes to the document, and they will see yours.

The Web is continually changing, so be aware that some of the specifics can change.

Source: Timothy O'Leary and Linda O'Leary, *Computing Essentials 2013, Introductory Edition*, pp. 92–93. Copyright © 2013 by The McGraw-Hill Companies, Inc. Reprinted by permission of The McGraw-Hill Companies.

Here is the same set of directions after they have been marked. Notice how much more clearly each step stands out.

CREATING AND SHARING A DOCUMENT ONLINE IN GOOGLE DOCS

Sometimes you need to collaborate with others on a document, presentation, or a spreadsheet. Or perhaps you need access to a document from both home and school. *Google Docs* is a free online resource that can address these needs. It is an online office suite that allows you to create and edit documents directly through a Web page with no additional software to install on your computer. *(Office suites* contain professional-grade word processing, spreadsheets, and more. Microsoft Office is an example.) Here is the procedure for creating and sharing a document online in Google docs:

① Visit http://docs.google.com. ② Follow the on-screen instructions to create a free Google account if you do not already have one.

③ Click the *Create new* button.

④ Select the type of document you want to create, such as a word processing document, presentation or spreadsheet. The new document is displayed and can be edited directly through the Web page.

⑤ To give others access to view and edit your document, click the *Share* button. Select *Share . . .*

⑥ Enter the e-mail addresses of the people to invite. ⑦ Optionally enter a brief message to the people you are inviting.

⑧ Click the *Share* button. The people you invited will receive an e-mail with instructions for accessing the document. You will be able to see any changes to the document, and they will see yours.

The Web is continually changing, so be aware that some of the specifics can change.

Source: Timothy O'Leary and Linda O'Leary, *Computing Essentials 2013, Introductory Edition*, pp. 92–93. Copyright © 2013 by The McGraw-Hill Companies, Inc. Reprinted by permission of The McGraw-Hill Companies.

OTHER THINGS TO KEEP IN MIND AS YOU PREPARE FOR TESTS BY APPLYING CORE COMPREHENSION SKILLS

Here are two helpful things you should know as you prepare for tests by applying core comprehension skills.

1. **When you study, choose the study techniques (underlining, highlighting, annotating, outlining, mapping, summarizing, making review cards or test review sheets) that (*a*) are appropriate to the type of material you are studying, (*b*) correspond to how you will be tested on the material, and (*c*) best suit your learning preferences.**

   For example, if you are dealing with complex material, you may prefer to use an outline to organize the information. If you are enrolled in a course in which the tests include essay questions, you may find it helpful to write summaries of important points in a chapter. You may want to use different techniques in different courses.

   Think about how you learn best. (See the section in Chapter 1 on learning preferences.) If you have a visual or kinesthetic preference, you will find maps and outlines especially helpful. If you have an auditory preference, you may want to rehearse the material by reading it or saying it aloud after you have written it down.

2. **Learn how to handle outline, summary, and mapped notes questions on standardized reading tests.**

   When you are taking a standardized reading test, you may be asked to choose the correct *outline* for all or part of a reading selection. You should rule out as incorrect answers that (*a*) have the information in the wrong order, (*b*) list main ideas or details at the wrong level (such as putting a detail at the level of importance of a main idea), (*c*) leave out main ideas, or (*d*) include incorrect information or information that did not appear in the passage. Compare the first item in each answer choice. If they are the same, drop to the next level. As soon as you encounter incorrect information in an answer choice, you can rule it out. This approach is more effective and efficient than reading each complete answer choice.

   When you are taking a standardized reading test, you may be asked to choose the correct *summary* for all or part of a reading selection. You should rule out as incorrect answers that (*a*) have the information in the wrong order, (*b*) include examples or other details, (*c*) leave out main ideas, or (*d*) include incorrect information or information that did not appear in the passage. A helpful strategy is to rule out answer choices that begin or end with the wrong information.

   When you are taking a standardized reading test, you may be asked to choose the correct *set of mapped notes* for all or part of a reading selection. You should rule out as incorrect answers that (*a*) have the information in the wrong order, (*b*) list details with a main idea that they do not support, (*c*) leave out main ideas or important details, or (*d*) include incorrect information or information that did not appear in the passage. Use the same strategy as for outlines: Compare the answer choices level by level, and rule out an answer choice as soon as you encounter the first bit of incorrect information.

Copyright © 2014 The McGraw-Hill Companies, Inc. All rights reserved.

Directions: Complete the chapter review cards for Chapter 11 by answering the questions or following the directions on each card.

Rehearsing Textbook Material

Card 1 Chapter 11: Preparing for Tests: Study-Reading, Rehearsal, and Memory

Copyright © 2014 The McGraw-Hill Companies, Inc. All rights reserved.

Underlining and Highlighting Textbook Material

Card 2 Chapter 11: Preparing for Tests: Study-Reading, Rehearsal, and Memory

Guidelines for Annotating Textbook Material

Card 3 Chapter 11: Preparing for Tests: Study-Reading, Rehearsal, and Memory

Guidelines for Outlining

Card 4 Chapter 11: Preparing for Tests: Study-Reading, Rehearsal, and Memory

Guidelines for Mapping

Card 5 Chapter 11: Preparing for Tests: Study-Reading, Rehearsal, and Memory

Copyright © 2014 The McGraw-Hill Companies, Inc. All rights reserved.

Guidelines for Summarizing

Card 6 Chapter 11: Preparing for Tests: Study-Reading, Rehearsal, and Memory

Guidelines for Following Written Directions

Card 7 Chapter 11: Preparing for Tests: Study-Reading, Rehearsal, and Memory

SELECTION **11.1**

Information Technology

Information Technology, the Internet, and You

From *Computing Essentials*

By Timothy O'Leary and Linda O'Leary

APPLYING THE CHAPTER 11 SKILLS

Selection 11.1, "Information Technology, the Internet, and You," appears on the *New Worlds* Online Learning Center (www.mhhe.com/newworlds). It is a complete chapter from an information technology textbook. The selection is accompanied by a Respond in Writing section. Your instructor will direct you about using it.

Unlike the reading selections in previous chapters, Selection 11.1 is accompanied by a 20-item practice quiz that your instructor may use. The quiz consists of questions an information technology professor would ask about the material. To prepare for the practice quiz, your instructor may direct you to use these Chapter 11 skills to organize the material:

- Outlining
- Mapping
- Summarizing

Preparing an outline, a map, or a summary provides an effective study tool you can use to rehearse the information and transfer it into long-term memory.

Copyright © 2014 The McGraw-Hill Companies, Inc. All rights reserved.

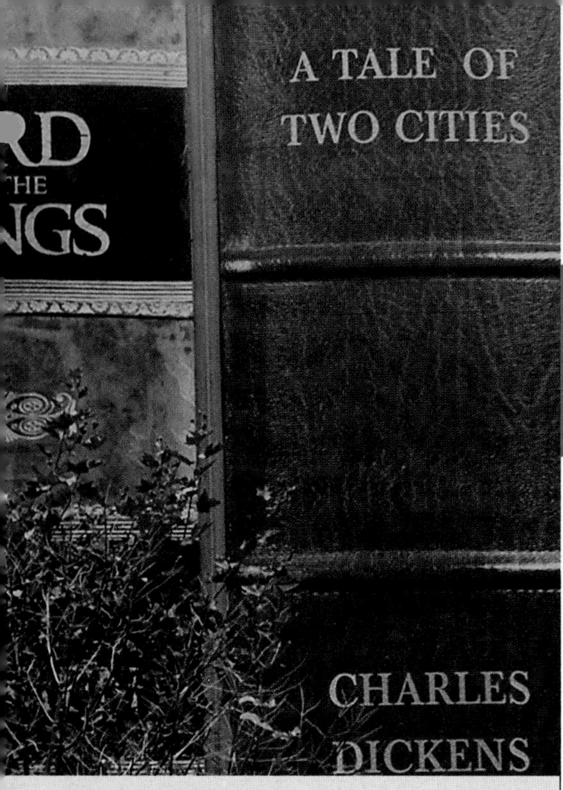

Essential Skills Review Tests

There are 10 Essential Skills Review Tests. Each consists of a short passage followed by multiple-choice items. The passages contain useful information that will expand your knowledge base. Most are from college textbooks, so they also provide excellent practice in dealing with the type of material students encounter in college courses.

The 10-item tests enable you to assess your progress in applying the following skills:

- vocabulary in context
- stated main ideas
- supporting details
- implied main ideas
- sentence relationships
- authors' writing patterns
- author's purpose, intended audience, point of view, and tone
- fact and opinion
- making inferences and drawing conclusions

Your instructor will direct you in using the tests. You may not have studied all the skills by the time you use each test. However, the tests can serve as a valuable introduction to skills you will be learning. They will also provide practice with vocabulary and comprehension skills you have already studied.

ESSENTIAL SKILLS REVIEW TEST 1

Directions: Read the passage below and then select the best answer for each question.

How to Make the Perfect Hard-Boiled Egg

By Lauren Torrisi

At first glance, hard-boiled eggs seem easy to make—just throw them in water and boil. While that sounds good in theory, chances are you won't get that perfectly cooked egg and easy-to-peel shell. We've nailed down the steps you need to take to have egg-cellent hard-boiled eggs in no time.

1. **Use older eggs.** Yup, you heard that right. In Harold McGee's book, *On Food and Cooking*, he says that the shells peel easily after several days of refrigeration due to the pH level of the albumen. If all you have are fresh eggs, McGee suggests adding 1/2 teaspoon of baking soda to the cooking water.
2. **Start with cold water.** Place eggs in a single layer at the bottom of a pan. Starting with cold water keeps the eggs from cracking; make sure that the water is about 1 inch above the eggs. Add a pinch of salt to the water to help make them easier to peel.
3. **Bring to a boil for a few seconds, then cover for 12 minutes.** Once the water has boiled on medium heat, turn off the heat and cover the eggs. They should be done after 12 minutes. To test the eggs, open one to make sure you have the desired consistency. Another test is to spin the egg on a table. Cooked eggs will spin quickly while uncooked eggs will spin slowly due to their liquid contents.
4. **Place the eggs in ice water.** Shocking the eggs in ice water stops them from continuing to cook. Once they are cool, remove them from the pan.
5. **Peel them under cool running water.** This makes the shelling easier if you're not decorating the eggs.

Source: http://abcnews.go.com/blogs/lifestyle/2012/04/how-to-make-the-perfect-hard-boiled-egg/ABC News; accessed 4/6/12.

_______ **1.** Which sentence is the *overall stated main idea* of the passage?

a. At first glance, hard-boiled eggs seem easy to make—just throw them in water and boil.
b. While that sounds good in theory, chances are you won't get that perfectly cooked egg and easy-to-peel shell.
c. We've nailed down the steps you need to take to have egg-cellent hard-boiled eggs in no time.
d. This makes the shelling easier if you're not decorating the eggs.

_______ **2.** What is the *relationship between these two sentences*? "At first glance, hard-boiled eggs seem easy to make—just throw them in water and boil. While that sounds good in theory, chances are you won't get that perfectly cooked egg and easy-to-peel shell."

a. The second sentence presents a contrast with something in the first sentence.
b. The second sentence continues a sequence begun in the first sentence.
c. The second sentence defines something mentioned in the first sentence.
d. The second sentence gives an example of something mentioned in the first sentence.

_______ **3.** With regard to selecting eggs to hard-boil, it is recommended that you use:

a. organic eggs only.
b. eggs you have had for a while.
c. smaller eggs rather than larger ones.
d. the freshest eggs possible.

_______ **4.** What is the *relationship between the parts of this sentence*? "Add a pinch of salt to the water to help make them easier to peel." (The second part starts after the word "water.")

a. comparison and contrast
b. definition and example
c. cause and effect
d. sequence

_______ **5.** "Cooked eggs will spin quickly while uncooked eggs will spin slowly due to their liquid contents." The preceding sentence presents:

a. facts.
b. opinions.
c. both fact and opinion.

_______ **6.** As used in item 4, *shocking* means:

a. taking by surprise.
b. coming into violent contact.
c. disturbing.
d. submerging in very cold water.

_______ **7.** Based on information in this passage, which of the following can be *concluded* with regard to hard-boiling fresh eggs?

a. They can be used if they are cooked longer.
b. They will peel more easily.
c. They will look better when decorated.
d. They can be used if baking soda is added to the water.

_______ **8.** The *author's purpose* in writing this passage is to:

a. instruct readers how to cook hard-boiled eggs properly.
b. inform readers about cooking with eggs.
c. persuade readers to stop hard-boiling eggs.
d. persuade readers to keep older eggs on hand.

_______ **9.** Whom does the author have in mind as the *audience,* or readers, of this passage?

a. chefs
b. gourmet cooks
c. home cooks
d. cookbook authors

_______ **10.** Overall, the information in the passage is organized using which *pattern*?

a. list
b. sequence
c. comparison and contrast
d. definition and example

ESSENTIAL SKILLS REVIEW TEST 2

Directions: Read the passage below and then select the best answer for each question.

Leading without Being Arrogant

1 Sometimes when groups form, no one wants to "lead." Perhaps that's because we've seen "leaders" who seemed dictatorial, who implied that no one else's work would be up to their high standards, and who generally antagonized the people unfortunate enough to have to work with them.

2 You don't have to be arrogant to be a leader. Here are some things that you can do to get your group started on the right track.

- **Smile.** Get to know the other members of your group as individuals. Invite members to say something about themselves, perhaps what job they're hoping to get and one fact about their lives outside of school.
- **Share.** Tell people about your own work style and obligations, and ask others to share their styles and obligations. Savvy group members play to each other's strengths and devise strategies for dealing with differences. The earlier you know what those differences are, the easier it will be to deal with them.
- **Suggest.** "Could we talk about what we see as our purposes in this presentation?" "One of the things we need to do is. . . ." "One idea I had for a project is. . . ." Presenting your ideas as suggestions gets the group started without suggesting that you expect your views to prevail.
- **Think.** Leaders look at the goal and identify the steps needed to get there. "Our proposal is due in two weeks. Let's list the tasks we need to do in order to write a rough draft."
- **Volunteer.** Volunteer to take notes or to gather some of the data the group will need or to prepare the charts after the data are in. Volunteer not just for the fun parts of the job (such as surfing the Web to find visuals for your PowerPoint presentation), but also for some of the dull but essential work, such as proofreading.
- **Ask.** Bring other people into the conversation. Learn about their knowledge, interests, and skills. If you do this, you'll have as much as possible to draw on as you complete your group projects.

Source: Kitty Locker and Stephen Kaczmarek, *Business Communication*, 5th ed., p. 320. Copyright © 2011 by The McGraw-Hill Companies, Inc. Reprinted by permission of The McGraw-Hill Companies.

Copyright © 2014 The McGraw-Hill Companies, Inc. All rights reserved.

_______ **1.** As used in paragraph 1, *dictatorial* means:

a. cooperative.
b. imposing one's will on others.
c. lazy and unmotivated.
d. skilled in dealing with others.

_______ **2.** In paragraph 1, the words "lead" and "leaders" are in quotation marks. It can be *inferred* that the authors do this to:

a. remind readers of the topic of the passage.
b. make them stand out as keywords.
c. make them match a word in the title.
d. indicate they do not reflect their true meaning.

_______ **3.** The *authors' purpose* in writing this passage is to:

a. instruct readers how to lead a group without acting superior.
b. inform readers about how to take control of any group.
c. persuade group members to participate more actively.
d. persuade group members to volunteer for unpleasant jobs.

_______ **4.** What is the *relationship of the parts of this sentence* in paragraph 2? "Volunteer not just for the fun parts of the job (such as surfing the Web to find visuals for your PowerPoint presentation), but also for some of the dull but essential work, such as proofreading." (The second part begins after the first comma.)

a. The second part adds information to that presented in the first part.
b. The second part presents the effect of something in the first part.
c. The second part continues a sequence begun in the first part.
d. The second part illustrates something mentioned in the first part.

_______ **5.** What is the *relationship between these two sentences* in the last bulleted item in paragraph 2? "Bring other people into the conversation. Learn about their knowledge, interests, and skills."

a. The second sentence presents a contrast with something in the first sentence.
b. The second sentence makes a comparison with something in the first sentence.
c. The second sentence gives the cause of something mentioned in the first sentence.
d. The second sentence clarifies something mentioned in the first sentence.

_______ **6.** Who is the *intended audience,* the people the authors have in mind as readers?

a. students who may need to work in groups
b. anyone who belongs to a professional group
c. anyone forced into leading a group
d. businesspeople who work on group projects

_______ **7.** Which of the following expresses the *overall implied main idea* of the passage?

a. Sometimes when groups form, no one wants to lead, but someone has to do it.
b. A group leader can do several things to avoid arrogance and get the group started on the right track.
c. A group leader who is not arrogant will learn as much as possible about the people in the group.
d. The most important thing about being a group leader is to present ideas as suggestions.

_______ **8.** Based on information in the passage, it is logical to *conclude* the authors believe that:

a. leadership is a quality some people are born with but that others do not have.
b. different groups require different leadership strategies.
c. it is possible to learn how to become a better group leader.
d. there are very few good leaders.

_______ **9.** According to information in the passage, smart group members:

a. volunteer for the more enjoyable jobs.
b. let others know about the obligations they have outside the group.
c. smile frequently.
d. tap each other's strengths.

_______ **10.** Which of the following describes the *overall organization* of the passage?

a. definition
b. list
c. sequence
d. contrast

ESSENTIAL SKILLS REVIEW TEST 3

Directions: Read the passage below and then select the best answer for each question. Since there are two fables, the paragraphs in them have been numbered consecutively.

Two Fables from Aesop

Aesop (ē′ säp) was a 6th-century Greek storyteller who is considered the author of *Aesop's Fables.*

The Old Woman and the Physician

1 An old woman having lost the use of her eyes, called in a physician to heal them, and made this bargain with him in the presence of witnesses: that if he should cure her blindness, he should receive from her a sum of money; but if her infirmity remained, she should give him nothing. This agreement being made, the physician, time after time, applied his salve to her eyes, and on every visit took something away, stealing all her property little by little. And when he had got all she had, he healed her and demanded the promised payment.

2 The old woman, when she recovered her sight and saw none of her goods in her house, would give him nothing. The physician insisted on his claim, and as she still refused, summoned her before the judge.

3 The old woman, standing up in the court, argued: "This man here speaks the truth in what he says, for I did promise to give him a sum of money if I should recover my sight, but if I continued blind, I was to give him nothing. Now he declares that I am healed. I on the contrary affirm that I am still blind. Before I lost the use of my eyes, I saw in my house various chattels and valuable goods. Now, though he swears I am cured of my blindness, I am not able to see a single thing in it."

Moral: He who plays a trick must be prepared to have one played on him: turnabout is fair play.

The Peacock and the Crane

4 A peacock spread its gorgeous tail and mocked a crane that passed by, ridiculing the ashen hue of its plumage. "I am robed like a king in gold and purple and all the colors of the rainbow, while you have not a bit of color on your wings."

5 "True," replied the crane, "but I soar to the heights of heaven and lift up my voice to the stars, while you walk below, like a cock, among the birds of the dunghill."

Moral: Fine feathers don't make fine birds: there are things far more important than appearances.

Source: Adapted from http://www.aesopfables.com/aesopsel.html; accessed 4/8/12.

______ **1.** As used in paragraph 1, *infirmity* means:

a. poor vision.
b. a frustration.
c. weakness.
d. a bodily ailment.

______ **2.** As used in paragraph 3, *chattels* refers to items that are:

a. extremely valuable.
b. used in the kitchen.
c. movable personal property.
d. used for decoration.

______ **3.** In paragraph 4, the peacock mocks the crane, "I am robed like a king in gold and purple and all the colors of the rainbow, while you have not a bit of color on your wings." The author intends the peacock's *tone* to be:

a. compassionate.
b. pessimistic.
c. arrogant.
d. apologetic.

_______ **4.** What is the *relationship of the parts of this sentence* in paragraph 4? "This agreement being made, the physician, time after time, applied his salve to her eyes, and on every visit took something away, stealing all her property little by little." (The second part begins after the first comma.)

a. The second part continues a sequence begun in the first part.
b. The second part makes a comparison with something in the first part.
c. The second part clarifies the first part.
d. The second part illustrates something mentioned in the first part.

_______ **5.** Which of the following is a *logical inference* about the first fable, "The Old Woman and the Physician"?

a. The doctor continued to take advantage of every patient whenever he could.
b. The doctor sold the things he stole.
c. From the beginning, the old woman did not trust the doctor.
d. The old woman outsmarted the thieving doctor.

_______ **6.** Based on the two passages, it is logical to *infer* that a *fable* is:

a. a short tale that teaches a lesson and may include animals as characters.
b. an untruth or a falsehood.
c. a story about supernatural or extraordinary persons or incidents.
d. a traditional tale about a hero or heroic event.

_______ **7.** The *author's intended audience* is likely to be primarily:

a. children.
b. writers.
c. parents.
d. scholars.

_______ **8.** What is the *relationship between these two sentences* in paragraph 3? "Now he declares that I am healed. I on the contrary affirm that I am still blind."

a. The second sentence adds information to that in the first sentence.
b. The second sentence presents a contrast with something in the first sentence.
c. The second sentence continues a sequence begun in the first sentence.
d. The second sentence illustrates something mentioned in the first sentence.

_______ **9.** "Fine feathers don't make fine birds: there are things far more important than appearances." The preceding sentence presents:

a. a fact.
b. an opinion.

_______ **10.** Based on the two passages, it is logical to *infer* that Aesop:

a. liked animals more than humans.
b. dreamed up fables because he was bored.
c. had insight into how humans behave and how they should behave.
d. knew his fables would be told for centuries to come.

Directions: Read the passage below and then select the best answer for each question.

Pink Slime

1 "Lean finely textured beef" (LFTB) or "boneless lean beef trimmings" (BLBT) sounds noncontroversial enough, right? Call the ground beef additive "pink slime," however, and it sounds much less attractive—and to most people, downright repulsive.

2 The term was first used by a microbiologist named Gerald Zimstein, who worked for the United States Department of Agriculture (USDA) Food Safety Inspection Service. In 2002, Zimstein objected to the USDA approving the use of pink slime, but the USDA approved it anyway.

3 Pink slime is used as an inexpensive filler in processed beef-based products, such as hamburger. It is inexpensive because it consists of salvaged beef parts: scraps and connective tissue, such as cartilage, tendons, and ligaments. By law, ground beef can contain up to 15% of pink slime without its being revealed on the label. In other words, ground beef that is 15 percent pink slime can still be labeled "100 percent ground beef."

4 Another point of controversy is that after being heated, the salvaged beef used to make pink slime is treated with ammonia gas or citric acid to kill bacteria. This is a process that some other countries, such as Canada, prohibit. The ammoniated beef scraps are finely ground and pressed into blocks. The blocks are flash frozen and then sold to supermarket and food chains as a beef filler.

5 In March 2012, *ABC News* reported that 70 percent of ground beef sold in the U.S. contained pink slime. Public outcry and consumer backlash were immediate and strong. As a result, many U.S. supermarket chains stopped selling products containing pink slime. Others continue to sell it, but now offer pink-slime-free meat as well. Several restaurant chains announced they would discontinue using products containing the filler.

6 In the U.S. there has been public demand to eliminate pink slime from meat served in school lunches. The USDA, which considers pink slime "meat," says it will give school districts the option of using meat with the filler. There has also been public demand for accurate labeling of meat that contains the filler so consumers can make informed choices.

7 The beef industry countered opposition to pink slime with a publicity campaign declaring that "Beef is beef" and "Dude, it's beef!" Perhaps, but before the ammoniated disinfecting process was invented, this "beef" could only be used in pet food and as a cooking oil ingredient. Dude, it's disgusting!

Source: Based on information at http://en.wikipedia.org/wiki/Pinkslime; accessed 4/5/12.

_______ **1.** Which sentence in paragraph 3 is the *stated main idea*?

a. first sentence
b. sentence 2
c. sentence 3
d. last sentence

_______ **2.** What is the *relationship between these two sentences* in paragraph 3? "By law, ground beef can contain up to 15% of pink slime without its being revealed on the label. In other words, ground beef that is 15 percent pink slime can still be labeled '100 percent ground beef.'"

a. The second sentence presents a contrast with something in the first sentence.
b. The second sentence makes a comparison with something in the first sentence.
c. The second sentence clarifies something mentioned in the first sentence.
d. The second sentence illustrates something mentioned in the first sentence.

_______ **3.** As used in paragraph 4, *salvaged* means:

a. rescued.
b. discarded, but saved for further use.

c. prime or first-quality.
d. having a pinkish color or tint.

_______ **4.** The information in paragraph 5 is organized using which *pattern*?

a. list
b. definition
c. cause and effect
d. comparison and contrast

_______ **5.** What is the *implied main idea* of paragraph 5?

a. After *ABC News* reported in March 2012 that 70 percent of ground beef sold in the U.S. contained pink slime, many U.S. supermarket chains stopped selling products containing pink slime.
b. Many U.S. supermarket chains stopped selling products containing pink slime, but others continue to offer both it and pink-slime-free meat.
c. In March 2012, when *ABC News* reported that 70 percent of ground beef sold in the U.S. contained pink slime, public outcry and consumer backlash were immediate and strong.
d. Many U.S. supermarket chains stopped selling products containing pink slime, and several restaurant chains announced they would discontinue using products containing the filler.

_______ **6.** The *author's tone* in paragraph 7, the last paragraph in the passage, can be described as:

a. supportive.
b. compassionate.
c. sentimental
d. disapproving.

_______ **7.** "In the U.S. there has been public demand to eliminate pink slime from meat served in school lunches." The preceding sentence presents:

a. a fact.
b. an opinion.
c. both a fact and an opinion.

_______ **8.** According to information in the passage, Canada prohibits:

a. ammoniated beef.
b. finely ground beef.
c. beef pressed into blocks.
d. flash-frozen beef.

_______ **9.** The *author's purpose* in writing this passage is to:

a. instruct readers how to tell if packaged ground meat contains pink slime.
b. persuade readers to lobby against pink slime in public school lunches.
c. inform readers about the history of, use of, and controversy surrounding pink slime.
d. persuade readers to boycott restaurants that use meat containing pink slime.

_______ **10.** What is the *author's point of view* regarding pink slime?

a. The author favors using pink slime.
b. The author opposes the use of pink slime.
c. The author favors using pink slime in school lunches but not in restaurants.
d. The author opposes accurate labeling of pink slime.

ESSENTIAL SKILLS REVIEW TEST 5

Directions: Read the passage below and then select the best answer for each question.

1 According to the National Sleep Foundation's 2009 Sleep in America Poll, 20% of American adults sleep an average of less than 6 hours per night. However, 7–9 hours per night are recommended in order to stay healthy and function as well as possible. Although many of us can attribute the lack of sleep to long work days and family responsibilities, as many as 70 million Americans suffer from chronic sleep disorders. These disorders are medical conditions that prevent them from sleeping well.

2 According to other National Sleep Foundation polls, more than 50% of adults report having trouble falling asleep or staying asleep—a condition called **insomnia.** The most common causes of insomnia are lifestyle factors, such as high caffeine or alcohol intake before bedtime; medical problems, such as a breathing disorder; and stress. About 75% of people who suffer from chronic insomnia report some stressful life event at the onset of their sleeping problems. In 2008, 56 million prescriptions for sleeping pills were filled in the U.S. at a cost of $4.5 billion.

3 Another type of chronic sleep problem, called **sleep apnea,** occurs when a person stops breathing while asleep. Apnea can be caused by a number of factors. However, it typically results when the soft tissue at the back of the mouth (such as the tongue or soft palate) "collapses" during sleep and blocks the airway. When breathing is interrupted, so is sleep: the sleeper awakens repeatedly throughout the night to begin breathing again. In most cases, this occurs without the sleeper's even being aware of it. However, the disruption to sleep can be significant, and over time acute sleep deprivation can result from apnea. There are several treatments for apnea, including the use of medications, a special apparatus that helps keep the airway open during sleep, and surgery.

Source: Paul Insel and Walton Roth, *Connect Core Concepts in Health,* 12th ed., Brief, p. 49. Copyright © 2012 by The McGraw-Hill Companies, Inc. Reprinted by permission of The McGraw-Hill Companies.

_______ **1.** As used in paragraph 1, *attribute* means to:

a. reveal.
b. deny.
c. discover.
d. regard as the cause.

_______ **2.** What is the *relationship between these two sentences* in paragraph 1? "According to the National Sleep Foundation's 2009 Sleep in America Poll, 20% of American adults sleep an average of less than 6 hours per night.However, 7–9 hours per night are recommended in order to stay healthy and function as well as possible."

a. The second sentence presents a contrast with something in the first sentence.
b. The second sentence gives an example of something mentioned in the first sentence.
c. The second sentence continues a series begun in the first sentence.
d. The second sentence defines a term presented in the first sentence.

_______ **3.** The *authors' purpose* in writing paragraph 2 is to:

a. instruct readers how to prevent insomnia.
b. inform readers about insomnia.
c. persuade readers with sleeping problems to request prescription sleeping pills.
d. persuade readers to learn to deal with stress more effectively.

_______ **4.** Which sentence in paragraph 3 is the *stated main idea*?

a. Another type of chronic sleep problem, called sleep apnea, occurs when a person stops breathing while asleep.
b. When breathing is interrupted, so is sleep: the sleeper awakens repeatedly throughout the night to begin breathing again.

Copyright © 2014 The McGraw-Hill Companies, Inc. All rights reserved.

c. However, the disruption to sleep can be significant, and over time acute sleep deprivation can result from apnea.
d. There are several treatments for apnea, including the use of medications, a special apparatus that helps keep the airway open during sleep, and surgery.

_______ **5.** What is the *relationship between the parts of this sentence* in paragraph 3? "There are several treatments for apnea, including the use of medications, a special apparatus that helps keep the airway open during sleep, and surgery." (The second part begins after the first comma.)

a. The second part contrasts with information presented in the first part.
b. The second part lists something mentioned in the first part.
c. The second part defines a term mentioned in the first part.
d. The second part completes a comparison begun in the first part.

_______ **6.** The information in paragraph 3 is organized using which *pattern*?

a. comparison
b. contrast
c. definition
d. sequence

_______ **7.** Based on information in the passage, which of the following would be a logical *conclusion*?

a. Stress management techniques could help those with sleep apnea.
b. Insomnia is declining among adults.
c. Sleeping pills should be prescribed for sleep apnea.
d. Lifestyle changes may benefit adults who have insomnia.

_______ **8.** Which of the following would be the *best title* for the passage?

a. Treating Insomnia and Sleep Apnea
b. Hooked on Sleeping Pills
c. Findings from National Polls
d. Sleep Problems

_______ **9.** "According to the National Sleep Foundation's 2009 Sleep in America Poll, 20% of American adults sleep an average of less than 6 hours per night." The preceding sentence presents:

a. a fact.
b. an opinion.

_______ **10.** According to information in the passage, the percentage of adults reporting trouble falling asleep or staying asleep is:

a. 20%.
b. more than 50%.
c. about 70%.
d. more than 75%.

ESSENTIAL SKILLS REVIEW TEST 6

Directions: Read the passage below and then select the best answer for each question.

OxyContin

1 A powerful narcotic that is presently sold legally is OxyContin. This drug, which is usually prescribed for cancer patients, has pushed aside marijuana, cocaine, and other narcotics as the drug of choice for addicts and teenage abusers. The active ingredient in OxyContin is a morphine-like substance called oxycodone, which is also found in the prescription drugs Percodan and Tylox. But unlike those drugs, which need to be taken in repeated dosages, OxyContin is a time-released formulation that is effective for up to 12 hours. Experts say, however, that addicts can achieve an intensely pure high by crushing the pills and snorting or injecting them. A telltale piece of paraphernalia among adolescent users is a pill crusher, sold by drugstores to help elderly people swallow their medication.

2 With the abuse of OxyContin on the rise, police in at least three states are reporting a record number of pharmacies being broken into. The homes of people with legitimate OxyContin prescriptions are being robbed, and home invasions are targeting the pills. These patients are often tracked down by relatives who know what is inside their medicine cabinets or by neighbors who hear them talk about their prescriptions. Illegal users are even accosting drugstore customers in parking lots on the hunch that they might be carrying this sought-after drug.

3 In an effort to deal with this growing problem, the manufacturer of OxyContin has developed a tamper-proof pill containing a newly designed polymer. This polymer makes the pill extremely difficult to crush for the purposes of snorting and injecting the drug. Moreover, when pill fragments are heated, the polymer turns into a gel-like substance. The FDA has stated that the benefits of this "tamper proof" pill are limited. Even so, because the new pill makes it more difficult to misuse OxyContin, the FDA calls it "advantageous."

Source: Adapted from Charles Swanson, Neil Chamelin, Leonard Territo, and Robert Taylor, *Criminal Investigation*, 11th ed., p. 552. Copyright © 2012 by The McGraw-Hill Companies, Inc. Reprinted by permission of The McGraw-Hill Companies.

_______ **1.** As used in paragraph 1, *telltale* refers to something that is:

a. worn out. b. revealing. c. startling. d. expensive.

_______ **2.** What is the *relationship between these two sentences* in paragraph 1? "A powerful narcotic that is presently sold legally is OxyContin. This drug, which is usually prescribed for cancer patients, has pushed aside marijuana, cocaine, and other narcotics as the drug of choice for addicts and teenage abusers."

a. The second sentence adds information to that in the first sentence.
b. The second sentence presents a comparison with something in the first sentence.
c. The second sentence continues a sequence begun in the first sentence.
d. The second sentence illustrates something mentioned in the first sentence.

_______ **3.** Which sentence represents the *implied man idea* of paragraph 2?

a. Certain types of crimes are increasing because of the rise in OxyContin abuse.
b. Police in at least three states report that a record number of pharmacies being broken into and that home invasions are targeting the pills.
c. Patients legitimately using OxyContin should not to mention it to relatives or neighbors.
d. To avoid being robbed in parking lots, legitimate OxyContin users should have their prescriptions delivered.

_______ **4.** The *authors' purpose* in writing paragraph 3 is to:

a. instruct readers how to identify tamper-proof OxyContin tablets.
b. inform readers about the manufacturer's effort to help prevent OxyContin abuse.

Copyright © 2014 The McGraw-Hill Companies, Inc. All rights reserved.

c. inform readers that the FDA believes the tamper-proof pills are highly effective.
d. persuade OxyContin users to buy only tamper-proof tablets.

_______ **5.** What is the *relationship between the parts of this sentence* in paragraph 3? "In an effort to deal with this growing problem, the manufacturer of OxyContin has developed a tamper-proof pill containing a newly designed polymer." (The second part begins after the comma.)

a. The second part of the sentence clarifies the first part.
b. The second part tells the result of something mentioned in the first part.
c. The second part presents an example of something mentioned in the first part.
d. The second part defines a term mentioned in the first part.

_______ **6.** According to the passage, which of the following is occurring as a result of OxyContin abuse?

a. More pharmacies are being broken into.
b. More home burglaries and invasions are targeting OxyContin.
c. Thieves are accosting people in parking lots who may have picked up an OxyContin prescription.
d. all of the above

_______ **7.** The *authors' tone* in this passage can be described as:

a. sentimental.
b. scornful.
c. unemotional.
d. arrogant.

_______ **8.** According to the passage, what is the effect of putting polymer in tamper-proof OxyContin tablets?

a. It makes them impossible to crush.
b. It makes them hard to crush and turns them to a gel when heated.
c. It prevents them from having any effect on a user.
d. none of the above

_______ **9.** According to the passage, teenagers use pill crushers with OxyContin tablets to:

a. make them easier to swallow.
b. make them dissolve faster in water.
c. snort or inject them.
d. conceal the substance more easily.

_______ **10.** According to information in the passage, oxycodone is:

a. the generic name for OxyContin.
b. the morphine-like active ingredient in OxyContin.
c. another name for OxyContin.
d. what OxyContin is called when it is crushed.

ESSENTIAL SKILLS REVIEW TEST 7

Directions: Read the passage below and then select the best answer for each question.

1 In 2008 federal officials investigated and arrested former NASDAQ chairman Bernie Madoff on charges of securities fraud. Madoff operated an asset management firm that, for decades, used the funds from new clients to pay profits and redemptions to existing clients. Often using his social networks to attract new investors, Madoff eventually defrauded his clients out of $64 billion, representing the largest, longest, and most widespread Ponzi scheme in history.

2 A *Ponzi scheme*, or *pyramid fraud,* involves recruiting people who are promised extraordinarily high returns on their money. The early investors are paid with money from later investors. The scheme always collapses because the recruitment of investors cannot be sustained and the perpetrators ultimately steal the funds for their personal use. With funds he fraudulently obtained, Madoff enjoyed a luxurious lifestyle that included a penthouse, yachts, and a French villa.

3 The number of dollars lost in the Madoff fraud is mindboggling. To place the $64 billion amount into perspective, compare the dollar loss in the preceding year due to crime. According to the FBI, there were 9.8 million crimes against property in the U.S. in 2007, which included about 2.2 million burglaries, 6.6 million larcenies, and about 1.1 million car thefts—totaling a mere $17.6 billion in losses. Put another way, the dollar loss for all property crimes in 2007 represented only a fraction (about 20%) of the total loss suffered by investors from the Madoff scheme! Even if 2007 was an "off year" for crime, to get a realistic picture of the magnitude of this crime, Bernie Madoff's fraud would essentially equal the monetary losses from all conventional property crimes against U.S. citizens for three years!

4 There has been some retribution and repayment of loss since 2008, and more may be coming. In 2009 Madoff pled guilty and was sentenced to 150 years in prison, the maximum sentence. In December 2010 federal authorities revealed that many of Madoff's victimized clients may regain about half of their losses as a result of seized property and assets by the federal government.

5 In the 1987 movie *Wall Street,* the fictional character Gordon Gekko soothingly intones at a stockholders' meeting, "Greed is good." Bernie Madoff's investment fraud was exposed the same year that the sequel, *Wall Street: Money Never Sleeps,* was released. In this movie, Gekko hawks his new book entitled *Greed Is Good!* The cynical nature and devastation of monetary loss from Bernie Madoff's investment fraud provide the backdrop to the movie, which highlights again one of the oldest and most successful cons, the Ponzi scheme.

Source: Adapted from Charles Swanson, Neil Chamelin, Leonard Territo, and Robert Taylor, *Criminal Investigation*, 11th ed., pp. 426–27, 662. Copyright © 2012 by The McGraw-Hill Companies, Inc. Reprinted by permission of The McGraw-Hill Companies.

______ **1.** What is the *relationship between these two sentences* in paragraph 1? "Madoff operated an asset management firm that, for decades, used the funds from new clients to pay profits and redemptions to existing clients. Often using his social networks to attract new investors, Madoff eventually defrauded his clients out of $64 billion, representing the largest, longest, and most widespread Ponzi scheme in history."

a. The second sentence presents a contrast with something in the first sentence.
b. The second sentence defines a term used in the first sentence.
c. The second sentence continues a sequence begun in the first sentence.
d. The second sentence illustrates something mentioned in the first sentence.

______ **2.** Which sentence in paragraph 2 is the *stated main idea*?

a. first sentence
b. sentence 2
c. sentence 3
d. last sentence

Copyright © 2014 The McGraw-Hill Companies, Inc. All rights reserved.

_______ **3.** As used in paragraph 3, *magnitude* means:

a. disgusting nature.
b. illegality.
c. great size.
d. evil.

_______ **4.** The *authors' purpose* in writing paragraph 3 is to:

a. instruct readers how to avoid becoming victims of Ponzi schemes.
b. inform readers about the vast extent of Madoff's fraud.
c. persuade readers that Madoff's crime was the worst in history.
d. persuade readers to urge the government to take Ponzi schemes more seriously.

_______ **5.** The *authors' tone* in paragraph 3 can be described as:

a. impassioned.
b. sympathetic.
c. solemn.
d. ambivalent.

_______ **6.** "The number of dollars lost in the Madoff fraud is mindboggling." The preceding sentence presents:

a. a fact.
b. an opinion.
c. both fact and opinion.

_______ **7.** As used in paragraph 4, *retribution* means something:

a. done to make up for a wrong doing.
b. required by law.
c. given in equal exchange.
d. done to ease the conscience.

_______ **8.** What is the *stated main idea* of paragraph 4?

a. There has been some retribution and repayment of loss since 2008, and more may be coming.
b. In 2009 Madoff pled guilty and was sentenced to 150 years in prison, the maximum sentence.
c. In December 2010 federal authorities revealed that many of Madoff's victimized clients may regain about half of their losses as a result of seized property and assets by the federal government.

_______ **9.** Based on information in the passage, it is reasonable to *infer* that:

a. the appropriate government agencies should make changes in how they monitor investment firms.
b. investors will not let greed cause them to make bad decisions in the future.
c. after Madoff's harsh sentence, money managers will no longer attempt investment fraud.
d. Madoff first studied other famous Ponzi schemes before he set his up.

_______ **10.** Which of the following would be the *best title* for the selection?

a. Greed
b. Bernie Madoff and the World's Biggest Ponzi Scheme
c. The Oldest Con: Ponzi Schemes
d. Bernie Madoff

Copyright © 2014 The McGraw-Hill Companies, Inc. All rights reserved.

ESSENTIAL SKILLS REVIEW TEST 8

Directions: Read the passage below and then select the best answer for each question.

The Decline in Marriage

1 The number of marriages in our society continues to decrease at the same time the number of singles and cohabiting couples increases. The number of marriages has reached its lowest level to date. The rate of marriage has declined from a high of 68% of the population in 1970, to 62% in 1980, to 52% in 2000. This decline in marriage has occurred across ethnic groups, but it has most affected African Americans. Only 36% of African American women and 41% of African American men are married, as opposed to 58% of White women and 60% of White men.

2 A second trend is an increase in the number of people who get divorced and choose not to remarry. The number of divorced people in the population has tripled from 3% in 1970 to 10% in 1996, but in the mid-1990s to mid-2000s, the U.S. divorce rate dropped by 17%. This slight decrease in the divorce rate, however, does not seem to have had an impact on the number of people choosing marriage.

3 A third major trend is the number of couples who are cohabiting. As of 2002, over 50% of women ages 19 to 44 have been in a cohabiting relationship for some time during their lives, compared to 33% in 1987. From 1970 to 2007, cohabitation increased by more than 1,000%, with about 10% of all couples cohabiting in 2007. Reasons people chose cohabitation over marriage are that people now are socially permitted to have sex outside of marriage, and there is greater equality between men and women, so women are choosing careers, education, or other opportunities over marriage.

4 As these statistics suggest, the popularity of marriage is decreasing. Although most individuals choose to marry at least once, it appears that fewer are choosing to remarry and instead either stay single or choose cohabitation over marriage. Marriage has been on the decline for the last two decades, and it appears that increasingly fewer people will choose to get married or to remarry in future years.

Source: David Olson, John DeFrain, and Linda Skogrand, *Marriages and Families*, 7th ed., p. 310. Copyright © 2011 by The McGraw-Hill Companies, Inc. Reprinted by permission of The McGraw-Hill Companies.

_______ **1.** As used in paragraph 1, *cohabiting* means:

a. engaged. b. long-term. c. living together. d. well-matched.

_______ **2.** What is the *relationship of the parts of this sentence* in paragraph 1? "Only 36% of African American women and 41% of African American men are married, as opposed to 58% of White women and 60% of White men." (The second part of the sentence begins after the comma.)

a. The second part presents a contrast with something in the first part.
b. The second part defines a term mentioned in the first part.
c. The second part continues a sequence begun in the first part.
d. The second part illustrates something mentioned in the first part.

_______ **3.** Which sentence in paragraph 3 is the *stated main idea*?

a. first sentence
b. sentence 2
c. sentence 3
d. last sentence

_______ **4.** The *authors' purpose* in writing this passage is to:

a. instruct readers how to decide whether to marry or to remain single.
b. persuade readers to consider marrying or remarrying.
c. inform readers about the decline in marriage, the causes, and projected trends.
d. inform readers about a major social problem the country is facing.

Copyright © 2014 The McGraw-Hill Companies, Inc. All rights reserved.

_______ **5.** Based on information in the passage, which of the following is a *logical conclusion*?

a. During the last 40 years, there have been significant changes in U.S. marriage, divorce, and remarriage rates.
b. Changes in U.S. marriage, divorce, and remarriage rates are the same for people of all races.
c. Although marriage is declining in the U.S., it is likely to regain popularity during the next two decades.
d. The reasons for the declining marriage, divorce, and remarriage rates in the U.S. are not understood.

_______ **6.** Overall, the information in this passage is *organized* as a:

a. comparison of marriage rates and remarriage rates.
b. set of contrasts between cohabitation and marriage.
c. series of events that lead to divorce.
d. list of trends associated with the decline in marriage.

_______ **7.** "Marriage has been on the decline for the last two decades, and it appears that increasingly fewer people will choose to get married or to remarry in future years." The preceding sentence presents

a. facts.
b. opinions.
c. both fact and opinion.

_______ **8.** Which of the following describes the *authors' position* on the issue of declining U.S. marriage rates?

a. They favor remarriage.
b. They oppose divorce.
c. They favor an increase in marriage.
d. They are neutral.

_______ **9.** According to information in the passage, the marriage rate in the U.S. was highest in which year?

a. 1970
b. 1980
c. 2000
d. 2002

_______ **10.** Which of the following is the *overall implied main idea* of the passage?

a. The number of people in the U.S. who divorce and choose not to remarry is increasing.
b. Declining marriage rates in the U.S. present a threat to our society.
c. Although most people in the U.S. marry at least once, the popularity of marriage is decreasing.
d. Greater gender equality between men and women has led to the decline in marriage.

ESSENTIAL SKILLS REVIEW TEST 9

Directions: Read the passage below and then select the best answer for each question.

Super Rich and Super Prepared

1 If you are a billionaire, what measures can you take to protect yourself, your family, and your property? According to *Forbes* magazine, quite a few. In a feature called "Billionaire Battle Plans," Steven Bertoni describes some extraordinary—and extraordinarily expensive—measures billionaires can take.

2 Armor-plated vehicles are essential. The super-rich customize them with panic buttons on the dashboard and tires that run when flat. Should the owner be forced into the car's trunk by an abductor, no problem: these vehicles can be equipped with cell phones and panic buttons in the trunk.

3 Tycoons can afford to hire the country's best personal-safety trainers to train them, their chauffeurs, and their bodyguards in self-defense techniques. Many moguls and their employees also take training in ways to elude vehicles that are pursuing them, such as doing J-turns and other car-chase-scene tricks.

4 To protect their estates, the mega-rich can have special cameras installed around their property. The cameras work even in the dark because they detect heat. If a camera picks up anything suspicious, such as the amount of heat given off by a person, it snaps a picture, triggers an alarm and notifies the police. Not only that, the system emails the homeowner the picture of the suspicious person. Although homeowners might be thousands of miles away, they can view it on their smart phone or tablet computer.

5 What if something apocalyptic happens and the only option is to get out of town? If you are a billionaire living in a big city, you are ready. You have a car—an SUV—on the street level, ready to go. It's packed with provisions, a satellite phone, information on escape routes, and radiation detectors. There are even fold-up bikes, should there be a need.

6 So where are the super-wealthy headed in their completely equipped SUVs? To their mountain estates or ranches which, of course, have been transformed into hideouts. Like the SUVs, these safe houses are equipped with everything the owners and their family might need for survival—comfortable survival. Along with stocks of necessary supplies, such as food and medicine, there are independent water sources, power generators, shortwave radios and satellite phones. Some mega-wealthy leave nothing to chance: should it come to it, they are prepared to cultivate crops and raise livestock at their secure retreats.

Luxury Doomsday Bunkers

7 Instead of equipping their own estates or ranches in case of a large-scale catastrophe, some mega-rich opt to buy doomsday bunkers. They see this as a necessity in case of a terrorist or nuclear event, abrupt global climate change, disruption to the world's oil supply, a pandemic, civil unrest, or a natural disaster, such as an earthquake or tsunami.

8 One developer has created a complex of doomsday domiciles in a decommissioned missile silo in the middle of a Kansas prairie. He bought it several years ago for $300,000, a steal. The 15-story silo is below ground and has nine-feet-thick walls. Anyone with $2 million can buy one of the 1,800-square-foot condos. (Two of the condos are half-floor, 900-square-feet units that go for less.) As of April 2012, four of the eight units had sold, two had sales pending, and two were available. Amenities include a custom residential interior, military-grade security, a theater, library, classroom, pool, and exercise facility. There is also a hydroponic garden, bar and lounge, general store, separate water and septic system, air filtration system, five-year per person food supply, medicines and a minor surgery center, and an in-house dentist and orthodontist. The structure operates on electricity, with off-the-grid wind-turbine, solar and generator power. Ahhh, home secure home.

Sources: Paragraphs 1–6 are based on Steven Bertoni, "Billionaire Battle Plans," *Forbes*, November 21, 2011, p. 24. Paragraphs 7–8: www.survivalcondo.com; accessed 4/12/12.

_______ **1.** Which sentence expresses the *implied main idea* of paragraph 1?

a. *Forbes* magazine published a piece called "Billionaire Battle Plans."
b. Only billionaires can protect themselves, their families, and their property.
c. If you are a billionaire, what steps can you take to protect yourself, your family, and your property?
d. There are extraordinary measures billionaires can afford that can protect them, their families, and their property.

Copyright © 2014 The McGraw-Hill Companies, Inc. All rights reserved.

_______ **2.** The information in paragraph 1 is organized using which *pattern*?

a. comparison and contrast
b. definition and example
c. cause and effect
d. sequence

_______ **3.** The *stated main idea* of paragraph 4 is:

a. To protect their estates, the mega-rich can have special cameras installed around their property.
b. The cameras work even in the dark because they detect heat.
c. If a camera picks up anything suspicious, such as the amount of heat given off by a person, it snaps a picture, triggers an alarm and notifies the police.
d. Not only that, the system emails the homeowner the picture of the suspicious person.

_______ **4.** As used in paragraph 5, *apocalyptic* describes something that is:

a. unexpected or unanticipated.
b. related to widespread devastation.
c. in another geographic region.
d. related to extreme wealth.

_______ **5.** What is the *relationship of the parts of this sentence* in paragraph 7? "Instead of equipping their own estates or ranches in case of a large-scale catastrophe, some multimillionaires and billionaires opt to buy doomsday bunkers." (The second part begins after the comma.)

a. The second part continues a sequence begun in the first part.
b. The second part makes a comparison with something in the first part.
c. The second part presents a contrast with something in the first part.
d. The second part illustrates something mentioned in the first part.

_______ **6.** What is the *relationship between these two sentences* in paragraph 8? "One developer has created a complex of doomsday domiciles in a decommissioned missile silo in the middle of a Kansas prairie. The 15-story silo is below ground and has nine-feet-thick walls."

a. The second sentence adds information to that in the first sentence.
b. The second sentence makes a comparison with something in the first sentence.
c. The second sentence continues a sequence begun in the first part.
d. The second sentence tells the cause of something mentioned in the first sentence.

_______ **7.** "He bought it several years ago for $300,000, a steal." The preceding sentence presents

a. facts only.
b. opinions only.
c. both fact and opinion.

_______ **8.** According to information in the passage, some mega-wealthy individuals have panic buttons installed:

a. in their wristwatches.
b. on the cameras surrounding their estates.
c. on the car dashboard and in the trunk.
d. at their mountain estates or ranches.

_______ **9.** The *author's purpose* in writing this passage is to:

a. instruct readers how to protect themselves from catastrophic manmade and natural disasters.
b. inform readers about measures billionaires take to protect themselves, their families, and their property.
c. persuade readers to take steps to protect themselves from large-scale disasters.
d. persuade readers that unless they are among the super-rich, there is little they can do to protect themselves and their families.

_______ **10.** Based on information in the passage, which of the following is a logical *inference*?

a. Billionaires fear for their safety and the safety of their family.
b. Billionaires go overboard in their concern about safety.
c. If there is a nuclear disaster, billionaires will perish along with everyone else.
d. Billionaires are foolish to go to the lengths they do to protect themselves against things that will probably never happen.

Copyright © 2014 The McGraw-Hill Companies, Inc. All rights reserved.

ESSENTIAL SKILLS REVIEW TEST 10

Directions: Read the passage below and then select the best answer for each question.

Decision Making and Unintended Pregnancy

1 When a woman suspects she is unintentionally pregnant, she should first confirm the pregnancy through a formal laboratory test. An examination by a doctor will help establish how long she has been pregnant. After pregnancy has been conclusively established, she can weigh her options carefully: carrying the child to term and keeping it, carrying the child to term and relinquishing it for adoption, or having an abortion. This is a decision that can greatly affect her life. A woman facing this difficult decision should then talk with several people she respects and trusts and who can remain calm and objective during the discussion.

2 Married couples commonly choose to keep an unplanned baby. However, an abortion remains an option for many married women, especially those who feel they already have as many children as they can care for properly. Couples who are not married may choose to get married. Many authorities, though, believe that pregnancy is not by itself a sufficient reason for marriage. Some young parents receive help rearing their babies from their own parents and other relatives while they complete their education and become more capable of assuming parental responsibilities. However, grandparents are often less than excited about becoming "parents" once again.

3 Adoption agencies today have difficulty finding babies for all the couples who wish to adopt. The high rate of abortion has contributed to this situation, along with society's generally negative attitude toward relinquishing babies for adoption. Social attitudes are reflected in the expression "giving up the child for adoption." The majority of adolescent mothers who carry their babies to term thus choose to keep them, despite the difficulties young mothers face in this situation. Adoption is seen as a viable alternative by many people, however. Some agencies are making an effort to ease the pain young mothers may feel by allowing them to have continued contact with the child and its adoptive parents.

4 Many people have strong feelings about the dilemma of unintended pregnancy and are eager to influence the decision in one direction or another. The individual or couple experiencing the dilemma, however, carries the responsibility for the decision. Whatever the decision, an unintended pregnancy is often a very lonely and stressful time in a woman's life.

Source: Adapted from David Olson, John DeFrain, and Linda Skogrand, *Marriages and Families*, 7th ed., p. A-22. Copyright © 2011 by The McGraw-Hill Companies, Inc. Reprinted by permission of The McGraw-Hill Companies.

_______ **1.** As used in paragraph 1, *conclusively* means:

a. temporarily.
b. partially.
c. recently.
d. definitely.

_______ **2.** The information in paragraph 1 is organized using which *pattern*?

a. comparison
b. contrast
c. definition
d. sequence

_______ **3.** Which of the following expresses the *implied main idea* of paragraph 1?

a. When a woman suspects she is unintentionally pregnant, she should first formally confirm the pregnancy and then weigh her options carefully since her decision can greatly affect her life.
b. There are several options for dealing with an unplanned pregnancy.
c. A woman facing an unplanned pregnancy should talk with several people she respects and trusts and who can remain calm and objective during the discussion.
d. A woman who thinks she may have become unintentionally pregnant should do nothing until she has seen a doctor.

Copyright © 2014 The McGraw-Hill Companies, Inc. All rights reserved.

_______ **4.** The *authors' purpose* in writing this passage is to:

a. instruct readers about how to put babies from unplanned pregnancies up for adoption.
b. inform readers about considerations and options related to unplanned pregnancies.
c. persuade readers to keep babies that result from unplanned pregnancies.
d. persuade readers to be more careful and avoid unplanned pregnancies.

_______ **5.** What is the *relationship between these two sentences* in paragraph 3? "Adoption agencies today have difficulty finding babies for all the couples who wish to adopt. The high rate of abortion has contributed to this situation, along with society's generally negative attitude toward relinquishing babies for adoption."

a. The second sentence presents a contrast with something in the first sentence.
b. The second sentence makes a comparison with something in the first sentence.
c. The second sentence presents the causes of something mentioned in the first sentence.
d. The second sentence illustrates something mentioned in the first sentence.

_______ **6.** As used in paragraph 3, *relinquishing* means:

a. abandoning.
b. preparing.
c. giving up.
d. celebrating.

_______ **7.** The *authors' tone* in this passage can be described as:

a. critical.
b. sympathetic.
c. irreverent.
d. pessimistic.

_______ **8.** "The individual or couple experiencing the dilemma, however, carries the responsibility for the decision." The preceding sentence presents

a. a fact.
b. an opinion.

_______ **9.** According to information in the passage, adoption:

a. is increasing in the United States.
b. should be required for young, unintentionally pregnant adolescents.
c. should always include ongoing contact between the birth mother, the child, and the adoptive family.
d. is still viewed negatively by society.

_______ **10.** What is the *authors' point of view* regarding unintended pregnancies?

a. Because unintended pregnancies present a difficult dilemma, individuals or couples involved should consider the options carefully to determine the decision that will be right for them.
b. Babies from unintended pregnancies should be put up for adoption, but the birth mother should be allowed ongoing contact with the child.
c. Family members should help in whatever way possible when a young woman becomes unintentionally pregnant.
d. Unintended pregnancies always create great stress and loneliness for a woman.

APPENDIX 1

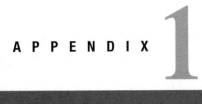

Glossary of Key Terms

IN THIS APPENDIX

Appendix 1 lists key terms from *New Worlds* with definitions. This listing will help you review material from this textbook and monitor your understanding of the concepts you have studied. The listing is alphabetical, and the chapter(s) in which the key term is presented is indicated.

addition pattern The author simply adds information. (*Chapter 7*)

affixes Word parts that are added to roots. Prefixes and suffixes are affixes. (*Chapter 2*)

annotating Writing explanatory notes in the margins of your textbook to organize and remember important information. (*Chapter 11*)

assessing your prior knowledge Determining what you already know about a topic. (*Chapter 10*)

audience (See *intended audience.*)

auditory preference A preference for hearing material to be learned. (*Chapter 1*)

average reading rate 200–300 wpm. Used for textbooks, newsmagazines, journals, and literature. (*Chapter 1*)

bar graph Chart in which the length of parallel rectangular bars is used to indicate relative amounts of the items being compared. (*Chapter 10*)

being selective as you read and study Focusing on main ideas and important supporting details. (*Chapter 1*)

box Supplementary material that is separated from the regular text. A box is also known as a *sidebar.* (*Chapter 10*)

cause-effect pattern Reasons (causes) and results (effects) of events or conditions are presented. (*Chapter 7*)

chapter introduction Textbook feature at the beginning of a chapter that describes the overall purpose and major topics. (*Chapter 10*)

chapter objectives Textbook feature at the beginning of a chapter, telling you what you should know or be able to do after studying the chapter. (*Chapter 10*)

chapter outline A list of chapter topics or headings in their order of appearance in the chapter. (*Chapter 10*)

chapter review cards Study tool and special textbook feature in *New Worlds*; a way to select, organize, and review the most important information in a chapter. (*Chapters 1–11*)

chapter summary Textbook feature in which the author consolidates most of the main ideas. (*Chapter 10*)

classification pattern Items that are listed are put into groups or categories. (*Chapter 7*)

comparison-contrast pattern Similarities (comparisons) between two or more things are presented, differences (contrasts) between two or more things are presented, or both. The comparison-contrast pattern is also known as *ideas in opposition.* (*Chapter 7*)

comprehension Understanding what you read. (*Chapters 3–6*)

comprehension monitoring Evaluating your understanding as you read and correcting the problem whenever you realize that you are not comprehending. (*Chapter 1*)

conclusion A logical outcome or judgment; often stated by the author at the end of a paragraph or a selection as the main idea. (*Chapter 9*)

context clues Words in a sentence or paragraph that help the reader deduce (reason out) the meaning of an unfamiliar word. (*Chapter 2*)

critical reading Gaining additional insights and understanding that go beyond comprehending the topic, main idea, and supporting details. Critical reading is also referred to as *critical reasoning* or *critical thinking.* (*Chapter 8*)

definition pattern Pattern presenting the meaning of an important term discussed throughout the paragraph. (*Chapter 7*)

definition-and-example pattern Definition with examples. (*Chapter 7*)

details (See *supporting details.*)

etymology The origin and history of a word. (*Chapter 2*)

fact Something that can be proved to exist or to have happened. (*Chapter 9*)

fallacies Implausible arguments using false or invalid inferences. (*Chapter 9*)

figurative language Words that create unusual comparisons or vivid pictures in the reader's mind. Figurative language is also called *figures of speech.* (*Chapter 2*)

flowchart A chart that shows steps in procedures or processes by using boxes, circles, and other shapes that are connected with lines or arrows. (*Chapter 10*)

formulated main idea (See *implied main idea.*)

generalization-and-example pattern Important concept, rule, or principle, followed by examples. (*Chapter 7*)

glossary A list of important terms and definitions from the entire textbook that is located near the end of a textbook. (*Chapter 10*)

graphic aids Tables, diagrams, graphs, and charts that present narrative information in an alternative format. (*Chapter 10*)

highlighting Technique for marking topics, main ideas, and definitions. (*Chapter 11*)

hyperbole Figure of speech using obvious exaggeration for emphasis or effect. (*Chapter 2*)

implied main idea A sentence formulated by the reader that expresses the author's main point about the topic. An implied main idea is also known as an *unstated main idea,* an *indirectly stated main idea,* and the *formulated main idea.* (*Chapter 5*)

inference A logical conclusion based on what an author has stated. (*Chapter 9*)

intended audience People an author has in mind as his or her readers. (*Chapter 8*)

intermediate goal Goal you want to accomplish within the next three to five years. (*Chapter 1*)

learning preference The modality through which an individual learns best. (*Chapter 1*)

line graph A diagram whose points are connected to show a relationship between two or more variables. There may be one line or several lines, depending on what the author wishes to convey. (*Chapter 10*)

list pattern A group of items presented in no specific order since the order is unimportant. The list pattern is also known as *listing pattern.* (*Chapter 7*)

location pattern Describes an object's position or location in space. Also called *spatial pattern.* (*Chapter 7*)

long-term goal Goal you want to accomplish during your lifetime. (*Chapter 1*)

long-term memory Permanent memory. (*Chapter 11*)

main idea A sentence that expresses both the topic and the author's most important point about this topic. (*Chapters 4–5*)

major details Details that directly support the main idea. Major details are also known as *primary details.* (*Chapter 6*)

mapping Informal way of organizing main ideas and supporting details by using boxes, circles, lines, arrows, etc. (*Chapter 11*)

metaphor Figure of speech suggesting a comparison between two seemingly dissimilar things, usually by saying that one of them *is* the other. (*Chapter 2*)

minor details Details that support other details. Minor details are also known as *secondary details.* (*Chapter 6*)

mixed pattern A combination of two or more patterns in the same paragraph. (*Chapter 7*)

monitoring your comprehension Evaluating your understanding as you read and correcting the problem whenever you realize that you are not comprehending. (*Chapter 1*)

opinion A judgment or belief that cannot be *proved.* (*Chapter 9*)

organizational patterns (See *writing patterns.*)

organizing as you read and study Arranging main ideas and supporting details in a meaningful way. (*Chapter 1*)

outlining Formal way of organizing main ideas and supporting details to show relationships among them. (*Chapter 11*)

overall main idea The general point of an entire selection (such as a section of a textbook chapter, a short reading selection, or an essay). (*Chapters 4–5*)

paraphrasing Restating an author's material in your own words. (*Chapter 6*)

patterns (See *writing patterns*.)

personification Figure of speech in which nonhuman or nonliving things are given human traits. (*Chapter 2*)

pie chart A circle graph in which the size of the "slices" represents proportional parts of the whole. (*Chapter 10*)

point of view An author's position (opinion) on an issue. Point of view is also known as the *author's argument*. (*Chapter 8*)

predicting Anticipating what is coming next as you read. (*Chapter 1*)

prefix Word part attached to the beginning of a word that adds its meaning to that base word. (*Chapter 2*)

preparing to read Previewing the material, assessing your prior knowledge, and planning your reading and studying time. (*Chapter 10*)

previewing Examining reading material (before reading it) to determine its topic and organization. (*Chapters 1 and 10*)

prior knowledge What you already know about a topic. Prior knowledge is also known as *background knowledge*. (*Chapter 1*)

propaganda devices Techniques authors use to unfairly influence the reader to accept their point of view. (*Chapter 9*)

purpose An author's reason for writing. (*Chapter 8*)

rapid reading rate 300–500 wpm. Used for fairly easy material; when you want only important facts or ideas; for leisure reading. (*Chapter 1*)

rehearsal Steps taken to transfer information into long-term memory. (*Chapter 11*)

rehearsing to remember information Saying or writing material to transfer it into long-term memory. (*Chapter 1*)

root Base word that has a meaning of its own. (*Chapter 2*)

scanning 1,500 wpm (words per minute) or more. Used to find a particular piece of information (such as a name, date, or a number). (*Chapter 10*)

sequence pattern A list of items presented in a specific order because the order is important. The sequence pattern is also known as *time order, chronological order, a process,* or *a series*. (*Chapter 7*)

short-term goal Goal you want to accomplish within three to six months. (*Chapter 1*)

short-term memory Temporary memory. (*Chapter 11*)

signal words Words that indicate the author's writing pattern. (*Chapter 7*)

simile Figure of speech presenting a comparison between two seemingly dissimilar things by saying that one of them is *like* the other. (*Chapter 2*)

skimming Reading at 800–1,000 wpm. Used to get an overview of material. (*Chapter 1*)

spatial pattern Describes an object's position or location in space. Also called *location pattern*. (*Chapter 7*)

SQ3R study system Textbook study system consisting of five steps: Survey, Question, Read, Recite, and Review. (*Chapter 1*)

stated main idea sentence The sentence in a paragraph that contains both the topic and the author's most important point about this topic. A stated main idea sentence is also known as the *topic sentence*. (*Chapter 4*)

statement-and-clarification pattern A general statement followed by additional information that clarifies the information in it. (*Chapter 7*)

study map (See *mapping*.)

study questions and activities Exercises, drills, and practice sections that direct your attention to or review information you will be expected to know. (*Chapter 10*)

study-reading process The three steps of preparing to read, asking and answering questions as you read, and reviewing by rehearsing the answers to your questions. (*Chapter 10*)

study-reading rate 50–200 wpm. Used for new vocabulary, complex concepts, technical material, and retaining details (such as material to be memorized, legal documents, and material of great interest or importance). (*Chapter 1*)

suffix Word part attached to the end of a root word. (*Chapter 2*)

summary Single-paragraph condensation of all the main ideas presented in a longer passage. (*Chapter 11*)

summary pattern A concluding paragraph that summarizes the section. (*Chapter 7*)

summary review cards Study cards that help you select, organize, and review the important information in a textbook chapter. (*Chapters 1–11*)

supporting details Additional information in the paragraph that helps you understand the main idea completely. Supporting details are also known as *support* or *details*. (*Chapter 6*)

table A systematic listing of data in rows and columns. (*Chapter 10*)

tactile preference A preference for writing material to be learned or for manipulating materials physically. (*Chapter 1*)

test review sheets Single sheet of paper consolidating and summarizing, on its front and back, the most important information to be covered on a test. (*Chapter 11*)

textbook feature Any device used by the author to emphasize important material or to show how it is organized. Textbook features are also called *learning aids*. (*Chapter 10*)

thinking critically to evaluate written material Using the additional skills of distinguishing between facts and opinions, and drawing logical inferences about what you have read. (*Chapter 9*)

three-step process for reading and studying college textbooks Step 1: Prepare to read; Step 2: Ask and answer questions as you read; Step 3: Review by rehearsing the answers to your questions. (*Chapter 10*)

tone Manner of writing (choice of words and writing style) that reveals an author's attitude toward a topic. (*Chapter 8*)

topic Word, name, or phrase that tells whom or what the author is writing about. The topic is also known as the *subject* or the *subject matter*. (*Chapter 3*)

transition words Words and phrases that show relationships among ideas in sentences, paragraphs, and longer selections. (*Chapter 7*)

underlining Technique for marking topics, main ideas, and definitions. (*Chapter 11*)

visual aids Photographs, diagrams, maps, and cartoons that supplement or illustrate narrative information. (*Chapter 10*)

visual preference A preference for seeing or reading material to be learned. (*Chapter 1*)

vocabulary aids Textbook devices that identify important terms and definitions. (*Chapter 10*)

word-structure clues Roots, prefixes, and suffixes that help you determine a word's meaning. Word-structure clues are also known as *word-part clues*. (*Chapter 2*)

writing patterns Ways authors organize the information they present. Writing patterns are also known as *organizational patterns, patterns of development,* and *thinking patterns*. (*Chapter 7*)

Copyright © 2014 The McGraw-Hill Companies, Inc. All rights reserved.

APPENDIX 2

Master Vocabulary List

IN THIS APPENDIX

Appendix 2 lists vocabulary words in the Vocabulary in Context and Word Structure quizzes that accompany the chapter reading selections. It will enable you to locate the vocabulary exercise in which each word appears. Vocabulary in Context words are in black; Word Structure ones are in color. Numbers in parentheses indicate the reading selection in which the vocabulary word occurs and are followed by the page numbers on which the word appears. In ***Part One,*** vocabulary words are ordered by reading selection. In ***Part Two,*** vocabulary words are listed alphabetically.

Part One

dictate (1.1) 31
dilapidated (1.1) 31
coalesce (1.1) 31
spewing (1.1) 31
consternation (1.1) 32
dictate (1.1) 32
predictable (1.1) 32
contradicts (1.1) 32
diction (1.1) 32
dictator (1.1) 32
edict (1.1) 33

prompts (1.2) 43
concise (1.2) 43
receptive (1.2) 43
accentuated (1.2) 43
rote memorization (1.2) 44
visualizes (1.2) 44
revise (1.2) 44
provisions (1.2) 44
visionary (1.2) 44
visionless (1.2) 44
vision (1.2) 45

systematic (1.3) 57
outweigh (1.3) 57
integrate (1.3) 57
vigilant (1.3) 57
fuel (1.3) 58
portable (1.3) 58
transporting (1.3) 58
reporters (1.3) 58
import-export (1.3) 58
deported (1.3) 58
support (1.3) 59

valleys (2.1) 113
adversity (2.1) 113
resilient (2.1) 113
thrive (2.1) 113
affirmations (2.1) 114
factors (2.1) 114
factory (2.1) 114
satisfaction (2.1) 114
manufacture (2.1) 114
malefactors (2.1) 114
benefactor (2.1) 115

epidemic (2.2) 123
sparked (2.2) 123
comprehensive (2.2) 123
common (2.2) 123
lion's share (2.2) 124
emotions (2.2) 124
demoted (2.2) 124
remote (2.2) 124
commotion (2.2) 124
promotion (2.2) 124
motive (2.2) 125

livestock (2.3) 133
profound (2.3) 133
perspective (2.3) 133
crude (2.3) 133
simulation (2.3) 134
progress (2.3) 134
regresses (2.3) 134
digress (2.3) 134
aggressive (2.3) 134
egress (2.3) 134
progression (2.3) 135

authoritarian (3.1) 167
judicious (3.1) 167
permissive (3.1) 167
authoritative (3.1) 167
temperament (3.1) 168
impose (3.1) 168
reposition (3.1) 168
transpose (3.1) 168
compose (3.1) 168
proposes (3.1) 168
repository (3.1) 169

poise (3.2) 177
groundless (3.2) 177
unrelenting (3.2) 177
diffused (3.2) 178
assailed (3.2) 178
rejection (3.2) 178
ejects (3.2) 178
dejected (3.2) 178
interject (3.2) 178
projector (3.2) 179
injection (3.2) 179

collectively (3.3) 186
denominations (3.3) 186
callous (3.3) 186
capitalize (3.3) 186
condolence (3.3) 187
respects (3.3) 187
spectacles (3.3) 187
retrospect (3.3) 187
spectator (3.3) 187
prospector (3.3) 187
specimen (3.3) 188

embrace (4.1) 217
stakeholders (4.1) 217
empathy (4.1) 217
resolve (4.1) 217
adopt (4.1) 218
autocratic (4.1) 218
automatically (4.1) 218
autopilot (4.1) 218
autonomous (4.1) 218
autodidact (4.1) 218
autobiography (4.1) 219

archaic (4.2) 227
lineage (4.2) 227
predestined (4.2) 227
reincarnation (4.2) 227
liberal (4.2) 228
prescribed (4.2) 228
transcribes (4.2) 228
subscribe (4.2) 228
scribe (4.2) 228
scribble (4.2) 228
inscribed (4.2) 229

misconception (4.3) 237
subtle (4.3) 237
jolts (4.3) 237
vulnerable (4.3) 237
sustained (4.3) 238
advocates (4.3) 238
vocal (4.3) 238
vocabulary (4.3) 238
vocation (4.3) 238
vociferous (4.3) 238
avocation (4.3) 239

commemorate (5.1) 274
flouted (5.1) 274
stark (5.1) 274
fitting (5.1) 274
incomparably (5.1) 274
commemorate (5.1) 275
remembrance (5.1) 275
memorize (5.1) 275
memorandum (5.1) 275
memoir (5.1) 275
memorable (5.1) 275

perpetrated (5.2) 282
white.collar crime (5.2) 283
vendor (5.2) 283
fictitious (5.2) 283
vulnerability (5.2) 283
involved (5.2) 284
revolves (5.2) 284
devolves (5.2) 284
evolves (5.2) 284
convoluted (5.2) 284
revolt (5.2) 284

species (5.3) 291
lethal (5.3) 291
strain (5.3) 291
unprecedented (5.3) 291
contain (5.3) 291
compelled (5.3) 292
propeller (5.3) 292
dispels (5.3) 292
expelled (5.3) 292
impels (5.3) 292
repels (5.3) 292

incentives (6.1) 328
banned (6.1) 328
mandatory (6.1) 328
glut (6.1) 328
surcharge (6.1) 329
innovative (6.1) 329
novice (6.1) 329
novel (6.1) 329
renovate (6.1) 329
novelty (6.1) 329
nova (6.1) 329

material (6.2) 336
ascetic (6.2) 336
enlightened (6.2) 336
intrinsically (6.2) 336
pacifist (6.2) 336
self.mortification (6.2) 337
mortuary (6.2) 337
post mortem (6.2) 337
mortician (6.2) 337
moribund (6.2) 337
mortal (6.2) 337

turmoil (6.3) 347
emigration (6.3) 347
hour glass (6.3) 347
metropolitan (6.3) 347
transient (6.3) 347
generation (6.3) 348
genetics (6.3) 348
genealogy (6.3) 348
generate (6.3) 348
ingenious (6.3) 348
progeny (6.3) 348

host (7.1) 406
latent (7.1) 407
acute (7.1) 407
chronic (7.1) 407
over-the-counter (7.1) 407
temporary (7.1) 408
extemporaneous (7.1) 408
contemporaries (7.1) 408
temporal (7.1) 408
tempo (7.1) 408
contemporary (7.1) 408

ratification (7.2) 415
disenfranchised (7.2) 415
shirk (7.2) 415
hovered (7.2) 415
rebounded (7.2) 415
include (7.2) 416
excluded (7.2) 416
occluded (7.2) 416
secluded (7.2) 416
precludes (7.2) 416
conclude (7.2) 416

reflect (7.3) 422
relatively (7.3) 423
retailer (7.3) 423
bulk (7.3) 423
perishable (7.3) 423
manage (7.3) 424
manual (7.3) 424
manuscripts (7.3) 424
manipulates (7.3) 424
manacles (7.3) 424
maneuver (7.3) 424

eclipsing (8.1) 468
guffawed (8.1) 468
sashay (8.1) 468
hoisted (8.1) 468
doused (8.1) 468
intending (8.1) 469
extends (8.1) 469
tenacious (8.1) 469
untenable (8.1) 469
distends (8.1) 469
attention (8.1) 469

detriment (8.2) 477
fundamentals (8.2) 477

Copyright © 2011 The McGraw-Hill Companies, Inc. All rights reserved.

muster (8.2) 477
intricacies (8.2) 477
perseverance (8.2) 477
dismissed (8.2) 478
transmission (8.2) 478
emission (8.2) 478
mission (8.2) 478
omission (8.2) 478
remission (8.2) 478

capital (8.3) 486
entrepreneur (8.3) 486
fiscal (8.3) 486
imperative (8.3) 486
contingencies (8.3) 486
confidence (8.3) 487
confide (8.3) 487
infidelity (8.3) 487
confidant (8.3) 487
bona fide (8.3) 487
Semper Fidelis (8.3) 487

suppress (9.1) 529
predominant (9.1) 529
differentiate (9.1) 529
stifled (9.1) 529
deludes (9.1) 529
conversation (9.1) 530
converts (9.1) 530
divert (9.1) 530
avert (9.1) 530
perverted (9.1) 530
extroverts (9.1) 530

explosively (9.2) 538
unabated (9.2) 538
plagued (9.2) 538
restrain (9.2) 538
attributes (9.2) 538
tortuous (9.2) 539
distorts (9.2) 539
contortionists (9.2) 539
torturous (9.2) 539
retort (9.2) 539
extortion (9.2) 539

provisional (9.3) 547
cohorts (9.3) 547
incompatibility (9.3) 547
embattled (9.3) 547
detachment (9.3) 547
independent (9.3) 548
interdependent (9.3) 548
pendulum (9.3) 548
pending (9.3) 548
suspend (9.3) 548
pendant (9.3) 548

euphoria (10.1) 603
alleviate (10.1) 603
acclaims (10.1) 603
murmuring (10.1) 603
progressive (10.1) 603
anonymous (10.1) 604
pseudonym (10.1) 604
synonyms (10.1) 604
antonyms (10.1) 604
homonyms (10.1) 604
heteronyms (10.1) 604

Part Two

accentuated (1.2) 43
acclaims (10.1) 603
acute (7.1) 407
adopt (4.1) 218
adversity (2.1) 113
advocates (4.3) 238
affirmations (2.1) 114
aggressive (2.3) 134
alleviate (10.1) 603
anonymous (10.1) 604
antonyms (10.1) 604
archaic (4.2) 227
ascetic (6.2) 336
assailed (3.2) 178
attention (8.1) 469
attributes (9.2) 538
authoritarian (3.1) 167
authoritative (3.1) 167
autobiography (4.1) 219
autocratic (4.1) 218
autodidact (4.1) 218
automatically (4.1) 218
autonomous (4.1) 218
autopilot (4.1) 218
avert (9.1) 530
avocation (4.3) 239
banned (6.1) 328
benefactor (2.1) 115
bona fide (8.3) 487
bulk (7.3) 423
callous (3.3) 186
capital (8.3) 486
capitalize (3.3) 186
chronic (7.1) 407
coalesce (1.1) 31
cohorts (9.3) 547
collectively (3.3) 186
commemorate (5.1) 274
commemorate (5.1) 275
common (2.2) 123
commotion (2.2) 124
compelled (5.3) 292
compose (3.1) 168
comprehensive (2.2) 123
concise (1.2) 43
conclude (7.2) 416
condolence (3.3) 187
confidant (8.3) 487
confide (8.3) 487
confidence (8.3) 487
consternation (1.1) 32
contain (5.3) 291
contemporaries (7.1) 408
contemporary (7.1) 408
contingencies (8.3) 486
contortionists (9.2) 539
contradicts (1.1) 32
conversation (9.1) 530
converts (9.1) 530
convoluted (5.2) 284
crude (2.3) 133
dejected (3.2) 178
deludes (9.1) 529
demoted (2.2) 124
denominations (3.3) 186
deported (1.3) 58

detachment (9.3) 547
detriment (8.2) 477
devolves (5.2) 284
dictate (1.1) 32
dictate (1.1) 31
dictator (1.1) 32
diction (1.1) 32
differentiate (9.1) 529
diffused (3.2) 178
digress (2.3) 134
dilapidated (1.1) 31
disenfranchised (7.2) 415
dismissed (8.2) 478
dispels (5.3) 292
distends (8.1) 469
distorts (9.2) 539
divert (9.1) 530
doused (8.1) 468
eclipsing (8.1) 468
edict (1.1) 33
egress (2.3) 134
ejects (3.2) 178
embattled (9.3) 547
embrace (4.1) 217
emigration (6.3) 347
emission (8.2) 478
emotions (2.2) 124
empathy (4.1) 217
enlightened (6.2) 336
entrepreneur (8.3) 486
epidemic (2.2) 123
euphoria (10.1) 603
evolves (5.2) 284
excluded (7.2) 416
expelled (5.3) 292
explosively (9.2) 538
extemporaneous (7.1) 408
extends (8.1) 469
extortion (9.2) 539
extroverts (9.1) 530
factors (2.1) 114
factory (2.1) 114
fictitious (5.2) 283
fiscal (8.3) 486
fitting (5.1) 274
flouted (5.1) 274
fuel (1.3) 58
fundamentals (8.2) 477
genealogy (6.3) 348
generate (6.3) 348
generation (6.3) 348
genetics (6.3) 348
glut (6.1) 328
groundless (3.2) 177
guffawed (8.1) 468
heteronyms (10.1) 604
hoisted (8.1) 468
homonyms (10.1) 604
host (7.1) 406
hour glass (6.3) 347
hovered (7.2) 415
impels (5.3) 292
imperative (8.3) 486
import-export (1.3) 58
impose (3.1) 168
incentives (6.1) 328
include (7.2) 416
incomparably (5.1) 274

incompatibility (9.3) 547
independent (9.3) 548
infidelity (8.3) 487
ingenious (6.3) 348
injection (3.2) 179
innovative (6.1) 329
inscribed (4.2) 229
integrate (1.3) 57
intending (8.1) 469
interdependent (9.3) 548
interject (3.2) 178
intricacies (8.2) 477
intrinsically (6.2) 336
involved (5.2) 284
jolts (4.3) 237
judicious (3.1) 167
latent (7.1) 407
lethal (5.3) 291
liberal (4.2) 228
lineage (4.2) 227
lion's share (2.2) 124
livestock (2.3) 133
malefactors (2.1) 114
manacles (7.3) 424
manage (7.3) 424
mandatory (6.1) 328
maneuver (7.3) 424
manipulates (7.3) 424
manual (7.3) 424
manufacture (2.1) 114
manuscripts (7.3) 424
material (6.2) 336
memoir (5.1) 275
memorable (5.1) 275
memorandum (5.1) 275
memorize (5.1) 275
metropolitan (6.3) 347
misconception (4.3) 237
mission (8.2) 478
moribund (6.2) 337
mortal (6.2) 337
mortician (6.2) 337
mortuary (6.2) 337
motive (2.2) 125
murmuring (10.1) 603
muster (8.2) 477
nova (6.1) 329
novel (6.1) 329
novelty (6.1) 329
novice (6.1) 329
occluded (7.2) 416
omission (8.2) 478
outweigh (1.3) 57
over-the-counter (7.1) 407
pacifist (6.2) 336
pendant (9.3) 548
pending (9.3) 548
pendulum (9.3) 548
perishable (7.3) 423
permissive (3.1) 167
perpetrated (5.2) 282
perseverance (8.2) 477
perspective (2.3) 133
perverted (9.1) 530
plagued (9.2) 538
poise (3.2) 177
portable (1.3) 58
post mortem (6.2) 337

Copyright © 2011 The McGraw-Hill Companies, Inc. All rights reserved.

Index

A

B

C

D

E

F

G

Copyright © 2014 The McGraw-Hill Companies, Inc. All rights reserved.

T

U

V

W

COMPREHENSION MONITORING QUESTIONS PRESENTED IN *NEW WORLDS*

Monitoring your comprehension means *evaluating your understanding as you read and correcting the problem whenever you realize that you are not comprehending.* You should monitor your comprehension whenever you read and study college textbooks. Asking yourself comprehension monitoring questions as you read will guide your reading and enhance your understanding. The comprehension monitoring questions that are presented throughout *New Worlds* are listed below.

Reading Comprehension Chapters 3–7

Determining the Topic: *"Who or what is this paragraph about?"*

Stated Main Idea: *"What is the most important point the author wants me to understand about the topic of this paragraph?"*

Implied Main Idea: *"What is the most important point the author wants me to infer about the topic of this paragraph?"*

Identifying Supporting Details: *"What additional information does the author provide to help me understand the main idea completely?"*

Recognizing Authors' Writing Patterns: *"What pattern did the author use to organize the main idea and the supporting details?"*

Critical Reading and Thinking Chapters 8–9

Determining an Author's Purpose: *"Why did the author write this?"*

Determining an Author's Intended Audience: *"Whom did the author intend to read this?"*

Determining an Author's Point of View: *"What is the author's position on this issue?"*

Determining an Author's Tone: *"What do the author's choice of words and style of writing reveal about his or her attitude toward the topic?"*

Determining an Author's Intended Meaning: *"What is the author's real meaning?"*

Evaluating Whether Statements in Written Material Are Facts or Opinions: *"Can the information the author presents be proved, or does it represent a judgment?"*

Making Inferences: *"What logical inference (conclusion) can I make, based on what the author has stated?"*

ASSIGNMENT SHEET AND PROGRESS RECORD, PART ONE

CHAPTER REVIEW CARDS, CHECKPOINTS, AND TEST YOUR UNDERSTANDING EXERCISES

Due Date		Review Cards, Checkpoints, and Test Your Understanding Exercises	Number of Items	Score
______	**Chapter 1**	Review Cards pp. 19–23	9 cards	______
______	**Chapter 2**	Review Cards pp. 81–82	3 cards	______
______		Test Your Understanding: Context Clues, Part 1 pp. 83–87	20	______
______		Test Your Understanding: Context Clues, Part 2 pp. 89–92	20	______
______		Test Your Understanding: Word Structure, Part 1 pp. 93–95	20	______
______		Test Your Understanding: Word Structure, Part 2 pp. 97–99	20	______
______		Test Your Understanding: Figurative Language, Part 1 pp. 101–03	20	______
______		Test Your Understanding: Figurative Language, Part 2 pp. 105–07	20	______
______	**Chapter 3**	Checkpoint: Determining the Topic pp. 151–52	5	______
______		Review Cards pp. 153–54	3 cards	______
______		Test Your Understanding: Determining the Topic, Part 1 pp. 155–57	5	______
______		Test Your Understanding: Determining the Topic, Part 2 pp. 159–61	5	______
______	**Chapter 4**	Checkpoint: Locating the Stated Main Idea pp. 201–02	5	______
______		Review Cards pp. 203–05	5 cards	______
______		Test Your Understanding: Locating the Stated Main Idea, Part 1 pp. 207–09	5	______
______		Test Your Understanding: Locating the Stated Main Idea, Part 2 pp. 211–12	5	______
______	**Chapter 5**	Checkpoint: Formulating an Implied Main Idea pp. 256–58	5	______
______		Review Cards pp. 259–60	3 cards	______
______		Test Your Understanding: Formulating Implied Main Ideas, Part 1 pp. 261–63	5	______
______		Test Your Understanding: Formulating Implied Main Ideas, Part 2 pp. 265–67	5	______
______	**Chapter 6**	Checkpoint: Identifying Supporting Details pp. 308–10	5	______
______		Review Cards pp. 311–12	3 cards	______
______		Test Your Understanding: Identifying Supporting Details, Part 1 pp. 313–17	5	______
______		Test Your Understanding: Identifying Supporting Details, Part 2 pp. 319–22	5	______
______	**Chapter 7**	Checkpoint: Recognizing Authors' Writing Patterns pp. 385–87	5	______
______		Review Cards pp. 389–93	9 cards	______
______		Test Your Understanding: Recognizing Authors' Writing Patterns, Part 1 pp. 395–98	5	______
______		Test Your Understanding: Recognizing Authors' Writing Patterns, Part 2 pp. 399–402	5	______
______	**Chapter 8**	Checkpoint: Reading Critically pp. 447–50	5	______
______		Review Cards pp. 451–53	5 cards	______
______		Test Your Understanding: Reading Critically, Part 1 pp. 455–59	5	______
______		Test Your Understanding: Reading Critically, Part 2 pp. 461–64	5	______
______	**Chapter 9**	Checkpoint: Thinking Critically pp. 510–12	5	______
______		Review Cards pp. 513–15	5 cards	______
______		Test Your Understanding: Thinking Critically: Fact and Opinion pp. 517–19	5	______
______		Test Your Understanding: Thinking Critically: Making Logical Inferences pp. 521–23	5	______
______	**Chapter 10**	Review Cards pp. 585–87	5 cards	______
______		Test Your Understanding: Interpreting Graphic Aids pp. 589–92		______
______	**Chapter 11**	Review Cards pp. 623–26	7 cards	______